DEADBALL STARS

OF THE
AMERICAN LEAGUE

DEADBALL STARS

OF THE

AMERICAN LEAGUE

By the Deadball Era Committee of

THE SOCIETY FOR AMERICAN BASEBALL RESEARCH

Edited by David Jones

Potomac Books, Inc.

ON THE COVER: The Detroit Tigers play the Chicago Cubs in Game 2 of the 1907 World Series, at Chicago's West Side Grounds. The Cubs won the game, 3-1.

Additional information about this volume and its companion *Deadball Stars of the National League* can be found at http://DeadballStars.SABR.org

Library of Congress Cataloging-in-Publication Data

Deadball Stars of the American League / written by the Deadball Era
Committee of the Society for American Baseball Research; edited by David Jones.
    p. cm.
  ISBN 1-57488-982-6
  1. Baseball players--United States--Biography. 2. American League of
Professional Baseball Clubs. I. Jones, David.Society for
American Baseball Research. Deadball Era Committee.

GV865.A1J65 2006
796.357092'2--dc22
[B]

                                2006010952

Potomac Books, Inc.
22841 Quicksilver Drive
Dulles, Virginia 20166

The Society for American Baseball Research
812 Huron Rd., Suite 719
Cleveland, OH 44115

ISBN 1-933599-01-4

First Edition
10 9 8 7 6 5 4 3 2 1

Hitting a home run in the days of sane baseball rules was an unusual feat. Now it is a daily incident and a joke. Safe to say that a large majority of baseball fans would be gratified to learn that the magnates had decided to supplant old-fashioned slugging matches with exhibitions of clever pitching, brilliant fielding, and scientific batting. Do away with the lively ball!

> Joe Vila, from a 1921 article
> in the *New York Sun*

I say the dead ball should be brought back. It would give the fans a game that is decided inside the park, not outside it. The dead ball makes for exciting catches in the outfield, eyelash plays at third on triples when the ball and the runner arrive at the same time, and more base stealing, which was an exciting part of the game.

> Ed Walsh, from a 1957 interview
> in *The Sporting News*

Keith Olbermann

FOREWORD

It almost wasn't the Deadball Era.

I can never think of the first decade of the American League without wondering if, in some parallel universe, the light bulb about the promotional value of home runs went off in 1901 instead of 1919—and if the citizens of that other world don't today revere Buck Freeman the way we revere Babe Ruth.

You'll meet Bucky inside these pages, as one of the sluggers with the first modern World Series winners, Boston in 1903. What he did in this universe's Deadball Era was atypical enough: he reached double-digits in homers for three years running, finishing second in the American League three times, and once leading the majors (with 13, in '03).

But it's how Freeman fared in 1899—and what nobody in baseball had the presence of mind to exploit over the subsequent few seasons—which ensured that the "bloop and a bunt" offense would prevail well into the twentieth Century.

In short, Buck Freeman had a Babe Ruth year in '99—and nobody noticed. It is undoubtedly the most unappreciated offensive season in baseball history. The fans didn't clamor for the long ball, and the owners didn't facilitate it, nor his swatting, by putting in a cork center. Nobody designed a stadium tailored to his strengths and anointed it "The House That Buck Built."

But they could have.

For the 1899 Washington Senators—the capitol's last National League team until the Expos moved there more than a century later—Buck Freeman, like Ruth a converted left-handed pitcher, slammed 25 home runs, when nobody else in baseball hit more than 12. There were other seasons of slugging anomaly in the 1800s. Four members of the 1884 Chicago White Stockings had hit 20 or more home runs—but the corner distances in their ballpark were only 180 and 196 feet.

Freeman did not have any such irregular advantages. The exact measurements of Washington's old National Park are lost to history, but the stadium seems to have been about the size of the later Griffith Stadium —a field so vast that the 1945 Senators (admittedly war-ravaged) would hit a total of one homer there all season.

Freeman hit 16 in roughly the same space—usually clearing not just the fence around the field, but also an outer one next to the sidewalks. On September 20th, 1899, he appears to have hit one ball into the street behind left field, and another into the one behind right.

We do have surviving outfield distances, and newspaper home run accounts for some of his nine road homers, and even today they are awe-inspiring. Buck pulled one in Brooklyn that went at least 400 feet, hit another to right in Boston that traveled about 430 feet, and in separate games at Chicago, he reportedly launched one to the clubhouse in left, and another into the center-field balcony (560 feet).

Still, somehow, in Buck Freeman, baseball recognized no sea change. The '99 Senators went out of business, Freeman was shuttled up to Boston, and he would play his last seven seasons in the Huntington Avenue Grounds, where a blast to dead center like the one to the balcony in Chicago would avail him nothing: the fence was an estimated 635 feet away.

There are fascinating players like Buck Freeman in every baseball era—guys you can't believe you've actually never heard much of before. But in the Deadball time covered by this exhaustively researched volume (and the counterpart National League volume), they seemed to have roamed the sport in packs.

As you meet Freeman, slow down and visit with some of his equally intriguing teammates in Boston: Nick Altrock, Lou Criger (still probably baseball's most famous "personal catcher"—Cy Young's), and the tragic Chick Stahl.

And don't forget to ponder that alternative universe where the Deadball Era ended in 1899, where they named the World Series MVP "The Buck Freeman Award," and where teenaged prospects still play in "Buck Freeman Leagues."

KEITH OLBERMANN
SABR MEMBER SINCE 1984

David Jones

INTRODUCTION

The Deadball Era (1901–1919) occupies a unique place in the historical imagination. Distinct from the chaotic, unruly brand of baseball played in the late nineteenth century—with its rising and falling leagues, vagabond franchises, and archaic rules—professional baseball during the first two decades of the twentieth century was relatively stable. The present two-league structure was formed in 1901 and codified in the sport's organizing apparatus in 1903. The same year, the American League, following the lead of the older National League, adopted the foul-strike rule, arguably the last rule change in baseball history to profoundly impact the way the game was played. Also in 1903, the Baltimore Orioles moved to New York and became the Highlanders, thus completing the familiar 16-franchise, 11-city format that would dominate the major league landscape for the next half century. With its organizational and playing structure in place, baseball finally settled into its destined role as the national pastime. In 1908, Jack Norworth penned "Take Me Out to the Ball Game," and indeed, throughout this period more and more fans went to the park: in 1901, the American and National Leagues drew slightly more than 3.6 million fans; by 1909, that figure had more than doubled. The parks they went to also changed over the ensuing years, as the old wooden grandstands gave way to majestic steel-and-concrete structures that would become familiar to generations of fans: Pittsburgh's Forbes Field and Philadelphia's Shibe Park, both opened in 1909; Chicago's Comiskey Park, debuted in 1910; New York's Polo Grounds, rebuilt in 1911; Detroit's Navin Field (later renamed Tiger Stadium) and Boston's Fenway Park, christened in 1912; and Chicago's Weeghman Park (now Wrigley Field), inaugurated in 1914.

To the present-day baseball fan, then, there is much about the Deadball Era that is familiar: the sport was dominated by the same two leagues, employed a rule-book similar to the modern version, and was played in parks that would be in use for much of the twentieth century, including two that are still in use as of this writing. But there was much that was different, too, particularly in regards to the way the game was played, and it is here that the Deadball Era presents the modern-day baseball researcher with its first enchantment. On the field, the Deadball Era's most notable feature, the one that gave the period its rather misleading name, was the lack of offense, particularly in comparison to the decades immediately preceding and following its reign. During the 1890s, offensive levels reached historic highs as pitchers struggled to adjust to the 60'6" pitching distance, implemented in 1893. In 1894, for example, the entire National League batted .309 and the average team scored 7.36 runs per game. (By comparison, in 2005 the average National League team plated 4.45 runs per contest.) Over the rest of the 1890s, offense declined somewhat, though even in its worst year, 1898, the average NL team scored 4.96 runs per game, a figure higher than any put up by either the American or National Leagues during the Deadball Era, with the exception of the 1901 American League. Following the Deadball Era, offense once again became ascendant, as Babe Ruth revolutionized the sport by hitting 54 home runs in 1920. On the strength of the long ball, offense surged throughout the 1920s and into the 1930s. In 1930, the average American League team scored 5.41 runs per game, a level higher than at any point during the Deadball Era, and much higher than the era's driest years, 1908 and 1909, when American League teams averaged just 3.44 runs per game.

So what, then, caused offense to sink so dramatically during the Deadball Era? First, we must clear up a common misconception: the decline in offense from 1901 to 1919 had nothing to do with the composition of the ball. In fact, the only major change to the ball that occurred during the era—the introduction of a cork center, which replaced the less elastic yarn center in use up to that time—caused offense to increase. The cork-center ball was officially adopted by the American League in 1911, when the average team's offensive output per game jumped by nearly a full run, to 4.61 runs per game, though offensive levels declined from this apogee over the rest of the decade.

On the other hand, the manner in which the ball was *treated* had much to do with the low tide of offense during the era. Whereas in the modern game baseballs are constantly being replaced by fresh specimens, during the Deadball Era the typical game featured only a few baseballs, and, sometimes, only one. Not surprisingly, the same ball, kept constantly in use, darkened considerably over the course of the game, making it harder for hitters to see. Also, especially prior to 1911, the ball became increasingly lumpy and misshapen over the course of the game, and as a result did not travel very far, even when well-struck.

Even this explanation, however, is less than satisfactory. After all, the same conditions applied to the game of the 1890s, when offense reached all-time highs. So what changed during the Deadball Era? I would argue that a confluence of several factors brought about the decline in offense so characteristic of the Deadball Era game. These are: 1.) the adjustment of a new generation of pitchers to the 60'6" pitching distance; 2.) the establishment of the aforementioned foul-strike rule; 3.) the invention of a number of new pitches, foremost among them the spitball; and 4.) the continuing evolution and improvement in fielding. By the beginning of the twentieth century, pitchers who had come of age when the mound was closer to home plate had mostly retired from the game, either through failure to adjust to the new pitching distance or because of old age. This was not the case in the 1890s, when many old-school pitchers struggled unsuccessfully to navigate the longer pitching distance. The importance of the foul-strike rule also should not be underestimated; prior to its implementation, crafty hitters had been able to foul off pitch after pitch without penalty. The foul-strike rule—which decreed that all foul balls would count as strikes (except for the third strike)—severely limited the usefulness of this strategy. At about the same time that hitters adjusted to this harsher reality, another set of circumstances emerged to confound their efforts. By 1904, pitchers throughout the game were using a new pitch, the spitball, that acted like a modern-day split-fingered fastball, diving as it approached the plate. Over the ensuing years pitchers added other gadgets to their arsenals, including the emery ball (see the biography of Russ Ford) and the shine ball (see Eddie Cicotte). By 1915, pitchers like Cicotte possessed a bevy of trick pitches that would make Gaylord Perry blush, and unlike Perry, often had

the added advantage of using a ball that had been in circulation for several innings. Finally, we should also remember that fielding continued to improve throughout this time period. By 1901, all fielders wore gloves (even if these gloves were quite small compared to the modern versions), and as a result, defensive play became more efficient. In 1910, the American League fielding percentage was .956; fifteen years earlier the National League figure had been .930.

So what, then, caused the Deadball Era to come to such a dramatic end in 1920, when Babe Ruth smashed 54 home runs for the New York Yankees? Three factors came together to bring an end to the deadball game: first, safety-minded officials implemented rules providing for a steady circulation of clean baseballs during the course of the game; second, league officials banned trick pitches, including the spitball; and third, Ruth demonstrated that talented sluggers could take advantage of the new rules to rewrite the record books.

The Deadball Era, then, is more of a historical accident than anything else, a brief burp in long-term trends that favored offense over pitching. Perhaps it is for this reason that so many baseball researchers have been so attracted to this time period. In recent years, it has become fashionable to discredit old tactics, such as the hit-and-run, stolen base, and the bunt, that emphasize one-run strategies over the big inning. This research is certainly valid, but if *ever* there was a period when it made sense to deploy these strategies, the Deadball Era was it. Along with a celebration of these tactics, deadball researchers are also drawn to the aesthetics of the sport during this time period, perhaps best represented in the photographs of Charles Conlon. Deadball Era baseball was played by young men who grew up working in coal mines and factories, and the restrictive measures of the reserve clause ensured that, for most of them, their financial prospects never strayed too far from their working class roots. For this reason, the sport lacked a certain veneer of respectability that it would later acquire, and the stories of Deadball Era ballplayers often carry a poignant tragedy largely missing from later eras, when athletes' fame made them more insulated from everyday social pressures. Thus, the Deadball Era is filled with men like Rube Waddell and Ed Delahanty, who essentially drank themselves into early graves; or Hal Chase and Chick Gandil, whose corruption destroyed careers and reputations. Of course, there were also good citizens too—men like Walter Johnson and Ray Schalk who resisted the pressures around them. For these men and many others, I hope this book provides as much insight into the kind of people they were as it does for the kind of baseball they played.

A collaborative project such as this one requires the hard work and dedication of literally hundreds of people, but there are a few at the top of the list who deserve special recognition. First I would like to thank Tom Simon, whose faithful, tireless stewardship of the National League volume provided the blueprint for the present book. Glenn LeDoux's beautiful designs enriched both volumes, and Jim Charlton's patience, encouragement, and occasional prodding kept the wheels moving forward. Eric Enders and Gunda Korsts worked hard to make sure that this book is as accurate and error-free as possible. My thanks also goes to all the members of the Society for American Baseball Research, and especially the SABR Board, particularly F.X. Flinn, for their unflinching support of this extensive project.

This book contains a lot of information and pictures, and I am particularly grateful to the wonderful staff at the National Baseball Hall of Fame Library for their help in providing us with many of them, particularly DEC member Gabriel Schechter, who provided a lot of files on very short notice. The photo department at the Hall of Fame supplied many of the images in the book; we also made frequent use of SABR's own photo archive, as well as the images of the Chicago History Museum. Additional images came from The Sporting News and Transcendental Graphics.

For the signatures that grace this book, I am particularly thankful to Paul Esacove, who, with the assistance of Kevin Keating, Doug Averitt, Harold Elsch, Mike Gutierrez, Dave Larson, Joe Murphy and Jim Stinson, supplied the vast majority that appear in these pages. Additional signatures came from James Elfers, Tom Hufford, Steve Steinberg, Dan O'Brien, and Robin Hicks-Connors at the Historical Society of Martin County Collection, Elliott Museum, in Stuart, Florida, who supplied hard-to-find examples of Bobby Veach and Ray Chapman signatures. I would also like to thank Keith Olbermann for writing the introduction.

I would like to thank Angelo Louisa for assembling the lineups that appear throughout this book, as well as the hard work of a phalanx of researchers who undertook the arduous task of going through every game of the Deadball Era, boxscore-by-boxscore, to assemble the lineups. They are: Paul Wendt (1901); Sheldon Miller (1902); Allan Wood (1903, 1918–1919); Matt Marini (1904–1905, 1914–1916); Richard Smiley (1906, 1909, 1917); Lenny Jacobson (1907); Dave Anderson (1908); Michael Foster (1910); Gabriel Schechter (1911); Angelo Louisa (1912), and R.J. Lesch (1913).

In this project I was also assisted by team editors who provided invaluable assistance in shepherding drafts of each of the 136 biographies to completion. Thanks go to Michael Foster (Boston), R.J. Lesch (Chicago), Steve Constantelos (Cleveland), Trey Strecker (Detroit), Eric Enders (New York), Norman Macht (Philadelphia), Stu Shea (St. Louis), and Tom Simon (Washington).

The 136 biographies that appear in this book were written by 89 individuals, and I would like to thank each one of them: Stephen Able; Vincent Altieri; David Anderson; Ray Anselmo; Mark Armour; Dennis H. Auger; John Bennett; Sam Bernstein; Robert W. Bigelow; Bill Bishop; Anthony Bunting; Charles Carey; David Cicotello; Steve Constantelos; Brian Cooper; Aaron Davis; Dan Desrochers; Nicole DiCicco; Jon Dunkle; Jim Elfers; Eric Enders; Jan Finkel; David Fleitz; David Fletcher; Michael Foster; Don Geiszler; Dan Ginsburg; Irv Goldfarb; Peter Gordon; Mike Grahek; Stanton Hamlet; Chris Hauser; John Heiselman; Dan Holmes; John Husman; Don Jensen; David Jones; Martin Kohout; Steve Krah; Bill Lamberty; John Leidy; Dan Levitt; Angelo Louisa; Norman Macht; Matt Marini; Wayne McElreavy; John McMurray; Paul Mittermeyer; T. Kent Morgan; Jim Moyes; Rod Nelson; Jim Nitz; Dan O'Brien; Marc Okkonen; Bob O'Leary; Elizabeth A. Reed; C. Paul Rogers III; John T. Saccoman; Kelly Boyer Sagert; Eric Sallee; Paul Sallee; Jim Sandoval; Joe Santry; Stuart Schimler; Scott E. Schul; Fred Schuld; Alex Semchuck; Tom Simon; Terry Simpkins; John Simpson; Doug Skipper; Richard Smiley; David Southwick; Lyle Spatz; John Stahl; Nathaniel Staley; Steve Steinberg; Brian Stevens; Trey Strecker; Tom Swift; Joan Thomas; Cindy Thomson; Richard Dixie Tourangeau; Scott Turner; Adam Ulrey; Paul Wendt; Christopher Williams; Allan Wood; and Paul J. Zingg.

Finally, I would like to thank my wife, Tracy, and my daughter, Anna, for their love and support during the planning, writing, and editing of this volume.

This book is dedicated to the memory of Lawrence Ritter, who passed away on February 15, 2004, just as *Deadball Stars of the National League* was being released. A friend and mentor to many within SABR, Larry was also an enthusiastic member of the Deadball Era Committee. Without his seminal work of oral history, *The Glory of their Times*, books such as this one might never have been written, and his work has served as inspiration to baseball researchers everywhere. What he once wrote of Sam Crawford, Rube Marquard, Davy Jones, Rube Bressler and others, we now say of him: "He, too, was honored in his generation, and was the glory of his times."

DAVID JONES
APRIL 2006

CONTENTS

Page numbers for this volume continue the pagination of *Deadball Stars of the National League*.
An index to both volumes is located at the end of this book.

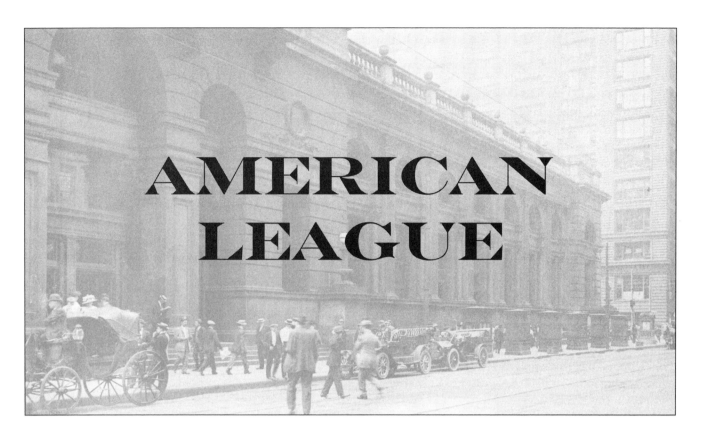

AMERICAN LEAGUE

T hough it eventually brought unprecedented stability to the national pastime, during the first two years of the twentieth century the American League wreaked havoc on the baseball landscape. During the final years of the nineteenth century, what would eventually be known as the American League, but was then called the Western League, had emerged under the steady guidance of league president Ban Johnson as the most successful minor league in the country. Not content to have his operation remain a humble serf in the established National League's fiefdom, prior to the 1900 season Johnson gave his circuit a new name more befitting of his ambitious designs. The following year Johnson's American League declared major league status and launched a full-scale war on the National League.

Though the American League initially lacked a franchise in New York, the nation's most populous city, by 1901 it boasted three teams in cities already occupied by the National League (Philadelphia, Boston, and Chicago) and three more teams in cities recently abandoned by the senior circuit (Baltimore, Washington, and Cleveland), to go along with Western League holdovers Detroit and Milwaukee.

More important, Johnson's constant raids on National League rosters guaranteed a steady crop of marquee talent for the new league. From 1901 to 1902 the American League successfully lured away superstars Napoleon Lajoie, Cy Young, Ed Delahanty, Jesse Burkett, Jimmy Collins, Bobby Wallace, and many more. In the latter season Johnson moved the Milwaukee franchise into a

A.L. ATTENDANCE (in millions) 1901–1919

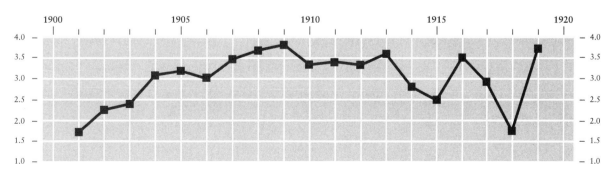

fourth National League city, St. Louis, and for the first time outdrew the National League at the gate.

Johnson's startling success forced the NL owners to the bargaining table, and prior to the 1903 season the two leagues forged a peace settlement, agreeing to honor each other's contracts and establishing a three-man National Commission to oversee the sport. That same off-season Johnson moved the Baltimore franchise to New York. The next American League franchise relocation would not occur for another 52 years.

Despite the 1903 peace settlement, the American League remained ascendant, outdrawing the National League at the gate in 16 of the next 17 seasons and capturing 10 of the first 15 World Series. For most of the Deadball Era Johnson also remained the most powerful figure in the sport, but by 1919 his influence began to decline. That autumn several members of the Chicago White Sox conspired to throw the World Series to the Cincinnati Reds. The public revelation of the Black Sox scandal the following fall embarrassed Johnson, brought the sport to its knees, and paved the way for the appointment of Judge Kenesaw Mountain Landis as baseball's first commissioner. Under Landis' strong leadership, and aided by the arrival of Babe Ruth with the New York Yankees, the American League, along with the rest of baseball, emerged from its greatest disgrace stronger than ever.

DAVID JONES

LEAGUE LEADERS
1901–1919

BATTING

GAMES
S. Crawford 2114
N. Lajoie. 1988
T. Cobb. 1929

RUNS
T. Cobb. 1416
E. Collins 1136
S. Crawford 1115

HITS
T. Cobb. 2713
N. Lajoie. 2521
S. Crawford 2466

RBI
S. Crawford 1264
T. Cobb. 1211
N. Lajoie. 1141

DOUBLES
N. Lajoie. 510
T. Cobb. 431
S. Crawford 402

TRIPLES
S. Crawford 249
T. Cobb. 210
J. Jackson 148
T. Speaker. 148

HOME RUNS
F. Baker. 80
S. Crawford 70
H. Davis 69

STOLEN BASES
T. Cobb. 765
E. Collins 564
C. Milan 481

BATTING AVERAGE
(2000+ plate appearances)
T. Cobb. 372
J. Jackson 352
T. Speaker. 338

PITCHING

GAMES
E. Plank 581
W. Johnson 544
E. Cicotte 465

WINS
E. Plank 305
W. Johnson 297
C. Young. 221

LOSSES
W. Johnson 191
G. Mullin 184
E. Plank 183

INNINGS
E. Plank 4227⅓
W. Johnson 4090⅔
G. Mullin 3451⅓

STRIKEOUTS
W. Johnson 2614
E. Plank 2099
R. Waddell 1965

WALKS
G. Mullin 1131
E. Plank 1018
W. Johnson 818

SHUTOUTS
W. Johnson 86
E. Plank 63
E. Walsh 57

ERA
(800+ innings pitched)
W. Johnson 1.65
E. Walsh 1.81
A. Joss. 1.89

STATS, LLC. A.L. ALL-STARS, 1901–1919

1901
C. Griffith, P
R. Miller, P
R. Patterson, P
C. Young, P
O. Schrecongost, C
B. Freeman, 1B
N. Lajoie, 2B
J. Collins, 3B
K. Elberfeld, SS
M. Donlin, OF
F. Jones, OF
S. Seybold, OF

1902
B. Bernhard, P
R. Donahue, P
R. Waddell, P
C. Young, P
O. Schrecongost, C
C. Hickman, 1B
N. Lajoie, 2B
L. Cross, 3B
G. Davis, SS
E. Delahanty, OF
B. Freeman, OF
S. Seybold, OF

1903
B. Dinneen, P
E. Moore, P
E. Plank, P
C. Young, P
H. Bemis, C
C. Hickman, 1B
N. Lajoie, 2B
B. Bradley, 3B
F. Parent, SS
S. Crawford, OF
P. Dougherty, OF
B. Freeman, OF

1904
J. Chesbro, P
E. Plank, P
R. Waddell, P
C. Young, P
J. Sugden, C
H. Davis, 1B
N. Lajoie, 2B
B. Bradley, 3B
F. Parent, SS
E. Flick, OF
W. Keeler, OF
C. Stahl, OF

1905
N. Altrock, P
E. Killian, P
E. Plank, P
R. Waddell, P
O. Schrecongost, C
H. Davis, 1B
D. Murphy, 2B
J. Collins, 3B
G. Davis, SS
S. Crawford, OF
E. Flick, OF
G. Stone, OF

1906
A. Joss, P
A. Orth, P
B. Rhoads, P
D. White, P
O. Schrecongost, C
H. Davis, 1B
N. Lajoie, 2B
F. LaPorte, 3B
G. Davis, SS
E. Flick, OF
S. Seybold, OF
G. Stone, OF

1907
B. Donovan, P
A. Joss, P
E. Killian, P
E. Walsh, P
N. Clarke, C
H. Davis, 1B
N. Lajoie, 2B
J. Collins, 3B
K. Elberfeld, SS
T. Cobb, OF
S. Crawford, OF
E. Flick, OF

1908
A. Joss, P
E. Summers, P
E. Walsh, P
C. Young, P
C. Schmidt, C
C. Rossman, 1B
N. Lajoie, 2B
H. Ferris, 3B
G. Schaefer, SS
T. Cobb, OF
S. Crawford, OF
D. Gessler, OF

1909
C. Bender, P
H. Krause, P
G. Mullin, P
E. Plank, P
B. Carrigan, C
J. Stahl, 1B
E. Collins, 2B
F. Baker, 3B
D. Bush, SS
T. Cobb, OF
S. Crawford, OF
T. Speaker, OF

1910
C. Bender, P
J. Coombs, P
R. Ford, P
W. Johnson, P
T. Easterly, C
J. Stahl, 1B
N. Lajoie, 2B
F. Baker, 3B
J. Knight, SS
T. Cobb, OF
D. Murphy, OF
T. Speaker, OF

1911
V. Gregg, P
W. Johnson, P
E. Plank, P
E. Walsh, P
O. Stanage, C
J. Delahanty, 1B
E. Collins, 2B
F. Baker, 3B
D. Bush, SS
T. Cobb, OF
S. Crawford, OF
J. Jackson, OF

1912
W. Johnson, P
E. Plank, P
E. Walsh, P
J. Wood, P
J. Lapp, C
S. McInnis, 1B
E. Collins, 2B
F. Baker, 3B
H. Wagner, SS
T. Cobb, OF
J. Jackson, OF
T. Speaker, OF

1913
C. Bender, P
C. Falkenberg, P
W. Johnson, P
R. Russell, P
J. Sweeney, C
S. McInnis, 1B
E. Collins, 2B
F. Baker, 3B
J. Barry, SS
T. Cobb, OF
J. Jackson, OF
T. Speaker, OF

1914
C. Bender, P
H. Coveleski, P
W. Johnson, P
D. Leonard, P
W. Schang, C
S. McInnis, 1B
E. Collins, 2B
F. Baker, 3B
D. Bush, SS
T. Cobb, OF
S. Crawford, OF
T. Speaker, OF

1915
W. Johnson, P
J. Scott, P
E. Shore, P
J. Wood, P
R. Schalk, C
J. Fournier, 1B
E. Collins, 2B
O. Vitt, 3B
R. Chapman, SS
T. Cobb, OF
T. Speaker, OF
B. Veach, OF

1916
H. Coveleski, P
W. Johnson, P
B. Ruth, P
B. Shawkey, P
L. Nunamaker, C
W. Pipp, 1B
E. Collins, 2B
L. Gardner, 3B
R. Peckinpaugh, SS
T. Cobb, OF
J. Jackson, OF
T. Speaker, OF

1917
J. Bagby, P
E. Cicotte, P
C. Mays, P
B. Ruth, P
W. Schang, C
G. Sisler, 1B
E. Collins, 2B
F. Baker, 3B
R. Chapman, SS
T. Cobb, OF
T. Speaker, OF
B. Veach, OF

1918
S. Coveleski, P
W. Johnson, P
C. Mays, P
S. Perry, P
S. O'Neill, C
G. Burns, 1B
E. Collins, 2B
F. Baker, 3B
R. Chapman, SS
T. Cobb, OF
B. Ruth, OF
T. Speaker, OF

1919
E. Cicotte, P
S. Coveleski, P
W. Johnson, P
A. Sothoron, P
W. Schang, C
G. Sisler, 1B
E. Collins, 2B
B. Weaver, 3B
R. Peckinpaugh, SS
T. Cobb, OF
J. Jackson, OF
B. Ruth, OF

1901–1919
C. Bender, P
W. Johnson, P
E. Plank, P
E. Walsh, P
C. Young, P
O. Schrecongost, C
H. Davis, 1B
E. Collins, 2B
F. Baker, 3B
D. Bush, SS
R. Chapman, SS
G. Davis, SS
T. Cobb, OF
S. Crawford, OF
T. Speaker, OF

LEAGUE STANDINGS 1901-1919

1901

Team	W	L	Pct.	GB
Chicago	83	53	.610	—
Boston	79	57	.581	4
Detroit	74	61	.548	8½
Philadelphia	74	62	.544	9
Baltimore	68	65	.511	13½
Washington	61	72	.459	20½
Cleveland	54	82	.397	29
Milwaukee	48	89	.350	35½

1902

Team	W	L	Pct.	GB
Philadelphia	83	53	.610	—
St. Louis	78	58	.574	5
Boston	77	60	.562	6½
Chicago	74	60	.552	8
Cleveland	69	67	.507	14
Washington	61	75	.449	22
Detroit	52	83	.385	30½
Baltimore	50	88	.362	34

1903

Team	W	L	Pct.	GB
Boston	91	47	.659	—
Philadelphia	75	60	.556	14½
Cleveland	77	63	.550	15
New York	72	62	.537	17
Detroit	65	71	.478	25
St. Louis	65	74	.468	26½
Chicago	60	77	.438	30½
Washington	43	94	.314	47½

1904

Team	W	L	Pct.	GB
Boston	95	59	.617	—
New York	92	59	.609	1½
Chicago	89	65	.578	6
Cleveland	86	65	.570	7½
Philadelphia	81	70	.536	12½
St. Louis	65	87	.428	29
Detroit	62	90	.408	32
Washington	38	113	.252	55½

1905

Team	W	L	Pct.	GB
Philadelphia	92	56	.622	—
Chicago	92	60	.605	2
Detroit	79	74	.516	15½
Boston	78	74	.513	16
Cleveland	76	78	.494	19
New York	71	78	.477	21½
Washington	64	87	.424	29½
St. Louis	54	99	.353	40½

1906

Team	W	L	Pct.	GB
Chicago	93	58	.616	—
New York	90	61	.596	3
Cleveland	89	64	.582	5
Philadelphia	78	67	.538	12
St. Louis	76	73	.510	16
Detroit	71	78	.477	21
Washington	55	95	.367	37½
Boston	49	105	.318	45½

1907

Team	W	L	Pct.	GB
Detroit	92	58	.613	—
Philadelphia	88	57	.607	1½
Chicago	87	64	.576	5½
Cleveland	85	67	.559	8
New York	70	78	.473	21
St. Louis	69	83	.454	24
Boston	59	90	.396	32½
Washington	49	102	.325	43½

1908

Team	W	L	Pct.	GB
Detroit	90	63	.588	—
Cleveland	90	64	.584	½
Chicago	88	64	.579	1½
St. Louis	83	69	.546	6½
Boston	75	79	.487	15½
Philadelphia	68	85	.444	22
Washington	67	85	.441	22½
New York	51	103	.331	39½

1909

Team	W	L	Pct.	GB
Detroit	98	54	.645	—
Philadelphia	95	58	.621	3½
Boston	88	63	.583	9½
Chicago	78	74	.513	20
New York	74	77	.490	23½
Cleveland	71	82	.464	27½
St. Louis	61	89	.407	36
Washington	42	110	.276	56

1910

Team	W	L	Pct.	GB
Philadelphia	102	48	.680	—
New York	88	63	.583	14½
Detroit	86	68	.558	18
Boston	81	72	.529	22½
Cleveland	71	81	.467	32
Chicago	68	85	.444	35½
Washington	66	85	.437	36½
St. Louis	47	107	.305	57

1911

Team	W	L	Pct.	GB
Philadelphia	101	50	.669	—
Detroit	89	65	.578	13½
Cleveland	80	73	.523	22
Chicago	77	74	.510	24
Boston	78	75	.510	24
New York	76	76	.500	25½
Washington	64	90	.416	38½
St. Louis	45	107	.296	56½

1912

Team	W	L	Pct.	GB
Boston	105	47	.691	—
Washington	91	61	.599	14
Philadelphia	90	62	.592	15
Chicago	78	76	.506	28
Cleveland	75	78	.490	30½
Detroit	69	84	.451	36½
St. Louis	53	101	.344	53
New York	50	102	.329	55

1913

Team	W	L	Pct.	GB
Philadelphia	96	57	.627	—
Washington	90	64	.584	6½
Cleveland	86	66	.566	9½
Boston	79	71	.527	15½
Chicago	78	74	.513	17½
Detroit	66	87	.431	30
New York	57	94	.377	38
St. Louis	57	96	.373	39

1914

Team	W	L	Pct.	GB
Philadelphia	99	53	.651	—
Boston	91	62	.595	8½
Washington	81	73	.526	19
Detroit	80	73	.523	19½
St. Louis	71	82	.464	28½
Chicago	70	84	.455	30
New York	70	84	.455	30
Cleveland	51	102	.333	48½

1915

Team	W	L	Pct.	GB
Boston	101	50	.669	—
Detroit	100	54	.649	2½
Chicago	93	61	.604	9½
Washington	85	68	.556	17
New York	69	83	.454	32½
St. Louis	63	91	.409	39½
Cleveland	57	95	.375	44½
Philadelphia	43	109	.283	58½

1916

Team	W	L	Pct.	GB
Boston	91	63	.591	—
Chicago	89	65	.578	2
Detroit	87	67	.565	4
New York	80	74	.519	11
St. Louis	79	75	.513	12
Cleveland	77	77	.500	14
Washington	76	77	.497	14½
Philadelphia	36	117	.235	54½

1917

Team	W	L	Pct.	GB
Chicago	100	54	.649	—
Boston	90	62	.592	9
Cleveland	88	66	.571	12
Detroit	78	75	.510	21½
Washington	74	79	.484	25½
New York	71	82	.464	28½
St. Louis	57	97	.370	43
Philadelphia	55	98	.359	44½

1918

Team	W	L	Pct.	GB
Boston	75	51	.595	—
Cleveland	73	54	.575	2½
Washington	72	56	.563	4
New York	60	63	.488	13½
St. Louis	58	64	.475	15
Chicago	57	67	.460	17
Detroit	55	71	.437	20
Philadelphia	52	76	.406	24

1919

Team	W	L	Pct.	GB
Chicago	88	52	.629	—
Cleveland	84	55	.604	3½
New York	80	59	.576	7½
Detroit	80	60	.571	8
St. Louis	67	72	.482	20½
Boston	66	71	.482	20½
Washington	56	84	.400	32
Philadelphia	36	104	.257	52

AMERICAN LEAGUE

Thomas Henry Connolly
Umpire, 1901–1931

The man who umpired the American League's first game as a major circuit, Tommy Connolly was also one of the greatest arbiters in baseball history. Beginning his umpiring career in 1894, Connolly was the cool-headed exception in an era when many umpires often resorted to ejecting players, managers, and fans in order to maintain control of the game. Small in physical stature, Connolly nonetheless earned the respect of his peers through his knowledge of the rules, fairness, and firm manner. "You can just go so far with Tommy," remarked Ty Cobb, one of the era's great umpire baiters. "Once you see his neck get red it's time to lay off."

Through his 52-year career with the American League, first as a field umpire for 31 years and later as the league's supervisor of umpires, Connolly oversaw dramatic changes in the game he loved and the way it was umpired. As the sport progressed from the one-man system to the modern-day four-man crew, the reputation of the umpiring profession improved; lowly regarded and subjected to ridicule at the beginning of the century, by the time of Connolly's retirement umpires were highly respected. As a role model for younger umpires and later a valuable scout for umpiring talent, Connolly deserves much of the credit for these changes.

Thomas Henry Connolly was born in Manchester, a smoky industrial city in the northwest of England, on December 31, 1870. As a young boy Connolly played cricket; he did not even see a baseball game until he arrived in the United States with the rest of his family in 1884. His father found work as a salesman for Catholic church supplies in Natick, Massachusetts, earning enough income to provide his family with a comfortable living. Eager to gain friends by learning the national pastime, Tommy became batboy for a local team and developed an interest in studying the rules of baseball, reportedly from reading editions of *The Sporting Life*. Unlike many early umpires, who took up the profession once their playing days were over, Connolly never played any organized baseball. Rather, his interest in the rules and devotion to the game led him to a successful umpiring career.

After serving as umpire for the YMCA club of Natick, Connolly's professional career began in 1894 in the New England League. Connolly remained with that league through the 1897 season, when he was hired by the National League on the recommendation of umpire Tim Hurst. Connolly worked two and a half years in the National League, during a time when umpiring in the major leagues was as much an ordeal as it was a job. He sat out a good part of the 1900 season due to multiple disagreements with National League president Nick Young, who had failed, Connolly felt, to support his on-field rulings. By the end of the year Connolly was officiating in the New York State League.

Fortunately for Connolly's umpiring career, Ban Johnson and his American League emerged as a major league in 1901, espousing the principles of on-field discipline and fair play that were so important to Connolly. Though he had never seen Tommy umpire, Connie Mack recommended that Johnson hire Connolly for the inaugural 1901 season. When Chicago hosted Cleveland in the first game in the AL's major league history, Connolly was behind the plate. Two years later he was chosen along with National League umpire Hank O'Day to umpire the 1903 World Series. He would go on to officiate seven more fall classics.

On the field Connolly was methodical and far from colorful. He would tell anyone who listened that no one ever bought a ticket to see an umpire. Connolly seldom resorted to ejections, demonstrating a degree of restraint unusual for his era. Reputedly he once went ten consecutive seasons without ejecting a single player, manager, or fan. Whether factual or not, the legend underscores how Connolly was perceived by players, managers, his fellow umpires, and the press. "Tommy had none of [Bill] Klem's histrionicism," Arthur Daley later observed. "In many respects he was the perfect umpire."

Connolly never failed to credit Ban Johnson for backing his rulings and stamping out the rowdyism that had so unsettled him during his tenure in the National League. "The American League ranks first in regard to umpires, to my mind, because Mr. Johnson, the president, had taken such a firm stand in the matter and supports his umpires to the letter," Connolly remarked after the 1907 season. "Rowdyism was rampant in the National League, and the officials were powerless. Now the example of the American League has compelled an entire change, and the prospects of the game were never better."

From 1901 to 1907 Connolly primarily worked games alone, and preferred to do so until the time came when the league hired enough umpires to allow for two-man and later three-man crews. Despite his preference, Connolly admitted later in his life that solo umpires had their hands full and often could not be in position to make a call. In describing play during the early days of the American League, Connolly said players took advantage of the single-umpire system by leaving base early on fly balls, cutting the second or third base corner to gain an edge, tripping base runners, and doing whatever else was required to gain an advantage. "An umpire just couldn't cover every base and everything that happened no matter how alert he was or how hard he tried," he admitted. "But we did the best we could. I have no regrets."

Like other veteran umpires of his era, he enjoyed a reputation as an excellent mentor for younger umpires, but Connolly would nurture young players as well. When Eddie Plank made his debut with the Philadelphia Athletics in 1901, the young pitcher was being heckled by the opposing dugout for not toeing the mound properly. Going out to the mound Connolly told the pitcher, "Son, there are right ways and wrong ways to pitch in this league. Let me show you the right way. I'll take care of that wrecking crew in the dugout and from what you've shown me today you'll be up here a long time."

Connolly retired as a field umpire in June 1931, when he was named American League umpire-in-chief by league president Will Harridge. Connolly's hiring came at a time when nearly every team in the league was unhappy with the quality of umpiring. To address the issue Connolly instituted many reforms, including scouting the minor leagues for umpiring talent. When a prospect was identified Connolly would often do the evaluation personally.

Upon his retirement after the 1953 season, Connolly was awarded a golden pass to major league games. When his schedule and health permitted he would often be seen at Fenway Park. He spent his final years in Natick, where he lived with two of his daughters. His 1902 marriage to Margaret Gavin had produced seven children, three daughters and four sons, before Margaret died in 1943.

In 1953 Connolly was selected to the Hall of Fame with fellow umpire Bill Klem, though illness prevented him from attending the induction ceremonies. Connolly lived to be 90 years old before dying of heart disease at his home in Natick, Massachusetts, on April 28, 1961. He was buried in St. Patrick's Cemetery, in Natick.

DAVID ANDERSON

AMERICAN LEAGUE

Byron Bancroft Johnson
President, 1901–1927

The most powerful figure of the Deadball Era, Ban Johnson's rise to prominence in the national pastime was as improbable as it was meteoric. Relying neither on athletic renown (his amateur catching career was abruptly cut short by a thumb injury) nor inherited wealth (he dropped out of law school to become a journalist), the talented Johnson maneuvered his way into the presidency of the Western League in 1893, then skillfully transformed the fledgling circuit into one of the most formidable minor leagues of the late nineteenth century. At the turn of the twentieth century, Johnson renamed the Western League the American League, declared major league status, and then succeeded in challenging the one-league supremacy of the National League. Johnson's triumph marked a turning point in baseball history, cementing the modern two-league system and setting the stage for the unparalleled financial successes of the coming years.

The catalyst for these momentous changes was a jowly, arrogant man whose outward demeanor seemed so cold, so unsympathetic, that one observer suggested that Johnson had been "weaned on an icicle." Autocratic and humorless, Johnson almost single-handedly administered the American League during his tenure, drafting schedules, signing players, and shifting franchises as he saw fit. Following the peace agreement with the National League in 1903, Johnson also became the most powerful force on the three-man National Commission that oversaw the sport, in the process making more than his share of enemies among the ownership ranks in both leagues. To writer Bob Considine, Johnson was "a ruthless dreamer who lived and died believing that baseball was perfected in order to serve him as a gigantic chess board on which to move his living pieces." Nonetheless, there is no denying his enduring impact on the sport. "His contribution

to the game," Branch Rickey once observed, "is not closely equaled by any other single person or group of persons."

Byron Bancroft Johnson was born in Norwalk, Ohio, on January 5, 1864, the fifth of six children of Alexander Byron and Eunice C. Fox Johnson. Shortly after Ban's birth, the family moved to Avondale, Ohio (then a Cincinnati suburb, though today it is within city limits), where A.B. Johnson served as a prominent school administrator.

After graduating from preparatory school Ban showed a lack of focus in his studies, bouncing around Ohio from Oberlin College to Marietta College to the University of Cincinnati Law School, where he would remain for less than two years. At Marietta the big, sturdy Johnson gained a reputation as a fearless catcher on the school team, manning his position without a glove, mask, or chest protector. Not surprisingly it was a thumb injury that ended his baseball career. At the time of the injury his experience consisted of a handful of games with the semipro Ironton, Ohio, team while on vacation from school.

When Johnson dropped out of law school midway through his sophomore year in 1886 to take a job as sportswriter at the Cincinnati *Commercial Gazette* at $25 a week, his father hit the roof. The paper's legendary editor, Murat Halstead, was finally able to convince Ban's father that journalism was an honorable profession. When sports editor O.P. Caylor left the Cincinnati paper to take a similar position in New York, Halstead named Johnson to the job.

Johnson soon earned a reputation for his knowledge of sports and willingness to speak his mind. From the beginning he did not back down from volatile topics of the day. For example, he was a champion of the Players League in 1890, which alienated (among others) Indianapolis Hoosiers owner John Brush. His strong opinions won him the friendship of others, however, such as star first baseman Charles Comiskey, who had joined the Players League.

When the Players League folded after 1890 and the American Association dissolved into the National League the following year, a new circuit, the Western League, was created in 1892. The progressive new league was the brainchild of Jimmy Williams, a Columbus, Ohio, attorney.

The circuit got off to a shaky financial start, however, and Williams was forced to close down the league in July 1892. In the fall of 1893 members of the disbanded league sought to rekindle the circuit, but Williams begged off, claiming he could no longer take charge of keeping the league afloat financially. Comiskey, remembering his old friend, suggested Johnson to committee members Denny Long of Toledo and James Manning of Kansas City. That November Ban Johnson was named president–secretary–treasurer of the Western League and given a salary of $2,500 a year.

To boost league attendance Johnson crusaded against rowdiness in the league, supporting his umpires with better pay and backing up their rulings on the field with stiff penalties for bad behavior. Under Johnson's able stewardship the league became increasingly profitable over the rest of the nineteenth century. In 1897 the circuit drew nearly one million fans, with the top clubs in Kansas City, Milwaukee, and St. Paul drawing better than some National League franchises.

When the National League voted to scale down from twelve to eight teams prior to the 1900 season, Johnson saw his big opportunity. Shifting the St. Paul club to Chicago and the Columbus franchise to Cleveland, he changed the league's name to the American League. The following year Johnson declared his organization a major league and abandoned the circuit's western roots, moving franchises into National League territories in Boston and Philadelphia, as well as into Baltimore and Washington, cities the National League had abandoned the year before.

The newly named American League waived the National League's $2,400 salary cap and enticed 111 players from the National League to jump to the new venture, including top stars Cy Young, Napoleon Lajoie, and John McGraw. Before the 1902 season Johnson transferred the Milwaukee club to St. Louis to compete head-to-head with the Cardinals, and continued his raid on National League rosters, coming away with more big-name players, including sluggers Ed Delahanty, Jesse Burkett, and Elmer Flick. The results were impressive: in 1902 the American League outdrew the National League by more than 500,000 fans. In the four cities home to franchises in both leagues, the upstart American League outdrew the National League in all of them by wide margins.

Clearly outmatched, the hapless National League owners finally sued for peace following the 1902 season. The resulting truce between the two leagues reaffirmed the principle of the reserve clause and the sanctity of contracts. A three-man National Commission was appointed to settle disputes; Johnson, National League president Harry Pulliam, and Cincinnati Reds executive Garry Herrmann (a friend of Johnson's) were picked for the new governing body. Though Herrmann was hardly Johnson's puppet, as he is often portrayed, his close relationship with the American League president did help Johnson to cement his power.

As chief executive of the American League, Johnson extended his efforts to eliminate rowdyism from the game. Supporting his umpires with a firm hand, Johnson swiftly punished players and managers who crossed the line. Johnson's tactics were not always successful. When Johnson and Baltimore manager John McGraw clashed over the skipper's unsportsmanlike behavior on the diamond during the 1902 season, McGraw jumped to the New York Giants and took many Orioles with him. Baltimore was able to complete the season only because owners from the other American League teams contributed players from their rosters. After the 1902 season Johnson moved the Orioles to New York, where they would in time become the most successful franchise in the history of the sport.

The American League grew and prospered under Johnson. He dealt with each problem firmly. Whether it was the Tigers striking over Ty Cobb's suspension in 1912 or floating loans to teams to strengthen the league, the obstinate Johnson usually got his way. He became so powerful that once, in 1910, he even changed the outcome of a batting race when the results did not suit him.

Indeed, it was Johnson's arrogant manner and dictatorial inclinations that eventually led to his downfall. During the last five years of the Deadball Era, four controversial rulings paved the way for the demise of the National Commission and fractured the ownership ranks of the American League into pro-Johnson and anti-Johnson camps.

In 1915 the National Commission ruled that George Sisler was the property of the American League's St. Louis Browns. As a 17-year-old, Sisler had signed a contract with the Akron club of the Ohio-Pennsylvania League. Akron was part of the vast farm system of Bobby Quinn and the Columbus Senators of the American Association. Sisler decided instead to attend the University of Michigan.

While he was in college, Sisler's contract was transferred to the parent club and Quinn sold it to the Pittsburgh Pirates. Sisler's coach at Michigan was Branch Rickey. Rickey became the manager of the Browns in 1913, and when Sisler was ready to turn pro, Branch represented the youngster in a legal battle to sign a contract with St. Louis. Rickey's argument was that because Sisler was a minor when he signed the Akron contract, his father's signature was required to make the contract binding. Johnson and Herrmann agreed, and Sisler became a Brown.

Barney Dreyfuss, owner of the Pirates, cried foul and vowed to destroy the National Commission. Cubs owner Charles Murphy, disgruntled after a Commission decision, was quoted by I.E. Sanborn in *The Sporting News* as saying he wanted the entire commission disbanded. It was the first nail in the coffin.

The next nail was driven in 1917, when Atlanta of the Southern Association sold pitcher Scott Perry's contract to the Braves. Perry jumped the team to play semipro ball. The National Commission ruled that Atlanta could resign Perry for $2,000. The Crackers then sold the journeyman pitcher to the A's. When Boston objected, the National Commission awarded Perry's contract to Philadelphia. Once again the American League had won a contract dispute, leaving some to wonder if the National League could ever win a case brought before the Commission.

Contract dispute number three came before Johnson in 1919, when the American League president awarded pitcher Jack Quinn to the Yankees instead of the Chicago White Sox. Johnson's action effectively ended a long friendship with his drinking buddy Comiskey. Gradually over the years the men who had shared the same Chicago office for nearly two decades became bitter enemies.

Later that season star pitcher Carl Mays of the Boston Red Sox jumped the team and refused to return. The Red Sox traded Mays to the Yankees after Johnson ruled that Mays first had to return to Boston and serve a suspension before he could be traded. Yankees owners Jacob Ruppert and Tillinghast Huston got a temporary restraining order allowing Mays to pitch for New York. Divided over the issue, the league split into the "Loyal 5" (St. Louis, Philadelphia, Cleveland, Detroit, and Washington) and the "Insurrectionists" (New York, Boston, and Chicago). The Insurrectionists controlled the five man Board of Directors and stripped Johnson of much of his power.

The owners met, voted in a new board, and reinstated Johnson. The New York owners then bombarded Johnson with lawsuits. Late that year things got so ugly that the Insurrectionists gave the league a one-week ultimatum. If an agreement could not be reached, the Yankees, Red Sox, and White Sox would join a 12-team National League. The 12th team would be the first of the Loyal 5 to jump; if none of them moved, the National League planned to place a team in Detroit. Finally, Frank Navin, the Detroit owner, brokered a peace agreement, albeit a tenuous one. Johnson now was required to answer to the owners.

A few months later a story broke centering on the suspicion that Comiskey's Chicago White Sox had thrown the 1919 World Series to gamblers. Johnson took some pleasure over his former friend's embarrassment. When he tried to ride in and save the situation, however, the owners balked. To restore integrity to the game, baseball's magnates decided to replace the National Commission with an all-powerful commissioner.

Judge Kenesaw Mountain Landis was chosen for the position. Landis had limited baseball experience, but he was every bit as stubborn as Johnson, who opposed Landis's appointment. Over the next several seasons Johnson had little interaction with Landis, concerning himself solely with league matters.

In 1927, however, enraged that his authority had been undermined by Landis in the Ty Cobb–Tris Speaker gambling scandal, Johnson locked horns with the commissioner. The judge responded with an ultimatum to the owners: Johnson or Landis. The American League owners voted 7–1 to strip Ban of his powers, but allowed him to retain his title.

After three meetings on July 8, 1927, at the Belmont Hotel in New York, a sick and sullen Johnson passed his scribbled resignation through his hotel door to Ruppert. His resignation would take effect at the end of the season.

Ban and his wife of over 30 years, Jane Laymon, retired to Spencer, Indiana. Their marriage had not produced any children. His retirement years were spent fund raising for Marietta College and promoting baseball in Mexico. In his final interview Johnson stated that major league baseball should extend coast to coast. Even near the end of his life, he was still 25 years ahead of his time.

Johnson died of diabetes on March 28, 1931, in St. Louis. He was buried in Riverside Cemetery in Spencer.

JOE SANTRY AND CINDY THOMSON

AMERICAN LEAGUE

CHARLES W. SOMERS
VICE PRESIDENT, 1901–1916

Once called the "good angel of the American League," Charles Somers was much more than simply one of the league's founding members—he was also its principal financier. An otherwise shy and unassuming man who had made his fortune in the coal business, Somers brought major league baseball back to Cleveland in 1901, and also helped the junior circuit establish clubs in Chicago, Philadelphia, and Boston. At one point the free-spending magnate was part owner of four of the league's eight franchises. "[Somers's] faith in Ban Johnson and his open checkbook were the legs upon which the American League learned to walk," writer Franklin Lewis observed in 1949. "Without them, there would be no American League today." Somers' enthusiasm for the national pastime also led to his downfall, however, as the magnanimous yet meddlesome owner failed to lift his Cleveland franchise into contention. Bankrupt by the end of his 16-year tenure, Somers was obliged to sell off his biggest star before his creditors forced him out of major league baseball for good in 1916.

Charles W. Somers was born on October 13, 1868, in Newark, Ohio, the only child of Joseph Hook and Philenia McCrum Somers. Joseph Somers worked in the coal-shipping business, and in 1884 the family moved to Cleveland, where Joseph established the J.H. Somers Coal Company. Under Joseph Somers's stewardship the company became very successful, opening numerous mines in Ohio and Pennsylvania. After attending business school Charles began working for his father, though he soon ventured out on his own. He later described his first years in the business world this way: "Kept store for my father. Went on the road as a salesman. Got into the coal business on my account. When I could not buy outright attractive mining properties, I managed to obtain them by lease. Kept at it

for ten years. Then sold out." At age thirty-one he was worth $1,000,000. The young millionaire returned to his father's coal operation as general manager.

The budding coal magnate had bigger dreams, and an avid interest in the national pastime. A fan of the Cleveland Spiders of the 1890s, Somers joined forces with John F. Kilfoyl, a local haberdasher who was interested in reviving major league baseball in Cleveland after the Spiders were contracted from the National League. Approached by Ban Johnson, Somers and Kilfoyl bought and moved the Grand Rapids, Michigan, team of the Western League to Cleveland in 1900.

Kilfoyl became the nominal president of the new club, and Somers served as vice president for both the Cleveland franchise and the American League. Using his quiet leadership and deep pockets, Somers strengthened the fledgling circuit at a critical moment in its history. In the first three years of the American League, Somers lent or spent close to $1 million on other American League franchises. He helped Connie Mack establish a team in Philadelphia and financed principal owner Ben Shibe with a substantial loan for a new ballpark. Shibe had been worried about investing in baseball in Philadelphia with so much National League opposition, but Somers wired Ban Johnson: "We will cure Shibe of his shyness. Tell Connie Mack to find the grounds and I'll put up the money."

Somers also lent Charles Comiskey money to build a new grandstand for his ballpark in Chicago, and when the Buffalo franchise was transferred to Boston, he funded the American League team there when no local purchasers came forward. Upon assuming control of the league's Boston franchise in 1901, Somers temporarily transferred his Cleveland ownership to Kilfoyl. During his two-year stewardship of the Boston Somersets (as sportswriters referred to the team), Somers lured stars

Jimmy Collins and Cy Young away from the National League, thereby immediately establishing a strong competitor for Boston's NL team. In 1902 Somers was able to reassume his co-ownership of the Cleveland franchise, after selling his Boston interests to Henry J. Killilea, a Milwaukee lawyer.

During the Somers era the Cleveland Naps (as they were known, after their manager and star second baseman Nap Lajoie) annually boasted one of the league's most talented rosters. A frustrating string of injuries and bad luck prevented the Naps from winning the pennant, however, and as the disappointing seasons mounted for the franchise, Somers became more actively involved in the club's day-to-day operations. In mid-1910 Kilfoyl sold his interest in the club, leaving Somers as the team's sole owner.

During the next six years Somers earned a reputation as one of the game's most meddlesome owners, as the Cleveland franchise cycled through six managers from 1909 to 1915, but finished with a winning record only twice. In 1912 Somers drew the ire of his players when he traded the team's popular manager, George Stovall, to the St. Louis Browns and replaced him with Harry Davis. Davis never had a chance to succeed with his disgruntled players. With the team in sixth place on September 1, Davis resigned and Somers hired 28-year-old center fielder Joe Birmingham as his playing manager.

The club's nadir came in 1914, when Cleveland finished in last place with a record of 51–102, and manager Birmingham's authority was publicly challenged by former manager Lajoie, who had resigned from that post in 1909 but continued as the team's second baseman. The following year Somers sold Lajoie to Philadelphia, and a poll by the sportswriters christened the franchise the Indians, but the changes did not bring success.

After the Indians got off to a slow start, Somers ordered Birmingham to play right fielder Joe Jackson at first base, a move that the manager resisted. Somers also criticized many of Birmingham's in-game decisions, declaring that the manager was using the hit-and-run too much and not bunting enough. Twenty-eight games into the season, Somers forced Birmingham's resignation and replaced him with Lee Fohl, but the disheartened club continued to struggle, finishing in seventh place.

Despite the club's on-field failures during this period, the franchise also enjoyed a few triumphs. In 1909 Somers renovated dilapidated League Park, replacing the old wooden structure with a steel-and-concrete edifice. In 1911 he successfully petitioned the Ohio General Assembly to allow for Sunday baseball, making Cleveland the third American League franchise (following St. Louis and Chicago) to host legal Sunday baseball. In 1912, under the advice of club vice president E.S. Barnard, Somers established the first farm system in baseball history, with franchises in Ironton (Ohio), Waterbury (Connecticut), Toledo (Ohio), New Orleans (Louisiana), and Portland (Oregon). Perhaps because the venture did not prove a success—although the system did eventually produce pitchers Jim Bagby and Stan Coveleski—Barnard and Somers's invention was largely ignored until Branch Rickey introduced the modern farm system with the St. Louis Cardinals in the 1920s.

By then, however, Somers had long since departed the major league scene. Financial difficulties proved to be the undoing for this self-made millionaire. An economic downturn in 1914 caused Somers's coal business and lake shipping investments to lose large amounts of money. This came at a bad time for Charles, who also had to pay his players higher salaries to compete with the Federal League. Even worse, that year the Tribe finished dead last both in the standings and at the turnstiles.

In January 1915, with Somers owing debts of $1.75 million, a consortium of his creditors took control of the Indians and his minor league clubs, though leaving Somers nominally in charge of team operations. Desperate for money, in August 1915 Somers traded Joe Jackson to Chicago for three players and $31,500 cash, but the infusion of money was not nearly enough to pay his debts. After the season the bankers gave Somers an ultimatum: "Get rid of the ball club or we'll get rid of it for you." Thus, early in 1916, Charles Somers, the man whom Ban Johnson would later credit for making "the American League's ambitious dreams become actual realities," was out of major league baseball.

Somers was divorced from his first wife, Cora, in 1906; later that year he married a 22-year-old model, Elsie J. Hubbard. After a second divorce he spent his post-baseball years with his third wife, the former Mary Alice Gilbert, and an adult daughter (Dorothy) from his first marriage.

Somers died at his island summer home at Put-in-Bay, Ohio, on June 29, 1934, after a lingering illness. He was buried at Lake View Cemetery in Cleveland. At the time of his death the 65-year-old Somers had rebuilt his personal fortune to more than $3 million.

FRED SCHULD

AMERICAN LEAGUE

FRANCIS "SILK" O'LOUGHLIN
UMPIRE, 1902–1918

In a crowded field of colorful characters, Silk O'Loughlin was among the most stylish and quotable umpires of the Deadball Era. During his 17 years as a major league umpire, O'Loughlin became known for the loud, clear voice with which he communicated his calls to the crowd. "The patrons of the game like to hear an umpire," he once explained. "I think, too, that it enlivens the game to have the decisions given in a sharp, brisk way." On the field O'Loughlin was a no-nonsense arbiter who stuck to his decisions and quickly ejected players and managers if they protested too vigorously. O'Loughlin was the first umpire to eject Ty Cobb from a game, when the Georgia Peach tried to stretch a triple into an inside-the-park home run, came up just a little bit short, and then dared to argue the call.

According to O'Loughlin, there was no such thing as a close call. "A man is always out or safe, or it is a ball or a strike," he declared. "The umpire, if he is a good man and knows his business, is always right. I am always right." Expounding further on his theology of umpiring, O'Loughlin once declared, "The holy prophets for religion and O'Loughlin for baseball, both infallible." A popular arbiter with fans and the press, Silk once ran (unsuccessfully) for the New York State Senate. Among his many claims to fame, O'Loughlin was behind the plate for seven no-hitters, a record unlikely ever to be equaled.

Francis O'Loughlin was born in 1870 in Rochester, New York, the sixth and youngest child of Irish immigrants Mary and Michael O'Loughlin. Michael, a railroad fireman, died when Frank was still a young boy, leaving Mary to raise the O'Loughlin clan. Frank spent a good part of his youth playing amateur baseball in the Rochester area. His curious nickname, Silk, was a moniker hung on him at an early age and referred to

his head of hair. O'Loughlin told a newspaper reporter from the *Rochester Evening Telegram* that "when I was a little duffer about five years of age my folks thought I was getting too old to wear the long silken curls that then hung artistically over my shoulders, so a relative snipped them off. Somebody called me 'Silk' and the name stuck. Now it is seldom any one calls me Frank." Other accounts say the curls were shorn by an aunt who did not like long hair on young boys, and the haircut angered some in the family, except his brother who teased, "Ta ta to the silken locks."

O'Loughlin's first umpiring experience came in an exhibition game between Rochester and a semipro team from Palmyra, New York, in 1895. The rivalry between the teams was heated, so finding a competent umpire was very important. O'Loughlin, nominated by an admirer, accepted the position. After the series of games both teams praised O'Loughlin's efforts. During the rest of 1895 and 1896, O'Loughlin umpired amateur and semipro baseball to, as he said, "get the necessary experience" to make it a full-time job.

His professional umpiring career began in 1897, when Ed Barrow, then president of the Atlantic League, tapped him. O'Loughlin worked in that league for most of the year and in the late season jumped to the New York State League in order to stay close to home. Moving up a few rungs in the minor league ladder, O'Loughlin umpired for the Eastern League from 1898 through 1901. Before the 1902 season American League president Ban Johnson came calling and O'Loughlin joined the new league, serving as one of its finest umpires for 17 seasons from 1902 through the war-shortened 1918 season.

As an umpire he was known for a loud and clear voice. O'Loughlin used his lungs to communicate his calls and believed it an important part of what he brought to the game. Around the American League, Silk was well-known for his patented "Strike Tuh!" and "He-z-zzz Out!" calls. Some observers credit him for developing arm signals as a means of communicating calls, but whether O'Loughlin, or any other umpire, actually can be credited for pioneering this device is uncertain.

What is certain is that O'Loughlin was also known as a sharp dresser, introducing creased trousers to his uniform. The crease was so sharp some players jokingly feared that getting too close would get them cut. Silk also was fond of a diamond ring that he wore on his right hand. He would sometimes refer to calling a base runner out by saying that he flashed the runner some cracked ice. Many players bitterly claimed O'Loughlin would call them out just so he could flash the ring.

O'Loughlin may have cut a fine figure on the field, but he was also superstitious, wearing a blue flannel shirt that dated back to his minor league days. He said he began wearing the lucky shirt back in 1898. During a game at Cortland in the New York State League, O'Loughlin incurred the wrath of fans, who after the game grabbed the ump and tossed him into a nearby river. The crowd wanted a confession, but O'Loughlin held his ground, saying the runner was out and the mob in turn made their point by holding Silk's head under water. With the help of a sympathetic farmer, O'Loughlin escaped, though wearing nothing but the shirt.

Silk was also concerned over the time of games and often suggested means to speed up play. O'Loughlin was known as a no nonsense man on the field, the only one of Johnson's umpires who could be called the tough cop on the beat. O'Loughlin said Ban Johnson helped make baseball a respectable profession by "eliminating rowdyism by giving his staff of umpires his unqualified support."

Silk's self-confidence and even arrogance as an umpire often rankled players and managers, who could be critical of his attitude. "O'Loughlin had a sharp tongue and a ready wit, which ball players tried to match, but invariably they came out second best," the *New York Times* once observed. "O'Loughlin was the best umpire in the business at squelching the freshness of the young players just graduated from the minor leagues." According to one story, when Clarence "Pants" Rowland first arrived in the major leagues as manager of the White Sox, O'Loughlin ejected him from a game for disputing a decision, saying, "What do you think this is—the Three Eye League? Remember, you are far away from Peoria now, Clarence."

If he was sometimes unpopular with players and managers, his flair for drama made him a darling of the media and the favorite umpire of many cranks during the Deadball Era. "Silk is a national institution," a wire service reporter declared in 1910. "His 'Strike Tuh!' is known from one end of the land to the other, and wherever it echoes it is known that Silk is still on the job and giving decisions behind the bat."

O'Loughlin married Agnes E. Swift in July 1905. After the war-shortened 1918 season Silk got a job as a security guard with the U.S. Justice Department, relocating to Boston and patrolling that city's munitions works and the shipyards where battleships were built. His brilliant umpiring career was tragically cut short in December 1918, when he and his wife fell victim to the influenza pandemic of 1918–1919. She recovered, but Silk did not, dying in Boston at age 48 on December 20 from complications of the illness that claimed the lives of hundreds of thousands of Americans (and millions of people worldwide).

On O'Loughlin's death umpire Billy Evans, a future Hall of Famer, noted that Silk was a great partner who worked every game as if it were his last. "Silk was a bundle of nerves," Evans said. "From the start of the game until the finish he was on edge. Baseball was a serious proposition for him." Silk O'Loughlin was buried in Holy Sepulchre Cemetery, in Rochester, New York. Agnes, upon her recovery, supported herself by running a boardinghouse in downtown Rochester.

DAVID ANDERSON

AMERICAN LEAGUE

William George Evans
Umpire, 1906–1927

Billy Evans had one of the most varied non-playing careers in baseball history. The third umpire to be inducted into the Hall of Fame, Evans umpired during most of the Deadball Era in the American League and from 1920 to 1927 augmented his umpire's salary by writing a syndicated sports column. After he retired as an umpire Evans served as general manager of the Cleveland Indians, farm director for the Boston Red Sox, and president of the Southern Association, before wrapping up his baseball career with a stint as general manager of the Detroit Tigers. He even served a year as general manager of the Cleveland Rams of the National Football League.

Known as Big Boy Blue or the Boy Umpire, Evans became, at 22, the youngest umpire to be hired by the majors when he joined the American League in 1906. Through his actions and on field judgment, Evans built a reputation as one of the fairest arbiters in the game. Unique among his peers, Evans openly admitted that he was fallible and could make mistakes. Having served as the man behind the plate for Walter Johnson's first major league game, Evans later confessed that Johnson's fastball sometimes came to the plate so quickly that he would close his eyes before making a call. "The public wouldn't like the perfect umpire in every game," he contended. "It would kill off baseball's greatest alibi— 'We wuz robbed.'" In 1947 his book *Umpiring from the Inside* was published. A superb umpire's manual, the book has withstood the test of time for its sound advice on the mechanics of umpiring and handling game situations.

Born in Chicago on February 10, 1884, Evans had a comfortable childhood. When he was still a young boy, the family moved to Youngstown, Ohio, where his father, a Welsh immigrant, worked as a superintendent in a Carnegie steel mill. Active in sports, Evans reportedly played football and baseball at Cornell University, although his name is conspicuously absent from Cornell football and baseball box scores of the era, and the

school's football records do not list him as ever being on the team.

Evans spent two and half years at Cornell studying law, before his father's death forced him to leave school. To help support his family Billy became a newspaper reporter for the Youngstown *Vindicator*, earning $10 per week. It was this line of work that led him to attend an outlaw Protective Association game between Youngstown and Homestead (Pennsylvania). When the regularly scheduled umpire failed to appear due to illness, Evans was persuaded to umpire the contest. He wound up working in the league for a few more days, and was then hired for $150 a month, a substantial increase from his newspaper salary. Between baseball seasons, he paid the bills by refereeing in the Ohio Polo League.

Evans umpired in the minors for just a couple of years in northeastern Ohio. In 1905 he stopped into a clothing store owned by St. Louis Browns manager Jimmy McAleer, who told Evans he had seen him umpire and liked what he saw. American League president Ban Johnson, acting on McAleer's advice, offered Evans $2,400 per year plus a $600 bonus to umpire in the American League. Evans said that looked like all the money in the world and claimed to break all speed records in getting his acceptance back to Johnson in a tersely worded telegram reply: "Yes and thanks!"

Evans quickly built a reputation as a "fair and square umpire" capable of handling any situation that arose on the diamond. He often said the trick of umpiring relied upon three talents: the ability to study human nature and apply the findings, the ability to be at the right angle to make a call, and the ability to bear no malice. Billy demonstrated this third skill in St. Louis in September 1907 when his skull was fractured by a bottle thrown by a 17-year-old fan after a controversial call. Immediately following the assault, Johnson came to St. Louis to announce he had hired an attorney and would prosecute the young offender. To his dismay, however,

Evans refused to press charges, saying the youth's parents were nice people and the kid had apologized for throwing the bottle. The incident sidelined Evans for the remainder of the season.

Evans was not a saint, however, and several times his stands led to post-game fights. In September 1921, for example, he was involved in a fist fight with Ty Cobb under the stands following a game. Cobb was irate over a call in the late innings. During the argument Cobb reportedly told Evans that he would whip him right at home plate, but would not do so because he knew he would be suspended. Evans invited Cobb to the umpires' dressing room for the post-game festivities. The brawl itself took place under the stands, with players from both teams forming a ring for the combatants. According to some accounts of the incident, many Detroit players rooted for Evans. Several witnesses later said the fight, which ended in a draw, was the bloodiest they had ever seen. Evans umpired the next game wearing bandages, and Cobb was suspended for the final two games of the season.

Among his colleagues Evans was well known as a mentor for young umpires, generous with his time and advice. Evans also became a strong advocate for the establishment of formal school training for umpires to meet the growing demand for officials. He was highly critical of organized baseball for doing little about the situation. Ironically, if the present day umpire school system had existed during the Deadball Era, Evans would probably have never gotten a chance to umpire in the major leagues. His umpiring philosophy sounds like something straight out of a handbook: "Good eyes, plenty of courage—mental and physical—a thorough knowledge of the playing rules, more than average portions of fair play, common sense and diplomacy, an entire lack of vindictiveness, plenty of confidence in your ability."

Evans could admit his mistakes, so long as no one expected the admission to change anything.

He once called a ball foul before it stopped rolling. When the ball struck a pebble and bounced back into fair territory, the manager of the team at bat rushed onto the field, cursing Evans and demanding he reverse his ruling. Billy responded, "Well, it would have been a fair ball yesterday and it will be fair tomorrow and for all years to come. But right now, unfortunately, it's foul because that's the way I called it."

Evans retired as an umpire in 1927 to become vice president and general manager for the Indians. During his years with Cleveland the team showed steady improvement on the field and Evans was credited with signing Tommy Henrich, Wes Ferrell, and Hal Trosky, among others. He left the Indians in 1935 because of a salary dispute, accepting a job as farm director for the Boston Red Sox. Evans was fired by owner Tom Yawkey in 1941, a year and a half after the club sold one of its prized prospects, shortstop Pee Wee Reese, to Brooklyn over Evans's objections. In June 1941 Evans became general manager of the NFL's Cleveland Rams, but lasted only one season, during which the Rams went 2–9. In December 1942 Evans was named president of the Southern Association. He remained in that position until 1946, when he took a job as executive vice president and general manager of the Detroit Tigers, a post he held until his retirement in 1951.

Evans was known as a good family man, though his baseball activities often kept him away from his Cleveland home. He married Hazel Baldwin in 1908 and the couple had one child, Robert, who enjoyed a successful career as a radio executive. Billy Evans died in Miami, Florida, on January 23, 1956, at age 71, after suffering a stroke while visiting his son. He was buried in Knollwood Cemetery in Mayfield Heights, Ohio.

DAVID ANDERSON

BOSTON

Between 1901 and 1919, the Boston Americans franchise won five world championships and led all American League clubs with 1,548 victories. Nevertheless, with six different owners and 12 managers in a 19-year span, the franchise was less a Deadball Era dynasty than a disparate series of talented teams that, from the outset, was graced by loyal fans who embraced them with passion and pride.

Thanks to the financial backing of Cleveland industrialist and first club owner Charles Somers, in 1901 Ban Johnson oversaw the establishment of a new American League franchise on new grounds on Huntington Avenue. Led by slugging outfielder-first baseman Buck Freeman and stalwart ace Cy Young, the club finished second and third in its first two seasons,

before capturing its first American League pennant under new owner Henry Killilea in 1903. That October, Boston defeated the Pittsburgh Pirates five games to three in the first modern World Series.

The franchise changed hands again in the spring of 1904, when *Boston Globe* founder Charles Henry Taylor purchased the club and installed his 28-year-old son, John I., as president. Following a second consecutive pennant in 1904, Boston sputtered to fourth in 1905, and then crashed into the AL basement in 1906. Many blamed the club's demise on Taylor, whose trades of popular players like outfielder Patsy Dougherty sparked outrage across the city; Taylor, conversely, blamed it on the old age of his men. Relying on a combination of trusted scouts and remarkable luck, over the next three

WINNING PERCENTAGE 1901–1919

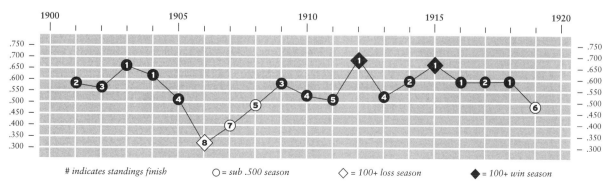

 # indicates standings finish ○ = *sub .500 season* ◇ = *100+ loss season* ◆ = *100+ win season*

years Taylor flushed away the remnants of the old team and assembled the new outfit, built around speed and youth. With Duffy Lewis in left, Tris Speaker in center, and Harry Hooper in right, the rechristened "Red Sox" boasted one of the greatest outfields of all-time. Aided by the emergence of hard-throwing right-hander Smoky Joe Wood, in 1912 the club celebrated the opening of Fenway Park by winning 105 games and besting the New York Giants in a thrilling eight-game World Series.

Though Wood fell victim to injury and Speaker was traded to the Cleveland Indians prior to the 1916 season, the Red Sox continued to rack up championships, winning the World Series in 1915, 1916 and 1918. They were aided by a new generation of pitchers, including Ernie Shore, Dutch Leonard, and Babe Ruth. But having won five world championships in their first 18 seasons, the Red Sox would not win another title for 86 years. In 1919, the club finished a disappointing sixth, despite Ruth's transformation into the game's most feared slugger. Following the season, owner Harry Frazee sold Ruth to the New York Yankees, ending the franchise's greatest era and setting the stage for a lifetime's worth of heartbreak.

MICHAEL FOSTER

ALL-ERA TEAM

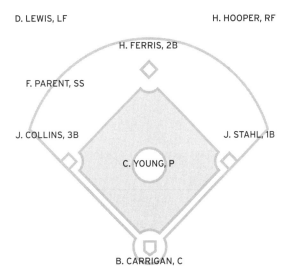

T. SPEAKER, CF

D. LEWIS, LF   H. HOOPER, RF

H. FERRIS, 2B

F. PARENT, SS

J. COLLINS, 3B   J. STAHL, 1B

C. YOUNG, P

B. CARRIGAN, C

TEAM LEADERS 1901–1919

BATTING

GAMES
H. Hooper 1508
D. Lewis 1184
L. Gardner 1123

RUNS
H. Hooper 897
T. Speaker 704
F. Parent 519

HITS
H. Hooper 1540
T. Speaker 1327
D. Lewis 1248

RBI
D. Lewis 629
T. Speaker 542
B. Freeman 504

DOUBLES
D. Lewis 254
T. Speaker 241
H. Hooper 216

TRIPLES
H. Hooper 113
T. Speaker 106
B. Freeman 90

HOME RUNS
B. Ruth 49
B. Freeman 48
T. Speaker 39

STOLEN BASES
H. Hooper 284
T. Speaker 267
H. Wagner 141

BATTING AVERAGE
(2000+ plate appearances)
T. Speaker 337
J. Collins 296
C. Stahl 290

PITCHING

GAMES
C. Young 327
J. Wood 218
G. Winter 213

WINS
C. Young 192
J. Wood 117
D. Leonard 90

LOSSES
C. Young 112
G. Winter 97
B. Dinneen 85

INNINGS
C. Young 2728⅓
G. Winter 1599⅔
B. Dinneen 1501

STRIKEOUTS
C. Young 1341
J. Wood 986
D. Leonard 771

WALKS
B. Ruth 425
J. Wood 412
D. Leonard 412

SHUTOUTS
C. Young 38
J. Wood 28
D. Leonard 25

ERA
(800+ innings pitched)
J. Wood 1.99
C. Young 2.00
E. Shore 2.12

TYPICAL LINEUPS 1901–1919

Though some in the Deadball Era came pretty close, no major league team uses an identical lineup and batting order over the course of an entire season. That was especially true during the war-muddled 1918 season, when many players were forced to "work or fight." For that reason we present two lineups for 1918: one for the first half and another for the second half.

1901

1. T. Dowd, LF
2. C. Stahl, CF
3. J. Collins, 3B
4. B. Freeman, 1B
5. C. Hemphill, RF
6. F. Parent, SS
7. H. Ferris, 2B
8. O. Schrecongost
   L. Criger, C

1902

1. P. Dougherty, LF
2. J. Collins, 3B
3. C. Stahl, CF
4. B. Freeman, RF
5. F. Parent, SS
6. C. LaChance, 1B
7. H. Ferris, 2B
8. L. Criger, C

1903

1. P. Dougherty, LF
2. J. Collins, 3B
3. C. Stahl
   J. O'Brien, CF
4. B. Freeman, RF
5. F. Parent, SS
6. C. LaChance, 1B
7. H. Ferris, 2B
8. L. Criger, C

1904

1. K. Selbach, LF
2. J. Collins, 3B
3. C. Stahl, CF
4. B. Freeman, RF
5. F. Parent, SS
6. C. LaChance, 1B
7. H. Ferris, 2B
8. L. Criger, C

1905

1. K. Selbach, RF
2. F. Parent, SS
3. J. Burkett, LF
4. J. Collins, 3B
5. C. Stahl, CF
6. M. Grimshaw, 1B
   B. Freeman, 1B–RF
7. H. Ferris, 2B
8. L. Criger, C

1906

1. J. Hayden, RF
2. F. Parent, SS
3. C. Stahl, CF
4. H. Ferris, 2B
5. J. Hoey, LF
   B. Freeman, RF–1B
6. M. Grimshaw, 1B
7. R. Morgan, 3B
8. C. Armbruster, C

1907

1. J. Barrett, LF
2. D. Sullivan, CF
3. B. Congalton, RF
4. B. Unglaub, 1B
5. H. Ferris, 2B
6. J. Knight, 3B
7. H. Wagner, SS
8. L. Criger
   A. Shaw, C

1908

1. J. Thoney, LF
2. H. Lord, 3B
3. A. McConnell, 2B
4. D. Gessler, RF
5. J. Stahl, 1B
6. D. Sullivan, CF
7. H. Wagner, SS
8. L. Criger, C

1909

1. H. Niles, LF
2. H. Lord, 3B
3. T. Speaker, CF
4. D. Gessler, RF
5. H. Wagner, SS
6. J. Stahl, 1B
7. A. McConnell, 2B
8. B. Carrigan, C

1910

1. H. Hooper, RF
2. H. Lord, 3B
3. T. Speaker, CF
4. J. Stahl, 1B
5. L. Gardner, 2B
6. D. Lewis. LF
7. H. Wagner, SS
8. B. Carrigan, C

1911

1. H. Hooper, RF
2. L. Gardner, 3B–2B
3. T. Speaker, CF
4. D. Lewis, LF
5. C. Engle, 1B–3B
6. H. Wagner, 2B
   R. Williams, 1B
7. S. Yerkes, SS
8. B. Carrigan
   L. Nunamaker, C

1912

1. H. Hooper, RF
2. S. Yerkes, 2B
3. T. Speaker, CF
4. D. Lewis, LF
5. L. Gardner, 3B
6. J. Stahl, 1B
7. H. Wagner, SS
8. B. Carrigan, C

1913

1. H. Hooper, RF
2. S. Yerkes, 2B
3. T. Speaker, CF
4. D. Lewis, LF
5. L. Gardner, 3B
6. C. Engle, 1B
7. H. Wagner, SS
8. B. Carrigan, C

1914

1. H. Hooper, RF
2. E. Scott, SS
3. T. Speaker, CF
4. D. Lewis, LF
5. H. Janvrin, 2B–1B
   D. Hoblitzell, 1B
6. L. Gardner, 3B
7. S. Yerkes, 2B
8. B. Carrigan, C

1915

1. H. Hooper, RF
2. H. Wagner, 2B
   E. Scott, SS
3. T. Speaker, CF
4. D. Hoblitzell, 1B
5. D. Lewis, LF
6. L. Gardner, 3B
7. J. Barry, 2B
8. H. Cady
   P. Thomas, C

1916

1. H. Hooper, RF
2. J. Barry, 2B
3. D. Lewis, LF
4. D. Hoblitzell, 1B
5. T. Walker, CF
6. L. Gardner, 3B
7. E. Scott, SS
8. P. Thomas, C

1917

1. H. Hooper, RF
2. J. Barry, 2B
3. D. Hoblitzell
   D. Gainer, 1B
4. D. Lewis, LF
5. T. Walker, CF
6. L. Gardner, 3B
7. E. Scott, SS
8. S. Agnew
   P. Thomas, C

1918 (first half)

1. H. Hooper, RF
2. D. Shean, 2B
3. A. Strunk, CF
4. G. Whiteman, LF
   B. Ruth, LF–P
5. S. McInnis, 1B
6. F. Thomas, 3B
7. E. Scott, SS
8. S. Agnew, C

1918 (second half)

1. H. Hooper, RF
2. D. Shean, 2B
3. A. Strunk, CF
4. B. Ruth, LF–P
5. S. McInnis, 1B
6. E. Scott, SS
7. G. Cochran
   J. Stansbury, 3B
8. S. Agnew, C

1919

1. H. Hooper, RF
2. O. Vitt, 3B
3. B. Roth
   A. Strunk, CF
4. B. Ruth, LF
5. S. McInnis, 1B
6. W. Schang, C
7. R. Shannon, 2B
8. E. Scott, SS

Jimmy Collins
BOSTON

JAMES JOSEPH COLLINS
THIRD BASEMAN, 1901–1907; MANAGER, 1901–1906

At the beginning of the Deadball Era, Jimmy Collins was considered baseball's greatest third baseman. Though small in stature, standing at just 5'7" and weighing but 160 pounds, his blazing speed and cat-like quickness helped him to revolutionize defense at the third sack, as Collins become the first to stymie the bunting attacks of opposing teams by playing in on the grass. One of the greatest bunters of the 1890s, John McGraw, described Collins as "the real pioneer of the modern style of playing third base" for his adeptness at handling bunts. Another observer, Ed Barrow, characterized Collins as "a sort of third base Hal Chase" for his alert, mobile brand of defense.

Fortunately for the Boston Americans, whom Collins managed to two American League pennants and one World Championship, the popular third baseman displayed more consistency and integrity than the infamous Chase, as he batted better than .300 five times during his 14-year major league career, and earned the respect and admiration of his fellow players for his honesty and commitment to the game. "He was very quiet in his manners and a favorite everywhere," wrote one observer. "He played his game, attended to his business and never scowled if getting what he might think is the small end. Collins was a model all players would do well to follow. It was no wonder that the umpires, one and all, spoke of him in enthusiastic terms. Collins showed that one does not need to be a rowdy or a kicker to achieve success on the diamond."

James Joseph Collins was born January 16, 1870, in Clifton, New York, a town just north of Buffalo which would change its name to Niagara Falls in 1881. He was the second of three sons of Anthony and Alice (O'Hare) Collins, Irish immigrants who had arrived in the United States in 1862. Anthony Collins worked as a police officer in Buffalo, eventually becoming a captain on the force. After graduating from Buffalo's St. Joseph College (which, despite its name, was a high school), Collins went to work for the Delaware, Lackawanna, and Western Railroad and played baseball with the North Buffalos in the Buffalo City League. It was with the North Buffalos that Collins's play caught the eye of Jack Chapman, manager of the Buffalo Bisons, then of the Eastern League. In 1893 Collins joined the Bisons, initially playing third base. But he was soon moved to the outfield, reportedly because he was "afraid of bunts."

After two fine seasons with Buffalo, Collins was sold to the Boston Beaneaters of the National League prior to the 1895 season. Collins started the 1895 season poorly however, hitting just .211 in his first 38 at bats before Boston loaned him to the Louisville club, subject to recall. During his 96-game tenure with the Colonels, Collins improved his hitting, posting a .279 mark with six home runs. More significantly, Collins resuscitated his defensive reputation, emerging as one of the game's brightest third basemen, at the vanguard of a style of play that would revolutionize how the position would be fielded for decades to come.

This dramatic change began during a game against the Baltimore Orioles and their vaunted bunting attack. After the Orioles bunting caused Louisville's regular third baseman to commit four errors, Collins was summoned from his right field position to play third, a position he had not manned since his minor league days. As reported by several newspaper accounts, the Orioles shortstop, Hughey Jennings, patted Collins on the back and told him that the Orioles weren't going to bunt any more that day. Collins's immediate response to Jennings was "that's all right, Hughey, bunt 'em down to me and I'll show you something." Collins had come to the conclusion that there was only one solution to the bunting game. A third baseman simply had to play in on the edge of the grass to give himself a chance against the "tap tactics of those fast guys." As the game progressed, sure enough, the Orioles' John McGraw dropped a bunt down the line. Collins raced in and threw underhand to quickly catch McGraw at first. Willie Keeler tried the same and Collins likewise nailed him at first. Four bunters in a row were thrown out by Collins before the Orioles quit bunting for the afternoon. Word of Collins' exploits against the Orioles quickly made its way around the league. Boston newspapers and fans clamored for his return to Boston from the Louisville club, and prior to the 1896 season Collins rejoined the Beaneaters.

In addition to providing stellar defensive play, Collins came up with career years in 1897 and 1898, batting .346 and .328, respectively, while leading the team in RBI each season and leading the entire league with 15 home runs in 1898. Thanks in large part to Collins's standout performances, the Beaneaters won back-to-back National League pennants. By 1900, the club had fallen on harder times, but Collins continued to shine, leading all third basemen in assists, putouts, and double plays, and posting a .304 batting average with a team-high 104 runs scored.

Given his stature as the game's best third baseman, Collins's defection to the Boston Americans prior to the 1901 season became a major source of controversy, as Collins accepted a lucrative offer that made him the manager of the new club and provided him with a $5,500 salary and a $3,500 signing bonus. In subsequent years his salary would be raised to $10,000, and he received 10% of the Americans' profits over $25,000. The deal made Collins one of the highest-paid players in the game, but Beaneaters owner Arthur Soden still tried to lure him back with a salary offer of $5,000, and when that failed, accused him of deserting the franchise. Collins responded to Soden's insults by accusing him and the other NL magnates of artificially suppressing salaries. "I would not go back now if they offered me the whole outfit," he told reporters during spring training. "These National League magnates have a way of frightening a man into believing that he has committed a crime, and unless a player has a good, stiff backbone, he will usually cave."

Once signed by the Americans, Collins went in search of other strong-willed players to fill out his roster, and came away with Cy Young, Buck Freeman, Chick Stahl, and pitcher Ed Lewis, among others. Freeman batted

.339 and slammed 12 home runs, Young won pitching's Triple Crown, and Collins batted .332 with 108 runs scored as the Americans finished in second place, four games behind the Chicago White Sox. In 1902, Boston finished third, as Collins, limited by injuries to 108 games played, finished with a .322 average. The following year, Collins managed Boston to its first American League pennant, as the team finished with a 91–47 record, a stunning 14½ games better than the second-place Philadelphia Athletics. More than anything else, Collins's team won with great pitching, by Young (28–9), Tom Hughes (20–7), and Bill Dinneen (21–13), who had jumped his contract with the Boston Nationals to join Collins's outfit prior to the 1902 season.

With the peace settlement between the two leagues in place by 1903, Boston owner Henry Killilea agreed to play a best-of-nine World Series against the National League champion Pittsburgh Pirates. After falling behind three games to one in the Series, the Americans stormed back to take four straight, thanks in large part to the brilliant pitching of Dinneen and Young. For the Series, Collins batted .250 with five runs scored and one RBI, but his greatest contribution was his managerial savvy. For instance, after 20-game-winner Tom Hughes pitched poorly in his Game Three start, Collins benched him for the rest of the Series and relied exclusively on Dinneen and Young. After the Series, rumors emerged that Hughes's irresponsible behavior had caused a falling out between him and Collins, with at least one reporter, Pete Kelley, intimating that Collins suspected Hughes of attempting to throw the Series. "[Hughes] made bad breaks at the time of the world's series," Kelly obliquely observed. "He didn't behave himself and lost his popularity." After the season, Collins promptly traded Hughes to the New York Highlanders for pitcher Jesse Tannehill. Following Boston's World Series triumph, Collins made his way home to Buffalo where a brass band and jubilant fans met him at the train station. From the station he was paraded to Buffalo's Iroquois Hotel for a gala celebration.

Boston captured the American League pennant again in 1904, winning 95 games to edge the second place Highlanders by 1½ games in the standings. Again, Boston's pitching led the way, as Young, Dinneen, and Tannehill all won more than 20 games. In fact, for the entire season Collins used only five pitchers, and his staff completed a major league record 148 games, meaning that Collins relieved his starters only nine times the entire season. Unfortunately, Collins never got the opportunity to test his stalwart pitching against the National League champion New York Giants, as McGraw refused to play the American League champions, whom he described as a "bunch of bush leaguers."

Following their 1904 triumph, the roof quickly caved in on the aging Americans, as the club slipped to fourth place in 1905 and last in 1906, thanks in large part to a club-record 20-game losing streak. The club's sudden decline may have been due in large part to Collins's overzealous use of his pitchers in 1904; by 1906, Young, Dinneen and Tannehill all posted ERAs roughly one run higher than their 1904 figures. The 1906 Americans used 12 pitchers, and finished last in the league with a 3.41 team ERA. After watching his team lose 79 of its first 115 games, Collins was replaced as manager by Chick Stahl. By that time, Collins had been sidelined by a knee injury.

Collins appeared in 41 games for Boston in 1907, before management traded him to the Philadelphia Athletics for John Knight. Collins remained with the Athletics through the 1908 season, when he batted just .217 at the age of 38. Dropped by Philadelphia after that poor showing, Collins completed his professional baseball career as a player–manager for Minneapolis in the American Association in 1909 and Providence in the Eastern League in 1910–1911.

Upon his retirement from the game Collins returned to Buffalo, where he joined his wife, Sarah Murphy, whom he had married in 1907. The couple had two daughters. Thanks to some investments in South Buffalo real estate, Collins amassed a considerable fortune, most of which he lost during the Great Depression. Nonetheless, he did manage to live comfortably on his pay while working for the Buffalo Parks Department. On March 6, 1943, at the age of 73, Collins succumbed to pneumonia. He was buried in Holy Cross Cemetery in Buffalo. Two years after his death, Collins was elected to the Baseball Hall of Fame by a special Old Timers Committee, after missing election in several previous BBWAA votes.

STANTON HAMLET

Louis Criger

BOSTON

LOUIS CRIGER
CATCHER, 1901–1908

Feisty, slender and packing a strong, accurate throwing arm, the smarts to call pitches for the winningest pitcher of all-time, and the resiliency to last despite facing many physical ailments, catcher Lou Criger was regarded by his peers as one of the best backstops of the Deadball Era. At 5′10″ (some sources say six feet) and 165 pounds, Criger made an inviting target for bigger opponents, but the slender receiver took the punishment and held his ground. "Many players tackled Criger because he looked like a weakling," said Louie Heilbroner, who managed Criger in St. Louis before the respected receiver jumped to the American League. "But Criger would fight any six men on earth in those days, and if someone didn't pull them apart, Lou would lick all six by sheer perseverance."

A 1910 newspaper account described Criger as having light chestnut hair, porcelain colored eyes, a countenance something like Julius Caesar's and so slight that he "looks anything but athletic." But looks can deceive, as Criger proved by using his arm and his cunning as weapons worthy of journalist praise. Wrote Boston writer and former player Tim Murnane, "Criger is the man who can turn back the fleetest base runner, a man who can nip the boys at first and third unless they are ever on the alert. Criger is the backstop that never drops a ball that he can reach, and who can throw harder and quicker to second than any catcher in the profession....I would like to see some one pick out the equal of Criger."

Louis Criger was born on February 3, 1872, on a farm just south of Elkhart, Indiana, to Charles Criger, a cooper originally from Mecklenburg, Germany, and Lovina (Stutsman) Criger. Lou had five brothers, one of whom, Elmer, pitched in the minor leagues, winning 22 games with Jackson of the Southern Michigan League in 1909 and earning a place with Los Angeles

of the Pacific Coast League. In 1890, Lou Criger pitched for the Elkhart Lakeviews. The following year, he moved behind the plate, where he became a mainstay for the newly-organized Elkhart Truths. After spending five seasons playing for Elkhart, Criger was signed by the Michigan State League's Kalamazoo Kazoos in 1895. The following year, Lou began the season with the Fort Wayne Farmers of the Inter-State League, splitting his time between left field and catcher and typically batting third or fourth in the lineup. One of his Fort Wayne teammates was R.C. Grey, whose brother Zane, a semipro player, went on to fame as an author of Western fiction. Criger joined the Cleveland Spiders at the end of 1896, going hitless in five at bats. He began the following year as a third-string catcher for the Spiders, but when he finally got a chance to play, he dazzled observers with his powerful throwing arm, gunning down all six would-be Louisville base stealers on June 22, 1897. Criger took great pride in his throwing; he often sounded like a pitcher when he discussed his technique. "Now the way I throw the ball, it rotates backward and has an upward tendency, while some catchers throw with the thumb exposed and that gives it the downward effect, like the billiard draw shot, a ball that hurts to catch," he explained to the *St. Louis Post-Dispatch* in 1909.

In 1898, Criger became the Spiders' primary receiver, appearing in 82 games behind the plate and batting a modest .279 with one home run for the season. That turned out to be the best offensive performance of the right-handed batter's career. A classic example of the good-field, no-hit catcher, Criger batted just .221 during his 16-year-career, and never collected more than 22 extra base hits in a single season. He played because of his stellar defensive work, and his close relationship with Cleveland ace right-hander Cy Young.

From 1897 to 1908, wherever Young went, Criger joined him: with Cleveland in 1897 and 1898, St. Louis in 1899 and 1900, and the Boston Americans from 1901 to 1908. During those twelve seasons, Young won 283 games, and Criger was behind the plate for most of them. As *Sporting Life* put it in 1908, "What battery still serving in the major leagues has more inseparable service than the firm of Young and Criger?" In 1910, Young called Criger "the greatest catcher that ever stood behind the plate." Catching the burly hurler took its toll. Recalled son Harold Criger in 1988, "I remember when the ball hit the mitt, it sounded like a pistol shot, and when dad was home, he soaked his hand in hot water, and it was red as fire. Sometimes he put a slice of beefsteak in his mitt for more padding, and Cy beat it to bloody shreds." After the two parted ways, Young talked to the *St. Louis Post-Dispatch* about what the 1909 season might be like without Criger. Said Young, "In Criger, St. Louis will get one of the greatest catchers that ever donned a glove. I've pitched to him so long than he seems a part of me, and I am positive no one will suffer from the departure more than I. Lou is a great student of the game and knows the weaknesses of every batter in the league. So confident am I of his judgment that I never shake my head. It means that I have to learn a great deal about the batters, features to which I had heretofore paid no attention."

Criger was behind the plate for some of Young's greatest games, including his perfect game at the Huntington Avenue Grounds on May 5, 1904, and his no-hitter against the New York Highlanders at Hilltop Park on June 30, 1908. Criger also caught all 20 innings of Young's famous duel with Rube Waddell on July 4, 1905. In 1903, the backstop was behind the plate for every game of Boston's eight-game triumph over the Pittsburgh Pirates in the first modern World Series. Twenty years after that success, Criger revealed that he had turned down a $12,000 offer from a gambler named Anderson to call "soft pitches" during the Series. In 1923, Criger, believing he was dying of tuberculosis, hired an attorney to file an affidavit with American League president Ban Johnson, who went public with the incident. Johnson, impressed with Criger's honesty, personally established a pension that helped Criger and other players after their playing days.

During his playing career, Criger endured his share of bumps and bruises, a subject about which the catcher was particularly sensitive. While recuperating from a damaged finger during the 1901 campaign, Criger told *Sporting Life*, "They are very solicitous about my health. Just tell them for me that I am feeling perfectly well. I am out of the game just now with a bad finger, but will be in all right, and think I am good for many more years of ball playing before I quit. Every now and then someone sends me a clipping in which it is stated that I am not well. It is extremely annoying, not only to me, but to my folks."

Nonetheless, Criger became so associated with injury that he later became a spokesman for the Elkhart-based Dr. Miles' Anti-Pain Pills.

With battery-mate Cy Young nearing the end of his career, Criger was traded to the St. Louis Browns in December 1908 for catcher Tubby Spencer and $5,000 (some sources say $4,000). In one season with St. Louis, Criger batted just .170 with two extra base hits in 212 at-bats. After the season, Criger was again traded, this time to the New York Highlanders for pitcher Joe Lake and outfielder Ray Demmitt. Criger appeared in only 27 games for the Highlanders and batted just .188. The following year he played briefly for Milwaukee of the American Association and was player–manager for Boyne City of the Michigan State League. In 1912, Criger returned to the American League as pitching coach for the Browns. The 40-year-old played in one game when both Browns catchers got hurt.

Criger, his wife—the former Belle Louise Wolhaupter, whom he married in 1893—and their six children lived in Elkhart until 1909, when the family moved 22 miles northeast to a 40-acre farm at Bair Lake, Michigan. There, he spent many an off-season hunting and fishing with his ball-playing friends. In 1914, Criger developed tuberculosis in his left knee, and the following year his leg had to be amputated above the knee. In failing health, Criger moved to Nevada in the early 1920s and in 1924 relocated to the arid climate of Arizona, spending winters in Tucson and summers in Flagstaff. The family ran a bakery in Tucson. In 1920 Criger's son Rollo, also a catcher, joined the St. Louis Cardinals but never appeared in a game.

Criger died on May 14, 1934 in Tuscon and was buried in Evergreen Cemetery in that city. A Northern Indiana SABR chapter was named for Criger in the spring of 1998.

STEVE KRAH

BOSTON

ALBERT SAYLES "HOBE" FERRIS
SECOND BASEMAN, 1901–1907

At 5′8″ and 162 pounds, slick-fielding second baseman Hobe Ferris looked the part of a light-hitting middle infielder, an initial impression supported by his lifetime .239 batting average and .265 on-base percentage. But looks can be deceiving, as Ferris was one of the hardest hitters in the junior circuit. Of the right-hander's 1,146 career hits, 28% of them went for extra bases, a ratio exceeded only by 10 other American Leaguers during the Deadball Era, and higher than such renowned sluggers as Ty Cobb, Frank Baker, Elmer Flick and Jimmy Collins. During his nine-year major league career, Ferris ranked in the league's top five in triples and home runs three times each. Defensively, Ferris was widely regarded as one of the best fielding second baseman of his time, and led the league in putouts twice, assists twice, and double plays once during his seven years with Boston. "At his best," the *Washington Post* observed in 1908, "[his defense] made Larry Lajoie look like a second-rater." A fierce competitor and notorious umpire baiter, the hot-tempered Ferris was later described by Fred Lieb as a "rough and tumble old time player that could take it and dish it out."

Most sources record Ferris as being born on December 7, 1877, in Providence, Rhode Island. However, the Rhode Island State Archives have no record of his birth in that state, and census records indicate that Albert Sayles Ferris was actually born in England, as were his parents, and immigrated to the United States in 1879. Having developed his baseball skills on the Providence sandlots, Ferris advanced to the next level by playing for a North Attleboro, Massachusetts team in 1898. One day the shortstop was missing, so Hobe, "with one side of his face swollen with a toothache," filled in and handled 22 chances perfectly, a feat that won him a starting position. Having kept himself in fine shape by playing polo during the off-season, Ferris reported to Pawtucket of the New England League in 1899. Despite an initial batting slump, Ferris finished with a .295 average and won accolades for his fielding. In 1900, the infielder joined Norwich in the Connecticut League, where he played shortstop and batted .292 with 31 extra-base hits.

Prior to the 1901 season, Ferris was drafted by the Cincinnati Reds, but instead opted to jump to the American League and play for the Boston Americans. That same offseason, shortstop Freddy Parent signed with the club, and Ferris shifted to second base.

It was initially a rough transition for Ferris, who committed 61 errors in 1901, the second-highest total by a second baseman in American League history. (That same year, Detroit second-sacker Kid Gleason committed 64 errors.) At the plate, the 23-year-old batted .250, drove in 63 runs, and led American League rookies with 15 triples.

The following year, Ferris again drove in 63 runs while smashing eight home runs (tied for seventh best in the league) and smacking 14 triples. His glove work also showed signs of improvement, as he committed 22 fewer errors in the field and showed brilliant range. In one June contest, Ferris recorded 11 putouts, and on another occasion he accepted 26 chances over two consecutive games.

But it was Ferris's numerous run-ins with umpires which garnered the most attention. In May, Ferris tangled with umpire Jack Sheridan and received a three-day suspension from American League president Ban Johnson. "Ferris deserves his suspension, and while it will hurt Collins' club, I am glad of it," wrote Peter Kelley of the *Boston Journal*. "We do not want any of the John McGraw biz in Boston, and the sooner that certain players become reconciled to that fact the better it will be for Boston baseball lovers. I hope this will be a lesson for Hobe, for if he behaves, he will make a big name for himself."

Ferris never reformed his ways, but he remained an integral part of the Boston club as it captured the 1903 American League pennant. In August, the second baseman's defense led to two victories in a doubleheader against St. Louis. "When the Browns broke into a rally Hobe cut them down with a triple play in one game and worked a double in the next that thrilled 19,000 fans," reported one observer. "Retiring five men on two chances is quite an achievement for one day." For the season Ferris batted an unimpressive .251, but swatted a career-high nine home runs and scored a career-best 69 runs. In the Americans' World Series triumph over Pittsburgh, Ferris recovered from a poor showing in the first game, in which he committed two errors (and briefly raised suspicions that Boston had thrown the game), to make a spectacular unassisted double play on a Honus Wagner line drive in Game Two, preserving a 3–0 Boston victory. In the eighth and final game, Ferris drove in all three Boston runs off Deacon Phillippe to secure the franchise's first world championship.

In 1904, Ferris slumped badly at the plate, as his batting average dipped to .213, but he figured prominently in Boston's narrow victory in the American League pennant race, as he scored from second base on a fly ball and error on the season's penultimate day to give Boston a 1–0 victory. It marked the final team triumph of Ferris's major league career, as the aging Boston roster unraveled from 1905 to 1907. Still in his prime, Ferris continued to post low batting averages while ranking among the league leaders in extra base hits and providing Gold Glove-caliber defense at second base. He also continued to make headlines whenever his nasty temper flared on the ball field, as occurred on September 11, 1906.

In that afternoon's game against the New York Highlanders at Hilltop Park, Boston outfielder Jack Hayden took a leisurely route on a fly ball hit to short right field, which Ferris himself failed to go after, resulting in an inside-the-park home run. Returning to the bench at the end of the inning, Ferris initiated a vile verbal attack on Hayden for what he perceived as lackadaisical play. Hayden, in turn, landed three stingers to Hobe's jaw. After their teammates separated

them, Ferris braced himself on a rail and thrust his foot into Hayden's face, knocking out several teeth. The fisticuffs continued and eventually both men were arrested. Neither player pressed charges, but in response to what one reporter called "the most disgraceful affair ever predicated by any ball players on the ball field," Ban Johnson suspended Ferris for the remainder of the season. For his part, Hobe declared, "I suppose I'm a fool for being in earnest and trying to win, but that is my way. I can't help it." Ferris lasted one more season in Boston, before owner John Taylor dealt him to the St. Louis Browns in a six-player trade. Explaining the move, Taylor suggested that Hobe had "outlived his usefulness."

Ferris enjoyed perhaps his best season as a professional in 1908, as he posted career highs in batting average (.270), on-base percentage (.291), and RBI (74). Because Jimmy Williams was already established at second base, Ferris shifted to third, where he combined with shortstop Bobby Wallace to form what one writer called "the stonewall defense." Hobe adjusted very well to his new position, as he led the league's third basemen in putouts, double plays, and fielding percentage. Browns manager Jimmy McAleer was effusive in his praise of Hobe. "I have been in the game a long while, but I have never seen a man play such remarkable ball for a team as has Ferris for us.... You never see him that he is not hustling."

The 1909 campaign, however, was a disappointment, as Ferris's average plummeted to .216. Hobe claimed he had a difficult time getting in shape, and as his season deteriorated, his frustration level spiraled to the point where a sportswriter sarcastically wrote that Ferris "has a sweet disposition when he is not getting his share of base hits." In one incident he hit a fly ball to left, and on his return to the dugout complained to Tom Hughes, the pitcher, "I ought to have killed that one." The Washington hurler retorted, "You hit like an old woman." Hobe applied "a few choice names to Hughes who was willing to stop the ball game while he got at Ferris. Umpire Egan, however, waved him back and prevented hostilities."

After the 1909 season, Ferris was released to Minneapolis of the American Association, where he produced respectable numbers for three seasons as his playing time gradually decreased. He spent the 1913 season with St. Paul in a utility role, before drawing his release. Ferris played one season for Wilkes-Barre of the New York State League before that club, too, released him. *Baseball Magazine* clarified the reasons for Hobe's decline: "Ferris is let out because he has slowed up both with arms and legs—finds it hard to make the throw to first, hard to stoop quickly for fast grounders."

By 1920, Ferris, his wife Helena and their daughter Natalie, had established roots in Detroit, where Hobe worked as a mechanic and occasionally played for semipro teams. As the years passed, however, Ferris became obese. On March 18, 1938, Hobe came across a newspaper account of ex-Tiger "Fatty" Fothergill's hospitalization. As he informed his wife of this story, Ferris died of a heart attack. He was 60 years old.

DENNIS H. AUGER

John "Bucky" Freeman

BOSTON

JOHN FRANK "BUCK" FREEMAN
RIGHT FIELDER, 1901–1907

The first legitimate home run hitter in baseball history, Buck Freeman escaped the coal mines of Northeastern Pennsylvania to become one of the premier sluggers during the first decade of the American League. Freeman won seven home run titles during his professional career, and his astonishing 25 homers for the Washington Senators in 1899 shocked the baseball world. After jumping to the Boston Americans, Freeman played a key role in that club's capture of the 1903 World Series and 1904 pennant. Umpire Tim Murnane called Freeman "the batting wonder of the age." The *Washington Post* agreed: "Modern base ball has never produced his like," a *Post* reporter wrote. "Even the eagle-eyed Anson, the slugging Brouthers of the falcon-eye, the mighty Tip O'Neill…all move back a niche in the game's history, and make room for one who is their master." Freeman broke the single-season home run records in the New England League, Eastern League, and American Association, while nearly doing the same in both the American and National leagues. During his peak from 1899 through 1905, Freeman led all major league players with 77 home runs, outdistancing his nearest competitor, Nap Lajoie, by 28.

John Frank Freeman was born on October 30, 1871, in Catasauqua, Pennsylvania, near Allentown, to Irish immigrants John and Annie Freeman. The elder John Freeman, born in Ireland at the height of the potato famine, emigrated to Pennsylvania in 1865. When young John was eight years old, the family moved to coal mining country near Wilkes-Barre, where first the father and later the son found work at what was reputed to be the largest coal breaker in the world. Young John lied about his age to get the job, and worked his way up from slate picker to – at age 12 – the more glamorous job of mule driver. Much to the dismay of his parents,

John found he liked baseball more than the mines, and starred as a pitcher on various local semipro teams. In 1891 the Washington Statesmen of the major league American Association gave Freeman a trial, but the 19-year-old southpaw quickly earned his release by walking 33 batters in five games.

Back in Wilkes-Barre, Freeman began pondering the sage advice given him a few years earlier by Bud Fowler, the first African-American player in professional baseball, who had reportedly witnessed the 16-year-old Freeman hit two home runs in an 1888 sandlot game. "I never gave batting a thought until Fowler tipped me off," Freeman said. "You have pretty good control of the ball for a left-handed pitcher, kid," Freeman claimed Fowler told him. "But batting is your hold. Keep on practicing with the stick. It will get you more money." Freeman pitched for Wilkes-Barre's Eastern League squad in 1893 before moving on to Haverhill, Massachusetts, where in 1894 he destroyed the New England League in his first season as a full-time hitter. Buck won the batting title at .386, while clubbing 34 home runs (including four in one game) and driving in a whopping 167 runs. After a brief stint with Detroit in 1895, the latter half of that year found Freeman in Toronto, where he would spend four seasons. Buck's "wicked bat made the hearts of the Eastern League pitchers quake with craven fear," according to one reporter. The free-swinging Freeman slugged 20 homers for the Toronto Canucks in 1897 and a league-record 23 in 1898.

At the conclusion of the 1898 Eastern League season, Toronto manager Arthur Irwin took over as skipper of the NL's Washington Senators. He took five of his best players with him to Washington, including Freeman, who was given a month to "make good" or be sent back to the minors. On September 14, after a seven-year absence from the major leagues, Buck made his National League debut and in his second at-bat, drove the ball deep into the right field bleachers for his first major league homer. Freeman impressed the Washington press corps by hitting the ball hard six times in eight at-bats during his debut doubleheader. "Freeman has a free, natural swing," the *Washington Post* reported. "His position at the bat indicates a natural hitter." Buck turned in a two-homer game five days later, and his .364 average and .523 slugging percentage during his 29-game trial eliminated any possibility of returning to Toronto.

Unlike almost every other hitter of the day, Freeman's batting style was to swing from the heels, and for the fences. Umpire Pop Snyder compared Freeman's batting approach to the pugilistic style of then-World Heavyweight Champion Bob Fitzsimmons. "When Fitz drives one of his pile-driver favorites into the enemy the blow is supported by the force of the body," Snyder said in 1898. "Freeman seems to push his full weight against the ball... he meets the ball about half way in a well-gauged, sweeping stroke. But his knack of meeting the ball is supported by a keen, correct eye for judging the angles." Freeman, an amateur boxer himself, was no doubt flattered by the comparison to the heavyweight champ.

In 1899 Freeman became the talk of baseball, clouting an unheard-of 25 home runs in his first full major league season. He also batted .318, slugged 25 triples, scored 107 runs while driving in 122, and even stole 21 bases during what still stands as one of the greatest rookie seasons in baseball history. Reds manager Buck Ewing called the rookie "one of the greatest batsmen that ever came into the League." John McGraw publicly lusted after Freeman's services, calling him "the best developer of heart disease among pitchers." Meanwhile, Irwin, Freeman's manager, claimed that half of Buck's homers had come on hit-and-run plays, and praised him as "one of the best natural batsmen I have ever seen." Not everyone was so pleased, however. The 1900 *Spalding Guide* virulently denounced Freeman without ever mentioning him by name, excoriating "sluggers" whose "sole object was to hit it out of sight." The *Guide* concluded that a good slap hitter was "worth a dozen of your common class of home-run hitters."

Although the *Washington Post* predicted that "his triumph at skirting the bases for homers will stand as a red-letter record for many a season to come," Freeman's 25 round-trippers were not technically the major league record. In 1884, Chicago's Lake Front Park boasted distances of 180 feet to the left field fence and 196 feet to right. Four White Stockings took advantage of these cozy dimensions to post 20-homer seasons, led by Ed Williamson with 27. Until 1899, they were the only four 20-homer seasons in major league history, and because of their illegitimate nature, Freeman's mark of 25 in 1899 was widely considered the standard until Babe Ruth arrived.

Freeman didn't need short porches to pad his home run totals; he was noted for holding distance records at several different ballparks. In 1899, Buck slugged what Ned Hanlon and others described as the longest home run ever hit at Brooklyn's Washington Park. "The ball sped far over a canvas awning in the right center corner of the lot," the *Washington Post* reported, "and was picked up by a small boy on the opposite side of the street, in front of a row of tenement houses half a block from the grounds." Although Freeman claimed the pitch was eight inches outside, he still had enough plate coverage to pull it to deepest right field. Meanwhile, in Louisville that year, a Freeman drive hit the wall of a distillery 50 feet behind the outfield fence. In Washington, he smashed two opposite-field drives off the distant left field scoreboard. On August 20, 1903, Freeman became the first man ever to hit the ball completely out of Chicago's South Side Park. And at Philadelphia's Columbia Park, he once hit a ball so far that it reportedly sailed out of the stadium, over several houses, and through an open second-story window.

As part of the National League's contraction from twelve teams to eight before the 1900 season, the Washington club went out of business. On February 9, 1900, owner J. Earl Wagner sold off eight of his best players, including Freeman, Bill Dinneen, and Shad Barry to the Boston Beaneaters for $8,500. Freeman, who made a point of never engaging in holdouts, immediately agreed to a $2,000 contract with Boston for 1900. Even the Boston papers called Washington's dumping of Freeman and the others "the rankest offense ever perpetrated on a sport-loving public."

Freeman batted a solid .301 in 1900, but did not get along with Beaneaters manager Frank Selee, who, like the *Spalding Guide*, abhorred Buck's power-hitting ways. "I know the Boston public like to see Freeman in the game, as he is likely to hit the ball very hard at times," Selee said. "But this style of play is not a winner, for when Freeman is dangerous the pitchers keep the ball away from him, and his hitting counts for little. He is a poor fielder, thrower, and base runner." Although previous observers in Washington had called Freeman's outfield defense "above average," Selee's comments were the start of a bad defense rap that would follow Freeman the rest of his career. Meanwhile, Boston's season spun out of control, with the franchise posting its first losing season in 14 years. "The Boston team is now playing every man for himself, and floundering about like a ship without a rudder," Tim Murnane wrote in the *Boston Globe*. The "Napoleon-like" Selee pounced upon Freeman as a scapegoat, leaving him off the traveling squad for a late-season road trip and insulting him in the press: "I have often thought of playing [Freeman] at first and trying Tenney in the outfield," Selee said, "but brains are needed in the infield."

It was no surprise, then, that Freeman chose to jump to the fledgling American League in 1901 rather than play for a manager who openly despised him. In March Buck signed a contract with the Boston Americans and rebounded to have one of his best seasons, ranking third in the AL batting race at .339 while finishing second to Nap Lajoie in homers (12), RBI (114), and slugging percentage (.520). Freeman also contributed several game-winning hits in the ninth or extra innings, helping the Americans to a second-place finish in their inaugural season. Freeman posted equally strong numbers in 1902, finishing second with 11 homers while leading the AL in extra-base hits (68) and RBI (121).

Ballplayers of Freeman's day shunned conditioning and weight training, often believing that it would make them muscle-bound and restrict their movements. "The successful ballplayer never hardens his muscles," Ty Cobb wrote in 1913. But Freeman was a notable exception. Indeed, he was a forerunner of the power-hitting workout gurus of the 1990s. A dedicated member of the local gym in his offseason home of Wilkes-Barre, Freeman kept himself in shape by walking 12 miles a day in addition to weightlifting, parallel bars, boxing, and other activities. "What work I have done as a batsman I owe in large measure to my exercise in the gymnasium," Freeman said, "which…developed the muscles that come into play when I hit the ball."

Freeman also carefully studied the mechanics of hitting, adapting his stance to get as much of his weight behind the swing as possible. "I gather myself for a swing, and, as a rule, take a forward step in order to place myself at such an angle that the whole weight of my body moves at once in the same direction as the bat." This approach to hitting was enhanced when Freeman began playing for Irwin, who spent long hours in Toronto teaching the dead pull hitter how to hit for power to the opposite field. Freeman was also an expert at intentionally fouling off pitches he didn't like—a practice which, though commonly accepted today, was illegal during Buck's career. On August 15, 1899, umpire Hank O'Day enforced the little-used rule against Freeman, calling a strike against him (foul balls did not yet count as strikes) for intentionally fouling off a Cy Young pitch.

In 1903 Freeman was the best hitter on Boston's World Championship team, winning his second consecutive RBI title with 104 while also pacing the league in home runs (13), extra base hits (72), and total bases (281). He thus became the first hitter ever to lead both the National and American leagues in home runs, later to be joined by Sam Crawford, Fred McGriff, and Mark McGwire. That October Freeman played a key role in helping Boston win the inaugural World Series, batting .290 with three triples in the eight-game Series. Freeman continued to bludgeon opposing pitchers in 1904, leading the league with 19 triples while finishing second in RBI (84) and tying for second in homers (7).

In 1905, however, the 33-year-old Freeman slipped dramatically, his batting average dropping 40 points to .240, while he failed to finish among the league leaders in home runs for the first time since 1898. In 1905 he also ended his impressive streak of playing 541 consecutive games and 5,431 consecutive innings, the latter a record which would stand until broken by Cal Ripken in 1985. In 1906 Freeman's downhill slide continued, as he posted a .302 on-base percentage with only one homer in 436 plate appearances. When Freeman started off the 1907 season 2-for-12, Boston gave up on him, selling him to the Washington Senators on April 24 for the waiver price of $1,000. But four days later, before Freeman played in a single game for Washington, the Senators sold him to Minneapolis.

Although the origin of his nickname is unknown, Freeman's popularity was such that later players with that surname were automatically dubbed "Buck". "Some day—but not in our generation," *Baseball Magazine* wrote in 1911, "it will be possible for a man named… Freeman to escape being called 'Buck.'" This phenomenon proved especially confusing in 1907, when there were three Freemans on the Minneapolis Millers, with the others dubbed "Buck II" and "Buck III" by the press. But the original Buck separated himself from the crowd, posting a .335 average while taking advantage of Nicollet Park's 279-foot right field fence to set a new American Association record with 18 homers. Freeman returned to Minneapolis in 1908, but his season ended in late July when he dislocated his right shoulder sliding into home plate. Despite playing only half a season, his 10 homers were still good enough to tie for the league lead.

Freeman recovered from the injury to serve as a player–manager in the outlaw Susquehanna League in 1910 and 1911, and in 1913 he embarked on a lengthy minor league umpiring career. After a game on August 9, 1913, the rookie arbiter was mobbed by 2,000 angry fans in Wilmington, Delaware. As a squad of a dozen policemen rushed him off the field, Buck was pelted with a hail of stones and bricks, several of them hitting him on the head. With Freeman still under police escort, the mob trailed him from the ballpark to a local saloon and then a trolley stop, where Freeman was finally able to board a car and escape safely. Unbowed by the riot, Freeman umpired for the next 13 years in the Tri-State League, Canadian League, International League, American Association, and even, apparently, a brief stint in the Negro Leagues. (An umpire named Buck Freeman is known to have worked the 1924 Negro League World Series. Since Freeman was an active minor league ump at the time, and since the Negro Leagues used white umpires then, it was almost certainly the same Buck Freeman.)

During his offseasons, though he didn't need the money, Freeman kept in shape by working as a stoker in the boiler room of a local silk mill. He spent much of his time cockfighting, and became well known as a breeder of fighting birds, keeping a flock of more than 100 gamecocks in his barn. Even a 1937 police raid on a cockfight at Freeman's home did not deter him. "I'd walk 20 miles to see a good cockfight," he once said. In October 1906, Freeman purchased the New Haven Blues of the Connecticut League; by 1910 the team had been renamed the Prairie Hens. After his retirement from umpiring, Freeman scouted for the St. Louis Browns from 1926 to 1933, then managed an outlaw team in Bloomsburg, Pennsylvania, for two years. After the 1935 season Freeman retired to the modest hillside home in the Georgetown section of Wilkes-Barre where he resided with his wife, the former Annie Kane (whom he had married in 1895), and their six sons. A well-known local institution, Freeman enjoyed regaling youngsters with tales from his playing days. "In Wilkes-Barre he was just like Babe Ruth," one of those youths recalled years later. "Every kid in town knew him." Buck Freeman died of a stroke in Wilkes-Barre on June 25, 1949, at age 77. He is buried at Evergreen Cemetery in nearby Shavertown.

ERIC ENDERS

BOSTON

ALFRED L. "FREDDY" PARENT
SHORTSTOP, 1901–1907

Sparkplug shortstop Freddy Parent, the "Flying Frenchman," led the Boston Americans with MVP-type seasons to the first modern World Series championship in 1903 and the American League pennant in 1904. An early American League star, Parent (along with teammate Buck Freeman) was its first iron man, playing in 413 consecutive games from the April 26, 1901, opener to September 25, 1903, surprising considering his aggressive playing style. Beset by injuries, including multiple head-beanings that hampered his play later in his career, Parent nevertheless ranked among the all-time American League leaders in several categories after its first decade, including second in games played and at bats, fourth in hits and sacrifice hits, and sixth in total bases.

Alfred (Frederick) L. Parent was born on November 25, 1875 in Biddeford, a predominantly textile community in southern Maine. He was the oldest of 10 children of Alfred, a fireman, and Celina (Paul) Parent, both French-Canadian immigrants. Freddy quit school at the age of 14 to labor in Biddeford's Laconia Mill harness shop for 65 cents a day. When not working, he enjoyed playing "scrub" ball in the city's back lots, captain of a team he helped organize. Parent moved to Sanford, Maine, at age 16, where he worked in the Goodall Worsted Company's weave-room and played amateur ball.

Parent married the former Fidelia LaFlamme in 1896 and had one child, Fred Jr. His "proposal" to the 16 year-old Fidelia included a conditional baseball provision: "I want to marry you, but I do not want to work in the mill. Okay?" The young Fidelia, aware of his baseball desire and potential, replied "yes." Thus began a 67-year relationship.

The 5'5", 148-pound (some sources say 5'7") Parent's introduction to league play was a secondary role on the Sanford town team. "Everybody pretty nearly told me I was too small to play baseball and that I would never make a player anyhow." Once given the opportunity to start at shortstop for the town's first team, he developed into a strong infielder. Parent stretched his playing time by playing on teams in Maine and New Hampshire over the next two years.

Parent's first professional season came in 1898 with New Haven in the Connecticut League. Boasting one of the league's top averages at .326, Parent helped New Haven to a second place finish. In July 1899, the short-handed St. Louis Perfectos of the National League recruited Parent from nearby New Haven while they played the New York Giants. The Brooklyn Superbas had expressed an interest in Parent to replace the injured Hughey Jennings, and maintained the initial rights to him after paying New Haven $1,000 for his release. But the team changed their plans, and the Perfectos got Parent on a trial basis for the same offer.

Parent started at second base for two games, contributing to a Perfectos victory in the first game and getting two hits overall. But he suffered a sprained ankle and the Perfectos subsequently released him, stating he needed more experience in the minors. Parent returned to New Haven and helped them win the 1899 Connecticut League championship, finishing second in the league in batting (.349) and third in runs scored (76).

In 1900, Parent played shortstop for the champion Providence Grays in the more advanced Eastern League, batting .287 with 23 stolen bases, 21 doubles, six triples and four home runs. In March of 1901, Parent signed with the Boston Americans, where the sturdy little shortstop's solid hitting, fielding, base stealing, and hustle endeared him to the Boston fans.

A right-handed batter, Parent was a dependable hitter. He was a wrist hitter, slapping balls to all fields. He hovered over the plate with an exaggerated piece of lumber, a wagon-tongue bat of suspicious weight. Known as an excellent bunter, Parent also showed some power. In 1901, he augmented a .306 batting average with 36 extra base hits. The following year his average dipped to .275, but he also cranked a career-best 31 doubles. Crowding the plate enhanced his bunting and opposite field hitting, but it also exposed him to being hit by pitches. He ranked sixth in the American League in times hit by pitch in the first decade, including multiple blows to the head.

Parent was also a snappy infielder. An unassuming player with great range, Parent was a "little general" on the field. He compensated for his size with keen instincts, quickness, and dexterity covering the ground. In 1902 he led the league with 492 assists, and also set an AL record by fielding 20 chances without an error in a 17-inning matchup against the Athletics. Recognized for his superior fielding skills, Parent at times ranked low in fielding percentages, possibly attributable to his ability to get to balls and being a risk taker. The *Washington Post* affirmed this view when reporting the 1904 fielding statistics: "But fielding averages really do not demonstrate the value of any player, for there is Fred Parent, probably the foremost shortstop in the country occupying a position next to last."

With Hobe Ferris and "Candy" LaChance, Parent was part of the early Boston Americans' dynamic double-play combination. Like the famous National League keystone duo of Johnny Evers and Joe Tinker, Parent and Ferris went years without speaking to one another. Whereas they demonstrated spontaneous and effective teamwork on the field, off-field their association was one of unspoken enmity. Fortunately, the proud and quiet Parent and hotheaded Ferris's baseball instincts outweighed their lack of verbal discourse, which translated into defensive brilliance.

Parent enjoyed his best seasons as a professional in 1903 and 1904, when Boston won back-to-back American League pennants. In 1903, Parent posted a .304 batting average, and registered career-highs in triples (17, tied for fourth best in the league) and RBI (80, eighth best in the circuit.) In the first modern World Series in 1903, Parent outshined the legendary Honus Wagner of the Pittsburgh Pirates, outplaying him in the field and notching a batting average nearly sixty points greater than Wagner's for the Series. A "two-way standout Parent made several sparkling plays—cutting off a half dozen hits with great plays," and ended the eight-game series with 28 assists. He established a record for most runs scored with eight, eventually broken by Babe Ruth 25 years later. The newborn American Leaguers, considered "soft touches" for the senior circuit stars, came back from a three-to-one deficit to win the best-of-nine series.

The following year, Parent again enjoyed an outstanding season, batting .291 with 85 runs scored and six home runs, tied for fourth best in the league. But he was simply a passive observer in his most famous at-bat of the season, when 41-game winner Jack Chesbro of the New York Highlanders unleashed a wild pitch in the ninth inning on the last day of the season to bring in the run that won the pennant for the Americans. Forgotten to most, Parent followed this most famous wild pitch with a base hit that would have scored the run otherwise.

His hitting effectiveness declined considerably after the 1904 season, however, as he batted just .234 and .235 in 1905 and 1906, respectively. Parent's average rebounded to .276 in 1907, despite two head beanings that year which caused him to become an early proponent of the batting helmet. During the season he began sporting a pneumatic head protector. "Those two blows which felled me had an effect of making me timid whenever I faced the pitcher, and instead of stepping into the ball I was pulling away, the result being that I did not hit up to my standard." He claimed he would wear the protective gear for the rest of his career. However, while the "bombproof" headgear provided him security and reassurance, it spurred hazing and timorous, chickenhearted jousting. In the spring of 1908, Parent claimed he was no longer shy at the plate and discarded the headgear.

Parent's salary battles with owners were epic, as he constantly challenged baseball's moguls. When he first signed with Boston, he demanded an extra $300, and got it. In 1904, he demanded Boston match Cincinnati's John Brush's offer of $4,000 per year. He got it. In 1907, Red Sox owner John Taylor was in dire financial straits and proposed cutting Parent's reported salary of $4,250. Freddy was determined to hold out for a "fancy" salary, and did so until mid-April. This stunt cost him his starting shortstop job and precipitated his trade to the White Sox. In October the Red Sox traded Parent to the White Sox in a three-way trade with the Highlanders who got Jake Stahl from the White Sox and sent infielder Frank LaPorte to the Red Sox.

Parent struggled at the plate during the next three seasons, posting batting averages of .207, .261, and .178 from 1908 to 1910. In 1911, Parent staged his final battle with major league ownership. Coming off a strong spring training, Parent tangled with Chicago owner Charles Comiskey over his pay. After playing three games for the White Sox, Parent was sold to the Baltimore Orioles of the International League. Parent's tenure with the Orioles gave him opportunities to extend his career, gain coaching experience, and influence his former team's purchase of the greatest player ever.

In 1914, Baltimore owner Jack Dunn signed 19-year-old Babe Ruth, regarded as a great pitching prospect, but one who required guidance and mentoring.

Parent was proud of his work with Ruth. "I coached Babe more than anybody else at the time. I remember he was pitching in the late innings of a close game and there were two outs and the bases loaded and a dangerous left-handed hitter was up. He got two strikes on him, and I ran out and told him to *waste* a pitch. The next pitch he threw right up the middle. Oh, gee, a triple. Babe comes in and I said, 'What happened?' He said, 'I threw one *waist* high, didn't I?'" Parent later noted, "I used to see him later, after he was a big star, and I'd ask him how his 'waist pitch' was. He did not like it much."

The Orioles, despite their star-studded lineup, faced stiff competition from the nearby Baltimore Terrapins of the newly formed Federal League. The day after his team played to an attendance low of just 17 fans, the financially-stricken Dunn began a fire sale. In July 1914, he visited Red Sox owner Joe Lannin and player–manager Bill "Rough" Carrigan in Washington. Dunn took Freddie along as a reference Carrigan would trust. Carrigan sought Parent's advice "as one of the Orioles master-minds at the time and I figured he could give me the dope." Parent told Carrigan that while Ruth lacked finish, "he can't miss with a little more experience." Carrigan concurred with Parent's advice, with Lannin and Dunn closing the deal.

Parent never lost his enthusiasm for baseball. After Baltimore, he played for a short stint with Toronto of the International League. He also returned briefly to organized ball as player–manager with the Springfield, Massachusetts Eastern League team in 1918 and Lewiston in the New England League in 1919. From 1922 to 1924, Parent was a successful head coach at Colby College, and later assisted

former teammate Fred Mitchell as junior varsity coach at Harvard from 1926 to 1928.

In 1936, Parent was presented a Lifetime Pass by the American and National leagues in appreciation of long and meritorious service to the game. In 1969, Parent was elected to the Maine Baseball Hall of Fame. An avid outdoorsman who loved to hunt and fish, Parent spent the rest of his life in his home state. After professional ball, Parent dabbled in a few ventures, including owning and operating a boarding home and running a gasoline filling station for a number of years. Along with former teammate Harry Lord, he once tried to purchase a minor league team in Portland. He also unsuccessfully ran for county sheriff.

As the last survivor of the 1903 World Series and one of the last nineteenth century players, during his later years Parent was often sought out for interviews by reporters, and proved to be a strong advocate for the Deadball Era style of play. He described modern baseball as a different game, using "a rubber ball," with rosters composed of "mostly Class A ballplayers, with only three or four major leaguers on a club." Parent also described modern players and game conditions as timid in comparison to his rough-and-tumble days. "People get real excited when someone throws a paper cup or something at a player. They didn't throw those kinds of things in my days. They threw beer bottles. And they aimed at your head."

Freddy Parent died on November 2, 1972, three weeks shy of his 97th birthday, in Sanford, Maine. He was buried in Saint Ignatius Cemetery, in Sanford.

DAN DESROCHERS

BOSTON

Charles Sylvester "Chick" Stahl
Center Fielder, 1901–1906; Manager, 1906

Prior to committing suicide under mysterious circumstances in the spring of 1907, Chick Stahl had forged a reputation as one of the best center fielders in the game over the course of a 10-year major league career. A lifetime .305 batter, the left-handed Stahl could also hit with power, and ranked among the league leaders in extra base hits numerous times. Among his teammates, the popular Stahl "possessed a pleasing personality that endeared him to all that came in contact with him." When the 34-year-old ballplayer ended his own life on March 28, 1907, his Boston teammates were overcome with grief. "Stahl was a king among men," said catcher Lou Criger. "He was the squarest man I ever knew. He had only one fault—he was too generous. I never saw him go back on a friend or a deserving acquaintance. In fact, he was often bunkoed because he believed in the goodness of all mankind."

Charles Sylvester Stahl was born on January 10, 1873 in Avilla, Indiana, the sixth child of Reuben and Barbara (Stadtmiller) Stahl, both devout Catholics of German descent. During Charles's early childhood, his father supported the growing Stahl clan as a peddler, but in 1885 the family moved to Fort Wayne, where Reuben found work as a carpenter. In an 1898 interview, Charles reported that he had 23 siblings. "We had just enough in our family to make a couple nines—eighteen boys and half a dozen girls."

Young Charles attended Catholic school and developed his baseball skills on Fort Wayne's vacant lots and diamonds south of the railroads. After playing for Brunswick, a local amateur team, in 1889 the teenager hurled for the Pilsener club in the City League. Between 1889 and 1894, Stahl also twirled for semiprofessional teams in Paducah, Kentucky, Decatur, Illinois, and Kalamazoo and Battle Creek, Michigan. During this period, the left-hander plied his sport in the dual role of pitcher and outfielder. Chick also worked in his father's carpentry business, but the latter wanted him "to tend store at Fort Wayne and give up baseball. But I took an inventory of the soft soap sale and the output of pickles to our customers, and I couldn't figure how I could turn out the revenue in the grocery business that came to me in baseball."

In 1895, Stahl signed a professional contract with Roanoke of the Virginia League. At his own insistence, Stahl became a full-time outfielder, and excelled at his new position, playing brilliantly in the field, posting a .311 batting average, and leading the league with 13 triples. It was a performance that attracted the attention of Buffalo of the Eastern League, who drafted the young outfielder prior to the 1896 campaign. Stahl continued to show improvement with his new team, finishing the year with a .340 average, 34 stolen bases, 52 extra-base hits, and a league-leading 23 triples and 130 runs scored. Based on Chick's "splendid hitting and excellent fielding," Sam Wise and Jimmy Collins advised Boston Beaneaters manager Frank Selee to draft him.

Selee planned to use Stahl in a utility role, but within a brief period of time the 24 year old was the club's starting right fielder. In 1897, he emerged "as the game's most outstanding frosh hitter." Not only did he lead all rookies in 11 hitting categories, he also paced Boston with a .354 average, a mark which remains the franchise record for rookies. Stahl also topped the Beaneaters with a .499 slugging percentage, helping the Boston offense score more than 1,000 runs and capture the National League pennant. Another crown awaited Boston in 1898, and even though Stahl's average declined to .308, his fielding talents were highlighted in the sports pages. In one descriptive account, the *Washington Post* wrote "the soubrette fancier from

Fort Wayne retrieved Tommy Leahy's fly in the eighth with the speed and celerity of a hound retrieving a jack rabbit." The Beaneaters fell from first in 1899 but the "Husky Hoosier," while hitting .351, produced career highs in hits (202), triples (19), homers (7), total bases (284), walks (72), on-base percentage (.426), stolen bases (33) and runs scored (122). On May 31, he went 6-for-6 in a nine-inning game against Cleveland, "five of which [were] very long drives."

Boston's fortunes tumbled in 1900 but Stahl still knocked in 82 runs, his second highest career total, and led all National League outfielders with a .968 fielding percentage. In 1901, his teammate and best friend Jimmy Collins signed with the American League's Boston entry to become that squad's player–manager. Because of religious tension on his previous team, the third baseman targeted talented Roman Catholic ball players to join the upstart club. Considered a devout Catholic and one of the National League's best outfielders, Chick fulfilled the criteria. The intra-city jumper became one of the Americans' main offensive threats while moving to center field, helping the squad to a second place finish. As for the character of this 5'10" 160 pound athlete, it was visibly demonstrated in a late August contest. After rookie umpire Joe Cantillon made a call that went against the home team, furious Boston fans assaulted him. Stahl and teammate Ted Lewis intervened, protecting Cantillon and escorting him off the field.

Although Chick had coached Notre Dame's college baseball team from January to April of 1900—leading them to a 15–2 record—his off-seasons were primarily spent in Fort Wayne. On the evening of January 26, 1902, while he was walking with a friend in his hometown, Louise "Lulu" Ortmann, a 22-year-old stenographer, approached him. Described as "a very handsome girl," she reached for a revolver, concealed in the folds of her dress, with the intent of killing him. The local police superintendent, who had been tipped off that the infuriated woman was stalking Stahl, arrived just in time to disarm and arrest her. In accounting for her actions, Miss Ortmann stated that she felt jilted by her "recreant lover." "Mr. Stahl, on the other hand, had nothing to say" and dropped any charges. This episode did not impact his 1902 season, as Stahl batted .323 with 92 runs scored and the Americans finished in third place.

In April 1903, Stahl injured his leg while sliding, limiting him to 77 games and a .274 average. Nevertheless, the Americans easily won the pennant. In the World Series against Pittsburgh, Chick was the only Boston player to hit .300, as he banged out 10 hits, including three triples, in 33 at-bats.

Chick's health improved in 1904, and the outfielder returned to his old form with a .290 batting average, 27 doubles, and a league-leading 19 triples, as the Americans captured a second consecutive pennant. Stahl also showcased his glove during Cy Young's perfect game on May 5 against Philadelphia. After the game Young expressed his gratitude for Stahl's play on a sinking line drive off the bat of Ollie Pickering "that Chick caught around his knees after a long run from center."

Along with many of his teammates, Chick's play declined precipitously in 1905, as he finished the year with a .258 batting average—by far the lowest of his career—and only 21 extra base hits. The following year, Stahl improved to .286 with four home runs and 51 RBI, while leading all American League outfielders in putouts and double plays. The Americans, however, won just 49 games, and Stahl became acting-manager of the club in late August, following the suspension of the increasingly disenchanted Jimmy Collins. One scribe wrote that Stahl was "the only man on the team who played his real game this season." In what turned out to be his last major league at-bat, he homered off Tom Hughes.

On November 14, 1906, Stahl married Julia Harmon at St. Francis De Sales Church in Roxbury, Massachusetts. The couple had met at a church function and she was described as "a pretty little brunette" and accomplished musician. Their honeymoon took them to Arkansas' Hot Springs and ended as guests of Jimmy Collins in Buffalo. The other significant event during this month was that Stahl, at the urging of owner John Taylor, and with the approval of his closest friend Collins, accepted the manager's position for the upcoming season.

In 1907, the "Chicks," as the team was nicknamed in deference to their manager, reported to Little Rock for spring training. It soon became evident that Stahl's personality and the position's requirements were incompatible. On March 25, with the team in Louisville, the manager abruptly resigned. Explaining his decision, he said, "This handling of a baseball team both on and off the field is not what it is cracked up to be. Releasing players grated on my nerves and they come so frequently at this time of the year that it made me sick at heart." On March 27, the team arrived at West Baden Springs, Indiana. Having agreed to serve as acting-manager until a replacement could be found, Stahl sent a telegram to his wife that night which read, "Cheer up little girl and be happy. I am all right now and able to play the game of my life."

On the morning of March 28, Stahl ate breakfast, checked the condition of the field and returned to his hotel room to put on his uniform. Jimmy Collins, who

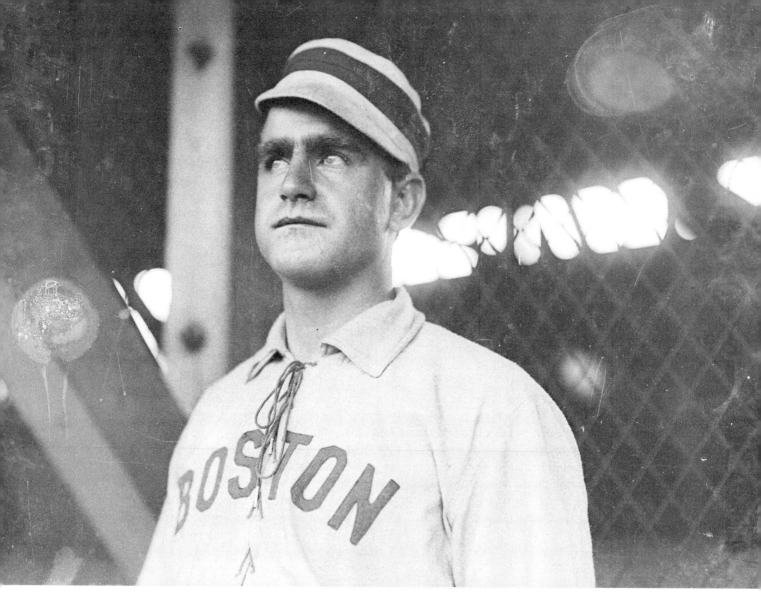

shared the suite, saw Stahl go into the next room for a moment, then stumble back toward Collins and fall onto his bed. The Boston manager had swallowed four ounces of carbolic acid which had been prescribed for a sore on his foot. There are a number of variations, but Stahl's last words were, "I couldn't help it. I did it Jim. It was killing me and I couldn't stand it, Jim." In another version Stahl simply said cryptically, "It drove me to it." Medical help arrived, but to no avail. Stahl suffered excruciating pain, dying in 15 minutes from poisoning. Since the death was ruled a suicide, a Catholic burial was denied. On March 31, the funeral rite, conducted by the Benevolent Order of Elks and the Fraternal Order of Eagles, took place at Stahl's mother's residence. The emotional state of the two women he had loved most "were pathetic in the extreme," according to one newspaper account. "The young bride of a few months was almost prostrated and the grief of the aged mother of the deceased was pitiful to behold." Five

former teammates—Criger, Buck Freeman, Bill Dinneen, Freddy Parent, and Jake Stahl (no relation)—attended, but Collins was too distraught to be present. The player's remains were conveyed to Lindenwood Cemetery "in one of the largest funeral corteges ever seen in Fort Wayne." Thousands marched to the burial place, where Congressman James Robinson gave the eulogy.

Why did Stahl commit suicide? Initially, baseball-related stress was identified as the cause of the tragic death, but soon other theories began to surface. Frederick P. O'Connell, a baseball editor for the *Boston Post* in 1907, contended that there was a non-baseball factor that led to his suicide. He wrote, "a great trouble was generally admitted" which was known to many. The truth was never known, as O'Connell developed pneumonia while in West Baden covering Stahl's funeral, and died there on April 21. Glenn Stout, a noted baseball historian, believes that "the trouble" refers to a brief affair that Stahl had with an anonymous woman in Chicago in 1906 and its aftermath. In March 1907, the woman, claiming she was carrying his child, threatened to blackmail Chick unless he married her. Unable to deal with the pressure and scandal, he ended his life. Stout's approach is factually problematic and lacks documentation. As he relates the blackmail theory, there is only one footnote. The reference is to Harold Seymour, who wrote, "There is reason to believe that a woman who asserted she was his pregnant wife hounded Chick Stahl into committing suicide." No documentation appears here either. Lastly, Stout cites David Voigt, another baseball historian, who accepts the theory in question. Voigt's documentation is limited to a 1959 quote from Al Stump, no different in content than what had already been stated and with no identifiable source. In short, all three respected historians provide an inconclusive theory based on questionable allegations.

The most significant contribution in examining Stahl's suicide has come from Dick Thompson. He uncovered a crucial March 30, 1907, story in the *Fort Wayne Journal-Gazette*. In an article that ran with the headlines, MEDITATED SELF-SLAYING, CHICK STAHL HAD OFTEN TALKED ABOUT SUICIDE, and BASE BALL PLAYER HAD ENTERTAINED DANGEROUS IDEAS ABOUT SELF-DESTRUCTION, the paper argued that Stahl had suffered from depression and suicidal ideation which had persisted from 1889 until the time of his death. The testimony was from close friends "who were not surprised at his suicide." Statements ranging from "Chick talked about killing himself several times" to "sometimes the slightest disappointment would sink him into almost a stupor of depression" appear to confirm he suffered from clinical depression.

This glimpse into Stahl's psyche helps us to understand his behaviors. For the sake of discussion, let us presume that his reputation as a womanizer was true. Clinically, it is not unusual for a depressed person to self-medicate emotional pain through unbridled sexual activity. Also, since baseball was an integral dimension to his identity, his perceived failing as a manager could have intensified his depression. There is still yet another element to the Stahl story. On March 30, 1907, a syndicated story appeared in newspapers. It related that David Murphy, an engineer from Fort Wayne, committed suicide by swallowing carbolic acid. Stahl was described as "an intimate friend of Murphy," and the latter left a note which read, "Bury me beside Chick." From a psychological perspective, this language and behavior strongly indicates that the relationship was not merely a Platonic one. Was Murphy delusional, resulting in an unreciprocated sexual obsession? Or, if it was mutual, was this Stahl's "dark secret"?

Chick had a strong Catholic faith. As one newspaper report following his death noted, "Stahl never forgot his religious duties during the baseball season. Only a week ago last Sunday, Stahl did his Easter duty in Little Rock. He never missed mass if it was possible for him to attend." To understand his behavior, it is important to realize that Jansenism, typically known for its ultra-rigid moral outlook and emphasis upon human nature as being corrupt, heavily influenced the nature of the Catholic Church during his life. As a result, Stahl would have been exposed to teachings about God's love and forgiveness, countered by sermons regarding sins of the flesh and the fires of hell, with suicide being the ultimate sin. The unresolved conflict between his beliefs and behaviors could have increased his inner turmoil and consequently his chronic depression. The healthy and unhealthy components of his persona were expressed during the last week of his earthly life. On the one hand, he had fulfilled his Easter duty, while on the other he committed suicide during Holy Week. As Thompson writes, "I think O'Connell did know the truth, but the truth was not that Stahl was responding to a blackmail threat. It was that he was responding to his own haunted emotions."

Speaking to his teammates after the ballplayer's death, Cy Young—named temporary manager in Stahl's absence—said, "It is mighty tough, boys. I never dreamed such a thing could happen. In fact, none of us could imagine Stahl doing away with himself. Players may come and go, but there are few Chick Stahls."

DENNIS H. AUGER

BOSTON

Denton True "Cy" Young
Right-handed Pitcher, 1901–1908

Along with that of Napoleon Lajoie, Cy Young's defection to the American League in 1901 generated instant credibility for the upstart circuit, as the league gained one of the game's greatest pitchers. Winner of 286 games in his first eleven seasons, Cy Young had established himself as a model of consistency and excellence, pitching more than 300 innings every year from 1891 to 1900, and ranking among the National League's top five in ERA six times during that span. Still, cracks were starting to show in the great pitcher's façade. At 34 years of age, Young had already entered the phase of his career when most pitchers start to break down. Indeed, in 1900, Young suffered through one of his worst seasons to date, failing to win 20 games for the first time since his rookie season, and pitching fewer innings than he had in any previous full season. Opposing batters attested that Young was more hittable than ever, and newspaper reporters began routinely affixing the adjective "Old" in front of his name. By all appearances, then, when the Boston Americans signed Young to a $3,500 salary, the acquisition represented more a public relations coup than a legitimate pitching upgrade.

As it turned out, Boston, not to mention the rest of the American League, got much more than it ever could have expected. During his eight years with the Red Sox, Young won 192 games, becoming the first pitcher in baseball history to pitch effectively into his forties. He won pitching's Triple Crown in 1901, and tossed the first perfect game in American League history. The many photos of Young that survive from this period portray a man advancing in years and gaining in weight. But as his girth expanded, his control sharpened; five times after 1900 he led the league in fewest walks per nine innings. And though his fastball lost some of its effectiveness, the wily Young more than made up for it with a pair of curveballs, one thrown overhand with a sharp break, the other thrown side-armed with a sweeping arc. Both pitches were delivered from a variety of arm angles; occasionally, Young even threw submarine-style to upset the batter's timing. In his continued mastery of opposing batters in the face of declining strength and advancing age, Young raised pitching to an art form, and earned his place in baseball's pantheon of all-time greats. "If I were asked who was the greatest pitcher the game ever knew, I would say Cy Young," Francis Richter wrote in 1910, when Young was 43 years old. "Cy is now…pitching as good ball today as he did twenty years ago."

Denton True Young was born on March 29, 1867, in Gilmore, Ohio, the oldest of five children of McKinzie Jr. and Nancy (Miller) Young. Gilmore was a small farming community located about 100 miles south of Cleveland, and the Young family was raised on a farm owned by McKinzie's father, McKinzie Sr. Cy's education stopped at the sixth grade so he could help his parents with farming chores, but it was also at this time that he discovered the game of baseball. Encouraged by their father, the Young boys played baseball every chance they got. Developing into a better pitcher than hitter, Denton would practice throwing during lunch breaks from farm work. In addition to practicing and playing in recreational games, he organized his own team in Gilmore, then in the summer of 1884 played on semipro teams in Newcomerstown, Cadiz and Uhrichsville, Ohio.

Believing he could make money playing the sport, plus having to make a living after his marriage to Robba Miller, Cy signed with Canton of the Tri-States League in 1890. After compiling a 15–15 record in his rookie season, the right-hander's contract was sold to the National League's Cleveland Spiders for $500. Young's quick ascendancy to the majors was the result of the emergence of the ill-fated Players League, which forced National League teams to dig deep into the minor leagues for any available talent.

Young pitched with the Spiders through the 1898 season, winning 30 games or more three times, and capturing the 1892 ERA title with a 1.93 mark. The following year, the pitcher's mound was moved back five feet to its present distance of 60′6″, and Young responded well, finishing the year with a 34–16 record and 3.36 ERA, third best in the league. Young was able to compensate for the increased distance with his terrific fastball. It had been the pitch that reportedly gave rise to his nickname, Cyclone (or "Cy" for short). Honus Wagner, who regularly faced Young in the National League toward the end of the decade, thought it the greatest fastball he had ever seen. "Walter Johnson was fast, but no faster than Rusie," Wagner observed. "And Rusie was no faster than Johnson. But Young was faster than both of 'em!" Another contemporary, Cap Anson, observed that when the 6′2″, 210-pound Young unleashed his speed, it seemed as if "the ball was shooting down from the hands of a giant."

When the syndicate of owners that controlled both the Cleveland and St. Louis franchises shifted Young to St. Louis in 1899, the pitcher's overpowering fastball began to lose some of its steam. He collected 26 wins that year, but only 19 in 1900, as a bruised rib suffered in a collision with the Giants' Ed Doheny caused him to miss significant playing time for the first time in his career. Additionally, as the summer progressed and Young suffered his share of tough losses, the normally quiet and reserved star uncharacteristically vented his frustration, charging into the stands on August 20 to confront a heckler who had accused him of quitting on the team. Young finished the year with a lackluster 19–19 record, and the Perfectos slumped into fifth place, 10 games below .500.

After the season ended, several St. Louis players defected to the American League, including catcher Lou Criger, Young's battery mate, who signed with Boston. Though he was hounded by Boston's owner, Charles Somers, for several weeks, the cautious Young did not sign with the Americans until the second week of March 1901. In declining to match Boston's offer of $3,500, St. Louis owner Frank Robison insisted that Young was just about "all washed up."

Young soon demonstrated otherwise. Though, like Napoleon Lajoie, he had the advantage of facing competition watered-down by the sudden addition of eight new major league teams, Young enjoyed one of the greatest pitching seasons in baseball history. He won pitching's Triple Crown, leading the league in wins (33), ERA (1.62), and strikeouts (158), to go along with his league-leading five shutouts. In 371⅓ innings, he also walked just 37 batters. When asked to explain his success, Young stated, "I have almost perfect control of the ball this year, and I try to keep it bumping over the plate. If two or three men get on bases, I put on a little more steam and shoot 'em over as fast as I can—but I try all the time to keep 'em over."

Over the next three seasons, the American League's talent pool expanded vastly as more players made the jump to the junior circuit, but Young remained unfazed by the new arrivals, leading the league in victories in 1902 and 1903, and finishing second in 1904. Though he began to rely more exclusively on his assortment of breaking pitches, Young's control remained as sharp as ever: in 1904, he walked just 29 men in 380 innings. His success helped the Americans win back-to-back pennants in 1903 and 1904, and though teammate Bill Dinneen stole the spotlight in Boston's eight-game victory in the first modern World Series, Young aided the cause with a 2–1 record and 1.85 ERA in the inaugural Fall Classic.

His greatest achievement, however, may have come on May 5, 1904, when Young pitched the first perfect game in American League history—just the third in all of baseball history, and the first from the 60′6″ pitching distance—against Rube Waddell and the Philadelphia Athletics. Prior to the game, Waddell, who had defeated Young in their previous encounter a weak earlier, taunted the old pitcher, promising to beat him again. After Young pitched his masterpiece and Boston won, 3–0, Cy uncharacteristically returned fire, shouting to Waddell, "How did you like that one, you hayseed?" It was his second career no-hitter (his first came in 1897); he would pitch a third in 1908, against New York.

Young's perfection against the Athletics came in the midst of a major-league record 24 consecutive innings in which the pitcher did not allow a single hit, as well as a scoreless innings streak that stretched to a then-major league record 45 innings. "And they said Uncle Cy was all in, did they?" observed Boston catcher Duke Farrell of his 37-year-old teammate. "He fooled them, didn't he?" Down the stretch, Young continued to impress, pitching shutouts in each of his last three starts to help the Americans to their narrow pennant victory over the New York Highlanders.

In the wake of Young's historic accomplishments, much of the baseball world began to acknowledge Young's unparalleled place in the pantheon of great pitchers. "Rusies have come and gone, in their turn, by Cy Young still pitches on," observed the *Detroit Tribune*. "Perhaps no ballplayer ever lived who paid stricter attention to business and who came out of a long series of honors showered on him with lesser opinion of himself and with such strict attention to temperate habits." For his part, Young placed no special emphasis on his remarkable durability and longevity. He downplayed the significance of his off-season conditioning program, which consisted mostly of splitting wood at his Peoli, Ohio, farmhouse. "It isn't any secret," Young said of his off-season activities, "just outdoor life, moderation, and a naturally good arm....I don't know that I take any better care of myself than any other pitcher does, it just happens, this thing of my lasting. It isn't the result of any system."

In an era when ballplayers were often regarded as dissolute, inveterate slackers, Young won praise for his clean living and moderate temperament. He prided himself on his work ethic, and reacted with indignation when accused of "easing up" with a big lead. "When you see me let any club make runs off my pitching on purpose," he charged, "come around and I'll give you a brand new hundred dollar bill." Easing up, he declared, placed the game "on the level with lawn tennis, tiddle-de-winks, or some other school girl frivolity." Later in life, Young articulated a personal philosophy for playing the game the right way by enumerating five rules of conduct: 1.) be moderate in all things; 2.) don't abuse yourself; 3.) don't bait umpires; 4.) play hard; and 5.) render faithful service to your employer. Adhering to this creed, Young continued to enjoy success long after other pitchers had left the game. Thus, Young's unbreakable career records (511 victories, 7,354⅔ innings, 749 complete games) were the product not just of exceptional talent and good

fortune, they were also the result of his own exacting standards.

As Young approached and then surpassed his fortieth birthday, he continued to rank among the game's best pitchers, thanks in large part to the wide assortment of breaking pitches and arm deliveries he employed to fool opposing batters. "If a right-hander crowded my plate," Young later said, "I side-armed him with a curve, and then, when he stepped back, I'd throw an overhand fastball low and outside. I was fortunate in having good speed from overhand, three-quarter, or side-arm. I had a variety of curves—threw a so-called screwball or indrop, too—and I used whatever delivery seemed best. And I never had but one sore arm." After enduring the worst season of his career in 1906, when he finished the year 13–21 with a terrible 3.19 ERA, Young came back strong in 1907 and 1908, winning 21 games in each season and posting ERAs of 1.99 and 1.26, respectively.

In February 1909, Young was traded to the Cleveland Naps for Charlie Chech, Jack Ryan, and $12,500 cash. Back in the city where he had started his big league career 19 years before, Young enjoyed one more solid season, going 19–15 with a 2.26 ERA at age 42. The following year, Young started only 20 games, finishing with a 7–10 record. Still, he resisted calls for him to retire from the game. "Quit the game, well, I guess not," he told one Cleveland reporter. "I'd be awfully lonesome, and you know this is a healthy game. I'll not quit until I have to."

In 1911, the 44-year-old Young fared even worse, going 3–4 with a 3.88 ERA in seven starts before drawing his release on August 15. He was quickly picked up by the Boston Braves of the National League, who wanted him, according to one writer, "just to draw the crowd." Young started 11 games for Boston down the stretch, going 4–5 with a 3.71 ERA. Despite much speculation that he would retire, Young attempted to hang on with the Braves for the 1912 season, remaining with the team out of spring training, and warming the bench for the first month of the campaign. But a chronically sore arm prevented him from ever taking the field; when he attempted to do so on May 23, he gave up after a brief warmup session, declaring, "It's no use. I'm not going on. These poor fellows have lost too many games already." Finally, at the age of 45, Young's major league career was officially over.

In retirement, Cy returned to his home in Peoli, where he lived out a quiet retirement on his farm, growing potatoes and tending to his sheep, hogs, and chickens. He and his wife Robba did not raise any children; their only offspring, a daughter, died a few hours after her birth in 1907, leaving, in the words of Young biographer Reed Browning, "an almost inexpungeable hole" in their lives. When Robba passed away in 1934, a grieving Young sold his farm. "Somehow, after she died I didn't want to live there any more," he explained. Elected to the Hall of Fame in 1937, Young was formally inducted with the Hall's first class at the museum's opening in 1939. Despite his frugal habits and status as a baseball legend, however, Young was beset by financial problems late in life. In 1935, he traveled to Augusta, Georgia, where he joined a group of baseball veterans looking to make some money during the Great Depression by playing exhibition games. When this venture failed, Young returned to Ohio, where he found work as a clerk in a retail store, and lived with a local couple, John and Ruth Benedum. He was still living with the Benedums when he died of a coronary occlusion on November 4, 1955, at the age of 88. He was buried in Peoli Cemetery. The next year, baseball instituted the pitching award that still bears his name.

DAVID C. SOUTHWICK

BOSTON

WILLIAM HENRY DINNEEN
RIGHT-HANDED PITCHER, 1902–1907

Before Sandy Koufax and Bob Gibson were hurling October masterpieces, Bill Dinneen set the standard for World Series excellence. In the 1903 World Series, the hard-throwing right-hander won three games for the Boston Americans against the Pittsburgh Pirates, including the first two shutouts in World Series history. For the Series, "Big Bill" struck out 28 batters in 35 innings, including Honus Wagner to end the Series. Dinneen's triumph in the inaugural World Series proved to be the highlight in a 12-year major league career which saw the right-hander win 170 games, but lose 177. After three consecutive 20-win seasons, in which Dinneen tossed 108 complete games in 113 starts, the overextended pitcher quickly lost his effectiveness and faded from the major league scene. Shortly following Dinneen's voluntary retirement at the age of 33, Alfred Spink wrote, "Bill realized that his pitching arm was gone, and though he might come back for an occasional contest, he could never again pitch ball in his old-time form. He did the wise thing and quit."

William Henry Dinneen was born in Syracuse, New York, on April 5, 1876, one of six children of Thomas and Katherine Dinneen, Irish immigrants who had migrated to the United States shortly before William's birth. The most controversial aspect of his life has been the spelling of his last name. Though many contemporary sources and reference works render his last name as "Dinneen," this retrospective will refer to him as "Dinneen," based on the fact that the latter is the spelling on his tombstone, death certificate, and in census records. Always a big kid for his age, Dinneen was one of the hardest throwers among his friends, and thus began pitching at an early age. While playing semipro ball in the Syracuse area, he signed a contract with Toronto of the Eastern League as a 19-year-old in 1895. "Big Bill" eventually filled out a 6′1″ frame with 190 pounds, and his fastball convinced the Toronto front office to hold onto him despite an 0–4 record in his first professional season. Following an 11–12 record in 1896, Dinneen flourished in 1897, posting a 21–8 record which led the Washington Senators to purchase him for the 1898 season.

In his two seasons with Washington, Dinneen won a combined 23 games with an ERA under 4.00. When the National League contracted from 12 teams to eight prior to the 1900 season, Dinneen was sold to the Boston Beaneaters. He posted the first of his four 20-win seasons in 1900, tying for second in the National League with 20 victories, as the Beaneaters finished in fourth place. After a 15-win season in 1901, Dinneen jumped to Boston of the American League, where he enjoyed his greatest success.

In his first three seasons with the Americans, Dinneen won 65 games, averaged more than 300 innings per season, and posted a 2.49 ERA. Dinneen was one of baseball's best pitchers from 1900 to 1904, finishing in the top 10 in his league each season in innings pitched, starts, complete games, and strikeouts, and finishing in the top five in victories in 1900 and from 1902 to 1904. In 1904, Dinneen set two American League records: most consecutive complete games (37), and most consecutive innings without being relieved (337⅔), as he finished every game he started for an entire season en route to a career high 23 victories. On the last day of the 1904 season the Pilgrims had a one-game lead over the New York Highlanders. With the Highlanders needing a doubleheader sweep, 41-game winner Jack Chesbro was sent to the mound in the first game. Boston manager Jimmy Collins went with Dinneen. Pitching on one day's rest, Dinneen was the winning pitcher as Chesbro's ninth inning wild pitch snapped a 2–2 tie and gave the Pilgrims their second consecutive American League pennant.

Probably because of all the innings he had piled up over the course of his career, Dinneen was never the same following his historic 1904 season. He did have one glorious afternoon on September 27, 1905, when Bill, who had not pitched the entire month because of a sore arm, hurled a no-hitter against the Chicago White Sox, striking out six. He won 12 games against 14 defeats in 1905, and fell to 8–19 in 1906 as he posted ERAs below the league average in both seasons. Less than four years after being carried off the field by the fans at Huntington Avenue Grounds as the 1903 World Series hero, Dinneen was traded to the St. Louis Browns in June 1907, for pitcher Albert Jacobson and $1,500.

Dinneen was a good athlete. He played in the field a fair amount, including center field four times, hit a respectable (for a pitcher) .192 for his career and stole 29 bases, including eight in 1901. His main two pitches were a fastball and a sharp curve, and he had textbook mechanics. *Baseball Magazine* praised his delivery: "A good step helps very much in pitching, and that it is essential to cultivate a powerful body swing, especially to follow the ball well with the arm and the body after it is delivered. Dinneen…has an especially stylish delivery in this respect, and should be a model for youth to imitate." Jimmy Collins rated six pitchers among the best he had ever seen. The list consisted of Dinneen and five Hall of Famers: Cy Young, Addie Joss, Jack Chesbro, Walter Johnson, and Ed Walsh.

After the trade to the Browns in 1907, *The Sporting News* noted, "Until 1906 [Dinneen] was rated as one of the fastest pitchers in the business, but fell off in his work." With the Browns, Dinneen rebounded and tied for the American League lead with four saves, despite spending just 70% of the 1907 season with the club, and posted 14 wins and a 2.10 ERA in 1908. In 1909, arm trouble limited Big Bill to a career-low 112 innings, during which he pitched very poorly. With 170 victories, he knew his career on the mound was finished. However, he did not want to leave the field, so the 33-year-old applied to become an umpire. American

League president Ban Johnson agreed to give Dinneen a one-month trial. His final game as a player was August 26, 1909, and less than three weeks later, on September 11, Dinneen joined the American League umpiring staff. The one-month trial resulted in a 28-year job that he held through the 1937 season, which means he was employed in the major leagues for 40 consecutive seasons.

Dinneen became the first person to play in a World Series and umpire in the Fall Classic, and is still the only person to pitch a shutout and umpire in the series. He umpired in eight different World Series, 45 games in all. He was on the field for Babe Ruth's called shot in 1932, and six years earlier he was the umpire who called Ruth out for attempting to steal second against Grover Cleveland Alexander to end the 1926 series. Among his other umpiring highlights, Dinneen was the home plate umpire for Ruth's 60th home run in 1927, the first All-Star Game in 1933, and five no-hitters. What type of reputation did Dinneen have as an umpire? In 1922, Dinneen ejected Ruth from a game. The following day, American League president Johnson wrote Ruth a letter stating, "Bill Dinneen was one of the greatest pitchers the game ever produced, and…is one of the cleanest and most honorable men baseball ever fostered."

After his retirement from umpiring, Dinneen continued to follow the game. To commemorate the fiftieth anniversary of the first World Series, the 77-year-old Dinneen threw out the first pitch prior to Game Two of the 1953 Series. As *The Sporting News* noted, "Many present remarked about the snap to the peg with which he started the second game. It wasn't an old man's fluffy toss." He lived in Syracuse his entire life, and was married to the former Margaret Quinn until her passing in 1949. The couple had four children, three sons and a daughter. Dinneen passed away on January 13, 1955, at the age of 78, due to a heart condition. He is buried at St. Agnes Cemetery in Utica, New York.

MATT MARINI

427

BOSTON

Garland "Jake" Stahl
First Baseman, 1903, 1908–1913; Manager, 1912–1913

Big, powerful, and deceptively fast, Jake Stahl parlayed the skills he first demonstrated as a college football star at the turn of the century into an even more successful career on the baseball field. At 6'2" and 195 pounds, the right-handed Stahl was one of the most intimidating sluggers of the Deadball Era's first decade. Though he hit just 31 home runs in his nine-year career, "there was no young player in the American League whom pitchers feared more," one writer later remembered. "In St. Louis today fans point to the left field fence and show where 'Jake put one over'—something that has not been done since." Pitchers often responded to the threat posed by Stahl by throwing at him—in 981 career games Jake was plunked 94 times; his 23 HBP in 1908 is the second highest single-season total of the century's first decade.

Yet Stahl's powerful bat was more than matched by his modest disposition, which some observers believed prevented him from realizing his full potential. "If Stahl could get a case of swelled head and begin to think he is really as good as he is, he would be the greatest of them all," Francis Richter declared in 1910. "Modesty has held him back and I have feared he would finish his career without finding out how good he is." Stahl did achieve lasting fame in 1912, when he managed the Boston Red Sox to their best regular season record in franchise history, and a World Championship. Yet even this victory came with its own bitter aftertaste: just nine months later, Red Sox management fired Stahl. It was the fastest dismissal of its kind in baseball history.

Garland Stahl was born on April 13, 1879, in Elkhart, Illinois, the third son of Henry and Eliza Stahl. Henry was a front-line Union veteran of the Civil War who survived the bloodbath at Shiloh, though Eliza lost a brother in the same battle. After the war, Henry and Eliza opened a thriving general store in Elkhart.

All of the Stahl's three sons and four daughters helped out at the store. In naming her third son, Eliza used the name of one of her brothers-in-law, Garland. In time, however, the young Garland was rechristened Jake by his schoolmates.

After graduating from high school and working in the family store, Stahl enrolled at the University of Illinois in 1899. In his second year, the Illinois football coach, George Huff, encouraged him to try out. Jake had his best year in college football as a junior in 1901, when he was named to the All-Western Conference football team. Huff also coached baseball at the University and encouraged Jake to join his highly successful squad. As the starting catcher, Stahl batted .441 his sophomore year, and in his senior campaign, led Illinois to a Western Conference championship.

Despite his considerable athletic accomplishments, Stahl also made a name for himself in the classroom. An outstanding student known for his efficiency and organizational skills, Jake graduated in 1903 with a law degree. That same spring, he made his major league debut with the Boston Americans. Appearing in 40 games as a reserve catcher, Stahl batted .239 with two home runs. In that year's World Series, however, Stahl rode the bench as manager Jimmy Collins went exclusively with a veteran lineup en route to the Americans' eight-game Series victory over the Pirates.

During the winter of 1903–04, Boston shipped Jake to the floundering Washington franchise. American League president Ban Johnson was in charge of the team until suitable owners could be found and converted Jake into a first baseman. He finished the year with a .262 batting average, three home runs, and 50 RBI. Even by Deadball Era standards, those numbers were not exceptional, yet Stahl led the woeful (38–113) Senators in all three categories.

In 1905, Johnson promoted Stahl to manager, replacing the deposed Patsy Donovan. At 26 years of age, Stahl became the youngest player–manager in American League history. Fielding essentially the same 1904 team that had lost 113 games, Jake led the 1905 squad to a 64–87 record. Washington climbed out of the American League cellar and into seventh place. For a short time early in the season, Jake even had the team in first place. When they came home from a successful western road trip, Washington gave the team a rousing parade. Though his batting average dipped to .250, Jake improved his game in every other respect, playing better defense at first base, and leading the team in hits (125), triples (12), home runs (5), RBI (66), and stolen bases (41). In the offseason, Jake married Jennie Mahan, the daughter of Henry Weston Mahan, a highly successful businessman. Flush with personal and professional success, Stahl had become, in the words of one observer, "popular with the players, and so well-liked by the club owners that it has been officially announced that he can retain his present berth until he voluntarily resigns."

In 1906, however, things fell apart for Jake and the Senators. Shortstop Joe Cassidy unexpectedly died of typhus at the beginning of the season, and the team went into a tailspin, finishing 55–95. On the field, Stahl also had his worst year, finishing with a .222 batting average and no home runs in 137 games. The frustrated Washington owners replaced Stahl as the manager to begin the 1907 season. Jake accepted the blame for the team's disappointing performance, noting, "If I'd been able to hit .300 this year, as many of my friends predicted, we'd have been up in the first division, but I was a frost." Jake asked to be traded back to Boston but Washington management declined, trading him instead to the Chicago White Sox. Stahl refused to report and spent the 1907 season playing semipro ball in Chicago.

In 1908, Chicago traded him to the New York Highlanders and this time Jake reported for duty. With Hal Chase manning first base, Jake spent several months attempting to play the outfield for New York, before the Red Sox purchased his contract in July and moved him back to first base. From 1908 to 1910, the hard-hitting Stahl anchored the Red Sox lineup. In 1910, Jake led the American League with 10 home runs, and ranked fourth best in RBI (77) and triples (16). Yet enigmatically, Jake responded to his best season as a major leaguer by announcing his retirement. In 1911, he left baseball to work in one of his father-in-law's Chicago banks.

After both he and his father-in-law, W. F. Mahan, became part-owners of the Boston Americans, Jake came out of retirement in 1912 to become the player–manager of a talented but uninspired Boston club. Replacing Patsy Donovan for the second time in seven years, Stahl effectively focused the roster's enormous potential and ran away with the American League pennant, winning 105 games and finishing 14 games ahead in the standings. On the field, Stahl had a solid year, batting a career-high .301 while splitting first base duties with Hugh Bradley and Clyde Engel. Facing the New York Giants in the 1912 World Series, Jake both outplayed the Giants' Merkle at first base and, according to Connie Mack, consistently out-managed John McGraw.

In 1913, Boston started slowly and Jake suffered a serious foot injury requiring the removal of part of a bone in his right foot. Although Stahl continued to manage the team, he could not play first base during his recuperation. Amid rumors that Stahl was interested in supplanting him, Boston president Jimmy McAleer blamed the club's poor performance on Jake's refusal to play, and demanded that he return to action. As the rift between McAleer and Stahl widened, the club split into factions, with Bill Carrigan, Duffy Lewis and Heinie Wagner opposing Stahl, and Tris Speaker, Joe Wood and Larry Gardner supporting their manager. Jake finally confronted McAleer in his Chicago hotel during a July road trip. Following a heated argument, McAleer demanded Stahl's immediate resignation. McAleer's action was condemned by much of the baseball community, including American League president Ban Johnson, who called the move "hasty and ill-advised." Carrigan replaced Stahl as manager, and in October Jake announced he was through with baseball.

He had good reason to be. At the expiration of his baseball contract, Stahl began his second career as a full-time banker. With his father-in-law serving as president, Jake became vice-president and board member of Washington Park National Bank in Chicago. Jake continued as vice president until 1917, when he served in World War I as a Second Lieutenant in the Army Air Bombing Division. He returned in 1919 to assume the presidency of Washington Park. During the years of his involvement, Stahl put in long hours at the bank, helping it to more than double its deposits in three years. But the hard work came with a heavy price: in 1920, Stahl suffered a nervous breakdown and was placed in a Monrovia, California, sanitarium. Though he spent two years in California, Stahl's health gradually worsened, and he contracted tuberculosis. With his wife and son at his bedside, Stahl died on September 18, 1922. He was just 43 years old.

JOHN STAHL

BOSTON

JESSE NILES TANNEHILL
LEFT-HANDED PITCHER, 1904–1908

He stood only 5′8″ and weighed just 150 pounds, but Jesse Tannehill was one of the most versatile players during the Deadball Era. Not only did the black-haired left-hander compile a 197–116 lifetime record and 2.79 ERA, the switch-hitter also played in the outfield 87 times and pinch hit in 57 games. A former saloon owner and a superstitious player who wouldn't shave on days he pitched, Tannehill had outstanding control and used his slow curve to routinely strike out twice as many as he walked, though he never did either with regularity and opted to let his defense make plays behind him. "I think Tannehill the greatest of living pitchers for the good reason that he was never rattled in his life," said his former minor league manager, Jake Wells. "No matter how hard his delivery may be, he never loses his head. I like a pitcher who can take punishment and pull himself together at a critical moment. Then don't forget that Tannehill is a good batsman."

Tannehill was proud of his hitting ability and boasted a lifetime average of .256, including a .336 mark in 1900. Tannehill also enjoyed capitalizing on his speed. For many years he bragged that he was one of the few pitchers to ever steal home.

Jesse Niles Tannehill was born on July 14, 1874, in Dayton, Kentucky, just across the Ohio River from Cincinnati. Tannehill was the middle child of William, a ship carpenter, and Julia Tannehill. Baseball was in the family genes. His father played for the Eagles of Dayton in the 1860s, one of the founding baseball clubs in the Cincinnati area, and Jesse's younger brother, Lee, enjoyed a ten-year career as a White Sox infielder. Jesse's baseball skills were first noticed on the Cincinnati sandlots, where Tannehill starred for the Cincinnati Shamrocks. The Cincinnati Reds signed Jesse and on June 17, 1894, he made his big league debut. Tannehill

finished the season 1–1 in five games with a 7.14 ERA. The next two years he posted 22 and 27-win seasons for Richmond of the Virginia League and helped them capture consecutive league titles. At the close of the 1896 season Pittsburgh drafted him.

Tannehill went 9–9 in his first full season in the majors, while filling in regularly in the outfield. He excelled so well that the Pirates considered making him a full time outfielder, but by the start of the 1898 season Tannehill was designated as a utility outfielder and pitcher. It was a role that he carried with him throughout his career. Tannehill blossomed as a pitcher in 1898, winning a career high 25 games. The wins continued and in four of his final five seasons with the Pirates he won 20 or more games.

On the mound, the short left-hander relied on an agonizingly slow curveball and razor-sharp control. Every year from 1897 to 1904, Tannehill ranked among his league's top five in fewest walks per nine innings pitched. He wasn't a big strikeout pitcher, either—he recorded only 940 strikeouts in more than 2,750 career innings—but his low walk totals still ensured him an annual spot among pitchers with the best strikeout to walk ratios. In 1901, he fanned a career-high 118 batters while walking just 36, and led the National League with a 2.18 ERA as the Pirates captured the pennant. Pittsburgh's dominance continued the following season as the Pirates won 103 games and clinched the pennant with a month left in the season. The Pirates' staff (Phillippe, Tannehill, Leever, Doheny and Chesbro) threw 21 shutouts, led the league in strikeouts, walked the fewest batters, and threw back-to-back two-hitters and back-to-back three-hitters.

Amidst Pittsburgh's success, rumors surfaced about players secretly negotiating with Ban Johnson to join the American League, with Tannehill believed to be one of the main catalysts. After a game in August, Jesse got

430

into an altercation with reserve Jimmy Burke. A scuffle occurred resulting in Tannehill dislocating his pitching shoulder. Tannehill went to a local hospital where the doctors administrated ether so his arm could be popped back into place. While under the anesthetic Tannehill told Pirates owner Barney Dreyfuss about conversations he had with Johnson. He even dropped the names of the other Pirates involved. Five days later at Tannehill's apartment, six Pirates were promised a $1,000 bonus for jumping leagues in 1903. Word got out and suspected ring-leader Jack O'Connor was suspended even though Tannehill reportedly told a friend that he was behind the meeting. When an exhibition game was set up after the season between the Pirates and a group of American League All-Stars, Tannehill did not participate. Dreyfuss, knowing Tannehill had already received a bonus from the American League, handed the pitcher his unconditional release and told him to take his baggage from Exposition Park at once. Along with teammates O'Connor and Jack Chesbro, Tannehill signed with the New York Highlanders.

Jesse's 1903 season was an unpleasant one, as the pitcher posted a mediocre 15–15 mark and clashed with manager Clark Griffith over the latter's suspension of O'Connor. Tannehill also complained that his struggles were the result of pitching at Hilltop Park. "The grounds are on a high bluff overlooking the river and the cold wind blows over the diamond morning, noon and night," said Tannehill. "A man would have to have a cast iron arm to pitch winning ball under these circumstances." His poor pitching was more likely the result of an arm problem that he suffered during the season. It was an injury that would nag him for the rest of his career, and prevent him from handling heavy workloads. Unhappy in New York, after the season Tannehill expressed interest in joining his hometown Cincinnati Reds. Instead the Highlanders traded the unhappy hurler to the Boston Americans for pitcher Tom Hughes.

The trade proved to be a winner for Boston. Tannehill went 21–11 with a 2.04 ERA in 1904 while Hughes struggled to a 7–11 mark before New York traded him in midseason. On August 17, Tannehill pitched the third no-hitter in American League history when he blanked the White Sox 6–0.

As it turned out, all the complete games wore on the veteran pitching staff, and Boston sank quickly in the standings. In 1905, the Americans finished a disappointing fourth, as Tannehill was the only starting pitcher to post a winning record (22–9). The following year, the Americans endured a 20-game losing streak on their way to a last-place finish, and Tannehill posted a mediocre 3.16 ERA, finishing the year with 13 wins and 11 losses. It was the only winning record on the team, though it would also be the last winning season of his career.

A sore arm limited Tannehill to just six wins the following season and after pitching in one game in 1908, he was traded to Washington. Boston management had become unhappy with him. On numerous occasions Tannehill mentioned that he would rather play in Washington for his hunting companion Joe Cantillon than anywhere else. Once Tannehill arrived in the nation's capital he wasn't shy about his happiness in leaving Boston. "I could not pitch in Boston. The weather there is hard on my arm and I could not get it going right," stated Tannehill. "It feels better already, though I have only been out of the town for a few hours." Despite the change in climate, Tannehill was unable to stay healthy for the Nationals, as a dislocated shoulder and displaced ribs limited him to two wins in 1908. The next season Tannehill pitched in only three games before being sold to Minneapolis of the American Association.

Offended by the pay cut and still bothered by recurring arm troubles, Jesse refused to report; instead he returned to Dayton and played for some local teams. Tannehill eventually joined the Millers when Cantillon was named manager in 1910, but once again his arm went back on him and he was given his unconditional release after pitching in eight games. Tannehill signed a contract to play for Cincinnati in 1911, but his major league return was short-lived. While Cincinnati suffered its worst opening day loss, 14–0 to the Pirates, Tannehill gave up six hits, seven runs (three earned), and walked three in four innings of mop-up work. After the game Jesse asked manager Clark Griffith for his release. Tannehill returned to the minor leagues later that season, playing in the Southern Association, first for Birmingham and later Montgomery.

In 1912, Tannehill signed on as an outfielder for South Bend of the Central League. Despite batting .285 in 59 games, Tannehill was given his unconditional release. Newspaper reports stated he was promoting discord on the team. He later played for Chillicothe (Ohio State League) and St. Joseph (Western League) before ending his playing career.

In his later years, Jesse worked in a Cincinnati machine shop. Tannehill died from a stroke at Speers Hospital in Dayton on September 22, 1956. Survived by his wife, the former Beulah Anderson, he was buried at Evergreen Cemetery in Southgate, Kentucky.

NATHANIEL STALEY

Bill Carrigan

BOSTON

WILLIAM FRANCIS CARRIGAN
CATCHER, 1906, 1908–1916; MANAGER, 1913–1916, 1927–1929

An excellent defensive catcher who provided the Boston Red Sox with above-average offense for his position, Bill "Rough" Carrigan batted .257 in 709 career games, and once finished as high as eighth in the American League in batting average. Behind the plate, the 5'9", 175-pounder compensated for his lack of size through sheer toughness. Confrontational by nature, Carrigan rarely backed down from a fight, and usually came out on the better end of his many scraps. From 1913 to 1916, Carrigan was one of the most successful player–managers of the Deadball Era, piloting the Red Sox to back-to-back world championships in 1915 and 1916. Following the latter season, the 32-year-old Carrigan, who Babe Ruth later called the best manager for whom he ever played, walked away from the game to spend time with family and his business.

Most sources indicate that William Francis Carrigan was born in Lewiston, Maine, on October 22, 1883, though the 1900 census places his birth year at 1884. William was the youngest of three children of John and Annie Carrigan, Irish Catholic immigrants who had arrived in the United States prior to the Civil War. According to census records, John supported the family as a deputy sheriff. During his youth, William worked on local farms when not playing sports, and was a star football and baseball player at Lewiston High. After high school, he moved on to the College of the Holy Cross in Worcester, Massachusetts. He starred as a football halfback for the legendary Frank Cavanaugh, who was later the subject of a movie (*The Iron Major*, starring Pat O'Brien) and a member of the College Football Hall of Fame. On the diamond Carrigan played for Tommy McCarthy, the baseball star of the 1890s, who converted his young charge from the infield to catcher, a position Carrigan would play the rest of his career.

In the spring of 1906 Carrigan was signed to a Red Sox contract by Charles Taylor, the father of Red Sox owner John I. Taylor. Carrigan joined the struggling Red Sox directly in the middle of the season, immediately catching the likes of Bill Dinneen and Cy Young. In this initial trial, he hit just .211 in 37 games, but impressed with his play behind the dish. He was sent to Toronto of the Eastern League the next season, where he batted .320, before rejoining the Red Sox in 1908. The right-handed hitting Carrigan was not a feared batsman, hitting just six lifetime home runs, but was soon one of the more respected members of the team. In 1908 he hit .235 as the primary backup to Lou Criger, but assumed the bulk of the innings for the next six seasons after Criger's departure to the Browns. His .296 average in 1909 was the highest of his career, and the eighth best in the league that season.

The well-mannered Carrigan earned the nickname "Rough" for the way he played. He was a well respected handler of pitchers, and had a fair throwing arm, but it was his plate blocking that caused Jimmy Callahan to say, "You might as well try to move a stone wall." On May 17, 1909, he engaged in a famous brawl with the Tigers' George Moriarty after a collision at home plate, while their teammates stood and watched. He had a fight with Sam Crawford a couple of years later, and maintained a reputation as someone who would not back down from a confrontation.

Fully entrenched as a regular by 1911, he had a fine season at the plate (.289 in 72 games) before suffering a broken leg on an awkward slide at second base on September 4. He caught the majority of the innings for the 1912 pennant winners, hitting .263, but was hitless in only seven at-bats in the Red Sox's World Series victory that fall.

In July 1913 the Red Sox were grappling with a series of injuries, fighting amongst themselves, and limping along in fifth place. Team president Jimmy McAleer fired manager Jake Stahl just months after his World Series triumph, and replaced him with his 29-year-old catcher. Carrigan liked Stahl, as did most of the team, and was reluctant to take charge of a team filled with veterans, many of whom were just as qualified for the job as he. McAleer convinced Carrigan to take it. The Red Sox were a team fractured along religious lines, as Protestants such as Tris Speaker, Joe Wood and Harry Hooper often crossed swords with the Catholics on the team, including Carrigan.

The club's new manager commanded respect through the unique brand of toughness he brought to the job. Wilbert Robinson, who managed against Carrigan in the 1916 World Series, later said that Carrigan was serious when it came to his pitchers dusting a hitter off: "When Carrigan told one of his pitchers to knock a man down and the batter didn't hit the dirt, the pitcher was fined." The team played better the rest of 1913, and finished second to Connie Mack's Athletics in 1914.

The most important event of the 1914 season was the purchase, at Carrigan's urging, of pitchers Ernie Shore and Babe Ruth from Baltimore. Although Ruth gave his skipper a lot of credit for his development as a player, Carrigan was humble in his own assessment: "Nobody could have made Ruth the great pitcher and great hitter he was but himself. He made himself with the aid of his God-given talents." Old "Rough" did allow that his protégé needed quite a bit of discipline, and Carrigan was there to provide it, even rooming with Ruth for a time. Carrigan caught Ruth in his pitching debut, on July 11.

Some might fault Carrigan for not seeing the potential of Ruth as a hitter. Given that the Red Sox were blessed with the game's best outfield in Duffy Lewis, Tris Speaker and Harry Hooper, and that Ruth soon developed into one of the game's best pitchers, it is understandable why Carrigan did not wish to mess with success. In 1915, Carrigan did use Ruth occasionally as a pinch-hitter, and Babe responded with a team-leading four home runs.

The next two seasons brought Carrigan and his team their back-to-back World Series triumphs. Against the Phillies in 1915, Carrigan famously did not pitch Ruth, which some took as a message to the Babe that the team did not need him to win. Carrigan always disputed this, claiming he wanted to avoid using left-handed pitchers against the heavily right-handed hitting Philadelphia club.

In early September 1916, Carrigan announced that he would be leaving baseball at the end of the season. He had actually wanted to quit after the 1915 Series, and had so told owner Joe Lannin, but his owner talked him into the one additional campaign. Carrigan later wrote, "I had become fed up on being away from home from February to October. I was in my thirties, was married and had an infant daughter. I wanted to spend more time with my family than baseball would allow." He retired to his hometown of Lewiston and embarked on careers in real estate (as co-owner of several movie theatres in New England) and banking. A few years later he sold his theatres for a substantial profit and became a wealthy man.

When Lannin sold the club to Harry Frazee prior to the 1917 season, Frazee drove to Lewiston to try to talk Carrigan into staying on. After that, an off-season did not go by without offers from major league teams to lure Carrigan back into the game. After a decade of trying, the Red Sox finally summoned Carrigan out of retirement in 1927 to manage the tail-end Sox. Offering proof that the players often make the manager, the Red Sox continued their struggles, finishing last for all three seasons during the second Carrigan regime, despite improving their record each year.

Carrigan was not happy with the way the players had changed in his time away. "These players didn't talk baseball. They talked golf and stocks and where they were going after the game." Players resisted practice, individual instruction, or talk of cut-off plays and other strategies. "Inside baseball had become a lost art," he felt. Interestingly, he thought baseball was too concerned with finding good citizens: "I'll take players who get arrested every night and win ball games two out of three afternoons to the best behaved second-division gang ever assembled."

Moving back to Lewiston for good, he continued a very successful banking career, joining the town's Board of Finance in 1938, and becoming president of Peoples Savings Bank in 1953. Through the years, he was a frequent guest at Fenway Park for ceremonies and reunions. He was named to the Holy Cross Hall of Fame in 1968.

Carrigan married the former Beulah Bartlett in 1915, and they had two daughters, Beulah and Constance, and one son, William Jr. Wife Beulah died in 1958, but Old Rough hung on until July 8, 1969, when he passed away at age 85 in his beloved Lewiston. He was buried in Lewiston's Riverside Cemetery.

MARK ARMOUR

BOSTON

TRISTRAM E. SPEAKER
CENTER FIELDER, 1907–1915

Tris Speaker, Ty Cobb's friendly rival as the greatest center fielder of the Deadball Era, could field and throw better than the Georgia Peach even if he could not quite match him as a hitter. Legendary for his short outfield play, Speaker led the American League in putouts seven times and double plays six times in a 22-year career with Boston, Cleveland, Washington and Philadelphia. Speaker's career totals in both categories are still major league records at his position. No slouch at the plate, Speaker's lifetime average, .345, is sixth on the all time list and no one has surpassed his career mark of 792 doubles. He was also one of the game's most successful player–managers. A man's man who hunted, fished, could bulldog a steer and taught Will Rogers how to use a lariat, Speaker was involved in more than his share of umpire baiting and brawls with teammates and opposing players. But when executing a hook slide on the bases, tracking a fly ball at the crack of an opponent's bat, or slashing one of his patented extra base hits, Speaker made everything he did look easy. "You can write him down as one of the two models of ball-playing grace," Grantland Rice wrote of the Grey Eagle. "The other was Napoleon Lajoie. Neither ever wasted a motion or gave you any sign of extra effort.... They had the same elements that made a Bobby Jones or the Four Horsemen of Notre Dame—the smoothness of a summer wind."

Tristram E. Speaker was born on April 4, 1888, in Hubbard, Texas, a railroad town of 500 people 70 miles south of Dallas, to a family that had relocated from Ohio just prior to the Civil War. His father, Archie, whose two older brothers had fought for the Confederacy, was in the dry goods business and died when Tris was ten. Tris's mother, Nancy Jane, whose brother also fought for the South, kept a boarding house. A born right-hander, young Tris taught himself to throw left-handed when he twice broke his right arm after being thrown from a bronco. Soon he began to bat left-handed as well. Tris played football in high school and was captain and pitcher on his high school baseball team. In 1905 Speaker entered the Fort Worth Polytechnic Institute (now Texas Wesleyan University), where he pitched for the Institute's baseball squad, as well as for the Nicholson and Watson semipro club in Corsicana. Tris picked up extra money working as a telegraph lineman and cowpuncher.

In 1906 Speaker wrote several professional teams asking for a tryout and was signed by Cleburne of the Texas League for $65 per month. Tris bombed as a pitcher—he lost six straight games and once reportedly gave up 22 straight hits, all for extra bases—but as an outfielder he hit .268 and stole 33 bases in 84 games. When the North and South Texas Leagues were consolidated in 1907, Speaker moved to Houston and hit a league-leading .314 with 36 steals in 118 games.

The Red Sox purchased Speaker's contract at the end of the 1907 season. He appeared in seven games for the big club, but hit only .158. Unimpressed with his play, the Red Sox did not send Speaker a contract for 1908. Speaker twice begged John McGraw for a chance to play for the Giants to no avail and was also rebuffed by several other major league clubs. Finally, Speaker paid his own way to Boston's Little Rock training camp to work out with the Red Sox. At the end of spring training, the Red Sox turned Speaker's contract over to Little Rock of the Southern Association as payment for the rent of the training field. There was one stipulation: if Speaker developed, Boston had the right to repurchase him for $500.

Speaker led the Southern Association in hitting in 1908 with a .350 average, stole 28 bases, and his outfield play drew raves. In a spring exhibition game

but one, won the Chalmers Award as the league's Most Valuable Player. He also batted .383, third in the league behind Cobb and Joe Jackson, and led the AL in doubles, home runs (tied), and on-base percentage. ("Spoke," one of Speaker's nicknames, came, ironically, from Speaker's teammate and rival Bill Carrigan, who would yell, "Speaker spoke!" when Tris got a hit.) To cap it off, in the World Series against the New York Giants, Speaker got a key hit in the tenth inning of the decisive eighth game after his harmless foul pop-up fell untouched between first baseman Fred Merkle and catcher Chief Meyers. Given a second chance, Speaker singled in the tying run.

Boston fans loved him. Speaker received $50 each time he hit the Bull Durham sign, first at Huntington Avenue and later at Fenway Park. He endorsed Boston Garters, had a two-dollar straw hat named in his honor, and received free mackinaws and heavy sweaters. Hassan cigarettes created popular trading cards of Speaker depicting him running the bases.

Despite the team's success on the field, tensions were often high in the clubhouse. Speaker and catcher Carrigan never got along and had several brawls. Speaker was often not on speaking terms with Duffy Lewis, who, like Carrigan, was Irish Catholic. (Religious differences had created cliques on the club, with Speaker siding with other Protestants such as Joe Wood and Larry Gardner). The atmosphere grew more complicated with the arrival of Babe Ruth in 1915. Ruth crossed Wood and Speaker never fully forgave him. In his book *Baseball As I Have Known It*, Fred Lieb claims that Speaker once told Lieb he was a member of the Ku Klux Klan. Although the Klan has always kept its membership rolls secret, Speaker's alleged membership is not surprising given that the Klan experienced a nationwide revival beginning in 1915, gaining much popularity with its anti-Catholic rhetoric. In addition, the Klan's national leader from 1922 to 1939, Imperial Wizard Hiram W. Evans, lived near Speaker in Hubbard.

Relations between the Grey Eagle and team president Joe Lannin were also far from warm. After the Red Sox Series victory in 1915, Lannin angered Speaker by proposing that the outfielder's salary be cut from about $18,000—higher at the time than that of Ty Cobb—to $9,000, since Speaker's batting average had declined three years in a row. (Lannin had raised Speaker's salary in 1914 to keep him from jumping to the Federal League's Brooklyn Club, which had offered Speaker a three-year contract for $100,000 to be its player–manager.) When Speaker held out, Lannin traded him to Cleveland for Sam Jones, Fred Thomas and $55,000.

Speaker received a massive outpouring of affection

against the Giants, sportswriter Sid Mercer recalled, Speaker "scooped up a grounder and threw out one of the fleet Giants on one of those automatic attempts to score from second on a single. It happened again the next day. That time he doubled a runner trying to score on a fly."

Despite interest from the Pirates, Superbas, Senators and, at last, the Giants, the Travelers sold Speaker back to Boston. Speaker hit only .224 in 31 games for the Red Sox, but was flawless in the outfield. Speaker further honed his outfield skills by working with Red Sox pitcher Cy Young. "When I was a rookie," Speaker later recalled, Young "used to hit me flies to sharpen my abilities to judge in advance the direction and distance of an outfield ball."

Speaker led Boston to World Championships in two of the next seven seasons, 1912 and 1915, hitting above .300 every year and perennially ranking among American League leaders in most offensive and defensive categories. With teammates Harry Hooper and Duffy Lewis, Speaker formed one of the best fielding outfields in history. During this period Speaker led AL centerfielders in putouts five times and double plays four times. Twice he had 35 assists, the American League record. In 1912, Speaker, playing in every game from the fans when he returned to Boston in a Cleveland uniform on May 9, and even mistakenly headed toward the Red Sox dugout at the end of one inning. Boston pitchers, meanwhile, complained that without Spoke in center, they could no longer groove fastballs when behind in the count, certain he would catch everything hit his way. The Red Sox won the World Series again, but Speaker became the idol of Indian fans and hit even better with his new club than he had in Boston. Overall, 1916 may have been Speaker's best season. He hit .386, to finally break Cobb's lock on the batting title, and led the AL in hits, doubles (tied), slugging and on-base percentage. Speaker's 35 stolen bases also ranked fifth in the league.

In the outfield, Speaker played so shallow that he was almost a fifth infielder. "At the crack of the bat he'd be off with his back to the infield," said teammate Joe Wood, "and then he'd turn and glance over his shoulder at the last minute and catch the ball so easy it looked like there was nothing to it, nothing at all." Twice in one month, April 1918, Speaker executed unassisted double plays at second base, catching low line drives on the run and then beating the base runner to the bag. At least once in his career Speaker was the pivot man in a routine double play. As late as 1923, after the advent of the lively ball forced Speaker to play deeper, he still had 26 assists. "I know it's easier, basically, to come in on a ball than go back," Speaker said later. "But so many more balls are hit in front of an outfielder, even now, that it's a matter of percentage to be able to play in close enough to cut off those low ones or cheap ones in front of him. I still see more games lost by singles that drop just over the infield than a triple over the outfielder's head. I learned early that I could save more games by cutting off some of those singles than I would lose by having an occasional extra-base hit go over my head."

Almost six feet tall and a sturdy 193 pounds, Speaker batted from a left-handed crouch and stood deep in the batter's box. He held his bat low, moving it up and down slowly, "like the lazy twitching of a cat's tail," according to an admirer, and took a full stride. "I don't find any particular ball easy to hit," he said. "I have no rule for batting. I keep my eye on the ball and when it nears me make ready to swing." Nevertheless, "I cut my drives between the first baseman and the line and that is my favorite alley for my doubles." He was a remarkably consistent batter. In 1912, Speaker set a major league record with three separate hitting streaks of 20 or more games, while his 11 consecutive hits in 1920 set a mark that went unsurpassed for 18 years. Speaker's major weakness as a batter was the slow, high, curve.

Speaker spent 11 seasons with the Indians, compiling a batting mark that averaged over .350. He paced the American League in doubles four straight seasons. As late as 1925, the year he married the former Mary Frances Cuddihy of Buffalo, the 37-year-old outfielder hit .389 in 117 games. The follow year, his final season with Cleveland, he hit .304 in 150 games.

As player–manager, Speaker piloted Cleveland to a 617–520 record (.543) between 1919 and 1926. The Indian club he took to the World Series in 1920 had been demoralized by the mid-season death of shortstop Ray Chapman. Speaker rallied the team and in the Series Cleveland defeated Brooklyn five games to two. Speaker was one of the first skippers to platoon extensively. In the Indians' championship year, he loaded up his batting order with right-handed hitters when a southpaw pitched, and vice versa. Speaker himself was the only left-handed hitter who faced left-handed pitchers. He did not believe his team should warm up in a batting cage, preferring his hitters to practice under real circumstances with a catcher behind the plate.

Following the 1926 season, Hubert (Dutch) Leonard, a disgruntled former teammate, accused Speaker and Cobb of fixing a game in 1919. Commissioner Kenesaw Mountain Landis cleared both men of the charges, but by that time AL president Ban Johnson, who believed the men guilty, had convinced Cobb and Speaker to resign in order to protect baseball's image. "Baseball in Cleveland and Tris Speaker have been synonymous for so long that a Speakerless team will seem contrary to natural law," lamented the *Cleveland Plain Dealer*. "What Mathewson was to New York, what Cobb was to Detroit, what Johnson was to Washington, Tris Speaker has been to Cleveland." In February 1927, Speaker signed with the Washington

Senators, where he hit .327. (When he returned to Cleveland for a farewell tribute from Indian fans in May of that year, Speaker was touched less by the gifts he received, said someone present, than the yells from the grandstand to "Hit it against the wall, Spoke!") Speaker finished his major league career with Cobb on Connie Mack's Philadelphia Athletics in 1928. He spent 1929 and 1930 as player–manager of the Newark Bears in the International League, where he hit .355 and .419 in limited play.

Although retired as a player, Speaker was far from through with baseball. With his wife, he had boxes at old League Park and later Municipal Stadium. Speaker was a broadcaster for the Cubs and White Sox in 1931 and then manager and part owner of the Kansas City Blues of the American Association. He was less successful as a bench manager, however, than when he was guiding his club from center field. "Speaker was possessed of a driving personality that seemed somehow to bring mediocre players up to his own level. That was the secret of his success," wrote one observer. "As long he was in uniform playing day in and day out he was a great manager. As soon as he quit playing, he lost his inspirational force. He became just another old timer in the dugout." The Kansas City venture was not successful and Speaker eventually returned to Cleveland as a broadcaster and scout. Meanwhile, newcomer Joe DiMaggio's graceful play in the Yankee outfield inevitably caused comparisons to Speaker. The proud Texan bristled at the suggestion that DiMaggio was a worthy successor. When asked about the Yankee Clipper in 1939, Speaker responded, "HIM? I could name fifteen better outfielders!"

In 1947, at the request of general manager Bill Veeck, Tris returned to uniform as a special coach, where he helped convert Larry Doby, who had played second base in the Negro Leagues, into a center fielder. After that, Speaker frequently visited Indians training camps to work with younger players. The Grey Eagle could "still spot a batter's weakness quicker than most of us," according to Al Lopez.

The Grey Eagle also capitalized on simply being Tris Speaker. A regular on the banquet circuit, he served as president of "Tris Speaker, Inc.," a wholesale wine and liquor firm in Cleveland, and later as a sales representative for a Detroit steel company. In 1936 he was chairman of the Cleveland Boxing and Wrestling Commission. In 1939 Speaker was president of the National Professional Indoor Baseball League, which had a club in every major league city except Washington, but the circuit lasted only one month. He kept busy hunting, fishing and flying (Tris had served as a naval aviator in the fall of 1918 and was commissioned a lieutenant) and kept in touch with old friends such as Ty Cobb, Joe Wood and Stan Coveleski. In 1953, Speaker had lunch in the White House with President Eisenhower.

Almost immune to injury when he played, Speaker suffered a series of health problems in his later years. In 1937, he fractured his skull and broke his left arm when he fell 16 feet from a second-story porch at his home. He also had a near-fatal perforated intestine and was hospitalized for weeks after a heart ailment in 1954. Speaker suffered a fatal coronary occlusion on December 8, 1958, while he and a friend pulled their boat on a dock after an afternoon fishing in Lake Whitney, Texas. He and Mary were on an extended vacation before hoping to head on to spring training.

Tris Speaker was buried in a cedar-shaded spot in Section 1, Block 2 of Fairview Cemetery in Hubbard, where Speaker's mother and father were interred and not far from the diamond where he once played as a boy. Speaker was elected to the Hall of Fame in 1937, one of the first eight players so honored. His plaque states that he was the "greatest centrefielder [sic] of his day."

DON JENSEN

Larry Gardner

BOSTON

WILLIAM LAWRENCE "LARRY" GARDNER
THIRD BASEMAN, 1908–1917

A career .289 hitter who was generally regarded during the second decade of the Deadball Era as the American League's finest fielder at third base, where his frequent acrobatics caused him to be known as the "diving third baseman," Larry Gardner also enjoyed a reputation as one of the era's best clutch players. As Boston sportswriter Tim Murnane put it, Gardner had "a way of rising to the occasion as a trout rises to a fly in one of his favorite Vermont streams." F.C. Lane named Gardner to his All-America Baseball Club no less than nine times, honoring him as the AL's first-team third baseman on four occasions – as often as Frank Baker. "In Boston and later in Cleveland, the fellow who really impressed me, especially when you needed a clutch hit, was Larry Gardner," recalled teammate Joe Wood. "Larry could play third base with the best of them. I wouldn't trade him for five Frank Bakers."

The third and youngest child of a shopkeeper of English-Canadian descent, William Lawrence Gardner was born on May 13, 1886, in Enosburg Falls, Vermont, a remote village in the foothills of the northernmost Green Mountains, just 16 miles from the Canadian border. In those days Enosburg Falls was the home of the world-famous Dr. B. J. Kendall Co., manufacturer of a horse liniment called "Kendall's Spavin Cure," making it one of the most prosperous and progressive villages in Vermont. Larry attended Enosburg Falls High School, serving as captain of the hockey club and star pitcher of the baseball team. During his senior year he batted .432 and pitched five shutouts in eight games, leading the team to a 7–1 record and an unofficial state championship. That summer Larry was playing shortstop for the Spavin Curers, his hometown's entry in the Franklin County League, when some players from the University of Vermont discovered him. With their encouragement, the 19-year-old Gardner enrolled at UVM in the fall of 1905.

Though freshmen baseball players usually played for the junior varsity or their class team, Larry Gardner was one of two first-year students to make the varsity, the other being his future Red Sox teammate Ray Collins. Usually playing third base and batting leadoff, Gardner hit safely in his first 10 games as a collegian but slumped over the last seven games, finishing the year at .269 with a team-leading nine stolen bases. That summer he became the regular right fielder for Burlington's team in the fast-paced Northern League, an outlaw circuit that included Eddie Collins among dozens of former and future major leaguers. Gardner moved to shortstop in his sophomore season at UVM and was batting .400 when he suffered a broken collarbone in a collision with the left fielder. He missed the rest of the college season but recovered in time for summer ball, playing for Bangor and earning All-Maine honors after leading the Maine State League with a .371 average.

Though Gardner had missed the last six games of the previous season, his UVM teammates had elected him team captain for 1908, and he was also elected president of the junior class. Against the toughest schedule it had played since the early 1890s, the UVM team finished 15–8–2 and was dubbed the champion baseball team of New England. "Capt. Gardner, the hardest hitting man on the team, has been batting at a .300 clip, and it would be hard to find a better shortstop," wrote the *Burlington Free Press*. Nonetheless the *Springfield Republican* named him the third baseman on its All-Eastern Nine, making room for Jack Barry of Holy Cross at shortstop. That summer Barry joined Connie Mack's Philadelphia Athletics, while Gardner, whom Mack also tried to procure, elected to sign with the Boston Red Sox, foregoing his final season of collegiate eligibility.

Gardner reported directly to the Red Sox after final exams, making his major league debut on June 25. Replacing an injured Harry Lord in extra innings, the 22-year-old rookie stroked a double in the 13th inning. Two days later Gardner appeared in the starting lineup at third base and went 0-for-4 with an error in a 7–6 loss to the New York Highlanders. Years later he remembered being "bunted to death" by Willie Keeler, who had two bunt singles among his four hits. That night Cy Young invited Larry to join him at the hotel bar and consoled him with the aid of a bottle of rye whisky. Though Gardner was batting an even .300 in three games, Boston owner John Taylor made him a proposition: stay with the club and gain experience by watching, or go to Lynn, Massachusetts, where there was a place open for a shortstop. Larry opted to play every day, reporting to the New England League club on July 15. He batted .305 in 61 games and showed "all the earmarks of another Harry Lord." The Red Sox invited Gardner to re-join the team in September, but he chose to return to UVM for the fall semester. "With a little extra money in my pocket, my senior year I lived the life of Reilly," he recalled.

Come spring, Gardner watched from the bleachers as Ray Collins led the UVM baseball team to a 13–9 record. Final exams ended in mid-June, but commencement festivities didn't start until June 26, so Larry went down to Boston and actually managed to get into a game. On June 23, 1909, after replacing Lord at third base, Larry tripled and scored in his only at-bat. A couple of days later he went back to Burlington for graduation, where he received his bachelor's degree in chemistry. Returning to Boston, Gardner spent most of the rest of the season as Lord's understudy, batting .297 with a .432 slugging percentage in only 19 games. He started 1910 on the bench as well, but a position opened up when second baseman Amby McConnell, a fellow Vermonter, injured his leg only 10 games into the season. Gardner batted .283 in 113 games and was called "one of the best second basemen in the country." His development allowed Boston to trade both McConnell and Lord to the Chicago White Sox.

Gardner opened the 1911 season at second base, but at midseason Patsy Donovan shifted him to third base, the position he played for the rest of his career. "Can it be possible that Larry Gardner has been out of position all this time?" wrote Ring Lardner. "He was certainly a success as a second sacker, but right now it would be hard to convince the uninformed observer that he hadn't been playing third base for years." A Hub sportswriter wrote, "Third base has not been played so well in Boston since the days when Jimmy Collins was in his prime." Gardner became famous for thwarting Ty Cobb's attempts to bunt for base hits. "I don't think Ty ever bunted for a hit against me because I found out his secret early," Larry said. "Cobb used to fake a lot of bunts, but I noticed that when he was really going to bunt, he always licked his lips. When I saw that, I'd start

in with the pitch. He never realized I'd caught on."

The 1912 season was a breakthrough year for both the Red Sox and Larry Gardner, who batted .315 with a team-leading 18 triples. In a meaningless game in Detroit on September 21, Gardner was injured diving for Donie Bush's grounder down the line. He tried to snag the ball with his bare right hand, but it hit the little finger, causing the bone to protrude through the flesh. Larry went home to Enosburg Falls to recuperate. Returning to Boston in time for the World Series, Gardner played with his fingers taped together and was a non-factor in the first three games. In Game Four, however, he blasted a single and a triple and scored two runs in Boston's 3–1 victory, and in Game Seven he hit Boston's only home run of the Series. But the game for which Gardner will always be remembered was the eighth and deciding game at Fenway Park, when he lofted a sacrifice fly to deep right field off of Christy Mathewson in the bottom of the 10th inning to drive home Steve Yerkes with the Series-winning run. "I was disappointed at first because I thought the ball was going out," Larry remembered, "but when I saw Yerkes tag up, then score to end it, I realized it meant $4,024.68, just about double my earnings for the year."

After signing a three-year contract that winter, Gardner batted .281 in 1913 but slumped to .259 and a career-low .258 over the next two seasons. In 1915 he rebounded to hit .308, fifth-best in the AL, despite playing with a dislocated big toe. With Tris Speaker gone to Cleveland in 1916, Gardner became the biggest bat in the Boston lineup. He enhanced his reputation as a clutch player by smashing two home runs in the 1916 World Series, the same number he had hit during the regular season. The first one came in Game Three at Ebbets Field. "I hadn't been hitting and was really mad," Larry recalled. "Jack Coombs was pitching for the Dodgers and he was a hell of a pitcher. He broke off a curve on me, a lefty hitter. I started to swing and tried to stop because I thought it was a bad pitch, but I was committed too far and had to go through with it. I even had my eyes shut. When I opened them, I saw the ball going over the wall." In Game Four, with two men on base and Boston down 2–0, Gardner hit a Rube Marquard fastball for an inside-the-park homer, giving the Red Sox a 3–2 lead they never relinquished. "That one blow, delivered deep into the barren lands of center field, broke Marquard's heart, shattered Brooklyn's wavering defense, and practically closed out the series," wrote Grantland Rice.

Gardner's batting average plummeted 43 points to .265 in 1917, giving the Red Sox the idea that he was slipping after a decade of service. On February 28,

1918, he and two others were traded to the Philadelphia Athletics for Stuffy McInnis. "The report that Gardner has passed the zenith of his career and is on the decline is all camouflage, probably designed to placate the Boston fans, with whom he was extremely popular," wrote one Philadelphia scribe. Even though the Red Sox won another World Series in 1918, they sorely missed the 32-year-old Gardner, who batted a solid .285 in 127 games for the last-place A's. "Gardner's absence last year almost cost the Red Sox the world's championship," wrote a Boston reporter. "The Sox tried out more than a dozen third sackers in an attempt to fill his shoes." (Actually, they tried nine, but none held a candle to Gardner.)

Continuing his youth movement, Connie Mack traded Gardner during the off-season to the Cleveland Indians, reuniting the veteran third baseman with his former teammates Tris Speaker and Joe Wood. Playing every inning of every game in 1919, Larry hit an even .300 and led the Indians with 79 RBI. In 1920 he did even better, batting .310 with a team-leading 118 RBI to help the Indians win their first AL pennant and World Series. Gardner's best season with Cleveland came in 1921, when he established career highs in batting average (.319), runs (101), hits (187), doubles (32), and RBI (120). Hampered by a series of nagging injuries, the 36-year-old Gardner tailed off to .285 in 137 games in 1922. He considered retirement but Speaker convinced him to return as a coach and occasional pinch

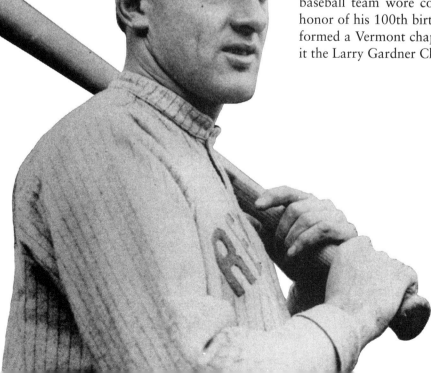

hitter. Larry played sparingly over his last two seasons in Cleveland, then played and managed for three years in the minor leagues with Dallas and Asheville. When Speaker got caught up in a gambling scandal and was sold after the 1926 season, many thought Gardner would replace him. Instead the Indians hired Jack McCallister, who had no previous major league playing or managing experience.

At that point Gardner left professional baseball and returned to his garage and automobile business in his old hometown of Enosburg Falls. His wife, Margaret, hated it there and was relieved in 1929 when Larry joined the UVM physical education department in the comparatively big city of Burlington. That same year Gardner became the head baseball coach, a position he held until 1951. He stressed sportsmanship over winning – his career record was 177–198—and prided himself on developing well-rounded students rather than specialized athletes. In addition to his coaching duties, Larry became UVM's athletic director in 1942. The Gardners and their two sons spent the school year in a comfortable brick cottage in Burlington, and their summers at a spectacular camp on a rocky bluff overlooking Lake Champlain. After retiring from the university in 1952, Larry fished even more frequently and worked a regular schedule at The Camera Shop in downtown Burlington. He kept in touch with several old teammates, especially his best friend on the Red Sox, Harry Hooper.

Larry Gardner died two months shy of his 90th birthday on March 11, 1976, at Larry Jr.'s home in St. George, Vermont. He left his body to UVM's Department of Anatomy, and his ashes were spread at St. Paul's Cathedral in Burlington. In 1986 the UVM baseball team wore commemorative sleeve patches in honor of his 100th birthday, and when SABR members formed a Vermont chapter in 1993, they elected to call it the Larry Gardner Chapter.

TOM SIMON

BOSTON

HOWARD ELLSWORTH "SMOKY JOE" WOOD
RIGHT-HANDED PITCHER, 1908–1915

Joe Wood's reign as one of the most dominating pitchers in baseball history lasted a brief two seasons, but it left an indelible impression on those who witnessed his greatness first-hand. "Without a doubt," Ty Cobb later recalled, "Joe Wood was one of the best pitchers I ever faced throughout my entire career." In 1911 and 1912, Smoky Joe Wood won 57 games for the Boston Red Sox, including a no-hitter against the St. Louis Browns on July 29, 1911, and an American League record-tying 16 straight wins in the second half of the 1912 campaign. He was by no means large or overpowering, standing 5'11¾" and weighing in at 180 pounds, but concealed in his lanky frame was one of the most overpowering fastballs of the Deadball Era. "I have seen a lot of speedy pitchers in my time," Red Sox catcher Tubby Spencer quipped in the spring of 1909, "but Joe Wood can make sparks fly better than anyone else I ever saw throw a ball." Three years later, Walter Johnson could only agree. "Can I throw harder than Joe Wood?" he asked a waiting reporter. "Listen, mister, no man alive can throw harder than Smoky Joe Wood."

Howard Ellsworth Wood was born in Kansas City, Missouri, on October 25, 1889, the second son of John and Rebecca Stevens Wood. The nickname by which he would be known for the rest of his life came to Howard by way of two circus clowns named Petey and Joey. "My folks thought it was all pretty funny, and after they came back home they started calling me and my brother Joey and Petey," Wood later explained. "My brother and I answered to 'Pete' and 'Joe' Wood from then on."

Joe Wood was not exaggerating when he once told an interviewer that, as a boy, his family was "always on the go." Generations of Joe's family had been content to farm the Pennsylvania lands colonial militia Private

Jonathan Wood had secured from the Public Domain after the close of the American Revolution, but for Joe's restless father, the prospect of remaining on the family farm for life was unthinkable. After completing his education at the University of Pennsylvania, John Wood moved to Ness City, Kansas, started his family, then moved again to Kansas City, where Joe was born. But no sooner had Joe entered the world before his father uprooted the family again in 1890, drawn north to Chicago by the promise of work and a safe haven with his wife's uncle.

In Chicago, John Wood became a successful attorney, amassing an estate approaching a quarter of a million dollars. But for Joe's father, an ample income and a successful legal career were simply not enough. Driven by a pair of itchy feet and the scent of Alaskan gold, in March of 1898 he sent his family back to Pennsylvania and ventured off into the Klondike. After eight months of prospecting he returned, half frozen and suffering from collywobbles, but his dream of striking it rich was undimmed. During the summer of 1900, he loaded his family and belongings aboard a covered wagon and headed west to Colorado, eventually settling in the tiny mining town of Ouray. Working out of the family's Fifth Street home, he renewed his legal practice and began publishing a weekly newspaper, the *Ouray Times*.

Drawn back to Ness City, Kansas, in 1905, the family fell on hard times when John Wood lost his substantial fortune on dubious land deals in Western Kansas. With Pete Wood preparing to enroll at the University of Kansas that fall, Joe—schooling now a thing of the past—passed the time working odd jobs and playing ball with the local Ness City club.

As the close of the 1906 season approached, baseball fans in Ness City learned from posters pasted on storefronts across town that the Ness City Nine was slated to take on an unusual opponent, the National Bloomer Girls out of Kansas City. Though they advertised themselves as an all-girls team, the popular bloomers outfit routinely augmented their strength by adding young boys, "toppers" as they were known, to the roster. Joe sparkled in a 23–2 trouncing of the visitors that afternoon, and at the close of the contest Bloomer owner Logan Galbraith offered him $21 a week to join the team for the duration of the summer.

After he closed out the summer with the Bloomers, Joe signed on as an infielder with the Three-I League Cedar Rapids Rabbits, managed by one time Baltimore Oriole Belden Hill. Reportedly "all full up" with infielders, however, in the spring of 1907 Hill unceremoniously scratched Joe from his roster and handed his contract, free of charge, to his friend Jason "Doc" Andrews, manager of the Western Association Hutchinson White Sox. Joe started the season playing the infield, but weeks into the campaign, the pitching-starved White Sox dispatched Joe to the mound. By late September his uncanny speed caught the attention of numerous scouts, among them George Tebeau, owner of the American Association Kansas City Blues. Tebeau purchased Joe's contract for $3,500 and ordered him to Association Park in Kansas City in March of 1908.

Joe's 7–12 record in 24 appearances with the mediocre Blues was nothing to gloat over, but his strong exhibition work against Joe Cantillon's Washington Senators back at spring training and a near perfect no-hitter in Milwaukee on the 21st of May were more than enough to attract big league interest. After a fair bit of contractual wrangling, Joe's contract was purchased by the Boston Red Sox, and on August 24, 1908, the 18-year-old made his big league debut at the Huntington Avenue Grounds. Joe was bested by Doc White and the Chicago White Sox, 6–4.

In the first instance of a pattern that would dog him for much of his career, in the spring of 1909 Joe suffered a foot injury during a hotel room wrestling match with his best friend, Tris Speaker, which knocked him out of action until mid-June. Joe pitched well on his return, notching 11 wins against seven defeats, and his strong work continued through the first half of 1910. But, once again, injury intervened, this time courtesy of a Harry Hooper line drive to the ankle during batting practice. Surgery to remove a blood clot would sideline Joe for better than a month.

On a club rife with cliques and infighting, Joe Wood was as rugged as they came. "He talked out of the corner of his mouth and used language that would have made a steeple horse jockey blush," Hugh Fullerton would recall years later. "He challenged all opponents and dilated upon their pedigrees." But for the underachieving 1910 Red Sox, Joe's rough demeanor off the field (not to mention his disappointing 12–13 finish) won him no praise among Red Sox brass. Exasperated by his club's disappointing fourth-place finish, at the close of the summer Boston owner John I. Taylor announced he had drawn up a list of so-called "malcontents" among his players, and Joe Wood's name, word had it, stood unceremoniously at the top of his list. Weeks later, rumors swirled out of Boston that Taylor was on the verge of shipping Joe, along with battery mate Bill Carrigan, out of Boston permanently.

Had Taylor traded Joe—and given the Red Sox owner's dubious track record, there is no evidence to suggest he was not serious—he would have single-handedly deprived Boston of one of the most electrifying summers of baseball on record. After nailing down 23 victories in 1911, in 1912 Wood rose to the very top of his game. Pitching in newly opened Fenway Park, he got off to a modest 3–2 start (twice defeated by Clark Griffith's Senators), but by the close of June his 16–3 mark placed him second in the AL to Philadelphia's Eddie Plank. Joe came up short, 4–3, against Plank on July 4, but from there he was literally unbeatable. On August 28 he tied down his 12th straight win, bringing him to within four of Walter Johnson's record of 16. "Gee," remarked *Boston Post* sportswriter Paul Shannon, as he watched Joe from foul territory one afternoon, "that boy throws smoke." A baseball sobriquet was born.

With the Red Sox bearing down on the pennant in early September, the stage was set for one of the most storied moments of the Deadball Era. "Up until that time Johnson had his sixteenth [straight win] and lost his seventeenth. I had about eleven [actually thirteen]," remembered Joe. "Well, old Foxy Clark Griffith comes in and says, 'Walter Johnson should have the right to defend his record of 16 straight,' so he challenged Joe Wood to meet Walter Johnson." On September 6 a circus-like crowd estimated at 35,000 packed every crevice of Fenway Park—filling the stands, outfield and even foul territory along the right and left field foul lines – and cheered wildly with every strike Joe burned across. One boy, hit by a foul ball behind home plate, had to be carried from the field; another reportedly "fainted from excitement" and had to be escorted from the stands. In the end, Joe prevailed 1–0, a victory made possible when back-to-back fly balls by Tris Speaker and Duffy Lewis (that would have been playable under ordinary circumstances) fell harmlessly into the crowd and were ruled as doubles. Nine days later, Joe tied Johnson's record with a 2–1 victory over St. Louis.

On September 20 in Detroit, an error by Red Sox shortstop Marty Krug (in addition to Wood's own mediocre pitching) deprived Joe of a 17th consecutive win, but he bounced back to win his final two starts of the summer to bring his record to 34–5, to go along with a 1.91 ERA and career-bests in innings (344), and strikeouts (258). He went on to win three more games against John McGraw's New York Giants in the World Series, capping his extraordinary summer with a 4–3 win in relief of Hugh Bedient in Game Eight on October 16.

Married to Kansas City, Missouri, native Laura O'Shea in the off-season, in the spring of 1913 Smoky Joe Wood stood atop the Majors. "I was the king of the hill," he recalled, "top of the heap, right along with the very best." But, once again, he was vexed by injury. The first mishap occurred in Detroit on July 18, 1913, when Joe slipped on the wet grass fielding a Bobby Veach infield grounder along the third-base line, breaking his thumb and (with exception of one inning of relief in September) ending his season. Joe was confident about a healthy return to the majors in 1914, but days before he was scheduled to depart for spring training, he was struck by an appendicitis that sidelined him another two months.

Wood went on to close out 1914 at a respectable 9–3, and in 1915 he led the AL with a career best 1.49 ERA, in just 157⅓ innings of work. To onlookers it was obvious that something was wrong with the erstwhile phenom. "Joe Wood has not been right since he was operated on for appendicitis," wrote the *Washington Post*. "At times...he has shown flashes of his former smoke, but it is uncertain what he can do..." Those fears were confirmed in early October when Joe was seen clinging to his shoulder in pain in his final start of the summer, a 3–1 loss to Walter Johnson. He did not factor into Boston's four-games-to-one World Series victory over Philadelphia two weeks later.

Refusing to accept a cut in pay, in 1916 Joe remained at home in Twin Lakes, Pennsylvania, working out at a New York University gymnasium while tending to his ailing arm under the care of New York Chiropractor A.A. Crucius. In February of 1917, his contract was sold to Cleveland for $15,000. "My arm is just as good as it ever was," he announced at camp a month after the sale. "I don't expect any trouble at all, provided I don't work it too fast now." Wood could not have been more mistaken. At his debut in Cleveland on May 26, he was shelled by the Yankees in eight innings of work, and three weeks later sportswriters revealed that, in all probability, he was through as a pitcher. "It is a wonder you have any arm left," Joe's physician, Dr. Robert Drury, scolded publicly. Wood refused Indian owner Jim Dunn's offer to keep him on in an advisory role and removed himself from the club payroll in early July.

The Deadball Era is replete with story upon story of pitchers whose careers were cut short by shoulders torn to shreds; rarely, if ever, did such men make or even contemplate a return to the diamond. Five months after leaving the Indians, however, Joe made the surprising announcement that he intended to attempt a return to the big leagues by converting himself from pitcher to outfielder. In the war-torn summer of 1918 he stepped into Cleveland's starting lineup, hitting a respectable .296 in 119 appearances. From 1919 to 1921 he was platooned with Elmer Smith (his best season coming in 1921 when he hit .366 in 66 games), and in 1920 he made his second and final World Series appearance, going 4-for-10 over four games in Cleveland's win over Brooklyn. He enjoyed another strong season with the Indians in 1922, hitting .296 in 142 games, but citing family obligations he opted not to return to baseball for 1923.

"Few players last 10 years in the Big Leagues, [and] fewer still reach such heights in their profession as Joe Wood," eulogized F.C. Lane near the end of Joe's career. "Joe Wood faced the most difficult task a player can be called upon to face and against all seemingly insurmountable handicaps he made good." Those qualities would serve Wood long after he left the game. Through his lifelong friend Tris Speaker, in 1923 Joe was hired by Yale University to coach the freshman nine and, one year later, he was promoted to coach the varsity. There was speculation that Wood's career at Yale might be in jeopardy in late 1926, when, along with Cobb and Speaker, he was accused of being one of three central figures in an alleged game-fixing scandal dating back to the 1919 season. But after an all night session, the Yale Board of Control declared it had "no evidence [which] discredits the honesty and integrity of his past record." Joe would remain with the University for another 15 years, amassing a coaching record of 283–228–1. At the end of his coaching career, Wood coached his son, Joe Wood, Jr, who went on to a brief major league career, pitching three games for the Boston Red Sox during the 1944 season. Two other sons, Stephen and Robert, played collegiate ball at Colgate. Wood and his wife also had one daughter, Virginia.

Citing "economic exigencies occasioned by war conditions," in March of 1942 the University dismissed Joe and two other University coaches. Wood then left New England for California, where he opened a golfing range with his brother, Pete. "I made more money in that seven years than I did my entire time playing and coaching baseball," he later recalled with a chuckle. Wood then returned to New England, and, by 1960, he was settled into comfortable retirement at 90 Marvel Road in New Haven, Connecticut.

Over the next quarter century, Joe looked on as his former teammates and adversaries, one by one, won induction into the Baseball Hall of Fame. Probably due to his frequent injuries and the fact that his record did not meet the Hall of Fame's requirement that a player's career be "outstanding for a long period of time," the Hall of Fame passed over Wood time and again. In January of 1985 Yale University president A. Bartlett Giamatti presented Wood with an honorary doctorate in Human Letters. At the ceremony, Joe wept uncontrollably.

Two months later, on March 25, 1985, Smoky Joe Wood died at the age of 95 while residing at a convalescent home in New Haven. He was buried in the Wood family ancestral grounds, in Shohola, Pennsylvania.

MICHAEL FOSTER

Ray W. Collins

BOSTON

RAY WILLISTON COLLINS
LEFT-HANDED PITCHER, 1909–1915

Ray Collins won a combined 39 games in 1913–14, and his career ERA of 2.51 is impressive even for the Deadball Era. Though big for his time (6'1", 185 lbs.), Collins didn't throw hard; his success was due to his corkscrew delivery, which one reporter described as resembling "an explosion in a leg and arm factory," and his remarkable control. "Ray Collins hasn't a thing," remarked Washington manager Clark Griffith, "yet he is one of the best pitchers in the American League—one of the two or three best left-handed pitchers in the business." Detroit manager Hughey Jennings concurred: "I class him as the best left-hander in the American League, with the possible exception of Eddie Plank." In 1915, however, the 28-year-old Collins suddenly and mysteriously lost his ability to pitch, forcing him to retire from professional baseball with a lifetime record of 84–62.

Ray Williston Collins was born on February 11, 1887, on his family's farm in Colchester, Vermont, seven miles north of Burlington. Ray wasn't kidding when he listed his nationality as "Yankee" on a 1911 *Baseball Magazine* survey. He was a ninth-generation descendant of William Bradford, second governor of Plymouth Colony, and his great-great grandfather, Capt. John Collins, was one of Burlington's original settlers and a close friend of Ethan Allen. Ray's father, Frank, was a dairy farmer who died of scarlet fever when Ray was 10 years old. Moving to Burlington with his mother, Electa, Ray attended the public schools and became captain of the Burlington High School tennis, basketball, and baseball teams.

Ray recalled his time at the University of Vermont as the four greatest years of his life. Though he lived at home, "Collie" became active in campus life, joining the Delta Psi fraternity and serving as chairman of the Kake Walk, a mid-winter blackface minstrel show that remained the highlight of UVM's social calendar into the 1960s. He also put his wide-ranging athletic talents to use, playing varsity basketball as a freshman and varsity tennis as a sophomore. Ray's greatest accomplishments came on the baseball diamond, where he and classmate Larry Gardner, his future teammate on the Red Sox, combined to make UVM one of the top college teams in the country. Collins gained honorable mention on the All-Eastern and All-New England teams as a freshman. Major league scouts followed him throughout his sophomore year, and towards the end of that season the New York Highlanders offered him $3,000 to turn professional. Collins turned down the offer, believing he was not yet ready for major league competition.

Gardner and Collins led UVM to the championship of the New England states in 1908, and both were named to the 1908 All-Eastern team. After the season Gardner signed with the Boston Red Sox, but Collins again shunned offers to turn professional. Taking over for Gardner as team captain, Collins pitched well as a senior, going out in a "blaze of glory," according to the *Burlington Free Press* headline, by striking out 19 Penn State batters in his last collegiate game—his 37th victory in 50 career collegiate starts. Half of the 16 major league clubs were interested in signing him, but Collins chose to follow Gardner to Boston. After coming to terms with Red Sox president John Taylor, Ray returned to Burlington and carried the class banner at commencement, closing the ceremony with a speech on behalf of the graduating class.

Leaving Vermont on July 12, 1909, Ray Collins joined the Red Sox in the midst of a western road trip. Eleven days later, he made his first career start, in the second game of a doubleheader against the Detroit Tigers, losing 4–2. Collins received a second chance against the Tigers on July 25, 1909, and tossed the first of his 19 career shutouts. Collins pitched only sporadically during the rest of the season, compiling a 4–3 record with a 2.81 ERA, but he'd proven that he was capable of competing in the majors without any minor league apprenticeship.

Collins became a regular in the Boston rotation in 1910, his 1.62 ERA ranking sixth in the American League and his 13 victories ranking second on the Red Sox, behind only Eddie Cicotte's 15. He got off to a 3–6 start in 1911, however, prompting rumors that he might be released. "Ominous rumblings agitate the atmosphere," wrote one Boston reporter. "The management holds, apparently, that a player who cannot pitch nine games and win, say, 15 or 20, is useless, dangerous, and ought to be abolished." Before the Red Sox did anything rash, Ray returned to form and won eight of his last 12 decisions, ending the year with a 2.40 ERA.

Ray missed the first two months of the 1912 season after suffering a spike wound to his knee during spring training. He didn't start a game until June 7, nor win one until June 22, but from that point on he was nearly invincible. A half-century later, his fondest memory of that pennant-winning season was pitching the first-place Red Sox to two victories in three days over the second-place Athletics at Shibe Park in early July. Collins went on to finish fifth in the AL in shutouts, pitching all four of them during the second half. By October Ray's record stood at 13–8 and his ERA at 2.53, fifth-best in the AL. He was considered Boston's second-best pitcher, behind only Smoky Joe Wood. After taking a no-decision in Game Two of the 1912 World Series, which ended up a 6–6 tie, Collins was slated to start Game Six, but the sky was overcast so Jake Stahl went with hard-throwing spitballer Buck O'Brien. The Giants shelled O'Brien for five runs in the first inning, after which Collins took over and pitched shutout ball. "Things might have been a little different had Collins been sent in from the first," Stahl admitted after the 5–2 loss.

In 1913 Collins posted a 19–8 record, his .704 winning percentage ranking fourth in the league. On August 29 Collins went head-to-head against Walter Johnson, who was riding a 14-game winning streak, and pitched 11 scoreless innings for the victory. Of the four games in which Collins and Johnson faced each other in 1913, three were decided by a score of 1–0, with the Vermonter prevailing twice. Coming off an excellent season, Collins expected a substantial increase in his $3,600 salary. He was disappointed when management offered only $4,500. Ray threatened to jump to the Federal League, but the Red Sox eventually met his demands and signed him to a two-year contract at $5,400 per year. He emerged as the staff's ace in 1914 when he became one of only three AL pitchers to reach the 20-win plateau, picking up his 18th and 19th victories on September 22 by pitching complete games in both ends of a doubleheader at Detroit's Navin Field.

That doubleheader victory proved to be the last highlight of Collins' major league career. As early as June 1915, newspapers began speculating that he would soon retire. Starting only nine games, the fewest since his rookie year, Ray finished at 4–7 with an abysmal 4.30 ERA. He didn't pitch a single inning in the 1915 World Series, and after the season the Red Sox expected him to take a cut in pay to $3,500. Rather than suffer that humiliation, Collins announced his retirement on January 3, 1916, stating that he was "discouraged by his failure to show old-time form." The newspapers made no mention of injury, and the cause of his sudden downturn remains a mystery.

With his economics degree and his college and baseball contacts, Collins received several job offers. Instead he elected to return to his family's farm in Colchester where he farmed in sweat-intensive, 19th-century fashion, walking behind a horse-drawn plow. Ray's mother moved back to the farm, and Ray and his wife, Lillian, raised five children. To make ends meet, the Collins family took in travelers in a precursor of today's bed and breakfasts, serving meals and talking baseball with their guests. They also sold a variety of maple products, with Ray collecting sap from a stand of sugar maples a mile north of the farmhouse. Neighbors had no idea that the family was struggling financially. To them Ray Collins was a pillar in the community—chairman of the draft board, the town's first zoning administrator, moderator of town meetings, and Colchester's representative in the Vermont legislature. He was also active in UVM alumni affairs, serving on the board of trustees that oversaw the school's transition from private to public university. Each year during reunions Ray hosted a get-together for the Class of '09 (Larry Gardner often attended), and it was during one of those Sunday brunches in 1969 that he suffered a stroke. His condition worsened until he died at Fanny Allen Hospital in Colchester on January 9, 1970. He was buried in Colchester's Village Cemetery.

Tom Simon

Harry Hooper

BOSTON

HARRY BARTHOLOMEW HOOPER
RIGHT FIELDER, 1909–1920

One of the best defensive right fielders in baseball history and one of the top leadoff hitters of the Deadball Era, Harry Hooper was also a team leader, superb practitioner of the inside game, and clutch hitter who played a key role in four Boston Red Sox world championships. As a product of rural California, but a college man who earned a degree in engineering, Hooper also symbolized baseball's transition, ongoing during the Deadball Era, from a game rooted in the eastern cities and played by professionals who were largely uneducated and illiterate, to a game that broadened its geographical horizons and expanded its social appeal through players like Hooper.

Although his play at times achieved the spectacular, Hooper eschewed flamboyance for simplicity, exaggeration for modesty. Possessing neither the crafted appeal of Christy Mathewson nor the raw excitement of Babe Ruth, Hooper practiced his profession quietly, skillfully, and confidently. More Everyman than Superman, he is a mirror of the game and its human touches in ways that his myth-encrusted contemporaries never can be. Though he never led the American League in any major statistical category, Hooper crafted a solid statistical resume that included 2,466 hits, 1,429 runs and 1,136 career walks, good for a lifetime .281 batting average and .368 on-base percentage. In 92 career World Series at-bats, Hooper batted a solid .293; in the 1915 Fall Classic he batted .350 with two home runs.

Harry Bartholomew Hooper was born on August 24, 1887 in California's Santa Clara Valley, the fourth and youngest child of Joseph and Mary Katherine Keller Hooper. In 1876, Joseph had left Canada's Prince Edward Island, slowly working his way westward through a series of jobs before landing in California, where he met Mary Keller, a German immigrant working as a housekeeper, and married her in 1878. Growing up on the family ranch, Harry first honed his athletic skills by tossing fresh eggs against the side of the family's barn. This merited little reaction from his parents, and Harry spent more time throwing various objects, challenging himself in distance and accuracy.

His first formal exposure to nine-man-a-side baseball came during a trip East with his mother. While visiting her family in Central Pennsylvania, Harry watched with great interest the Lock Haven team play. He capped the trip with a visit to relatives living in New York City, and a chance to see his first Major League game. The Brooklyn Bridegrooms played the Louisville Colonels, and although the home team lost, Hooper's dedication and love of the game solidified. Just before he and his mother began the long journey back to California, he received from his uncle something he later called "the best of all" his boyhood treasures: a bat, ball, and well-worn fielder's glove.

Harry Hooper's formal baseball career began when he left the family's farm in August 1902, for the high school attached to Saint Mary's College of California, then located in Oakland. Although Hooper originally arrived for a two year secondary program, the Christian Brothers who ran the school quickly recognized his mathematical aptitude, and encouraged his parents to consider allowing him to complete the full baccalaureate program, which would stretch his time at the school from two years to five. Consistent with the emerging sense of education as a means to economic opportunity, Harry's parents agreed to the school's request. At roughly the same time, he earned a place on the secondary school's new baseball team.

Working his way up through the four teams at the school, Hooper earned a place as a starting pitcher on the junior varsity as a collegiate sophomore, but his stature—he stood slightly over five feet at the time—and pitching velocity limited his chance to earn a spot on the varsity squad. The top team's head coach suggested a switch to an outfield position, which Hooper accepted. It assured him the starting left field spot on the College's varsity nine at the start of the 1907 season, a team regarded by many as one of collegiate baseball's finest in the pre-World War I era. With a roster that contained six future big leaguers, Hooper played alongside catcher Eddie Burns, third baseman Joe Hamilton, pitcher Harry Krause, plus outfielders Charlie Enwright and Mickey Thompson, on a team that completed a 27-game season with a perfect record. Among that year's victims were Stanford University, the University of California, a Pacific Coast League all-star team, and the Chicago White Sox, who the Phoenix faced in an exhibition game prior to the start of the major league season.

Hitting for a .371 average during his senior season, Hooper drew the attention of several organized ball representatives, and signed his first contract—for 10 days—to play with the Alameda club of the California League, where he teamed with Duffy Lewis for the first time; the two had been schoolmates but not teammates at St. Mary's. Ironically, the short length of the contract was Hooper's idea. Focused primarily on his engineering career, he agreed to play only for the time between the end of the Phoenix's season and his graduation date. His strong play during the short stretch earned Hooper a contract with the Sacramento club, which he agreed to accept with the proviso that Sacramento's owner arrange a surveying position for him, which was done.

Late in the 1908 season, after hitting .347, scoring 39 runs, and stealing 34 bases in 68 games, Hooper earned the tag "Ty Cobb of the State League," and an offer from his manager, Charlie Graham, who also served as a scout for the Boston Red Sox. Initially when approached about the possibility Hooper recalled saying he thought baseball "was a sideline to engineering to make enough money for a living." Graham persisted and Hooper agreed to meet with Red Sox owner John Taylor, who soon would be in the area to observe several prospects for his team. At their meeting at a Sacramento saloon, the two agreed to a contract that would pay the 21-year-old Hooper $2,800 for the 1909 season, approximately $1,000 more than he would have made combined through his California baseball play and his job with the Western Pacific Railroad.

Harry Hooper's career with the Boston Red Sox began on March 4, 1909, when he arrived in Hot Springs, Arkansas, for the team's training camp. The Red Sox of 1909 represented a team in transition. Following the demise of the championship clubs of 1903 and 1904,

owner Taylor aspired to build a pennant contender with young pitchers, power hitting, and speed on the bases. The rotation included Joe Wood, Eddie Cicotte, and Frank Arellanes. Other than shortstop Heinie Wagner, no member of the squad had two complete seasons with the team.

Harry Hooper's major league debut came on April 16, in Washington, D.C., during the team's second series of the season. Called upon to start in left field and bat seventh, Hooper lined a single in his first at-bat that also notched his first RBI. That day he went 2-for-3 at the plate, with "a clever steal in the ninth," three flies caught including "a superb running back catch" that saved a triple, and one assist when he threw out Gabby Street at home. During the first month of the season, he played occasionally, always fielding well.

A natural right-handed hitter and fielder while at Saint Mary's, the 5'10" 168-pound Hooper experimented with switch hitting. Playing in an era when manufacturing runs one at a time mattered more than sheer power, Hooper decided to take advantage of his abilities and reduce one step from the batter's box to first base by making the move to full-time left-handed hitting. His hard work and dependable play, especially in the field, made personnel decisions easier for the club's management. By the season's midpoint, Hooper firmly held the fourth outfield position, and often entered games in the late innings because of his defensive skills. The squad finished the year in third place, 9½ games behind Detroit, but also 25 games over .500. Hooper recorded a .282 average in 81 games, while completing the transition from one side of the plate to the other.

The Red Sox that assembled in Hot Springs in March 1910 had reason to be optimistic about the coming season. Most of the lineup returned, with Hooper virtually assured one outfield spot. With Tris Speaker secure in center, the only question was whether it would be right or left on a day-to-day basis. The arrival of another veteran of the Saint Mary's Phoenix in camp, George "Duffy" Lewis, largely settled the issue. The outfield trio of Tris Speaker, Harry Hooper in right and Duffy Lewis in left made its debut on April 27. Through the course of that season—when they hit a combined .296—and the next five, the "Million Dollar Outfield" played more than 90% of Boston's games. After batting .267 in 1910, Hooper improved to an impressive .311 average in 1911, scored 93 runs and posted a .399 on-base percentage. The club, however, failed to finish better than fourth in either season.

Despite his .242 batting average, Hooper was an integral piece of the 1912 pennant-winners, ranking second on the team with 98 runs scored, 66 walks, 29 stolen bases, and 12 triples. In that year's World Series against the New York Giants, Hooper elevated his play, batting .290 for the Series and making several crucial plays at bat and in the field. In Game One, Hooper rapped a game-tying double in the seventh inning to secure a 4–3 Boston victory. After taking a 3–1 lead in the Series, the Red Sox saw the Giants even things at three each. Despite numerous base runners for both teams, the Giants held a slim 1–0 lead in the seventh inning of the deciding game, which would have been greater if not for Hooper's catch of Larry Doyle's drive to the right field fence, robbing him of a home run. In the tenth inning of Game Eight, Hooper hit "a sure triple" that Fred Snodgrass caught, but it advanced Clyde Engle to third, from where he scored the series-winning run on a sacrifice fly. Hooper's "paralyzing catch" in the final game earned him accolades in the press, but John McGraw paid an even higher compliment when he labeled the Californian "one of the most dangerous hitters in a pinch the game has ever known." In the next day's *Boston Globe*, Speaker called Hooper's catch "the greatest, I believe, that I ever saw."

Coming off the championship year, Hooper married Esther Henchy, a 20-year-old banker's daughter from nearby Capitola, California, but remained dedicated to his off-season training. Although the Red Sox struggled as a team in 1913 and 1914, Hooper personally improved his offensive output, hitting .288 in 1913 and scoring 100 runs, and batting .258 with 85 runs scored in 1914. On May 30, 1913, Hooper hit home runs to lead off both games of a double-header, a feat not equaled until Rickey Henderson did it 80 years later.

In 1915 the Red Sox returned to championship form and began a stretch of success where the team played the best, and most consistent, baseball in the major leagues. Between 1915 and 1917, the team won at least 90 games each season , and likely would have done so again in 1918 if World War I had not shortened the season. The successes came through the team's effective use of the strategies of the era. Rather than power hitting and home runs, the Red Sox won by manufacturing runs, playing strong defense, and, most of all, getting solid pitching. In fact, during the four-year stretch, the team never featured more than one hitter with an average of .300 or higher. As Hooper wrote, "With the best pitching staff and the best defensive outfield...we played for one run—tried to get on the scoreboard first and then increase our lead."

In 1915, Hooper's average dipped to .235, but he compensated by collecting 89 walks, fifth best in the league, and posting a respectable .342 on-base percentage. Once again, he saved his best work for

the World Series, when he helped Boston finish off Philadelphia in five games with a .350 batting average and two home runs, both of which came in the final game of the Series, making Hooper only the second player in World Series history to homer twice in the same game. (Both homers bounced into Baker Bowl's temporary stands; today they would be considered ground-rule doubles.)

After another championship in 1916, and a disappointing second-place finish nine games behind the Chicago White Sox the following year, Hooper's Red Sox entered the 1918 season in a tenuous position. Although Boston's roster suffered fewer losses to the military and war-related industries than other teams, the lineup managed a woeful team average of .249, the second-worst in the American League; Hooper posted a .289 average and a .405 slugging percentage (second on the team to Babe Ruth in both categories). He also helped the team to another pennant in a war-shortened season (126 games) that ended with a dramatic labor challenge during the World Series.

During the Fall Classic against the Chicago Cubs, Hooper demonstrated his clear thinking and effective leadership, representing his fellow players' concerns in a manner that preserved the integrity of baseball, while also exposing some of the inherent weaknesses of baseball's ruling system. Due to wartime travel restrictions, the teams played the Series in a 3–4 format, with the first games in Chicago (ironically at Comiskey Park). The rest of the games took place at Fenway. The Red Sox returned home enjoying a 2–1 lead, but all was not well. For several war-related reasons, attendance and gate receipts during the regular season and World Series in 1918 fell well below pre-war levels. However, at this time the players' post-season bonuses came from gate receipts and the owners would not guarantee a minimum payment. The two teams, traveling on the same train, appointed four representatives, including Hooper, to speak to the governing National Commission and press their case. Specifically, the teams sought a guarantee of $2,600 each for the winners and $1,400 for the losers, with 10% going as a donation to the Red Cross. The National Commission begrudgingly listened, and agreed to consider the matter, but made no promises.

With Boston leading three games to one, the players delayed the start of the fifth game by more than one hour in an attempt to secure concessions from the Commission. Although Hooper negotiated an end to the strike, and secured a verbal promise from Ban Johnson of no reprisals, he forever regretted not securing the guarantee in writing. After Boston won the Series 4–2, its last for 86 years, the players received the smallest financial awards in World Series history ($1,108.45 for each Red Sox player and $574.62 for each Cub). In December the Boston players all received letters from John A. Heydler, acting president of the National League and a Commission member. It informed them that, "Owing to the disgraceful conduct of the players in the strike during the Series…(the players) would be fined the World Series emblems that were traditionally awarded to the winners." Although a modest symbol, the emblems—really lapel pins—became a symbol of the lack of respect accorded the players in the years before a strong players union and free agency.

Harry Hooper's career with the Boston Red Sox ended on March 4, 1921, when Boston owner Harry Frazee thwarted a holdout by trading him to the Chicago White Sox for Shano Collins and Nemo Liebold. Hooper posted some of the best offensive seasons of his career during his five years with the White Sox. In 1921 he batted .327; the following year he notched career highs in runs scored (111), home runs (11) and RBI (80). In 1924, he posted a career-best .328 batting average and .413 on-base percentage. In 1925, his last major league season, Hooper batted .265. Playing in his final major league game on October 4, 1925, Hooper went 1-for-4 with a double.

Upon his retirement, Hooper returned to California and worked in real estate for one year before accepting a job as player–manager with Mission (San Francisco) in the Pacific Coast League. Hooper lasted one year with the club, batting .282 in 81 games and guiding the Missions to a disappointing 86–110 record. Let go after the season, Hooper returned to the real estate business for a few years while also playing minor league baseball in nearby Marysville and Santa Cruz, then became coach of the Princeton baseball team in September 1930. Hooper stayed at the post for two years, posting a 21–30–1 record before Depression-era finances forced the college to cut back on Hooper's salary, leading to his resignation. He once again returned to the real estate business in California, survived the Depression, and became wealthy in his old age. He also served as postmaster of Capitola for over twenty years. His greatest honor came in 1971, when the Veteran's Committee elected him to the Baseball Hall of Fame. Hooper was also one of the inaugural inductees when the St. Mary's College Athletic Hall of Fame was established in 1973; his son John, a center fielder during the 1940s, was inducted four years later. Harry Hooper died at the age of 87 on December 18, 1974, following a stroke. He was laid to rest in an above-ground crypt in the center of Aptos Cemetery, in Aptos, California. He was survived by two sons and a daughter.

PAUL J. ZINGG AND
ELIZABETH A. REED

BOSTON

GEORGE EDWARD "DUFFY" LEWIS
LEFT FIELDER, 1910–1917

For decades after they last played together, the Red Sox's outfield of Duffy Lewis, Tris Speaker and Harry Hooper, who toiled next to each other for six years in the Deadball Era, was often considered the greatest in baseball history. Although all three, especially Speaker, were fine hitters, their reputation was due largely to their exceptional defensive play. Lewis, the left fielder and the only one of the three not in baseball's Hall of Fame, was long remembered for the way he played the incline at the base of Fenway Park's left field wall, a slope of grass that bore the name "Duffy's Cliff." Hooper thought Lewis was the best of the three "at making the back hand running catch at balls hit over his head." A powerful left-handed batter, the 5'10", 170-pound Lewis typically batted behind Speaker in the cleanup position, and often ranked among American League leaders in home runs and RBI.

George Edward Lewis was born April 18, 1888, in San Francisco to George and Mary Lewis. He was the youngest of three children, following Agnus by four years and Edward by two. Young George acquired his lifelong nickname, Duffy, from his mother's maiden name. On April 18, 1906—Duffy's 18th birthday—the infamous earthquake and fire ravaged his hometown. "I thought the whole world was coming to an end," he later said. Lewis attended and played baseball at St. Mary's College for one year, before signing with the Alameda team in the California League in 1907. In mid-1908 he joined the Oakland Oaks, and he continued his apprenticeship the next year, playing 200 games and batting .279 in 1909. John I. Taylor, the Red Sox owner, first discovered Lewis playing for Yuma, Arizona, in the Imperial Valley League during the winter of 1908–09, and in September 1909 drafted Lewis's contract from the Oaks. After the 1909 season, Taylor went west and signed Lewis himself.

Lewis joined the Red Sox in spring training at Hot Springs, Arkansas, in 1910. He apparently did not take too kindly to the treatment accorded to rookies, refusing, for example, to limit his time in the batting cage or to back down from confrontations with his fellow players. Tris Speaker, in particular, did not take to Lewis's outspoken and cocky demeanor, leading to a prickly relationship that lasted throughout their many years as teammates. Lewis also irritated his new manager, Patsy Donovan, who fined and then benched the brash rookie. Duffy played in 149 games his rookie season, hitting .283 with eight home runs, only two fewer than the league-leading figure, and 29 doubles, which placed him third in the league.

In 1911 Lewis's average climbed to .307, a career-high, and his seven home runs tied for fourth in the circuit. After the season Lewis was to be wed to Eleanor Keane, a young baseball fan he had met at Huntington Avenue Grounds. But at the urging of Red Sox owner Taylor, Lewis broke off the engagement two days before the wedding and headed back to California. Keane was the third woman with whom Lewis had broken off an engagement, but a month later the couple reconciled and were married in San Rafael, California.

When Boston's Fenway Park was built in 1912, the 10-foot embankment in deep left field was one of its most interesting trademarks. Lewis covered this ground for six years, and became its master. "I'd go out to the ballpark mornings," he later told a sportswriter, "and have somebody hit the ball again and again out to the wall. I experimented with every angle of approach up the cliff until I learned to play the slope correctly. Sometimes it would be tougher coming back down the slope than going up. With runners on base, you had to come off the cliff throwing." The slope remained until l933, when Fenway Park was thoroughly renovated.

In 1912, Lewis's 284 batting average was solid, but it was his 109 RBI, tied for second in the league, that contributed the most to his first championship team. In the famous duel between Walter Johnson and Smoky Joe Wood on September 6, Lewis's bloop double down the right field line against the Big Train plated the only run of the contest. Although the Red Sox won a classic World Series over the Giants that fall, Lewis hit just .188 and made a costly error in the second game.

Lewis's frosty relationship with Speaker continued. During the summer of 1913 things deteriorated when Speaker continually knocked Lewis's cap off his head, revealing Duffy's heavily receding hairline. Finally, when Speaker persisted one time too many, Lewis threw his bat at his teammate, hitting him in the shins hard enough that Speaker had to be helped from the field. This friction did not affect their play on the field, as they helped form what may have been the best defensive outfield in baseball history. In 1913 the three accounted for an astonishing 84 assists, including 29 by Lewis.

Lewis hit .298 with 90 RBI in 1913 as the Red Sox dropped to fourth place, and, after resisting the advances of the Federal League to jump his team, managed just .278 the following year.

Lewis hit .291 in 1915, and made up for his sub-par 1912 Series performance by hitting .444 in the 1915 Fall Classic, driving in five of the 13 runs the Red Sox scored in their five-game triumph. He drove in the game winner off Pete Alexander in the bottom of the ninth of the third game, plated the winning run on a double in the fourth contest, while also making game-saving catches in both games. He also blasted a long drive that bounced into the center field bleachers for a game-tying home run off Eppa Rixey in the finale. Of Lewis's stellar defense, the *Boston Globe*'s Tim Murnane wrote, "the all-around work of the modest Californian never has been equaled in a big Series."

Speaker was traded to the Indians before the 1916 season, for two players and $55,000. Manager Bill Carrigan experimented briefly with Lewis in center field before Duffy moved back to his familiar cliff in left. Lewis slumped to .268 in 1916, but on his return to the World Series, he hit .353 (6-for-17). The following season Lewis hit .302 with a team-leading 167 hits.

Lewis spent the 1918 season in the United States Navy, missing out on his team's 1918 World Series championship while serving as player–manager of a Naval baseball team at Mare Island, California, near his hometown. Discharged from the service, in December 1918 he was traded to the Yankees, along with Dutch Leonard and Ernie Shore, for $15,000 plus Frank Gilhooley, Al Walters, Slim Love and Ray Caldwell. After being dealt, Lewis initially considered quitting unless he was given a larger contract. Once he reported, he hit .272 with seven home runs (more than his previous five seasons combined, thanks to the Polo Grounds' short porch) and a team-high 89 RBI. In 1920, he found himself fighting for playing time (.271 in 107 games) after the acquisition of Babe Ruth and the debut of rookie Bob Meusel. After the season he was traded to the Senators, for whom he hit .186 in just 27 games.

Early in the 1921 season, Lewis joined Salt Lake City of the Pacific Coast League, where he played through the 1924 campaign. He hit a league-high .401 in 1921, and took over as manager the next three years, in which he hit .362, .358, and .392 in the famed hitters' paradise. In 1925, he was the player–manager of Portland in the PCL, hitting .294 for the Beavers. He finished his baseball career with Mobile, Jersey City and Portland (Maine) in 1926 and 1927, acting as manager at both Mobile and Portland.

His finances wiped out by the stock market crash, Lewis was a coach for the Boston Braves from 1931 to 1935, and may have been the only man to have witnessed Babe Ruth's first home run (when he was Lewis's teammate in 1915) and last (when Ruth was playing out the string for the 1935 Braves). In 1936 he became the traveling secretary of the Braves, a post he held for 26 years. His motto was "Pay another buck and travel first class," and he became renowned around the league with bellhops and waiters as a big tipper.

Lewis was often called upon to return to Fenway Park, and appeared in several old-timers games. He attended a celebration of the park's 50th anniversary in 1962 along with many of his 1912 teammates. In 1975, the 87-year-old Lewis threw out the first ball on Opening Day, in honor of the team's 75th season, and again before the famous sixth game of that season's World Series.

Lewis spent his later years in retirement in Salem, New Hampshire, with Eleanor. They had no children. He spent much of his time at Rockingham Park, a nearby horse track, where he had his own suite. A dapper dresser, he was said to own 72 suits. Lewis died in Salem on June 17, 1979, three years after his beloved wife. At the time of his death he had no known living relatives and no money, and was buried in an unmarked grave in Holy Cross Cemetery in Londonderry, just outside of Salem. In 2001, a collection was taken up to pay for a stone, engraving and upkeep on the plot.

MARK ARMOUR

BOSTON

HUBERT BENJAMIN "DUTCH" LEONARD
LEFT-HANDED PITCHER, 1913–1918

A hard-throwing, spectacularly talented left-hander who posted the best single-season earned run average in American League history in 1914, Dutch Leonard was also one of the Deadball Era's most controversial figures. At nearly every stop along his journey in professional baseball, Leonard feuded with management over his salary, and at one point was even suspended from Organized Baseball for nearly three years for refusing to report for work. Regarded as a selfish, cowardly player by many of his contemporaries, Leonard frittered away much of his major league career, alternating periods of brilliance with long bouts of inertia. "As a pitcher, he was gutless," Hall of Fame umpire Billy Evans once declared. "We umpires had no respect for Leonard, for he whined on every pitch called against him." After exiting the game in 1925, Leonard touched off one of the biggest scandals in baseball history when he accused Ty Cobb and Tris Speaker of conspiring to throw a baseball game in 1919. Commissioner Kenesaw Mountain Landis dismissed the charges, and Leonard retired to his California ranch, where he earned millions of dollars growing grapes.

Hubert Benjamin Leonard was born on April 16, 1892, in Birmingham, Ohio, the youngest of six surviving children of David and Ella Hershey Leonard. For a time David worked as a real estate agent in Toledo, before moving the family to California in the early 1900s and finding work as a carpenter. While Hubert's older siblings became accomplished musicians (a brother, Cuyler, eventually made a name for himself as a composer and trumpet soloist), Hubert gravitated toward the pitching mound. In 1911, "Dutch" (a moniker hung on him during his childhood because he "looked like a Dutchman") pitched for the highly regarded St. Mary's College team while attending classes there.

He was spotted by a scout for the Philadelphia Athletics, who signed him during the 1911 campaign. With the Athletics rotation already loaded with the likes of Jack Coombs, Eddie Plank, Chief Bender and Cy Morgan, Leonard never appeared in any games. The following year, Leonard joined the Boston Red Sox for spring training, but developed a lame arm and failed to make the team. Sent to Worcester of the New England League, Leonard was bombed in one of his first outings and shortly thereafter abandoned the club. He showed up at Boston team headquarters and complained to club president Jimmy McAleer that "I didn't get any support. It's a rotten league. I won't play there any more." Still sensing promise in the young left-hander's arm, Boston sent Leonard to Denver of the Western League, where he overcame a midseason suspension for insubordination to win 22 games and strike out 326 batters in 241 innings of work. The following spring Leonard made the Red Sox squad out of spring training and joined the rotation.

Darkly-complexioned and built "more like a football player than a baseball player" according to F.C. Lane, the stocky 5'10½" Leonard relied on the classic combination of an overpowering fastball and sharp-breaking curve. Later in his career he mixed in the spitball, and in 1920 became one of the "grandfathered" pitchers allowed to continue throwing the pitch after it was made illegal. In his rookie season with the 1913 Red Sox, Leonard posted a 14–16 record and 2.39 ERA in 259⅓ innings of work. His biggest problem was his control: for the season he struck out 144 batters but also walked 94. All in all, it was a solid performance by the 21-year-old southpaw, but it gave little indication of the dominance he would achieve the following year.

Leonard's historic 1914 campaign was cut short by a wrist injury in early September, but in the 36 games in which he pitched, including 11 in relief, the left-hander posted an astounding 0.96 ERA, the lowest mark in the twentieth century and the second best all-time, behind Tim Keefe's 0.86 recorded for the 1880 Troy Haymakers of the National League. (Keefe's record was established in just 105 innings, good enough to qualify for the record only because his team played just 83 games that season.) Leonard pitched 224⅔ innings in his record-setting summer, striking out 176 (giving him a league-best strikeout rate of 7.05 per nine innings) and lowering his walk total to 60 while hitting eight batters. For the season, he allowed just 24 earned runs (10 unearned) and won 19 games against five defeats.

He didn't win his first game of the season until his fourth start, a 9–1 victory on May 4 against Philadelphia. After dropping a game to Washington on May 30 to run his record to 4–3, Leonard did not lose another game until August 13, running off a 12-game winning streak during which he struck out 91 batters in 116 innings. Despite his microscopic ERA, Leonard did not enjoy any long scoreless inning streaks or periods of noteworthy invincibility. Rather, he remained thoroughly consistent throughout the season, shutting out his opponents in seven of his starts and allowing just one run in 10 other outings. He surrendered more than two runs in a game just four times all season, and never allowed more than four runs in any start.

Because Leonard's season was curtailed by injury, the pitcher failed to reach many of the milestones that were most noted at the time. He failed to win 20 games, and except for ERA (which had only been an official American League statistic since the previous season) did not lead the league in any major pitching category. For this reason, Leonard's 1914 performance went largely unheralded in the press. Even Leonard regarded his work that year as incomplete. As he later told F.C. Lane, "If I hadn't broken my wrist I think I would have done very well that year."

Nonetheless, Leonard's 1914 season did raise expectations for the 1915 campaign, which would prove to be a resounding success for the Boston franchise but a turbulent year for its ace southpaw. After receiving a raise in salary to $5,000 per year, Leonard reported to the team out of shape, and started only three games in the first six weeks of the season. In late May, Leonard was suspended by the club for insubordination. According to newspaper reports, Leonard accused club owner Joseph Lannin of undermining manager Bill Carrigan's authority and generally mistreating his players. Leonard did not return to the starting rotation until early July, though he finished the season strong, posting a 15–7 record and 2.36 ERA. For the second consecutive year, Leonard led the American League in strikeouts per nine

innings pitched, with 116 strikeouts in 183⅓ innings. He rounded out his season in impressive fashion, beating Philadelphia's Pete Alexander in Game Three of the World Series, 2–1.

Leonard proved more durable over the next two seasons for the Red Sox, throwing a combined 568⅔ innings in 1916 and 1917, and winning 34 games against 29 defeats. Although his strikeout rate continued to fall and he was no longer considered one of the game's overpowering pitchers, Leonard did pitch his first no-hitter in 1916, a 4–0 shutout over the St. Louis Browns on August 30. That autumn, Leonard also won his second and final World Series start, pitching Boston to a 6–2 victory over Brooklyn in Game Four. In 1918, Leonard pitched a second no-hitter, a 5–0 shutout victory, this time over the Detroit Tigers on June 3. His season came to an end a few weeks later when he circumvented the draft by joining the Fore River (MA) Shipyard team, for whom he won three games.

Prior to the 1919 season Leonard was included in the trade which also sent Ernie Shore and Duffy Lewis to the New York Yankees. Unlike Shore and Lewis, however, Leonard never appeared in a Yankee uniform and became a salary holdout. According to one report, Leonard demanded that his entire 1919 salary be deposited into a savings account, a request which infuriated New York owner Jacob Ruppert. "No man who doesn't trust my word can pitch for my team," Ruppert declared. In late May, the rights to the still-unsigned Leonard were sold to the Detroit Tigers for $10,000.

Now relying more on the spitball, Leonard spent the next three seasons with the Tigers, posting a modest 35–43 record. Prior to the 1922 season, Leonard again became tangled in a salary dispute, this time with Detroit owner Frank Navin, who refused to meet the pitcher's demands. Leonard in turn violated the reserve clause in his contract by jumping to Fresno of the independent San Joaquin League, an act which led to his suspension from Organized Baseball. After two years with Fresno, in which he compiled a 23–11 record, Leonard won his reinstatement and returned to the Tigers late in the 1924 season. Appearing in nine games for Detroit, Leonard went 3–2 with a 4.56 ERA.

In 1925 Leonard started 18 games for the Tigers, posting a solid 11–4 record despite a pedestrian 4.51 ERA. However, the pitcher feuded constantly with manager Ty Cobb, who had long disliked Leonard and would later claim that the southpaw was one of only two players he ever intentionally spiked during his career. As Cobb later explained, "Leonard played dirty—he deserved getting hurt." According to Cobb

biographer Charles Alexander, Cobb punished Leonard by deliberately overusing him, even after the team physician warned that the work could do permanent damage to the pitcher's arm. When Leonard protested that his arm hurt, Cobb castigated him in front of the entire team, exclaiming, "Don't you dare turn Bolshevik on me. I'm the boss here."

Matters finally came to a head on July 14, when Leonard suffered the most brutal loss of his career, surrendering 12 runs and 20 hits to the Philadelphia Athletics. Despite the pounding, Cobb kept Leonard in the game for the full nine innings. Even Connie Mack, the opposing manager, pleaded Cobb to take Leonard out of the game, reportedly saying, "You're killing that boy." Cobb laughed at the suggestion. Later that month, he placed Leonard on waivers and pulled strings to make sure that no other team claimed him. Leonard was particularly hurt that Tris Speaker, manager of the Cleveland Indians and a former teammate, passed on him. Once Leonard had cleared waivers, Cobb traded him to Vernon of the Pacific Coast League, but Leonard characteristically refused to report. With that, his professional baseball career came to an end.

Throughout his career Leonard had invested his money wisely, and by the time of his retirement operated a lucrative grape ranch just east of Fresno. But embittered by the manner in which he had been treated, Leonard quickly focused on exacting his revenge. Early in the 1926 season, Leonard told American League president Ban Johnson that on September 24, 1919, he had conspired with Cobb, Speaker and Indians outfielder Joe Wood to place bets on the following day's game against the Cleveland Indians, which Speaker had promised to lose in order to help the Tigers finish in third place. (It was Cleveland's first game after being eliminated from the pennant race.) The Tigers did win the game, 9–5, and Leonard, who did not play in the game, bet $1,500 on the outcome, receiving a modest $130 for his winning bet. To back up his story, Leonard produced two letters, one from Cobb and one from Wood, written shortly after the 1919 season, in which both made reference to the bets, though neither letter specifically stated what the bets had been for or whether the Indians had deliberately lost the game, as Leonard claimed.

Nonetheless, when presented with the letters, Johnson informed both Cobb and Speaker that their days in the American League were over, and after the 1926 season convinced both to resign their respective managerial positions and retire from the game. However, commissioner Kenesaw Mountain Landis, a long-time foe of Johnson's, saw the matter differently and decided to launch his own investigation. He asked Leonard to come to his office in Chicago to answer questions, but the ex-pitcher declined the invitation. Cobb, Speaker, and Wood, in turn, declared their innocence of the game-fixing charges and demanded an opportunity to face their accuser. With Leonard stubbornly refusing to leave his California ranch, the public sided with the accused stars. "Only a miserable thirst for vengeance actuated Leonard's attack on Cobb and Speaker," Billy Evans declared. "It is a crime that men of the stature of Ty and Tris should be blackened by a man of this caliber with charges that every baseballer knows to be utterly false."

Faced with a lack of evidence corroborating the game-fixing charge (indeed, Cobb, who supposedly had played the game to win, went only 1-for-5 at the plate with two steals that day, while Speaker, who was supposedly throwing the game, went 3-for-5 with two triples), as well as Leonard's unwillingness to come to Chicago, Landis publicly cleared Cobb and Speaker of any wrongdoing prior to the 1927 season, and Cobb signed with the Philadelphia Athletics, where he concluded his Hall of Fame career, while Speaker was sold to the Washington Senators.

Leonard, meanwhile, spent the rest of his days turning his grape ranch into a multimillion dollar enterprise. For a time he lived with his wife, Sybil Hitt, a vaudeville dancer known professionally as Muriel Worth. The marriage, which produced no children, ended in divorce in 1931. With the money from his grape-growing business, Leonard enjoyed a comfortable retirement in his lavishly-furnished home, which sat on a 2,500-acre plot of land. Among his most prized collections was a record collection totaling 150,000 discs.

Leonard remained in good health until 1942, when he suffered a heart attack. To the end of his life he remained reluctant to discuss the details of his controversial career. As a nephew later told sportswriter Joseph E. Simenic, "Many times we pleaded with him to sit down and put it on a recording—the highlights of his career—but he never felt in the mood and when he was not in the mood he was not about to do anything regardless of what it might be."

Dutch Leonard died in Fresno of a cerebral hemorrhage on July 11, 1952. To his heirs (a sister, four nephews, and a niece) he left an estate totaling more than $2.1 million. He was buried in Mountain View Cemetery, in Fresno.

DAVID JONES

Babe Ruth

BOSTON

George Herman "Babe" Ruth
Left-handed Pitcher, 1914–1919

During his five full seasons with the Boston Red Sox, Babe Ruth established himself as one of the premier left-handed pitchers in the game, began his historic transformation from moundsman to slugging outfielder, and was part of three World Series championship teams. After he was sold to the New York Yankees in December 1919, his eye-popping batting performances over the next few seasons helped usher in a new era of long-distance hitting and high scoring, effectively bringing down the curtain on the Deadball Era.

George Herman Ruth was born to George Ruth and Catherine Schamberger on February 6, 1895, in his mother's parents' house at 216 Emory Street, in Baltimore, Maryland. His father owned a saloon at 406 Conway Street, where the family also resided; the spot is now center field at Oriole Park at Camden Yards. With his father working long hours in his saloon and his mother often in poor health, Little George (as he was known) spent his days unsupervised on the waterfront streets and docks, committing petty theft and vandalism. Hanging out in his father's bar, he stole money from the till, drained the last drops from old beer glasses and developed a taste for chewing tobacco. He was only six years old.

Shortly after his seventh birthday, the Ruths petitioned the Baltimore courts to declare Little George "incorrigible" and sent him to live at St. Mary's Industrial School For Boys, a reform school run by Xaverian Brothers on the outskirts of the city. The boy's initial stay at St. Mary's lasted only four weeks before his parents brought him home for the first of several attempted reconciliations; his long-term residence at St. Mary's actually began in 1904. But it was during that first stay that George met Brother Matthias.

"He taught me to read and write and he taught me the difference between right and wrong," Ruth said of the Canadian-born priest. "He was the father I needed and the greatest man I've ever known." Brother Matthias also spent many afternoons tossing a worn-out baseball in the air and swatting it out to the boys. Little George watched, bug-eyed. "I had never seen anything like that in my life," he recalled. "I think I was born as a hitter the first day I ever saw him hit a baseball." The impressionable youngster imitated Matthias's hitting style—gripping the bat tightly down at the knobbed end, taking a big swing at the ball—as well as his way of running with quick, tiny steps.

When asked in 1918 about playing baseball at St. Mary's, Ruth said he had little difficulty anywhere on the field. "Sometimes I pitched. Sometimes I caught, and frequently I played the outfield and infield. It was all the same to me. All I wanted was to play. I didn't care much where." In one St. Mary's game in 1913, Ruth, then 18 years old, caught, played third base (even though he threw left-handed) and pitched, striking out six men, and collecting a double, a triple and a home run. That summer, he was allowed to pitch with local amateur and semipro teams on weekends. Impressed with his performances, Jack Dunn signed Ruth to his minor league Baltimore Orioles club the following February.

Though he was a bumpkin with minimal social skills, at camp in South Carolina Ruth quickly distinguished himself on the diamond. That spring, the Orioles played several major league teams. In two outings against the Phillies, Ruth faced 29 batters and allowed only six hits and two unearned runs. The next week, he threw a complete-game victory over the Philadelphia Athletics, winners of three of the last four World Series. Short on cash that summer thanks to the Federal League's invasion of Baltimore, Dunn sold Ruth to the Red Sox on July 9, along with pitcher Ernie Shore and catcher

Ben Egan, for $30,000.

On July 11, 1914, less than five months after leaving St. Mary's, Babe made his debut at Fenway Park: he pitched seven innings against Cleveland and received credit for a 4–3 win. After being hit hard by Detroit in his second outing, Ruth rode the bench until he was demoted to the minor leagues on August 18, where he helped the Providence Grays capture the International League pennant. Ruth returned to Boston for the final week of the 1914 season. On October 2, he pitched a complete game victory over the Yankees and doubled for his first major league hit.

Babe spent the winter in Baltimore with his new wife, Boston waitress Helen Woodford, and in 1915 he stuck with the big club. Ruth slumped early in the season, in part because of excessive carousing with fellow pitcher Dutch Leonard, and a broken toe—sustained by kicking the bench in frustration after being intentionally walked—kept him out of the rotation for two weeks. But when he returned, he shined, winning three complete games in a span of nine days in June. Between June 1 and September 2, Ruth was 13–1 and ended the season 18–8. However, despite his fine season, Ruth was benched in the World Series; his 2.44 season ERA was the worst among Boston's five spectacular starters.

In 1916, Ruth won 23 games and posted a league-leading 1.75 ERA. He also threw nine shutouts—an American League record for left-handed pitchers that still stands (it was tied in 1978 by the Yankees' Ron Guidry). In Game Two of the World Series, Ruth pitched all 14 innings, beating the Brooklyn Dodgers 2–1. Boston topped Brooklyn in the series four games to one.

Ruth's success went straight to his head in 1917, and he began regularly arguing with umpires about their strike zone judgment. Facing Washington on June 23, Ruth walked the first Senators batter on four pitches. Feeling squeezed by home plate umpire Brick Owens, Ruth complained and was promptly ejected, after which he stormed off the mound and punched Owens, striking a "glancing blow behind the ear." After Ruth was ejected, Ernie Shore came in to relieve. The baserunner was thrown out trying to steal and Shore retired the next 26 batters for an unofficial perfect game. Ruth got off lightly with a 10-day suspension and a $100 fine. He ended the year with a 24–13 record, completing 35 of his 38 starts, with six shutouts and an ERA of 2.01. Ruth's 35 complete games have been topped only once since then, by Bob Feller in 1946.

Although Ruth didn't play every day until May 1918, the idea of putting him in the regular lineup was first mentioned in the press during his rookie season. Calling Babe "one of the best natural sluggers ever in the game," Washington sportswriter Paul Eaton thought Ruth "might even be more valuable in some regular position than he is on the slab—a free suggestion for Manager [Bill] Carrigan." The Boston Post reported that summer that Babe "cherishes the hope that he may someday be the leading slugger of the country."

In 1915, Ruth batted .315 and topped the Red Sox with four home runs. Bobby Roth led the AL with seven homers, but he had 384 at-bats compared to Babe's 92. Ruth didn't have enough at-bats to qualify, but his .576 slugging percentage was higher than the official leaders in the American League (Jack Fournier .491), the National League (Gavy Cravath .510) and the Federal League (Bennie Kauff .509).

With the Red Sox offense sputtering after the sale of Tris Speaker in April 1916, the suggestion to play Ruth every day was renewed when he tied a record with a home run in three consecutive games. Ruth hated the helpless feeling of sitting on the bench between pitching assignments, and believed he could be a better hitter if given more opportunity. In mid-season, with all three Boston outfielders in slumps, Carrigan was reportedly ready to give Babe a shot, but it never happened. Ruth finished the 1917 season at .325, easily the highest average on the team. Left fielder Duffy Lewis topped the regulars at .302; no one else hit above .265. Giving Ruth an everyday job remained nothing more than an entertaining game of "what if"—until 1918.

The previous summer, the United States had entered the Great War; many players had enlisted or accepted war-related jobs before the season began. Trying to strengthen the Red Sox offense, about two weeks into the season, manager Ed Barrow, after discussions with right fielder and team captain Harry Hooper, penciled Ruth into the lineup. The move came only a few days after a Boston paper reported that team owner Harry Frazee had refused an offer of $100,000 for Ruth. "It is ridiculous to talk about it," Frazee said. "Ruth is our Big Ace. He's the most talked of, most sought for, most colorful ball player in the game." Later reports revealed that the offer had come from the Yankees.

On May 6, 1918, in the Polo Grounds against the Yankees, Ruth played first base, subbing for the injured Dick Hoblitzel, and batted sixth. It was the first time he had appeared in a game other than as a pitcher or pinch-hitter and the first time he batted any spot other than ninth. Ruth went 2-for-4, including a two-run home run. At that point, five of Ruth's 11 career home runs had come in New York. The Boston Post's Paul Shannon began his game story, "Babe Ruth still remains the hitting idol of the Polo Grounds." Three days later, on May 9, Ruth had one of the most extraordinary games of his career, going 5-for-5 in the cleanup spot with three doubles and a triple, while also pitching a 10-inning complete game, losing 4–3 to reliever Walter Johnson.

Barrow also wanted Ruth to continue pitching, but Babe, enjoying the notoriety his hitting was generating, often feigned exhaustion or a sore arm to avoid the mound. The two men argued about Ruth's playing time for several weeks. Finally, after one heated exchange in early July of 1918, Ruth quit the team. He returned after a few days and, after renegotiating his contract

with Frazee to include some hitting-related bonuses, patched up his disagreements with Barrow.

"I don't think a man can pitch in his regular turn, and play every other game at some other position, and keep that pace year after year," Ruth said. "I can do it this season all right, and not feel it, for I am young and strong and don't mind the work. But I wouldn't guarantee to do it for many seasons."

Ruth then began what is likely the greatest nine- or ten-week stretch of play in baseball history. From mid-July to early September 1918, Ruth pitched every fourth day, and played either left field, center field or first base on the other days. Ruth's double duty was not unique

during the Deadball Era—a handful of players had done both—but his level of success was (and remains) unprecedented in modern baseball. In one ten-game stretch at Fenway, Ruth hit .469 (15-for-32) and slugged .969 with four singles, six doubles and five triples. He was remarkably adept at first base, his favorite position. On the mound, he allowed more than two runs only once in his last 10 starts. The Colossus, as Babe was known in Boston, maintained his status as a top pitcher while simultaneously becoming the game's greatest hitter.

Ruth's performance led the Red Sox to the American League pennant, in a season cut short by the owners because of a work-or-fight order and dwindling attendance. All draft-age men were under government order to either enlist or take war-related employment—in shipyards or munitions factories, for example—which led not only to star players being lost to the war effort, but also to paltry turnouts of less than 1,000 for many afternoon games that summer.

Ruth opened the World Series on September 5 against the Chicago Cubs with a 1–0 shutout. He pitched well in Game Four, despite having bruised his left hand during some horseplay on the train back to Boston, and his double drove in what turned out to be the winning runs. However, Ruth was used almost exclusively as a pitcher during the Series. In order to neutralize Ruth, the Cubs started only left-handed pitchers against the Red Sox; manager Barrow responded by inexplicably benching baseball's best hitter.

Still, Ruth's pitching performances, together with his extra-inning outing in 1916, gave him a record of 29⅔ consecutive scoreless World Series innings, one of the records Ruth always said he was most proud of. His streak was finally bested by Whitey Ford of the Yankees in 1961. Ruth established a record as the first pitcher in baseball history to pitch in at least 10 regular seasons and post a winning record in all of them.

While with the Red Sox, Ruth often arranged for busloads of orphans to visit his farm in Sudbury, Massachusetts, for a day-long picnic and ball game, making sure each kid left with a glove and autographed baseball. When the Red Sox were at home, Ruth would arrive at Fenway Park early on Saturday mornings to help the vendors—mostly boys in their early teens— bag peanuts for the upcoming week's games.

"He'd race with us to see who could bag the most," recalled Tom Foley, who was 14 years old in 1918. (Ruth was barely out of his teens himself.) "He'd talk a blue streak the whole time, telling us to be good boys and play baseball, because there was good money in it. He thought that if we worked hard enough, we could be as good as he was. But we knew better than that. He'd

stay about an hour. When we finished, he'd pull out a $20 bill and throw it on the table and say 'Have a good time, kids.' We'd split it up, and each go home with an extra half-dollar or dollar depending on how many of us were there. Babe Ruth was an angel to us."

To management, however, Ruth was a headache. His continued inability—or outright refusal—to adhere to the team's curfew earned him several suspensions and his non-stop salary demands infuriated Frazee. The Red Sox owner had spoken publicly about possibly trading Ruth before the 1919 season, when Babe was holding out for double his salary and threatening to become a boxer. However, Ruth and Frazee came to terms and the Babe's hitting made headlines across the country all season long. He played 111 games in left field, belted a record 29 home runs, and led the major leagues in slugging percentage (.657, 127 points better than runner-up George Sisler), on-base percentage (.456), runs scored (103), RBI (114) and total bases (284). He also drove in or scored one-third of Boston's runs. But while Ruth also won nine games on the mound, he slumped badly there, going from a spectacular 6.8 hits allowed per nine innings to a decidedly pedestrian 10.0. The rest of the staff fell victim to injuries and the defending champs finished in the second division with a 66–71 record.

The sale of Ruth to the Yankees was announced after New Year's 1920 and although it was big news, public opinion in Boston was divided. Many fans were aghast that such a talent would be cast off, while others, including many former players, insisted that a cohesive team (as opposed to one egomaniac plus everyone else) was the key to success.

"[T]here is no getting away from the fact that despite his 29 home runs, the Red Sox finished sixth last year," Frazee said. "What the Boston fans want, I take it, and what I want because they want it, is a winning team, rather than a one-man team that finishes in sixth place." Frazee also called Ruth's home runs "more spectacular than useful."

He also intimated that the Yankees were taking a gamble on Ruth. It was a statement he would be later ridiculed for, but at the time the Yankees felt the same way. The amount paid ($125,000, plus a $300,000 loan) was astronomical, Ruth ate and drank excessively, frequented prostitutes, and had been involved in several car accidents. It would have surprised no one if, for whatever reason, Ruth was out of baseball in a year or two.

Amidst this speculation over his future, on February 28, 1920, Babe Ruth left Boston and boarded a train for New York. He was still only 25 years old.

ALLAN WOOD

BOSTON

CARL WILLIAM MAYS
RIGHT-HANDED PITCHER, 1915–1919

Carl Mays is best remembered for throwing the pitch that led to the death of Cleveland shortstop Ray Chapman in August of 1920. But he also had a career record of 207–126 and a 2.92 ERA over fifteen seasons, and remains one of the best pitchers not honored in the Hall of Fame. Throwing with a submarine motion so pronounced that he sometimes scraped his knuckles on the ground while delivering the ball, Mays looked "like a cross between an octopus and a bowler," *Baseball Magazine* observed in 1918. "He shoots the ball in at the batter at such unexpected angles that his delivery is hard to find, generally, until along about five o'clock, when the hitters get accustomed to it—and when the game is about over."

Perhaps the most disliked player of his era, Mays was once described by F.C. Lane as "a strange, cynical figure" who "aroused more ill will, more positive resentment than any other ballplayer on record." A noted headhunter even before the Chapman beaning, Mays refused to apologize for how he pitched. "Any pitcher who permits a hitter to dig in on him is asking for trouble," he once said. "I never deliberately tried to hit anyone in my life. I throw close just to keep the hitters loose up there." One teammate said Mays had the disposition of a man with a permanent toothache. Throughout his professional career, Mays had trouble making friends—even on his own teams. "When I first broke into baseball, I discovered that there seemed to be a feeling against me, even from the players on my own team," Mays said after a few years in the big leagues. "I always have wondered why I have encountered this antipathy from so many people wherever I have been. And I have never been able to explain it, even to myself."

Carl William Mays was born on November 12, 1891, in Liberty, Kentucky, one of eight children. The family soon moved to Mansfield, Missouri, where Carl's father William was a traveling Methodist minister. After his death when Carl was 12 years old, Mays's mother moved the family to Kingfisher, Oklahoma. It was there that Carl met his cousin, John Long, a catcher who introduced him to the game of baseball.

In 1912, Mays signed with Boise, Idaho, in the Class D Western Tri-State League, for $90 dollars a month; he finished the season 22–9 with a 2.08 ERA. He played the next season in Portland, Oregon, and in 1914 was drafted by the Providence Grays, a team the Detroit Tigers owned in the International League. During his stay with Providence, the Grays were sold to Red Sox owner Joe Lannin.

Mays's 24 victories led Providence to the 1914 IL pennant; in the final month of the season, he was ably assisted by Babe Ruth, who had made his debut in Boston that summer. The two young men were called up for the final week of the Red Sox's season, but Mays did not appear in any games.

Mays joined the Red Sox staff in 1915 and made his debut on April 15. During the Red Sox's pennant-winning season, he was used mostly in relief, appearing in 38 games. He went 6–5, with a 2.60 ERA, and (though the statistic hadn't been invented yet) led the league with seven saves. He did not appear in the World Series.

Mays's abrasive personality grated on opponents. In his rookie season, Mays often sparred with Detroit's cantankerous outfielder Ty Cobb. In one game, after Mays threw high and inside on Cobb, the Tiger laid down a bunt along the first base line for the sole purpose of spiking Mays and cutting his leg. Though bitter rivals— the Red Sox and Tigers battled for the American League pennant that season—the men held a grudging respect for each other's single-minded pursuit of victory.

In 1916, Mays split his time between the rotation (24 starts) and bullpen (20 other appearances), winning 18 games and posting a 2.39 ERA. In that fall's World Series against Brooklyn, Mays recorded a save in Game One—bailing out Ernie Shore by recording the final out with the bases loaded and the tying run on third—and was the losing pitcher in Game Three, the Red Sox's only loss in the series.

In 1917, Mays became a star. His 1.74 ERA was the third-lowest in the major leagues, and he ranked among the top five in the American League in fewest walks and hits allowed per nine innings, and lowest opponents' batting average and on-base percentage. But Mays also hit a league-high 14 batters and earned a reputation as a headhunter that dogged him for the rest of his life. "Mays is a low-ball pitcher," one opponent noted. "How does it happen that when he puts a ball on the inside it generally comes near the batter's head?"

Mays would often berate his fielders for making errors behind him. "I have been told I lack tact, which is probably true," he said. "But that is no crime." Late in his career, Mays praised another pitcher: "This fellow has no friends and doesn't want any friends. That's why he's a great pitcher." He could have easily been talking about himself.

Yankees infielder Roger Peckinpaugh said Mays threw " a very 'heavy' ball. It sinks and when you catch it, it feels heavy enough to almost go through your glove." Horace Ford, who batted against Mays in the National League, said that hitting Mays's fastball "was like hitting a chuck of lead. It would go clunk and you'd beat it into the ground."

Mays got an incredible amount of outs via ground balls, especially with the Red Sox. From 1916–18, he recorded 117, 118 and 122 assists, which remain the top three season totals in

Red Sox history. In 1918, Mays, then 26 years old, was the ace of the Boston staff, winning 21 games with a 2.21 ERA. He tied Walter Johnson for the league lead with eight shutouts and tied Scott Perry for the lead with 30 complete games. He finished fifth in strikeouts and fifth in fewest hits allowed per nine innings. He also hit 11 batters, the second-highest total in the league.

Mays started and completed Games Three and Six of the 1918 World Series against the Cubs; Boston won both games by a 2–1 score. Eight days after he pitched the Red Sox to the World Series championship, Mays married Marjorie Fredricka Madden, a graduate of the New England Conservatory of Music whom he had met at Fenway Park during his rookie season.

But things went downhill for Mays in 1919. While he was at spring training, his farm house in Missouri burned to the ground; he suspected arson. During a Decoration Day series in Philadelphia, when Athletics fans were pounding on the roof of the visitors' dugout, Mays threw a baseball into the stands, hitting a fan in the head. He also ran into a lengthy streak of bad luck on the mound, as the slumping Red Sox gave him almost no run support. Over a 15-day period in June, Mays lost three games by a combined score of 8–0. The last straw came on July 13, during a game against the White Sox. When Eddie Collins tried to steal second base, catcher Wally Schang's throw hit Mays in the head. At the end of the inning, the pitcher stormed off the mound, left the team and headed back to Boston.

Mays told sportswriter Burt Whitman that he needed to make a fresh start with another team. "I'm convinced that it will be impossible for me to preserve my confidence in myself as a ballplayer and stay with the Red Sox as the team is now handled," he said. "The entire team is up in the air and things have gone from bad to worse. The team cannot win with me pitching so I am getting out.... Maybe there will be a trade or a sale of my services. I do not care where I go." On July 30, the Red Sox traded Mays to the New York Yankees for Allan Russell, Bob McGraw, and $40,000 in cash.

A fierce legal battle ensued, as enraged American League president Ban Johnson attempted to block the trade. Several days before Mays was dealt, Johnson had privately suspended Mays and issued a secret order to all eight American League clubs prohibiting them from acquiring the pitcher until his suspension had been served. Johnson feared that Mays's actions could set a bad precedent for the league, by giving players the power to subvert the reserve clause and force trades simply by refusing to play for their clubs. "Baseball cannot tolerate such a breach of discipline," Johnson said of Mays's abandonment of the Red Sox. "It was up to the owners of the Boston club to suspend Carl Mays for breaking his contract and when they failed to do so, it is my duty as head of the American League to act."

The league's owners fractured over the matter, with five franchises (Cleveland, Detroit, Washington, St. Louis and Philadelphia) siding with Johnson, while three (New York, Chicago and Boston) defied him. Because the three "Insurrectionist" clubs held control over the league's five-man board of directors, Johnson was forced to back down from his stance on the issue, particularly after the three clubs began holding meetings with the National League to discuss the formation of a new 12-team circuit. Mays reported to New York, and the incident marked the first time in his long tenure as AL president that Ban Johnson had been outmaneuvered on a major issue. Mays pitched in 13 games for the Yankees in the second half of 1919, posting a sterling 1.65 ERA. Mays won 26 games for New York in 1920 and in 1921, he led the American League in both wins (27) and saves (7). He also hit .343 that year. Mays batted .268 over his career and, despite his reputation, was hit by a pitch just four times in 15 years—and only once after 1918.

On August 16, 1920—a dark, overcast day at the Polo Grounds—Mays hit Indians shortstop Ray Chapman in the temple with an inside fastball leading off the fifth inning. A loud crack resounded through the stadium, and Mays, thinking the pitch had hit Chapman's bat, fielded the ball and threw it to first base. Chapman was helped off the field, but collapsed in the clubhouse; after a late-night operation on his fractured skull, he died early the following morning. As Chapman staggered off the field, Mays pointed out to the umpires a scuff mark on the baseball which he claimed had caused the pitch to sail inside. Later that day, Mays would also claim the ball was wet from the rain that had fallen earlier. A few hours after Mays was informed of Chapman's death, he told a Manhattan District Attorney: "It was a little too close, and I saw Chapman duck his head in an effort to get out of the path of the ball. He was too late, however, and a second later he fell to the grounds. It was the most regrettable incident of my career, and I would give anything if I could undo what has happened." Almost all other witnesses to the incident, however, reported that Chapman never moved an inch and probably never saw the ball.

Sorrow over Chapman quickly turned to anger against Mays. Several teams, including the Red Sox, Tigers and Browns, sent petitions to league president Ban Johnson, demanding Mays be thrown out of baseball. Mays spent a week in seclusion, then returned to the mound on August 23. Yankee fans were supportive— a clearly nervous Mays defeated Detroit 10–0 at the Polo Grounds—but there was an increase in calls for a boycott of any game pitched by Mays.

He made three starts in New York before his first appearance on the road, on September 3, in a relief stint at Fenway Park. He was greeted with a mixture of boos and cheers, but by the time he had pitched the second game of a doubleheader the following day, most of the crowd was on his side. He decided, however, not to accompany the Yankees on a road trip to Cleveland later that week.

In the 1921 World Series against the Giants, Mays pitched three complete games without allowing a walk, but he was charged with two losses as the Yankees lost the series. According to sportswriter Fred Lieb, there were suspicions Mays may have lost those two games on purpose. In *The Pitch That Killed*, Mike Sowell details the concern among several writers and Commissioner Kenesaw Mountain Landis after Mays's meltdown in Game Four. Sowell also quotes Yankees co-owner Cap Huston as saying many years later that Mays and others (possibly Joe Bush) had deliberately lost World Series games in both 1921 and 1922. Lieb believed the unanswered questions about those series were what really kept Mays out of the Hall of Fame.

The rumors also were a likely reason that, despite Mays's 65 wins in three years, the Yankees tried to dump him before the 1923 season. That didn't work, so manager Miller Huggins simply refused to use him. Mays appeared in only 23 games for the Yankees in 1923, and at the end of the season was sold to Cincinnati. He pitched for the Reds for five years—rebounding to a 20–9 record in 1924—and ended his career in 1929 with the New York Giants.

After his retirement from the major leagues, Mays pitched in the Pacific Coast League and American Association for two seasons, then worked as a scout for 20 years for the Cleveland Indians and the Milwaukee and Atlanta Braves. He died on April 4, 1971, in El Cajon, California at age 79, and was buried in River View Cemetery in Portland, Oregon. He was survived by a second wife, Esther, and two children.

ALLAN WOOD

BOSTON

EDWARD GRANT BARROW
MANAGER, 1918–1920

Most famous for his wildly successful tenure in the New York Yankees front office from 1920 through 1945, Ed Barrow left his mark on the Deadball Era as well. Though he never played a game of professional baseball, the ubiquitous Barrow was a key participant in the careers of countless players and a major actor in many of the era's biggest controversies. The man who scouted Fred Clarke and Honus Wagner, moved Babe Ruth from the pitcher's mound to the outfield, and managed the Red Sox to their last world championship of the twentieth century also experimented with night baseball as early as 1896, helped Harry Stevens get his lucrative concessions business off the ground, and led an unsuccessful campaign to form a third major league with teams from the International League and American Association. In his official capacities, he served as field manager for both major and minor league teams, owned several minor league franchises, and served as league president for the Atlantic League (1897–1899) and the International League (1911–1917).

Hot-tempered and autocratic, over the years Barrow crossed swords with Kid Elberfeld, Frank Navin, Babe Ruth and Carl Mays, among many others. Harry Frazee, owner of the Red Sox during Barrow's managerial tenure with the club, jokingly referred to his skipper as "Simon," after Simon Legree, the infamous slave-driver from *Uncle Tom's Cabin*. "Big, broad-shouldered, deep-chested, dark-haired and bushy-browed, [Barrow] had been through the rough-and-tumble days of baseball," Frank Graham later wrote. "Forceful, outspoken, afraid of nobody, he had been called upon many times to fight, and the record is that nobody ever licked him."

Edward Grant Barrow was born on May 10, 1868, in Springfield, Illinois, the first of four sons of Effie Ann Vinson-Heller and John Barrow. John and Effie had met in Ohio after the Civil War, and the young couple had decided to head west for the greener land-grant pastures of the newest state in the Union, Nebraska; Edward's birth had come during that arduous journey. The Nebraska land the Barrows settled proved unproductive, and the family left for Iowa after six bleak years.

The family finally put down roots near Des Moines. At sixteen Ed went to work as the mailing clerk for a local paper, and when later promoted to city circulator, Barrow found himself in charge of the newsboys. A large, strapping, generally good-natured but hot-tempered lad who had some ability as a boxer, Barrow surely had the right attributes for his new job. A baseball enthusiast as well, Barrow pitched on a town team, but his playing career quickly ended when he critically injured his arm pitching in a cold rain. His baseball spirit remained intact, however, and he soon organized and promoted his own town teams. After accepting a more senior position at another paper, Barrow discovered future Hall of Fame outfielder Fred Clarke among his newsboys and recruited him for his ballclub.

After a brief foray into the cleaning business and time as a hotel clerk, in 1895 Barrow returned to baseball when he bought into the Wheeling franchise in the Inter-State League. At mid-season when the league collapsed, Barrow moved his franchise into the Iron & Oil League. Baseball management now in his blood, Barrow acquired (with a partner) the Paterson, New Jersey, franchise in the Atlantic League for 1896. Just after his acquisition of the Paterson club, Barrow signed the player he would later call the greatest of all-time, Honus Wagner. The following year, Barrow sold Wagner to the major league Louisville club for $2,100, a high price for the time. Later that year Barrow himself sold out.

The contentious Atlantic League elected Barrow as president for 1897, and for the next three years until the league folded after the 1899 season, Barrow oversaw the inter-owner squabbles, dealt with numerous player disputes, and managed the umpires. As league president during the Spanish-American War, he championed a number of marketing gimmicks to help keep the fans' interest: he brought in a woman, Lizzie Stroud (she played under the last name Arlington), to pitch and heavyweight champions John L. Sullivan and James Jeffries to umpire. Another heavyweight, Jim Corbett, often played first base in exhibitions, mostly in 1897.

For 1900 Barrow purchased a one-quarter interest in the Toronto franchise in the Eastern League and became its manager. With little inherited talent, Barrow brought the club home fifth in his first year. Barrow acquired some better players for the next season, including hurler Nick Altrock, and finished second. Despite losing a number of players to the fledgling American League, Barrow's club captured the pennant in 1902.

With the tragic suicide of new Detroit Tigers skipper Win Mercer in January 1903, Detroit owner Sam Angus hired Barrow as manager on the recommendation of AL president Ban Johnson. Bolstered by two contract jumpers from the NL, pitcher Bill Donovan and outfielder Sam Crawford, Barrow brought the team in fifth, a 12 ½ game improvement over the previous year. In one of the year's most notorious controversies, Barrow was forced to suspend star shortstop Kid Elberfeld in June after some outlandishly lackadaisical play. (Elberfeld, upset at not being named team captain, was supposedly throwing games as a ploy in order to obtain his release from the Tigers.) The St. Louis Browns were reportedly tampering with Elberfeld and encouraging him to maneuver for his release. The Giants, too, were likely interfering with the unhappy Elberfeld. Barrow claimed he would see Elberfeld out of baseball before sending him to one of these two teams, and charged "that in three of the last six games lost to St. Louis, Elberfeld made a muff, fumble or wild throw at the moment of a critical stage." Ban Johnson intervened and engineered a trade of Elberfeld to the new AL franchise in New York.

After the season Angus sold the franchise to William Yawkey after first offering it to Barrow and Frank Navin. The latter, soon promoted to secretary-treasurer, ingratiated himself with Yawkey, becoming his right-hand man. Barrow continued his effort to improve the club by adding several players that would contribute to the Tigers' pennant three years later, including third baseman Bill Coughlin, shortstop Charlie O'Leary, and outfielder Matty McIntyre. Not surprisingly, however,

Navin and Barrow, both young, ambitious, and egocentric, could not co-exist, and with the Tigers at 32–46 Navin gladly accepted Barrow's resignation.

Following his stint in Detroit, Barrow began a two-year odyssey managing in the high minors. Montreal, in the Eastern League, recruited Barrow right after his resignation to come finish out the 1904 season as their manager. For 1905 he was hired by Indianapolis in the American Association, and 1906 found him back in Toronto. Disheartened with his baseball career after his first-ever last-place finish that year, Barrow left baseball to help operate Toronto's Windsor Hotel.

Four years later in 1910 Montreal offered Barrow the manager's post and a chance to get back into baseball. Barrow happily accepted, and after the season he was elected league president. In recognition of the two Canadian franchises, Barrow persuaded the Eastern League to change its name to the International League (IL) prior to the 1912 season.

In January 1912 Barrow married Fannie Taylor Briggs, whom he had met in Toronto many years earlier. It was the second marriage for both and would last until Barrow's death many years later. The couple would raise one daughter, Audrey. In his many autobiographical writings, Barrow never mentioned his first wife.

When the Federal League (FL) challenged Organized Baseball as a self-declared major league in 1914, the most severe hardship fell upon the high minors, particularly Barrow's IL, which lost numerous players to the upstart league. The FL also placed teams in the IL's two largest markets, Buffalo and Baltimore, significantly affecting attendance. Barrow, his hands full managing the various financial crises and potential franchise moves, tried to obtain major league status for his league or some eight team amalgamation of the IL and the other affected high minor league, the American Association. Not surprisingly, nothing ever came of these efforts.

After holding the league together through the difficult 1914 season, 1915 proved even worse. The FL now invaded Newark as well, and with Canada now fully engaged in World War I, the Toronto and Montreal franchises operated under wartime conditions. Before and during the season, moves and rumors of moves of IL franchises dominated league business. The financial strain forced the Jersey City and Newark (transferred to Harrisburg) owners to forfeit their franchises to the league, leaving Barrow to run both clubs until new owners could be found.

With the collapse of the FL after 1915, the IL received a brief respite in 1916, but 1917, with America now also engaged in the First World War, brought severe financial hardship back to many of the franchises. Barrow again battled to hold his league together, while at the same time striving to create a third major league of four IL and four AA franchises. After four extremely difficult years, a number of disagreements and bad feelings had developed between the authoritarian Barrow and several franchise owners. When the owners voted to drastically cut his salary from $7,500 to $2,500, Barrow happily jumped to the Boston Red Sox managerial post offered by owner Harry Frazee.

The Red Sox were less affected by war losses than most teams, and Barrow successfully guided the club to the pennant despite a showdown with his star player, Babe Ruth, in July. Earlier in the year, on the advice of outfielder Harry Hooper, Barrow had shifted Ruth to the outfield to take full advantage of his offensive potential. But when hurler Dutch Leonard left the team due to the war, Barrow looked to Ruth to pitch. Ruth begged off due to a sore wrist. The tension between the two erupted in July when Barrow chastised Ruth after swinging at a pitch after being given the take sign. When Ruth snapped back, the argument escalated, and Ruth left the club and returned to Baltimore, threatening to join a shipbuilding team. Ruth of course soon realized he'd gone too far and wanted to come back. Hooper and Frazee helped mediate and appease the furious, stubborn Barrow. The chastened Ruth ended up pitching a number of games down the stretch. Owing to complications from the war, in mid-year the season was shortened and adjusted to end on Labor Day, at which point the Sox found themselves 2½ games ahead of the Cleveland Indians. In the World Series the Sox defeated the Chicago Cubs four games to two.

Falling attendance and much lower receipts than anticipated from the World Series put added financial burdens on Frazee. Prior to the 1919 season, he sent two players (Duffy Lewis and Ernie Shore) to the Yankees for $15,000 and four lesser players. During the ensuing season, Barrow became embroiled in two player controversies. The Babe spent the start of the season living the high life beyond even his own standard. Once, on a tip, Barrow burst into Ruth's room at 6:00 A.M. right after the latter had snuck back in and caught Ruth hiding under the covers with his clothes on. The next morning in the clubhouse Ruth confronted and threatened to punch Barrow for popping into his room. Barrow, well tired of Ruth's shenanigans, ordered the rest of the players onto the field and challenged Ruth to back up his threat. Ruth backed down, donned his uniform, and joined the others. Barrow and Ruth eventually reached an unconventional detente: Ruth would leave a note for Barrow any time he returned past curfew with the exact time he came in.

The other hullabaloo began when star Boston pitcher Carl Mays refused to retake the mound after a throw by catcher Wally Schang to catch a base stealer grazed Mays' head. Barrow intended to suspend the dour Mays, until Frazee quickly quashed any suspension so as to possibly trade him. After listening to several offers, Frazee traded Mays to the Yankees for two players and $40,000. Johnson voided the sale and suspended Mays, arguing Frazee should have suspended him, and that a player should not be able force a favorable outcome through insubordination. The Yankee owners went to the courts, which upheld the sale. Boston finished the 1919 season tied for fifth, 20½ games back.

That offseason, when Frazee sold Ruth to the Yankees, Barrow grimly told him that "you ought to know you're making a mistake." Frazee tried to placate Barrow by promising him that he would get some players in return for Ruth, but Barrow snapped back, "There is nobody on that ball club that I want. This has to be a straight cash deal, and you'll have to announce it that way."

Without Ruth there was little Barrow could do in 1920 and the club finished 25½ games back with a record of 72–81. The death of Yankee business manager Harry Sparrow during the 1920 season created an opportunity for Yankee owners Jacob Ruppert and Tillinghast Huston to bring in a strong, experienced baseball man to run the team. A natural yet brilliant hire, Barrow fit his role perfectly. When Ruppert bought out Huston in 1923, Barrow borrowed around $300,000 to buy a 10% interest in the club.

During Barrow's tenure with the Yankees, the team won a staggering 14 pennants and 10 championships. Still a brilliant evaluator of talent, Barrow brought in stars such as Lou Gehrig, Earle Combs, Tony Lazzeri, Lefty Gomez, Bill Dickey, Joe DiMaggio, and Yogi Berra, among many others, to cement the Yankee dynasty. When Ruppert died in 1939, Barrow became club president, a title he held until the Ruppert trust was forced to sell the team in 1945. After the sale, the 77-year-old Barrow finally retired.

During his lifetime he had survived various health problems, but in December 1953 at age 85 Barrow passed away, following several years of convalescence at his home in Port Chester, New York, just north of New York City. His death came just three months after his election to the Baseball Hall of Fame. He was buried in Kensico Cemetery in Valhalla, New York, within a stone's throw of Lou Gehrig's grave.

DAN LEVITT

CHICAGO

In Chicago "baseball is a religion rather than a sport," wrote sportswriter Joe S. Jackson, "and a man is a West Side or a South Side rooter rather than a member of any sect or even of any political party." During the formative years of the American League, the Chicago White Sox, owned and operated by Charles Comiskey, challenged the supremacy of their National League rivals from their first season in town, building their church and establishing themselves in the hearts and minds of their congregation over the next two decades—and yet the close of this period saw the club in disgrace, mired in the worst scandal in baseball history. Chicago, the White Sox, and baseball would never be the same afterward.

Playing in an old park, the South Side Grounds, under an old name, the White Stockings, the South Siders won the first American League pennant in 1900. When the American League declared itself a major league in 1901, the White Stockings romped to the AL's first major league pennant under pitcher–manager Clark Griffith. After new manager Jimmy Callahan's team fell to seventh place in 1903, Fielder Jones took over as manager of the club and rebuilt the team around pitching and defense. Following strong finishes in 1904 and 1905, the club captured another pennant in 1906, despite a team batting average of just .230. Facing their cross-town rivals in that year's World Series, the "Hitless Wonders" upset the heavily favored Cubs in six games behind the strong pitching of aces Nick Altrock, Ed Walsh, and Doc White.

WINNING PERCENTAGE 1901–1919

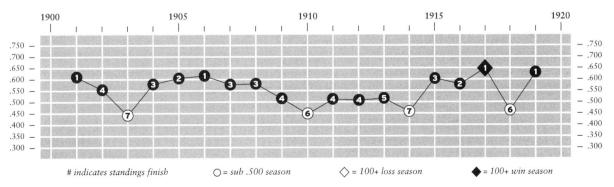

# indicates standings finish   ◯ = sub .500 season   ◇ = 100+ loss season   ◆ = 100+ win season

Midway through the 1910 season, in the wake of three more winning and profitable seasons, the club moved into a new concrete-and-steel structure, Comiskey Park, to rave reviews. The White Sox themselves were not as successful: the club was in decline, and the pitchers found it harder to carry the weak-hitting attack. After the club finished a disappointing sixth in 1910, Comiskey overhauled his charges. Phasing in new talent such as Ray Schalk, Eddie Collins, Joe Jackson, Buck Weaver, and Eddie Cicotte, the club began its climb back to the first division. After a second-place finish in 1916, the 1917 club, sometimes considered the best White Sox team ever, won 100 games during the regular season and took the fall classic from the New York Giants in six games.

It seemed as if Comiskey's young club would establish themselves as a winner for years to come, but poor team chemistry and resentment over Comiskey's cost-cutting and salary-slashing measures came home to roost in 1919. Eight "Black Sox" players met with gamblers before the World Series, and seven of them arranged to throw several games in exchange for cash. The story, the details of which are still debated hotly, became public toward the end of the 1920 season. The White Sox, subsequently stripped of several star players and disgraced before their fans, would not return to the World Series for 40 years.

R. J. LESCH

ALL-ERA TEAM

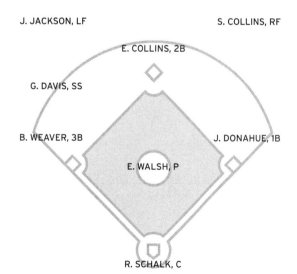

F. JONES, CF

J. JACKSON, LF   S. COLLINS, RF

E. COLLINS, 2B

G. DAVIS, SS

B. WEAVER, 3B   J. DONAHUE, 1B

E. WALSH, P

R. SCHALK, C

TEAM LEADERS
1901–1919

BATTING

GAMES
S. Collins.........1202
F. Jones..........1153
B. Weaver........1103

RUNS
F. Jones...........693
B. Weaver.........521
S. Collins..........502

HITS
F. Jones..........1151
S. Collins.........1104
B. Weaver........1100

RBI
S. Collins.........478
F. Isbell...........447
G. Davis..........377

DOUBLES
S. Collins.........209
B. Weaver.........164
F. Isbell...........154

TRIPLES
S. Collins...........94
F. Isbell............62
B. Weaver..........61

HOME RUNS
H. Felsch..........24
P. Bodie..........20
B. Weaver.........19

STOLEN BASES
F. Isbell..........250
F. Jones..........206
E. Collins.........194

BATTING AVERAGE
(2000+ plate appearances)
J. Jackson........327
E. Collins........307
D. Green.........284

PITCHING

GAMES
E. Walsh.........426
D. White.........360
J. Scott..........317

WINS
E. Walsh.........195
D. White.........159
E. Cicotte........135

LOSSES
E. Walsh.........125
D. White.........123
J. Scott..........113

INNINGS
E. Walsh.......2946⅓
D. White.......2498⅓
E. Cicotte........2019

STRIKEOUTS
E. Walsh.........1732
D. White.........1067
J. Scott...........945

WALKS
J. Scott..........609
E. Walsh.........608
D. White.........542

SHUTOUTS
E. Walsh..........57
D. White..........42
J. Scott...........26

ERA
(800+ innings pitched)
E. Walsh........1.81
E. Cicotte.......2.10
F. Smith.........2.18

TYPICAL LINEUPS 1901–1919

1901

1. D. Hoy, CF
2. F. Jones, RF
3. S. Mertes, 2B
4. F. Isbell, 1B
5. F. Hartman, 3B
6. F. Shugart, SS
7. H. McFarland, LF
8. B. Sullivan, C

1902

1. S. Strang, 3B
2. F. Jones, CF
3. D. Green, RF
4. G. Davis, SS
5. S. Mertes, LF
6. F. Isbell, 1B
7. T. Daly, 2B
8. B. Sullivan
   E. McFarland, C

1903

1. D. Holmes, LF
2. F. Jones, CF
3. D. Green, RF
4. J. Callahan, 3B
5. F. Isbell, 1B
6. G. Magoon, 2B
7. L. Tannehill, SS
8. E. McFarland
   J. Slattery, C

1904

1. D. Green, RF
2. F. Jones, CF
3. J. Callahan, LF
4. G. Davis, SS
5. J. Donahue, 1B
6. F. Isbell, 1B-2B
7. L. Tannehill, 3B
8. B. Sullivan, C
   G. Dundon, 2B

1905

1. F. Jones, CF
2. D. Holmes, LF
   F. Isbell, 2B–RF
3. G. Davis, SS
4. J. Callahan, LF
5. J. Donahue, 1B
6. B. Sullivan, C
   D. Green, RF
7. L. Tannehill, 3B
8. G. Dundon, 2B

1906

1. E. Hahn, RF–LF
2. F. Jones, CF
3. F. Isbell, 2B
4. G. Davis, SS
5. J. Donahue, 1B
6. P. Dougherty, LF
   B. O'Neill, RF
7. B. Sullivan, C
8. L. Tannehill, 3B

1907

1. E. Hahn, RF
2. F. Jones, CF
3. F. Isbell, 2B
4. J. Donahue, 1B
5. G. Davis, SS
6. P. Dougherty, LF
7. G. Rohe, 3B
8. B. Sullivan, C

1908

1. E. Hahn, RF
2. F. Jones, CF
3. P. Dougherty, LF
4. J. Anderson, RF
5. G. Davis, 2B
   J. Donahue, 1B
6. F. Parent, SS
7. B. Sullivan, C
8. L. Tannehill, 3B

1909

1. E. Hahn
   D. Altizer, RF
2. F. Parent, SS
3. F. Isbell, 1B
   W. Cole, CF
4. P. Dougherty, LF
5. B. Purtell, 3B
6. L. Tannehill, 3B–SS
7. J. Atz, 2B
8. B. Sullivan, C

1910

1. R. Zeider, 2B
2. F. Parent, CF
3. P. Meloan, RF
4. P. Dougherty, LF
5. C. Gandil, 1B
6. B. Purtell, 3B
7. L. Blackburne, SS
8. F. Payne, C

1911

1. M. McIntyre, RF
2. H. Lord, 3B
3. J. Callahan, LF
4. P. Bodie, CF
5. A. McConnell, 2B
6. L. Tannehill, SS
7. S. Collins, 1B
8. B. Sullivan, C

1912

1. M. Rath, 2B
2. H. Lord, 3B
3. J. Callahan, LF
4. P. Bodie, CF
5. S. Collins, RF
6. R. Zeider, 1B
7. B. Weaver, SS
8. W. Kuhn, C

1913

1. M. Rath, 2B
2. H. Lord, 3B
3. S. Collins, RF
4. H. Chase, 1B
5. P. Bodie, CF–LF
6. L. Chappell, LF
7. B. Weaver, SS
8. R. Schalk, C

1914

1. B. Weaver, SS
2. L. Blackburne, 2B
3. R. Demmitt, LF
4. S. Collins, RF
5. J. Fournier, 1B
6. P. Bodie, CF
7. R. Schalk, C
8. J. Breton, 3B

1915

1. E. Murphy, RF
2. B. Weaver, SS
3. E. Collins, 2B
4. J. Fournier, 1B–LF
5. S. Collins, OF–1B
6. H. Felsch, CF
7. R. Schalk, C
8. L. Blackburne, 2B

1916

1. S. Collins, RF
2. B. Weaver, 3B
3. E. Collins, 2B
4. J. Jackson, LF
5. J. Fournier, 1B
6. H. Felsch, CF
7. R. Schalk, C
8. Z. Terry, SS

1917

1. N. Leibold
   S. Collins, RF
2. B. Weaver, 3B
3. E. Collins, 2B
4. J. Jackson, LF
5. H. Felsch, CF
6. C. Gandil, 1B
7. S. Risberg, SS
8. R. Schalk, C

1918 (first half)

1. N. Leibold, LF
2. E. Murphy, RF
3. E. Collins, 2B
4. H. Felsch, CF
5. B. Weaver, SS
6. C. Gandil, 1B
7. S. Risberg
   F. McMullin, 3B
8. R. Schalk, C

1918 (second half)

1. E. Murphy, RF
2. N. Leibold, LF
3. E. Collins, 2B
4. C. Gandil, 1B
5. S. Collins, CF-RF
6. B. Weaver, SS
7. F. McMullin, 3B
8. R. Schalk, C

1919

1. N. Leibold, RF
2. E. Collins, 2B
3. B. Weaver, 3B
4. J. Jackson, LF
5. H. Felsch, CF
6. C. Gandil, 1B
7. S. Risberg, SS
8. R. Schalk, C

CHICAGO

JAMES JOSEPH "NIXEY" CALLAHAN
UTILITY, 1901–1905, 1911–1913; MANAGER, 1903–1904, 1912–1914

Often referred to today as Nixey, even though he rarely went by that moniker during his career, Jimmy Callahan was one of the most colorful and versatile figures of the Deadball Era. Equally at home on the pitcher's mound, the infield, the outfield, the stage, the manager's bench, or in the business world, Callahan won 99 games as a pitcher and batted .273 as a hitter in a 13-year major league career interrupted by a five-year stint as the operator of one of the era's most successful semipro teams. In the off-season of 1913–14, Callahan put his organizational skills to use as one of the chief promoters of the Chicago White Sox–New York Giants world tour. In all his pursuits, Callahan was one of the game's most respected and admired figures. As *Baseball Magazine* observed in 1909, "He is bright and brainy, and a hustler. No one has a larger personal following or carries with him so many good wishes for success."

James Joseph Callahan was born to Irish immigrants in Fitchburg, Massachusetts, on March 18, 1874. Jimmy lost his father at an early age, and by 14 left school to support his mother as a sewing machine boy in a clothing mill, earning 75 cents a day.

During this period Nixey (a childhood nickname he abandoned later in life, although local papers continued to use it throughout his career) also apprenticed himself to a plumber. Over the next two years, Jimmy's athletic ability began to attract attention at mill ball games. At 16 he was promised a dollar if he won a game at Lake Whalon, Massachusetts, against another local team. Jimmy won the game and the dollar and soon began pitching regularly for Pepperell, Massachusetts, one of the best semipro teams in the state.

Because his plumber employer frowned on such moonlighting on the diamond, he played under the name of William Smith. The alias was discovered after

three years and Callahan was dismissed from his apprenticeship. That proved to be no real hardship, however, because by this time he was earning between $30 and $40 a game pitching for Pepperell, and once recorded 22 strikeouts in a single game.

At the age of 19 he was spotted by Arthur Irwin, manager of the Philadelphia Phillies. Irwin signed Callahan and brought him south. Jumping into the Phillies lineup in 1894, he appeared in nine games, compiling a 1–2 record with a terrible 9.89 ERA. "They didn't pay me enough salary to wreck them or make me," Callahan later joked to John J. Ward of *Baseball Magazine*. "That way they could afford to take a chance with such a green youth as myself. I pitched a few games but I wasn't a Walter Johnson with speed or a Christy Mathewson with skill so at the end of the season they decided that Philly would muddle along as best it could without my services. In short, they wished me well, propelled me gently through the door and carefully closed the door in my face. I was alone in the wide world."

What would have been a moment of profound doubt and loss of self-esteem to most rookies became a bolt of inspiration for Jimmy Callahan. Realizing there were plenty of jobs to be had in the minor leagues, he wrote a letter to the Springfield Maroons of the Eastern League informing them that he "was a player of rare promise." The ploy worked and he was given a starting position on the team.

Jimmy certainly lived up to his own billing, winning 32 out of the 41 games he started, helping Springfield to the pennant. When not pitching, Callahan played the outfield and second base. Kansas City of the Western League drafted Jimmy off of Springfield's roster in 1896. He lasted one season with the Blues before being bought by the Chicago Colts of the National League prior to the 1897 season.

Callahan impressed the Colts not only with his pitching, but also with his running ability. Before the season was out he had pitched and played second, third, short, and the outfield. Although he was not a particularly good base stealer, Callahan developed a reputation as perhaps the fastest man from home to first in the game, and the papers referred to him as the "sprinter–twirler." John McGraw later concluded that Callahan's remarkable speed actually hurt him on the field. "Time after time," McGraw recalled, "when a grounder was hit his way, Callahan darted at it with such terrific speed that he couldn't check himself over the ball, but overran, and the hit went on unhindered."

During the 1899 season, McGraw also characterized Callahan's method of pitching as an imitation of teammate Clark Griffith, who relied on a polished delivery and excellent control, rather than raw speed and strikeouts, to retire hitters. When Callahan first arrived in Chicago, McGraw declared, "he was a green stripling with plenty of mechanical ability, but lacking the artistic veneer, the finish and cleverness of Clark Griffith. Jimmy became an apt pupil of Grif's, and you will notice that his style of delivery is a reproduction of Grif's." Indeed, like his mentor, Callahan was a durable pitcher for the Colts, completing all but three of his starts in his four years with the team. Like Griffith he also relied heavily on his defense, never posting more than 77 strikeouts in an individual season.

Prior to the 1901 season he became one of the first players to jump to the upstart American League, following Griffith's lead and signing with the Chicago White Sox. Although Callahan missed the first few weeks of the 1901 season with a broken bone in his forearm, he recovered to post a sparkling 15–8 record with a 2.42 ERA. He was just as impressive at the plate, where the right-handed batter hit a career-best .331 for the season, with 11 extra-base hits in 132 plate appearances. The combination of Griffith and Callahan on the pitching mound helped Chicago win a second consecutive American League pennant, taking the flag by four games over Boston.

The following season, Callahan slumped to a 16–14 mark with a subpar 3.60 ERA. But he also pitched the best game of his career, a no-hitter against the Detroit Tigers on September 20. In what marked his final hurrah as a major league pitcher, Callahan set down the Tigers in just one hour and 20 minutes, becoming the first American Leaguer to toss a no-hitter. Named manager of the White Sox in 1903, Callahan pitched in just three games, posting a terrible 4.50 ERA. Callahan transitioned to third base, where he registered a poor .895 fielding percentage but batted a solid .292. Under

Callahan's leadership the Sox finished a disappointing seventh.

Callahan remained Chicago's manager for the first 42 games of the 1904 season before he was replaced by Fielder Jones. Nonetheless, he went on to play in 132 games for the White Sox that year, batting .261 and splitting his time between left field and second base. In 1905 he appeared in 93 games, mostly in left field, and finished the year with a .272 average and 26 steals.

Despite that performance, the following year Callahan resigned from the White Sox and became a semipro magnate. Seeing how much money Comiskey cleared as owner and president of the White Sox, Jimmy realized there was tons of money to be made off the game of baseball. He bought the Logan Squares semipro team and their stadium at the corner of Diversey and Milwaukee in the Logan Square section of Chicago. The club very quickly established itself as one of the finest if not the premier semipro baseball team in the country. At the end of the 1906 season, Callahan's club (with a line-up augmented by several major leaguers, some of whom played under assumed names) beat both participants in that year's World Series, the White Sox and the Cubs.

Callahan's business venture did not endear him to Organized Baseball. The Logan Squares were declared outlaws by Ban Johnson and major league teams faced fines or censure if they played the Logan Squares club. Walter Johnson was once fined $100 for pitching in an exhibition game against them. Such machinations did little to curb the enthusiasm Chicago had for the local boys. On August 27, 1910, Callahan's club won the first night game ever played at Comiskey Park, defeating the Rogers Park semipro club 3–0 under portable lights, with Callahan himself driving in two of the three runs. Callahan amassed quite a nice bit of money in his role as stadium owner and team president.

After a few years, however, attendance started to lag and Callahan began looking for an opportunity to get back into Organized Baseball. He ran into Comiskey during the winter of 1910. Commy offered him the job of president of the White Sox, but Callahan, then nearing 37 years of age, convinced him that he was not through as a player. To return to the majors, he had to get his name cleared from the ineligible list. This was accomplished by paying a fine of $700. His return to baseball in 1911 was one of the era's most remarkable comeback stories. In a season Callahan considered his best in the major leagues, Jimmy played left field and hit .281 in 121 games, while also posting career highs in hits (131), home runs (3), RBI (60), and stolen bases (45). Not bad for a man who had been out of the majors for five years.

During the off-season he added stage performer to his repertoire, taking a turn in front of the floodlights in Chicago as a monologist. His specialty was telling funny Irish stories, complete with the brogue. It was not great theater, but it satisfied his audience.

So impressed was Comiskey with Callahan's 1911 performance that he re-appointed him manager of the club in 1912. The club finished in fourth place that year with a 78–76 record, and Jimmy, in his last full season as a player, batted .272 in 111 games. The following year manager Callahan confined himself to the bench for all but six contests, and the White Sox again won 78 games, although the club dropped to fifth place.

From October 1913 to March 1914 Callahan's White Sox and the New York Giants took their baseball teams on a world exhibition tour. Along with Comiskey and McGraw, Callahan was a major force behind the tour, putting up an undisclosed amount of money to help pay the teams' traveling expenses. The teams first barnstormed across the United States and then set out for Japan, China, Hong Kong, the Philippines, Australia, Ceylon (now Sri Lanka), Egypt, Italy, France, and Great Britain, with a personal side trip to Ireland. As far as

Callahan was concerned the best parts of the tour were the teams' visit with the Pope and the game in London, played before 20,000 fans, including King George V.

The tour was wearying, however, and the White Sox got off to a flat start in 1914 and finished the year tied for sixth. Just before Christmas 1914 Callahan was bumped up to the White Sox front office to make room for Eddie Collins, whom Comiskey had just acquired, to serve as player-manager. (Collins didn't want the job, however; it later ended up going to Pants Rowland.) The Pirates selected Callahan as manager in 1916. He led the team to a sixth-place finish. Callahan was dismissed midway through the 1917 season with the Buccos mired in last place.

Following his baseball career, Callahan became one of Chicago's most successful contractors, building the entire waterworks for the Great Lakes Naval Station. On October 4, 1934, Callahan died of natural causes while visiting friends in Boston. Survived by his wife, the former Josephine Hardin, two sons and a daughter, Callahan was buried in St. Bernard's Cemetery in his hometown of Fitchburg.

JAMES E. ELFERS

Chas a Comiskey
CHICAGO

CHARLES ALBERT COMISKEY
OWNER, 1901–1931

One of the most influential figures in the history of the sport, Charles Comiskey's 55-year odyssey through professional baseball ran the gamut from captain of one of the greatest teams of the nineteenth century, league-jumper during the 1890 players' rebellion, chief architect of the American League's emergence in 1901 as a major league, long-time owner of one of the league's most successful franchises, the Chicago White Sox, and a central figure in the 1919 Black Sox scandal. During his long association with the game, Comiskey was regarded at various points as a labor radical, a visionary executive, and a domineering patriarch who lavished money on his ballpark and the press while underpaying his best players. Baseball, Comiskey once wrote, "is the only game that is complicated enough to be always interesting and yet simple enough to be always understood." Ultimately, the same can be said of the Old Roman himself.

Charles Albert Comiskey was born in Chicago on August 15, 1859, at the corner of Union and Maxwell Streets, one of seven children of John Comiskey, an Irish immigrant, and his wife Mary, a native New Yorker. Charles's father served at various times as county board clerk, assistant county treasurer, and representative of the seventh and eighth wards on the Chicago city council, a resumé that may have given young Charley valuable experience in the ways of backdoor local politics, which he would later put to use in the halls of the American League's offices.

It was not long before Charley discovered baseball, spending as much time as he could on the old Garden City grounds on Chicago's West Side, enjoying the fledgling game with his neighborhood friends. James T. Hart recalled just before the 1917 World Series how his boyhood pal was already the unspoken leader during their sandlot days in Chicago. He "seldom went to school more than two months a year," recalled Hart. "He was the captain of our team. He played all positions, and when any of us were sick, or our parents kept us at home to do the chores, Charley was ready at a moment's notice to serve as utility man." Hart also remembered how difficult it was for the team to obtain bats and balls, often using the broken castoffs of older players. "When our team played we would compete on the proposition that the losing team would forfeit a bat.... When we were threatened with a loss, Comiskey would start a row with the umpire or the opposing players and break up the game before we lost our bats. He was the foxiest kid in Chicago."

From Father O'Neill's Holy Family parochial school, through religious colleges in Chicago and Kansas, Comiskey never let his studies interfere with his principal outdoor recreation. Charley developed into a fairly skilled hurler, but the elder Comiskey objected to his son's obsession with baseball and quickly signed him up as an apprentice to a local plumber. Arguments ensued and in 1876, at the age of 17, Comiskey left home to play third base for an independent team in Milwaukee at $60 per month. His manager, Ted Sullivan, became a scout for Comiskey in later years.

The following season Comiskey moved on to pitch for Elgin, Illinois. A right-handed thrower and hitter who stood approximately six feet tall, Comiskey's repertoire included a solid fastball and an assortment of curves. Elgin did not lose in any of his starts all season, despite facing fairly tough competition from around the Chicago area. From there Charley shifted to the Dubuque (Iowa) Rabbits, where he was reunited with Sullivan. Once again a utility man, Comiskey played first, second, and the outfield, as well as pitching. Possibly more important, Sullivan also employed Comiskey as a representative of his successful news agency, where

Charley's 20 percent commission dwarfed his baseball salary. Comiskey stayed with Sullivan's Dubuque club for four seasons, helping the team win one Northwest League pennant.

With Charles Radbourn and Laurie Reis on the same pitching staff, however, Comiskey turned full time to first base, where, as legend has it, he revolutionized the position. According to most accounts, Comiskey did not "hug the bag," as was the habit of contemporary first basemen; instead, Charley positioned himself closer to second, enabling him to cut off grounders hit toward right field. He practiced with his pitchers in the morning, making sure they became adept at covering first base whenever he snagged a ground ball. In recent years some historians have claimed that this approach was already in practice well before Comiskey applied it with Dubuque. Even if he was not the first, the story is nonetheless an early indication of Comiskey's keen baseball instincts and his penchant for leadership.

The big leagues finally beckoned following an exhibition game in St. Louis in 1882, when Chris Von der Ahe, owner of the St. Louis Browns of the newly formed American Association, offered Comiskey a contract. Although Von der Ahe originally suggested that Comiskey not ask for too much money in his contract terms, Charley found that by the second paycheck his salary was a lot higher than what he had signed for. Comiskey never forgot the gesture, and was said to be one of the old man's benefactors when Von der Ahe lost his fortune later in life.

When Von der Ahe and his manager Sullivan had a dispute late in the 1883 season, the Browns owner chose Commy as his new skipper. Charley responded by piloting his team to four straight American Association pennants, and won the world's championship in 1886, beating Cap Anson's Chicago White Stockings of the National League in six games.

Although he carried a reputation as an excellent team leader and solid defensive player, Comiskey was a poor hitter. For his career he batted .264 with 29 home runs and 419 stolen bases. Perhaps his best season came in 1887, when he batted .335, scored 139 runs, drove in 103 runs and stole 117 bases. Far more typical, however, was his showing the previous year, when he batted .254 with 95 runs scored, 76 RBI, and 41 stolen bases.

In 1890, in a bold move, Comiskey jumped to the Chicago club of the maverick Players League, only to return to the Browns at the end of the season when the Players League disbanded and peace was declared. The first baseman's desertion caused friction between him and Von der Ahe, however, and in 1892 Comiskey signed with the Cincinnati Reds of the National League, where

he spent the next four seasons as the club's manager. His annual salary was $7,500, but his promised share of the club's profits never materialized, as there were none to be had.

Prior to the 1894 season, his last as an active major league player, the 34-year-old Comiskey was advised by his doctors that he was "threatened with tuberculosis." To aid his health, Comiskey headed for the warmer climes of the South, scouting for new players along the way. Reportedly it was on this trip that Commy hit upon the idea of a new league featuring clubs from the Western states. Upon his return, Comiskey immediately contacted Ban Johnson, the sports editor of the *Cincinnati Commercial Tribune*, asking if he would be interested in helping to lead this new venture. Although Johnson was already embroiled in a feud with Comiskey's boss with the Reds, John T. Brush, Comiskey's well-honed powers of persuasion helped convince Brush to campaign for Johnson to become the first president of the newly-formed Western League. The plan worked, and Johnson took over control of the Western League, quickly transforming it into one of the best circuits in the country.

Comiskey, meanwhile, spent the 1894 season with Cincinnati, fulfilling his obligations to Brush. After the season Comiskey purchased the new league's Sioux City Cornhuskers and moved it to St. Paul. There he built his first ballpark, at a cost of $12,000. After five seasons in Minnesota, Comiskey was granted permission by the National League to relocate his franchise to Chicago, on the condition that he could not use the name Chicago for his relocated ball club. Therefore, recalling perhaps his finest moments as a player, Comiskey decided on "White Sox," honoring the team his Browns had beaten for the 1886 championship.

Meanwhile, Johnson and Comiskey positioned the Western League to challenge the monopoly of the established National League. In October 1899 the league changed its name to the American League. Prior to the 1901 season, with franchises now placed in Washington, Baltimore, Philadelphia, Boston, Cleveland, Detroit, Chicago, and Milwaukee, the circuit declared major league status. Quickly gaining credibility with the public, the American League was heralded by *The Sporting News* as being devoid of the "cowardly truckling, alien ownership, syndicalism…jealousies, arrogance…mercenary spirit, and disregard of public demands" that the National League had become infamous for. Comiskey and Johnson were making a favorable impression with baseball fans, and the National League knew it. The ugly war between the leagues, rife with player-jumping, franchise-shifting, and acrimony on both sides,

CIII.

finally concluded with the establishment of the National Commission in 1903.

During the first years of the new century, Comiskey built his club into one of the best in the country. The White Sox captured the 1901 American League pennant behind the strong pitching of manager Clark Griffith and an offense powered by outfielders Fielder Jones and Dummy Hoy. After falling to seventh place in 1903, Comiskey's White Sox gravitated toward the top of the standings again, with strong finishes in 1904 and 1905 and a second pennant in 1906, led by pitchers Ed Walsh, Nick Altrock, Doc White, and Frank Owen, and with the Hitless Wonders offense (potent, despite the name) featuring Frank Isbell, George Davis, and Jones, now serving as the club's player–manager. Although the team would not win another pennant for 11 years, Comiskey built his franchise into one of the most financially successful in the country. At the end of the century's first decade, the White Sox showed a ten-year profit of $700,000, highest among recorded earnings during that time. He turned some of those profits into the world tour, taken with the New York Giants following the 1913 season.

From the beginning of his tenure Comiskey established a reputation as an owner passionately involved in the day-to-day affairs of his club. Comiskey was never afraid to express his opinions about the game from his private box. Reporters shared numerous stories of Comiskey railing at his team over bonehead plays or games tossed away. "Sitting next to him at a game, one is likely to be nudged in the ribs, or have his toes stepped on as Comiskey 'pulls' on a close play," stated *Baseball Magazine*.

Nor was Comiskey afraid to spend money on his team or his ballpark. By the time of its opening on July 1, 1910, the cost of Comiskey Park and its grounds totaled $750,000, a remarkable amount for the time. Additional seating in subsequent seasons raised the cost to over a million. Commy was also the only owner at this time to own his entire club, grounds, and all the equipment. And, although he did everything he could to hold down his players' salaries, Comiskey spent large sums of money putting together his second great team of the Deadball Era. In December 1914 Comiskey purchased second baseman Eddie Collins from the Philadelphia Athletics for a reported $50,000. Less than a year later, he acquired Cleveland slugger Joe Jackson for three players and $31,500.

Throughout his reign, Comiskey polished his reputation as a benevolent monarch. Beginning in 1900, he handed out free grandstand tickets to 75,000 schoolboys each season. He constantly professed love for the fans and when it rained at his ballpark the occupants of the bleachers were permitted to enter the higher-priced sheltered sections without extra charge. "Those bleacherites made this big new plant possible," announced Comiskey. "The fellow who can pay only twenty-five cents to see a ball game always will be just as welcome at Comiskey Park as the box seat holder." He later claimed to have given away a quarter of a million tickets to servicemen, and followed that by donating a reported 10 percent of his 1917 home gate receipts to the Red Cross, an amount totaling about $17,000. Comiskey regularly allowed the city of Chicago to use his park for special events, often free of charge. The owner's benevolence also extended to the press, whom he regularly feted with roasts and free drinks.

Although Comiskey spent lavishly on his park, his city, and his fans, he squeezed every dime he could out of his players. Long before the 1919 scandal erupted, Comiskey's team was already known as the Black Sox— for their dirty uniforms, a result of Comiskey's efforts to cut down on laundry bills. Most league players received four dollars a day on the road to cover hotels and meals, but the Sox got only three. Most importantly, Comiskey underpaid many of his best players, including three men who later turned against him—star pitcher Eddie Cicotte, Jackson, and third baseman Buck Weaver.

During the course of the Deadball Era Comiskey's once-amicable relationship with Ban Johnson disintegrated into open warfare. According to legend, the discord erupted in 1905, when Johnson sent Comiskey a load of fresh fish on the same day that he suspended outfielder Ducky Holmes for an altercation with an umpire the day before. Comiskey, who had already given his extra outfielder, Jimmy Callahan, the day off when the suspension was handed down, was irate. "What does he want me to do?" he bellowed. "Put one of these bass out in the left field?" (Versions of this story abound: some sources say the incident occurred in 1907, and involved Fielder Jones, not Holmes.) A further series of disagreements set the stage for 1919, when two scandals rocked the league and irrevocably split Comiskey and Johnson.

In July 1919 Boston pitcher Carl Mays abandoned the Red Sox and demanded a trade. Johnson ruled that the temperamental pitcher could not be traded until disciplinary action was taken, but Boston owner Harry Frazee ignored the edict and dealt Mays to the Yankees, only to see Johnson suspend Mays. The Yankee owners responded by securing an injunction allowing Mays to play. League owners immediately took sides: Frazee, Yankee owners Jacob Ruppert and Tillinghast Huston, and Comiskey were labeled The Insurrectionists, while most of the remaining American League moguls sided with Johnson. As part of the Insurrectionists, Comiskey even pursued a proposal to have his club join the National League, but an uneasy truce was brokered the following winter and the plan never got off the ground.

By then the Black Sox scandal hung like a dark cloud over the sport. Many historians believe that Comiskey was aware of the plot to throw the World Series as early as Game One and did nothing to stop it. Johnson helped fuel such accusations, and Comiskey threw the burden of the scandal back on Johnson. "I blame Ban Johnson for allowing the Series to continue," he announced. "If ever a league president blundered in a crisis, Ban did."

Comiskey himself certainly knew of the fix after the Series ended. Indeed, one of his players, Joe Jackson, tried to return his share of the payoff, only to be turned away. As rumors of the fix spread throughout the sport, Comiskey responded by publicly offering $10,000 to anyone with knowledge of the fix. The announcement was a public relations move, intended to make Comiskey appear nobly dedicated to uncovering the truth, no matter the cost. When St. Louis Browns infielder Joe Gedeon did come forward with information, however, Comiskey turned him away and never paid the $10,000.

By the end of the 1920 season, details of the plot did start to emerge, as several conspirators confessed to their involvement. Even though the eight accused Black Sox were acquitted in court of the conspiracy charges filed against them (in part because the confessions mysteriously disappeared, a turn of events many suspect Comiskey himself of engineering), the revelation of the scandal effectively ruined Comiskey's franchise. The eight accused players were banned from the game for life, and after 1920 the White Sox never again finished in the first division during Comiskey's lifetime.

Charles Comiskey died of heart complications at his lakeside estate in Eagle River, Wisconsin, on October 26, 1931, at the age of 72, and was buried in Calvary Catholic Cemetery in Evanston, Illinois. He was survived by a son. His wife, Nan Kelly, whom he had married in 1882, preceded him in death in 1922. The Comiskey family continued to control the Chicago White Sox until 1959, when they were bought out by a consortium led by Bill Veeck Jr.

IRV GOLDFARB

Frank Isbell

CHICAGO

CHI.

A prematurely bald and round-faced Irishman, Frank Isbell was a fixture of the Chicago White Sox for the first decade of their existence. Best remembered as the second baseman of the 1906 Hitless Wonders, Isbell spent most of his career as a versatile utility player—one of the few men to have played all nine positions in the major leagues—before becoming a minor-league manager and magnate. As a young ballplayer, Isbell's acute sensitivity about his already receded hairline earned him the unappreciated nickname of Bald Eagle.

William Frank Isbell was born to John Isbell, a blacksmith, and Julia Lawton Isbell on August 21, 1875, in Delevan, New York, 40 miles south of Buffalo. Little is known about his childhood. The young Isbell played semipro baseball as a pitcher and outfielder around Minneapolis in 1895, including a brief stint with the Macalester College team, where the 5′11″, 190-pound right-handed thrower was dubbed The Tall Pine by his teammates. The following year Isbell began his professional career as a pitcher for Charles Comiskey's St. Paul club in the Western League. A left-handed batter, he hit .365 for the Saints during the 1896 season, and Comiskey tried him out in the outfield and various infield positions throughout the year.

Drafted by Jim Hart for the Chicago Orphans in 1898, Isbell became a hero before appearing in a single major league game. On April 16, 1898, the grandstand at Sportsman's Park in St. Louis burned down during a game, injuring dozens. Isbell, taking tickets at the ballpark gate, witnessed a fleeing family leave an infant behind as their home across from the ballpark erupted in flames. Isbell ran into the burning house, grabbed the baby, and carried it to safety. During his stay with the club he appeared in 45 games as a utility infielder and spot starter, batting .233 in 159 at-bats while posting a 4–7 record with a 3.56 ERA in 81 innings pitched. In August he was returned to St. Paul for pitcher Bill Phyle. Two years later, when Comiskey transferred the St. Paul club to Chicago in the new American League, Isbell followed the Old Roman and was the regular first baseman for the White Sox from 1900 to 1903. In 1901 he led the league with 52 stolen bases while batting .257 with three home runs, 70 RBI, and 93 runs scored. That year he also established an American League record, since equaled but never surpassed, by leaving 11 men on base during a contest against Cleveland on August 10.

Over the next three seasons Isbell struggled at the plate, posting low on-base percentages with little power. When first baseman Jiggs Donahue arrived in 1904, Isbell moved around the diamond to various positions and was eventually installed at second base. That year was also his worst as a major leaguer: he hit just .210 with a .255 on-base percentage and only 14 extra-base hits in 314 at-bats. The following season, Isbell played part time as a second baseman and outfielder and had a breakout hitting season, attaining career highs in batting average (.296), on-base percentage (.335), and slugging percentage (.440). The performance was good enough to earn Isbell a full-time position in 1906 as the club's second baseman.

Throughout his career, Isbell earned the reputation of a dependable "all-around man" on the diamond. "As a utility man there has seldom been a player in the class of 'Izzy,'" wrote a contemporary scribe. "He has been all around the 'circuit,' from first base to the outfield." For Isbell, the talented utility man was "a jewel, something to be desired almost above all else." "When you are a baseball Jack-of-all-trades," Isbell explained, pointing to the Cubs' Arthur "Solly" Hofman as a prime example, "you must needs be a hitter and a base-runner. For you are sure to be called on." On two occasions when both Chicago catchers were injured, Isbell even donned the mask and went behind the plate. Over ten major league seasons, Isbell batted .250, with a .289 on-base percentage, and logged 619 games at first base, 351 at second base, 23 at third base, 17 at pitcher, 15 at shortstop, 2 at catcher, and 103 at the various outfield positions, with an overall .974 fielding percentage.

Typically batting third during Chicago's pennant-winning 1906 season, Isbell emerged as one of the best hitters on the "Hitless Wonders." That year he led the team in hits (153), triples (11), stolen bases (37), and batting average (.279), and although his .352 slugging percentage was not significantly better than the American League's .318 mark, playing in the cavernous South Side Park, Isbell trailed team leader George Davis by just .003 in that category on the strength of his 124 singles, 18 doubles, and 11 triples. Isbell saved his best performance for the last two games of the 1906 World Series. He had slumped through the first four games of the Series, and manager Fielder Jones lashed out at Isbell's dismal 1-for-16 performance, but Izzy rebounded, hitting four doubles and driving in two runs in Game Five and knocking out three hits in Game Six to salvage a .308 Series average as the Sox upset their West Side rivals. Isbell's World Series records for most hits in two consecutive games (7) and most extra-base hits in a game (4) still stand.

Isbell's production dropped off in 1907, his batting average falling to .243 in 125 games. Accidentally spiked by teammate Patsy Dougherty during an off-day workout on August 26, 1907, Isbell asked Comiskey for his unconditional release so that he could fulfill a dream of managing the Wichita team in the Western Association. Several reports indicate that the Old Roman was willing to grant Isbell his release, but other major league clubs would not waive him. In any case Comiskey refused, and the following spring Isbell became a salary holdout, and spent the first two months of the 1908 season working out on his Wichita farm. He finally reported back for duty in June to once again serve as the club's first baseman, a position he held through the 1909 season. He posted a .247 batting average in 84 games in 1908, as Chicago narrowly missed another American League pennant. In 1909, his final season in the major leagues, Isbell struggled at the bat, posting a horrible .224 batting average in 120 games. The following January Isbell was granted his release.

Upon leaving the major leagues, Isbell returned to Wichita, where he enjoyed hunting and fishing. In addition to playing first base Isbell was the manager and part-owner of the Western League's Wichita Jobbers for two seasons, transferring the franchise to Pueblo, Colorado, midway through the 1911 campaign. In 1912 Isbell moved to Des Moines, Iowa, in the Western League, where he was manager as well as president and part-owner of a team controlled by Comiskey. After three years in Des Moines, he returned to Wichita as president of the Jobbers club from 1915 through 1926,

serving as manager for the 1917 campaign. His Wichita team won the Western League pennant in 1915. Isbell retired from the Wichita club in 1926 and then operated for several years as a freelance scout before accepting the presidency of the Topeka Senators, also of the Western League, in 1931. During his tenure as a Western League magnate, Isbell developed future talent for the White Sox and other major league clubs, tirelessly boosting young players he felt deserved a chance in the big leagues.

After his retirement from baseball, Isbell worked in the Wichita recreational department and managed a local filling station. In 1940 he was elected to the post of Sedgwick County Commissioner by a wide margin. Isbell's friend, Fred J. Mankoff, recalled that "all those kids whom Frank allowed to occupy the so called 'Kid Bleachers' free, were now voters.... It was surprising, who [sic] these grown up 'Kids' went to bat for Frank." Married twice, Isbell had one son with his first wife, Addie Baker, who died in 1929.

Isbell died on July 15, 1941, at age 65, after suffering a heart attack. He was buried in Wichita's Old Mission Cemetery.

TREY STRECKER

479

Fielder Jones

CHICAGO

FIELDER ALLISON JONES
CENTER FIELDER, 1901–1908; MANAGER, 1904–1908

Best remembered today as the no-nonsense manager of the world champion 1906 Chicago White Sox, Fielder Jones was also a superb left-handed hitter who excelled at getting on base and scoring runs, and an excellent defensive center fielder who twice led the American League in putouts. In 1906 Jones became the first outfielder in American League history to record an unassisted double play. As a manager, Jones earned a reputation as a stern taskmaster, regularly fining and suspending his players for bad conduct on and off the field. A brilliant tactician, he was one of the first managers to position his outfielders according to the hitter. Jones was also one of the fiercest umpire-baiters of the Deadball Era. As the *New York Times* once observed, "He wore a path from centre [*sic*] field to the diamond as he ran in to argue umpires' decisions and called balls and strikes. He was banished often for kicking."

Jones became a prominent advocate for players' rights, frequently feuding with his owner, Charles Comiskey, and becoming an outspoken critic of the reserve clause. Beneath the tough exterior, Jones could be an easy touch; throughout his career he bailed out a number of old players experiencing financial difficulties, with no expectation that he would ever be repaid.

A committed cigar smoker and fancy dresser who liked the newest gadgets, Jones was known to pull out his harmonica to entertain teammates and friends. He was also a superb checkers player—the Portland *Oregonian* once excitedly reported that the great Christy Mathewson, also a noted checkers player, would be coming to town to play an exhibition series against Jones. Unfortunately, this showdown between the two most noted checkers players of the era never happened.

Fielder Allison Jones was born on August 13, 1871, in the village of Shinglehouse, Pennsylvania, near the New York border. He was the second child of Benjamin F. and Laura Parmenter Jones. Both parents came from area pioneer families. Jones was named for his uncle, Fielder Alsor Jones, a much-decorated Union Civil War general. Jones's father, also a Union army officer, contracted lung disease while in a Confederate prisoner-of-war camp and died when Fielder was two.

Jones's first taste of Organized Baseball came as a catcher with the Shinglehouse town team, where he formed an all-Jones battery with his brother Willard. Jones then followed Willard into the engineering and surveying business, eventually working his way west to join his brother in Portland, Oregon. He decided to give baseball a try, making his professional debut with Portland in the Oregon State League in 1893. The following year he returned east, playing in the New York State League for Corning in 1894 and Binghamton in 1895. When the league folded in midseason, he was picked up by Springfield (Massachusetts) of the Eastern League, and proceeded to hit .399 in 50 games. That drew notice from Brooklyn, who signed him for the 1896 campaign.

Jones reported to Brooklyn but did not play much at first; the Bridegrooms had a solid outfield in place. When John Anderson was injured in May, Jones replaced him and remained an outfield fixture for the rest of his time in Brooklyn. He hit .354 that year, sixth-highest average ever by a rookie. Back in Shinglehouse, the local paper breathlessly reported that Jones was making the astounding sum of $11 per day. By the end of the season, Jones was drawing notice around the league. *The Sporting News* reported, "he is a young man yet, with fine habits, and is very modest and unassuming. He has a bright professional future before him." They were certainly right about the bright future, but Jones would prove to be anything but modest and unassuming. After the 1898 season, he married Mabel

Schaney, a local girl from the Shinglehouse area. They eventually had one child, Cecil.

Jones, who hit left but threw right, demonstrated a powerful and accurate throwing arm, ranking near the top of the league in assists year after year. Although his rookie season would prove to be his best offensively, Jones continued to be a solid and consistent .300 hitter throughout the first half of his career. The Bridegrooms, however, were perennial bridesmaids. That all changed in 1899, when ownership machinations brought Ned Hanlon to the Bridegrooms as manager.

Hanlon, despite being in command of that infamous gang of rowdies in Baltimore, was a smart baseball man; he is credited with being the prime influence on Jones's managing style, with its emphasis on strategic innovation. The team, now called the Superbas, won the National League pennant in 1899 and repeated as champions in 1900.

Jones, never shy about getting paid, jumped early to the American League, signing for the 1901 season with Comiskey's White Sox, the defending league champions. He was a prize catch, 29 years old and at the top of his game. Also coming to the Sox was Billy Sullivan, the Boston Nationals catcher, who would become Jones's lifelong friend and also his successor as White Sox manager. Arriving from the cross-town Chicago Orphans was pitcher Clark Griffith, who not only managed the team to a second consecutive AL pennant, but led the pitching staff as well. Griffith was another of those "brainy" managers who would be an influence on Jones, who in 1901 led the regulars in batting average (.311), on-base percentage (.412), runs (120), and hits, as well as outfield assists.

Jones remained a solid offensive presence in 1902, batting .321 with a .390 on-base percentage, but the team slipped to fourth place and after the season Griffith was reassigned by Ban Johnson to the league's new New York franchise and replaced by another player–manager, Jimmy Callahan.

The White Sox continued to slide, finishing seventh in 1903. Jones tried to return to the National League with the New York Giants for 1904, but the two leagues, at peace by this time, declared he must remain in Chicago. The Sox played indifferent baseball in 1904. Callahan, who was not firmly in control, resigned in June and Jones was named manager, although Callahan continued to play the outfield alongside Jones. The team, in fourth place when Jones took over, turned around, rising briefly to the league lead in August before finishing third, six games out. Jones's Chicago teams would remain in pennant contention throughout his tenure as manager.

The White Sox continued their improvement under Jones in 1905, climbing to second place. Although he would continue as the regular center fielder through 1908, his age and the stress of managing caused Jones's offense to fall off further. In the context of the Deadball Era, however, he remained a productive player, ranking in the top five in walks every year from 1905 to 1908.

The famous 1906 "Hitless Wonders," well-known for their league-low .230 batting average, took a cue from their manager and generated offense by finding other ways to get on base. Their 453 walks were far and away the most by any team in the league, helping them to score 570 runs, third most in the circuit, despite playing in the pitcher's haven of South Side Park. Jones's squad was adept at manufacturing runs—a critical skill in the low-offense environment in which they played. The 1906 White Sox had two of the league's top five base stealers and two of the top five in sacrifices. As the *Chicago Tribune* later observed, "A White Sox rally at that time was described as a base on balls, a sacrifice, a stolen base, and a long fly." More important, however, Chicago's fine pitching staff was at or near the top of every pitching category, with staff aces Ed Walsh, Doc White, and Nick Altrock backed up by the league's premier defense.

In addition to Jones's continued sterling play in center, the Sox also boasted exceptional defenders at nearly every position, particularly catcher (Billy Sullivan), third base (Lee Tannehill), and shortstop (George Davis). In that year's World Series the Sox upset the 116-win Cubs in six games by playing their style of ball, as the South Siders hit just .198 for the series, but drew 18 walks and held the Cubs to a .196 average.

The team slipped to third in 1907, 5½ games back. They repeated their third-place finish in 1908, but remained in the fight until the end, finishing only 1½ games behind the Tigers. After the 1908 season, Comiskey was ready to talk contract with Jones. At this point Fielder, always a savvy money man who had invested his money wisely, was interested in buying into the team, but Commy rebuffed him. Despite a large salary offer, Jones announced that he was moving to Portland, Oregon, to manage his business interests. While it was undoubtedly part negotiating ploy, Jones was in fact serious. Despite entreaties from Comiskey and Ban Johnson, he stayed put. Jones's lifelong friend and soon to be fellow Oregonian Billy Sullivan took over the team. In a newspaper interview in March, Jones claimed that he was in Portland because his financial interests demanded it. He said he might own a big league club someday, and that there were no hard feelings between he and Comiskey. There was another reason for his apparent retirement.

Known only to his family, Jones was feeling the effects of the heart problems that would eventually kill him.

Jones was not quite done with baseball, however. In 1909 he was named treasurer of the Northwestern League, a six-team circuit in Oregon, Washington, and British Columbia. In 1910 he served as coach of the Oregon Agricultural College (now Oregon State University) team, which won the Northwest Intercollegiate Association championship. When Jones arrived in Corvallis, he was described as the game's greatest baseball wizard and a practitioner of scientific baseball. "He was seen," according to the local paper, "strolling the diamond like a well-dressed bulldog, his right hand clutching a bat as if he were about ready to smash something," After the college season, he played for Chehalis of the Washington State League, leading the circuit in batting at the age of 38 while openly flouting the reserve clause that still bound him to the White Sox.

In returning to Portland, Jones had also rejoined his brother. Willard, always considered somewhat of a scoundrel by the family, had served a term in 1903 in the Oregon legislature, but had since run afoul of the law in a land fraud scheme that also implicated U.S. Senator John H. Mitchell. Willard's political connections must have remained solid, however, because he received a pardon from President William Howard Taft in 1912. That same year, Fielder Jones was named president of the Northwestern League; by all accounts he brought order to the circuit, which had suffered a chaotic 1911 season. Peace in the league was short-lived, however, and Jones was consistently at odds with one or another faction of the league's owners. Fed up with the warring owners, Jones resigned the league's presidency on August 16, 1914, in order to take over as manager and part-owner of the Federal League's St. Louis Terriers, replacing Three Fingered Brown.

The 1914 Terriers were a poor team, and the arrival of Jones did not help. The team was in seventh place when he took over, and they had sunk to the basement by season's end, posting a 12–26 record under Jones. They reversed their fortunes in 1915, and the Terriers battled to the wire, losing the pennant by a single percentage point.

When the Federal League collapsed after the 1915 season, Terriers owner

Phil Ball was allowed to buy the American League Browns; he then merged the Terriers with the Browns. Jones became the manager, moving incumbent Branch Rickey to the front office. In 1916 Jones brought the team home in fifth place, a little over .500. With insinuations by Ball and the league that some players were dumping games, and a countering libel suit by the players, 1917 proved to be a tumultuous year, and the team fell to seventh, finishing only 1½ games out of the cellar. Oddly, Jones won a $500 prize from AL president Ban Johnson for having the best "drilled" team, a gimmicky appeal to patriotism during World War I.

In 1918 Phil Ball was pressured to run a more taut ship, something Jones had experienced before, with Charles Comiskey. Furthermore, the players were not happy with Jones or Ball, and there were still accusations of lying down on the part of the players. On June 13, a day after watching his team blow a 4–0 ninth inning lead against the Senators, Jones walked out on the team for good, with barely a goodbye. He was done with Organized Baseball.

Jones returned to Portland to tend to his businesses. His heart condition remained a concern, and he lived at a more relaxed pace. Jones rejoined his brother Willard and was again near Billy Sullivan, with whom he jointly owned nut orchards in McMinnville, Oregon. The 1920 census lists his occupation as timber salesman. He remained active in the local baseball scene, and was seen often at local events. He could sometimes be found holding forth in the downtown clubs with his friends.

Jones took ill at a meeting of local baseball boosters in February 1934 and was hospitalized. He died on March 13 at age 62 of congestive heart failure. His funeral attracted more than 300 people, including many prominent baseball figures. "[Jones] ranks right with McGraw and Connie Mack," former Cleveland manager George Stovall said. "He had an inspiring personality and his teams played flashing, dashing, smart baseball. You had to keep your eyes and ears wide open to play baseball under Fielder Jones. The morale of his ballclubs was wonderful. They never were beaten no matter the score." Jones was cremated and his remains were entombed in Portland Memorial Mausoleum.

PAUL ANDRESEN

"Billy" Sullivan

CHICAGO

WILLIAM JOSEPH SULLIVAN
CATCHER, 1901–1912, 1914; MANAGER, 1909

Although he was considered "never very strong in stick work," his Deadball Era contemporaries believed that Billy Sullivan's "brilliant performances behind the bat…more than offset his weak hitting." His paltry .213 lifetime batting average is the second worst all-time (next to Bill Bergen) among players with at least 3,000 at-bats, but Sullivan developed a reputation as a brainy backstop with an uncanny ability to handle pitchers. Described by Ty Cobb as the best catcher "ever to wear shoe leather," Sullivan was "the best man throwing to bases in the American League," and "no man in the business [knew] more about getting the best work from a pitcher and holding an infield together." Sullivan also revolutionized the way his position was played: he is credited as the first catcher to position himself directly behind the batter and also as the inventor of an inflatable chest protector.

William Joseph Sullivan was born on a farm near Oakland, Wisconsin, on February 1, 1875, the son of Irish immigrants. He first displayed his potential as a ball player at Fort Atkinson High School, where he starred in the infield. As a high school student, Sullivan played shortstop until an accident disabled his team's regular catcher. Without any previous experience, the young Sullivan was put in to catch, where his work behind the bat attracted the attention of the local town team's manager. Afterward, he caught for an independent team in Edgewater, Wisconsin, before he broke into the professional ranks with the Western Association's Cedar Rapids (Iowa) Bunnies in 1896.

The next year the 5′9″, 155-pound right-hander played for Dubuque, Iowa, where he caught 124 consecutive games. Purchased from Dubuque by Tom Loftus, Sullivan worked behind the plate for Columbus, Ohio, of the Western League in 1898. The next year

he was transferred with his team to Grand Rapids, Michigan, where he hit .306 in 83 games before being sold to the Boston Beaneaters at the end of the season. Catching 66 games for Boston in 1900, Sullivan slugged eight home runs, fifth in the National League. It was the only time in his career he would make the top ten in any hitting category.

Before the 1901 season an offer of $2,400 enticed him to jump to the White Sox, where he caught the American League's first game as a major league, Chicago's 8–2 victory over Cleveland on April 24, 1901. Despite his impressive hitting for the Beaneaters in 1900, once in American League company Sullivan's offense quickly disappeared, as it did for most of the era's backstops. He batted .245 in his first season with the White Sox, a pedestrian average that would prove to be the highest of his American League career. From 1903 to 1912 he never batted higher than .229 in any season, and finished as low as .162. His abysmal hitting was coupled with a shortage of power and an inability to get on base via other means—for his career he finished with a .254 on-base percentage and a .281 slugging percentage. Sullivan was particularly dreadful in his only postseason appearance. In the 1906 World Series against the Chicago Cubs, he went hitless in 21 at-bats, including nine strikeouts. However, he caught every inning of every game and guided his pitchers to a collective 1.33 ERA in the Sox's six-game victory.

Somehow, the White Sox seemed a better team with the scrappy, resourceful Sullivan in their lineup. With Sullivan as their primary catcher, the White Sox won two pennants (1901 and 1906) and narrowly missed two others (1905 and 1908), while never finishing lower than fourth place. By contrast, in the two seasons in which Sullivan was injured, 1903 and 1910, the club finished in the second division both times, more than 30 games out of first place. During his years in uniform, Sullivan was particularly important in steadying Chicago's stalwart pitching rotation, which included the likes of Ed Walsh, Doc White, and Nick Altrock. Four times a league leader in fielding percentage, Sullivan placed himself directly behind the batter. In 1908 Sullivan was issued a U.S. Patent for an inflatable, contoured chest protector, which protected his body better and, thanks to hinging, allowed more freedom of movement than the normal model.

On October 24, 1905, Sullivan married Mary Josephine O'Sullivan, who had emigrated from Ireland five years earlier. The marriage lasted 59 years until his death. A clean-living player who did not swear, drink, or smoke, Sully replaced Fielder Jones as Chicago's playing manager in 1909, piloting the club to a 78–74 record and a fourth-place finish. It was Sullivan's only season as manager; the next year, Hugh Duffy took the helm and Sully returned to catching full time.

On August 24, 1910, Sullivan caught three baseballs thrown by Ed Walsh off the top of the Washington Monument as a publicity stunt, duplicating Washington catcher Gabby Street's feat from two years earlier. Contemporary reports estimated that the balls sped at 161 feet per second toward Sullivan's pancake mitt. Remarkably, despite gusty winds, Sullivan caught three of the eleven balls Walsh threw. Despite this stunt, Sully declined to attempt to catch a ball dropped from an airplane, saying he "might as well try to stop a bullet."

Sullivan was often sidelined by injuries. An errant foul tip broke his throwing hand in 1901. The next year he required an emergency appendectomy. He was hit by a pitched ball in 1904 and knocked unconscious. During the 1906 pennant chase, he reinjured his throwing hand. Perhaps the most serious injury Sullivan faced was a battle with the blood poisoning he contracted in 1910, after stepping on a rusty nail during a spring training trip. Following the dubious advice of a quack physician, he received a nearly lethal dose of turpentine and almost lost a leg before receiving appropriate medical care. "This Sullivan man is a real hero," the *Atlanta Constitution* wrote after the 1908 campaign. "He begged permission to catch the final game in Cleveland although two rows of stitches had been removed from his right thumb only the day before.... The nature of his injury must have made his work agony, but he stuck to his job."

In 1912, with Sullivan's performance and endurance declining, young backstop Ray Schalk emerged as his successor. Sullivan spent the 1913 and 1914 seasons as a Sox coach, assisting manager Jimmy Callahan, teaching Schalk, and managing the B squad in spring training. Chicago owner Charles Comiskey had promised Sullivan lifetime employment with the team as a reward for his years of service, but broke that promise on February 15, 1915, when he unconditionally released the shocked Sullivan. After trying and failing to land a job as an AL umpire, Billy joined the Minneapolis Millers where he coached, batted .215, and caught 105 games of "fine ball," as they won the American Association pennant. Released by Minneapolis at the end of the year, he appeared in a single game as a player–coach with Detroit in 1916.

At the end of the 1916 season, the 41-year-old Sullivan accepted his release and retired to a 20-acre apple, walnut, and filbert farm outside Newberg, Oregon, where he spent the rest of his life with his wife, Mary. During the 1917 season, Sully attempted to catch on with Portland of the Pacific Coast League and Seattle of the Northwestern League, but he was unsuccessful.

Upon his retirement, Sullivan paid tribute to four of the foremost pitchers he caught. According to Sully, "Kid Nichols, of the old Boston Nationals, possessed the greatest speed; Ed Walsh was the peer of the spit ball pitchers; Jim Scott tops all the curve ball experts, and for all-around mixing and slow ball delivery there never was a man who excelled 'Doc' White."

Although one son, Joseph, a second baseman and captain on the University of Notre Dame team, turned down an offer from the White Sox in order to pursue a law career, Billy Sullivan, Jr., began his own 12-year major league career with the White Sox in 1931, playing with Chicago, Cincinnati, Cleveland, the St. Louis Browns, Detroit, Brooklyn, and Pittsburgh. When Billy caught for Detroit in the 1940 World Series, the Sullivans became the first father and son to have played in the fall classic. Baseball dopesters frequently remarked that if Billy, Sr., could hit like his son, and if Billy, Jr., could field like his father, they would be "the best catcher in the history of the game."

Sullivan died of a heart ailment on January 28, 1965, eight days after the death of his Chicago batterymate, Nick Altrock, and just four days shy of his 90th birthday. He was buried in St. James Catholic Cemetery in McMinnville, Oregon.

Trey Strecker

CHICAGO

GEORGE STACEY DAVIS
SHORTSTOP, 1902, 1904–1909

Known as Gorgeous George for his graceful play and blond locks, George Davis established himself as one of the game's most well-rounded players during his 20 seasons in the major leagues. At the plate, the switch-hitting Davis was a model of consistency, batting better than .300 every year from 1893 to 1901. In the field the shortstop was steady and reliable, leading his league in fielding percentage four times. On the basepaths the 5'9", 180-pounder was a constant threat, swiping 616 bases in his career, the third most ever by a player whose primary position was shortstop, behind Honus Wagner and Bert Campaneris. John McGraw described Davis as "an exceptionally quick thinker," a reputation which led to his spending the 1901 season and parts of the 1895 and 1900 campaigns as the manager of the New York Giants, where some claim Davis taught Christy Mathewson his famous fadeaway pitch. Despite his many achievements, however, Davis vanished from sight after his career ended and died in obscurity.

George Stacey Davis was born on August 23, 1870, in Cohoes, New York, the fifth of seven children of Irish immigrant Abraham Davis and his Welsh wife, Sarah. According to the 1880 census, Abraham supported his family as a machinist. Baseball was becoming very popular in the Albany area during George's childhood, and Cohoes newspapers place the lad on tavern-sponsored teams as early as 1886. According to these sources, even at this young age Davis was already a switch-hitter.

Davis spent the 1889 season with an Albany semipro team. The following year, the Cleveland Spiders of the National League, looking to replace players who had jumped to the upstart Players League, signed Davis on the recommendation of Albany manager Tom York. Still just 19 years old at the start of the 1890 season, the rookie answered the call by hitting a solid .264, with six home runs, 73 RBI, 22 stolen bases, and 35 assists in the outfield, playing mostly center. The following year, Davis proved that his promising debut had been no fluke, as he batted .289 with 115 runs, 50 extra-base hits, and 42 stolen bases. Davis's excellent and versatile defense allowed Cleveland manager Patsy Tebeau to bounce him between the outfield, third base, second base, and even the pitcher's box (albeit only for three abominable appearances in which the right-handed thrower yielded seven earned runs in four innings of work).

Prior to the 1893 season, New York Giants manager John Montgomery Ward traded heralded veteran utility man Buck Ewing for the young Davis, 22 years old and just off a subpar year in which he had batted .241. Ward moved Davis to third base and the switch-hitter, aided by the new 60'6" pitching distance, hit an impressive .355 with 119 RBI and a career-high 27 triples. He also set a major league record with a 33-game hitting streak, although the mark would be broken by both Bill Dahlen and Billy Hamilton the next year. The New York fans embraced their new player and Ward became a mentor to Davis, who grew a handlebar mustache that resembled Ward's, making it difficult to tell the two apart.

In 1895 the Giants' majority holder Andrew Freedman took control of the franchise as Ward retired to make use of his new law degree. Freedman jumped on 24-year-old Davis as a replacement because of his intelligence and well-spoken demeanor, making him the youngest manager in major league history at the time. The Giants struggled under Davis, however, going 16–17 before the manager was relieved of his duties.

The Giants' second manager of the 1896 season was third baseman Bill Joyce, who moved Davis to shortstop. Davis became a true leader of the infield and shone with his wide range and above-average arm. In

1897 Davis was spectacular at the plate: he batted .353 with career highs in RBI (136) and stolen bases (65). He also excelled in his first full season at short, ranking third in the league in fielding percentage at .926 while leading the league in putouts (337) and double plays (67). Davis's offensive numbers declined in 1898 in line with the entire league and in 1899 he was hampered with injuries. Despite a solid .337 average that year, Davis managed just one home run and 57 RBI for the season.

Prior to the 1900 season the Giants' new manager, Buck Ewing, appointed Davis as field captain, but before long dissension infested the Giants clubhouse. The team split into two cliques, one consisting of leftover New Yorkers, the other of Ewing imports. After a terrible early July road trip the Giants fell to 21–41, forcing Ewing to resign under pressure. Ewing cried foul, accusing Davis of conspiring to steal his job. Following Ewing's resignation Davis was named manager of the club, which finished in last place despite posting a solid 39–37 record under Davis.

After a horrid 52–85 season in 1901, it was apparent that Davis would not be returning as manager of New York. Like many other players at the time, he ignored the reserve clause and signed a contract with the White Sox drawn up by his lawyer, John Montgomery Ward. Freedman did not contest the move because he wanted to replace Davis anyway. In his first season in

the American League, Davis batted a solid .299, drove in 93 runs, and stole 31 bases.

In the winter of 1902 John T. Brush took over control of the Giants and named John McGraw as manager midway through the 1902 season. After the campaign McGraw, looking to fill the club's gaping hole at shortstop, acquired Davis's signature on a two-year contract to play for New York. The move threatened to destroy the new peace treaty which had been forged between the two leagues that winter. White Sox owner Charles Comiskey threatened legal action. Davis went to Ward, who argued (rather disingenuously, considering that he had helped Davis jump his New York contract the previous year) that the reserve clause in Davis's 1901 Giants contract constituted a legal hold on the ballplayer's services for the 1902 season, thus overruling any claim the White Sox had. Ward declared that Davis was entitled to rejoin the Giants per the new contract. Comiskey counterattacked by first securing an injunction from an Illinois court, which prevented Davis from playing baseball for any team other than the White Sox in that state. In July Comiskey obtained another injunction, this one from the U.S. Court of Appeals, which prohibited Davis from playing for any team anywhere other than the White Sox. The National League owners, weary of the dispute, instructed Brush to give up his rights to Davis. In all, the shortstop played only four games for New York that year. and none for Chicago.

Davis returned to a hostility-free White Sox team in 1904 and, corresponding to a league-wide freefall in offense, batted just .252, although he also swatted 43 extra-base hits and swiped 32 bases for the season. Defensively, Davis continued his excellent work, leading all American League shortstops in putouts, assists, double plays, and chances per game.

After finishing third in 1904 Chicago improved to second place in 1905, as Davis, now 34, batted a solid .278. In 1906 the veteran was the best offensive performer for the famous Hitless Wonders, finishing the year with a .277 batting average and leading the team in doubles (26), slugging percentage (.355), and RBI (80).

Davis missed the first three games of that year's World Series because of illness. After going 0-for-3 in Game Four, he rebounded nicely in the critical final two games of the Series, stroking three doubles and a single, and collecting six RBI.

The 1906 championship marked the last hurrah for Davis, as age and injuries caused his average to steadily decline in 1907 and 1908. By 1909 he was a part-time player, appearing in just 28 games and batting only .132. At the end of the season, the White Sox granted Davis's request to be released.

Davis managed the Des Moines (Iowa) Western League team in 1911 but, much like his major league managerial career, he was not successful, finishing in last place with a 49–113 record. Davis then managed a Manhattan bowling alley from 1911 through 1913 and was featured in a New York paper looking clean-shaven and fit, a star bowler at age 43. From 1913 to 1918 Davis was coach at Amherst College in Massachusetts, during which time he also scouted for the Yankees (in 1915) and the Browns (in 1917). He was last mentioned in the press as selling cars in St. Louis in 1918.

Davis then vanished from public view until 1968, when Hall of Fame historian Lee Allen discovered his death certificate. Davis had been admitted to Philadelphia General Hospital in 1934 and three weeks later was transferred to a mental hospital in the city. He died on October 17, 1940, at age 70. The cause was paresis—insanity produced by syphilitic alteration of the brain that leads to dementia and paralysis. His wife, Jane Holden Davis, signed the death certificate and buried him 24 hours later just outside of Philadelphia in an unmarked grave in Fernwood Cemetery. Davis's family would not learn of his death until years later.

Davis received his due recognition when the Veterans Committee voted him into the Hall of Fame in 1998. Thanks to the George Davis chapter (now defunct) of the Society of American Baseball Research (SABR) and the Century Monument Company, George Stacey Davis now has a stone at his gravesite.

NICOLE DiCICCO

CHICAGO

GUY HARRIS "DOC" WHITE
LEFT-HANDED PITCHER, 1903–1913

At 6'1" and only 150 pounds, rail-thin Doc White spent 13 seasons in the big leagues and won 189 games, thanks in large part to a drop ball that consistently fooled hitters and a fastball that kept them honest. Although he once led the league in fewest walks allowed per nine innings pitched, White ensured that opposing hitters never got too comfortable against him by hitting 41 batters in his first three seasons in the majors, and mixing in a change-of-pace to disrupt the batter's timing. "The days of standing in the center of the diamond and depending on your speed alone to take you through are gone," White wrote, "and to expect to be able to pitch balls past the batters of this generation before they can get their bats around, as is commonly expressed, is ridiculous." His greatest achievement came in 1904 when he tossed five consecutive shutouts, a major league record not broken until Don Drysdale pitched six straight shutouts in 1968.

Guy Harris White was born the seventh son of a seventh son on April 9, 1879, in Washington, D.C. His father, George White, was a powerful businessman in the nation's capital, and at the time of Guy's birth owned the city's only iron foundry. An older son, Charles Stanley White, became one of Washington's most prominent physicians, and the youngest child was also urged to go into the medical profession. Along the way Guy White developed a secondary interest in playing baseball, at which he excelled for Washington's Central High. During his high school years, White also met his future wife, Iva Martin, with whom he enjoyed a marriage of more than 50 years until her death in 1955.

With his studies still coming first, White enrolled at Georgetown University in 1897. He joined the baseball team in the spring of 1898 and quickly became its star pitcher and outfielder. The highlight of his college career came in a game against Holy Cross in 1899,

when he struck out the first nine batters, thus earning the attention of professional scouts. White stuck to the books, however, working hard toward a degree in dentistry until the end of his junior year in 1900. That summer he joined the Fleischmann's Mountain Athletic Club, a semipro team that also featured future major leaguers Red Dooin and George Rohe. It was with the FMAC that White was discovered by Roy Thomas, star center fielder for the Philadelphia Phillies, who urged his owner John Rogers to sign the young left-hander.

Rogers inked White to a contract for $1,200, with a promise of a $200 bonus if he had a good season. Without a day of minor league experience, the young left-hander stepped into the rotation of a strong veteran team boasting three Hall of Famers in its starting lineup. White more than met the challenge all season long, winning his debut with a six-hitter against Brooklyn and 14 games total for the season. Always a good-hitting pitcher, White batted .276 and helped his team to a 19–1 victory on June 24 with four hits, including an inside-the-park home run. In 1902 the Phillies slumped badly and White's 16–20 record reflected it; however, he finished second in the National League with 185 strikeouts, including four in one inning against Brooklyn on July 21 (the first documented time this had been accomplished since the advent of the 60'6" pitching distance).

Despite his burgeoning big league career, White returned to Georgetown to finish his studies. He received his dentistry degree in 1902 and opened a dental practice in Washington after the season. That off-season, however, he became the object of a bidding war between the Phillies and Chicago of the nascent American League. Chicago offered White a raise to jump to the new league, which he quickly accepted. Philadelphia then tried to keep White by tripling Chicago's offer. Before he could jump back, a peace settlement was forged between the two leagues, part of which stipulated that White should go to Chicago.

In his first season in the American League, White won 17 games, leading the Chicago staff, and his 2.13 ERA ranked fourth in the league. A highlight came on September 6 when he pitched a 10-inning one-hitter against Cleveland. The college-educated White also earned the respect of some of his rough-and-tumble teammates by continuing to rank among the league leaders in hit batsmen. After the season he again returned to his dental practice, which had now earned him the nickname "Doc." (Previously he had been known as Harry White, after his middle name.)

The White Stockings had struggled in 1903, but contended for the pennant all season long in 1904. Doc White played an important role in the pennant race, winning 16 games with a sterling 1.78 ERA. Although slight of stature, the lefty threw a hard fastball and also relied on a sinker and spitball to get him out of trouble. In September he single-handedly kept the team in contention with a shutout streak that remained a baseball record for the next 64 years.

The streak began on September 12, when White shut out Cleveland 1–0. Four days later he took a no-hitter into the eighth inning at St. Louis in another 1–0 victory. On September 19 he had an easier time with Detroit, shutting them out 3–0 on just two hits.

With the White Stockings trying to hang on in the pennant race, White pitched his fourth straight shutout, defeating the Philadelphia Athletics 4–0 on September 25. On September 30, shutout number five came courtesy of the first-place New York Highlanders, again by a 4–0 total. With staff mainstay Frank Owen hurt, White took his turn in the rotation and agreed to start both ends of a doubleheader against New York on October 2. His streak of 45 consecutive scoreless innings finally came to an end in the first inning of the opener, when Willie Keeler scored from second on a single by Jimmy Williams. White then shut the Highlanders out for the rest of the game to win 7–1. In the nightcap, the exhausted lefty finally gave out, losing 6–3.

It had been a magnificent stretch of pitching and endurance, but it contributed to renewed calls (unheeded for many more years) for baseball to do something to help the game's overmatched hitters. Even White's own manager, Fielder Jones, called for the spitball his ace often used to be banned from the sport. "If baseball legislators want to do any legislating this winter let them pass a rule against the spit ball," Jones argued. "There is no way the batter can get at that ball and the pitcher is already too strong for him."

By 1905, White had established himself as one of the game's elite pitchers. He posted a 17–13 record, and his ERA of 1.76 ranked second in the league. The multitalented pitcher was also drawing attention for his off-the-field exploits. Loquacious and bright, he proved to be a prime resource for newspaper reporters seeking interviews. White's "Words of Wisdom" columns appeared in the *Chicago Tribune*, offering his thoughts on a variety of baseball subjects, including the use of the mud ball (too dangerous), college players (ironically, he felt they should go to the minor leagues first), and the inability of left-handed batters to hit left-handed pitching (not enough practice). He was well respected by both the ownership, who asked him to help design the team's uniforms, and his teammates, who in 1912 chose him to represent Chicago at the first formative meetings of the short-lived players union.

After two years of near misses, the White Stockings won the American League pennant in 1906, setting up a showdown with the cross-town powerhouse Chicago Cubs. White enjoyed another strong season, winning 18 games and leading the American League with a 1.52 ERA. Doc had not pitched much at the end of the season, due to illness and arm fatigue, and was hit hard in a 7–1 loss in Game Two. White's next appearance came in relief in Game Five, when he pitched three scoreless innings to hold down an 8–6 victory and give the Sox a 3–2 edge in the Series. Pitching on no days rest, White got the start in the sixth game, and coasted to an 8–3 complete-game victory to nail down the championship.

Although White's ERA rose to 2.26 in 1907, Doc enjoyed another outstanding season, walking just 38 batters in 291 innings and notching a career-best 27 victories. In another remarkable streak, White also pitched 65⅓ consecutive innings without allowing a walk. The streak ended on September 11 with an intentional pass to the .250-hitting Tom Jones, who was batting eighth in the lineup that day. The free pass loaded the bases with one out, and White then proceeded to strike out pitcher Barney Pelty before inducing a ground ball from Harry Niles and escaping the inning unscathed. Following the game the *Chicago Tribune* (apparently unaware of the streak, which established an American League record that lasted for the next 55 years) commended White for the decision, marveling, "Some brains!"

Although overshadowed in 1908 by his teammate Ed Walsh, White won 18 games and helped keep the White Sox in an exciting pennant race that went down to the season's final day. Chosen to start over a well-rested Frank Smith, who had been feuding with manager Jones, White went to the mound against Detroit on October 6 with a chance to give the team a tie for the pennant. Working with only a day's rest, White could not get out of the first inning of a 7–0 loss that cost the team the championship.

Off the field White had stopped practicing dentistry and become active in his church, where he displayed yet another talent by leading the church choir in song and on the piano. He collaborated with Chicago newspaper columnist Ring Lardner on two songs, providing the music for Lardner's words. The first, a sentimental ditty entitled "A Little Puff of Smoke, Good Night" became quite popular in 1910 and is still held in high regard by fans of the genre. The second, 1911's "Gee It's A Wonderful Game," celebrated his baseball roots. During White's later baseball years in California, he extended his church work to include a short vaudeville tour in which he performed spirituals and popular songs.

Over the first eight years of his career, White's slender frame had absorbed a punishing workload: he had pitched more than 250 innings five times. By 1909 the strain began to manifest itself, and White managed to pitch only 177 innings on his way to an 11–9 record. Despite 15 victories the following season, Doc's ERA jumped nearly a run to 2.66, and continued to increase every year for the rest of his career. After the 1913 season, in which he appeared in only 19 games and posted a 3.50 ERA, White retired as an active major league player, although he did pitch for Venice and Vernon in the Pacific Coast League in 1914 and 1915.

Although his playing career had ended, White continued to work in baseball. He became interim manager of Vernon during the 1915 season, and worked in a front-office job there in 1916. He then became part-owner of the Dallas franchise in the Texas League, for whom he pitched one game in 1917.

After the league suspended play due to World War I, White served as a YMCA director with an aviation unit in Dallas. He ran the Waco franchise in 1919, and then managed Muskegon (Michigan) in the Central League in 1920. After leaving pro ball, White returned to his old school, Central High in Washington, accepting a position as a coach and physical education teacher in 1921. He continued in this post for the next 28 years, while also serving as a pitching coach for the University of Maryland and as a basketball coach at Wilson Teachers College (now the University of the District of Columbia).

White retired from his coaching positions at age 70 in June 1949. In 1968 Don Drysdale's successful run at his record brought Doc into the limelight one last time. Bedridden and living with his daughter in Silver Spring, Maryland, White was too weak even to leave his bed or come to the phone to answer requests for interviews—although he did telegram Drysdale to congratulate him on breaking his record.

On February 17, 1969, White died in Silver Spring, just a few weeks shy of his 90th birthday. He was buried at Oak Hill Cemetery in Washington, DC.

JOHN BENNETT

CHICAGO

Frank Elmer Smith
Right-handed pitcher, 1904–1910

Frank Elmer Smith, known during his playing days as the Piano Mover because he used to boast that he could "carry a baby grand up four flights of stairs without a rest," was a mainstay of the Chicago White Sox pitching staff between 1904 and 1909, winning 104 games for the club during that span. Relying on a drop ball, curve, and occasional spitball, Smith hurled two no-hitters for the White Sox, the only pitcher in franchise history to do so, and led the American League in both innings pitched and strikeouts in 1909.

Smith, who during his prime stood a shade under 5'11" and weighed in at a hefty 194 pounds, was born in Pittsburgh on October 28, 1879, to a family whose original name was Schmidt. He briefly attended and coached at Grove City College before he signed on with his first professional team in Erie, Pennsylvania, in 1900.

After a stint with the Raleigh Senators of the Virginia–North Carolina League in 1901, Smith was promoted to Birmingham (Alabama) in the Southern League for the 1902 season, where he acquired the nickname Nig due to his dark complexion. Smith was a terrific power pitcher for Birmingham, and was described as "a big hulk" who had tremendous back and shoulder muscles "super induced by his piano pulling proclivities." During every off-season Smith worked as a furniture mover for his father and this contributed to his prowess on the mound. Eventually he caught the attention of Charles Comiskey and was drafted by Chicago for the 1904 season.

Smith won 16 games for the White Sox in his rookie campaign, a season in which he acquired a new pitch, the spitball. Along with Ed Walsh, Smith was tutored on the pitch by Elmer Stricklett, a minor league prospect for the White Sox. Stricklett showed Walsh and Smith how to put spit on the ball and throw it like a fastball, producing a pitch with tremendous speed but little rotation, giving it the effect of a knuckleball.

At times able to master the spitball, Smith had a brilliant season in 1905, when he went 19–13 with an ERA of 2.13. On September 6 that year the White Sox traveled to Detroit for a doubleheader against the Tigers on a Wednesday afternoon; 3,500 fans in Bennett Park watched the White Sox defeat the Tigers 2–0 in the first game, and then saw Smith throw just the fifth no-hitter in American League history. Smith was staked to an eight-run lead thanks to five walks, five errors, and one hit in the top of the first inning. Detroit's starting pitcher, Jimmy Wiggs, was replaced by George Disch for the second inning but the White Sox pounded out 11 hits and seven runs over the next eight innings. Meanwhile the Piano Mover was putting together a gem. He struck out eight and walked three and retired the last 17 Tiger batters in order to preserve the no-hitter. The 15–0 drubbing of the Tigers remains the most one-sided no-hitter in AL history.

The first ever one-city World Series, between the White Sox and their cross-town rivals, the Cubs, highlighted the 1906 season. Smith contributed very little to the team that year, posting a 5–5 record in 13 starts, and in fact was kept out of the rotation by Sox manager Fielder Jones for weeks at a time so that Smith could conquer his problems controlling the spitter. Late in the season, The Piano Mover was able to get his spitter over the plate. He was used mostly in relief down the stretch and saw no action in the White Sox's World Series triumph. He returned to form the following year, however, as he compiled a 23–10 record while striking out 139 batters in 310 innings pitched. Chicago, however, lost the pennant to Detroit during the final week of the season.

Conflicts with Comiskey and Jones led to Smith deserting the ball club and returning home to Pittsburgh on June 14, 1908. Always the sensitive type, Smith was offended by Comiskey's constant criticism of his lack of control and outraged by Jones's insinuation that he was drinking too much. The *Chicago Tribune* reported that "prior to departing for Pittsburgh, Piano Smith went in to give Mr. Comiskey a hard call down. Before Smithy could open his flow of language the boss said, 'You've been threatening to quit for two years. Now then, pack up your duds and dig and I don't care if you never come back.' The pianist was peeved because he was asked to practice control and other things." Comiskey felt that Smith had an obligation to follow team rules regardless of his personal issues. Comiskey "declares he is the boss, and that Smith, if he has gone, has left because he would not obey orders," reported the *Tribune* on June 21. The White Sox were in first place at the time of Smith's departure.

As the White Sox headed for home after an east coast trip late in July, rumors persisted that Smith was going to rejoin the team. On July 25, 1908, the *Chicago Tribune* reported that "according to the dope, Mr. F. Smith, the prodigal piano mover is about to burst upon the job once more. He was to have met the team at Cleveland with his mouth wide open for a feed of the justly celebrated husks. Smith so often declared he never would return that Jones applied reverse English to the declaration and told Smith to come on as far as Cleveland, anyhow. Moving the kind of pianos they have at Allegheny, Pa., sounds poetical and all that, but, strong as he is, the esteemed Smithy couldn't kick in $125 per week at the job. Moving a baseball with saliva on it is much easier, the distance is shorter, as a rule, and there is no expense on the side for horse feed and axle grease."

After Smith was reunited with Ed Walsh the pitching tandem kept the Sox afloat for the rest of the season, combining for 43 starts and often relieving each other late in games. Smith won 11 games after he returned and despite injuring a finger on his pitching hand trying to stop a hot shot in Cleveland on September 13, pitched his second career no-hitter a week later. Smith held the visiting Philadelphia Athletics hitless through nine innings before Chicago finally pushed across a run in the bottom of the ninth. Frank Isbell led off for Chicago and reached first on a grounder deflected by first baseman Danny Murphy. After Isbell advanced to third

Connie Mack ordered intentional walks to the next two Chicago batters, George Davis and Freddy Parent. On the third outside lob to Parent, the infielder "grasped his bat as near the tip of its handle as he dared, and reached for that ball." One account had Parent stepping across the plate, but his tapper to second baseman Scotty Barr resulted in Isbell scoring the game's only run on a close play at home, giving Smith his second career no-hitter in a thrilling 1–0 win. The season ended on a sour note, however, as the White Sox lost the pennant on the final day to finish in third place.

Under new manager Billy Sullivan, Smith hit his stride in 1909. He pitched 365 innings with an ERA of 1.80, striking out 177 batters. He finished 25–17 that year, his most wins in the majors. Smith's 1910 season began with an opening day one-hitter against St. Louis, but his better days were behind him and on August 11 he was traded to the Boston Red Sox, who had high hopes for him. The Red Sox owner, John I. Taylor called Smith the "hope" of the team and felt that the 1911 season "depends on Frank Smith to live up to his reputation" and prove himself one of the game's best pitchers. Taylor even offered a bonus to Smith for winning a certain percentage of games. Smith never responded. He appeared in only five games for the Red Sox, who, frustrated with his drinking, washed their hands of him and sold him to the Cincinnati Reds on May 11, 1911, for $5,000.

Smith did pitch in 42 games for the Reds, compiling a record of 11–15 in 1911 and 1912, but in June of the latter year Cincinnati sold him to Montreal, where he finished out the season. In 1914, at the age of 34, he joined the Baltimore entry in the upstart Federal League and pitched reasonably well, posting a 14–12 record before he hooked on with the Federal League Brooklyn Tip Tops. There he finished out his career in 1915 with a 5–2 record in 63 innings pitched.

After he retired from baseball Smith returned to the moving business in Pittsburgh. He died in his home on November 3, 1952, at the age of 73. Smith had succumbed to complications of Bright's disease, a chronic kidney ailment known today as nephritis. He was survived by his wife, Rena Shriner Smith, his son Frank, Jr., two grandchildren, and two great-grandchildren. He is buried in Minersville Cemetery in Pittsburgh.

SAM BERNSTEIN

CHICAGO

EDWARD AUGUSTINE WALSH
RIGHT-HANDED PITCHER, 1904–1916

From 1907 to 1912 "Big Ed" Walsh tested the limits of a pitcher's endurance like no pitcher has since. During that stretch the spitballing right-hander led the American League in innings pitched four times, often by staggeringly large margins. He hurled a total of 2,248 innings, 300 more than any other pitcher in baseball. He started 18 more games than any other pitcher, and led the American League during that stretch in games finished and saves (a retrospective statistic: saves would not be tracked for another 60 years). His finest season came in 1908, when Walsh became the last pitcher in baseball history to win 40 games, and hurled an incredible 464 innings, 73⅓ more than any other pitcher in baseball.

A fierce competitor, Walsh wanted the heavy workload that the White Sox foisted upon him. He also fielded his position with as much agility as any pitcher in the history of the game. During his six-year stretch of historic greatness, Walsh accumulated 963 assists, an amazing 344 more than any other pitcher in baseball. He fielded bunts like a territorial animal. Once, when a new third baseman came in for a bunt with a runner on second, Walsh got to the ball but could not make a play to third because it was uncovered. Walsh then turned to the third baseman and said, "If you do that again, I'll kill you. On bunts on that side of the field, you stay where you belong."

Although he finished his career with the lowest ERA (1.82) in baseball history, Walsh's arm could not withstand the overuse, and by 1913 the Iron Man pitcher was a shadow of his former self. Despite winning an impressive 182 games before his 32nd birthday, Walsh finished his career short of 200 wins.

Edward Augustine Walsh was born on May 19, 1882—although census records place his year of birth variously as 1880 or 1881—in Plains, Pennsylvania, one of 13 children (ten boys and three girls) of Michael and Jane Walsh. Edward's father was a native of Ireland who emigrated to the United States in 1866, where he found work as a shoemaker and married Jane, a heavy-set Welsh immigrant who had crossed the Atlantic in 1854. Edward's mother was active in the local Catholic church choir, and often sang old Irish folk songs to her children. Ed attended parochial school until the age of 12, when he began work as a slate-picker in the Plains mines for the Lackawanna Coal Company, earning 75 cents a day. For an additional $1.25, Ed also drove mule-drawn coal carts in the mines.

At age 18 he enrolled at Fordham University but left after only two days: he hated the wild students and grown men who were his roommates. Returning to Pennsylvania, Walsh began his baseball career as a pitcher for the Miner-Hillard Milling Company in Miners Mills, Pennsylvania, in 1901. In July 1902 Walsh signed his first professional contract, agreeing to terms with the Meriden Silverites of the Connecticut League for $150 per month. Walsh posted an impressive 16–5 record in Meriden before Wilkes-Barre of the Pennsylvania State League picked him near the end of the season. After winning only one of four decisions for Wilkes-Barre, Walsh was sold back to Meriden, where he spent the first part of the 1903 season, until his skills caught the attention of Newark of the Eastern League. He finished out the 1903 campaign with Newark, notching a 9–5 record. In the off-season the Chicago White Sox purchased his contract for a mere $750.

Throughout his minor league career the 6'1", 193-pound Walsh—whose height, unusual for the time, earned him the moniker Big Ed—relied exclusively on a fastball and curve. During 1904 spring training with the White Sox in Marlin Springs, Texas, Walsh roomed with spitballer Elmer Stricklett, the same pitcher who had inspired Jack Chesbro to start experimenting with the pitch the year before. Stricklett taught Walsh the spitter, but the big right-hander did not start using the pitch for two years. As a spot starter and reliever for the White Sox in 1904 and 1905, Walsh went 14–6 with a solid 2.37 ERA. It was not until the 1906 campaign, when the White Sox captured their second American League pennant in six major league seasons, that Walsh began to use the spitter on a regular basis.

Although pitching with a weakened right arm for part of the 1906 season, Walsh put up his best regular season numbers to date, posting a 17–13 record with a 1.88 ERA, seventh best in the league, and a league-leading 10 shutouts. He saved his best work for the World Series, when he beat the cross-town Chicago Cubs twice in two starts, allowing only one earned run (and five unearned) in 15 innings of work and striking out 17 batters, including a then-Series record 12 in a Game Three shutout.

On the heels of his World Series triumph, Walsh put together his first 20-win season in 1907. In a reflection of his competitive nature, he also began to change his approach on the mound. "Early in my career I eased up in the first few innings to save myself, but I found I couldn't get back into stride after once letting up," he later explained. "After that, I threw hard all the time. I threw my best to every hitter I faced and I found I had the strength to go all the way."

In 1908 Walsh put together his masterpiece season, compiling 40 wins against just 15 losses, with a 1.42 ERA (including a league record-breaking 11 shutouts) in 464 innings pitched. Pushing himself to the limit, during one nine-day stretch Walsh pitched five times, including a four-hitter on October 2 that he lost to Addie Joss, who threw a perfect game. Walsh's pitching kept the White Sox in the AL's thrilling four-way pennant race until the last day of the season; the club finished in third place, 1½ games behind the front-running Detroit Tigers. For the season Walsh struck out 269 batters, a career best, and walked only 56 men, giving him the fourth lowest walk rate in the majors that year.

Not surprisingly, at the time Walsh's spitball was considered the most effective pitch in baseball. Walsh disguised the pitch by going to his mouth before every delivery, regardless of what he was going to throw. When he did throw the spitter, according to Alfred Spink he moistened a spot on the ball between the seams an inch square. "His thumb he clinches tightly lengthwise on the opposite seam, and swinging his arm straight overhead with terrific force, he drives the ball straight at the plate," Spink wrote. "At times it will dart two feet down and out, depending on the way his arm is swung."

In a 1913 article for *Baseball Magazine*, Walter Johnson called Walsh's delivery "about the most tantalizing in baseball" for the way it arrived at the plate: "with such terrific speed, and unerringly dives just as if it knew what it was about and tried to dodge the hitter's bat...." For all practical purposes the pitch was the Deadball Era equivalent of the split-fingered fastball; it was absolutely devastating to batters accustomed to seeing mostly fastballs and curves. "I think that ball disintegrated on the way to the plate and the catcher put it back together again," Sam Crawford later joked. "I swear, when it went past the plate it was just the spit went by."

When batters did reach base, Walsh often picked them off with the game's most deceptive move to first base. In a motion that would probably be ruled a balk today, Walsh lifted his shoulder slightly, as if beginning his motion to throw home, before swinging around and firing the ball to first. Clyde Milan, one of the era's best base stealers, declared the move "at least a half balk," but Walsh got away with it anyway.

In 1909 Walsh's numbers dipped, as he recovered from the heavy workload of the year before. Starting in only 28 games, he finished the year with a 15–11 mark in 230⅓ innings, less than half his 1908 total. Although his 1.41 ERA was nearly identical to his 1908 mark, Walsh's strikeout rate fell slightly while his walk rate nearly doubled. The explanation for this sudden bout of "wildness" was that he was tipping his pitches. Specifically, the Cleveland Naps believed they had deciphered when he was going to throw the spitter: he had a habit of ticking the bill of his cap prior to unleashing a wet one. Word spread quickly around the league, and hitters started to lay off the spitter, which usually dropped out of the strike zone. When Walsh learned what was happening, he changed his style.

In 1910 Walsh finished with 18 wins against 20 losses, but the losing record was deceptive: Walsh's 1.27 ERA was the best of his career and also good enough to lead the league. In 1911 Walsh's ERA rose nearly a full run, to 2.22, but he received better run support and won 27 games against 18 defeats in 368⅓ innings pitched. In 1912 he again won 27 games, tossed six shutouts, collected a league-record 10 saves, and finished the year with a 2.15 ERA in 393 innings of work.

The first sign that his powerful right arm was about to give up on him came in the Chicago city series at the end of the 1912 season. In one outing against the Cubs Walsh took a line drive off his jaw. He went on pitching, but after the game his arm felt weak. Looking back, Walsh blamed himself for his sudden decline. "It was my fault I didn't continue in the majors longer than I did," Walsh

said. "My arm was played out after the 1912 season—it needed a rest." Instead, Walsh began the 1913 season still trying to fulfill his role as the staff's workhorse. He started 14 games, going 8–3 with a 2.58 ERA, but often required long periods of rest between starts. After lasting just five innings against the Philadelphia Athletics on July 19, Walsh was shelved indefinitely, and he left the team to have his arm examined by Bonesetter Reese in Youngstown, Ohio. Reese looked over Walsh and declared that he had a "misplaced tendon" in his right shoulder. According to the *New York Times*, Reese fixed the pitcher in three minutes and declared he would be better than ever the following season.

It did not happen. Over the next three seasons Walsh pitched sparingly for the White Sox, starting only nine games from 1914 to 1916 and winning five. During that time he rejected a lucrative offer from the Federal League, and at one point contemplated becoming an outfielder. During the 1916 season Walsh appeared in only two games, pitching 3⅓ innings. His most notable achievement came off the field, in late July, when he rescued two girls from drowning in Lake Michigan. Let go by the White Sox at the end of the season, Walsh made a brief appearance with the Boston Braves in 1917, going 0–1 with a 3.50 ERA in 18 innings of work.

During World War I Walsh worked in a munitions factory. Thereafter he pitched briefly for Milwaukee of the American Association in 1919, Bridgeport (Connecticut) of the Eastern League in 1920, and finally with a semipro club in Oneonta, New York, in 1921. He spent the first half of the 1922 season as an umpire for the American League, but Walsh hated the job, mainly because he did not like calling strikes. "I remember when I wanted every pitch to be a strike," he said.

For the next several years he served as a coach for the White Sox, and after that was a battery coach at Notre Dame, where his son pitched. Ed Walsh, Jr., spent parts of four seasons in the major leagues; his most notable achievement came

in 1933, when as a pitcher for the Oakland Oaks of the Pacific Coast League he halted young Joe DiMaggio's 61-game hitting streak. Tragically, the younger Ed died suddenly of rheumatic fever in 1937. That same year, Ed's other son, Bob, also a graduate of Notre Dame, gave up baseball when he was almost hit by a line drive while playing for the Richmond club in the Piedmont League.

The Great Depression hit Walsh hard. His $14,000 investment in a showplace on Hanover Road in Meriden went belly-up and for six years he worked for the Works Progress Administration, conducting a baseball school through the agency's recreational program. Toward the end of the decade Walsh became a chemical engineer and worked at a filtration plant for the Meriden municipal water department. When he was not working Walsh indulged his love for golf, and became the course professional in Meriden.

To the end of his life, Walsh pushed for the spitball to be legalized. He once said, "Everything else favors the hitters. Ballparks are smaller and baseballs are livelier. They've practically got pitchers wearing straitjackets. Bah! They still allow the knuckleball and that is three times as hard to control."

Walsh was inducted into the Baseball Hall of Fame on July 21, 1947, and was the only one of that year's 15 inductees to attend the ceremony. He and his wife Rosemary struggled to make ends meet. By the late 1950s Walsh had contracted cancer. The disease was devastating; his weight dropped from 200 pounds to less than 100. To help pay his medical bills, the White Sox held an Ed Walsh Day at Comiskey Park in 1958, raising nearly $5,000 for his care.

Ed Walsh died on May 26, 1959, two weeks after his 77th birthday (or 78th or 79th, depending on the source). He was buried in Forest Lawn Memorial Gardens in his adopted hometown of Pompano Beach, Florida.

STUART SCHIMLER

CHICAGO

PATRICK HENRY DOUGHERTY
LEFT FIELDER, 1906–1911

It would be hard to spend time studying the American League's first decade without running into the brawny and brawling figure of left fielder Patsy Dougherty. With his moonface and cleft chin, the powerfully built (6′2″, 190 pounds—large for his day) second-generation Irish-American Dougherty was a major contributor to the first two American League world champions and to three other pennant contenders in his ten-year career. While never the best of flycatchers, he made up for his defensive deficiencies with hard work, fighting spirit, plenty of stolen bases, and uncanny left-handed clutch hitting. In his decade in the bigs his red-hot bat was matched only by his curly red hair and the shamed faces of opposing pitchers whose bids for no-hitters he denied.

Patrick Henry Dougherty was born on October 27, 1876, in Andover, New York, the seventh of eight children. His father, Michael Dougherty, had emigrated from Ireland during the Great Famine and settled in Allegany County in southwestern New York, where he managed to parlay a small farm into a small fortune during the 1880s oil boom in the region. By the 1890s the family had moved to Bolivar, another town in the area, where Patsy's older brother Francis helped establish the State Bank of Bolivar. There Patsy played high school baseball with Frank Gannett (who soon founded what would become the Gannett newspaper chain, which now includes *USA Today*), and later joined a town team.

From 1896 to 1901 Dougherty took a Cook's tour of minor league ball clubs in the Northeast: first Bristol, Connecticut, then Dayton, Ohio; Canandaigua, New York; Homestead, Pennsylvania; and finally three years with Bridgeport, Connecticut, where he would live for over a decade. Starting out as a pitcher who played the outfield on off days, his hitting and speed soon made him more valuable as an outfielder who occasionally pitched. After the 1901 season he headed west to chase flies, pitch, and bat leadoff for the Columbias, a Los Angeles–based winter league team. The Columbias' manager was Jimmy Collins, skipper and third baseman of Boston in the American League, who thought enough of Dougherty's hitting to bring him east as Boston's new left fielder.

On April 19, 1902, Dougherty made his first appearance in a Boston Americans box score. Although he would miss almost thirty games that season to minor injuries, he was in the lineup enough to lead the Hub nine in batting (.342, fourth in the American League) and on-base percentage (.407, third in the league), and to keep the team in the pennant race despite losing Collins, catcher Lou Criger, and pitcher George Winter for long periods. Defense was his one weakness: he compiled an .899 fielding percentage, worst of any regular major league outfielder.

Coming into 1903 expectations for Dougherty were high, and he responded with his finest year, leading the American League with 107 runs scored and 195 hits and leading the pennant-winning Boston squad with 35 stolen bases and a .331 batting average (both third in the American League). In the first modern World Series that October against National League champion Pittsburgh, he hit homers in the first and sixth innings in Game Two, then contributed two triples, a single, and three RBI in Game Five, leading Boston to the first two of its five victories on the way to a world championship.

Behind the curtain of a brand-new pennant, trouble was brewing. After the 1903 season American League president Ban Johnson transferred ownership of the Boston club to *Boston Globe* publisher Charles Taylor, who turned it over to his business-failure of a son, John I. Taylor. Dougherty and the younger Taylor soon were at odds over how much a third-year man who had led his team twice in batting should get paid. They eventually settled, but the relationship was permanently soured.

There was one remaining moment of glory for Dougherty in Boston. On May 2, 1904, in Philadelphia, he led off the fourth inning with an infield single off the Athletics' Rube Waddell. It was the last baserunner Waddell allowed that day, as the Rube defeated Jesse Tannehill and Boston 3–0 on a one-hitter. But Waddell made a grave error: taunting Cy Young to pitch against him the next time he was scheduled. On May 5 Dougherty would crash into the left field fence in Boston's Huntington Avenue Grounds to catch a seventh-inning foul fly—aiding Cy Young's perfect game against Waddell and the A's.

On June 17, Dougherty was shipped to the New York Highlanders for utility man Bob Unglaub, who at the time of the deal was hospitalized with alcohol poisoning and would play only nine games for Boston that year. Although it was never proven, the deal may have been part of Ban Johnson's ongoing project to strengthen the young league's base in New York City; he had earlier engineered the transfers of shortstop Kid Elberfeld and pitcher Long Tom Hughes to the Highlanders, and Taylor may have seen Johnson's plan as a way to jettison a player who was in his doghouse. Taylor, for his part, maintained that Dougherty was dealt because of his poor defense, and *The Sporting News* reported that "his traits as an individual made him unpopular with Manager Collins and his team mates. He refused to obey instructions and…became involved in quarrels with his fellow players."

But the Beantown fans and press were not buying it, instead citing the contract problems and making aspersions as to Taylor's intelligence or lack thereof. "That President Taylor has made a great mistake is the way I dope it out," *The Sporting News*'s Boston correspondent, Johnny Hallahan, averred. "If we admit that Pat Dougherty is not a crack outfielder, that he has fallen off with the stick considerably, that he has shown some sign of indifference, that, it seems to us, covers all that can possibly be said against him…Dougherty's weakness on the field never did the team any harm, and if his batting was a good cause for considering a deal, it seems to me to be a very poor excuse." As a side note, the *Boston Herald*, reporting the deal, ran the headline DOUGHERTY AS A YANKEE—the first instance in print of the New York American League team being referenced with that nickname.

Dougherty wasted no time in making sure that Taylor—and Taylor's team—regretted the move. On June 25, in his first game against his old mates, he nailed Cy Young for three hits as the Highlanders won 5–3. New York won again two days later, 8–4, with Dougherty tattooing Tannehill for three more safeties. The teams met again on July 11 as Dougherty had a four-hit game to help New York beat Taylor's nine 10–1.

On Friday, October 7, in New York, with Boston leading New York in the American League pennant race by half a game, Dougherty made the Hub nine pay once again, with a fifth-inning double, a seventh-frame bunt single, and two runs scored as the Highlanders won 3–2 and regained the league lead. The scene then shifted to Boston, however, because New York owner Frank Farrell (who had not thought his team would be in contention in October) had months earlier rented Hilltop Park out to Columbia University for a football match on the 8th. The oversight proved deadly, as Boston won both ends of a doubleheader in their home park, 13–2 and 1–0. The Highlanders lost the pennant in a doubleheader back in New York on October 10.

Despite the midseason trade and last-day disappointment, Dougherty had put together another strong year, again leading the league in runs scored (with 113, he was the only big leaguer to crack 100) and contributing 181 hits and 21 steals between the two cities. Although he did not hit .300 again (his average for the year was .280), it was more a result of a league-wide drop in offense than any actual slump.

The real slump came in 1905, when not only did the American League's batting average keep falling, but the Highlanders slid to a sixth-place finish. Dougherty hit only .263 with 56 runs that year, and fielded below .900 for the second time (.898). The troubles continued into 1906, as he not only ended up in a protracted contract wrangle with the Highlanders' manager Clark Griffith, but got into a fistfight with him as well. (Contemporary reports assessed the blame for the fisticuffs equally, the Old Fox having been known to lose his cool on occasion.) With his batting average at .192 and his relationship with his skipper a shambles, Dougherty jumped the team after 12 games and joined Lancaster, Pennsylvania, in the outlaw Tri-State League. He was subsequently suspended by Ban Johnson.

Fielder Jones, now managing and playing center field for the Chicago White Sox, was in desperate need of another bat for his Hitless Wonders. On July 6 he bought Dougherty's contract from New York and smoothed things out with Johnson to allow the jumper to return to the American League. Although Dougherty suffered the worst offensive season of his career, his .233 average with Chicago was still higher than the team's .230 overall mark. In fourth place in early August, the White Sox rode Dougherty, Ed Hahn, and young hurler Ed Walsh to a 19-game winning streak (a league

record until it was broken by the 2002 Oakland A's) and into first, ironically taking the pennant away from the Highlanders in the process. Dougherty had only two hits (in 20 at-bats) in the White Sox's World Series upset of the cross-town Cubs, but he had one of only two hits off Three Fingered Brown in a 1–0 loss in Game Four.

With Chicago, Dougherty moved from the leadoff spot to sixth in the batting order, and quickly showed that he was up to his new responsibilities. In 1907 he led the Sox in batting (.270) and slugging (.315), as well as steals (33), and kept the team in contention into the final week of the season. But the still-Hitless Wonders were unable to catch the bats of Ty Cobb and Sam Crawford, and Chicago finished in third place, 5½ games behind Detroit. This set the stage for the wild 1908 race, as Detroit, Chicago, and Cleveland battled into the season's last weekend before the Tigers clawed out a bare half-game winning margin over Cleveland. The White Sox were again third, but only 1½ games back. Dougherty, now batting third in the order, finished the season with a team-best .278 batting average, .326 slugging percentage, and .367 on-base percentage. His 47 stolen bases led the entire league.

Throughout the last weeks of the 1908 race, Dougherty made his presence known to opposing pitchers, both at bat and on the bases. On September 24 his seventh-inning single was the only hit off New York's Joe Lake, the second no-hitter he prevented in his career. (He would make a habit of this, also swatting the only safeties off Washington's Dolly Gray on August 28, 1909, in a 6–4 Chicago win—Gray giving up Patsy's single and eight walks in a bizarre second inning for all six Sox runs—and off Detroit's Ed Summers on July 29, 1910.) On October 4 he kept the Tigers from clinching. With runners on second and third in the first inning, he grounded to second base, but the throw was botched by Detroit first baseman Claude Rossman, allowing the lead runner to score and Dougherty to reach first. Later that same inning, he scored the third run on a double steal when second baseman Red Downs muffed a throw from the catcher. The rally provided all the runs in Chicago's 3–1 victory.

In 1909 Dougherty more or less *was* the Sox offense, leading the South Side nine in batting (.285), slugging (.391), runs (71), RBI (55), doubles (23), triples (13), hits (140), walks (51), steals (36), and homers (1, in a four-way tie). Only one other regular batted over .240, however, and Chicago slipped to fourth, 20 games out of the lead.

In 1910 the White Sox attempted a full-fledged youth movement in preparation for the opening of Comiskey Park in July, leaving the 33-year-old Dougherty as the oldest regular. Once again he proved to be the club's steadiest offensive contributor, leading the team with a .248 batting average, 43 RBI, and 110 hits. But the season was an overall disappointment for Patsy, who lost over 20 games to "malarial attacks" and saw the Sox (with a team .211 average) sink to a distant sixth. His health problems continued into 1911, holding him to 76 games, although he was able to take advantage of the new cork-centered baseball to rap out a .289 average.

Dougherty, seeing that his time on the field was more or less up due to his health, decided to retire following the 1911 season. According to the *Chicago Tribune*, he was "reported to be one of the wealthiest players in the game," having invested in oil wells back in Allegany County and business properties in Bolivar, atop a general thriftiness; he had kept playing ball for love of the game. Patsy had a job lined up as well, as clerk at the State Bank of Bolivar, still presided over by his older brother Frank.

Dougherty let no dust collect on him in his post-flychasing years. He worked for almost thirty years at the bank, eventually rising to the post of assistant cashier. He and his wife, Florence, whom he married in 1904, had five children; the last, William, died in infancy. In 1916 he returned to the game when he was elected president of the class D Inter-State League, an eight-team circuit of New York and Pennsylvania squads, including one in nearby Olean. The league was on shaky ground, however; three of the teams folded in mid-year and the league itself closed up at season's end, not to be revived until 1932.

By the late 1930s Dougherty was a grandfather, and in failing health. He soldiered on at the bank, but the end came with a fatal heart attack at age 63 on April 30, 1940. A lifelong devout Catholic, he was buried at Saint Mary Catholic Cemetery in Bolivar.

Ray Anselmo

James Scott

CHICAGO

JAMES SCOTT
RIGHT-HANDED PITCHER, 1909–1917

In between two world championship seasons in 1906 and 1917, the Chicago White Sox franchise fell back to the middle of the pack in the American League, but they were always competitive, thanks to the unheralded and hard-luck hurling of a burly right-handed pitcher from Wyoming, Jim "Death Valley" Scott. At 6'1" and more than 200 pounds, Scott often used his large frame to deceive base runners with perhaps the best pickoff move of any right-handed pitcher during the Deadball Era, and confused batters with a bevy of pitches and pitching deliveries. An intelligent craftsman who liked to experiment on the mound, Scott often threw with what he called a "clockspring" delivery; toward the end of his career he even tinkered with a pitch, which he called the "X-ball," that involved the use of mineral water and a camel's-hair shirt. "Jim admits he does not know what the ball will do or what will happen to it," the *Chicago Tribune* explained, "but he means to find out." Despite notching only two winning seasons, Scott ended his major league career with a 2.30 ERA, still the 17th lowest figure in baseball history.

James Scott, the third of five children of George and Kitty Scott, was born in the frontier mining town of Deadwood, Dakota Territory, on April 23, 1888, a dozen years after Wild Bill Hickok was murdered in a saloon there. George worked for the U.S. Weather Bureau in the region and moved his family twice by the time Jim was five years old, finally settling in Lander, Wyoming, in 1894, where he also ran a telegraph office and a photography studio. Jim attended public schools in Lander, and by his own account, had his future all planned out. After finishing school in Lander, Scott was set to enroll at Nebraska Wesleyan University and become a physician; however, baseball intervened and Scott never finished his schooling.

Scott had played part-time at third base for a local team coached by Bill McMahon, a former professional player. At one such game in 1907 against an army team, Scott was asked to take the pitching mound after the team's starter had been knocked out. In his own words, Scott knew nothing about pitching but to "fire the ball over and pitch a curve when I felt like it." However, the beginner was good enough to shut down the team the rest of the way, earning the attention of James P. Cantillon, a local railroad official whose brother Joe managed a team in Des Moines in the Iowa State League.

Cantillon convinced his brother to offer Scott a tryout in Des Moines. The young pitcher left school and reported to the team in Iowa, showing up dressed in overalls and tennis shoes. Decidedly unimpressed, Joe Cantillon let Scott hang around for a couple of weeks before sending him packing. Undaunted, Scott traveled 60 miles to Oskaloosa, Iowa, where he talked his way onto the local ball club. As fate would have it, his first start was a shutout win against Des Moines. Cantillon then attempted to talk Scott back on his team by claiming he was still under contract. Jim ignored him, posting a 4–0 record against the Joe Cantillon-managed Washington Senators in 1909.

Next stop for Scott was the Western Association, where he won 30 games for Wichita and set a league record with 16 strikeouts in a game. Scott was able to dominate opposing batters by a combination of a hard curveball and a tricky spitball. His exploits caught the eye of several big league scouts, and prior to the 1909 season the Chicago White Sox purchased his contract for $2,000.

Scott rolled into Chicago with high expectations and a brand new nickname: Death Valley Scott. The moniker was earned in part due to confusion over Scott's place of birth, and also because Jim supposedly arrived in Chicago on the same train as Walter Scott, better known as "Death Valley Scotty," an infamous Western prospector and con man who had tricked several wealthy patrons into investing thousands of dollars in a Death Valley gold mine that did not exist. For his part Jim Scott always viewed his nickname with a mixture of befuddlement and amusement. "I have never been in Death Valley in my life," he told *Baseball Magazine* in 1916. "Odd about nicknames, isn't it?"

Scott's major league debut on April 25, 1909, was an auspicious one. Scott dazzled the capacity crowd by shutting out the St. Louis Browns 1–0, striking out six, and getting his first major league hit as well. This started him on the way to a fine rookie season, winning 12 games and posting a 2.30 ERA in 250⅓ innings.

The White Sox struggled in 1910, falling to sixth place largely due to an offensive attack that ranked near the bottom of every league category. Scott's 8–18 record reflected the lack of support, as he posted a 2.43 ERA, slightly worse than league average. Despite the losing record, Scott's pitching drew the respect of both opponents and the media. He mixed in a screwball and spitball with his harder pitches, and used his clockspring delivery to further confuse opposing hitters. He possessed an excellent pickoff move, and also frequently worked in relief between starts, leading the team that season with 18 relief appearances. In 1911 the team improved to a tie for fourth place, and Scott posted a 14–11 record with a 2.39 ERA.

The 1912 season started well for Scott, as he pitched an entire 15-inning scoreless tie against Washington on April 20. The extended outing, however, led to a case of rheumatism that limited the pitcher to just six games over the season. In 1913 he recovered to become a staff ace and record a remarkable season. Scott started 38 games, completing 25, and relieved in 10 others to throw a total of 312⅓ innings. He also achieved a rare feat by winning and losing 20 games in the same season. Scott's 1.91 ERA was third best in the American League.

After taking part in the world tour of 1913–14, Scott returned to the White Sox and slumped to 14–18 with a below-average 2.84 ERA. The highlight of his ill-starred season came on May 14, when he took a no-hitter against the Washington Senators into extra innings, before surrendering a run in the bottom of the tenth to lose, 1–0. After the season Scott joined teammate Buck Weaver on a vaudeville tour. The act's best result was a romance that blossomed between Scott and coperformer Harriet "Hattie" Cook, whom he married in 1917. In so doing, he became brother-in-law to Weaver, who was married to Hattie's sister Helen.

Scott's luck improved along with the White Sox in 1915. Under new manager Pants Rowland, the big

right-hander had the second-best season of his career. Supported by an improved offensive attack (the Sox scored 230 more runs than the previous season), Scott won 24 games with a 2.03 ERA and tied Walter Johnson for the league lead in shutouts with 7. Although Scott struggled with a 7–14 record in 1916—though with a still creditable 2.73 ERA—the team improved to second place and seemed poised for greatness in 1917.

The White Sox did go on to win their second World Series championship in 1917, but unfortunately for Scott he was not around to be part of it. His 1917 season did have one highlight when he stopped Ty Cobb's 35-game hitting streak on July 6, and his 1.87 ERA was the best of his career; however, events outside the diamond led to the end of his major league career. The patriotic Scott was one of the first major league players to enlist after the United States declared war on Germany, leaving the team to report to training in San Francisco.

Offered the chance to try out for the White Sox again in 1919, he turned down the opportunity. Baseball still had its hold on Scott, however, and he headed west to pitch for the San Francisco Seals in the Pacific Coast League. Joining the team in late May, Scott remained with the Seals through the 1924 season, winning 96 games, pitching a no-hitter, and helping the Seals to Pacific Coast League championships in 1922 and 1923. After the 1924 season Scott moved on to the New Orleans Pelicans in the Southern Association, winning 31 games for two more championship clubs before retiring following the 1927 season.

Settling permanently with his family in Los Angeles, he began working fulltime for RKO and Republic Studios. Scott served as the best boy, or chief electrician, working mainly on westerns, and later was promoted to head property man. According to some reports during the mid-1930s, "Death Valley" Scott also spent time as a leader of a religious cult in the California desert, working as an evangelist. Details are sketchy, but it is possible that Scott was involved with the religious ministries of popular evangelist Aimee Semple McPherson, whose Foursquare Gospel mission was based in Los Angeles.

Scott continued to work in the motion picture industry until 1953, when he retired shortly after the death of his wife. The always heavy Scott began to experience heart troubles, suffering a heart attack in 1956. Seeking a cure in the desert air, he traveled to Jacumba, California, for a vacation in April 1957. On the morning of April 7 Scott suffered a massive heart attack and was found dead in his hotel room by a maid. He was buried next to Hattie in Inglewood Park Cemetery in Inglewood, California.

JOHN BENNETT

CHICAGO

Edward Victor Cicotte
Right-handed pitcher, 1912–1920

Although he did not invent the pitch, Eddie "Knuckles" Cicotte was perhaps the first major league pitcher to master the knuckleball. According to one description, Cicotte gripped the knuckler by holding the ball "on the three fingers of a closed hand, with his thumb and forefinger to guide it, throwing it with an overhand motion, and sending it from his hand as one would snap a whip. The ball acts like a 'spitter,' but is a new-fangled thing." Cicotte once estimated that 75 percent of the pitches he threw were knuckleballs. The rest of the time, the right-hander relied on the fadeaway, slider, screwball, spitter, emery ball, shine ball, and a pitch he called the "sailor," a rising fastball that "would sail much in the same manner of a flat stone thrown by a small boy."

Whether he was sailing or sinking the ball, shining it or darkening it, the 5′9″, 175-pound Cicotte had more pitches than a traveling salesman. "Perhaps no pitcher in the world has such a varied assortment of wares in his repertory as Cicotte," *The Sporting News* observed in 1918. "He throws with effect practically every kind of ball known to pitching science."

The most famous pitch Cicotte ever threw was the one that nailed Cincinnati Reds leadoff man Morrie Rath squarely in the back to lead off the 1919 World Series, a pitch that signaled to the gamblers that the fix was on. Following his confession to his role in the scandal one year later, Cicotte was banned from the game for life, a punishment that perhaps denied the 208-game winner a spot in the Hall of Fame.

Edward Victor Cicotte (pronounced SEE-cot) was born June 19, 1884, in Springwells, Michigan, into a large family of French heritage. He was the son of Ambrose and Archangel (Drouillard) Cicotte. Al Cicotte, who pitched in the major leagues for five seasons, was

Eddie's brother Alva's grandson. By the time Eddie was 16 years old, his father had died, forcing his mother to support her large family as a dressmaker. Leaving school early, Eddie also took up work as a box maker to help pay the family bills.

Cicotte began his baseball career as early as 1903, according to some sources, playing semipro ball in the Upper Peninsula of Michigan. In 1904 he pitched for Calumet (Michigan) and Sault Ste. Marie (Ontario) in the Northern Copper League, posting a record of 38–4 with 11 shutouts. Based on that dominating performance, Cicotte earned a tryout with the Detroit Tigers in the spring of 1905. The Tigers determined that he was not yet ready for the majors and optioned him to Augusta (Georgia) of the South Atlantic League, where he compiled a record of 15 wins against nine losses.

Near the end of the season Detroit promoted Cicotte to the American League, where he made his major league debut on September 3, allowing one run in relief and getting tagged with the loss in a 10-inning game. Two days later Cicotte earned his first major league win, a complete-game victory over the Chicago White Sox. He finished the year 1–1 with a 3.50 ERA, but would not return to the major leagues for another three seasons.

Cicotte began 1906 with Indianapolis of the American Association, where he posted a 1–4 record in 72 innings before landing with Des Moines of the Western League. Cicotte blossomed with his new team, registering an 18–9 record. The following season Cicotte pitched for Lincoln, also of the Western League, going 21–14. Impressed by the young hurler's arsenal of pitches, the Boston Red Sox purchased Cicotte's contract for $2,500 at the end of the 1907 season.

During his five-year-stint with the Red Sox, Cicotte lost nearly as many games as he won, and frequently found himself in trouble with Red Sox owner John

Taylor, who accused the pitcher of underachieving. "He was suspended without pay so much of the time that it was like having no job," the *Chicago Tribune*'s Sam Weller wrote of Cicotte's Boston career. On a club that consistently failed to meet expectations, Cicotte often became the scapegoat, and in 1911 Taylor tried to secure waivers on his inconsistent pitcher, only to pull back when another team made a claim. "[Taylor] wouldn't like the way I was working, or perhaps the opposition had made one or two hits," Cicotte later charged. "Taylor never liked me; I never liked him, and it was seldom that I went through a game without having him comment upon it."

After Cicotte started the 1912 season with a 1–3 record and 5.67 ERA in six starts, the Red Sox—though no longer owned by Taylor—had finally seen enough. On July 22 the team sold Cicotte's contract to the Chicago White Sox, where the 28-year-old right-hander began to mature into one of the game's best pitchers. With Boston, Cicotte had won 51 games against 46 losses. Over the next 8½ seasons with the White Sox, Eddie would win 156 games against 102 losses.

The biggest reason for this improvement was Cicotte's gradual mastery of his expansive pitching repertoire. As his command over the knuckleball improved, Cicotte's walk rate dramatically decreased: from 1912 to 1920 Eddie ranked among the league's ten best in walks per nine innings seven times, leading the league in 1918 and 1919, when he walked a combined 89 men in 572⅔ innings. Cicotte also fully exploited the era's liberal regulations regarding the doctoring of the ball.

In this regard his most infamous pitch was the "shine ball," in which Cicotte rubbed one side of the ball against the pocket of his right trouser leg, which had been filled with talcum powder. As Fred Lieb later explained it, the pitch "worked like an emery ball that had been roughened, in reverse. When pitched against air currents, the natural side of the shined ball became rough in contrast, and the sphere wobbled on its way to the batsman." Flustered opponents protested to league president Ban Johnson that the pitch should be outlawed, but Johnson ruled the pitch legal in 1917, and it would remain so until February 1920. Thanks to the knuckleball, the shine ball, the emery ball (ruled illegal by Johnson in 1914), and other trick pitches, Cicotte struck out a fair number of batters, placing in the top ten in strikeouts per nine innings three times, even though his fastball probably could not break a pane of glass. Asked to explain his success, Cicotte chalked it up to "head work," adding that it "involves an ability to adapt pitching to certain conditions when they arise

and perhaps use altogether different methods in the very next inning."

In 1913 Cicotte enjoyed his first standout season in the major leagues, posting an 18–12 record to go along with a 1.58 ERA, second best in the American League. That off-season Pittsburgh of the newly formed Federal League attempted to sign Cicotte, but White Sox owner Charles Comiskey was able to secure the pitcher's loyalty through a three-year contract. In the first year of his contract, Eddie managed only an 11–16 record, although his 2.04 ERA was fifth-best in the league. After a mediocre 13–12 campaign in 1915, Cicotte finally hit his stride in 1916, when he split time between the starting rotation and bullpen, posted a 1.78 ERA, won 15 out of 22 decisions, and registered five saves.

The following year Cicotte moved back to the starting rotation and enjoyed the best season of his career as the White Sox captured their first pennant in 11 seasons. Cicotte led the way, ranking first in the league in wins (28), ERA (1.53), and innings pitched (346⅔). Eddie also tossed seven shutouts, including a no-hitter against the St. Louis Browns on April 14, the first of six no-hitters pitched in the major leagues that season. In that year's World Series Cicotte contributed one win to Chicago's six-game triumph over the New York Giants.

Despite the breakthrough season, Comiskey offered his star pitcher only a $5,000 contract, much less than pitchers of the same caliber earned for other teams. Perhaps bitter over his meager salary, in 1918 Cicotte failed to produce an encore suitable to his dominant 1917 campaign; he wrenched his ankle in early May, limping his way through the season to a mediocre 2.77 ERA and a co-league-leading 19 losses. It was not a performance to inspire Comiskey to hand out a raise, and by the time the 1919 season opened, financial troubles weighed heavily on Cicotte. According to the 1920 census, Cicotte was the head of household for a family of 12, including his wife, Rose, and their three children, his wife's parents, Eddie's brother and wife, and a brother-in-law and his wife and child. To make room for his large family, Cicotte took out a $4,000 mortgage on a Michigan farm.

Despite the financial worries, Cicotte regained his 1917 form, pitching the White Sox to their second pennant in three years. Once again, Eddie led the American League in victories (29) and innings pitched (306⅔, tied with Jim Shaw). His 29–7 record also was good enough to lead the league in winning percentage (.806), and his 1.82 ERA ranked second. In August, however, first baseman Chick Gandil approached Cicotte about throwing the World Series. After thinking

it over for several weeks, Eddie agreed to the scheme, telling Gandil, "I'll do it for ten thousand dollars. Cash. Before the Series begins."

Contrary to conventional wisdom, Cicotte's abysmal performance in the 1919 World Series was not a complete surprise to informed observers. Throughout September, reports surfaced that the overworked Cicotte was suffering from a sore shoulder. Prior to the first game of the Series, Christy Mathewson noted, Cicotte "has had less than a week [just two days, in fact] to rest up for his first start.... And that may not prove to be enough. If he blows up for a single inning it may cost the White Sox the championship, for I think the first battle is going to have a very strong bearing on the outcome, especially if the Reds win it."

With at least six of his other teammates in on the fix, Cicotte led the way in blowing the first game, surrendering seven hits and six runs in just 3⅔ innings of work, and fueling Cincinnati's winning rally by throwing high to second base on what should have been an inning-ending double play ball. The performance was so bad that it generated renewed speculation that Cicotte was suffering from a dead arm. For his second start, in Game Four and with the Sox trailing two games to one, Eddie pitched more effectively, holding the Reds to just five hits and two unearned runs, both coming in the fifth inning on two Cicotte errors, including one inexplicable play in which Eddie muffed an attempt to cut off a throw from the outfield, allowing the ball to go to the backstop and a Cincinnati runner—who had already stopped at third—to score. The miscues were enough to ensure the Sox lost the game, 2–0. Afterwards, Chicago manager Kid Gleason declared, "They shouldn't have scored on Cicotte in 40 innings....There wasn't any occasion for Cicotte to intercept that throw. He did it to prevent Kopf from going to second. But Kopf had no more intention of going to second than I have of jumping in the lake."

Although Eddie had received his $10,000 prior to the start of the Series, many of his fellow conspirators had not received the money promised them by the gamblers, so prior to Cicotte's third start, in Game Seven, the players decided to play the game to win. Accordingly, Cicotte put forth his best effort of the Series, allowing just one run on seven hits in a 4–1 Chicago victory. Lefty Williams threw the following game, however, giving Cincinnati the world championship.

Despite the persistent rumors that swirled around the club that off-season, Cicotte re-signed with Chicago for 1920 and put forth another excellent season, posting a 21–10 record with a 3.26 ERA.

On September 27, 1920, the *Philadelphia North American* ran a story in which Billy Maharg, one of the gamblers in on the Series fix the previous fall, testified to his role in the affair and specifically named Cicotte as the man who initiated the plot. The next day Eddie met with Comiskey and admitted to his role in the scandal. "Yeah—we were crooked," he sobbed in the owner's office. "We were crooked." Before Cicotte could unburden himself any further, however, Comiskey cut him off, barking, "Don't tell me! Tell it to the Grand Jury!"

That very day Cicotte did appear before the grand jury, becoming the first player to confess. When asked why he had taken the gamblers' money, Cicotte blamed Gandil, shortstop Swede Risberg, and utility infielder Fred McMullin for hounding him about it for weeks prior to the Series. "They wanted me to go crooked. I don't know. I needed the money. I had the wife and kids. The wife and kids don't know about this. I don't know what they'll think."

Although he and the other seven accused players would be acquitted of conspiracy charges the following year, Eddie Cicotte's major league baseball career ended with his confession. For the next three years Eddie played with several of his banned teammates for outlaw teams in Minnesota and Wisconsin, and also in Bastrop, Louisiana, where he pitched under the alias Moore. Although some of the other Black Sox continued to play outlaw ball, by 1924 Cicotte had moved on with his life. Eddie worked as a Michigan game warden and managed a service station before finding a job with the Ford Motor Company, where he remained until his retirement in 1944.

During the last 25 years of his life, Cicotte raised strawberries on a 5½-acre farm near Farmington, Michigan. In a 1965 interview with Detroit writer Joe Falls, Eddie said that he lived his life quietly, answering letters from kids who sometimes asked about the scandal. He agreed that he had made mistakes, but insisted that he had tried to make up for it by living as clean a life as he could. "I admit I did wrong," he said, "but I've paid for it the past 45 years."

Eddie Cicotte died on May 5, 1969, at Henry Ford Hospital in Detroit. His death certificate listed his occupation as baseball player, Chicago White Sox. He was buried in Park View Cemetery in Livonia, Michigan.

JIM SANDOVAL

CHICAGO

RAYMOND WILLIAM SCHALK
CATCHER, 1912–1928; MANAGER, 1927–1928

In an era when the common impression of a baseball catcher was a sturdy player with bulging shoulders, a husky framework, and brute strength, the 5′7″(many sources say 5′9″), 155-pound Ray Schalk did not convey an imposing figure behind the dish. However, as John C. Ward wrote in *Baseball Magazine* in 1920, "Schalk is unquestionably the hardest working catcher in baseball as he is doubtless also the brainiest, the nerviest, the most competent. He presents the unique distinction of performing more work than any other catcher and at the same time performing it better. Both in quantity and in quality of service Ray Schalk is unquestionably the premier backstop in baseball."

Raymond William Schalk was born in Harvel, a small village in central Illinois, on August 12, 1892, the fifth of six children of Herman and Sophia Schalk, German immigrants who had arrived in the United States in 1875. Herman supported his family as a day laborer in Litchfield, 20 miles away, where his children, including Ray, attended public school. As a youngster, Schalk worked as a newsboy and carried the *Chicago Tribune* and the weekly *Litchfield News*. Ray was captain of the Litchfield basketball team, but left high school at the end of his second year to learn the printer's trade. Two years later he traveled to Brooklyn to study how to operate the linotype machine. After mastering its intricacies, Schalk returned home in 1910, but found his desire to progress in his chosen field was not matched by career advancement. Rather, it was Schalk's participation in local baseball games that soon earned him the promotion he was looking for.

First a member of the town team, he soon moved up to semipro ball for the sum of $2 a game. From there he quickly progressed on to Taylorville, Illinois, in the Class D Illinois–Missouri League, where he caught 47 games, batted .387, and earned $65 a month. Later in the 1911 season, the 18-year-old moved up to the Milwaukee Brewers of the American Association and appeared in 31 games. Returning to Milwaukee for the 1912 campaign, he batted .271 in 80 contests, attracting so much attention for his aggressive approach to the catching position and his feisty on-field leadership that he was purchased by the Chicago White Sox for $10,000 and two other players.

August 11, 1912 (the day before his 20th birthday), was both Ray Schalk's first visit to a major league park and his first appearance in a big league game. He had just arrived by streetcar minutes before the first game of a doubleheader against the Philadelphia Athletics and manager Jimmy Callahan told the rookie, "Young man, here's your pitcher, Doc White. You're the catcher." In his first at-bat, Schalk grounded out to Frank Baker, but did manage to get a hit later in the game against Chief Bender. Reflecting back on the experience nearly fifty years later, Schalk reminisced, "You think of no-hit games and playing in the World Series, but that first game was my greatest day."

Schalk played 23 games for the White Sox in 1912, batting a respectable .286, but it was his energy, willingness to learn, and outright desire that made the biggest impression on his coaches and teammates. The electric Schalk soon became the favorite of Sox coach Kid Gleason, who helped the young backstop hone his skills. "We'd start a game at 3:00 P.M., but he'd have me out practicing at 9:30 in the morning. We'd work on catching the double steal, he had me chasing from behind the plate to field bunts, and running under pop flies. He taught me to crouch over and make myself a target on the throws from the outfield. He taught me to give, or yield with the catch, to never hold the ball high when making a throw—to cock my hand by my ear. He was a tireless worker." And Schalk was undoubtedly an indefatigable student.

The diminutive Schalk, weighing a scant 148 pounds in his first season, was thought at first too small to catch Chicago ace Ed Walsh's sharply breaking spitball; however, with the help of Gleason, he was soon handling Walsh better than Billy Sullivan, Bruno Block, or Red Kuhn. Even more difficult than catching Walsh was backstopping Ed Cicotte, who had more pitches than a carnival barker. Said Schalk about Cicotte, "He had every type of pitch, including a knuckler, fadeaway,

slider, screwball, spitter, emery ball, and shine ball."

More important than handling the ball was Schalk's ability to handle his pitchers. Wrote John Sheridan of *The Sporting News* in 1923, "Schalk at all times insists that his pitcher shall have and use his stuff, that he shall be able to control it, and that he should use it whenever the catcher calls for it. The manner in which Schalk handles his pitchers must be of inestimable value to his team. He, more than any catcher that I can remember, makes a pitcher work up to the mark all the time. No catcher that I have known made or makes the pitcher work right, stand right on the rubber and use a correct motion, hold runners close to base, better than said Schalk. As a manager of young pitchers, Schalk stands head and shoulders above the others of all time."

Although it might be inferred that Schalk earned his nickname Cracker because he cracked the whip over his White Sox hurlers, the moniker was actually hung on him by Sox outfielder Shano Collins. Collins saw a resemblance between Schalk's physique when viewed from behind and a cracker box. The nickname stayed with the popular Schalk long after his playing days ended.

Revered by his teammates for his intelligent, nervy play and aggressive style on the diamond, his easy disposition made him a favorite off the field as well, and Cracker's youthful looks made for some interesting horseplay. One rainy day in 1915 in Washington, Cicotte, Walsh, and Collins were enjoying their favorite beverages in a tavern when Schalk entered the bar wearing a cap and raincoat. He sidled up to the trio, but before he could order his own beer the bartender growled, "We don't allow no school kids in this joint." Schalk suggested to his teammates that they identify him, but they gave no hint of recognition and instead congratulated the bartender for enforcing the policy which forbade little boys from pestering men at their amber.

Another off-field adventure drew the ire of owner Comiskey. Looking to use the Chicago skyline's newly constructed Tribune Tower for a promotional stunt, a movie company came upon the idea of having Schalk catch a ball thrown from the top of the Tower—a distance of 463 feet. Smiling for the cameras, the Cracker caught the third ball tossed. "Didn't sting me any more than one of those high fouls Ruth used to hit," he later said. Comiskey caught wind of the stunt and was irate when Schalk arrived at the ballpark later that day. Comiskey chided Schalk of the consequences had his star catcher misjudged the ball. Schalk's unadorned response—"But I didn't misjudge it"—did not placate the Old Roman.

Schalk played the catching position like a fifth infielder. He is credited with being the first catcher to back up infield throws to first base and outfield throws

to third. His speed, alertness, and prowess led to his claim of being the only major league catcher to make a putout at every base. His first putout at second base occurred in 1918 against St. Louis in Chicago. On a hit-and-run the Brownies' Ray Demmitt sped past second as Joe Jackson made a great catch in deep left off the bat of Joe Gedeon. Schalk, in the middle of the diamond, ran to second to take the relay from Sox shortstop Swede Risberg and slapped the tag on Demmitt. Putouts at first were more common, because Schalk would often follow runners to first on hits to right field. Chick Gandil, the first baseman, would decoy himself away from the bag, drawing the runner into a wide turn at first. Right fielder Eddie Murphy would then peg the ball back to Schalk at first to tag out the unsuspecting runner.

Over his 18-year career (1,757 games with the White Sox and 5 with the New York Giants in 1929), Schalk participated in more double plays (226) than any other backstop in history, and his lifetime total of 1,811 assists ranks second all-time behind nineteenth-century backstop Deacon McGuire. Schalk led the American League in fielding percentage and putouts eight times each, both figures tops among catchers. He also arguably holds the record for career no-hitters caught, with four (historians having dismissed Jim Scott's gem of May 14, 1914, as he lost his no-hitter in a losing effort in the tenth inning). In 1916 Schalk established the single-season stolen base record for catchers with 30, a mark not broken until 1982, when John Wathan swiped 36 bags. Although his lifetime batting average was just .253, the lowest of anyone elected to the Hall of Fame as a position player, Schalk was considered an excellent bunter, both for the base hit and sacrifice. The Cracker was a frequent selection to *Baseball Magazine*'s All-Star American League Team, and was named by both Ty Cobb and Babe Ruth to their own personal all-time all-star teams.

From 1913 to 1926 Schalk caught nearly 80 percent of the White Sox's contests. His durability was legendary—broken fingers, deep spike lacerations, and sprained ankles did not sideline him. During one game against the Tigers in 1922, Schalk was knocked unconscious by a foul tip. Trainer William "Doc" Buckner of the White Sox resorted to artificial respiration and use of oxygen to revive him. Recounted Buckner, "As soon as he got his breath and collected his senses, he immediately wanted to get back behind the plate."

In 1920 the Cracker backstopped 151 of the 154 games for the second-place White Sox. Schalk maintained he would have caught the full 154 but for an extremely hot sun on a no-Sunday baseball off-day in Philadelphia. Related Schalk, "I went over to Atlantic

City that Sabbath and frisked on the sand too much and too long. When I got back to Philly that night, I looked more like a boiled lobster than any human I ever saw." It was a sunburn—not cracked knuckles, charley horses, or aching dogs—that kept Schalk from catching every game in 1920.

Schalk's best season was probably 1922, when he batted .281, one point below his career best of .282 in 1919. In that 1922 campaign Schalk hit four of his career 11 home runs, stole 12 bases in 16 attempts, hit for the cycle on June 27 (the next White Soxer to do so was Jack Brohamer in 1977), and drove in 60 runs. He led the league in putouts and chances while committing only eight errors, tying the American League record for fielding percentage at .989. He finished third in voting for the 1922 American League Most Valuable Player Award.

Ray Schalk's silence regarding the Black Sox scandal of 1919 and his status as one of the honest men of the Series (in which he batted .304) are well known. Schalk knew something was amiss when both Cicotte and Lefty Williams continually crossed him up on pitches. Regarding the penalties doled out to the conspirators, Schalk did not disagree with the banishments, but later portrayals of the eight as vicious criminals bothered him. In a discussion with Ed Burns of the *Chicago Tribune* in 1940, Schalk conveyed his compassion: "As long as I live, I'll never forget the day Charles A. Comiskey come into the clubhouse and told eight [*sic*] of the boys they had been exposed and were through forever. It was a shocking scene and my mixed emotions never have been straightened out since I watched several of the ruined athletes break down and cry like babies. I never have worried about the guys who were hard-boiled, but those tears got me."

Pennant purgatory followed the Sox after the revelation of the Series fix in late 1920. The dismissal of seven players (Gandil had retired after the 1919 fiasco) wore a large hole in the Pale Hose that left the lineup talent threadbare for years. Schalk's keen efforts on and off the diamond helped bring respectability back to the club. In addition to his MVP-caliber year in 1922, Schalk was responsible for discovering future Hall of Famer Ted Lyons in March 1923 at Baylor College in Waco, Texas. Lyons joined the club later that year in St. Louis, and would collect a franchise-record 260 victories for the Chisox.

The respect and regard for Schalk's knowledge of the game led him to succeed his friend Eddie Collins as White Sox player–manager in November 1926. But Schalk's lenient style led to his forced resignation in July 1928. Expecting to retain his contract as a catcher at an estimated $15,000 (his managerial salary had been $25,000), Schalk—who had only one plate appearance that year—was distressed when Comiskey cut his pay to $6,000. Schalk considered litigation, but a lawsuit was never filed.

Instead, Schalk joined the New York Giant coaching staff with John McGraw in 1929, appearing as a player in five games that year. Back in Chicago again, he became a coach for the Cubs in 1930 and 1931, then went east to manage the Buffalo Bisons in the International League from 1932 to 1940. Later in 1940 Schalk returned to Milwaukee of the American Association, 28 years after he had last played for the club.

It was in these later years that Schalk operated a popular bowling and pool hall establishment in Evergreen Park, Illinois. Ray was also one of the founders of Baseball Anonymous, an organization whose charge was to assist indigent ballplayers. In 1965, after assistant coaching at Purdue University for 18 years, Ray Schalk finally retired from baseball at the age of 72.

Through all his years of following the game of baseball, Schalk would never fail to call and congratulate the catcher of a no-hitter. Schalk always remained popular with Chicagoans, and was invited to catch the first ball of the 1959 World Series, thrown out by Red Faber.

In 1955 Schalk was named to the Baseball Hall of Fame by the Veterans Committee. Fittingly, he was inducted to the Hall on the same day as Ted Lyons, the man he had discovered 32 years earlier. At the ceremony, Schalk thanked his wife, the former Lavinia Graham, as his strongest supporter, saying, "Whatever I've accomplished, I owe to Mrs. Schalk." The Schalks celebrated their 50th wedding anniversary on October 25, 1966. The couple had two children and several grandchildren. When Ray Schalk died of cancer at age 77 on May 19, 1970, the White Sox and California Angels observed a moment of silence prior to their contest in memory of the Hall of Famer. He was buried at Evergreen Cemetery in Evergreen Park.

BRIAN STEVENS

CHICAGO

GEORGE DANIEL "BUCK" WEAVER
SHORTSTOP, THIRD BASEMAN, 1912–1920

Best known as the third baseman banned from Organized Baseball for his knowledge of the 1919 World Series fix in which he did not participate, Buck Weaver spent most of his nine-year major league career as a shortstop, converting full-time to the third sack only in 1917. Initially a right-handed batter, Weaver learned to switch hit after a poor rookie season, and from there he made his mark as one of the American League's most resourceful players, twice leading the circuit in sacrifices, and using his excellent range to reach balls that escaped most of his peers.

Nelson Algren once described Weaver as a "territorial animal...who guarded the spiked sand around third like his life." Despite his competitiveness, the infectious Weaver, nicknamed The Ginger Kid, was also one of the most popular players of his day, known for an ever-smiling, jug-eared face that mimicked a Halloween Jack. Throughout the 1910s Weaver steadily improved his game, enjoying his best season in 1920, just before he was permanently banished from the game he loved. An optimist by nature, Weaver spent the rest of his life fighting to restore his name.

George Daniel Weaver was born on August 18, 1890, in Pottstown, Pennsylvania, the fourth of five children of Daniel and Sarah Weaver. Located 41 miles northwest of Philadelphia, Pottstown had become one of the centers for the state's emerging iron industry, and Daniel Weaver supported his family by working in one of the area's iron furnaces. By late nineteenth-century standards the heavily unionized iron industry paid good wages, and George Weaver's childhood was a contented one. Not very interested in school, Weaver turned his attention to baseball, where his energy and natural athletic talent were noticed at an early age by fellow players, coaches, and scouts. Veteran minor leaguer Curt McGann was so fascinated by Weaver's passionate

style of play and his upbeat, positive attitude that he nicknamed him Buck, a name in Chicago that would soon be synonymous for sympathy.

Buck began his professional career in 1908 with Mt. Carmel, Pennsylvania, of the outlaw Atlantic League, batting approximately .243 (the stats are incomplete) and splitting his time between shortstop and second base. After a year of semipro ball, in 1910 Weaver joined Northampton, Massachusetts, of the Connecticut State League, where he caught the eye of Philadelphia Phillies manager Red Dooin, who signed Buck to a $175 per month contract and farmed him out to York (Pennsylvania) of the Tri-State League. In the fall of 1910 superscout Ted Sullivan of the Chicago White Sox bought Buck's contract for $750 and assigned him to the San Francisco Seals of the Pacific Coast League.

Far from home for the first time, Weaver enjoyed an excellent season with the Seals in 1911, batting .282 in 182 games and drawing praise for his defensive skills. The performance was good enough to elicit an invitation to the spring training of the Chicago White Sox in 1912, but just as Buck made his way to the White Sox camp in Waco, Texas, tragedy struck: his mother succumbed to illness. Buck faced a tough personal choice: attend his mother's funeral or attend spring training. A telegram from his father persuaded Buck to go to camp instead of returning for the funeral.

Upon his arrival in Waco, Weaver initially told no one of his mother's death. When the *Chicago Tribune* learned what had happened, the newspaper published a feature article on the young recruit, applauding his grit. "Not a man on the squad displayed as much enthusiasm," *Tribune* reporter Sam Weller observed. "He has confessed that later when he was alone in his room he couldn't help but weep over the matter.

510

However, he knew he could do no good by going home and he was determined to make good as a ball player and couldn't afford to quit the training squad."

Despite the pain engendered by his mother's death, Weaver impressed the White Sox with a superlative camp, winning the starting shortstop job out of spring training. Irv Sanborn dubbed Weaver The Ginger Kid after Buck gamely played with an injured left hand wrapped in bandages. "Buck hasn't a thing against him but his age," Weller observed. "He is only twenty years old now and lacks only in experience. In his fielding he looks every bit as fast as [Donie] Bush of Detroit."

However, as Weaver's performance during the 1912 season demonstrated, Buck was not as ready for the big leagues as the White Sox hoped or the beat writers imagined. Playing in 147 games, Weaver batted just .224 with nine walks, and led the league with 71 errors at shortstop. Knowing that his position on the Chicago White Sox roster was not secure, he spent the entire off-season learning how to become a switch hitter. Heading into the 1913 season with new ammunition, Buck was able to raise his batting average from .247 to .272 in the last month of the season. Despite excellent range, Weaver's defense remained problematic, as he again led the league with 70 errors—although he also led the circuit in putouts and double plays.

Following the 1913 season, Buck joined the world tour organized by Charles Comiskey and John McGraw, one of only a few White Sox players to make the trip. The touring party traveled 38,000 miles over a span of 17 weeks, not returning to Chicago until the following March. The lengthy trip may have sapped Buck's strength for the 1914 season, as his batting average dipped to .246, with a .279 on-base percentage. Despite this poor showing, Buck had become the leader of the White Sox and was appointed team captain after Harry Lord jumped to the Federal League.

In a 1915 poll of Chicago White Sox fans, Weaver was voted the most popular member of the team, but the next two seasons would be rough ones for him. After spending most of the spring of 1915 recovering from surgery to remove his adenoids and tonsils, Weaver batted .268 and scored 83 runs. The following season, however, his batting average dipped to an abysmal .227, and Weaver began splitting his time on the field between shortstop and third base. At the end of the season, Buck filed for bankruptcy when his Chicago billiard hall operation went broke. At the time, the newspapers reported that he had no other assets. Like most of his teammates, Weaver's baseball salary paled in comparison to his American League peers.

Nonetheless, following the 1916 season Weaver, along with teammates Eddie Collins and Joe Jackson, publicly promised owner Charles Comiskey that they would capture the 1917 American League pennant. This they did, thanks in large part to a superlative season from Weaver, one of the best of his career. Switched to third base to make room for new shortstop Swede Risberg, Weaver proved an instant sensation at his new position, displaying excellent range, an adeptness at scooping up bunts down the third base line, and leading the league in fielding percentage. "In stopping men coming around the bases, going after a fly ball, and digging in for hard chances Buck has few equals in the major leagues," *Baseball Magazine* observed after the season.

In that year's World Series, Weaver batted an impressive .333, but committed four errors in the field. In the postgame celebration that followed Chicago's championship-clinching victory in Game Six, Buck "danced around in a manner which indicated he had completely lost himself," the *Chicago Tribune* reported. "He tossed his cap into the air and followed with his sweater and a dozen bats and three or four hats that belonged to the spectators, and if there had been anything within reach it, too, would have gone into the air."

The war-shortened 1918 season was a successful one for Buck, as he returned to shortstop and batted an even .300, the first time he crossed that threshold in his major league career. At season's end, Weaver went to Beloit, Wisconsin, where he worked as a mechanic in the Fairbanks–Morse manufacturing plant and played for their semipro baseball team. The experience was an eye-opener for him, as he found that he made more money for the plant than he had earned playing for the White Sox. As the 1919 season approached, Buck demanded a raise from Comiskey, and negotiated a three-year-contract worth $7,250.

For the 1919 season Weaver returned to third base and enjoyed another outstanding season, smashing a career-high 45 extra-base hits and batting .296. As the White Sox surged toward the pennant, some of Buck's teammates, disgruntled over the shabby treatment they had received at the hands of Comiskey and looking for a big payday, began conspiring to throw the upcoming World Series. That September, Weaver attended two meetings regarding the proposed fix. Buck was skeptical that the scheme could work, telling his teammates and the gamblers present that throwing the World Series "couldn't be done."

Weaver approached the World Series unsure of his teammates' intentions. Rumors were rampant that the fix was on, but Buck wanted no part of it. Declining the advances of his crooked teammates, Weaver played his best in the Series, batting .324 with four doubles

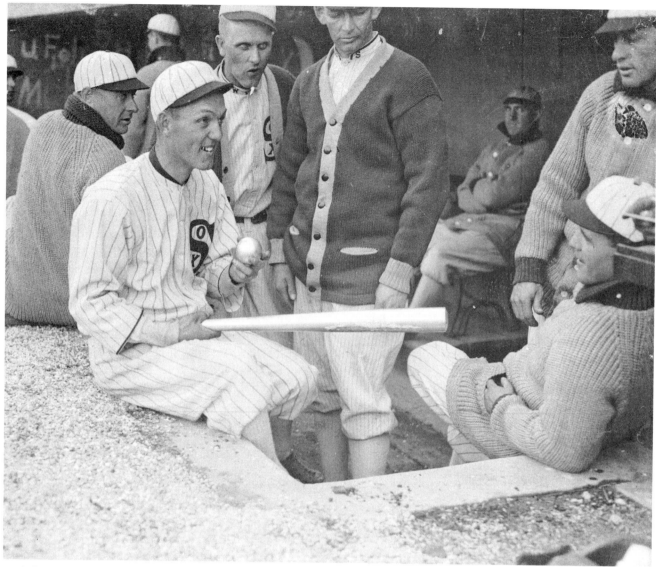

and four runs scored in Chicago's eight-game loss to the Cincinnati Reds. In the wake of the Sox's stunning defeat, sportswriters suspicious of the outcome alluded to the role of the seven conspirators, but often went out of their way to praise Weaver's efforts. "Though they are hopeless and heartless, the White Sox have a hero," the *Cincinnati Post* declared. "He is George Weaver, who plays and fights at third base. Day after day Weaver has done his work and smiled. In spite of the certain fate that closed about the hopes of the Sox, Weaver smiled and scrapped. One by one his mates gave up. Weaver continued to grin and fight harder."

Weaver's 1920 season, which would prove to be his last in the major leagues, was also his finest. Over 151 games, Buck posted career highs in batting average (.331), on-base percentage (.365), slugging percentage (.420), runs (102), hits (208), and doubles (34). Still only 29 years old and a nine-year veteran, Weaver was at the top of his game, leading Chicago in its fight for

a second consecutive pennant. But it all came crashing down on September 28, after Joe Jackson and Eddie Cicotte confessed to their role in the Black Sox scandal when gambler Billy Maharg alleged in the press that eight members of the White Sox had thrown the Series. Immediately after Maharg's allegations were published, Comiskey had suspension letters hand delivered to the eight accused players, including Weaver.

When Weaver was served his suspension letter by White Sox employee Norris "Tip" O'Neill, he instantly marched to Comiskey's office and declared his innocence. He was the only player of the eight accused to do so. *Collyer's Eye* later reported that Comiskey promised Weaver—separate from the other seven players—that he would be reinstated to baseball if he was acquitted in the Cook County trial.

Although Buck requested a separate trial from the other seven players, he was forced to sit with his Black Sox teammates during the proceedings. Judge Hugo

Friend, presiding over the trial, all but declared Buck innocent by saying he would not allow a conviction to stand against him if the jury ruled that way. Three hours of deliberation on August 2, 1921, returned a verdict of not guilty for all players accused. The following day, however, the new commissioner of baseball, Kenesaw Mountain Landis, released his famous statement banning all eight of the accused for life, "regardless of the verdict of juries." One clause in the statement was specifically targeted at Weaver: "…no player that sits in conference with a bunch of crooked players and gamblers where the ways and means of throwing games are discussed and does not promptly tell his club about it, will ever play professional baseball."

Alongside his lifetime banishment of Bennie Kauff, Landis's ruling in the Weaver case ranks as the harshest punishment he ever imposed on a player. Unlike the other Black Sox, Weaver had not accepted any money to throw the Series, and there is no doubt that he played the games to win. His crime was simply his silence, and in this respect there was little to distinguish Weaver's actions from others who had also known about the fix and yet had done nothing to stop it.

But there was a method to Landis's cruelty. By making an example of Weaver, Landis sent a message to the rest of Organized Baseball that any player who learned of a fix was guilty in the eyes of baseball unless he immediately reported it. The effect of this policy is readily apparent: prior to Weaver's banishment baseball authorities usually discovered game-fixing schemes only after the fact. Following the ban, some attempted conspiracies were brought to light before they ever unfolded on the field, thanks to the honesty of players frightened by the Weaver precedent. In 1922, for instance, New York Giants pitcher Phil Douglas was banned for life after Cardinals outfielder Les Mann reported Douglas's efforts to extract money from the Cardinals in exchange for Douglas abandoning the Giants. In 1924 Jimmy O'Connell and Cozy Dolan, two other members of the Giants, were banned for life after they tried to give Phillies shortstop Heinie Sand $500 to throw a game. Sand immediately reported the bribe offer. In this light Weaver's suspension, and the object lesson it imparted to the rest of Organized Baseball for years to come, was one of Landis's most successful moves as commissioner.

All of this was small consolation to Weaver, his family, and the legion of Chicago fans who wanted to see him reinstated. Within a year of the 1921 verdict banning him from baseball for life, Buck submitted the first of many petitions to Commissioner Landis. He was turned away every time. He collected the signatures of 14,000 fans, hired a New York City attorney, and tried to get the courts to intervene. It was all to no avail.

Buck was the only Black Sox player to remain in Chicago after his banishment; he lived there with his wife, the former Helen Cook. After spending several years playing in the semipro circuit, Buck took a job with the city of Chicago as a day painter. He also tried his hand in the drugstore business. With his pharmacist brother-in-law William Scanlon, he opened six drugstores on Chicago's south side. Noticing Buck's business sense, Charles Walgreen, whose drugstore empire was about to skyrocket, asked Scanlon and Weaver to join him as junior partners. They rejected the offer—but then the Depression hit and Scanlon and Weaver were forced to close their stores. In an ironic twist, he later made his living with money from gamblers, working as a betting clerk at a racetrack.

Into his old age, Weaver continued to pursue every avenue to clear his name and return to the good graces of Organized Baseball. His final petition came in 1953, when he again requested reinstatement from Commissioner Ford Frick. In the letter, now prominently displayed at the Baseball Hall of Fame, Buck pleaded, "You know…the only thing we have left in this world is our judge and the 12 jurors and they found me not guilty. They do some funny things in baseball."

Weaver received no response.

Shortly before his death, Buck was interviewed by Chicago author James T. Farrell about his banishment. The good-natured man who had once exuded joy and optimism in all he did had clearly been embittered by his ordeal. "A murderer even serves his sentence and is let out," Buck observed. "I got life." On January 31, 1956, Weaver died of a heart attack at the age of 65; his body was found on West 71st Street by a Chicago policeman. He was survived by his wife and buried in Chicago's Mt. Hope Cemetery.

DAVID J. FLETCHER

CHICAGO

EWELL ALBERT "REB" RUSSELL
LEFT-HANDED PITCHER, 1913–1919

With superb control and a rising fastball, left-hander Reb Russell rose to stardom with one of the best rookie pitching performances of the Deadball Era, notching 22 victories and tossing eight shutouts for the Chicago White Sox in 1913. A typical Russell start featured few walks, few strikeouts, few runs, and many balls hit in the air as pop-ups to the infielders or soft flies to the outfielders. "Russell gets out of a lot of tight places on his nerve," commented White Sox manager Jimmy Callahan. "Three men on the bases, with none out, is a situation that fails to shake him. In fact, it is in the pinches that he shows to advantage." After an arm injury cut short his pitching career, Reb returned to the big leagues in 1922 as a slugging outfielder with the Pirates in another impressive debut season. Although he was a bit naïve when he entered the big leagues, Reb's eagerness to learn and calm demeanor helped him to polish his rough edges both on and off the field. By 1915 the pitcher, who had once been a major source of inspiration for Ring Lardner's Jack Keefe (*You Know Me, Al*), had become a mainstay of high society, holding forth on such topics as music, literature, and psychology.

Ewell Albert Russell was born on March 12, 1889, on a farm near Albany, Mississippi, the second of three children of Tobias and Naomi Russell. When he was one year old his family moved to Texas and eventually settled on a 100-acre farm located eight miles outside Bonham, an agricultural center of 5,000 people in North Texas and a key stop on the Texas and Pacific Railroad. Russell attended primary school and helped his father on the farm, but he developed a passionate love of baseball and could often be found ignoring his chores while playing ball on a crude diamond in the nearby town of Telephone. At 15 he left the farm for good and got a job driving teams for the railroad.

In May 1912 Russell signed to pitch for Bonham of the Texas–Oklahoma League at a salary of $75 a month. Despite using "nothing but curves," he impressed scouts by striking out many while walking few. Following his success in Bonham, Russell's contract was purchased by the Fort Worth Panthers of the Texas League. At Fort Worth, a line drive off his thumb removed the curveball from his arsenal and he had to rely on his fastball and change-up. While posting a 4–4 record in 13 games for the seventh-place Panthers, Russell was spotted by White Sox scout and former major league pitcher Harry Howell, who liked what he saw and recommended the young pitcher to owner Charles Comiskey. After the 1912 season the White Sox drafted Russell for $1,200.

The 5'11", 185-pound Russell arrived at camp in the spring of 1913 with great speed, exceptional control, confidence, coolness under pressure, and a willingness to learn. He also arrived with barely any money in his pocket and little knowledge of major league hitters. Although he had success early in camp based strictly on his fastball, coach Kid Gleason helped him add a curveball to his arsenal with a new grip which generated a sharp break. The White Sox initially intended to farm him out to the Pacific Coast League for more seasoning, but Gleason successfully argued against it and, to the surprise of many, Russell made the club.

On April 18 Russell made his major league debut and justified Gleason's confidence in dazzling style. With the White Sox trailing Cleveland 4–0, Russell was inserted in the seventh inning and proceeded to retire nine of the ten batters he faced, including five strikeouts. Russell's fine performance earned him a spot in the starting rotation, where he quickly blossomed into one of the league's best pitchers. "That boy has everything," Callahan marveled. "He has speed, he has curves, he has control, he has nerve, he has strength. What more

514

could I ask for?" Russell, now called Reb or Tex by the papers, finished the season with 22 wins, a 1.90 ERA, and a league-leading 52 games pitched. He also set an American League rookie record with 316⅔ innings pitched, and his eight shutouts tied the AL rookie record established by Russ Ford three years earlier. Demonstrating a knack for winning close ballgames, Russell also set a major league record by winning five games by the score of 1–0. As an early indication of his hitting skills, Russell also connected for three triples during the season, and hit his first major league home run on June 16 against the Washington Senators. After the season, on October 14, Russell married Charlotte Benz, a cousin of his Sox roommate Joe Benz, and relocated to her hometown of Indianapolis.

On May 26, 1914, Reb was in the midst of a shutout when he collided with Yankee first baseman Les Nunamaker while attempting to get on base. The collision resulted in injuries to his left ankle and hip and kept him out of action for three days. Upon returning to the mound Russell was no longer effective and was hit hard. The combination of the injury and an increase in his weight led to a loss of velocity on his fastball and less break on his curve. By the end of the season, when his ERA had risen a full run to 2.90, doubts arose as to whether he would ever be effective again.

Reb reported to spring training in 1915 grossly overweight, and new White Sox manager Pants Rowland threatened to cut him from the team. Under Rowland's direction, Reb underwent an intensive program of hot mud baths and extensive workouts. Reb also immediately went on a diet consisting solely of lettuce with French dressing, side orders of lemon ice, and pickles. By early March he had dropped nearly 40 pounds and was back near his playing weight. By mid-March he had regained his form, and Sam Weller reported in the *Chicago Tribune* that "Russell let loose more speed than he has shown in a year and his curveball, which disappeared so mysteriously last season, was seen to crack sharply across the plate several times." His job was safe. Splitting his duties between the starting rotation and the bullpen, Reb turned in a fine season, winning 11 games and pitching 3 shutouts.

In 1916 Reb reported to camp already in shape and so impressed Rowland that he was chosen as the club's opening day starter against Detroit. After getting shelled by the Tigers he was relegated to relief duties, where he regained his manager's confidence by contributing a number of solid outings. He spent the rest of the season shuffling between the rotation and the bullpen, and was the workhorse of the staff, leading the team in innings pitched (264⅓) and victories (18) while posting a 2.42

ERA. Russell also led the league with the fewest walks per nine innings pitched, as he allowed just 42 free passes on the season. A turbulent four years into his big league career, many observers still considered him to be the best left-handed pitcher in baseball next to Babe Ruth.

Such comparisons did not stand up for long. Reb's first attempts to throw a curveball in the spring of 1917 left him unable to straighten his left arm. X-rays revealed the presence of "two fibrous growths in Reb's left arm just above the elbow." To combat this malady, the doctor prescribed "exercise and heavy lifting." Once again Reb began the season in a relief role, but spent the year going back and forth between the bullpen and starting rotation. With the White Sox in the midst of a tight pennant race against defending champion Boston, Reb pitched some of the best games of his career. In August Russell won several important games for Chicago, including a shutout against the Red Sox. He finished the year with a 15–5 record and a sparkling 1.95 ERA, and once again led the league with the fewest walks per innings pitched. Nevertheless, the arm injury took its toll and the White Sox could never be sure about whether he would be able to pitch on a given day. His one start in that year's World Series was a disaster, as Reb failed to get a single out before being removed from the game.

Reb did not sign his 1918 contract until early April, and was used sparingly during the first two months of the season. Back in the starting rotation by mid-June, Russell was not as effective as he had been in previous years, displaying uncharacteristic wildness and often losing his effectiveness late in games. Starting 15 games, he finished the year 7–5 with a 2.60 ERA. The following year Reb was not impressive in spring training and barely made the team. After facing two Red Sox batters and not recording an out in his only appearance, Reb was removed for good. Released to Minneapolis of the American Association, he finished the year playing center field, and hit nine home runs, more than twice as many as anyone else on the team.

In 1920 Reb attempted one last comeback as a pitcher for the White Sox, but could not make the team. He returned home to Indianapolis, where he found work in a garage as an auto assembler. Later that season, the Minneapolis Millers traveled to Indianapolis and were in emergency need of an outfielder. Reb agreed to fill in, and came through with a couple of hits in the game. The Millers decided to sign him and he went on to have a great season at the plate, hitting .339 with six home runs and 41 RBI in 85 games. He did even better in 1921, leading the Millers in batting (.368), home runs

(33), and RBI (132), while also posting a 1.64 ERA in five games on the mound.

After clouting 17 homers for the Millers in his first 77 games of 1922, Russell was picked up by the Pittsburgh Pirates in July. As part of a right field platoon with Clyde Barnhart, Russell rapidly became one of the most feared hitters in the National League and finished the season with 12 home runs, 75 RBI, and a .368 average in 60 games. The following year, however, Reb failed to follow up on that sensational 1922 campaign, batting .289 with nine home runs and 58 RBI in 94 games. Given his limited defensive abilities, this performance was not enough to hold his spot in the starting lineup, and by the end of July Russell was benched. He finished the season with the team, but received scant playing time in the last two months.

After being released by the Pirates, Reb returned to the American Association, where he emerged as one of the league's best hitters. With Columbus from 1924 to 1925, Russell smashed 55 home runs and drove in 247 runs while splitting time between the outfield and first base. From 1926 to 1929 he played for Indianapolis, winning a batting title in 1927 at .385. Released by Indianapolis in 1929, Russell finished out his minor league career with Quincy, Illinois, of the Illinois–Indiana–Iowa League and Mobile and Chattanooga of the Southern League. His lifetime minor league batting average was .330.

When his minor league career ended, Reb got a job as a security guard at the Kingan and Company meat packing plant in Indianapolis and worked there until retiring in 1959. During that time, he played for a number of local semipro teams, including the Sterling Beers, which were managed by Clyde Hoffa, a relative of labor leader Jimmy Hoffa.

Russell died at age 84 on September 30, 1973, two weeks short of his 60th wedding anniversary, in an Indianapolis nursing home and was buried in St. Joseph Cemetery in Indianapolis. He was survived by his wife and two children.

RICHARD SMILEY

CHICAGO

URBAN CLARENCE "RED" FABER
RIGHT-HANDED PITCHER, 1914–1933

Urban "Red" Faber, one of the last pitchers to legally throw a spitball, persevered through illness and injury, a world war, and the Black Sox scandal to win a place in the National Baseball Hall of Fame. But he had to toil in the minor leagues for several seasons before learning the pitch that brought him major league success. "I never resorted to the spitter until I was obliged to," Faber later said. "I nearly ruined my arm throwing curves." Wetting the tips of the first two fingers on his right hand, Faber threw the spitter from a variety of arm angles, befuddling batters with the pitch's late-breaking downward movement. "A batter cannot guess with Faber," Goose Goslin later remarked. "His only chance is to close the eyes and hope bat meets ball." To get the consistency required to throw his spitter, Faber was known to chew a combination of slippery elm and tobacco, although he preferred the latter. "And I don't chew [tobacco] because I like it either," Faber explained. "In fact, I never chew except when I am pitching."

The right-hander played his entire 20-year major league career with the White Sox, one of the league's strongest teams before the Black Sox scandal but a perennial also-ran afterward. Faber won 254 games—a total that Ray Schalk, Faber's long-time battery mate and friend, contended might have reached 300 had the team not been decimated by scandal.

Urban Clarence Faber (some references incorrectly list his middle name as Charles), was born on his parents' farm near Cascade, a tiny community in northeast Iowa, on September 6, 1888. The second of four children of Nicholas and Margaret Grief Faber, he was of Luxemburger descent. German was the primary language in the Faber home and at the Catholic elementary school that the Faber children attended. In 1893 the family moved into Cascade, where Nicholas operated a tavern and then opened the Hotel Faber. With his real estate holdings and successful hotel, Nicholas Faber became one of Cascade's most affluent citizens. The Fabers could afford to send their children to out-of-town prep schools and colleges, and for several years preceding World War I they lived off Nicholas's investment income.

The red-haired Faber apparently had a sporadic and unspectacular high school baseball career. He attended prep academies associated with colleges in two Mississippi River communities: Sacred Heart, in Prairie du Chien, Wisconsin, and then St. Joseph's in Dubuque, Iowa. In 1909, when he was 20 and studying at a Dubuque business school, he joined the college varsity of his prep alma mater, St. Joseph's. The institution, now Loras College, has no record of Faber taking any college classes there; however, there is ample documentation of Faber's dominance over college batters in 1909, when St. Joseph's went undefeated in its half-dozen games. The highlight was Faber's 22-strikeout performance against St. Ambrose College, which mustered only three hits.

Faber's performance for St. Joseph's and for semipro clubs caught the attention of Clarence "Pants" Rowland, former owner of Dubuque's minor league team and an acquaintance of Chicago White Sox owner Charles Comiskey. (Rowland was between baseball jobs at the time, managing a hotel bar in Dubuque.) Rowland encouraged Faber to sign with the Dubuque Miners, who were struggling in the Class B Three-I (Indiana–Illinois–Iowa) League. Joining the team with two months left in the 1909 season, Faber went 7–6. In August 1910, during his first full season as a professional, Faber threw a perfect game against Davenport; only one ball reached the outfield. The Pittsburgh Pirates bought his contract the next day.

Faber made the Pirates' 1911 opening day roster, but

manager Fred Clarke never used him and in mid-May sent him to Minneapolis of the American Association. Within days of his arrival in Minnesota, Faber entered a distance-throwing contest and injured his pitching arm. During his short stay in Minneapolis, Faber had a career-changing experience: teammate Harry Peaster taught him the finer points of the spitball, which at the time was a legal pitch. Within weeks, the sore-armed Faber was shipped to Pueblo (Colorado) of the Western League. The young Iowan worked on his spitter over the next 2½ seasons in Pueblo, and then two years in Des Moines (Iowa) of the Western League. In the closing weeks of the 1913 season, White Sox owner Comiskey bought Faber's contract for 1914.

Faber's off-season was abbreviated. In October 1913 Comiskey, at the urging of Rowland, belatedly added Faber to the White Sox roster for the around-the-world exhibition tour with the New York Giants. The rookie-to-be performed adequately on the domestic leg of the tour, but Comiskey planned to drop Faber from the squad before departure for Japan, Australia, the Mideast, and Western Europe. At this point, however, Faber caught another break: just hours before the teams embarked on their Pacific crossing, Giants pitcher Christy Mathewson withdrew from the tour because he feared becoming seasick. Comiskey and Giants Manager John McGraw made an agreement: Faber was loaned to the Giants to take Mathewson's place.

Mathewson must have felt vindicated in his decision. A powerful storm nearly wrecked the tourists' ship as it crossed the Pacific, and all the passengers experienced bouts of seasickness. None suffered more than Matty's replacement: Faber was too ill to leave the ship for a day or two after its arrival in Japan. Eventually, Faber took regular turns pitching against his future team. In the finale in London, with King George V in attendance, Faber pitched tenaciously for 11 innings but took the loss. As they headed back to the United States, McGraw failed to convince Comiskey to sell him Faber's contract.

After a no-decision start and a handful of relief assignments, the 6'2", 180-pound rookie forged into the national spotlight in June 1914. On June 1 Red pitched all 13 innings in a 2–1 loss to Detroit. Six days later, he earned his first career victory with a three-hit shutout of the Yankees. Ten days after that, he came within three outs of no-hitting the defending World Series champion Philadelphia Athletics (an infielder's slow work on a bouncer allowed the only hit). He cooled off in the second half of the season—a sore elbow sidelined him for the better part of a month—and finished 10–9 with a league-average 2.68 ERA.

Before the 1915 season, Comiskey installed Rowland as White Sox manager, and Faber responded by elevating his game to new heights, posting a 24–14 record with a 2.55 ERA. Although the spitball was part of his repertoire, Faber also relied on his fastball and curve. He said that just the knowledge that he might unleash a spitter at any time was enough to keep most batters guessing. His forte was getting hitters to swing early in the count and beat the ball into the ground. That skill was best demonstrated on May 12, 1915, in Comiskey Park, where he required a then-record-low 67 pitches to defeat Washington. Faber pitched less in 1916 due to injury, but he improved to 17–9 with a 2.02 ERA for a team that lost the pennant by two games.

Faber earned a reputation as a battler, and he held his own against the game's greatest hitters. During one at-bat against Faber, Ty Cobb found himself on the ground on three consecutive knockdown pitches. Faber's combination of competitive fire and a pleasant personality made him popular with White Sox fans and management. Comiskey, who owned a Wisconsin game preserve, named a moose after his young pitcher. In September 1916 the moose escaped. It startled a couple of local youths, one of whom happened to be carrying a rifle. When word of the incident reached the Chicago newspapers, headline writers had some fun. One headed an article, SHOOTS RED FABER, PRIDE OF COMISKEY! MOOSE, NOT PITCHER.

In 1917 Faber posted a career-best 1.92 ERA, winning 16 games for the White Sox en route to their first pennant in 11 seasons. In the 1917 World Series against New York, Faber tied a series record with three victories. He won Game Two, lost Game Four, won Game Five in relief, and then closed out the host Giants with a complete-game victory in Game Six. His pitching performance overshadowed his baserunning blunder in Game Two, when he tried to steal third while it was occupied by teammate Buck Weaver. ("It would seem that the well-known pencil for which this young athlete is named, is not the only Faber that has a lump of rubber at its upper end," the *Chicago Tribune*'s Irvin S. Cobb quipped.)

With World War I raging as the 1918 season opened, it appeared likely that major leaguers would be drafted into military service. As a 29-year-old bachelor, Faber was virtually certain to be conscripted. He won his first four decisions, enlisted in the Navy, and lost his farewell game. Although he told reporters that he wanted assignment to a submarine—apparently forgetting the seasickness of his world tour—Faber served his entire tour at Great Lakes Naval Base, near Chicago. A chief yeoman, he supervised recreation programs and pitched for the base's team for the duration of the war.

Back in a White Sox uniform for 1919, Faber, like many Americans that year, suffered from influenza—he was weak and underweight—and with arm and ankle injuries. After a layoff of several weeks he made only two appearances in the final month of the regular season and remained on the bench throughout the tainted 1919 World Series. Ray Schalk long contended that the Black Sox scandal would have been impossible had Faber been healthy; the conspirators would not have had enough pitching to succeed.

After the 1920 season the 32-year-old Iowan married Milwaukee-born Irene Margaret Walsh, then of Chicago. They met by accident—literally. He was a bystander who came to her assistance after an auto collision. The couple had no children, and she (though 10 years younger) experienced ongoing health problems that reportedly included dependency on painkillers. A Faber relative described their marriage as unhappy. There were whispers that she became romantically involved with White Sox outfielder Johnny Mostil, and that Mostil's 1927 suicide attempt occurred after Faber confronted him about the affair. (More likely, Mostil became despondent when he learned that his longtime girlfriend had thrown him over for a teammate, Bill Barrett, whom she subsequently married.) The Fabers remained married until March 1943, when Irene died of a cerebral hemorrhage at age 44.

The advent of the lively ball coincided with Faber's best three-season performance (1920–1922), when he went a combined 69–45 and led the league in ERA in 1921 and 1922. He was among the 17 grandfathered pitchers permitted to throw the otherwise banned spitball for the duration of his career. In 1921, when the White Sox were a shambles after the Black Sox indictments, Faber's 25 wins (against 15 losses) represented 40 percent of all the team's victories. He followed that with his third consecutive 20-win season (21–17).

After 1923, however, it was clear that Faber's days of dominance were behind him; age, injury, and White Sox ineptitude took their toll. He suffered his first losing season (9–11) in 1924, when he got a late start after elbow surgery. As early as the mid-1920s, sportswriters started predicting Faber's retirement. But Red remained generally effective and kept returning, season after season. He explained his longevity by noting that the spitball exerted less stress on his arm. Faber showed occasional flashes of his old form, as when he registered his third and final career one-hitter in 1929.

In 1932 new manager Lew Fonseca took him out of the starting rotation, and Faber's record tumbled to 2–11. By 1933, his 20th season in the majors, Faber (3–4) was the American League's oldest regular player—he turned 45 that fall—and its second-to-last legal spitballer. (Another grandfathered spitballer, Burleigh Grimes, pitched 18 innings for the 1934 Yankees.) After posting a 5–15 record the previous two seasons, Faber was upset with his 1934 contract offer from the White Sox, who wanted to cut his pay by one-third, to $5,000. He secured his release and hoped to join another major league team, but there were no takers. He closed his career with a 254–213 record.

In retirement, Faber tried his hand at selling cars and real estate before acquiring a bowling alley in suburban Chicago. Early in the 1946 season, Ted Lyons became White Sox manager and hired Faber as pitching coach; they lasted three seasons. In April 1947 the 58-year-old Faber married Frances Knudtzon, a 29-year-old divorcée. They became parents the next year with the arrival of their only child, Urban C. Faber II. In the mid-1950s the Cook County (Illinois) Highway Department hired Faber; he worked on a survey crew until he was nearly 80. Exactly 50 years after his rookie season, in 1964 he was inducted into the National Baseball Hall of Fame.

A lifelong smoker—he took up the habit at age eight—Faber suffered heart and respiratory problems in his final years. He died at home on September 25, 1976, at age 88. His grave marker in Chicago's Acacia Park Cemetery cites his Navy service but makes no mention of his baseball glory.

BRIAN COOPER

CHICAGO

Oscar Emil "Happy" Felsch
Center fielder, 1915–1920

With his trademark grin and sunny disposition, Happy Felsch quickly scaled the ladder of fame in the national pastime, winning over fans and opponents alike with his hard hitting and brilliant fielding. By the end of the Deadball Era, the fleet-footed, rifle-armed Felsch was widely regarded as one of the greatest center fielders in the game. Babe Ruth thought him "far superior to Cobb on the defense," adding, "Felsch was a greater ball hawk than Speaker, and what an arm he had!" In his last major league season, Felsch placed in the top five in the American League in doubles, triples, home runs, and slugging percentage, while leading all outfielders in double plays and recording 25 assists. Just when his performance was reaching new heights, however, the revelation of his role in the Black Sox scandal brought his promising career to a premature and ignoble end. In the decades following his banishment, the open and gregarious Felsch was the only tainted player eager to discuss his role in the scandal, and his assistance proved crucial to historian Eliot Asinof's classic book on the subject, *Eight Men Out*. "I shoulda knew better," Felsch admitted to Asinof. "I just didn't have the sense I was born with. It matters. It still matters."

Oscar Emil Felsch, who grew up to be arguably the best baseball player ever produced by Milwaukee's north side, was born on April 7, 1891, in a working-class neighborhood, one of 12 children of German immigrants Charles and Marie Felsch. (Most sources list his birthdate as August 22, 1891, but his death certificate and other legal documents show the April 7 date.) Charles worked as a carpenter to support his family. Oscar, after proceeding no further than the sixth grade, took up work as well, finding employment as a $10-per-week factory laborer and shoe worker. The lack of formal education would come to haunt Felsch in later years, when he had to match wits with wily baseball executives, gamblers, lawyers, and college-educated teammates.

The broad-shouldered Felsch, listed at heights between 5'9" and 5'11" and weights of 160 to 190 pounds over his playing career, first appeared on the Milwaukee baseball scene in 1911, playing shortstop and third base for a semipro club sponsored by a local clothier. The following year, Oscar played with four semipro teams throughout Wisconsin, including Sewell's, Manitowoc, Wisconsin Rapids, and Stevens Point. His easygoing nature, wonderful smile, and love of baseball made the family nickname, Happy, a perfect fit. Newspapers adopted the sobriquet as early as 1912.

In 1913 Felsch made his Organized Baseball debut with the Milwaukee Mollys of the Class D Wisconsin–Illinois League. In early August the Milwaukee Brewers of the American Association signed Felsch, after the young right-handed hitter posted a .319 batting average with 18 home runs for the Mollys. Against the tougher competition of the American Association, Happy, now playing primarily in the outfield, struggled to a .183 average with two home runs in 26 games.

The following year, however, Felsch showcased his major-league potential both at the plate and in the outfield. He set home run distance records in Milwaukee (over 500 feet at Athletic Park) and Kansas City, and led the American Association in round-trippers with 19, while also collecting 41 doubles, 11 triples, and 19 stolen bases for the repeat-champion Brewers. In the outfield Happy demonstrated his prowess with great range and a rifle arm. The Senators, Cubs, White Sox, Giants, and Reds all pursued him, and on August 8, the Sox acquired Felsch for $12,000 plus two players. The Brewers were delighted that Chicago allowed their "fence breaker" to remain in Milwaukee for the duration of 1914. Felsch, declared the greatest Brewer ever by their business manager, Lou Nahin, then signed a two-year contract with Chicago at a salary of $2,500 per year.

The rookie made his major league debut on April 14, 1915, in St. Louis with two singles, a stolen base, and an error. The 1915 White Sox started their steady ascent toward the top of the American League by rising from sixth to third place with a 93–61 record, thanks to the addition of energetic 36-year-old manager Clarence "Pants" Rowland and four new position players, including Eddie Collins, Shoeless Joe Jackson, and Felsch. Now playing center field, Felsch struggled at the plate, as a nagging leg injury suffered early in the season limited his effectiveness. He finished his rookie year with a .248 batting average, three home runs, and 16 stolen bases in 121 games.

A healthy Felsch returned for the 1916 campaign and made good on his potential, posting a .300 batting average and belting a team-high seven home runs, tied for third in the American League. His .427 slugging percentage was sixth-best in the circuit. Felsch also led all outfielders with a .981 fielding percentage while recording 19 assists.

Things got even better for Happy in 1917, when he led all outfielders in putouts, with 440, finished fifth in the American League with a .308 batting average, and tied for second in RBI, with 102. This made Felsch the first player in White Sox history to reach the century mark in runs batted in. For *Chicago Tribune* reporter James Crusinberry, the timeliness of Felsch's hits was more impressive than their quantity. "It seems that Felsch doesn't get into a hitting mood unless there is a good cause," Crusinberry observed, "such as walking up with two out and some mates on the runway."

Already one of the game's brightest young stars, Felsch's performance in the 1917 World Series would make him a nationally recognized hero. The first game of the Series, played at Comiskey Park on Saturday, October 6, was decided by a "loud and vicious clout from the trusty bludgeon of Felsch" when "Milwaukee's famous beef and brawn" hit a long home run to deep left field, giving the Sox a run in a game they eventually won, 2–1, over the New York Giants. The center fielder also made a sensational one-handed cutoff play of a Giant double, preventing a round-tripper. Chicago captured the Series, four games to two. In addition to his World Series check of $3,666 (almost matching his salary of $3,750), the popular star received many presents, including a gold watch, a set of silverware, and $100 worth of shares in American Aircraft.

Despite having captured their first championship in 11 seasons, the 1917 campaign was not an altogether pleasant one for the Sox, with the clubhouse torn in two by the arrival of shortstop Swede Risberg and first baseman Chick Gandil. Although both players were welcome additions to the starting lineup, they helped form divisive clubhouse cliques through their crude manners and connections to gamblers. Felsch, an easygoing free spirit who never fit in with his more educated teammates, started fraternizing with the boisterous, card-playing Risberg–Gandil group, which was often in conflict with the more learned Ray Schalk–Eddie Collins faction. As the animosity between the two groups began to grow, the seeds of discord that would lead to the 1919 scandal were already being sown.

In the meantime Felsch, like many other major leaguers, took a break from major league baseball following the U.S. entry into World War I. Complying with the government's "work or fight" edict, Felsch accepted a job with the Milwaukee Gas Company for $125 per month plus earnings from weekend semipro ball with the Kosciuskos of the Lake Shore League.

Despite the divisions within the team, in 1919 the White Sox captured their second pennant in three seasons, and Felsch enjoyed the best defensive year of his career, as he led the league with 32 outfield assists, tied a major league record with four assists in a single game, set a major league record with 12 chances accepted on June 23, and established a major league record that still stands with 15 outfield double plays. At the plate, Felsch contributed to Chicago's powerful offense with a .275 average, seven home runs, and 86 RBI. All things considered, the 27-year-old Felsch had made a smooth transition back to major league life.

And yet, when Gandil approached Felsch in late September and asked him to participate in the conspiracy to throw the World Series, the happy-go-lucky outfielder agreed. Why? As Felsch later told reporter Harry Reutlinger, "I had always received square treatment from [Comiskey] and it didn't look quite right to throw him down. But when they let me in on the idea, too many men were involved. I didn't like to be a squealer and I knew that if I stayed out of the deal and said nothing about it they would go ahead without me and I'd be that much money out without accomplishing anything." In the end, Felsch's eagerness to please his teammates got the best of him.

Happy played poorly in the Series, producing only a .192 batting average with one extra-base hit and botching catches in Games Five and Six. White Sox manager Kid Gleason, suspicious of Felsch's play, demoted him to right field for Game Seven. After the Series had ended Felsch took home a loser's share of $3,154, in addition to the $5,000 he received from Gandil, which was only half the amount he had been promised when he agreed to participate in the fix.

Despite the ugly rumors and growing scandal that surrounded the eight Black Sox and the entire sport during the 1920 season, Felsch put together the best year of his career, reaching career highs in batting average (.338), on-base percentage (.384), slugging percentage (.540), hits (188), doubles (40), triples (15), home runs (14), runs (88), and RBI (115)—but it all came to an end on September 27, when gambler Billy Maharg exposed the fix in an interview with a Philadelphia newspaper. Two days later, Felsch verified his role in the plot in an interview with Reutlinger, admitting that he accepted $5,000 but denying that he had played to lose. Nonetheless, Felsch already sensed that his days in the major leagues were at an end. "I got five thousand dollars," Happy told Reutlinger. "I could have got just about that much by being on the level if the Sox had won the Series. And now I'm out of baseball—the only profession I ever knew anything about, and a lot of gamblers have gotten rich. The joke seems to be on us." Later news reports of the scandal, meanwhile, alleged that Felsch had tripled his money by betting on Cincinnati to win Game Two, and that his agreement to participate in the fix had led to marital discord between he and his wife, Marie.

Following Felsch's acquittal in the subsequent trial and the lifetime banishment imposed by Commissioner Landis, Felsch joined up with several other Black Sox to form a barnstorming team. Their efforts generally went for naught, however, as ballpark operators and opposing teams were afraid of the consequences of any association with the tainted players. In 1923 Felsch and his wife opened a grocery store in Milwaukee, living on site for about a year as they attempted to proceed with the stark reality of their new lives. In 1924 Felsch discovered that playing ball—albeit an outlaw version in south-central Wisconsin—was more fitting and profitable than selling food. Competing against African-American, Native American, and House of David teams unconcerned with the threat of a Landis blacklisting, Felsch helped the Twin City (Sauk City and Prairie du Sac) Red Sox to a 33–20 record, batting .365.

In 1925 Felsch joined fellow conspirator Swede Risberg in Scobey, Montana, where the pair earned $600 a month plus expenses as they guided their club to a 30–3 record in a nasty environment of heavy gambling and drinking. Playing before crowded ballparks in Montana, Canada, and the Dakotas, Risberg and Felsch endured opponents' taunts—and responded with brawling—about their descent from the big leagues to a "cow pasture."

Though he returned to Milwaukee for the winter, Felsch continued to play outlaw ball in Montana, Saskatchewan, and Manitoba through 1930. In 1932 Hap, now 40 years old, joined a Milwaukee sandlot team, although the hometown Brewers prohibited Felsch's "contaminated" presence at a Borchert Field all-star game. Nonetheless, Felsch soldiered on. Although well past his prime, Happy continued to play in the area for several more years, shifting to first base as his weight climbed to 200 pounds and varicose veins developed.

In the mid 1930s Felsch ran a tavern on Milwaukee's West Center Street, which quickly became a gathering place for sandlot players and managers. According to a report in the *Milwaukee Journal*, "Happy served free peanuts and kept the bowls on the bar full. The crunch of shells underfoot mingled with baseball talk that often lasted far into the night. He seldom became angry when questioned—even about the Black Sox scandal—but found that silence was most effective in ending a distasteful subject."

By 1943 Happy left the saloon business and worked as an assembler, watchman, and crane operator. Card playing, bowling, hunting, fishing, smoking, and coffee drinking were his favorite pastimes when he was not listening to the Milwaukee Braves on the radio. In 1952 Oscar and Marie, parents of three and eventual grandparents of 11, entered their final home on the second floor of a flat at 2460 N. 49th Street. This was where *Eight Men Out* author Eliot Asinof conducted his pivotal interview with Happy. Expressing contempt for the tight-fisted Comiskey and his fawning sportswriters, Felsch nonetheless admitted, "God damn, I was dumb, all right. Old Gandil was smart and the rest of us was dumb." In contrast to the other surviving Black Sox, who either stonewalled or refused Asinof's inquiries, Felsch struck Asinof as forthright, charming, and articulate. Although the interview lasted for three hours, per Asinof's recollection in a 1999 interview, Happy actually wanted the author to stay longer, as the conversation appeared to be liberating for him. Asinof was so appreciative of Felsch's openness that he dedicated his book *Bleeding Between the Lines* to Felsch's memory.

In poor health in his later years, the 73-year-old Felsch succumbed to a coronary blood clot due to arteriosclerosis on August 17, 1964, at Milwaukee's St. Francis Hospital. Felsch was cremated and his remains entombed in the Gardens of the Last Supper Mausoleum at Wisconsin Memorial Park in Brookfield, Wisconsin.

JIM NITZ

Claud Lefty William

CHICAGO

CLAUDE PRESTON "LEFTY" WILLIAMS
LEFT-HANDED PITCHER, 1916–1920

Despite posting a career ERA (3.13) slightly higher than the league average (3.10), Lefty Williams notched the highest winning percentage in White Sox history during his five years with the club, winning 81 games against just 44 losses. The 5′9″, 160-pound left-hander possessed an average fastball and a curve that he could effectively locate in the strike zone. A fly-ball pitcher, he used Chicago's excellent outfield defense to full advantage and rode Chicago's stellar offense to back-to-back 20-win seasons in 1919 and 1920. No more than an average starting pitcher, Williams achieved greater fame than his skills warranted through his involvement in the 1919 Black Sox scandal. He threw his three games in the Series, thereby becoming the first pitcher in baseball history—and still the only starting pitcher—to lose three contests in a single fall classic.

Claude Preston Williams was born in Aurora, Missouri, on March 9, 1893, son of William and Mary Williams. While he was still a child, his parents moved 30 miles to Springfield, Missouri, where Williams began playing baseball. As a left-hander, Williams immediately took to pitching. He mastered the curveball at a young age, using it to fool other kids in games played in vacant lots.

Williams's mastery of the curve brought him local notoriety and he soon began playing with the Springfield team of the semipro Missouri–Kansas League. In 1912 he joined Morristown (Tennessee) of the Appalachian League, posting an 18–11 record and a league-leading 224 strikeouts. The following year Williams joined the Nashville Volunteers of the Southern Association, and once again won 18 games. Near the end of the season, the Detroit Tigers purchased his contract. He made four starts for the Tigers at the end of the 1913 season, going 1–3 with a 4.97 ERA. The young left-hander made one more start for the Tigers in May 1914, allowing five unearned runs in one inning. Sent to Sacramento of the Pacific Coast League, Williams went 13–20 with a 2.05 ERA in 276 innings of work.

Williams spent the 1915 season with the Salt Lake City Bees of the PCL, and finally started coming into his own as a pitcher. In 418⅔ innings of work Williams struck out a league-high 294 batters, en route to 33 victories, also tops in the league. After the season the Chicago White Sox purchased his contract.

Despite his diminutive size Williams seemed to have little difficulty handling heavy workloads, even though he relied on a pitch (the curveball) that was taxing on the arm. Williams had a robust upper body, with broad shoulders and neck, which earned him the nickname "the biggest and littlest man in baseball."

Williams was an immediate success with the White Sox, showing excellent command of his curveball as he established himself as a stalwart of the Sox pitching staff. He started more games than any other pitcher for the White Sox in 1916, compiling a 13–7 record with 138 strikeouts in 224⅓ innings pitched. Nonetheless, he was not overpowering. For the season Williams compiled a 2.89 ERA, highest on the team and slightly higher than the league average. To be successful the slender lefty relied on good run support from the Chicago offense (which included Eddie Collins, Happy Felsch, and Joe Jackson) and stellar defense, especially from his outfielders, as Williams used his curve to coax hitters into sending harmless fly balls into the vast outfield of Chicago's Comiskey Park. "Outside of Eddie Plank, no left-hander in the American League makes as close a study of his batters or pitches more intelligently to them than Williams," Eddie Collins observed after Lefty's inaugural season with the White Sox. In June 1916, Williams married Lyria Wilson, a manicurist he had met in Salt Lake City the previous summer.

In 1917 Williams became even more dependent on his defense and run support, as he struck out just 85 batters in 230 innings and posted a subpar 2.97 ERA. Nonetheless, he established a club record by winning nine games in a row to start the season, before tailing off to finish the year with a solid 17–8 ledger for the White Sox. Williams's late-season struggles relegated him to the bullpen for the World Series, and he appeared in only one game in relief in Chicago's victory over the New York Giants.

Despite the immense talent of this squad, the members of the team did not get along well. Differences in geographic roots, education, and salaries created rifts among many of the White Sox players. On a team filled with strife the soft-spoken, often morose Williams was nonetheless able to befriend a teammate. On the road Williams roomed with Joe Jackson, a South Carolina native, and the two players and their wives often spent time together. Their marital status inadvertently created conflict with Comiskey. Following the United States' entry into World War I, Jackson opted to play baseball in the Navy shipyards rather than make himself eligible for the military draft. In June Williams and catcher Byrd Lynn, also married, chose to follow Jackson into the shipyards rather than risk being sent overseas away from their spouses.

With a lineup essentially identical to that of the 1917 White Sox, Chicago marched to the American League pennant in 1919. Williams combined with pitcher Eddie Cicotte to provide a dynamic pitching tandem, Williams contributing 23 wins over the course of the season to go with Cicotte's 29. Williams posted his only full-season ERA better than the league average, and his strikeout rate also climbed, as he fanned 125 batters in 297 innings of work.

Poised to be an asset in the club's quest to win a second World Series in three years, Williams instead joined six of his teammates in accepting money from gamblers to throw the Series. With a salary that did not exceed $500 per month, Williams was one of the lowest paid players on the club, and particularly susceptible to the promise of a $10,000 payoff. He proved instrumental in the success of the fix, agreeing to participate before Jackson and Felsch did. It was also Williams who personally delivered a payment of $5,000 to Jackson after Game Four of the Series.

Of course, his greatest contribution to the scheme came on the field, where he artfully threw his first two starts against the Cincinnati Reds. In Game Two he coasted through the first three innings before allowing three walks, a single and a triple in the fourth inning to give Cincinnati three runs, which proved to be all they needed in a 4–2 victory. In his next start in Game Five, Williams actually held the Reds hitless through the first four innings, then again eased up, allowing four runs in the sixth frame to provide the Reds with a lead they would not relinquish.

With Chicago trailing four games to three in the best-of-nine series, Williams took the mound for Game Eight. He wasted no time in throwing the contest, surrendering four runs in the first inning before Chicago manager Kid Gleason removed him from the game. Williams had faced just five batters, retiring only one. Chicago went on to lose the game 10–5. In the end Williams received $5,000 for his role in the fix. In *Eight Men Out*, author Eliot Asinof writes that Williams had planned to try to win the eighth game until receiving a visit from a gambler's henchman named Harry F., who threatened to harm Williams's wife unless Williams lost the game in the first inning. However, Asinof later admitted fabricating this tale as a means of thwarting potential plagiarizers. The story, which was also a pivotal scene in director John Sayles's film version of the book, is fictional.

Williams was again a big winner for the White Sox in 1920, notching 22 victories against 14 defeats for the season, despite an unimpressive 3.91 ERA. Like his teammates who were involved in the 1919 fix, Williams's season came to an end on September 27, following gambler Billy Maharg's revelation of the fix to a Philadelphia newspaper. Soon afterward, Cicotte became the first player to confess to the Cook County grand jury, and Williams himself confessed the following day.

After his 1921 acquittal in trial but banishment from the game, Williams played on various barnstorming teams with his disgraced teammates, eventually moving to Arizona where he played in the outlaw Copper League in 1926 and 1927.

Williams and Lyria eventually continued west to Laguna Beach, California, where Lefty started a nursery and landscaping business, and like many of the other banned players, maintained his silence about the affair. Williams and his wife—the couple had no children—remained in Laguna Beach until Williams died at age 66 on November 4, 1959. He was buried in an unmarked grave in Memorial Park in Anaheim, California.

JON DUNKLE

CHICAGO

CHARLES AUGUST "SWEDE" RISBERG
SHORTSTOP, 1917–1920

Charles August "Swede" Risberg, the slick-fielding, rifle-armed shortstop best known for his complicity in the Black Sox scandal, was born on October 13, 1894, in San Francisco, the youngest of three children of a Swedish-born lumberman and his Danish wife. Although little is known about his childhood, Risberg was raised in San Francisco, which then had a population of approximately 350,000, and his formal education apparently ended in the third grade. When asked in later years why he had dropped out of school so soon, Risberg supposedly replied that he had refused to shave.

After winning wide acclaim as a semipro pitcher in the Bay Area, the 17-year-old Risberg got a tryout in spring training in 1912 with the Vernon (California) Tigers of the Pacific Coast League. The *Los Angeles Times* reported that "the youngster looks like a fixture," but Risberg managed to pitch in only one game for the Tigers that year. In 1913 he spent the year in Class D leagues, pitching for Spokane, Washington, of the Northwestern League, before moving on to Ogden, Utah, of the Union Association, where he was converted to shortstop. Returning to Ogden in 1914, the 19-year-old shortstop batted .358, which earned him another chance with the PCL Tigers at season's end. He soon became a full-time utility man for the Tigers, playing 175 games in 1915 and 185 in 1916 despite indifferent hitting performances, and spending time at first base, second base, shortstop, the outfield, and occasionally the pitcher's mound.

Risberg's strong arm was both an asset and a liability; his throwing ability garnered praise, but once, in a fit of anger, Risberg punched an umpire who called a third strike on him.

After two years of minor league play, Risberg's contract was purchased by the Chicago White Sox for $4,000. Swede—who stood 6 feet tall and weighed 175 pounds, making him one of the biggest shortstops in the game—replaced 129-pound Zeb Terry on the team.

Risberg's transition to the major leagues was not smooth. A newspaper article written in June 1917 revealed that Risberg suffered from "the worst case of homesickness in the history of the Sox aggregation," adding that "he would gleefully toss up his chances for fame and lucre, and take the first train back to the Pacific Coast, where he knows everybody and is known by everybody. He misses the soft blue skies of California. He wants to be back where the sun shines and his wife can cheer him on from the grand stand." Risberg—a right-handed "marvel at shortstop"—even asked that Comiskey send him home, but the request was denied.

Risberg's 1917 batting average of .203 was far from spectacular but, because of his defensive skills, he played in 149 games that year for the Sox. Late in the season Risberg went into a slump, and he therefore pinch hit only twice when the Sox beat the New York Giants in the 1917 World Series. Heading into the 1918 season, White Sox manager Pants Rowland told Risberg he would have to hit better if he wanted to keep his job.

The year 1918 was chaotic for professional baseball. Under the "work or fight" order, players were not exempt from war duties. Though he batted an improved .256, Risberg found his playing time reduced, appearing in 82 of Chicago's 102 games before leaving the team on August 8 and heading home to San Francisco. Risberg told Comiskey and the press he would enlist in the Army upon his arrival, but instead found work in an Alameda, California, shipyard owned by Bethlehem Steel. Risberg's job was termed essential and enabled him to avoid the draft, but it consisted largely of playing baseball, as he batted .308 for the shipyard ballclub.

Risberg returned to the Sox in time for the pennant-winning 1919 season, and in September received good press in the *Atlanta Constitution*, which labeled him a "miracle man" who had "blossomed out as a wonder" after making four plays that were "phenomenal." His fielding was "brilliant" and more than one big leaguer, according to this article, claimed that Risberg possessed the "greatest throwing arm of any infielder in the big show."

Darker undertones, however, stalked Risberg and the White Sox during the 1919 season. Risberg, along with many of his teammates, resented the comparatively low wages being paid by Comiskey. The team was also split into two factions—the more educated players, including second baseman Eddie Collins, and the rougher group, led by former boxer and current first baseman Arnold "Chick" Gandil—which added to the tension. Risberg, who hated Collins and sided with Gandil, agreed to throw the 1919 World Series in exchange for payoffs from gamblers. In addition, Risberg assisted Gandil in organizing the scheme, collecting money from the gamblers, delivering it to teammates, and helping to convince Joe Jackson to participate.

Risberg reportedly took home $15,000 for his role in the conspiracy. He also sent a telegram before the Series to his friend, Browns infielder Joe Gedeon, informing Gedeon that the Series was fixed and advising him to bet on Cincinnati. A year later Gedeon informed on Risberg to the White Sox, hoping to collect a $10,000 reward offered by Comiskey for information on the fix. Gedeon didn't get the reward, but was later banned from baseball for his prior knowledge.

Risberg played horribly in the Series, hitting only .080 (2 for 25) and chalking up four errors. Perhaps to cover up the reasons behind his poor performance, Risberg claimed to have a cold during the Series. In the 1921 trial a team trainer testified that he had, indeed, given Risberg cold medicine before Game One.

After his acquittal on conspiracy charges and banishment from Organized Baseball, Risberg enjoyed a lucrative 11-year career playing outlaw ball in Minnesota, Wisconsin, the Dakotas, Montana, and Manitoba. According to Risberg's wife, Agnes, he also played ball in Chicago in 1922 under the name of Jack Maples. Although he and Happy Felsch unsuccessfully sued Comiskey for back wages in 1923, Risberg did comparatively well playing outlaw ball; his son Robert later reported that his father earned more money playing in outlaw leagues than he ever had playing for Comiskey.

When not playing ball, Risberg ran a dairy farm in Blue Earth, Minnesota. In 1922 his wife filed for divorce, citing cruelty and neglect. In court Agnes stated that the couple had been happy when Risberg was playing in the Pacific Coast League, but not during his major league career. As for the game-fixing scandal, Agnes said that Risberg grew fond of saying, "Why work, when you can fool the public." The divorce was granted in December 1922; Agnes received custody of their two children. Her request for alimony was denied, however, because Swede had fled the jurisdiction of the court.

In December 1926, Commissioner Kenesaw Mountain Landis contacted Risberg to garner testimony about a gambling scandal involving Ty Cobb and Tris Speaker. Although adding nothing to that case, Risberg testified that in September 1917 the Detroit Tigers deliberately lost four games to the White Sox. Risberg added that two weeks after the games he and Gandil collected $45 each from Sox players, and forwarded the money to players in Detroit. Many other witnesses contradicted the reason for the payment however, saying that it was thanks for playing well against Boston. When only Gandil and Hap Felsch backed Swede's story, Landis dismissed the charges. The case resulted in strong anti-betting edicts, a statute of limitations on game-fixing allegations, and the abolition of the common practice of teams rewarding other clubs with "gifts" for defeating pennant rivals. Will Rogers attended the crowded hearings in Landis's Chicago office and said of Risberg, "It was just that bottled-up hate against everything that made him think he hadn't had a square deal in the game, and he exaggerated the incident."

In his later years Risberg's health suffered as he developed osteomyelitis in his knee. The condition, which was apparently caused by a spike wound, forced Risberg to walk with a pronounced limp. The leg eventually became infected and had to be amputated.

In 1962 Risberg moved back to California, where he owned a tavern that he named after himself. Eliot Asinof described Risberg at nearly seventy as "balding and gray, his pale face relatively free of creases." When approached, Risberg "seemed pleasant enough, although uninterested, as if sensing there was nothing in it for him." Once the former ballplayer realized Asinof's intent to interview him, though, "His look was so cutting, so full of suspicion," and Risberg claimed not to remember anything about the events that had transpired so long ago.

Risberg died on October 13, 1975, his 81st birthday, in a convalescent home in Red Bluff, California, the last of the "Eight Men Out" to die.

KELLY BOYER SAGERT AND ROD NELSON

DETROIT

onsidered the American League's weak sister when the junior circuit became a major league in 1901, fortuitous events both on and off the field helped to transform Detroit into one of the game's strongest franchises by the end of the Deadball Era. Off the field, Henry Ford's innovations revolutionized the automobile industry and vastly expanded Detroit's working class; on the field, the acquisition of Ty Cobb for $700 brought the Tigers three consecutive American League pennants and gave the team the game's most exciting star. In 1905 Detroit had finished dead last in the American League in attendance; 14 years later the club ranked first in the league.

On April 25, 1901, the Detroit Tigers made their debut as a charter American League franchise at Bennett Park, an 8,500-seat ballpark on the northwest corner of Michigan and Trumbull avenues, named after Charlie Bennett, the popular Detroit catcher of the 1880s. The home team scored ten runs in the ninth for a stunning 14–13 comeback win in front of an overflow crowd of 10,000 spectators.

Before long, however, league officials lamented the club's dismal attendance figures, and in 1902 Ban Johnson arranged financial support to move the team to Pittsburgh for the 1903 season. The plan collapsed when the National League allowed the junior circuit to locate a franchise in New York and Johnson agreed to keep the American League out of Pittsburgh. As part of the peace pact, outfielder Sam Crawford, who jumped to Detroit from Cincinnati after the 1902 campaign,

WINNING PERCENTAGE 1901–1919

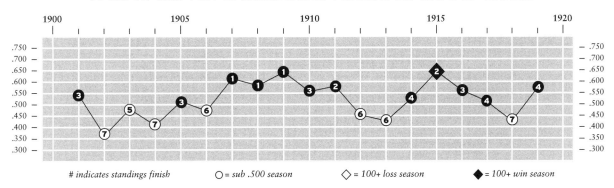

 # indicates standings finish   ◯ = *sub .500 season*   ◇ = *100+ loss season*   ◆ = *100+ win season*

remained with the Tigers, where he roamed the outfield for 15 seasons.

Eighteen-year-old Ty Cobb joined the club in 1905, and Hughey Jennings became manager in 1907, the year before Frank Navin took over as the club's president. Together Navin, Jennings, and Cobb drove the Tigers to three consecutive pennants and three World Series defeats. In 1907 the Tigers set a franchise attendance record of 297,079, and Wild Bill Donovan established the team record for winning percentage (.862). In 1909 Cobb became the first player in franchise history to win the Triple Crown.

After the 1911 season Navin demolished Bennett Park to construct Navin Field, a $300,000 concrete-and-steel ballpark that sat 23,000, nearly three times the capacity of the old grounds. The new park opened on April 20, 1912, securing the Tigers' future at the corner of Michigan and Trumbull.

Despite boasting the game's best all-around player, the Tigers failed to capture a pennant through the Deadball Era's second decade. In 1915 they finished 2½ games behind Boston, becoming the first American League club to record 100 victories and not win the pennant. According to Bill James's win shares system, the 1915 Tigers sported the greatest outfield (Bobby Veach, Cobb, and Crawford) of all time. Indeed, five of James's top ten outfields belong to the deadball Detroiters. Nevertheless, the Tigers did not win another flag until 1934.

TREY STRECKER

ALL-ERA TEAM

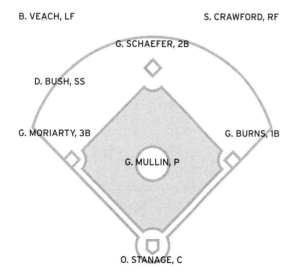

T. COBB, CF

B. VEACH, LF   S. CRAWFORD, RF

G. SCHAEFER, 2B

D. BUSH, SS

G. MORIARTY, 3B   G. BURNS, 1B

G. MULLIN, P

O. STANAGE, C

TEAM LEADERS 1901–1919

BATTING

GAMES
S. Crawford 2114
T. Cobb.........1929
D. Bush.........1627

RUNS
T. Cobb.........1416
S. Crawford 1115
D. Bush.........1085

HITS
T. Cobb.........2713
S. Crawford 2466
D. Bush.........1499

RBI
S. Crawford 1264
T. Cobb.........1211
B. Veach 636

DOUBLES
T. Cobb..........431
S. Crawford 402
B. Veach 216

TRIPLES
S. Crawford 249
T. Cobb..........210
B. Veach 92

HOME RUNS
S. Crawford 70
T. Cobb..........67
H. Heilmann.......22

STOLEN BASES
T. Cobb..........765
D. Bush..........377
S. Crawford 317

BATTING AVERAGE
(2000+ plate appearances)
T. Cobb..........372
S. Crawford 309
B. Veach 304

PITCHING

GAMES
G. Mullin 435
H. Dauss.........269
B. Donovan.......261

WINS
G. Mullin 209
B. Donovan.......141
H. Dauss.........125

LOSSES
G. Mullin 179
B. Donovan........96
H. Dauss..........92

INNINGS
G. Mullin 3394
B. Donovan..... 2137⅓
H. Dauss.......1869

STRIKEOUTS
G. Mullin 1380
B. Donovan.......1079
H. Dauss.........739

WALKS
G. Mullin 1106
B. Donovan.......685
H. Dauss.........591

SHUTOUTS
G. Mullin 34
B. Donovan........29
E. Killian..........19

ERA
(800+ innings pitched)
H. Coveleski 2.34
E. Killian.........2.38
E. Summers.......2.42

TYPICAL LINEUPS 1901–1919

1901

1. D. Casey, 3B
2. D. Holmes, RF
3. J. Barrett, CF
4. K. Gleason, 2B
5. K. Elberfeld, SS
6. D. Nance, LF
7. P. Dillon, 1B
8. F. Buelow, C

1902

1. D. Harley, LF
2. K. Elberfeld, SS
3. D. Casey, 3B
4. J. Barrett, CF
5. D. Holmes, RF
6. K. Gleason, 2B
7. P. Dillon, 1B
8. D. McGuire
   F. Buelow, C

1903

1. J. Barrett, CF
2. B. Lush, LF
3. S. Crawford, RF
4. C. Carr, 1B
5. S. McAllister, SS
6. H. Smith, 2B
   H. Long, SS
7. J. Yeager, 3B
8. F. Buelow
   D. McGuire, C

1904

1. J. Barrett, CF
2. M. McIntyre, LF
3. C. Carr, 1B
   R. Robinson, UT
4. S. Crawford, RF
5. E. Gremminger, 3B
6. B. Lowe, 2B
7. L. Drill
   B. Wood, C
8. C. O'Leary, SS

1905

1. D. Cooley, CF
2. C. Lindsay, 1B
3. M. McIntyre, LF
4. S. Crawford, RF-1B
5. B. Coughlin, 3B
6. G. Schaefer, 2B
7. C. O'Leary, SS
8. L. Drill, C

1906

1. D. Jones, CF
2. G. Schaefer, 2B
3. S. Crawford, RF
4. M. McIntyre, LF
   T. Cobb, OF
5. B. Coughlin, 3B
6. C. Lindsay, 1B
7. C. O'Leary, SS
8. B. Schmidt, C

1907

1. D. Jones, LF
2. B. Coughlin, 3B
3. S. Crawford, CF
4. T. Cobb, RF
5. C. Rossman, 1B
6. G. Schaefer
   R. Downs, 2B
7. B. Schmidt, C
8. C. O'Leary, SS

1908

1. M. McIntyre, LF
2. G. Schaefer, SS
3. S. Crawford, CF
4. T. Cobb, RF
5. C. Rossman, 1B
6. B. Coughlin, 3B
7. B. Schmidt, C
8. R. Downs, 2B

1909

1. M. McIntyre, LF
2. D. Bush, SS
3. S. Crawford, CF
4. T. Cobb, RF
5. C. Rossman, 1B
6. G. Moriarty, 3B
7. G. Schaefer, 2B
8. B. Schmidt
   O. Stanage, C

1910

1. D. Jones, LF
2. D. Bush, SS
3. T. Cobb, CF
4. S. Crawford, RF
5. J. Delahanty, 2B
6. G. Moriarty, 3B
7. T. Jones, 1B
8. O. Stanage, C

1911

1. D. Jones, LF
2. D. Bush, SS
3. T. Cobb, CF
4. S. Crawford, RF
5. J. Delahanty, 1B-2B
6. G. Moriarty, 3B
7. D. Gainer, 1B
   C. O'Leary, 2B
8. O. Stanage, C

1912

1. D. Jones, LF
2. D. Bush, SS
3. T. Cobb, CF
4. S. Crawford, RF
5. B. Louden, 2B
6. G. Moriarty, 1B
7. C. Deal, 3B
8. O. Stanage, C

1913

1. D. Bush, SS
2. O. Vitt, 2B
3. S. Crawford, RF
4. T. Cobb, CF
5. B. Veach, LF
6. D. Gainer, 1B
7. O. Stanage, C
8. G. Moriarty, 3B

1914

1. D. Bush, SS
2. G. Moriarty, 3B
3. T. Cobb, CF
4. S. Crawford, RF
5. B. Veach, LF
6. M. Kavanagh, 2B
7. G. Burns, 1B
8. O. Stanage, C

1915

1. D. Bush, SS
2. O. Vitt, 3B
3. T. Cobb, CF
4. S. Crawford, RF
5. B. Veach, LF
6. G. Burns, 1B
7. R. Young, 2B
8. O. Stanage, C

1916

1. D. Bush, SS
2. O. Vitt, 3B
3. T. Cobb, CF
4. B. Veach, LF
5. S. Crawford
   H. Heilmann, RF
6. G. Burns, 1B
7. R. Young, 2B
8. O. Stanage, C

1917

1. D. Bush, SS
2. O. Vitt, 3B
3. T. Cobb, CF
4. B. Veach, LF
5. H. Heilmann, RF
6. G. Burns, 1B
7. R. Young, 2B
8. O. Stanage, C

1918 (first half)

1. D. Bush, SS
2. O. Vitt, 3B
3. T. Cobb, CF
4. B. Veach, LF
5. H. Heilmann, RF
6. L. Dressen, 1B
7. R. Young, 2B
8. A. Yelle, C

1918 (second half)

1. D. Bush, SS
2. B. Jones, 3B
3. T. Cobb, CF
4. B. Veach, LF
5. A. Griggs
   H. Heilmann, 1B
6. G. Harper, RF
7. R. Young, 2B
8. O. Stanage, C

1919

1. D. Bush, SS
2. R. Young, 2B
3. T. Cobb, CF
4. B. Veach, LF
5. H. Heilmann, 1B
6. I. Flagstead, RF
7. B. Jones, 3B
8. E. Ainsmith, C

DETROIT

James Erigena Barrett
Center fielder, 1901–1905

Jimmy Barrett arrived in the majors with a brilliant one-month trial in 1899 and for five years performed as a scintillating outfielder, a superior batter, and the speed darling of fans in Cincinnati and Detroit. Before injuring his knee in 1905, Barrett was called the finest throwing outfielder and the fastest man to first base in his league. During his five healthy seasons he led the majors in outfield games, putouts, and double plays by small margins and collected 30 more assists than any other outfielder in baseball. Upon his retirement, the *Washington Post* observed that Barrett "could go back as fast and as far on a fly ball as any man in the game....He was a wonder at throwing, and none can remember where Barrett made the wrong play after grabbing the ball; he always knew where to throw it." Foot speed was crucial to Barrett's offensive production. With superior bunting ability and the lefty's advantage, it made him a great slap hitter. The way he beat out grounders and bunts drew comparisons of a young Barrett to Willie Keeler and, later, a young Ty Cobb to Barrett.

James Erigena Barrett was born on March 28, 1875, in Athol, Massachusetts, near Vermont, and he lived in that region until moving to Detroit as the Tigers' biggest star. His father died when he was four years old and his mother when he was six, and Jimmy was raised by several uncles. Listed at 5′7″ and 170 pounds, he was probably shorter. At 21 he played in Brattleboro, Vermont, 20 miles from Athol—professionally, by one later report. When the New York State League expanded to Utica and Oswego in 1898, Barrett applied to both clubs. Oswego's manager, George Sayers, received more than 800 letters and selected Barrett as one of three shortstops among only nine fielders on a team of 18 that would be cut to 12 after practice. Barrett impressed quickly, especially with his throwing, but he could hit

and run, too, smacking two triples and a homer in an exhibition against the Cuban Giants. Writer Fred Fayette called him a sure major leaguer within two years.

After six errors in two games Barrett was shifted to third. In a month at third and a month back at short, he committed about one error per game. When the New England League went out of business after Independence Day, Sayers picked up two men from its Taunton, Massachusetts, team, putting one of them at shortstop and moving Barrett to right. From there Barrett developed into one of the league's best players, leading the league in games, at-bats, and hits while finishing ninth in batting average (.332) and slugging almost .500. He notched 20 assists in 53 outfield games and made speed his trademark.

No National League club drafted him that fall, so when Barrett became available to the Class A minors on January 1, George Stallings selected Barrett for Detroit of the Western League. The young outfielder starred for the 1899 Tigers, scoring 117 runs and batting .331. At the end of August Stallings sold Barrett to Cincinnati, and Jimmy made his major league debut two weeks later.

Joining the team a few days after Sam Crawford, Barrett was an immediate sensation. Installed as the club's right fielder and leadoff batter, he scored 30 runs in 26 games while hitting .370 with a .477 OBP. Barrett secured the leadoff and right field roles the next spring, but moved to center after 30 games and finished the year with 114 runs scored and 44 steals, both third-best in the league, and a .316 batting average with 72 walks.

Besides his statistical achievements, Barrett's speed and aggressive style contributed to his popularity with fans and thus to his stature in the lucrative labor market that soon opened with the emergence of the American League as a major league. He was most popular in

Detroit, which quickly signed him for $3,000 ($600 above the NL ceiling). For the next four seasons Barrett remained a fixture as the club's center fielder, eventual leadoff batter, and best overall player. He led the Tigers in runs and walks each year, three times led the club in on-base percentage, and twice led the team in homers.

Barrett's best season came in 1903. He led the league in walks and on-base percentage (.407), ranked fourth with a .315 average, tied for third with 95 runs, and led in assists for the second time in three seasons. Still, manager Ed Barrow thought Barrett too cocky—"didn't think too much of his ball playing," according to reports—and in 1904 tried to trade him to the New York Giants for Art Devlin, though the deal was vetoed by Tigers' secretary Frank Navin. Barrett survived the controversy to post another outstanding season, when he once again led the league in outfield assists and in walks. Under the new 154-game schedule Detroit played ten ties, of which eight were replayed, for a total of 162 games. Barrett played every single game, establishing a major league record that would remain out of reach until the season expanded to 162 games in 1961.

On April 26, 1905, Barrett went down with a twisted knee, an injury from which he tried to come back too soon, according to one observer. "If the kneecap had been broken he might have been saved many playing days but as it was a sprain it caused Barrett to be careless. He got back into the game before the injury had properly healed, and there was a recurrence." Although his "torn knee tendons [were] still in bad shape" on June 19, in early July he returned to the lineup. But before long his leg gave out again, relegating Barrett to a part-time role and forcing the Tigers to call up an 18-year-old Ty Cobb at the end of August. In Barrett's absence the team charged to third place, generating optimism for 1906. That off-season the Tigers also secured Davy Jones, a dominating player in the American Association and another capable center fielder. In the Tigers' now-crowded outfield the limping Barrett became expendable. One of five outfielders on the official roster at the beginning of the 1906 campaign, he practiced with the team but did not play.

Cincinnati finally reacquired its 1899 phenom by conditional purchase in May 1906, for an amount variously reported as either $2,500 or $3,500. Cincinnati never paid a dime, however, returning Barrett to Detroit after

Jimmy, looking slow, went hitless in 12 at-bats. A few days later Barrett agreed to become player–manager for Dayton of the Central League, where he served less than a month before drawing his release. Three weeks later, Barrett signed with Rochester of the Eastern League, where, remarkably, he played 74 games in 74 days, batting .277 and scoring 42 runs. After the season the Boston Red Sox picked him up for two years at a $3,000 salary with a $2,000 bonus.

Reinjuring his bad knee prior to the 1907 season, Barrett went home and rejoined the Red Sox only upon their arrival in Detroit late in May. He served as the team's regular left fielder for the next four months, running the bases cautiously and generally fitting in well on a weak team. He hit .244 with enough walks and extra-base hits to be an average batter in the trough of the Deadball Era. For 1908, however, the Red Sox acquired several promising outfielders. Barrett's leg was still unreliable, and he was let go on May 15.

Within a week Barrett was back in the Eastern League with Providence, then in last place. His season came to an abrupt end on August 17, however, when he reinjured his leg sliding into home. His .251 average and 55 runs in 82 games were not bad, but he was not reserved for 1909.

Barrett finished his professional career with three years in Milwaukee. Joining the Brewers late in June 1909, he was the regular left fielder for a month, then a sub. The following spring he won a regular outfield job. Hitting .400 and scoring 19 runs in 21 games, he slowed moderately before his season was ended on June 12, once again by leg injury, after a painful slide into home. He went home to rest.

Named manager of the club for 1911, Barrett guided the team to a fifth-place finish while occasionally playing center. The club did not rehire him for 1912, so he was a free agent.

In February 1913 he announced his retirement in Detroit. He became senior partner in the real estate firm Barrett & Walsh with one of his in-laws and died in their office of a stroke on the morning of October 25, 1921, at age 46. Former teammates served as pallbearers when he was buried in Mount Olivet Cemetery. His wife, the former Margaret Walsh (whom he had married in 1904), inherited an estate worth more than $400,000.

PAUL WENDT

DETROIT

GEORGE JOSEPH MULLIN
RIGHT-HANDED PITCHER, 1902–1913

Powerfully built, and with a fearful fastball and biting curve that Johnny Evers once referred to as a "meteoric shoot," George Mullin was Detroit's stalwart right-handed pitcher for 12 years. He was nicknamed Wabash George or Big George, in reference to his 6'0", 188-pound frame, though his weight routinely fluctuated throughout his career. A double threat, Mullin also earned a reputation as a batter to be feared, finishing his career with an impressive .262 batting average. During his prime with the Tigers Mullin established himself as one of the game's best cold-weather pitchers, an asset that served him well in Detroit's frigid climate. As Alfred Spink once observed, Mullin was "one of the few veteran twirlers who is able to jump right in at the start of the season and do good work."

George Joseph Mullin was born in Toledo, Ohio, on July 4, 1880, one of five children of Irish immigrants Martin and Helen (Kelly) Mullin. As a youngster George worked part-time as a messenger boy and attended St. John's Jesuit Academy in Toledo. By 1898 Mullin was engaged in semipro ball and over the next three years played for Wabash and South Bend in Indiana. In 1901 Mullin signed his first professional contract with Fort Wayne of the Western Association. Big George became a workhorse for his new club, hurling 367 innings en route to a 21–20 mark. After the season Mullin signed a contract with Brooklyn of the National League, but broke the agreement before ever appearing in a Superbas uniform, as he accepted a more lucrative offer from the Detroit Tigers.

Mullin was 21 when he entered the major leagues on May 4, 1902, at Bennett Park in Detroit. A week later he made his debut start at home against Chicago, surrendering nine runs over 8⅓ innings in a no-decision against the White Sox. In an early display of his hitting prowess, Mullin also cracked three doubles in the game. A regular in the Detroit rotation for the rest of the season, Mullin's rookie campaign was mixed: he pitched himself to a 13–16 record in 30 starts, but also batted .325 (which would remain a career high) in 120 at-bats.

A crafty pitcher, Mullin had a full arsenal, with more than just his excellent stuff. Like Mark Fidrych, the Tigers pitcher of the late 1970s, Mullin perfected a number of eccentric strategies to gain an advantage over hitters. At critical times Mullin chose the stall: he distracted the batter with tactics of walking off the mound, loosening or tightening his belt, fixing his cap, retying his shoes, and removing imaginary dirt from his glove. Mullin also incessantly talked to himself, to batters, and to fans of opposing teams who would heckle him when he engaged in his act. Mullin was also superstitious and believed that the team mascot, Ulysses Harrison, an African-American orphan whom the players nicknamed Li'l Rastus, brought him good luck.

In 1903 Mullin achieved a breakthrough performance with a 19–15 record and 2.25 ERA, though wildness caused him to lead the league in walks, with 106. He continued to lead the circuit in free passes every year through 1907, but during that time he also developed into one of the league's most durable pitchers. He led the league in innings pitched with 347⅔ in 1905, and in September 1906 he started and won both ends of a doubleheader against Washington. Mullin ran off a string of three consecutive 20-win seasons from 1905 to 1907—although during that span he also lost 20 games twice, in 1905 and again in 1907. In his first taste of the fall classic, against the Chicago Cubs in 1907, Mullin lost both his starts despite pitching two complete games and notching a sterling 2.12 ERA.

The following year Mullin struggled to a 17–13 mark, with a poor 3.10 ERA, but overcame his difficulties to capture the Tigers' only victory in the 1908 World Series, an 8–3 complete-game victory in Game Three.

The 1909 season proved to be the superlative achievement of his career. Trimming off 40 pounds during the off-season, Mullin pitched a one-hitter against Chicago on opening day as the first act in what proved to be a personal 11-game winning streak to start the season. His first loss of the year, 5–4 to the Athletics, came on June 16. Mullin finished the season 29–8 with a 2.22 ERA, leading the league in wins and winning percentage (.784). He was second in innings pitched, with 303⅔, and gave up only 78 walks, a sign of his improved control.

Returning to the World Series for the third straight year, Mullin drew the Game One starting assignment, losing to Babe Adams of the Pittsburgh Pirates at Forbes Field by a score of 4–1. With Pittsburgh leading 2–1 after three games, Mullin started Game Four in Detroit against the Pirates' Lefty Leifield. Mullin limited Pittsburgh to five hits and pitched a 5–0 complete-game shutout, squaring the Series at two games apiece. The teams returned to Pittsburgh, where Babe Adams won his second game of the Series, 8–4. Facing elimination in Game Six at Detroit, Mullin started his third game and gave up three runs in the first inning before settling down to pitch seven straight innings of shutout ball in a 5–4 Detroit victory.

After Detroit starter Bill Donovan was knocked out of the box early in the decisive Game Seven, Tigers manager Hughey Jennings turned to Mullin, but he was unable to hold the Pirates and Pittsburgh cruised to an 8–0 victory. Despite the poor performance, Mullin finished the Series with an impressive 2–1 record and 2.25 ERA in 32 innings pitched, the latter still a major league record for a seven-game series. Detroit, however, would not return to the World Series for another 25 years, and Mullin never again pitched in the postseason.

With his career-year behind him, Mullin pitched two distinguished seasons out of the next three. He posted winning records of 21–12 and 18–10 in 1910 and 1911, respectively, but fell to 12–17 in 1912, his last full season with Detroit. Despite being out of condition for most of the season, Mullin achieved a number of milestones in 1912. On May 21 he faced Walter Johnson at Washington and outdueled him 2–0 for his 200th career victory. On June 22, with the Tigers trailing Cleveland 11–3 with two outs in the bottom of ninth, Jennings chose Mullin to pinch-hit for Cobb, who had gone to the clubhouse. Mullin ended the game with an out.

In disfavor with management and in decline as a pitcher, Mullin was placed on waivers by Detroit in June. Still unclaimed three weeks after the team's decision, Mullin was vindicated in the second game of a July 4 doubleheader against the St. Louis Browns at Navin Field. He gave himself a birthday gift of a no-hitter, striking out five and walking five. Mullin iced his performance by delivering three hits and driving in two runs in the 7–0 victory.

Following a feeble 1–6 start to the 1913 season, albeit with a much improved 2.75 ERA, Mullin was purchased by the Washington Senators on May 16. He posted a 3–5 record for the year before Washington assigned him to Montreal of the International League. After finishing out 1913 with the Royals, Mullin jumped to Indianapolis of the Federal League in 1914, where he went 14–10. Although he finished his Organized Baseball pitching career in 1915 at Newark in the Federal League with a 2–2 mark, Mullin continued to participate in semipro baseball as manager and pitcher for various clubs in Indiana and Ohio until 1919. His last position was assistant manager and coach of a club in Rockford, Illinois, of the Three-I League in 1921.

Mullin's pitching career, while impressive, was certainly influenced by his lack of weight control and conditioning. Dapperly dressed, with black hair and blue eyes, he was also the most gregarious of players, enjoying the social life and celebrity of being a major leaguer. All the same, Mullin achieved a set of admirable pitching marks. Over 14 seasons he was 228–196 (.538) with a 2.82 ERA. A 20-game winner five times in six seasons, he also achieved the distinction (twice) of winning and losing 20 in the same season (1905 and 1907). Mullin still holds four single-season Detroit pitching records for a right-hander, all set in 1904: most games started (44), most complete games (42), most innings pitched (381⅓), and most games lost (23). His 209 victories as a Tiger rank second in franchise history.

After baseball Mullin returned to Wabash, Indiana, where he lived and worked as a police officer. He died at age 63 on January 7, 1944, after a long illness that wasted his robust body to 100 pounds. He was survived by his wife of 43 years, Grace (Aukerman) Mullin, and one daughter, Mrs. Beatrice Rish of Detroit. He was buried in Falls Cemetery in Wabash.

DAVID CICOTELLO

DETROIT

FRANCIS J. NAVIN
SECRETARY, 1902–1908; PRESIDENT, 1908–1935

Known as Old Stone Face for his colorless and stoic demeanor, Frank Navin controlled the destiny of the Detroit Tigers for three decades, becoming one of the game's most influential owners and important power brokers. During his lengthy tenure as Tigers president, Navin was, at various times, an implacable foe of the American League's strong-willed president, Ban Johnson, and later an important ally and confidant for Commissioner Kenesaw Mountain Landis, who sometimes called Navin as much as 20 times in a single day. Like Charles Comiskey and Clark Griffith, Navin relied on his franchise as his sole source of income, and like those owners he developed a reputation for being tight-fisted and autocratic. Navin "kept an accounting of the day's receipts in his vest pocket," historian Joe Falls once wrote. "He was the owner, general manager, business manager, farm director, and publicity man, and, if things got busy, he'd be down in the booth selling tickets on the side."

Francis J. Navin was born on April 18, 1871, in Adrian, Michigan, the youngest child of Irish immigrants Thomas and Eliza Crotty Navin. Located 70 miles southwest of Detroit, Adrian served as a railroad hub, linking the Michigan Southern and Erie & Kalamazoo lines. To support his family, Thomas Navin worked on the railroad, though his children developed loftier ambitions. Frank's older brother, Thomas Jr., entered law school and became a successful Detroit attorney and prominent politician, until he was convicted of forgery and sent to prison for his part in an embezzlement scheme while serving as mayor of Adrian. Initially following in his brother's footsteps, Frank earned a law degree at the Detroit College of Law (now Michigan State University Law School) and ran unsuccessfully for justice of the peace, but then abandoned the legal and political professions for more mundane work selling insurance and keeping the books for Detroit insurance agent Samuel Angus. When Angus purchased the Detroit Tigers in 1902, Navin became the club's business manager, handling the day-to-day affairs of the franchise.

After the 1903 season Angus put the team up for sale and it was purchased by millionaire William C. Yawkey, who insisted that Navin be retained to run the business end of the franchise. Yawkey died suddenly, and the ownership fell to his son, William H. Yawkey, who had little genuine interest in baseball and also leaned heavily on Navin. Yawkey bankrolled the enterprise but remained in the background, and Navin became president by proxy until 1908, when Yawkey sold him almost half the club and Navin officially became team president. Upon Yawkey's death in 1919, Navin finally became half-owner of the Tigers, as the Yawkey estate sold him the 15 shares necessary to get up to 50 percent ownership. The remaining 50 percent was sold to automobile magnates Walter O. Briggs and John Kelsey, with Navin continuing in his role as team president.

While he immersed himself in the business of running a ball club, Navin also acquired a thorough knowledge of the game itself, becoming a keen judge of baseball talent. In his own introverted and uncharismatic style, he quietly turned the mediocre Tigers into a pennant winner in a few short years. From 1903 to 1905 he assembled the nucleus of the Tigers' first pennant-winning clubs, luring outfielder Sam Crawford and pitcher Bill Donovan away from the National League, acquiring pitcher Ed Killian and third baseman Bill Coughlin, and purchasing 18-year-old outfielder Ty Cobb from Augusta of the South Atlantic League for $700.

Another big coup for Navin was the signing of Hughey Jennings as manager prior to the 1907 season. After manager Bill Armour had seemingly lost control of the club in 1906, Navin happened to attend a minor league game between Newark and Baltimore to scout some Newark prospects and was immediately attracted to the managing style of Baltimore pilot Jennings. Baltimore owner Ned Hanlon demanded $5,000 from the Tigers for Jennings, but because Baltimore had signed Jennings to a player contract before naming him manager, Navin shrewdly drafted him as a player, paid the standard $1,000 draft price, and then installed the fiery ex-shortstop as manager.

Under Jennings's leadership the Tigers won three consecutive American League pennants from 1907 to 1909, while the penny-pinching Navin kept the team's payroll among the lowest in the big leagues. After the 1907 season, for instance, Navin paid his two best players, Ty Cobb and Sam Crawford, a combined $8,000 in salary—considerably less than many players of comparable stature earned. "Paying a ball player his worth pained Old Stone Face deeply," Ty Cobb later remembered. Cobb claimed that, following his 1911 holdout, Navin attempted to rewrite his contract, which was supposed to be for $10,000, at a lower figure. When Cobb threatened to make Navin's deceit public, the owner "fiddled with his pen and harrumphed a few times and finally restored the $10,000 sum."

Despite his penurious ways, Navin managed to earn the respect of his players. In May 1912, when Cobb was suspended indefinitely for attacking a fan in the stands, Navin backed his players in their refusal to play until the ban was lifted—although he avoided paying the standard fine for failing to field a team by instructing Jennings to hire a group of collegiate and semipro players for $10 each. The resulting farce (the newly-minted Tigers lost their only game 24–2) infuriated Ban Johnson, but may have helped persuade the American League president to lighten Cobb's suspension to only 10 days.

By 1912, with Ty Cobb drawing fans both at home and on the road, Navin and Yawkey had raked in $365,000 in profits, and the franchise that Navin had once bought into for a few thousand dollars was now worth an estimated $650,000. The owners invested much of their earnings back into the franchise, constructing a new steel-and-concrete stadium on the site of old Bennett Park following the 1911 season. The new structure at Michigan and Trumbull avenues played host to the Tigers for the next 88 seasons, and was first known as Navin Field. Over the 1923–24 off-season Navin improved the park by adding a second deck to the grandstand and installing a press box, which provided reporters covering Tigers games with the closest view of the action of any park in baseball.

Navin provided first class amenities for the fans and reporters who came to watch the Tigers, but he failed to bring another pennant winner to Detroit. After a disastrous seventh-place finish in 1920, Jennings resigned (after 14 years at the helm), leading Navin to install Cobb as the club's new manager. Despite having one of the best-hitting clubs in baseball, the Cobb-led, Cobb-dubbed Tygers of 1921–1926 made only one serious challenge, when in 1924 they finished a close third behind Washington. Manager Cobb publicly blamed Navin for his reluctance to purchase needed pitching to fill out a championship roster, and by 1926 the Cobb–Navin honeymoon was over. In the wake of a budding game-throwing scandal involving Cobb and Tris Speaker, a disappointed Navin replaced the Georgia Peach with former Tiger George Moriarty.

By 1931 Navin had lost much of his personal fortune through a combination of the stock market crash and accumulated gambling losses, and thereafter came to rely on his wealthiest partner, Briggs, to finance the club. It was Briggs's cash that overcame sagging gate receipts to trade for high-salaried players such as outfielder Goose Goslin and catcher–manager Mickey Cochrane.

Under Cochrane's leadership the Tigers captured the American League pennant in 1934 and finally won their first world championship in 1935, in six games over the Chicago Cubs. The normally reserved Navin was beside himself with joy when Cochrane crossed the plate with the winning run of the Series and, uncharacteristically, he joined in the post-game locker room celebration. A little over a month later, on November 13, 1935, he collapsed from a heart attack while riding his favorite horse, Masquerader, at the Detroit Riding and Hunt Club. His body was later found by a search party.

Dead at age 64, he left behind a wife, Grace Shaw Navin, but no children. Following a funeral attended by dozens of baseball notables and hundreds of ordinary fans, he was buried at Mount Olivet Cemetery, in Detroit.

MARC OKKONEN AND DAVID JONES

Samuel E Crawford
"Wahoo Sam"

DETROIT

SAMUEL EARL CRAWFORD
RIGHT FIELDER, 1903–1917

Sprung from fertile Midwestern farm soil, for nearly two decades Sam Crawford swept over the major league baseball landscape like a storm blowing across his native Nebraska's prairie. One of the Deadball Era's most consistent performers, the powerful Crawford never led his league in slugging percentage, but from 1901 to 1915 he finished in the top ten each year but one. During that span the left-hander paced the circuit in triples six times, on his way to establishing a career record for three-baggers that has not been eclipsed in the nearly nine decades since his historic career came to an end.

Standing an even six feet tall and weighing 190 pounds, Crawford was generally regarded as the strongest hitter of his day. "While we are no sculptor, we believe that if we were and were looking for a model for a statue of a slugger we would choose Sam Crawford for that role," F.C. Lane of *Baseball Magazine* wrote in 1916. "Sam has tremendous shoulders and great strength. That strength is so placed in his frame and the weight so balanced that he can get it all behind the drive when he smites a baseball." Crawford was much more than a one-dimensional slugger, however. Playing in the era's cavernous parks Crawford had to leg out even the longest of his drives. In addition to his 309 career triples, the Nebraskan also holds the record for the most documented inside-the-park home runs in a single season, with 12 in 1901.

Samuel Earl Crawford was born on April 18, 1880, in Wahoo, Nebraska, one of four children of Stephen and Ellen Ann (Blanchard) Crawford. Crawford's family had emigrated from Scotland through Canada. His father fought in the Civil War and used his military pension for a number of commercial ventures, including a general store and real estate speculation. Although Sam was widely regarded as articulate, well-read, and

eloquent during and particularly after his playing days, he abandoned formal education after the fifth grade to work as an apprentice barber.

Crawford's trade would make for a great story in later years. National columnist Charles Dryden, in a mock interview with Crawford, had the slugger talk of building his renowned natural strength by "whacking the wind-whipped whiskers of Wahoo." It became apparent early that Crawford was not fully committed to the razor. He began playing baseball at a young age, and quickly showed a talent for the game. Honing his skills playing one-old-cat with North Ward schoolmates, he joined a team formed by Snakes Crawford (likely no relation), which toured eastern Nebraska, challenging town teams for the purse on a daily basis.

The Wahoo contingent, Crawford recalled years later, "made Cedar Bluffs, Fremont, West Point, Dodge…Schuyler …wherever there was a ball team we challenged them for a game." Wahoo won most of those, traveling on a lumber wagon behind a team of horses with a tent and cook stove for subsistence. "We were ballplayers on a trip and loved it." Crawford eventually landed with Killian Brothers, a local team "who had big league uniforms. We all wanted to play for Killian Brothers and get one of those uniforms," he wrote. One local crank recalled years later that Crawford earned a suit of clothes from Killian's mercantile for promising not to smoke.

Crawford moved to West Point, Nebraska, in 1898, his first gig drawing a salary to play ball, and then landed jobs barbering and playing baseball in the small Nebraska towns of Wymore and Superior. In the spring of 1899 a pitcher named John McElvaine recommended Crawford to a Chatham, Ontario, club in the Canadian League. The young outfielder tripled in his first game with Chatham (his only safety in four tries) and registered six putouts in left field. He hit .370 in 43 games, moving to Columbus and later Grand Rapids in the Western League after Chatham folded.

Crawford hit .328 with 13 triples and five homers in 60 Western League games that summer, and on August 1 and 2, 1899, played in an exhibition series against the Detroit Wolverines. Batting third and playing left field, Crawford doubled in the first game and knocked out three singles in the second for manager Tom Loftus. Loftus also tried him out as a pitcher that season, and Crawford split two decisions.

After Grand Rapids fell out of the pennant race, Crawford's contract was sold to Cincinnati, making him, at age 19, the youngest player in the major leagues. Crawford batted .307 to close the 1899 season, hitting seven triples with a homer in his first 31 major league games. The Reds played an unusual Sunday doubleheader in Crawford's major league debut on September 10, 1899. He made the day a memorable one, cracking a pair of singles in four tries against the Cleveland Spiders in game one, and walloping his first major league triple and two other safeties off Louisville's Bert Cunningham in the nightcap.

From 1899 through 1902 Crawford played 403 games for the Reds, collecting 495 hits, including 60 triples, 56 doubles, and 27 home runs. After batting just .260 in 1900, his first full season in the majors, Crawford put together one of his most successful major league seasons in 1901, batting .330 with a major league-leading 16 home runs and 104 RBI, tied for third-best in the National League. In 1902 he maintained a .333 average, second-best in the league, and smacked 22 triples (tied for the league high). Oddly, Crawford hit only three home runs that season and just 18 doubles, one of five times during his career that he ended a season with more triples than doubles.

After the 1902 campaign Crawford jumped his contract with the Cincinnati Reds and signed with the Detroit Tigers. Crawford immediately became a fixture in the Tiger outfield, appearing in 137 or more games every year for the next 13 years, during which he batted better than .300 eight times. Crawford's main defensive position was right field, except for three years (1907–1909) when he manned center and the Tigers won three consecutive pennants. Contemporary reports suggest that Crawford was considered a fairly good outfielder. Although he never led the league in assists, Crawford consistently threw out between 16 and 24 baserunners each season from 1900 to 1907. Not a particularly fast runner, Crawford covered the outfield terrain more than adequately, and even if he never led the league in putouts, he was consistently in the top ranks.

Crawford's stardom owed itself not to his fielding, but his slugging, and it was here that he distinguished himself with the Tigers, becoming one of the sport's acknowledged long-ball threats. Like Frank Baker, Crawford eschewed the scientific approach to hitting advocated by other luminaries of the game. Put quite simply, Crawford believed that hitting success was simply a matter of seeing the ball and hitting it very hard. "My idea of batting is a thing that should be done unconsciously," he once explained. "If you get to studying it too much, to see just what fraction of a second you must swing to meet a curved ball, the chances are you will miss it altogether."

Applying this pared-down philosophy, Crawford became a steady run producer for the Tigers. He ranked among the American League's top ten in RBI every year from 1903 to 1915, and paced the circuit in 1910, 1914, and 1915 (tied with teammate Bobby Veach). During that 13-year span he led the league in triples five times, in extra-base hits four times, and in doubles, home runs, and runs scored once each. Despite his slugging, Crawford was a consistent contact hitter. Batter strikeout totals were not recorded in the American League until 1913, but in that season Crawford struck out only 28 times in 609 at-bats, less than half as often as the average AL batter. For a top slugger he also seldom walked, particularly during his prime. From 1903 to 1910 Crawford drew no more than 50 walks in any season.

During his first three seasons with the Tigers, Crawford was undisputedly the team's best player, but the disappointing Tigers twice lost more games than they won. Things began to change in 1906 with the emergence of the brash young Southerner Ty Cobb, who by 1907 had propelled the Tigers to the first of three consecutive American League pennants, permanently supplanted Crawford as the team's best player, and made for himself a slew of enemies within the clubhouse, including the normally easygoing Crawford. Cobb "came up with an antagonistic attitude, which in his mind turned any little razzing into a life-or-death struggle," Crawford recounted for Lawrence Ritter in *The Glory of their Times* years later. "He came up from the South, you know, and he was still fighting the Civil War. As far as he was concerned, we were all damn Yankees before he even met us."

Despite, or perhaps because of, his disagreements with Cobb, Crawford remained one of the game's most respected figures, admired for his honesty, intelligence, and endurance. Crawford "is a man of most exemplary habits, remarkable disposition, and is an example that it would be well for any man in any profession to follow,"

Detroit owner Frank Navin wrote in 1915. "He has always been a gentleman on and off the field. I have never had any occasion to worry in the least about his condition."

From the close of the 1909 Series until Crawford's departure in 1917, Detroit slipped from serious contention. The Tigers finished within 10 games of first only twice, in 1915 and 1916. Crawford continued to produce at a furious clip through most of that time, however, leading the league in triples four times (1910 and 1913–1915). He batted over .310 five years in a row (1910–1914).

Crawford's major league career ended almost as suddenly as it began. After productive seasons in 1915 (.798 OPS with a league-leading 112 RBI) and 1916 (.760 OPS in just 100 games), he limped to a .173 batting average and a .473 OPS in 104 at-bats in 1917 before retiring from the major leagues.

Crawford did not go quietly. He was released from his contract in 1917 after two years of complaining about his meager salary and Cobb's individualistic style of play, two sore points with Crawford ever since Cobb had begun stealing headlines and drawing a larger salary a decade earlier. Like so many players whose days in the majors were finished, Crawford migrated west, settling in Peco, California, and closing his professional career with four productive seasons with the Los Angeles Angels of the Pacific Coast League, leading the league in hits in 1919 and triples in 1920.

When his playing days were completely over, Crawford made a living raising walnuts—but also struggled to stay active in the game. He was head baseball coach at the University of Southern California from 1924 to 1929, posting a 55–33 record and establishing the Trojans as one of the premier college programs in the nation. He became a Pacific Coast League umpire in 1935, retiring from the post in 1938 after the death of his wife of 37 years, the former Ada Lattin. Crawford remarried widow Mary Blazer in 1943.

In his later years the gentle slugger known for his quiet swing lived a reclusive existence, immersing himself in literature and philosophy, until rediscovered by Lawrence Ritter in a Baywood Park, California, laundromat. Crawford proved to be one of the most memorable subjects in Ritter's classic *The Glory of Their Times*, interspersing memories of Rube Waddell, Dummy Hoy, and Walter Johnson with quotes from Robert Ingersoll and George Santayana in his inimitable plain-spoken manner. "No, I don't have a telephone," he explained. "If I had a lot of money I wouldn't have one. I never was for telephones. Just don't like them, that's all. Anybody wants to talk to you, they can come to see you. I do have a television over there—it was a gift—but I never turn it on. I'd rather read a book."

Crawford's relationship with Cobb remained complicated throughout their lives. The two partially reconciled at Harry Heilmann's funeral near Detroit in 1951, and many consider Cobb's campaign on his former outfield mate's behalf as a primary factor in Crawford's induction to the Baseball Hall of Fame in 1957. Cobb nonetheless complained for the remainder of his days about Crawford's role in the hazing that the Georgia Peach endured in 1905 and 1906. Crawford, in turn, was anxious to lay blame for the tension in the Tiger clubhouse at Cobb's feet. As he told Ritter, "We weren't cannibals or heathens. We were all ballplayers together, trying to get along. Every rookie gets a little hazing, but most of them just take it and laugh. Cobb took it the wrong way."

Sam Crawford died at age 88 on June 16, 1968, in Hollywood Community Hospital, following a stroke. On the day Crawford died the college program that he had brought to prominence, USC, won its fifth national championship. He was survived by his widow and two children from his first marriage, and was buried in Inglewood Park Cemetery in Inglewood, California.

BILL LAMBERTY

Wm. Donovan

DETROIT

WILLIAM EDWARD DONOVAN
RIGHT-HANDED PITCHER, 1903–1912, 1918

A hard-throwing and durable right hander, Wild Bill Donovan harnessed his lively curveball, volatile temper, and busy social life well enough to become a 25-game winner first in the National League and then again in the American League. Genial and engaging, Donovan was called Smiling Bill by sportswriters and was a fan favorite—though umpires frequently found cause to eject him. Regarded as a "slant ball artist" and a "big game pitcher," Donovan drew, and often won, key matchups during Detroit's run of three consecutive World Series appearances from 1907 to 1909. His 25–4 mark in 1907 was the best winning percentage in the American League, and by 1912 he had compiled 185 major league victories, 140 of them in 10 years with the Tigers.

"Donovan is a giant and pitches, hits and fields equally well," Alfred Spink wrote in 1910. "When in good shape Donovan has fine speed, a wonderful break on his fastball and is one of the best fielding pitchers in the country." After a three-year sojourn in the minors, Donovan came back to the big leagues as a player–manager with the floundering New York Yankees, where he enjoyed little success at either vocation. Donovan resurrected his managerial career in the minors, and appeared to be on the fast track back to the majors when a wreck of America's most famous train ended his life.

William Edward Donovan was born October 13, 1876, in Lawrence, Massachusetts, the sixth child of carpenter Jeremiah Donovan and his wife, Mary. Young Bill played locally in Lawrence, and later in Waverly, New York. Donovan made his National League debut at age 21 on April 22, 1898, with Washington, where he split time as a pitcher and position player. He was unsuccessful at either. In 39 games as an outfielder, infielder, and pitcher, he batted just .165, though he hammered two homers. In 17 games as a hurler he compiled a 1–6 record, gave up 69 walks in 88 innings, and was dubbed Wild Bill, both for his erratic control and for his explosive temper.

In 1899 he landed in Brooklyn, which won pennants that year and in 1900. Donovan barely contributed, posting 1–2 records each season. Farmed to Hartford of the Eastern League in 1900, Bill appeared headed for release, but manager Ned Hanlon brought Bill back to Brooklyn. He was rewarded when Donovan developed in 1901, leading the National League with 25 wins against 15 losses and posting a 2.77 ERA. He also led or tied for the league lead in games pitched, saves, and walks. He finished 17–15 in 1902.

For 1903 Ban Johnson and the American League came calling, and Donovan jumped to Detroit just before the two leagues reached a peace treaty. The 5'11", 190-pound curveball artist posted identical 17–16 marks in his first two seasons in the Motor City. On March 4, 1905, he married Nellie Stephen, of Windsor, Ontario, and the couple lived with extended family on Trumbull Avenue, not far from Bennett Park. Donovan improved to 18–15 in 1905, but in 1906, suffering from a sore arm, he slumped to 9–15. He led a player revolt to oust manager Bill Armour, a move that angered Johnson.

Under new manager Hughey Jennings, Wild Bill bounced back in a big way. Donovan enjoyed his finest season in 1907, when he posted a 25–4 record with a 2.19 ERA, despite missing the first six weeks of the season because he was not "in shape" to pitch. In the campaign's most crucial series, Donovan escaped two bases-loaded jams to defeat Philadelphia, 5–4, on the last Friday in September. Then, after two days off, he came back on Monday to pitch all 17 innings of a tie game, the last 10 brilliantly, to keep Detroit in first place. In the Tigers' five-game loss to the Chicago Cubs in that year's World Series, Donovan pitched all 12 innings of Game One, which ended in a 3–3 tie, and lost Game Four, 6–1.

Donovan was brilliant again in 1908. He started late once again, and was suspended twice for umpire-baiting, but still won 18 of 25 decisions, including six by shutout, posted a 2.08 ERA, and issued just 53 walks in 242⅔ innings. He pitched 25 complete games—and was ejected on five occasions. He was 8–1 against the other three pennant contenders in one of baseball's greatest races, and he shut out the White Sox on the final day of the season in a winner-take-all match to clinch the AL flag. In the World Series Donovan lost twice to Chicago's Orval Overall, who allowed just one run in 18 innings, and the Tigers fell four games to one.

Wild Bill suffered from a sore arm again in 1909, but won eight of 15 decisions, including four by shutout. He was effective down the stretch as the Tigers held off the emerging Philadelphia Athletics by 3½ games and returned to the World Series for the third straight year. He went the distance in a 7–2 Game Two win, but gave up the first two runs in an 8–0 loss in Game Seven.

Sore arm behind him, Donovan won 17 games in 1910 and 10 games in 1911, but he started and won just one game in 1912, when he served as a scout. Navin farmed Donovan to Providence of the International League for managerial experience. Leaving his wife, Nellie, behind, Wild Bill became a part-owner of the Providence club the following year and appeared in 17 games as a pitcher in 1913 and 1914. That summer, the franchise was sold to Boston, and Donovan managed young Babe Ruth.

Donovan's work at Providence was rewarded when he was named manager of New York's floundering franchise in 1915. Early in the season Nellie sued Donovan for a divorce, which he did not contest. Wild Bill pitched 33⅔ innings, mostly on trips to Detroit, and guided the Yankees to a fifth-place finish. He continued to draw ejections and suspensions for arguing in 1916, and the Yankees climbed into fourth place.

In 1917, New York—dubbed the Donovanites—suffered a series of injuries and slipped to sixth. Ban Johnson orchestrated a transfer of St. Louis Cardinals manager Miller Huggins to New York, which resulted in the unpopular ouster of Smiling Bill.

Donovan spent the 1918 season as a coach for Jennings in Detroit, and also pitched in two games, winning one, to close out his major league career with a record of 186–139 and an ERA of 2.69. His playing career at an end, Donovan took over the Jersey City team in the International League and led the Skeeters in 1919 and 1920. After two seasons at Jersey City, owner William Baker tabbed Donovan to manage the woeful Philadelphia Phillies in 1921. The team started slowly, and in mid-July, Wild Bill was summoned to Chicago to testify at the Black Sox trial. Baker suggested that because of his familiarity with many of the figures in the case, Donovan surely "knew too much" about the 1919 World Series fix, and dismissed his manager. However, Wild Bill had been a favorite of Kenesaw Mountain Landis when he pitched for Detroit, and the new commissioner, after an investigation, ordered Baker to apologize and sent Donovan a letter that cleared him completely.

In 1922 New Haven owner George Weiss, later a Hall of Fame executive with the Yankees, hired Donovan on the advice of Ty Cobb, a shareholder in the club, and was rewarded with an Eastern League pennant and a postseason win over International League champion Baltimore. Donovan piloted the New Haven squad again in 1923, but the defending champs were clipped by Hartford and phenom Lou Gehrig.

In December newspapers speculated that Clark Griffith would name Donovan Washington's manager during baseball's winter meetings in Chicago. On Saturday, December 8, Wild Bill and Weiss departed Grand Central Station aboard the Twentieth Century Limited, the New York Central Railroad's flagship fast train to the Windy City.

Donovan stayed in his sleeping compartment in the forward part of the second section's final car, a Pullman observation–sleeper. Weiss, the younger man, had allowed Donovan the lower berth, and was already asleep in the top bunk. At 1:30 in the morning on December 9, in heavy fog and rain, the leading section of the Twentieth Century slammed into an abandoned automobile at a grade crossing at Forsyth, New York, 25 miles east of Erie, Pennsylvania. The second section of the train stopped behind the first, to examine the damage and remove the burning automobile, while the lead section resumed its journey. The trailing third section, attempting to catch up, bore down on the second, and the veteran engineer ran through a series of stop signals and smashed into the back of the second section, telescoping and splitting the rear car. Donovan was killed instantly, one of nine people to die, and arguably the most famous person ever killed in an American train wreck. Weiss suffered a serious back injury and a lacerated thigh.

Donovan was laid to rest in Holy Cross Cemetery in Yeadon, Pennsylvania, near Philadelphia.

DOUG SKIPPER

DETROIT

EDWIN HENRY KILLIAN
LEFT-HANDED PITCHER, 1904–1910

Remembered in Detroit as the pitcher who won both games of a doubleheader to effectively clinch the 1909 pennant, Ed Killian was also the stingiest pitcher in baseball history when it came to the home run. In his entire big league career the left-hander surrendered just nine homers, and he once went nearly four full seasons without allowing a single round-tripper. A flashy fielder and competent hitter, Killian was especially fond of the hidden-ball trick, which he and teammate Charley O'Leary successfully performed on several occasions.

Edwin Henry Killian was born in Racine, Wisconsin, on November 12, 1876, to wheelwright Andrew Killian and the former Etta Harliss, both German immigrants. As a youngster Killian was strong and thick-chested, and he became a stalwart pitcher for amateur and semipro clubs in Wisconsin and northern Illinois. In 1902 Killian signed his first professional contract with Rockford of the Three-I League. By the next season the 26-year-old southpaw was in the majors with Cleveland, winning three of eight starts in a late-season audition.

Standing a shade below six feet tall, Killian had a large jaw and big ears and bore a striking resemblance to Johnny Evers. Unlike Evers, however, Killian had broad shoulders, a barrel chest, and long arms. Arriving in the big leagues a little older than most other rookies, Killian had a confidence that other players new to the majors lacked and, perhaps in consequence, he often quarreled with teammates.

In February 1904 the Detroit Tigers, in need of left-handed pitching after selling Ed Siever to the St. Louis Browns, acquired Killian and pitcher Jesse Stovall for outfielder Billy Lush. With the Tigers, Killian pitched regularly, earning 14 wins against 20 defeats while posting a 2.48 ERA. For the season he hurled more than 330 innings and did not allow a home run, using an effective sinker to induce groundballs. Never a great strikeout pitcher, Killian relied heavily on his defense to convert hit batted balls into outs. On May 11, 1904, Killian hurled 14 innings of shutout ball against the Red Sox before Cy Young defeated Killian, 1–0.

Killian, who earned the nickname Twilight Ed for his tendency to pitch extra-inning games into the early darkness, enjoyed a fine season in 1905. That year he had 23 wins, including a league-leading eight shutouts.

The 1906 campaign was frustrating for Killian, as he saw his win total cut by more than half. After losing to Jack Chesbro and the Highlanders on August 2, 1906, 11–1, at Detroit's Bennett Park, Killian was furious at the lack of run support he was receiving. A week later he arrived at the park drunk, tore apart the clubhouse, and abandoned the team. Manager Bill Armour slapped Killian with a $200 fine and ordered the surly pitcher to remain in Detroit when the team embarked on their road trip August 14. Unrepentant, Killian did not start again until September 19, a game in which, finally, his teammates plated nine runs.

The outburst was typical of Killian's reaction to adversity. When things were going well, Killian was a valuable member of the team, but when things went sour, Killian was often at the center of a storm. For example, when young Ty Cobb played his first full season with Detroit in 1906, Killian joined other veterans in hazing the sensitive and high-strung rookie. It was Killian and his good friend, left fielder Matty McIntyre, who locked Cobb out of the shower during spring training in Augusta, infuriating the young Georgian and setting the stage for a season filled with in-fighting. Describing the Tigers 1906 season, historian Marc Okkonen wrote that the team was "beset by injuries, dissension, and a visible absence of spirit . . . something had to give for 1907."

That something was not Killian but McIntyre, who was benched, lost his job, and suffered a season-ending injury. With the contentious McIntyre out of the lineup, and with Cobb winning his first batting title, Detroit captured its first pennant. Killian returned to his winning ways, earning 25 wins behind a 1.78 ERA. Just about the only thing to go wrong for Killian, who also hit .320 for the season, came on August 7, when Philadelphia's Socks Seybold hit a home run to beat the lefty. It was the first homer allowed by Killian since September 18, 1903, 1,001 innings earlier.

In the first of a series of postseason disappointments, manager Hughey Jennings chose to use the sore-armed Killian out of the bullpen in the 1907 fall classic. In Game Three against the Cubs in Chicago's West Side Park, Killian relieved Siever (since reacquired by Detroit) with the Tigers trailing 4–0. He pitched four innings of one-run ball and did not get a decision. The Cubs defeated the Tigers in five games. After the Series, with a loser's share of $1,892 now in his pocket, Killian married Lottie McAzee, a flower girl at Detroit's Hotel Brunswick.

In 1908 the Tigers battled Chicago and Cleveland for the AL flag. Entering the season-ending three-game series in Chicago against the White Sox, Detroit held a 1½ game lead over the Naps and a 2½ game margin over the Sox. Killian started the first game, and more than 22,000 fans swarmed into South Side Park to see the contest. Uncharacteristically wild, Killian allowed three runs in the first without surrendering a hit, but settled down to mow down the Sox. Unfortunately, as had happened before in his career, Killian received little offensive support. Chicago's Doc White stymied the Tigers, and despite allowing just one hit, Killian lost the game, 3–1. Detroit did win the final game of the series to earn its second straight flag. Killian started Game One of the 1908 World Series but was roughed up by the Cubs, surrendering four runs in less than three innings. It was his last World Series appearance as the Tigers were once again beaten by the Cubs in five games.

Killian's 1909 season was bittersweet. He did not join the rotation until May, due to an unspecified arm injury. The ailment limited Killian to 19 starts for the season, but when he did pitch he was very effective, posting a 1.71 ERA and three shutouts to go along with 11 victories. In September, perhaps because the reduced number of starts had left Killian well-rested, Detroit manager Hughey Jennings relied heavily on Killian's left arm as the Tigers once again made a push for the pennant. After Twilight Ed lost yet another hard-luck game (to Walter Johnson, 2–0), the Tigers held a 2½ game lead on Philadelphia. With less than a week left in the season, Jennings started Killian in the first game of a doubleheader against Boston. Killian took a no-hitter into the eighth inning before allowing a single, eventually winning the game 5–0. Twenty minutes after that game ended, Jennings ran Killian out to the mound again to pitch the second game. The lefty again shackled Boston, winning the game 8–3 and effectively securing the pennant for the Tigers.

In a strange twist Jennings abandoned Killian in the 1909 World Series, passing over his late-season hero in the rotation. Jennings opted to start Ed Summers despite the fact that the pitcher had just overcome a bout with dysentery, and after the Series loss to the Pirates Jennings was roundly criticized by pundits. "His next and greatest mistake," the *Reach Guide* wrote the following spring, "was to take another chance with Summers in the fifth game, with Killian and [Ed] Willett ready and eager for the fray."

Killian sat on the bench and watched Detroit lose its third straight World Series. In 1910 Killian was the odd man out in the Tiger rotation and did not earn his first start until a month into the season. He was inconsistent at first, and then ineffective, losing his last three decisions before being sold to Toronto of the Eastern League on August 1. He had started nine games and won four, with a 3.04 ERA.

Set adrift from major league baseball, Killian went 2–6 in 10 games with Toronto in 1910 and spent the first part of the 1911 campaign there before moving on to Nashville of the Southern Association. In 1912 he began the season with the International League's Buffalo Bisons, but quickly drew his release and pitched the rest of that summer and the next for a semipro club in Detroit.

After his playing career Killian settled in Detroit, where he lived with his wife. Revered for his career as a Tiger, Ed worked odd jobs and took advantage of the free drinks and meals that adoring fans sent his way. Killian was hired as a mechanic by the Ford Motor Company in the early 1920s, and stayed there until he fell ill from cancer in early 1928. He died at age 51 on July 18, 1928, his wife earning a generous pension from Tigers owner Frank Navin, who called Killian the "finest left-hander ever to wear a Detroit uniform." Killian was buried in Woodlawn Cemetery in Detroit.

DAN HOLMES

DETROIT

Praised for his outfield defense and savvy base running skills, Matty McIntyre was the starting left fielder and leadoff hitter on two Detroit Tiger pennant-winning teams. Although a broken ankle in 1907 somewhat diminished his defensive abilities, McIntyre was still able to contribute with the bat upon his return and was considered to be among the best left-handed batters facing left-handed pitching. In 1908 he led the major leagues in runs scored and was part of one of the greatest outfields of all time along with Ty Cobb and Sam Crawford. Long a nemesis of Cobb and long rumored to be on the trading block, McIntyre was nonetheless a popular player on the teams for which he played, and he led a number of all-star teams to Cuba during his off-seasons.

Matthew W. McIntyre, one of seven sons of Irish immigrants James McIntyre and Bridget Larkin, was born on June 12, 1880, in the village of Pawcatuck near Stonington, Connecticut. Early in his childhood his family moved to Staten Island, where he attended primary school. He learned baseball on the Staten Island sandlots late in his boyhood and rapidly demonstrated skill in the sport. In June 1901 Augusta (Maine) of the New England League signed him on to play left field. Quickly taking over the third batting spot, McIntyre hit .292. Upon the disbanding of the Augusta team, Connie Mack signed McIntyre to play for the Philadelphia Athletics in their inaugural year, and the young outfielder made his major league debut on July 3, 1901.

Although McIntyre batted a solid .276 in 82 games with the Athletics, he was "not considered fast enough" to stay in the majors and was turned over to Newark, Philadelphia's unofficial farm team in the Eastern League. He spent all of 1902 in Newark, playing left field, hitting in the middle of the order, and batting .256. After the season ended he was traded to Buffalo of the

Eastern League, where he continued to play left field. Hitting over .400 at midseason, McIntyre started to get noticed in the press. He finished 1903 with a .342 average and was drafted in September by the Tigers.

McIntyre was so impressive at the Tigers' 1904 spring training camp that one season preview called him a "find." He quickly lived up to this billing with good base running, solid fielding, and "reliable" hitting, going on to bat .253 in 152 games while batting second in the lineup. A Detroit newspaper elaborated on this success, noting, "The sensation of the team, and the one man who stands head and shoulders above anything taken from the minor league this year, is left fielder McIntyre. He is developing into a grand baseball player in every department. He seems to have the faculty of bunting and beating out his bunts, or of hitting the ball to the farthest end of the lot. The general opinion in this city seems to be that McIntyre, with one more year in the big league, will have Willie Keeler skinned in every manner. On the bases he has shown wonderful speed and the same is true of his fielding."

McIntyre enjoyed another solid season in 1905, batting .263 and moving into the leadoff position late in the year. He also started to develop an ability to hit left-handers. Former teammate George Moriarty recalled that "Matty reversed the order by requesting the southpaws to only throw the 'hook' when he was in batting practice. He also sought out kid pitchers who threw left-handed, and after regular batting practice he biffed their slants all over the lot. As a reward Matty was never yanked out of the lineup in a pinch when he faced a left-hander. His intensive batting-practice program made him one of the greatest left-handed batsmen who ever faced a southpaw."

Due to the late August addition of Ty Cobb to the Tiger outfield, 1905 turned out to be a pivotal year for

McIntyre. Within a week the two were at odds. In the bottom of the ninth inning of a close game against the White Sox, Cobb overzealously pursued a fly ball that was in McIntyre's territory, which caused McIntyre to drop the ball and nearly lose the game. The play contributed to McIntyre's taking a quick dislike of Cobb. Their feud escalated the following year, as McIntyre actively participated in hazing of the brash rookie and Cobb fought back.

McIntyre started off the 1906 season in fine form, garnering praise from manager Bill Armour for a number of spectacular catches, but then quickly fell out of Armour's favor. In late June the manager roasted him for not chasing a ball down to the fence. McIntyre's refusal to return to the field led to his being suspended for "indifferent work." In response he fired off a telegram to the *Washington Post* in which he expressed his desire to play in Washington. He also prepared letters to the National Commission, demanding his right to play, and threatened to jump to an outlaw league. The Tigers in turn announced that all offers to trade for or purchase McIntyre would be declined. During the suspension McIntyre showed up every day at the park and practiced with the Tigers, announcing his intent to "play his best ball for the club." The Tigers, however, would not reinstate him until he formally reported and asked to play. The issue was settled when McIntyre gave in just before the team departed for a long road trip. After the suspension, rumors of dissension among Tiger players began appearing in the press and McIntyre's poor relationship with Cobb was brought to light. McIntyre finished the season batting .260 with a career-best 29 stolen bases, but whispers of his imminent departure were rampant.

Early in 1907 Chicago, Boston, and Washington made offers for McIntyre, which the Tigers turned down. Reportedly due to his inability to get along with Cobb, McIntyre refused to sign a contract with the Tigers until just before opening day. His season lasted only 20 games, as he broke an ankle sliding feet first into first base while attempting to avoid a collision with Boston's Bob Unglaub in a May game. While he was recovering from his injury, the Tigers used McIntyre to scout players in the minor leagues.

McIntyre returned to the field in 1908 and enjoyed his best season at the plate, helping the Tigers defend their American League championship. In the last and pennant-deciding game of the season, at Chicago, his first-inning single off Doc White sparked a four-run rally that secured the title for the Tigers. Many observers thought that McIntyre was as valuable as any player on the team. Serving as the perfect leadoff hitter, he led the league with 105 runs scored and 258 times on base, posting a .392 OBP.

His last years with the Tigers were not productive. After recovering from a battle with appendicitis, McIntyre posted a poor .244 average in 1909 and was limited to three at-bats in the World Series. Both his baserunning and defensive abilities seemed to be hindered by the ankle that he had broken back in 1907. In the off-season he managed a team, made up mostly of Tiger players, that played a series of games in Cuba. The experience was so positive for him that he repeated the trip in subsequent years. His 1910 season echoed his 1909 campaign, and he gradually lost playing time to Davy Jones. With the franchise tiring of McIntyre's annual salary holdouts, the club finally agreed to sell him to the White Sox for between $2,000 and $3,000.

McIntyre was well-received by the White Sox and quickly became a crowd favorite as he turned in a stellar year at the plate. Playing most of his games in right field, McIntyre scored 102 runs in 1911 and posted a career-best .323 average. That off-season he returned to Cuba—not as a barnstormer, but as a full-fledged member of the Cuban Winter League's Almendares team, a squad that also included Cuban pitching legend José Méndez.

The following year, however, McIntyre was a shadow of his former self, reporting late to the club and batting just .167 in 84 at-bats. In September McIntyre was sold to San Francisco of the Pacific Coast League, where he batted .336 but declined a contract offer for the following season. Returning east, he hooked on with Providence of the International League, where he played for two seasons. In 1914 the Providence team won the International League title behind the pitching of Carl Mays and Babe Ruth as well as the hitting of McIntyre, who posted a .310 average.

McIntyre took over as manager of the Lincoln (Nebraska) Tigers in the Western League for the 1915 season. Late in the 1916 campaign he was engaged as manager of the Mobile Sea Gulls in the Southern Association, where he remained until a franchise shake-up in May of 1917. He returned to Detroit later that year, where he played for local semipro clubs "more for the pleasure which it could afford him [better] than any baseball franchise could."

Following a siege of influenza, McIntyre died at age 39 on April 2, 1920, in St. Mary's Hospital, suffering from Bright's disease, a kidney ailment known today as nephritis. Survived by his wife, the former Grace Kennedy, McIntyre was buried in St. Peter's Cemetery on Staten Island.

RICHARD SMILEY

DETROIT

TYRUS RAYMOND COBB
CENTER FIELDER, 1905–1926; MANAGER, 1921–1926

Perhaps the most competitive and complex personality ever to appear in a big league uniform, Ty Cobb was the dominant player in the American League during the Deadball Era, and arguably the greatest player in the history of the game. During his 24-year big league career Cobb captured a record 11 (or 12) batting titles, batted over .400 three times, and won the 1909 Triple Crown. Upon his retirement he held career records for games played (3,035), at-bats (11,434), runs (2,246), hits (4,189), total bases (5,854), and batting average (.366). Cobb also retired with the twentieth-century record for most career stolen bases, with 892.

Having adopted an aggressive, take-no-prisoners style of play that mirrored his fiery temperament and abrasive personality, Cobb dominated the game in the batter's box and on the base paths. At the plate the 6′1″, 175-pound left-handed swinger often gripped the bat with his hands several inches apart, but usually brought them back together during his swing. A powerful hitter, Cobb led the league in slugging percentage eight times, and paced the circuit in doubles three times and triples four times. He was also a scientific hitter who liked to beat out bunts and infield grounders for base hits. After 1920 Cobb became a passionate defender of the Deadball Era-style of play, derisively mocking the "swing crazy" batters of the modern game who had neglected the inside strategies mastered by him.

Tyrus Raymond Cobb was born December 18, 1886, in The Narrows, Georgia, the first of three children of William Herschel Cobb, a school teacher, and Amanda Chitwood Cobb, who came from a prominent Georgia family. Young Ty developed a passion for baseball, and by the time he was 14 he was playing on the Royston, Georgia, town team. Cobb soon became a standout on the team and began to focus his energies on baseball, a development that did not please his father.

The elder Cobb was an educated man, and wanted his son to be a professional. Young Ty, however, although highly intelligent, did not enjoy his studies, and his father's efforts to interest him in law or medicine were unsuccessful. Cobb nonetheless loved, respected, and even idolized his father. W.H. Cobb was by far the most influential person in Ty's life. As Cobb related much later, "My father was the greatest man I ever knew. He was a scholar, state senator, editor, and philosopher. I worshiped him. He was the only man who ever made me do his bidding."

In 1904 Cobb, encouraged by a Royston teammate who had had a failed professional tryout, contacted teams in the newly formed South Atlantic (Sally) League. He received a response from the Augusta (Georgia) Tourists, inviting Cobb to spring training provided the boy pay his own expenses, and offering him a contract for $50 per month, contingent on Cobb's making the team. For young Tyrus this was a dream come true, a chance to play professional baseball. His father tried to talk him out of the decision, but finally relented, telling his son, "You've chosen. So be it, son. Go get it out of your system, and let us hear from you."

Cobb was released just two games into his stay with Augusta, but immediately received an offer from a semipro team in Anniston, Alabama. Cobb called his father, who advised him, "Go for it. And I want to tell you one other thing—don't come home a failure." These words were to have a great impact in shaping the life and baseball career of Ty Cobb. Cobb played well with Anniston, and by August he received a telegram from Augusta asking him to rejoin the team.

The year 1905 was to be a fateful one for Cobb. He reported to Augusta for spring training, and got the chance to play in two exhibition games against the

Detroit Tigers. The Tigers trained in Augusta, in return for an option to purchase one player from the Augusta team at a later date. Cobb made an impression on the Tigers with his talent and his aggressive, even reckless, style of play.

Augusta got off to a poor start, and Cobb's play was uninspiring. In July, however, veteran George Leidy replaced Andy Roth as manager and took Cobb under his wing. He told young Ty that he was wasting his talent, and schooled him in the finer points of the game. Cobb became the league's best hitter, and Detroit and other teams began to take notice. The tutelage of Leidy was the turning point in Cobb's career.

Unfortunately, August 1905 brought a tragedy and a major turning point in Ty Cobb's life. On the evening of August 8, W.H. Cobb had left home, announcing to his wife that he was going to their farm and would not be back that night. As it turned out, the elder Cobb suspected his wife of infidelity, and he returned to the house with a pistol later that night. Shortly after midnight he climbed up onto the porch roof and attempted to enter the bedroom through a window. Exactly what happened next is unknown, but Amanda Cobb put two bullets into her husband, killing him. She claimed to have mistaken her husband for a burglar. A coroner's inquest ordered her arrest on the charge of manslaughter. A grand jury indicted her, but at trial in March 1906 she was eventually acquitted.

After a week of mourning and taking care of family business, Ty Cobb rejoined his team. Before the month was out the Tigers exercised their option and purchased Cobb for $700. Normally, this would have been a great moment, the realization of a dream, but the shadow of the tragedy hung over the teenager. In his autobiography Cobb wrote, "In my grief, it didn't matter much....I only thought, Father won't know it."

Cobb made his big league debut on August 30, 1905. He appeared in 41 games that season, compiling a modest .240 batting average. During this first season he got the typical rookie hazing. This was perhaps poor treatment, given his state of grief. Between that and the fact that this was his first time out of the South, Cobb was unable to deal with the hazing, which led to resentments with his teammates that lasted many years.

The 1906 season was a hard one for Cobb from the outset. In spring training, while his mother's trial was ongoing, he continued to feud with his teammates. Cobb found his hats ruined and his bats cut. In his autobiography Cobb described the ostracism and hazing by his teammates as "the most miserable and humiliating experience I've ever been through."

On the field Cobb played well, winning the center field job against strong competition; however, the stress wore him down, and he was out of the lineup the second half of July and all of August with what may have been an emotional and physical collapse. He returned in September, and finished the season with a .316 batting average in 98 games.

These events of 1905 and 1906 changed Cobb forever. Already strong willed and competitive, Cobb became a loner, at war with the world. His relations with teammates eventually improved, and Cobb did make some lasting friendships, but his will to succeed at any cost never changed. Late in life, when asked by Al Stump why he fought so hard in baseball, Cobb explained, "I did it for my father....I knew he was watching me and I never let him down."

The 1907 season marked Cobb's arrival as a superstar. The Georgian led the league in hits, RBI, and batting average, carrying the Tigers to their first American League pennant. He and the team repeated the performance the next two seasons, and Cobb added his only home run title in 1909 to take the Triple Crown. He also led the league in stolen bases in 1907 and 1909. The Tigers lost all three World Series, the first two to the powerful Chicago Cubs and the third in a seven-game thriller to the Pittsburgh Pirates. Over these 17 World Series games (the only ones in which he would appear), Cobb had an undistinguished .262 batting average with nine RBI and four stolen bases.

During this period Cobb began to develop a reputation for controversy. In August 1908 he left the team for six days, in the middle of a tight pennant race, to marry Charlie Lombard in Augusta. In August 1909 Cobb slid into third on a close play, slightly cutting the arm of Philadelphia Athletics third baseman Frank Baker. Although Cobb was within his rights, emotions ran high in Philadelphia, and Cobb received death threats when the Tigers played in Philadelphia in mid-September. Meanwhile, in a more serious matter, Cobb got into a fight in Cleveland with George Stanfield, a hotel night watchman and an African-American. In the aftermath a warrant was issued for Cobb's arrest and Stanfield filed a civil suit. The criminal charges were settled after the season was over, with Cobb pleading guilty to assault and battery, for which he paid a $100 fine, and the civil suit was settled out of court.

During and after his career Ty Cobb was involved in a number of violent altercations. Some of the best known of these incidents were with African-Americans. In recent years concern over Cobb's racial attitudes has often diminished his reputation.

Cobb certainly did not oppose racial segregation in baseball or elsewhere, and all evidence shows that

his attitudes were typical of his times and his Georgia upbringing. Years later he took a somewhat different view, however. In an Associated Press article dated January 29, 1952, Cobb came out in favor of integration in baseball, stating, "Certainly it is O.K. for them to play. I see no reason in the world why we shouldn't compete with colored athletes," but went on to qualify his statement by adding, "as long as they conduct themselves with politeness and gentility." Later, Cobb wrote to Al Stump that segregation was a "lousy rule."

Cobb's style of play relied more on strategy, daring, and quick thinking than pure talent. He was always one step ahead of the opposition, doing the unexpected, especially on the base paths. In *The Glory Of Their Times*, Larry Ritter quoted Sam Crawford, who did not like Cobb, as saying, "He didn't outhit the opposition and he didn't outrun them. He outthought them!" Cobb dominated the Deadball Era both through his performance and his style of play. Runs were hard to come by, and Cobb was always looking for an edge. At bat he studied pitchers, learning their weaknesses. On the base paths he was always the aggressor, trying to create opportunities. Cobb later told of how he sometimes ran the bases recklessly in one-sided games to plant fear in the minds of the opposition, which led to errors in close games where a momentary hesitation by an opposing fielder could prove decisive. When on the bases, Cobb would kick the bag—not because it was a habit, which everyone assumed, but because by kicking it toward the next base he could pick up a few precious inches if he decided to steal a base.

By 1910 Cobb was recognized as the biggest star in the American League; however, he remained unpopular with his teammates and opposing players for his attitude and rugged style of play. This led to another major controversy—an attempt to fix the 1910 American League batting title. Cobb and Cleveland's popular star Napoleon Lajoie were locked in a tight race for the American League crown. The Browns manager, Jack "Peach Pie" O'Connor, who hated Cobb, decided to make sure that Lajoie caught up with Cobb; in a season-ending doubleheader between St. Louis and Cleveland, he ordered rookie third baseman Red Corriden to "play back on the edge of the [outfield] grass." Lajoie responded by dumping seven bunt singles down the third base line, as part of an 8-for-8 day that seemingly gave him the title.

Cobb's teammates wired Lajoie their congratulations, but the press railed against the obvious fraud. American League president Ban Johnson investigated the matter, but, in typical fashion for baseball officials of that day, decided to sweep the scandal under the rug. The official figures, however, ended up showing that Cobb had won the batting championship, thanks to one game's results being counted twice. The clerical error was discovered only years later, and who should be considered the 1910 AL batting champion is still a matter of controversy. Lajoie has the higher average, but Cobb is still recognized by Major League Baseball as the official batting champion.

Another major controversy in Cobb's career occurred in 1912, and it led to the first players' strike. During a game in New York on May 15 of that year, Cobb was subjected to vicious and unrelenting taunting from the fans, especially a disabled man named Claude Lueker, who for several years had made sport of heckling Cobb whenever the Tigers visited Hilltop Park. Finally, unable to stand the abuse and urged on by his teammates, Cobb went into the stands and attacked Lueker. When he was informed of the incident, Ban Johnson suspended Cobb indefinitely. Despite their dislike for Cobb, his teammates were outraged, and announced that they would not play again until Cobb was reinstated. After a one-game farce in which the Tigers fielded a team of semipro players, the matter was resolved when Cobb's suspension was reduced to ten days.

Cobb continued to excel on the field throughout the decade, clearly becoming the game's dominant player, and in the opinion of most contemporaries the greatest player in baseball history. The 1911 season was one of his finest, as he batted .420 and led the league in runs, hits, doubles, triples, RBI, slugging percentage, and stolen bases. He regularly led the league in batting, and was at or near the top of most offensive categories.

In addition to his success on the field, the second decade of the twentieth century brought economic affluence to Ty Cobb. He was the game's highest-paid player, aided by his almost annual holdouts and the 1914–1915 Federal League war. Cobb also made money outside baseball, including investments in cotton in the commodities market, and he became an early investor in both Coca-Cola and United Motors (which later merged with General Motors). Cobb's investments made him a rich man, and they outlasted the Great Depression. At the time of his death in 1961 his estate was estimated at $12 million.

Despite Cobb's continued excellence, the Tigers generally finished far out of first place after 1909. Detroit fans and management wanted Cobb to succeed his long-time friend and boss, Hughey Jennings. In 1921 Cobb finally accepted and became the player–manager of the Tigers. The team improved under Cobb, but other than in 1924 the Tigers were not a real factor in the pennant race under his leadership. He did, however, have a great deal to do with the development of Tigers hitters, especially future Hall of Famer Harry Heilmann.

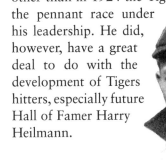
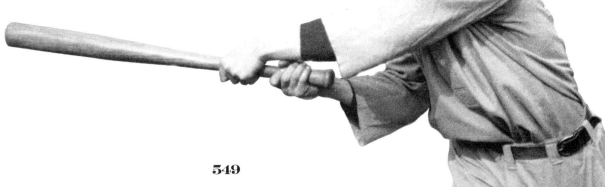

In 1926 the Tigers fell to sixth place in the American League, but they had a respectable 79–75 record, so it was a surprise when, on November 3, 1926, Cobb announced that he was stepping down as manager of the Tigers and retiring from baseball. Soon thereafter, player–manager Tris Speaker of the second-place Cleveland Indians announced that he was also stepping down and retiring from the game. A few weeks later, the reason was made public: former Detroit pitcher Hubert "Dutch" Leonard claimed that he, Cobb, Speaker, and Cleveland outfielder Joe Wood had fixed a game between Detroit and Cleveland on September 25, 1919.

Had it been Leonard's word alone, it is unlikely that the charge would have been taken seriously. Cobb, who was supposed to benefit from the fix, went only 1-for-5, albeit with two runs scored and two steals, while Speaker, supposedly throwing the game, had three hits in five trips to the plate, including two triples. (Wood and Leonard did not play in the game.) However, Leonard supplied two letters written to him in the fall of 1919, one from Wood that clearly indicates that bets were placed (although Wood states that Cobb did not bet) and one from Cobb himself, indicating that an attempt to bet was made, but that it did not work out.

While there was strong evidence that bets were placed or, in the case of Cobb, a bet was attempted, there was no evidence of a fix other than Leonard's word, and he refused to travel to Chicago to face Cobb and Speaker at a hearing. It was also common knowledge that Leonard nursed a grudge against the two stars. On January 27, 1927, Landis ruled that Cobb and Speaker were not guilty, stating, "These players have not been, nor are they now, found guilty of fixing a ball game. By no decent system of justice could such finding be made."

In the aftermath Cobb threatened a lawsuit, and enlisted the help of several prominent politicians to launch an investigation into Organized Baseball, but then he received a lucrative offer from Connie Mack, Philadelphia owner and manager. Mack was one of the few men in baseball that Cobb truly admired and respected, and Ty agreed to join the Athletics, playing with that club for two seasons before announcing his second and final retirement.

Cobb's life after baseball was less rewarding than his career as a player. Secure financially, he led a life of leisure, but his family life was less than ideal. After a number of rifts he and Charlie Cobb were divorced in 1947, and Cobb's relationship with his five children was strained. He married Frances Fairburn in late 1949, but by 1956 this marriage also ended in divorce.

Ty Cobb's health began to fail him in the late 1950s, and he became an alcoholic. Realizing that he was in decline, he finally agreed to do what he had always refused to consider: write his autobiography. He teamed up with Al Stump on *My Life in Baseball— The True Record*, which was published posthumously. In summing up his life to Stump, Cobb stated, "I had to fight all my life to survive. They all were against me...tried every dirty trick to cut me down. But I beat the bastards and left them in the ditch."

Ty Cobb died at age 74 on July 17, 1961, in Emory Hospital in Atlanta, of prostate cancer. He was buried in Rose Hill Cemetery in his hometown of Royston, beside his parents and his sister.

DAN GINSBURG

DETROIT

HERMAN A. "GERMANY" SCHAEFER
SECOND BASEMAN, 1905–1909

Always willing to entertain the crowd, Germany Schaefer's antics as a player and coach helped pave the way for later baseball clowns. An infielder with decent range and an average bat, Schaefer had impeccable timing, and more than once delighted fans with clutch performances, including legendary homers off Rube Waddell and Doc White. He gained his greatest notoriety for "stealing first base," a maneuver that led to a rule change.

Herman A. Schaefer was born on February 4, 1877, to German immigrant parents in Chicago in the South Side's Levee District. This rough neighborhood was world-famous for prostitution and vice, including a patchwork of ethnic gangs which often served as a violent backdrop for Schaefer's youth. Nevertheless, Schaefer had an enjoyable childhood, gravitating to the game of baseball, which he and other neighborhood kids played in sandlots and in the streets. By the time he was 18 Schaefer's defensive skill and slugging prowess gained attention. A right-handed hitter and thrower with solid shoulders and short legs, the 5′9″ Schaefer was quick and agile on the diamond.

After a few years playing semipro ball in Chicago, Schaefer signed on with a semipro club in Sioux Falls, South Dakota, in 1898. His outstanding play with that team spurred an offer from Kansas City of the Western League, where he suited up for parts of two seasons, mostly at shortstop. In 1901 his contract was acquired by St. Paul of the same league, and after a solid performance he was purchased by the Chicago Cubs late in the season. He made his major league debut on October 5, 1901, and banged out three hits in five at-bats in two games.

Back with the Cubs in 1902, the 25-year-old Schaefer played third base, but lost his job in midseason due to a terrible .196 batting average. He did partake in a bit

of history on September 13, when he played third base in the game that featured Joe Tinker, Johnny Evers, and Frank Chance together for the first time in what would become their legendary infield spots. After the season, however, the Cubs returned Schaefer to St. Paul, where he spent another season before the Saints released him in February 1904. Schaefer then signed with Seattle of the outlaw Pacific Coast League, but after the PCL reached a peace agreement with Organized Baseball, a dispute broke out over his services and he was ultimately assigned to Milwaukee of the American Association. In his lone season with the Brewers, Schaefer honed his defensive skills, improving his range and accuracy while also perfecting several daring baserunning plays that he would later use in the majors. One Milwaukee observer described Schaefer: "He was a well-built chap, wearing an astonishing pair of shoulders, and showed rare speed and fighting ability."

In 1905 the struggling Detroit Tigers were in desperate need of middle infielders. Schaefer, purchased from Milwaukee, joined the team and fit in immediately, most notably with infielder Charley O'Leary, a fellow Chicago native. The two were best friends both on and off the field, and later briefly teamed in a vaudeville act. In his first season with the Tigers, Schaefer proved his worth. "Herman Schaffer [sic], second baseman and principal prop of the Detroit infield, is one of the few ball players whose value to a team is not shown by statistics," wrote one observer. In 1905 Schaefer led American League second basemen in putouts, while hitting .244 with nine triples.

The Prince, as he was often called because of his flashy showmanship on the field, always enjoyed performing in front of his hometown crowd, and on June 24, 1906, he turned in one of the most memorable games of his career. Schaefer was called on to pinch hit with two outs in the ninth, a runner on base, and his Tigers down by a run. According to teammate Davy Jones in *The Glory of Their Times*, Germany announced to the crowd: "Ladies and gentlemen, you are now looking at Herman Schaefer, better known as 'Herman the Great,' acknowledged by one and all to be the greatest pinch-hitter in the world. I am now going to hit the ball into the left field bleachers. Thank you." Facing Chicago's Doc White, Schaefer proceeded to hit the first pitch into the left field bleachers for a game-winning homer. As he made his way around the diamond, Germany supposedly slid into every base, announcing his progress as if it were a horse race as he went around. "Schaefer leads at the half!" and so on. After hook-sliding into home he popped up, doffed his cap, bowed, and said, "Ladies and Gentlemen, this concludes this afternoon's performance. I thank you for your kind attention." Newspaper accounts of the game confirm the essential (and dramatic) baseball details, but not the fanciful embellishments offered by Jones.

Once, while facing Rube Waddell, one of his favorite targets for verbal abuse, Schaefer reportedly launched a long home run out of Philadelphia's Columbia Park and razzed the left-hander as he trotted around the bases. Carrying his bat with him, Schaefer pretended it was a gun, "shooting" Rube as he moved from bag to bag. Among Schaefer's other supposed antics: during a steady rain he once appeared at the plate wearing rubber boots and a raincoat, and he once ventured to the plate sporting a fake black mustache. In both instances his outlandish behavior reportedly resulted in his ejection. Schaefer was also a master of the hidden-ball trick, which he performed in the 1907 World Series.

In 1907 Schaefer was named captain of the Tigers and helped the team to back-to-back pennants. Germany was one of the few Tigers who befriended Ty Cobb, and he was a key figure in the Tigers late-season drive to win the 1907 pennant. Despite his popularity in Detroit, late in 1909 Schaefer was traded to Washington, for whom he played through 1914. In 1911 he enjoyed his finest offensive season, batting .334 in 125 games. During his last few years with Washington, Germany spent more time in the coach's box than on the field. He was an accomplished sign-stealer and heckler, qualities integral to coaching during the era. One publication described Schaefer as "next to Hughey Jennings, the best grass-puller in captivity."

On at least one occasion Schaefer stole first base. On August 4, 1911, in the bottom of the ninth, Schaefer stole second, hoping to draw a throw and allow teammate Clyde Milan, who was on third with the potential winning run, to steal home. White Sox catcher Fred Payne did not fall for the gambit, however, so Schaefer, now on second, took his lead toward the first-base side of the bag and promptly stole first on a subsequent pitch. Sox manager Hugh Duffy came out to argue, and while Duffy jawed with umpire Tommy Connolly, Schaefer scampered for second again. This time Schaefer got caught in a rundown, as had been his intention, and Milan dashed for home, where he was nipped to end the inning. Schaefer and his teammates then argued unsuccessfully that the play should be nullified because the White Sox had ten players on the field, although Duffy had not been an active player since 1908. The official scorer credited Schaefer with only one stolen base, but he "had a perfect right to go from second back to first," umpire Connolly insisted after the game. It has been widely reported that Schaefer also stole first base on another occasion, against Cleveland in 1908, although the details usually given are contradictory and the incident is almost certainly a fabrication.

Schaefer continued to fine-tune his crazed antics as a player–coach. Umpire Silk O'Loughlin chased him from a game in Chicago on June 8, 1912, for eating popcorn in the coach's box, and Schaefer also began to perform tricks, like tight-rope walking the foul line and using two bats to "row across the grass." His performances were later incorporated by baseball clowns Nick Altrock and Al Schacht. While he enjoyed drawing laughter, Schaefer defended his comedic coaching as important to team success. "Is humorous coaching of value to a team? I think so. It is valuable for two reasons. It keeps our fellow in good spirits, and it sometimes distracts the opposing players. . . . I guess [Clark] Griffith thinks so also, for he encourages me in my tomfoolery," Schaefer told *The Sporting News* in 1912.

After a stint with Newark in the Federal League in 1915, Schaefer served as player and coach for the Yankees in 1916 and the Indians in 1918. Ever the comedian, when the First World War broke out, Schaefer announced he would change his name to Liberty Schaefer, much as sauerkraut had been renamed liberty cabbage.

John McGraw hired Schaefer as a scout in 1919, but when Germany was taking a train through upstate New York on May 16, he died suddenly of a hemorrhage in Saranac Lake. The 42-year-old had been battling pulmonary tuberculosis. A bachelor, Schaefer was survived by a sister and buried in Chicago's Saint Boniface Cemetery.

DAN HOLMES

DETROIT

David Jefferson Jones
Left fielder, 1906–1912, 1918

In his interview with Lawrence Ritter for his classic, *The Glory of Their Times*, Davy Jones described the kaleidoscope of players who enlivened the Deadball Era. "Baseball attracted all sorts of people in those days," he explained. "We had stupid guys, smart guys, tough guys, mild guys, crazy guys, college men, slickers from the city, and hicks from the country." At times Jones himself could seem a bit like all of the above. A rare collegian who possessed a law degree and later went on to a prosperous career in pharmacology, the intelligent Jones could also be quick-tempered and impulsive. He had run-ins with umpires, managers, players, and fans, and once even bounced a knife-wielding robber from his drugstore. During his first years in the pros he jumped so many contracts that the press nicknamed him the Kangaroo. When he finally settled down with the Detroit Tigers, the fleet-footed and pesky Jones became one of the game's best (though oft-injured) leadoff hitters.

David Jefferson Jones was born on June 30, 1880, in Cambria, Wisconsin (about 40 miles north of Madison), to Welsh immigrants. His father was a city street commissioner. Davy attended elementary school in Cambria and high school in nearby Portage, where he lettered in baseball, football, and track. A very fast runner, Davy used his speed to earn money in foot races.

After graduating from high school, Jones worked on the railroads for a short time before enrolling at Dixon College in northern Illinois in the fall of 1899. His skill in sports had earned him a scholarship to Dixon, where he studied law, eventually completing a two-year degree program. In 1901, during his final year at Dixon, the baseball team traveled to Rockford for a couple of exhibition games with the local minor league club. After helping to drub the professionals on successive days, Davy was persuaded to sign a contract and report to Rockford upon completion of the college season.

Appearing in 77 games for Rockford in 1901, Davy won the Three-I League batting title with an average of .384 and attracted the attention of big league scouts. His eventual debut in the major leagues was not without a bit of controversy, however. Rockford sold him to the Chicago National League club, but Jones jumped his first contract, electing to stay closer to home and finish the 1901 season with the American League's Milwaukee Brewers, where he batted .173 in 52 at-bats.

When the Brewers moved to St. Louis after the 1901 season, Jones claimed free agency, saying his AL contract contained language that prevented the transfer of a player to a new city without his consent. The young lawyer signed with Chicago, which still owned his rights within Organized Baseball. Soon, however, he jumped back to St. Louis (later claiming he was bulldozed into signing), but played in only 15 games with the Browns in 1902 before jumping back to Chicago after Orphans owner James Hart offered him a 50 percent raise and a $500 signing bonus. Davy left his Browns teammates without a word on the morning of May 14 and was patrolling center field for the Cubs that afternoon. Though a major leaguer for barely a month all told, Davy was quickly gaining a reputation for jumping contracts whenever a better offer came along. All told, he had walked out on four different contracts in a nine-month span. The *Chicago Tribune* referred to him as a "rubber-leg," and Chicago fans even quit teasing fellow outfielder Jimmy Slagle, another noted jumper, out of deference to Jones. As Jones himself said later, "a contract didn't mean anything in those days."

When healthy Davy was Chicago's starting center fielder, but injuries and illness cut into his playing time. In August 1902 he contracted typhoid fever and did not return to the lineup, missing the final 43 games; in 1903 he missed only nine games and hit .282. During a Fourth of July doubleheader in 1904, however, he collided with Pittsburgh catcher Harry Smith and suffered a broken leg. Upon his return to the lineup in mid-August, his play was greatly hampered by the injury. Although he played in most of the club's remaining games, with limited speed and mobility Davy's average dipped and his outfield range (he was now in right field) vanished. When the leg failed to show improvement the following spring, he was sold to the American Association's Minneapolis Millers just prior to Chicago's departure for spring training in Los Angeles.

Jones played center field for the 1905 Millers. Under the tutelage of manager W. H. Watkins, his base running and defense greatly improved as he recovered from the leg injury and learned to harness his tremendous speed. His .346 average placed second in the league, and his overall play attracted the attention of Detroit's Frank Navin and Bill Armour, who had come to scout catcher Boss Schmidt. The Tigers bought three Minneapolis players—Jones, Schmidt, and pitcher Ed Siever—after the Millers played a doubleheader in Toledo.

Reporting to the Tigers in 1906, Davy moved into the starting center field role. Injured in late August Jones appeared in 84 games for Detroit, batting .260 but drawing 41 walks for a .347 OBP, second-best on the team after Ty Cobb. The Tigers finished a disappointing sixth in the league. Davy enjoyed his finest season in 1907, as the Tigers captured their first American League pennant. Switched to left field and batting leadoff, Jones posted a .357 OBP and scored 101 runs, second-best in the American League. Davy also swiped a career-best 30 bases, tied for eighth in the league. In that year's World Series Jones performed well against the team that had discarded him, batting .353 with a .476 OBP, but the Tigers lost to the Chicago Cubs in five games.

Despite the solid year, Jones sat on the bench for much of the 1908 season as Matty McIntyre, the Tiger veteran whom he had displaced in 1907, reclaimed left field. The result was Jones's most unsatisfying season to date. Appearing in only 56 games, often only as a pinch hitter or runner, he batted a mere .207. The following season Davy once more was forced to defer to McIntyre, playing in only 69 games, but when he did play he was far more valuable to the Tigers than in 1908, scoring 44 runs. In the World Series against the Pirates, it was McIntyre who was relegated to the bench and Davy started every game. Despite scoring six runs in the seven games and bouncing a homer into the stands to lead off Game Five, Davy batted only .231 as the Tigers lost their third straight World Series.

Detroit failed to capture another pennant, but Davy remained a valuable part-time player for the Tigers from 1910 through 1912, though his combative temperament caused numerous headaches for Tigers management. In June 1910 Jones got into a fistfight with his former St. Louis manager, Jimmy McAleer, then managing the Washington club, and was handed a fine and week-long suspension. In May 1912 Jones served as a catalyst for Cobb's famous brawl with a fan in New York's Hilltop Park. After Cobb endured several innings of vitriolic abuse from a spectator, Jones reportedly said to Cobb, "If you don't go up to knock that guy's block off, I'm going to do it!" When Cobb charged into the stands to confront the heckler, Jones helped to prevent onlookers from interfering.

In mid-June, before the Cobb commotion had cooled, Davy got into another tangle, this time with umpire Billy Evans in Philadelphia. Disagreeing with Evans's pitch calling, Jones challenged him to a fight after the game. When Evans came to the Tigers' dressing room, he was reportedly intercepted and roughed up by several of Davy's teammates. Both were fined, and Jones received another suspension.

Wearying of the controversy, the Tigers decided that Jones's best playing days were behind him and after the 1912 season sold him on waivers to the Chicago White Sox. Davy appeared in only 12 games for Chicago in 1913 before he was sold to Toledo. Refusing to report and take a pay cut, he eventually agreed to terms and became one of the American Association's top hitters. Prior to the 1914 season, however, the 33-year-old Kangaroo jumped to the Pittsburgh Rebels of the newly formed Federal League. Jones played passably for the Rebels in 1914, scoring 58 runs in 97 games before injuring his ankle. Davy appeared in only 14 games in 1915 before being released. He made one final, brief appearance in a Tigers uniform, playing the outfield in the last game of the 1918 season.

His baseball career over, Davy earned a Ph.G. in Pharmacy from the University of Southern California and moved back to Michigan, where he became licensed as a pharmacist and worked in his drug stores for the next 40 years.

Davy's first marriage, to Mae W. Maynard, lasted 52 years and produced two children. After her death in 1955, Jones married his high school sweetheart of 60 years earlier, whom he had been forced to break up with because he was a ballplayer. They moved to Milwaukee in the late 1950s and later to Mankato, Minnesota. Jones died of a heart ailment at his home in Mankato, on March 30, 1972, at the age of 91.

MIKE GRAHEK

DETROIT

HUGH AMBROSE JENNINGS
MANAGER, 1907–1920

In 1907 38-year-old Hughey Jennings became the sixth manager in seven years for the downtrodden Detroit Tigers. Aided by a young phenom named Ty Cobb, Jennings proceeded to lead the Tigers to three consecutive pennants in his first three seasons with the club. Although he never won another pennant after 1909, Jennings continued to manage the Tigers through the 1920 season, accumulating a .538 winning percentage and guiding the club to 10 first-division finishes in 14 seasons. Despite having to deal with the temperamental Cobb during his tenure with Detroit, Jennings was the most colorful, animated, and cheerful manager in the game. He sported a boyish, infectious smile on his freckled Irish face. Umpire Tim Hurst called it "the grin that echoed." During the game he was constant motion, continually hollering his signature "Ee-yah!" and "Attaboy" from his third-base coaching box while plucking the grass bare. Perhaps not surprisingly, given his gift of gab, in the off-season Jennings was a highly regarded trial lawyer in his hometown of Scranton, Pennsylvania. He achieved all this success despite a string of freak accidents—including three separate, serious head injuries—unparalleled in the history of the sport.

Hugh Ambrose Jennings was born on April 2, 1869, in Pittston, Pennsylvania, the ninth of 12 children of a miner's family. He grew up in Moosic, near Scranton, and near the mouths of the anthracite coal pits of the region. As a youngster he dropped out of school at about age 12 and became a breaker boy in the mines, picking slate from coal for 90 cents a day, but he played baseball whenever he could. Young Hughey was soon the 90-pound catcher for the Anthracites, representing The Patch (so called after Stark's Patch, the section of Moosic that his family lived in). Jennings also played for town teams in Minooka, Avoca, and Pittston. Against his father's wishes, in 1889 Hughey signed for $5 a game with a semipro team in Lehighton, Pennsylvania, leaving the mines behind. He performed so well that the club agreed to pay him $50 a month for the 1890 season.

In June he signed his first professional contract with Allentown (Pennsylvania) of the Eastern Interstate League. In his first three professional games he played right field, shortstop, and catcher, respectively. On July 1 he even pitched, losing against Altoona 6–3. In his first game as a catcher, Jennings attempted to show off his rocket arm, throwing from behind the plate to try to catch a runner stealing second base. Unfortunately, the throw nailed the batter in the back of the head and knocked him cold. The club folded on July 5 and Hughey soon found himself back with Lehighton, where he began the 1891 season. Distinguishing himself early in the year, Jennings was signed by the Louisville Colonels of the American Association as a fill-in for injured first baseman Harry Taylor. Unfortunately, the club did not have a uniform that even remotely fit the slight Jennings. The one they gave him was so large it seemed he was encased in about three large pillowcases. Sam Crane, the sportswriter for the *New York Journal*, wrote that Hughey's red head stuck up through his uniform "like a red peony in a field of chrysanthemums."

When Taylor returned from injury Jennings switched to shortstop, where he finished the season as the regular, playing 70 games at the position. He batted .292 in 360 at-bats as a 22-year-old rookie. The following year, Jennings played shortstop all season for the Colonels, who were absorbed into the National League when the American Association folded. Hughey slumped to .222 and committed 90 errors for a .907 fielding percentage in 152 games at shortstop for the ninth-place Colonels.

After an even slower start in 1893, Jennings was dealt with Harry Taylor to the Baltimore Orioles for another shortstop, the highly regarded "Voiceless Tim" O'Rourke. Jennings broke through in 1894, taking over at shortstop and batting a lusty .335 as a key element in the first of three straight National League pennants by the Orioles juggernaut put together by manager Ned Hanlon. Jennings flourished under Hanlon, taking to Ned's brainy, do-anything-to-win style. Under Hanlon, Jennings learned scientific baseball: the bunt, the hit-and-run, and the stolen base. As one of the Orioles' famous Little Big Four (along with John McGraw, Willie Keeler, and Joe Kelley), he also learned about intimidating opponents, baiting umpires, and even cheating, if that's what it took to win.

Jennings became roommates and fast friends with McGraw while with the Orioles. They hit grounders to each other and worked to make themselves better players. Both lamented their lack of education and so began spending the winters taking classes at St. Bonaventure College and helping with the baseball team there in exchange for their tuition. It was at St. Bonaventure that McGraw worked with Jennings to correct his habit of stepping in the bucket when he swung. Pitching to him in the college's batting cage with a screen set behind Hughey so he could not step away from the plate, McGraw conditioned Jennings to step into inside pitches.

With the Orioles, Jennings became the top shortstop in baseball, both offensively and defensively. He hit .386 in 1895 and an amazing .401 in 1896 to finish second in the league. Jennings would do anything to get on base and in 1896 was hit by pitches 51 times, a major league record that still stands. In 1897 Hughey was in the midst of another fine year when fastballer Amos Rusie quick-pitched him (faking a throw to first and throwing an in-shoot home) and struck Jennings near the temple, laying him out flat at the plate. His skull was reportedly fractured and, according to one account, he was unconscious for four days. Even after that life-threatening beaning, Jennings continued to crowd the plate and was hit by pitches 46 times in 1898, leading the league in the category for a fourth consecutive year. For his career Hughey was plunked by pitches a major league record 273 times (including a record three in one game on three different occasions).

In 1899 Jennings ended up with Brooklyn when Hanlon and Baltimore owner Harry Von der Horst purchased a controlling interest in that club while retaining their stock in the Orioles. After 11 games at shortstop, however, Hughey blew out his arm and could no longer play the position. The ever-conniving Hanlon

tried to trade Jennings to Pittsburgh, but Hughey was an honest man and wrote the Pirates that he was damaged goods. Hanlon then tried to return Jennings to the Orioles, but after only two games Hughey was back with Brooklyn.

As a part-time first baseman Jennings contributed to two consecutive pennants for the Superbas. He adapted to his new position quite well—by July 1900 *Sporting Life* was calling him "the best fielding first baseman ever"—but Jennings was nonetheless on the downside of his playing career. After a midseason 1901 squabble in which four different teams in two leagues claimed rights to his services, the Philadelphia Phillies prevailed, purchasing Jennings to play first base and provide leadership. Despite rumors that Jennings would take over as manager for Billy Shettsline, it did not happen. Hughey played for the Phillies in 1901 and 1902, after which he was essentially finished as a major league player at the age of 33.

During the autumn of 1899 Hughey began attending the Cornell Law School in the off-season, still intent on improving his education. Law school was a high enough priority that Jennings refused to report to the Superbas in 1901 until June, so that he could complete the spring term at Cornell, which hastened his sale to the Phillies. He coached the Cornell baseball team as well, in exchange for his tuition. One winter evening in 1904, Jennings decided to take a swim in Cornell's darkened indoor pool. Unaware that maintenance had drained the pool, he dove in, seriously injuring himself with a lacerated scalp, two badly sprained wrists, and many abrasions. Fortunately, Jennings recovered completely, but after he became a manager he was frequently reminded of his ill-fated dive. When he would fuss at a player for a bonehead play, the player would often reply, "At least I never dove into an empty pool."

Although Jennings fell two semesters short of graduating from Cornell, he passed enough classes to take the bar exam. He was admitted to practice in Maryland in 1905 and in Pennsylvania in 1907, when Jennings moved to Scranton and began practicing law with his brother, W.A. Jennings. Hughey became a very accomplished and respected trial lawyer, defending accused murderers on several occasions.

After two seasons with the Phillies, Jennings rejoined Brooklyn in 1903, but stayed with the team for only six games. Hanlon still controlled the now minor league Baltimore Orioles of the Eastern League, and he sent Hughey to take over as manager for his old Oriole teammate Wilbert Robinson. Jennings stayed on as the Orioles manager for four years, leading them to a fourth-place finish, followed by two seconds and a third in 1906. He still played shortstop or second base when his health allowed and hit .328 in limited action in 1903 and .292 in 332 at-bats in 1904. He was still plagued by more than his fair share of injuries. For example, in 1905 he was hit by a pitch that broke his arm. After returning to action several weeks later, he broke it again in a base path collision.

After the 1906 season Tigers secretary Frank Navin wanted to purchase Jennings to manage his team. Hanlon demanded $5,000 for Jennings. Navin declined to pay that much and then, under the rules in force, simply drafted Jennings as a player from the Orioles for $1,000. Hughey inherited a sixth-place club led by the veteran "Wahoo Sam" Crawford, with a promising pitching staff and a 20-year-old firebrand outfielder named Ty Cobb. Cobb was in so many scrapes with teammates during spring training that Jennings almost traded him. Instead he gave Cobb more freedom at the plate and the green light to steal. Young Tyrus responded by becoming a full-fledged star, winning his first batting title and leading the league in hits, RBI, slugging percentage, and stolen bases.

The rest of the Tigers also responded well to Jennings's able leadership. Led by 25 wins apiece from "Wild Bill" Donovan and Ed Killian and 20 from George Mullin, Detroit won its first pennant by 1½ games over the Philadelphia Athletics—with virtually the same team that had finished deep in the second division the year before. The Tigers also won pennants the following two years, giving Jennings a record three pennants in his first three years as manager. He also lost three straight World Series, however, coming up short against the Chicago Cubs in 1907 and 1908, and the Pittsburgh Pirates in 1909.

Although generally cheerful and enthusiastic, Jennings as manager would do anything to win, a definite carryover from his playing days with the Orioles. He baited umpires and opposing players, and even resorted to buying rubber snakes and jack-in-the boxes when A's man-child Rube Waddell pitched against the Tigers. Because Rube was a southpaw, Hughey would station himself in the first base coaching box with the toys and yell, "Hey, Rube, look at this," while he popped the jack-in-the-box or wiggled the rubber snake. On another occasion, when Waddell was pitching for the St. Louis Browns, Jennings and his players brought several dogs into their dugout to distract Rube, who loved animals. Jennings even took a dog out to his third base coaching box. (It did not work—Waddell defeated the Tigers 7–1.)

Jennings's famed, piercing "Ee-yah" yell could be heard all over the ballpark. His characteristic pose from his coaching box was with arms spread, hands balled in fists, and right leg hoisted high like some imagined Native American rain dance. His shrill yell became one of baseball's historic trademarks. (It may have contributed to the rallying cry of the U.S. Marines in World War I; a recruiting poster of the time is blazoned with "E-e-e-yah-yip.") Hughey claimed to have contributed 'attaboy' to the language as well, a contraction of "That's the boy," as a way to applaud a good play.

There are two stories for the origin of Jennings's "Ee-yah." One is that it originally came from Johnnie Williams, a pitcher from Hawaii. Jennings was enamored with the yell and learned from Williams that it was Hawaiian for "Look out." The fact that Williams was not with the Tigers until 1914 casts some doubt on that version. The other, more likely story is that it started out simply as "That's the way," which evolved in yells to "Way-yah," and then to its final "Ee-yah."

Jennings constantly picked blades of grass and chewed on them until the area around the coaching box was bare. His signs were just straightforward words like 'bunt' or 'steal' mixed into his chatter. With his constant motion, characteristic poses, and grass plucking, the opposition never caught on. He also perfected a shrill whistle, of the two-fingers-in-the-mouth variety, which annoyed opposing teams throughout the league.

It is not surprising, given his background with the old Orioles, that Jennings favored smart, aggressive ballplayers. Jennings did not suffer fools lightly and could be quite acerbic and sarcastic with his own players, particularly in his later years as manager. He once said about one of his players, "If that guy's brains were made of nitroglycerin and they exploded, the bust wouldn't muss his hair. Give me a man who can think and with arms and legs, and I'll make a ballplayer of him."

Even though Cobb continued to flourish under Jennings, winning 12 batting titles in 13 years and setting stolen base records, the Tigers never again won a pennant for Old Ee-yah after 1909. In fact, although they finished second twice, the only years they came close were 1915 (when they finished in second, 2½ games behind the Boston Red Sox) and 1916 (when they came in third, four games behind the same Red Sox).

Jennings's favoritism toward Cobb, whom he generally allowed to set his own rules, was a frequent cause of discord on the club, and his handling of pitchers sometimes drew criticism. Still, he enjoyed a deserved reputation as one of the best managers in the game. Bill James identifies Jennings as one of the very first to platoon players, beginning with his catchers in the 1907 World Series. In 1911 he platooned left-handed hitting Davy Jones with right-handed hitting Delos Drake in left field for most of the season.

Off the field Jennings invested wisely and, with his off-season law practice, became quite comfortable financially. He was so respected that he became a director of several banks. Nonetheless, he never lost touch with his breaker-boy beginnings. During the off-season he would sometimes visit the mines near where he grew up and offer the miners rides home or groceries for their families. He also married a girl from his hometown, Elizabeth Dixon, in 1897; however, she died of complications from childbirth after only 13 months of marriage, leaving him with a young daughter. After the 1911 season Jennings married Nora O'Boyle.

His proclivity for accidents returned. On December 1, 1911, he was seriously injured while driving an automobile that veered off a slick bridge, fell ten feet, and pinned Jennings in the current of the Lehigh River, rendering him unconscious and injuring his three passengers. Narrowly escaping drowning, Jennings was able to recover from two broken legs, a broken arm, and yet another head injury, which doctors described as a "concussion of the brain."

Jennings continued to manage the Tigers through the second decade of the century but, either through bad luck, bad judgment, or a combination of both, failed to develop or secure top-flight pitching. In 1920 the club lost its first 13 games and limped home in seventh place, 37 games behind Tris Speaker's pennant-winning Cleveland Indians. Although Frank Navin was reluctant to replace Jennings after 14 years at the helm, Jennings had become increasingly unpopular with the players. After the season Jennings resigned by mutual consent and shortly thereafter Navin named Cobb manager.

Old pal John McGraw quickly called, however, and asked Hughey to join him in New York as his number one coach with the Giants. Jennings accepted and coached for the Giants during their run of four consecutive pennants from 1921 to 1924, often taking over as manager during McGraw's frequent absences (caused by persistent sinusitis and other maladies). In 76 games as Giants manager Jennings posted a remarkable .697 winning percentage, nearly 150 points higher than McGraw's during those seasons.

McGraw's sinuses were particularly bad in 1925, and Jennings managed the club for large chunks of the season. Although armed with seven future Hall of Famers, the Giants finished second, 8½ games behind the Pittsburgh Pirates. The grueling season took a real toll on Jennings and he became moody, distracted, and easily upset as the season wore on. That winter he entered the Winyah sanatorium in Asheville, North Carolina, where he was diagnosed with tuberculosis. He was unable to rejoin the Giants for the 1926 season.

On July 19, 1927, the Giants celebrated McGraw's Silver Jubilee, to honor his 25 years as manager. Jennings attended and was sitting alone in the stands in a drizzle during the ceremony when some fans recognized him. Immediately the fans began a "We Want Jennings" clamor and would not subsist until Hughey, aided by a cane and looking far beyond his 57 years, unsteadily made his way down to the playing field to home plate amid a huge cheer.

It would be his last public appearance. In the winter of 1927–28 Jennings contracted meningitis and died at his Scranton home on February 1, 1928; he was buried in St. Catherine's Cemetery in nearby Moscow. Jennings was posthumously elected to the Hall of Fame in 1945.

C. Paul Rogers III

DETROIT

OWEN JOSEPH "DONIE" BUSH
SHORTSTOP, 1908–1921

One of the greatest defensive shortstops of the Deadball Era, Donie Bush used quick feet and soft hands to lead the American League in assists seven times and putouts three times, and his 425 putouts in 1914 established an American League record and tied a major league mark which has never been broken. At the plate the diminutive 5'6", 140-pound switch-hitter used all his tools to set the table for Detroit's powerful offense. Although he batted just .250 with little power during his career, Bush scored more than 100 runs four times, thanks to his patience at the plate and ability to work the count. Bush led the league in walks five times during his 16-year career, including every season from 1909 to 1912. Bush was also a gifted bunter, leading the league in sacrifices twice, and an excellent base-stealer, swiping 404 bags in his career and stealing 40 or more bases in a single season four times. Despite these achievements, Bush's offensive skills remained largely overlooked in an era when fans and commentators focused mostly on batting averages. "Just why fans have relegated Bush to the 'poor-hitting class' is beyond me," *Baseball Magazine's* J. C. Kofoed remarked in 1915. "Donie gets on base, and scores more often than any of his slugging mates on the Detroit club."

Owen Joseph Bush was born on October 8, 1887, in Indianapolis. His father died at any early age, and Bush was cared for by his mother. Still in his teens, the pint-sized Hoosier left his mother and his Indianapolis pals for the woodlands of southern Canada. Bush first displayed his skills in 1905 with Sault Ste. Marie in the Class D Copper Country League. He split the 1906 season among three teams in the lower minors: Saginaw, Michigan, and Dayton and Marion, Ohio.

Bush landed closer to home with the South Bend (Indiana) Greens to start the 1907 campaign. Here he found his stride. Displaying excellent defensive skills, Bush also began hitting better, and finished the season with a .279 batting average and a reputation as the best all-around shortstop the Central League had ever seen.

Along with his ownership of the Tigers, Frank Navin held a minority interest with the South Bend club. After the 1907 season Navin sold Bush to the Indianapolis Indians of the American Association, with the stipulation that the Tigers would retain the first option on Bush's services. When veteran Tiger shortstop Charley O'Leary was sidelined with an injury late in the 1908 pennant race, Navin quickly summoned Bush from Indianapolis. The normally tightfisted Tiger owner shelled out $6,000 to purchase Bush, a princely sum for the era, but one that would prove to be a major bargain for Navin and the Tigers. When the sale was announced, a telegraphic error had the Tigers purchasing a Donie Bush from Indianapolis—the "Donie" being a mis-transcription of Ownie, the name by which his closest friends knew him. The accidental moniker would stick with Bush throughout his baseball career.

Bush's impact was felt immediately. Making his debut with the Tigers on September 18, 1908, Donie proved to be the extra spark that would take Detroit to their second American League pennant in a row. In addition to giving Navin's crew a defensive stopper, Bush was also a pleasant surprise at the plate. Appearing in the final 20 tension-packed games of the season, Bush batted .294 and swiped the first two of his 400 stolen bases while wearing a Tiger uniform.

Navin's only regret in signing Bush for the stretch run was that he did not call up Bush before September, which would have made the shortstop eligible for the upcoming World Series against the Cubs. Bush was sidelined, and the Tigers lost the Series in five games.

In 1909 Bush proved that his superior play down

the stretch in 1908 had been no fluke. The scrappy Bush led all American League shortstops with 567 assists, establishing a new AL record. At the plate Bush drew a major league-leading 88 walks, and also led the majors with 52 sacrifices, which remains the fourth-highest total in major league history. Bush combined his solid .273 average with a stellar .380 OBP, and he scored 114 runs, second in the league to teammate Ty Cobb. After the season Alfred Spink described Bush, "the midget shortstop," as "one of the best players that ever filled that position.... Bush, the grand little Detroit short-stop, has in a single year won a reputation that other stars well may envy. No member of the Tiger nine is more respected by opposing teams." The Tigers won their third consecutive American League pennant, but once again fell short in the World Series, losing to the Pittsburgh Pirates in seven games. Bush batted .318 for the Series, with a .483 OBP (though he also committed five errors in the field).

It was to be Bush's only appearance as a player in the World Series. Over the next decade Donie continued to set the table for Detroit's powerful offense. Although his batting average steadily declined from 1910, when he batted a respectable .262, to 1916, when he batted just .225, Bush continued to find ways to get on base and score runs. He led the league in walks every year from 1909 to 1912, and again in 1914. (His highest walk total in the major leagues actually came in 1915, when he drew 118 free passes, but that figure was one short of Eddie Collins's league-leading mark.) Thanks to his remarkable ability to find ways to get on base, Bush ranked among the league leaders in runs scored every year from 1909 to 1915. In 1917, when his batting average rebounded to a solid .281, Bush led the American League in runs scored for the only time in his career, with 112.

Meanwhile, Bush continued to distinguish himself in the field and on the base paths. He regularly ranked among the leaders in most major fielding categories, and in 1914 tied a major league record, which has yet to be broken, with 425 putouts. After the 1915 season *Baseball Magazine* declared Bush the greatest shortstop in the American League. "Since Jack Barry moved over to second base, 'Donie' is the best man in his position that the American League can boast," J.C. Kofoed declared.

Although Donie continued to get on base and score runs through the end of the Deadball Era, Detroit management concluded that his speed and defensive skills were on the wane and in August 1921 waived him to the Washington Senators, where he finished his career as a part-time player. Washington owner Clark Griffith

instantly took a liking to Bush's knowledge of the game and installed Donie as the team's manager for the 1923 season. Bush improved Washington's position from sixth to fourth place, but inexplicably was not retained for 1924. Griffith looked like a genius when his new skipper, Bucky Harris, piloted the Senators to their first and only world championship.

Donie returned to his hometown of Indianapolis to take over the reins of the local American Association club. Three straight second-place finishes earned Bush a return trip back to the big leagues, where he served as manager of the Pittsburgh Pirates. Bush piloted the Pirates to the National League championship, but had the misfortune to run into the 1927 New York Yankees, who swept Pittsburgh in the World Series. Bush's most controversial move as manager came that year, when he benched future Hall of Famer Kiki Cuyler for the rest of the season and the World Series after Cuyler failed to perform a take-out slide on a double-play ball during an August 6 game. Donie continued to manage the Pirates for two more seasons. He had two more managerial stints in the big leagues after that, with the Chicago White Sox (1930–1931) and the Cincinnati Reds (1933), but in both cases was saddled with mediocre talent and finished in the second division.

Bush returned to the minor leagues, where he briefly managed the Louisville Colonels and Minneapolis Millers of the American Association. With Minneapolis, Bush was credited with helping a young Ted Williams become a more complete ballplayer: in 1938, the year he was managed by Bush, Williams's batting average went up 75 points.

Upon hearing of the death of his former skipper in 1972, Williams had kind words of praise for Donie: "I've been in the game for 36 years and nobody has any closer affection to my heart than Ownie." Williams remembered Bush as "fiery as a man could be... a man who tried to be tough but was as soft as a grape."

Bush, who never married and had no children, was a pillar of strength in Indianapolis for three decades, from 1941 until his death. First as a manager, and then as president of the local American Association club, Bush was known as Mr. Baseball in his hometown. In 1967 the city fathers in Indianapolis renamed the local ballpark Bush Stadium in his honor. When he died at age 84 on March 28, 1972, shortly after attending spring training as a White Sox scout, the funeral hearse led a procession one final time around Bush Stadium before the body was driven to Holy Cross Cemetery for burial.

JIM MOYES

DETROIT

JAMES CHRISTOPHER DELAHANTY
SECOND BASEMAN, 1909–1912

Remembered mostly in connection with his more famous older brother, Jim Delahanty was a fine player in his own right, and one of the most well-traveled hitters of the Deadball Era. During a professional career that lasted nearly two decades, the free-swinging right-hander played for 15 different clubs, including eight in the major leagues. This extensive itinerary notwithstanding, Delahanty bore an excellent reputation within his profession. "Delahanty is looked upon as one of the 'classy' boys of the American League," Alfred Spink wrote in 1910. "He is a most graceful fielder and a congenial sort of a fellow both on and off the field." Second base was his primary position, but during his career the versatile Irishman filled every position on the diamond except catcher, and he finished his career with an excellent .283 batting average in 1,186 career games.

James Christopher Delahanty was born on June 20, 1879, in Cleveland, the second youngest of five brothers, each eventually a major leaguer (although Jim never got to play on the same big league team with any of them). Jim was a distant 12 years younger than his famous brother Ed, and growing up followed more in the footsteps of his other older brothers, Joe and Tommy, who made names for themselves on the Cleveland sandlots. In the mid-1890s Jim's famous last name got him a tryout with the Fort Wayne (Indiana) club of the Inter-State League. Jim did not make a good impression on the club, and subsequently returned to Cleveland to play semipro ball. After writing to the Lima, Ohio, entry in the Northwest Ohio League requesting a tryout, Delahanty made the team as a third baseman.

Dubbed the Yellow Kid after a popular cartoon of the time, Jim's play at Lima led his brothers to encourage him to try for a higher level of competition. In 1898 he played for Montgomery of the Southern League.

The league folded, so Jimmy hooked up with brother Tommy in Allentown. Playing shortstop with Tommy at second base, Jim impressed manager Billy Sharsig with his sandlot scrappiness and superior range. When Joe's contract was purchased from the Paterson, New Jersey, club three weeks later, Allentown (Pennsylvania) featured three Delahantys in the infield.

The Allentown brother act was broken up in the 1900 season with the demise of the Atlantic League. Jim's contract was sold to Worcester (Massachusetts) of the Eastern League, where he hit .281 in 80 games at short and third. After the season the Chicago Orphans outbid three other National League teams for his services, but Jim opened the 1901 season with just a .190 average in 17 games at third base before being benched. The rookie then broke his kneecap and came down with malaria, and in late June was sent home for the rest of the season. The following winter Chicago sold him to the New York Giants.

In no small part because of his last name, Jim Delahanty's arrival at the Polo Grounds in late March for spring practice merited a mention in the *New York Times*. In his brief tenure with the Giants, however, Jim was a disappointment. Named the club's opening day starting right fielder, he appeared in just seven games, batting .231 before drawing his release in early May. Delahanty then hooked on with Little Rock of the Southern Association, where he played third, batted a robust .328 in 101 games, and led the league in triples. He continued with Little Rock in 1903, and was returning home to Cleveland to recuperate from a cracked shoulder blade when brother Ed died, falling from a bridge into the Niagara River. Jim rejoined Little Rock later in the year, finishing the campaign with a league-best .382 batting average.

Jim's showing in the Southern Association prompted

another big league trial, this time for the Boston Beaneaters of the National League. He appeared in a combined 267 games over the next two years, playing primarily third base (in 1904) and left field (in 1905), and batting a combined .272 with 115 RBI.

In January 1906 Cincinnati manager Ned Hanlon traded Al Bridwell to Boston for Delahanty. The deal met with some skepticism in Cincinnati, where Bridwell had become a fan favorite, but Delahanty won the starting third base job from Hans Lobert and Mike Mowrey and put in a fine season, as he batted .280 with a stellar .371 OBP in 115 games. Despite that success, Delahanty's stay in Cincinnati was short-lived. That December, owner Garry Herrmann sold the infielder to the St. Louis Browns for $1,500.

Delahanty lasted only 33 games with the Browns, contributing a disappointing .221 batting average with only three extra-base hits before St. Louis sold him to the Washington Senators on June 11, 1907. Shifted to second base full time, Delahanty found the new environs to his liking, batting .292 in 108 games for Washington. The following year Delahanty put in another fine season, batting .317 in 83 games, though his campaign was marred by nagging injuries and an ugly incident in his hometown of Cleveland on August 4. In a game that Washington lost 7–5, Delahanty and teammate Otis Clymer were ejected for arguing with umpire Silk O'Loughlin. According to reports, Delahanty responded to the ejection by unleashing a torrent of profanity that could be heard throughout the park. American League president Ban Johnson responded by suspending Delahanty, fining him $50, and banning him from the Cleveland park for one year. Not surprisingly, Delahanty considered the ruling unfair and excessive. "O'Loughlin's decisions were way off and I told him so, and when he put me out of the game I grew sore and said things to him, but I did it quietly and no one in the stands heard it," Delahanty insisted.

To be fair to the other contenders in that year's hotly contested pennant race, Washington manager Joe Cantillon decided that if Delahanty could not play in Cleveland, he also would not play him in Detroit, Chicago, or St. Louis, a decision that resulted in Delahanty missing 14 games in addition to the 13 Johnson had suspended him for. At the start of the next season, Johnson lifted the Cleveland ban.

Jim remained with Washington through August 1909, when he was traded to the Detroit Tigers for Germany Schaefer and Red Killefer. Delahanty played 46 games down the stretch for the eventual AL champs, and appeared in all seven World Series games, leading the Tigers with a .346 average, including five doubles, in a losing cause. After the Series Alfred Spink remarked that Del's "aggressive playing, desperate base running and timely bingling was probably one of the real features of this series."

After another solid campaign in 1910 Delahanty put together the best season of his career in 1911 (thanks in part to the new cork-centered baseball) as he stayed healthy all year and batted .339 with career highs in on-base percentage (.411), slugging percentage (.463), runs (83), hits (184), doubles (30), triples (14), and RBI (94). The 32-year-old Delahanty had lost several steps in the field, however, so manager Hughey Jennings also played Delahanty at first base 71 times during the season.

As good as his 1911 season was, it marked Delahanty's last hurrah in Detroit. The following August, despite having posted a solid .286 batting average and .397 OBP for the season, Delahanty was given his unconditional release. Newspaper reports at the time stated that "injuries and illness" were the motivating factors for the decision, but another report suggested that "his too close touch with the revolt spirit after last season's famous Ty Cobb incident caused his undoing and he dropped out." Perhaps Delahanty's actions in supporting the Tigers' strike following Cobb's suspension for attacking a fan in May, coupled with his $4,000 salary, led the Tigers to release him.

In any event, Delahanty hooked on with the Minneapolis Millers of the American Association, where he remained through the beginning of the 1914 season, when he signed with Brooklyn of the upstart Federal League. Appearing in 74 games for the Tip-Tops, Delahanty batted a solid .290 with a .372 OBP. He finished out his big league career in 1915 with the Tip-Tops, appearing in 17 games and batting .240 before drawing his release. His professional career concluded that autumn with Hartford of the Colonial League, an independent minor league affiliated with the Federal League, where he led the circuit in batting (.379) and managed the team to a league championship.

After his playing career ended Delahanty moved back to Cleveland, where he lived with his wife, Hester, and daughter, Eunice, and worked as a truck driver for the Cleveland Street Repair Department. He died at St. John's Hospital in Cleveland after a prolonged illness on October 17, 1953, at age 74, and was buried in Cleveland's Calvary Cemetery.

JOHN T. SACCOMAN

DETROIT

GEORGE JOSEPH MORIARTY
THIRD BASEMAN, 1909–1915; MANAGER, 1927–1928

Fiery and temperamental on the playing field but friendly and reserved off it, George Moriarty was one of the most colorful characters of the Deadball Era, gaining fame at various times as a third baseman, umpire, manager, poet, newspaper columnist, and songwriter. Famed for his leadership abilities, penchant for brawling, a strong arm at third base, and an unparalleled knack for stealing home, Moriarty manned the hot corner for Detroit from 1909 through 1914. Almost universally well-liked, Moriarty was "a fine type of man, the kind of man anyone would like to meet…deservedly popular wherever he goes," *Baseball Magazine* reported in 1912. "Moriarty…was always likely to come through in the pinch," Detroit sportswriter Joe S. Jackson wrote in 1915. "As a third baseman he had a wonderful whip and as a base runner he was daring, and especially dangerous after he had reached third base….He knows the game thoroughly and is aggressive. His one handicap, as said, has been that he is not a hard hitter."

George Joseph Moriarty was born in Chicago on June 7, 1884, to John J. Moriarty and the former Catherine Stevens, whose home had burned in the great fire of 1871. (The family name may originally have been rendered Moriarity, a spelling George used until he reached the major leagues.) The elder Moriarty was a semipro catcher, a childhood friend of Charles Comiskey, and a driver on Chicago's streetcar line for 58 years. George grew up near the stockyards on Chicago's South Side, and, after dropping out of school following the sixth grade, became a noted ballplayer in the city's notoriously competitive semipro leagues.

George signed his first professional contract at age 16 in 1901, batting .263 for Davenport (Iowa) and Rock Island (Illinois) during the first of three seasons he would spend in the Three-I League. After spending 1902

and 1903 with Bloomington, Joliet, and Springfield in Illinois, Moriarty took a job with the Oliver Typewriter Company in late 1903, playing third base on the renowned company team. In an exhibition game against the Cubs, Moriarty had the good fortune to start a triple play at third base. Cubs manager Frank Selee decided to give Moriarty a one-game tryout on the last day of the 1903 season. The press noted the 19-year-old was "palpably nervous," and he went 0-for-5, though acquitting himself well in the field. The performance was enough for him to break camp with Chicago in 1904, but after going hitless in four games he was farmed out to Little Rock of the Southern Association, then sold outright a few weeks later to Toledo of the American Association.

It was in Toledo that Moriarty began to earn a reputation as a brawler. One day in 1905 Indianapolis manager Ed Barrow was riding Moriarty mercilessly, but the young third sacker began shouting comebacks that were more clever than Barrow's insults. Barrow charged, and Moriarty beat him to a pulp. Former big leaguer Willie McGill, who witnessed the incident, afterward called Moriarty "the fightingest kid I ever saw."

After Moriarty led the league with 51 steals in 1905, Toledo sold his contract to the American League's New York Highlanders. Moriarty proved a capable utility player for New York in 1906, batting only .234 but filling in at five different positions: first, second, third, left, and center. Defensively, he impressed one writer as "as cool a man for his age—twenty-one—as ever stood at the third corner, and he handles the hardest hits with the greatest ease." In 1907 Moriarty became a full-time utility player, garnering 474 plate appearances while playing seven positions—everything except pitcher and catcher. He also blossomed as a hitter. His .277 average, .320 OBP, and .336 slugging percentage were all better than the league average; the first two would remain career highs. Moriarty filled the same super-utility role in 1908, though his average fell to .236. After that season George received the good news that the last-place Highlanders had sold him to the reigning American League champs, the Detroit Tigers.

Installed as Detroit's regular third baseman in 1909, Moriarty helped them win another pennant with a .273 average and good defense at third. In the Tigers' thrilling World Series loss to Pittsburgh, he batted the very same .273, collecting six hits and scoring four runs. A spike wound sustained in Game Six required 15 stitches, but Moriarty was nonetheless in the starting lineup for Game Seven.

At six feet tall and about 190 pounds, the right-handed batting Moriarty was a large player for his time. "He was a weak hitter," sportswriter Joe Williams once wrote, "but he had that rare something in his makeup which produces leadership, that divine spark that invests mediocrity with might." He was also willing to brawl with anyone who cared to challenge him. Once the young Ty Cobb wanted to fight Moriarty, and George promptly handed Cobb a baseball bat. "A fellow like you needs a bat to even things up when fighting an Irishman," Moriarty told him. Cobb backed down.

Off the field, Moriarty's personality was just the opposite. He was considered a gentleman who never used profanity, "soft spoken and gentle in manner." On road trips to Boston he spent most of his leisure time socializing with Jesuit priests from nearby College of the Holy Cross.

Moriarty lit a fire under the Tigers with his daring baserunning exploits, which included an uncanny ability to steal third base and, most especially, home plate. One writer made the unlikely claim that Moriarty stole home "almost as often as other players pilfered second base." The numbers vary widely, depending on who tells the story. Over one unspecified two-year period he was said to have successfully stolen home 14 times in 17 attempts, while other sources credit him with 14 thefts of home in a single season. Moriarty himself claimed to have done the deed 17 times in 1908 and 1909 combined. Anecdotes aside, Moriarty is documented to have stolen home at least 11 times, although the actual number is almost certainly larger.

Moriarty's most famous attempt to steal home resulted in an out. On May 16, 1909, with two outs in the bottom of the ninth and his Tigers losing 3–2, Moriarty attempted to steal home with the game-tying run. Boston catcher Bill Carrigan not only tagged Moriarty out to end the game, but also spit tobacco juice on him, saying, "Don't ever try to pull that on a smart guy." Moments later Carrigan was lying on his back, having been flattened by a Moriarty punch. After the game the Boston catcher had to disguise himself as a groundskeeper to escape the mob of angry Detroiters waiting for him outside Bennett Park.

On May 28, 1909, shortly after this incident, *Detroit News* editorial writer William J. Cameron published a tribute to Moriarty's choice of risk over inertia, titled "Don't Die On Third," that was syndicated nationwide. In its day Cameron's editorial was more famous than either of two popular contemporary pieces, Jack Norworth's "Take Me Out to the Ball Game" and Franklin P. Adams's "Baseball's Sad Lexicon." Thousands of copies were reprinted, and for the rest of his life Moriarty would carry the unwieldy nickname of The Man Who Won't Die On Third.

From 1911 through 1916 Moriarty served as field captain of the Tigers and managed the club whenever skipper Hughey Jennings was not present; however, he would never again hit as well as he had in 1907 and 1909. The Tigers plummeted from the 1909 pennant to sixth place by 1912, and Moriarty's batting followed the same downward spiral. He hit between .239 and .254 every year from 1910 through 1914, providing the Tigers with solidly below-average offense but, most observers agreed, with excellent defense at third base. "No third baseman ever whipped a ball across the infield with more speed or accuracy," wrote H. G. Salsinger of the *Detroit News*. Moriarty was also a quick thinker on the field. On April 24, 1911, he started a triple play by intentionally dropping a pop-up after the infield fly rule had been called, then throwing out the two confused base runners.

In 1915 the 31-year-old Moriarty gave up his third base job to Ossie Vitt and spent the year assisting Jennings as a player–coach. That November the Tigers gave Moriarty his unconditional release. After going 1-for-5 as a pinch hitter for the Chicago White Sox in early 1916, Moriarty again received his release and was named manager of the Memphis Chicks in May. Suffering from typhoid fever, he guided the club to a sixth-place finish in the Southern Association. In 1917 he found his true calling, when he embarked on what would become an illustrious 22-year career as an American League umpire.

"Mr. Moriarty has always been a fiery, spirited individual who never hesitated to speak his piece," Joe Williams once wrote in the *New York World-Telegram*. "Indeed, the only indictment I have ever had against Mr. Moriarty is that he writes poetry—not only writes it, but recites it." The charge, alas, was true. Moriarty had long been an amateur poet, getting published here and there, and in 1918 he began writing a nationally syndicated newspaper column that frequently featured his poetry. Moriarty's literary specialty was elegies; he composed tribute poems upon the deaths of John McGraw, Miller Huggins, Lou Gehrig, fellow umpire Silk O'Loughlin, and others. A poem written after Frank Chance's death was engraved on the Peerless Leader's tombstone. Also a talented vocalist and songwriter, Moriarty had several of his musical compositions published by the Remick Music Corporation, including "Bonehead Plays," "Mississippi Moon," and "It's a Long Road to Dublin." He also wrote a regular column, "Calling Them," for *Baseball Magazine*. The quality of his literary work is debatable, but he was certainly a better writer than most other grammar school dropouts.

In 1927 Moriarty resigned his umpiring position and replaced Cobb as Tigers manager. A teetotaler, Moriarty attended church every Sunday and expected his players to do the same. He piloted the Tigers to fourth- and sixth-place finishes before resigning when his two-year contract ended and returning to the American League umpiring staff.

In a famed incident that almost cost him his career, on Memorial Day of 1932 Moriarty fought four members of the Chicago White Sox simultaneously. Moriarty called a pitch by Sox hurler Milt Gaston ball three instead of strike three, and Gaston gave up a game-tying triple on the next pitch, eventually losing the game. When the White Sox heckled Moriarty as he walked off the field, he shouted back: "I'll fight the whole White Sox team!" The 47-year-old umpire was promptly attacked by four White Sox, some scarcely half his age: Gaston, Charlie Berry, Frank Grube, and player–manager Lew Fonseca. Moriarty sustained cuts, bruises, and a broken hand, but fought them to a draw. "Mr. Moriarty must be slipping," columnist Joe Williams quipped. "I can remember when he used to take on whole ball clubs as a warmup." Gaston was suspended for ten days by American League president Will Harridge, the other three players were fined, and Moriarty was given a public reprimand.

Rumored to be on the chopping block because of the fight, Moriarty saved his job by embarking on a goodwill tour on behalf of the American League that off-season, lecturing and reciting his poetry at schools, American Legion banquets, and the like. Using dramatic gestures as he spoke, Moriarty, according to one observer, "makes the dishes rattle when he pounds home a point. Has power to compel attention by his appearance, as well as his voice. Might be taken for a ship's captain, a chief of police or a major of marines." The lecture tour was well-received, so much so that league owners found it impossible to fire Moriarty, as they had planned. It did not hurt that he was also an excellent umpire; a 1935 poll of AL players conducted by *The Sporting News* named him "hands down" the best umpire in the league.

Moriarty has the distinction of ejecting three players from World Series play, more than any other umpire. In Game Three of the 1935 Series, he berated and then booted the Cubs' Charlie Grimm, Tuck Stainback, and Woody English for, among other things, excessive heckling of Hank Greenberg. For that stunt Moriarty was fined $200; he had violated Kenesaw Mountain Landis's rule against ejecting players from World Series games without the commissioner's prior approval.

Moriarty retired from umpiring after the 1940 season, joining the American League public relations staff as a traveling lecturer. During World War II he rejoined the Tigers as what was called a master scout and held the post through 1958, discovering a handful of future big leaguers, including Harvey Kuenn.

Moriarty married Ada Stone in 1905; they had one son, George, Jr. The marriage ended sometime between 1920 and 1936—whether due to death or divorce is unclear—and Moriarty remarried Mary Allen in 1936. They also had one child, David, before they were divorced in a lively 1943 trial during which Mrs. Moriarty accused her husband of domestic violence.

Moriarty's grandson, the Fulbright Scholar and actor Michael Moriarty, would later play the lead role in one of the most acclaimed baseball films of all time, *Bang the Drum Slowly* (1973). Michael Moriarty also starred on television's *Law & Order*, playing Assistant District Attorney Ben Stone—or ADA Stone, his grandmother's maiden name.

After his scouting career ended Moriarty retired to Coral Gables, Florida, where he died of kidney cancer on April 7, 1964. He was 79 years old and was buried in Saint Mary Catholic Cemetery in the south Chicago suburb of Evergreen Park. The headline over his *Sporting News* obituary read BATTLING MORIARTY—UMP WHO LOVED TO FIGHT.

ERIC ENDERS

DETROIT

OSCAR HARLAND STANAGE
CATCHER, 1909–1920, 1925

Inconspicuous yet ever-present, from 1911 to 1915 Detroit catcher Oscar Stanage was the most durable backstop in the American League, appearing behind the dish in 560 games, 125 more than any other American League catcher. In 1911 Stanage caught 141 games for the Tigers, the most of any American League catcher during the Deadball Era, and also totaled 212 assists, an American League record that has never been broken. Three years later Stanage was credited with 190 assists. When Stanage left the Tigers after the 1920 season, sportswriter H.G. Salsinger observed, "No backstop ever had the ability to outguess the opposition on the hit and run and squeeze play that Stanage had. He threw fast and accurate, but always a light ball. He never moved faster than he had to but he always got there. His lack of wasted motion made him a favorite with pitchers, for he was an easy man to pitch to and he had the ability to steady the twirlers."

Oscar Harland Stanage was born on his father's ranch in Tulare, California, on March 17, 1883. The son of Thomas W. Stanage, a prosperous rancher–farmer, and his wife, Charlotte, young Oscar attended school at Stockton High School, graduating with the class of 1905. Standing close to six feet tall and tipping the scales at approximately 180 pounds, the 22-year-old Stanage was a star in the early rough-and-tumble era of high school football at Stockton High.

Stanage also starred on his high school baseball team, and after graduation played with the local Stockton team of the California League. It was while catching for this club that he first caught the attention of major league scouts, signing with the St. Louis Cardinals in early 1906. Before he ever appeared in a St. Louis uniform, however, Stanage was dealt to the Cincinnati Reds for pitcher Carl Druhot. Stanage made only one plate appearance with the Reds in May 1906 before he

was dealt again, this time to the Newark Sailors of the Eastern League. He remained with Newark for three seasons, posting anemic batting averages but earning rave reviews for his defense behind the plate. The Detroit Tigers, still smarting from catcher Boss Schmidt's inept defensive performance in the 1907 World Series, purchased Stanage's contract in August 1908.

Stanage did not appear in any games for the Tigers that first year, but in 1909 he competed for the starting catching position on the club and, in one of the first instances of platooning in baseball history, eventually shared those duties with Schmidt. Appearing in 77 games that year, Stanage batted a solid .262 (which was 53 points better than Schmidt) and dazzled observers with his cannon throwing arm. Making the only World Series appearances of his career, Stanage played in two contests in the Tigers' seven-game defeat to the Pittsburgh Pirates.

The following year Stanage's batting average dipped to .207, but he earned the lion's share of the time behind the dish. He firmly supplanted the outgoing Schmidt in 1911, when he caught 141 games for the Tigers and threw out a league-record 212 baserunners. On the flip side Oscar also committed a league-record 41 errors during the campaign. For the season the right-handed Stanage batted a respectable .264 with a career-best 51 RBI.

He continued his solid hitting in 1912 as he appeared in 121 games and batted .261. In August of that year Cincinnati Reds owner Garry Herrmann wrote to Tigers president Frank Navin, trying to unload catcher Larry McLean. Herrmann was quickly rebuffed by Navin, who replied, "As long as Stanage continues to do all the catching on our club, which he has been doing so for the past two years, there is no room for any other catcher on our club, especially for a high class man like McLean." Navin's closing words to Herrmann pretty much summed up the Tigers' failure to win an American League pennant during the Deadball Era after 1909: "If only you had a pitcher to offer, we would be glad to take the matter up with you, but judging from the box scores you are as bad off for pitchers as our Detroit club."

In 1917 Stanage demonstrated his loyalty to Navin when Oscar signed his contract in early January, thereby violating an agreement he had signed with the Baseball Players Fraternity. When Stanage was expelled from the Fraternity for his action, he remarked that he was well pleased with the salary offered him and added: "I quit the Fraternity because I couldn't see what good it was doing me."

Quietly filling the role of everyday catcher on the club, Stanage earned the respect of management and teammates for his toughness and ability to handle pitchers. Hughey Jennings had such high regard for Stanage's knowledge of the game that midway through the 1914 season Stanage assumed the role of pitching coach for the Tigers.

Although not well known as a baseball pugilist, Stanage over the years also earned the off-field respect of his teammates, including the club's brawling superstar, Ty Cobb. When Cobb and Buck Herzog squared off in a legendary spring training brawl in 1917 each man was granted a teammate to bring into the room to make sure everything was all square. Cobb selected Oscar Stanage, and Herzog was represented by Heinie Zimmerman.

Cobb had a reputation as being especially hard on rookies. One of the yannigans Cobb targeted for abuse was the pint-sized third baseman Ossie Vitt, who joined the Tigers in 1912. In a 1938 feature article in *The Sporting News*, Vitt recounted how Cobb treated him unmercifully until Stanage stepped in. According to Vitt, Stanage (called Big 'O' by his teammates) told Cobb, "If you don't lay off little 'O' Big 'O' is going to hit you so hard he will drive you right back to Georgia." Not wanting to incur the wrath of Stanage, the Georgia Peach never again harassed Vitt during their seven years as Tiger teammates.

Stanage's long tenure with the Tigers came to an end in 1920. His duty-battered body had begun to crack during the 1918 campaign, when the catcher was twice sidelined with a broken finger. Always the consummate team player, Stanage wanted to retire before the 1920 campaign got underway, but the Tigers, who were very weak in the catching department, induced him to return for one final year.

After the 1920 campaign Stanage was traded to Los Angeles of the Pacific Coast League, where he joined former teammate Sam Crawford. The next year he appeared in nearly 100 games for the Sacramento Senators of the same circuit. Traded to the PCL's Salt Lake City Bees before the 1923 season, Stanage chose instead to sign with the Visalia (California) Pirates in the outlaw San Joaquin Valley League. In 1924 Stanage surfaced with the Toronto Maple Leafs of the International League. He was summoned back to Detroit before the 1925 season, where he worked as a coach under manager Cobb for one season, while also appearing in three final games for the Tigers at the age of 42. Stanage, who never batted higher than .264 in any individual season, finished his major league career with a .234 batting average and just eight home runs.

In 1926 Stanage served as player–manager of the Evansville (Indiana) Hubs of the Three-I League, guiding the team to a fifth-place finish. The next year, Oscar returned to the major leagues as a bench coach for the Pittsburgh Pirates, under former teammate Donie Bush. Stanage remained with Pittsburgh through the 1931 season, after which he retired from baseball for good.

Stanage spent the remainder of his life in Detroit, where one of his post-baseball working jobs was as a night watchman at the corner of Michigan and Trumbull, site of Briggs Stadium. One could only imagine the many fond memories Stanage recalled while walking his rounds in the old landmark during the early 1950s.

The catcher who had received very little media attention during his career, died at age 81 on November 11, 1964, when all the Detroit newspapers were on strike. Thus, his passing was scarcely recorded, and his burial place is unknown. His first wife, Della, had died in 1950. Stanage was survived by his second wife, the former Mabel N. Mason, whom he married in 1952, and four children from his first marriage.

JIM MOYES

DETROIT

GEORGE AUGUST "HOOKS" DAUSS
RIGHT-HANDED PITCHER, 1912–1926

George "Hooks" Dauss used to tell other retired ballplayers in the St. Louis area that he was never a great pitcher, nor had he ever pitched any memorable games, but he was proud that he did manage to win quite a lot of games in his 15-year major league career with the Detroit Tigers. Often overshadowed by the offensive stars in Detroit's outfield, which during Dauss's career included future Hall of Famers Ty Cobb, Sam Crawford, and Harry Heilmann, Dauss gradually emerged as the workhorse of the Tigers pitching staff in the latter part of the Deadball Era. He won more than 20 games three times and eventually eclipsed George Mullin as the winningest pitcher in Tigers history, with 222 victories.

Despite being of average height and looking a bit frail at 168 pounds, the right-handed Dauss was remarkably durable and versatile, pitching over 200 innings for 11 years in a row and making 150 relief appearances during his career, closing out games in 121 of them. He pitched 245 career complete games, finishing in the top ten in the league nine times. Nicknamed for his best pitch, Hooks (or Hookie) used excellent control of his signature curveball to compensate for only an average fastball. Dauss was known to have an easygoing nature, even on the mound, yet he led the league in hit batsmen three times and still ranks in the all-time top 30 in that category.

George August Daus was born in Indianapolis on September 22, 1889, to Annie and John Daus, a local machinist. As a child George—who later added an extra 's' to his surname—attended the local elementary school with his brothers Raymond and Edward, and later spent a year studying at the Manual Training High School in Indianapolis, where he attracted some local attention as a talented right-handed pitcher on their baseball team. The next year, at age 19, he landed a spot on his first

professional team, South Bend (Indiana) in the Central League. Aggie Grant, the manager of the South Bend team, thought Dauss was "too small" and released him before ever allowing him to pitch in a game. Before he left the team, however, Dauss convinced Grant to let him pitch an exhibition game against Duluth (Minnesota) of the Northern League. He pitched a shutout and Duluth promptly signed him for the 1909 season.

Dauss went 19–10 for Duluth in 37 games that year, and then was ejected in the first inning of the Minnesota–Wisconsin League championship game for (uncharacteristically) arguing balls and strikes. Apparently, several of Dauss's teammates agreed with him and they subsequently kicked and beat the umpire, before they too were ejected. At season's end Duluth sold his rights to St. Paul of the American Association, but he was subsequently returned to Duluth to play in 1910 and then was sent to Winona (Minnesota) of the same league in 1911. At the end of the 1911 season the Pittsburgh Pirates bought his rights, but sent him back to St. Paul for the 1912 season, where he defeated the Pirates in a preseason game. He went on to post a disappointing record of 12–19 that year, despite having a low ERA. It was while pitching for St. Paul in 1912 that Dauss impressed Tiger scout "Deacon" Jim McGuire. Detroit bought his rights in late August.

Dauss would not have to wait long to make his major league debut. On September 28, 1912, Dauss overcame nervous wildness to win his first major league game. He walked eight batters and hit three others, but gave up only four hits in a darkness-shortened 6–2 win over Cleveland. His performance impressed his catcher, Oscar Stanage, and was enough to convince manager Hughey Jennings to install him into the regular rotation in 1913.

In his first full season in the major leagues, Dauss

won 13 games, tied for the second most on the team, and posted an excellent 2.48 ERA. After the season his performance drew the attention of the Federal League team forming in his hometown of Indianapolis. Tiger owner Frank Navin wisely came to terms with Dauss before he could accept the Hoosiers' offer, and Dauss rewarded him in 1914 with an 18-win campaign in which he pitched more than 300 innings for the first time in his career. That year Dauss finished fifth in the American League with 150 strikeouts, and led the majors by hitting a career-high 18 batters. He also made ten relief appearances and tied for the league lead in saves, with four.

The 1915 season was the closest Dauss ever came to being on a pennant-winning team. Dauss, Harry Coveleski, and Jean Dubuc made up an impressive pitching trio, contributing 63 wins as the Tigers went on to win 100 games for the first time in team history, finishing only 2½ games behind the Boston Red Sox. Also for the first time, Dauss led the team in wins with 24 and once again pitched over 300 innings. He posted an excellent ERA of 2.50 and often pitched in relief when needed.

1915 was also a watershed year for Dauss personally. He married Ollie Speake in midseason, without missing his start in the pitching rotation. When the team arrived in St. Louis on May 29, Dauss quietly slipped away to attend a double ceremony where both Ollie and her sister Jessie were married. Later that afternoon, he beat the Browns at Sportsman's Park, 7–1.

As he moved into the prime of his career, Dauss became known as a good fielding pitcher, topping 100 assists four times, usually with a fielding percentage among the league leaders. He was also a weak hitter, however, managing only a .189 batting average for his career. In a game against the Senators in 1916, Dauss banged out a ninth-inning walk-off triple to defeat a young pitcher named Sam Rice, who would one day be inducted into the Hall of Fame as an outfielder. Rice was so discouraged that he lost the game to "probably the worst hitting pitcher in baseball" that he decided to give up pitching altogether.

In 1916 the Tigers once again battled the Red Sox for the pennant, but fell four games short. Coveleski won 21 games and Dauss was right behind him with 19 wins, but the Tigers' brief period of pitching depth was all but over. After 1916 Dubuc was sold to the minors and Coveleski won only four more games before retiring.

Even though Dauss posted a career-best 2.43 ERA in 1917 and won 17 games, his team slid into mediocrity.

In the war-shortened season of 1918, for the first time in his career Dauss lost more games than he won, laboring for a Tiger team that finished in seventh place. In 1919 Dauss rebounded with a 21–9 record, as the Tigers finished in the first division with a winning record; however, in 1920 they sank back to seventh place again and Dauss lost 21 games, despite posting a respectable 3.56 ERA. Like many pitchers of the late Deadball Era, Dauss saw his ERA rise with the introduction of the lively ball in 1920. In fact Dauss's ERA after 1920 was higher by almost a full run per game than it had been up to that point.

1921 brought another major change: Ty Cobb replaced Hughey Jennings as the Tigers manager. Cobb has often been criticized for his erratic use of his pitching staff, and his use of Dauss as both a starter and a reliever produced somewhat disappointing results over the next two years—although Jennings had used him the same way. In 1923, however, erratic use turned to overuse, as Dauss became perhaps the only Tiger pitcher Cobb had any confidence in. It also marked the last big statistical year for Dauss; he won 21 games and pitched a grueling 316 innings in a career-high 50 games. In 1924 Cobb wanted to use Dauss mostly in relief, but the inconsistency of Detroit's starting pitching caused him to spot-start Dauss throughout the season before reinserting him into the starting rotation in 1925.

In the spring of 1926 Dauss developed a sore arm for one of the few times in his career. Increasingly during that season, he experienced the symptoms of an irregular heartbeat. Despite his health problems, he still led the league with 11 relief wins. When his heart ailment was fully diagnosed at the end of the season, Dauss decided it was time to hang up his spikes.

Dauss retired to his 320-acre farm near his wife's hometown of St. Louis. Limited in how much manual labor he could perform, his brother-in-law provided the day-to-day management of the farm. Dauss eventually took a job at Pinkerton's National Detective Agency office in St. Louis, where his co-workers described him, true to form, as "likeable, dependable and sturdy."

Eventually his heart condition worsened, and on July 27, 1963, he died at age 73 of a ruptured aorta after an extended illness. He was buried at Sunset Memorial Park in the St. Louis suburb of Affton, Missouri, and was survived by his wife and two brothers.

BOB O'LEARY

DETROIT

Robert Hayes Veach
Left fielder, 1912–1923

As the cleanup hitter on one of the strongest offensive teams of his day, Bobby Veach was one of the truly great RBI men of the late Deadball Era, easily leading the major leagues in runs driven in over the 12 years that he was a full-time player (1913–1924). Veach drove in over 100 runs in a season six times, hit 30 or more doubles eight times, and smacked ten or more triples ten years in a row. Veach played for 14 major league seasons in all and hit .300 or better ten times, finishing with a lifetime .310 batting average.

Veach was known to be easygoing, steady, and unassuming, characteristics that put him in stark contrast to, and at times at odds with, the volatile Ty Cobb playing next to him in the outfield. At 5'11" and a slim 165 pounds, Veach was small for a power hitter, but as baseball writer Fred Lieb noted, he "packed a terrific punch for his size." A right-handed fielder who batted from the left side, Veach was a full and free swinger. He rarely altered his picturesque swing to adjust to pitchers, slumps, or game situations. For this reason he was remarkably consistent offensively, although he sometimes struggled to execute situational hitting staples like the hit-and-run. Although regarded as awkward in the field and on the basepaths while in the minor leagues, Veach was always blessed with a strong and accurate arm and good natural speed as a runner. In time he worked hard to make himself an accomplished fielder (he recorded over 300 putouts six times and over ten assists 11 times) and base stealer (he swiped 195 bases in his career).

Robert Hayes Veach was born in Island, Kentucky, on June 29, 1888, one of three sons of Mark and Sarah Veach. Like many ballplayers of his day, Veach was of Irish descent and the male members of his family were coal miners. His father moved the family to Madisonville, Kentucky, when Veach was 12 years old, and he played his first organized baseball game at the relatively advanced age of 13. The following year Veach quit high school to join his father, and eventually his brothers, working in the mines. Later, even while in the minor leagues, Veach continued to work there during the winters. Working in the mines for almost all of his teenage years undoubtedly strengthened Veach, but it may have left him little time to develop other baseball skills. When he was 17 years old, Veach moved to Herrin, Illinois, and began his professional career playing semipro baseball in the old Eastern Illinois Trolley League. He made very little money, but showed enough promise to be signed five years later as a pitcher by the Peoria Distillers of the Three-I League.

A few games into the 1910 season, Peoria farmed Veach out to the Kankakee, Illinois, team in the Northern Association, where he reportedly posted a 10–5 record as a pitcher. The next year Veach was back with Peoria, who moved him to the outfield to take advantage of the power he showed as a hitter. The move was successful, and Veach finished the year hitting .297.

During this time Peoria employed Charlie Barrett, a former scout for the St. Louis Browns, as a fundamentals coach. Barrett helped to polish Veach's fielding and baserunning skills. In 1912 Veach's batting average improved to .325 before he was sold to Indianapolis of the American Association. There, he hit .285 during a brief two-month stay until the Detroit Tigers purchased the 24-year-old and added him to their late-season roster.

When Veach arrived in Detroit in late 1912, the Tigers had been platooning left fielders for a number of years, trying to find a player who could both hit and field. The aging Davy Jones made the majority of starts in 1912, but, hitting leadoff, had driven in only 24 runs in 99 games that year. When Veach hit .342 and drove in 15 runs in just 23 games at the end of 1912, manager Hughey Jennings knew he had found the third piece of his outfield. In later years Veach remarked how kind Jennings had been to him and how patient he was in developing his skills as a ballplayer. Over the next two years Veach established himself as an everyday player, hitting over .270 and driving in an average of 68 runs a year. Baserunners also learned about his powerful arm as he started a string of nine consecutive seasons with 14 or more outfield assists.

Despite his small size, Veach swung the bat like a powerful slugger, down at the end of the handle, and with similar results. "Years ago I choked up on the bat," Veach later explained to F.C. Lane of *Baseball Magazine*. "Choking up has the effect of shortening the bat and it seemed reasonable to suppose that the shorter the bat the more quickly you could swing to meet the ball. In theory this was sound, but in practice I found it wouldn't work. Most of the really good hitters swing from the handle of the bat." Veach was a free swinger with a long, beautiful stroke; he put his shoulders, and not just his wrists and arms, into each of his swings. Despite this aggressive approach, Veach walked more often than he struck out, and never ranked among the league leaders in the latter category.

By 1915 Veach was just entering his prime, and his offensive performance placed him near the top of the league. He hit .313 that year and tied Sam Crawford for the league lead in RBI with 112. He also led the league in doubles with 40, was second in extra-base hits, and third—on both his team and the AL—in hits and total bases. 1915 also marked the last full productive year of Crawford's career, and it was clear that Veach was poised to take over as the man counted on to drive in key runs for the Tigers. The team was an offensive juggernaut and roared to a 100-win season, which left them only 2½ games short of the pennant. From 1916 to the war-shortened 1918 season, Veach continued his assault on AL pitchers, hitting over .300 in 1916 and 1917, leading the league in RBI in 1917 and 1918, and finishing among the league leaders in hits, doubles, and triples each year.

In 1919 the Tigers rebounded with a winning season and Veach had one of the best years of his career. He posted a .355 batting average, second only to Cobb in all of baseball, and the highest total of his career. In addition he led the league in hits (191, tied with Cobb), doubles (45), and triples (17). As the Deadball Era ended, Veach's hitting style seemed tailor-made for the free-swinging offensive era that followed it, and yet 1920 saw the 32-year-old Veach's offensive production dip slightly as he batted .307 and drove in 113 runs.

On September 17, 1920, against the Red Sox, he had one of the best games of his career, collecting six hits and hitting for the cycle. When Jennings stepped down as the Tiger manager at the end of the season, however, and Cobb was named to replace him, life as a Tiger would never be the same for Veach.

Veach was just not Cobb's type of player. It had bothered Cobb for years that Veach did not seem to take baseball very seriously and was known to joke with opposing players, even pitchers, something Cobb could not tolerate. Determined to wipe the ever-present smile off Veach's face, Cobb instructed Harry Heilmann to yell insults at him throughout the 1921 season to make him angry. The ploy may have worked, because Veach's offensive numbers improved in almost every category in 1921. In fact the Tigers starting outfield had a season for the ages, banging out 641 hits for a .372 batting average and driving in 368 runs. Veach also led the league in outfield putouts with 384, showing how far he had come as a fielder. The team's pitching, however, was once again too weak to contend for a pennant and the Tigers finished with a losing record. At the end of the season Cobb refused to admit that he had instigated the year-long hazing, though he had promised Heilmann to do so. When Heilmann tried to explain, Veach did not believe him and carried a grudge for many years.

In the winter and spring leading

up to the 1922 season, Cobb tried to trade Veach to the Yankees for shortstop Everett Scott, but the Yankees would not budge, despite the early suspensions of sluggers Babe Ruth and Bob Meusel. Veach responded to his manager's lack of confidence in him by almost mirroring his excellent 1921 season, collecting 202 hits, driving in 126 runs, and recording 375 putouts. Despite this continued excellence at the plate and in the field, Cobb continued to try to replace his 34-year-old left fielder. Veach hit .321 in 1923, but had only half his normal 600 at-bats, due partly to injuries and partly to increased playing time for talented newcomer Heinie Manush. In January of 1924 Cobb sold Veach to the last-place Red Sox for an undisclosed amount of cash.

Veach was not happy about how his Tiger career had ended, nor the prospect of going to the team with the most anemic offense in the league. After an initial holdout he joined his Red Sox teammates before spring training and ended up having a decent season, driving in 99 runs and hitting .295. At his first game back in Detroit on May 18, the local fans thanked Veach for his years as a Tiger by presenting him with a diamond ring. Veach returned the favor that same year, arranging a try-out with Detroit for future Hall of Fame second baseman Charlie Gehringer, whom he had spotted in a sandlot game.

The 1924 season was to be Veach's last as a major league starter. In May 1925, after only five at-bats, he was traded to the Yankees, who later sold him to the Senators in August for the waiver price. Used almost exclusively as a bench player, he had the distinction in 1925 of pinch hitting for Babe Ruth in one game and also of breaking up Ted Lyons's bid for a no-hitter with two outs in the ninth in another. Finally, by ending the year with the Senators, he was able to play in his first and only World Series. Characteristically, although he had only two plate appearances, he drove in a run.

From 1926 to 1929 Veach played for the Toledo Mud Hens of the American Association. In his first three years with Toledo, he averaged 157 games a season, hit over .360 each year and won the batting crown in 1928 with a .382 average at age 40. Moving to the Jersey City Skeeters in the International League in 1930, he played in only 75 games.

Veach retired from baseball for good after the 1930 season and settled down in the Detroit area with his wife of over 20 years, Ethel Clare Schiller Veach, and their sons. Returning to the other profession he knew well, he purchased an interest in a coal company in 1933 and was the sole owner two years later. In 1943 he was hospitalized and had a serious abdominal operation. He was never completely healthy again and died at home two years later on August 7, 1945, from what may have been lung cancer. Survived by his wife and sons, he was entombed in the White Chapel Memorial Cemetery in Southfield, Michigan.

BOB O'LEARY

DETROIT

HARRY FRANK COVELESKI
LEFT-HANDED PITCHER, 1914–1918

Several years before his younger brother Stanley embarked on a Hall of Fame career, Harry Coveleski established the family name as the Giant Killer who, as an unheralded rookie with the Philadelphia Phillies, defeated the New York Giants three times in five days to deny John McGraw's squad the 1908 National League pennant. A few years after his auspicious debut, the left-handed Coveleski drifted out of the major leagues and become an object lesson in the unpredictable vagaries of the sport, his case "frequently cited as that of a player who had showed excellent promise only to prove a flivver," according to *Baseball Magazine*. Coveleski, however, with a rising fastball, sharp-breaking curve, and an endurance first developed working in the coal mines of Pennsylvania, returned to the major league spotlight to enjoy three standout seasons for the Detroit Tigers from 1914 to 1916. The undisputed anchor of the league's most beleaguered pitching staff, Coveleski won 20 or more games and pitched at least 300 innings in three consecutive seasons. "Other pitchers on the Tiger club may grow wild and give an unbelievable number of free passes to first," John J. Ward noted in *Baseball Magazine* during the 1916 season. "Others may be hit to all corners of the lot; but Coveleskie, though he has his off days like all the rest, is a steady, consistent performer whose work is uniformly good."

Coveleski was born Harry Frank Kowalewski on April 23, 1886, in Shamokin, Pennsylvania, one of five sons of Polish immigrants Anthony and Ann Kowalewski. When Harry entered professional baseball he anglicized his name to Coveleskie, as would his brother Stan; the final 'e' was not dropped until after his retirement. The father worked as a coal miner in Shamokin and, like the other sons, Harry left school at the age of 12 to work in the mines, where he toiled as a slate picker for $3.75

per week. He was nicknamed Donkey Boy because he was also responsible for driving the mules that carried supplies into and out of the mines.

Given the grueling nature of his work, one would expect Coveleski to have been more eager to escape the mines. In fact he fell into professional baseball almost by accident. While he was pitching for the Bunker Hills, a sandlot team in Shamokin, a scout for the St. Louis Cardinals spotted the left-handed Coveleski and signed him to a contract for Kane (Pennsylvania) of the Inter-State League in 1907. The league disbanded after Harry won four and lost seven. He then joined the independent Wildwood (New Jersey) Ottens, where his brother John played the infield.

His performance in New Jersey was impressive enough to catch the attention of the Philadelphia Phillies, who signed Coveleski to a $250 per month contract on September 3, 1907. Harry appeared in four games for the Phillies that year, pitching 20 innings and allowing no earned runs.

Standing six feet tall and weighing 180 pounds, Coveleski initially threw with a side-arm motion. At the beginning of the 1908 season, the Phillies optioned the young left-hander to Lancaster (Pennsylvania) of the Tri-State League, where Coveleski converted to an over-the-top pitching motion. The change paid immediate dividends, as Coveleski enjoyed a banner season for Lancaster, finishing the year 22–15 with 232 strikeouts in 304 innings.

Near the end of the 1908 season, the Phillies recalled him, whereupon Coveleski forever etched his name in the game's lore by beating the injury-depleted New York Giants three times in the span of just five days. On September 29, with New York tied for first place, Coveleski tossed a six-hitter at the Polo Grounds, shutting out the Giants 7–0. Two days later, Harry allowed only four hits against the Giants, winning 6–2.

Promised $50 by manager Bill Murray if he would work against the Giants again on October 3, Harry accepted the assignment against Christy Mathewson and won, 3–2, knocking McGraw's club into third place. The Giants did not go down easily. They had a runner on third in the ninth with nobody out, but Coveleski retired the side. The newly-minted Giant Killer had virtually single-handedly prevented the Giants from capturing the National League pennant. Assessing the youngster's stuff after the season, Chicago Cubs pitcher Rube Kroh told *The Sporting News* that Coveleski "has plenty of speed, all that any pitcher wants, and he has a great curved ball. His fast ball has a jump on it."

Despite his extraordinary showing at the end of the 1908 season, Coveleski failed to pay off on his considerable promise. Over his next two seasons in the NL, the Giant Killer won only seven more games, just one of them against the New York Giants, as arm troubles limited his effectiveness. After going 6–10 in 1909, Coveleski was dealt to the Cincinnati Reds. Harry lasted only one month into the 1910 season before Cincinnati optioned him to Birmingham (Alabama) of the Southern Association. The Reds recalled Coveleski in September, but the left-hander was shelled in two of three starts and sold to the Southern Association's Chattanooga Lookouts at the end of the season.

Over the next three seasons in Chattanooga, the lefty rediscovered his game. In 1913 Coveleski pitched 32 complete games for the Lookouts, including seven shutouts, en route to a 28–9 record with an ERA well under 2. Branch Rickey of the St. Louis Browns tried to land Coveleski, but the Detroit Tigers beat him to the punch, purchasing the left-hander's contract for the 1914 season.

Coveleski, presumed to be washed up four years earlier, surprised the baseball world with his 1914 comeback, finishing second in the league with 22 victories and leading the Tigers staff with a 2.49 ERA in 303⅓ innings pitched. During his days in the minor leagues, Coveleski had developed a reputation as a pitcher who could be thrown off his game by taunts, and throughout the 1914 season teams tried to unnerve the left-hander by humming the song, "Silver Threads Among the Gold." (The reasons behind Coveleski's aversion to the song remain unknown.) According to the *Washington Post*, the New York Yankees performed this routine to excellent effect. "For a few innings [Coveleski] performed in great style," the *Post* reported of one contest. "And then of a sudden there came from the Yankees' bench: 'Darling, I am growing old / Silver threads among the gold.'" When Coveleski looked up, "the singing ceased. When he took up pitching again it resumed. Sometimes the strains came in solo order. Then it was a duet. Now it rolled out in a chorus.…The air became filled with the music—and Coveleskie was through for the day."

Despite the taunts, in 1915 Coveleski put up another good season, almost identical to his 1914 effort, winning 22 games and posting a 2.45 ERA. In 1916 he was even better: his 1.97 ERA ranked fourth in the league and he pitched a career-best 324⅓ innings, finishing the season with a record of 21–11. For the three-year span of 1914–1916, Coveleski had won 65 games against only 36 defeats, and tossed 940⅓ innings. The heavy workload proved too great for his well-traveled left arm, however, and, according to newspaper reports, his wing "went back on him" during 1917 spring training. Coveleski struggled through 11 starts, winding up with a record of 4–6 before he was shelved for the season. He managed only one start in 1918 before drawing his release.

In the ensuing years Coveleski tried to extend his playing career in the minor leagues, making several unsuccessful comeback attempts with Little Rock in Arkansas, Altoona in Pennsylvania, and Oklahoma City and McAlester in Oklahoma. In 1922 he accepted a job as a plainclothesman for Ford's River Rouge plant in Michigan. Two years later, he returned to Shamokin, where he lived with his wife, the former Cecilia Glassie, and their only child, William. In 1926 he began a four-year stint with the Shamokin police force. After leaving the squad in 1930 he operated a café, and was fined for serving alcohol in violation of the prohibition laws. To pay off the fine, Harry took a job as a watchman in a silk mill, eventually earning enough money to once again open his own place, a tavern he called The Giant Killer.

Coveleski died on August 4, 1950, at the age of 64. He was buried in St. Stanislaus Cemetery, in Shamokin, Pennsylvania.

JOHN HEISELMAN

PHILADELPHIA

I t was the best of teams; it was the worst of teams. The Philadelphia Athletics won six of the first 14 American League pennants and three world championships. Then they finished last—way down out-of-sight last—for the next seven years. In 1916 they won 36 and lost 117, and finished 40 games out of seventh place. Their .235 winning percentage that year is still the lowest in the league's history.

When the minor American League assumed major status and invaded the east in 1901, league president Ban Johnson gave the franchise in the nation's third-largest city to Connie Mack. In a shrewd public relations move, Mack adopted the name of the last Philly team to win a pennant, the 1883 American Association Athletics. When he arrived in January 1901, the 38-year-old former catcher had three months to find local financial backing, a place to play, and a team of players. He found the first in Ben Shibe, built the second and called it Columbia Park, and acquired the third in the traditional way of invaders: raiding those who had what he needed.

Mack lured away the cross-town Phillies' star second baseman, Nap Lajoie, and half their pitching staff. He brought first baseman Harry Davis out of retirement, and acted on a tip to acquire 25-year-old left-hander Eddie Plank. After finishing fourth in their inaugural season, on Opening Day 1902 the A's had most of the fruits of their Phillies raids taken away by

WINNING PERCENTAGE 1901–1919

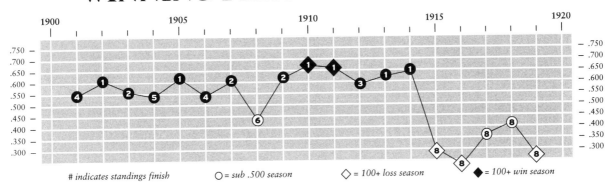

# indicates standings finish   ◯ = sub .500 season   ◇ = 100+ loss season   ◆ = 100+ win season

a state supreme court ruling. Mack scrambled to fill the holes and surprised everybody by winning the pennant. The new Athletics, featuring fireballing left-hander Rube Waddell, were now the baseball toast of the town. Three years later, they won a second AL pennant before falling to the New York Giants in five games in the World Series.

Saddled with an aging roster, Mack set out to rebuild. Given a completely free hand by Ben Shibe, he did what he enjoyed most: finding rough stones as green as emeralds on high school, sandlot, and college grounds and polishing them into stars. By 1910 the Athletics, led by young stars Frank Baker, Eddie Collins, Jack Barry, Rube Oldring, and Jack Coombs, were world champions. Two more titles followed in 1911 and 1913, but Mack's dynasty crumbled after the 1914 World Series, when the Athletics were swept by the Boston Braves.

His team's harmony torn by Federal League overtures, his payroll soaring and attendance falling, Mack sold Collins to the White Sox prior to the 1915 season. Ready to build a new winning machine, over the next few years Mack dealt away the remains of his old one. For the rest of the decade he searched the sandlots and campuses for a new vein of nuggets, but with no success. It looked as if he would never find them again. And then…but that's a story for another era.

NORMAN MACHT

ALL-ERA TEAM

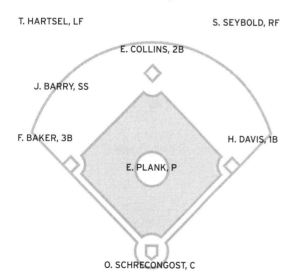

R. OLDRING, CF

T. HARTSEL, LF

S. SEYBOLD, RF

E. COLLINS, 2B

J. BARRY, SS

F. BAKER, 3B

H. DAVIS, 1B

E. PLANK, P

O. SCHRECONGOST, C

TEAM LEADERS 1901–1919

BATTING

GAMES
H. Davis 1,413
D. Murphy 1,412
R. Oldring. 1,188

RUNS
H. Davis 811
E. Collins 702
T. Hartsel 686

HITS
H. Davis 1,500
D. Murphy 1,489
R. Oldring. 1,222

RBI
H. Davis 761
D. Murphy 664
F. Baker. 612

DOUBLES
H. Davis 319
D. Murphy 279
S. Seybold 213

TRIPLES
D. Murphy 102
F. Baker. 88
E. Collins 83

HOME RUNS
H. Davis 69
S. Seybold 51
F. Baker. 48

STOLEN BASES
E. Collins 370
H. Davis 223
T. Hartsel 195

BATTING AVERAGE
(2000+ plate appearances)
E. Collins 338
F. Baker. 321
S. McInnis 313

PITCHING

GAMES
E. Plank 524
C. Bender 385
R. Waddell 251

WINS
E. Plank 284
C. Bender 193
R. Waddell 131

LOSSES
E. Plank 162
C. Bender 102
R. Waddell 82

INNINGS
E. Plank 3,860⅔
C. Bender 2,602
R. Waddell 1,869⅓

STRIKEOUTS
E. Plank 1,985
R. Waddell 1,576
C. Bender 1,536

WALKS
E. Plank 913
C. Bender 614
J. Coombs. 606

SHUTOUTS
E. Plank 59
R. Waddell 37
C. Bender 36

ERA
(800+ innings pitched)
R. Waddell 1.97
C. Morgan 2.15
C. Bender 2.32

TYPICAL LINEUPS 1901–1919

1901

1. D. Fultz, CF
2. H. Davis, 1B
3. L. Cross, 3B
4. N. Lajoie, 2B
5. S. Seybold, RF
6. M. McIntyre, LF
7. D. Powers, C
8. J. Dolan, SS

1902

1. T. Hartsel, LF
2. D. Fultz, CF
3. H. Davis, 1B
4. L. Cross, 3B
5. S. Seybold, RF
6. D. Murphy, 2B
7. M. Cross, SS
8. O. Schrecongost
   D. Powers, C

1903

1. T. Hartsel, LF
2. O. Pickering, CF
3. H. Davis, 1B
4. L. Cross, 3B
5. S. Seybold, RF
6. D. Murphy, 2B
7. M. Cross, SS
8. O. Schrecongost
   D. Powers, C

1904

1. T. Hartsel, LF
2. O. Pickering, CF
3. H. Davis, 1B
4. L. Cross, 3B
5. S. Seybold, RF
6. D. Murphy, 2B
7. M. Cross, SS
8. O. Schrecongost, C

1905

1. T. Hartsel, LF
2. D. Hoffman, CF
3. H. Davis, 1B
4. L. Cross, 3B
5. S. Seybold, RF
6. D. Murphy, 2B
7. J. Knight
   M. Cross, SS
8. O. Schrecongost, C

1906

1. T. Hartsel, LF
2. B. Lord, CF
3. H. Davis, 1B
4. S. Seybold, RF
5. D. Murphy, 2B
6. O. Schrecongost, C
7. M. Cross, SS
8. J. Knight, 3B

1907

1. T. Hartsel, LF
2. S. Nicholls
   M. Cross, SS
3. S. Seybold, RF
4. H. Davis, 1B
5. D. Murphy, 2B
6. J. Collins, 3B
7. R. Oldring, CF
8. O. Schrecongost, C

1908

1. T. Hartsel, LF
2. R. Oldring, CF
3. E. Collins, 2B
4. D. Murphy, RF
5. H. Davis, 1B
6. J. Collins, 3B
7. S. Nicholls, SS
8. O. Schrecongost
   D. Powers, C

1909

1. T. Hartsel, LF
   R. Oldring, CF–LF
2. B. Ganley, CF
3. E. Collins, 2B
4. D. Murphy, RF
5. H. Davis, 1B
6. F. Baker, 3B
7. J. Barry, SS
8. I. Thomas, C

1910

1. T. Hartsel, LF
2. R. Oldring, CF
3. E. Collins, 2B
4. F. Baker, 3B
5. H. Davis, 1B
6. D. Murphy, RF
7. J. Barry, SS
8. J. Lapp
   I. Thomas, C

1911

1. B. Lord, LF
2. R. Oldring, CF
3. E. Collins, 2B
4. F. Baker, 3B
5. D. Murphy, RF
6. S. McInnis, 1B
7. J. Barry, SS
8. I. Thomas, C

1912

1. B. Lord, RF
2. R. Oldring, CF
3. E. Collins, 2B
4. F. Baker, 3B
5. S. McInnis, 1B
6. A. Strunk, LF
7. J. Barry, SS
8. J. Lapp, C

1913

1. E. Murphy, RF
2. R. Oldring, LF
3. E. Collins, 2B
4. F. Baker, 3B
5. S. McInnis, 1B
6. A. Strunk, CF
7. J. Barry, SS
8. J. Lapp
   W. Schang, C

1914

1. E. Murphy, RF
2. R. Oldring, LF
3. E. Collins, 2B
4. F. Baker, 3B
5. S. McInnis, 1B
6. A. Strunk, CF
7. J. Barry, SS
8. W. Schang, C

1915

1. E. Murphy, RF
2. J. Walsh, CF
   A. Strunk, CF–RF
3. R. Oldring, LF
4. W. Schang,
   3B–C–CF–LF
5. N. Lajoie, 2B
6. S. McInnis, 1B
7. J. Lapp, C
8. L. Kopf, SS–3B

1916

1. W. Witt, SS
2. J. Walsh, RF
3. A. Strunk, CF
4. W. Schang, LF
5. N. Lajoie, 2B
6. S. McInnis, 1B
7. C. Pick, 3B
8. B. Meyer, C

1917

1. C. Jamieson, RF
2. A. Strunk, CF
3. P. Bodie, LF
4. R. Bates, 3B
5. S. McInnis, 1B
6. W. Schang, C
7. W. Witt, SS
8. R. Grover, 2B

1918 (first half)

1. C. Jamieson, RF
2. R. Oldring, LF
3. T. Walker, CF
4. G. Burns, 1B
5. L. Gardner, 3B
6. R. Shannon, SS
7. J. Dugan, 2B
8. W. McAvoy
   C. Perkins, C

1918 (second half)

1. C. Jamieson, RF
2. M. Kopp, LF
3. T. Walker, CF
4. G. Burns, 1B
5. L. Gardner, 3B
6. W. McAvoy
   C. Perkins, C
7. J. Dykes, 2B
8. J. Dugan, SS

1919

1. W. Witt, 2B-LF
2. F. Thomas, 3B
3. T. Walker, CF
   B. Roth, RF
4. A. Strunk, RF
5. G. Burns, 1B–RF
6. M. Kopp, LF
7. J. Dugan, SS
8. C. Perkins, C

PHILADELPHIA

HARRY H. DAVIS
FIRST BASEMAN, 1901–1911, 1913–1917

Several years before Babe Ruth revolutionized the game with the home run, during a period when hitting a baseball was likened by some to swatting a cabbage, Harry Davis was one of the country's most feared sluggers. Known today primarily for leading the American League in home runs four consecutive seasons, the right-handed Davis was as apt to win games with his brains as he was with his bat.

Handpicked by Connie Mack, he was the heart and soul of the early Philadelphia Athletics teams that dominated the newly-formed American League, winning six titles and three World Series. Davis really had two separate major league careers: one before 1900 and the other after; one as an itinerant player without a steady team or position, the other as the cornerstone of a dynasty. He was credited by the Philadelphia press with being a significant portion of the brains behind the A's success, and as a player, coach, manager, and scout, Davis was one of the most respected and admired figures in baseball.

Harry Davis was born in Philadelphia on July 19, 1873, the oldest of two boys. His father, John, was a shoemaker, and his mother, Mary, took in wash. Christened simply Harry Davis, he added the middle initial H later in life to differentiate himself from the numerous other Harry Davises in and around Philadelphia. Considering there was a notorious gangster in Ohio named Harry Davis, another in politics, and a prominent Pennsylvania theater owner with the same name, it is no wonder he wished to more clearly identify himself.

His father died of typhoid when he was five and his mother, unable to provide for the family, applied in September 1879 to send Harry to Girard College, the famous Philadelphia elementary and high school for disadvantaged and orphaned boys. He was eventually accepted, and enrolled on January 3, 1882. There he excelled in business and accounting and became interested in baseball. At the time Girard College was a fertile source of baseball talent, eventually sending several players to the major leagues, including Moose McCormick and Johnny Lush. While there, Davis primarily caught and played the outfield. During his years at Girard Harry also was given the nickname Jasper by his schoolmates, a name by which he would be familiarly known for the rest of his life.

Harry graduated from Girard in June 1891 and that summer caught for the Bank Clerks' Athletic Club in the Amateur League of Philadelphia. He later played in the Philadelphia area with the Pennsylvania Railroad club and in the Suburban League with Riverton before signing his first professional contract with Providence of the Eastern League. He batted .412 in a five-game trial before being dispatched to Pawtucket in the New England League. An immediate success, he batted .369 to rank second in the circuit. The following year, playing and managing part-time for Pawtucket, he won the league batting title with a .391 average and was subsequently purchased by the New York Giants.

Harry joined the Giants after the minor league season ended and made his major league debut with them on September 21, 1895, getting three hits against Boston, including a bases-loaded triple. Davis drove in five runs in his team's 13–12 victory. In the wake of a disappointing season for the Gothamites, the papers were full of glowing reports about Davis. O.P. Caylor of the *New York Herald*, never known for his reserve, bubbled, "He is the find of the season. Davis is highly intelligent, quick-witted, cool as a veteran and a natural ball player. If he does not turn out to be a second Mike [King] Kelly, indications are worthless. [He] will be the idol of the Polo Grounds patrons."

Spending most of his time in left field, Davis got off

to a good start at the plate in 1896 and was on a pace to drive in over 100 runs. Although he was regarded as a good fielder, with a strong and accurate arm, Harry's fielding was in fact subpar. Only 22, he also suffered from rheumatism and for these reasons, apparently, the Giants were willing to give him up despite the initial ballyhoo. During a doubleheader on July 25 he was traded to the Pittsburgh Pirates, along with $1,000, for Jake Beckley. Mack, who was Pittsburgh's manager at the time, immediately proclaimed Davis to be the everyday first baseman. The trade was not well received in Pittsburgh: the popular Beckley, despite an uncharacteristically poor year in 1896, proved productive for several years thereafter, but Davis was a dud with the Pirates, batting .190 over 44 games.

Davis improved to bat .305 in 111 games for the Pirates in 1897, and also emerged as one of the team's main power sources, connecting for a league-leading 28 triples—which remains the fifth-highest total in major league history—while hitting only 10 doubles, a statistical peculiarity no one has ever matched.

On March 1, 1898, before heading to spring training with the Pirates, Harry was married to Eleanor Hicks of Philadelphia. Together they would have two sons, Harry Jr. and Eugene.

The next two seasons were marked by injuries and frustration. When healthy, Harry produced, but leg and ankle injuries often forced him out of the lineup. The Pirates sold him to Louisville in July 1898; hitting only .217 for the Colonels, he was released on September 10. Picked up by Washington in October, he appeared in one game for the club before the season ended. The next year was no better; Harry appeared in only 18 games for the Senators in 1899, hitting .188, and was released to Providence of the Eastern League in May.

The rest of 1899 and all of 1900 were spent back in Providence. Harry performed very well, hitting over .300 and leading the league in doubles both seasons. In 1899 he led the league in steals, with 70. When 1901 rolled around bidding wars with the American League decimated the Providence roster, and Harry, who was not signed by the new major league, decided he had had enough of professional baseball. He returned to Philadelphia and took a job with the Pennsylvania Railroad. It was not long before Mack, now managing the Philadelphia American League franchise, contacted him about playing first base for the Athletics. After some convincing, Harry agreed and joined the team on May 22 in Chicago. Off to a terrible start, the A's turned it around to finish with a winning record. Harry hit over .300 and remained the A's starting first baseman for nine more seasons. On July 10, against Boston, he hit for the

cycle for the only time in his career.

In 1902 Harry batted over .300 again and led the league in doubles as the Athletics won their first pennant. On August 13, 1902, several years before Germany Schaefer made it popular, he stole first base against the Tigers. Late in the game, Dave Fultz was on third and Harry on first. Harry took off for second, in an attempted double steal, and got into a rundown. Fultz edged off third until he finally drew a throw, but dove back in safely, and Harry wound up on second. Before anyone realized what was happening, Davis ran back to first, making it easily without a throw. Then, before Tigers pitcher George Mullin could deliver a pitch, Harry was off again for second. Mullin threw to second and Fultz dashed for home, beating the throw in. Harry was safe at second again, and both men were credited with a stolen base.

In 1903 Davis's production increased slightly by several measures, but his overall production was down as injuries kept him out of over 30 games. He began to find his home run stroke, however, equaling his previous season's total of six in over a hundred fewer at-bats. The following year he led the American League for the first time with ten, beginning a run of four consecutive home run titles. The A's finished fifth in 1904, but the following year they edged out the White Sox for their second AL crown. Besides leading in homers, Harry paced the league in runs, doubles, and RBI, and finished tied for fifth with a career-high 36 stolen bases. In his first World Series, against John McGraw's New York Giants, he and the rest of the A's were stymied by Christy Mathewson, losing in five games.

Harry earned a reputation over the years as a thinking man's ballplayer—a teacher and a gentleman. Playing for Mack, who discouraged his players from kicking and fighting, had a lot to do with creating this image, but Harry was full of fire, too, and not afraid to say what was on his mind. Back in his early days with the Giants, O.P. Caylor wrote that Harry "blossomed into a kicker of class A. He can give McGraw two jumps, a hundred words, and beat him in a canter. Harry has a voice that puts [Patsy] Tebeau's to shame, and when he isn't denouncing the rascality of the umpire to the latter's face, he is talking to himself about human depravity in general."

Harry was a team leader, and after the sale of Lave Cross following the 1905 season Mack named him captain of the Athletics. He had become Philadelphia's leader on the field and was widely recognized as Mack's lieutenant. Off the field, he took promising players under his wing, boarding them in his own house. From future Hall of Famers (such as Eddie Plank and Eddie Collins) to rookies (such as Billy Orr), many players could cite Davis as a big influence on their careers.

Davis had his best season in 1906, but the next few campaigns saw Harry's offensive numbers decline as the A's finished up and down in the standings. Although he led the league in home runs again in 1906 and 1907, his power began to dwindle in the latter year. After posting slugging percentages better than .400 every season from 1901 to 1906, Davis never again cleared the .400 barrier, and his extra-base hit totals shrank as his speed vanished.

Philadelphia was back on top in 1910, but Harry, now 36, was reaching the end of the line. With most of his power gone, he hit only one home run. Another Girard College alumni, Ben Houser, was being groomed to take his place at first base. Under Harry's tutelage Houser fielded well, but struggled at the plate, and Harry wound up playing most of the season. The A's won their first pennant since 1905 and, with Davis batting a robust .353 in the World Series, won their first world championship, beating the Cubs in five games.

The 1911 season would be Harry's last real hurrah with the Athletics as a player, although it did not get off to a promising start. Harry struggled mightily at the plate in the early season, starting out 2-for-28 as the A's stumbled out of the gate in April. It was early May before the team reached .500. On May 3, at the Hilltop Grounds in New York, Harry hit his last home run, a long drive into the center-field bleachers, as the A's beat the Highlanders. Fittingly, Jack "Stuffy" McInnis, the A's young recruit who would soon take Davis's place, also homered in that game.

The torch was passed, though no one knew it at the time. McInnis, now remembered for the high quality of his fielding at first base, played himself into a regular position because of his bat. His work at shortstop for the A's was abysmal, but he was hitting well over .400 and Harry was not hitting a lick. By early June McInnis was the regular first baseman and Davis's playing days were virtually over. Harry, ever the professional, handled the move with class, tutoring McInnis on the finer points of play around first, and the youngster eventually developed into one of the finest fielders in history. The A's began winning and took the pennant going away.

In late September McInnis was hit on the wrist by a George Mullin pitch and could not play regularly in the World Series. Mack was forced to rely on his aging lieutenant to play first, and there was talk before the Series that this would be a major disadvantage for the A's. Although he hit only .208, Harry acquitted himself nicely, driving in five runs with timely hits to tie teammate Home Run Baker for the Series lead, as the A's

PHILA.

won their second consecutive championship, beating McGraw's Giants. With two outs in the bottom of the ninth in the final game of the Series, Davis initiated a symbolic changing of the guard, leaving the field before the final out so McInnis could be at first base when the championship was won. Davis got a standing ovation from his home fans for the classy gesture, and McInnis made the final putout to clinch the title. After the series, Christy Mathewson tipped his cap to the veteran, and the Giants players insisted that Davis's ingenious sign stealing contributed heavily to the A's victory. Harry had fun with the Giants' claims, admitting most of the sign stealing was a bluff. "Any time we got three or four hits," he said later, "we would give the [Giants] some hint that we were getting their signals. They argued, I guess, that if old Harry Davis could get a hit he must know what was [coming.] Half the time…we were doing nothing of the kind."

With back-to-back championships, his playing skills waning, and his successor in place, Harry decided, to no one's surprise, that the time was right for a career change. In early August, a report surfaced that Davis had agreed to manage the Cleveland Naps in 1912, taking George Stovall's place. Harry refused to talk about it during the season, saying he had not signed any contract, but the consensus was that a deal was in place. After the Series, Harry immediately left for Cleveland and the rumors were soon confirmed.

Despite his impressive resumé and the respect he commanded from his fellow players, Davis's managerial tenure was not a successful one. His first managerial moves did not go over well with the hometown fans. He traded the popular but light-hitting George Stovall, whom Davis had replaced as manager, to the St. Louis Browns for Lefty George, a 4–9 pitcher who never won another game in the American League. Some viewed this as a sign of insecurity, but Harry said he wanted left-handed pitching. It wound up leaving the Naps with a gaping hole at first base for the entire season. Then, in a move that had many scratching their heads, he appointed Ivy Olson team captain, thereby alienating the many fans of Harry's former teammate, Nap Lajoie. The club was beset by injuries and when it did not perform well, Davis was critical to the press and accused his players of quitting on him. The press and the public, in turn, roasted him for the moves he made and maintained that

Stovall, had he remained, would have done better. Gus Fisher, a catcher whom Harry waived during spring training, claimed Davis's "ivory-skulled work…[was] directly responsible for the poor showing." Finally, in early September, with the Naps mired in sixth place, Harry resigned, citing severe criticism as one of the main factors, and Joe Birmingham took over.

Harry signed back on as a coach with his old team for 1913, amid speculation that he would eventually take Mack's place. This, of course, never happened, but with Davis back on the payroll, the A's proceeded to win another world championship, beating the Giants once more, four games to one. Harry, who batted .353 in seven games during the season, did not play in the World Series. The A's celebration, however, was delayed and subdued by news of the death of Harry's eldest son, Harry Jr., the day after the team returned to Philadelphia. The 13-year-old died suddenly of an undetected liver condition reportedly exacerbated by the excitement of the Athletics' victory. The $100,000 infield of McInnis, Baker, Eddie Collins, and Jack Barry, with pitchers Eddie Plank and Chief Bender, were pallbearers at the boy's funeral and joined in mourning Harry's loss.

From 1914 to 1917 Harry continued to serve as a coach for Mack, occasionally appearing in games, mostly as a pinch hitter. After the 1917 season Harry retired temporarily when he was elected to the Philadelphia city council, but he was back by mid-1919 and remained with the A's as a coach and a scout until 1927.

During and after his playing career Harry had many business endeavors. He owned a scrap iron business, was a clerk in the municipality of Philadelphia, and owned a bowling alley later in his career. He also enjoyed bowling, golfing, and trapshooting. In his later years he worked as a foreman for the Burns Detective Agency, guarding the rotogravure plant at the *Philadelphia Inquirer*.

Harry Davis died of a stroke at his home in Philadelphia on August 11, 1947. Upon learning of his death, Connie Mack lamented, "All baseball will miss him. He was a great hitter and fielder, but above all, he was a team player." He is buried at Westminster Cemetery in Bala Cynwyd, Montgomery County, Pennsylvania.

MIKE GRAHEK

Connie Mack

PHILADELPHIA

CONNIE MACK
MANAGER, 1901–1950

He was called the Tall Tactician, the Wise Old Owl, and was the original Mr. Baseball. A stately, dignified gentleman admired by players, fans, umpires, and writers, he was usually addressed as Mr. Mack out of respect, and he and the Philadelphia Athletics were linked so closely that the team was commonly called the Mackmen.

Connie Mack founded the Philadelphia Athletics in 1901, managed the team through 1950, and was a part owner during the franchise's entire 54-year existence in the City of Brotherly Love. Mack skippered some of the Deadball Era's best—and worst—teams. The Athletics won six pennants and three World Series in the American League's first 14 years as a major league, then finished dead last for seven straight seasons. Mack built a second dynasty in the Roaring Twenties and dismantled it during the next decade. An astute but frugal businessman, he persisted through two world wars and the Great Depression before he finally surrendered his spot in the dugout at age 87, after 67 years in baseball as a player, manager, and executive.

For half a century Mack sat ramrod straight on Philadelphia's bench—his tall, thin frame clad in a dark blue business suit and a starched white shirt—and directed his outfielders with a wave of his scorecard. A superb judge of talent, he was a brilliant strategist, a patient teacher, and a father figure to his players. "Connie Mack. There was a wonderful person," former pitcher Rube Bressler told Lawrence Ritter in an interview for *The Glory of Their Times.* "He really respected his fellow man. If you made a mistake, Connie never bawled you out on the bench, or in front of anybody else. He'd get you alone a few days later, and then he'd say something like, 'Don't you think it would have been better if you'd made the play this way?' And you knew damn well it would have been

better. No question about it. He knew what he was talking about. Never raised his voice.…In my opinion, Connie Mack did more for baseball than any other living human being—by the example he set, his attitude, the way he handled himself and his players.…He was a true gentleman, in every sense of the word."

Cornelius McGillicuddy was born December 22, 1862, in East Brookfield, Massachusetts, the third of seven children of Irish immigrants Michael and Mary McKillop McGillicuddy. Except in legal documents, the family was known as Mack. Connie arrived during the Civil War while his father was away with the 51st Massachusetts Infantry. A tall, thin boy dubbed Slats by his friends, Connie began to play baseball at an early age. He dropped out of school at 14, worked in a local shoe factory, and became the catcher for the town team. In 1884, at age 21, he embarked on a minor league career that included stops at Meriden in the Connecticut State League and Hartford in the Eastern League.

Purchased by Washington of the National League, the 6′2½″ (some sources say 6′1″), 150-pound right-handed catcher made his big league debut on September 11, 1886. In 1887 and 1888 Mack was the Nationals' regular backstop, though he also played first base, second base, all three outfield positions and even once at shortstop. Mack was a leader in the rebellion that led to the formation of the Players League in 1890. He invested his savings of $500 in the Buffalo club and caught 112 games. When the Players League collapsed after one season, Mack signed contracts with two different teams: Boston of the American Association and Pittsburgh of the National League. Baseball's Board of Control, called upon to resolve the snafu, awarded Mack to Pittsburgh, and he spent the next six seasons in the Smoky City.

His wife of five years, the former Margaret Hogan, died in 1892, leaving him with three infant children. He did not remarry until 1910, when he began his second family with Katherine Hallohan; they had four girls and a boy.

A broken leg diminished Mack's playing skills in 1893, and in 1894, he was named player–manager. The Pirates finished seventh that year, seventh again in 1895, and climbed to sixth in 1896, but disagreements with management led to Mack's dismissal.

Mack moved to Milwaukee, became manager and part-owner of the city's Western League club, and formed a friendship with league president Ban Johnson. Johnson transformed the circuit into the American League, which invaded eastern cities before the 1901 season and declared major league status. Johnson granted Mack the new Philadelphia franchise, and sent him to Benjamin Shibe, part owner of the A.J. Reach Company, which manufactured baseball equipment. Shibe invested in half the stock, Mack owned 25 percent, and two sportswriters, Frank Hough and Sam Jones, held the rest until 1912, when Mack bought out the writers.

Johnson placed the franchise in America's third-largest city to compete against the National League's established Phillies, but the Athletics possessed no ballpark and no players. Mack solved the first problem by leasing a vacant lot and commissioning construction of Columbia Park. To solve his second problem, Mack turned his attention on his cross-town rivals. With a salary offer of $4,000, Mack lured second baseman Napoleon Lajoie from the Phillies, along with pitchers Chick Fraser, Bill Bernhard, and Wiley Piatt. Lajoie was the American League's best player in 1901, leading the league in batting average (.426), slugging percentage, runs, doubles, home runs (14), and RBI (125). Fraser won 22 games, Bernhard won 17, and 25-year-old lefty Eddie Plank won 17. Mack also added Harry Davis, Socks Seybold, and Lave Cross to the fold. Still, the Athletics managed just a 74–62 record and finished fourth in the league, nine games behind Clark Griffith's Chicago White Sox.

Mack again set his sights on the Phillies. This time, he signed outfielder Elmer Flick, pitcher Bill Duggleby, and shortstop Monte Cross. At the start of the 1902 season, however, the Athletics suffered a severe setback when the Pennsylvania Supreme Court reversed a lower court, and an injunction prevented Lajoie, Fraser, and Bernhard from playing for the A's. The ruling, valid only in Pennsylvania, also affected Flick and Duggleby (Monte Cross was not named). Fraser and Duggleby returned to the Phillies, but Lajoie, Flick, and Bernhard were awarded to Cleveland by Ban Johnson, and avoided Pennsylvania when their team played there.

With half his team pulled out from under him on opening day, Mack rebuilt in a hurry. He signed

catcher Osee Schrecongost (released by Cleveland), picked up slugging second baseman Danny Murphy from the minors, and lured mercurial left-hander Rube Waddell (whom he had managed in Milwaukee) from the California League. Waddell joined the A's in mid-June, and posted a 24–7 record with a 2.05 ERA and 210 strikeouts the rest of the way. Plank, a 20-game winner for the first time, and Seybold, who hit 16 home runs (an AL record until Babe Ruth hit 29 in 1919) led the Athletics to their first pennant. Ironically, the court decision against Mack may have won him the 1902 pennant. Relieved of the burden of facing several of the league's best players while at home, the A's posted a 27–36 road record but a monstrous 56–17 mark in Philadelphia, the second-biggest home-road differential in baseball history.

With the two leagues still months away from a peace agreement that would pave the way for the first modern World Series the following year, much of the National League regarded Mack's championship club with disdain. John McGraw, upon jumping from the AL Baltimore Orioles to the NL New York Giants during the season, derisively labeled the Athletics "a white elephant." Rather than smart under the insult, Mack adopted the pachyderm as the team's symbol. The Mackmen finished second in 1903, 14½ games behind Boston, despite 20-win seasons by Plank and Waddell and 17 victories from newcomer Albert "Chief" Bender. The Athletics closed the gap to 12½ games in 1904, but finished fifth.

With much the same squad, the Athletics outdistanced the Chicago White Sox by two games in 1905. The Mackmen faced the Giants, and had to do it without Waddell, who was injured. Christy Mathewson tossed three shutouts to wrap up the Series, and McGraw, who clad his squad in new black uniforms, earned his first world championship.

The A's slipped to fourth in 1906, finished 1½ games behind Ty Cobb's Tigers in 1907, and a distant sixth in 1908. That season, however, Mack began to build his first dynasty, providing playing time for 21-year-old second baseman Eddie Collins, 21-year-old infielder Jack Barry, and 22-year-old third baseman Frank Baker. With the three youngsters in the lineup and the Athletics playing their home games at newly-built Shibe Park, Philadelphia finished second in 1909.

With a solid lineup and a veteran pitching staff, the Mackmen won their first World Series in 1910. Jack Coombs won 31 games, Bender 23, and Plank 16 as Philadelphia steamrolled first the American League, then the Chicago Cubs, 4–1, in the fall classic. "Connie Mack, the astute gentleman who sits on the bench for the

Philadelphia Athletics and pilots his 'White Elephants' to victory, is one of the marvels of baseball," *The Sporting Life*'s Jack Morse wrote. "Above everything else, he instilled the spirit of team play."

The Tall Tactician instilled the spirit of team play because he "understood the need to handle each man as an individual," Mack biographer Norman L. Macht wrote. "He demonstrated his confidence in them by giving them the responsibility of creating ways to win.... He focused on his objectives, told his men what he wanted to accomplish, and suggested ways they might achieve them. He then left it to them to carry out the mission. He didn't do all their thinking for them. He didn't signal their every move or call pitches from the bench...they called their own infield defensive alignment. They flashed their own hit-and-run, steal and double steal signs. Sometimes the batter initiated the sign, sometimes the base runner.... Using his scorecard, on which he kept score with a pencil, Mack deployed his outfielders. He knew his pitchers' strengths and opposing hitters' tendencies, and put them together to position the outfield."

Mack preferred that his players be smart, and preferred that they be educated. He traded away Joe Jackson, who was illiterate, during the 1910 season, and relied on Coombs, Plank, and Bender to carry the Athletics to a second straight World Series win in 1911. That year 20-year-old first baseman Stuffy McInnis stepped into the starting lineup, along with Collins, Barry, and Baker, to complete what came to be known as the $100,000 Infield. Once again, the Mackmen squared off against McGraw's black-clad Giants. This time, Bender won twice, Coombs and Plank each picked up a victory, and the Athletics prevailed 4–2 as their third sacker hit two key round-trippers and earned the moniker of Home Run Baker.

The Mackmen slipped to third in 1912, but bounced back to finish 6½ games ahead of Walter Johnson's Washington Senators in 1913. For a third time the World Series matched Mr. Mack and Muggsy, and for the second time, the Athletics won, 4–1, as the 38-year-old Plank outdueled Mathewson in the finale and Bender won two more World Series games.

Under Mack's patient tutelage Philadelphia cruised to its fourth American League title in five years in 1914 behind the $100,000 Infield and the pitching of Bender, Plank, 21-year-old Bullet Joe Bush, 23-year-old Bob Shawkey, 20-year-old Herb Pennock, and 19-year-old Rube Bressler. As tranquil as the season appeared, there were storm clouds on the horizon. World War I erupted in Europe, an event that shortened future seasons and reduced box office revenues. The Federal League began operations in eight cities, and its well-financed owners dangled cash in front of major leaguers. The Boston Braves, mired in last place on July 18, arose like a cyclone in the summer heat, stormed past the rest of the National League, and demolished the Athletics in a stunning World Series sweep.

Mack blamed the loss on the lure of Federal League money distracting his players. "I felt it was the most unhappy season I ever experienced," Mack later told sportswriter Fred Lieb. "In view of conditions which existed on my ball team, the beating we took from the Braves in the 1914 World's Series was not surprising. The Federal League was after our players from the spring to the World's Series, and the season was one of trouble and unpleasantness." The off-season would be no more enjoyable. Unable—and unwilling—to meet his players' payroll demands, Mack disassembled his dynasty. After the Feds lured away Plank and Bender, Mack released Coombs, and in a stunning move sold Collins to the White Sox. He refused to renegotiate a three-year contract Baker had signed in 1914, and Baker retired to his family farm and played semipro ball for a year before the equally stubborn Mack traded him to the New York Yankees at the strong urging of Ban Johnson.

When the 1915 season started, Mack hoped that Bressler, Bush, Shawkey, and Pennock could offset the loss of his veteran pitchers, but they were not ready. Although the latter three combined for 631 career wins, they went just 14–27 for the Athletics in 1915. Before the season ended, Mack sent Shawkey to the Yankees and Pennock and Barry to the Red Sox. The scuttled squad lost 109 games, and finished 58½ games behind the Red Sox, even though Lajoie (now 40) returned to the fold. A year later, Nap closed out his career on an even more dismal Athletics squad that finished 36–117. The Athletics finished last for seven straight seasons, including the final five of the Deadball Era.

The Mackmen escaped the cellar in 1922 with a seventh-place finish, and by 1925 Mack had assembled a new generation of stars. In 1929 he returned to the top with a team that featured Jimmie Foxx, Al Simmons, Mickey Cochrane, and Robert "Lefty" Grove. The retooled Athletics won three consecutive AL pennants from 1929 to 1931, and world championships in 1929 and 1930.

Mack's second dynasty ended much like the first. The Depression struck the city of Philadelphia severely. Despite the league's highest payroll, attendance plummeted. Mack sold and traded off his stars to owners with deeper pockets, and his team returned to the nether regions of the American League. Between 1935 and 1950 the Athletics finished last ten times, and as high as fourth just once. Still, Mack was regarded as baseball's Grand Old Man. He defeated McGraw in the first All-Star Game in 1933, and in 1937 was elected to the Baseball Hall of Fame, along with his old nemesis, McGraw, and his old friend, Ban Johnson.

Mack, who had assembled two dynasties by discovering and developing talented young players, was later unable to compete with teams that had built minor league systems. He also never employed an African-American player and fared poorly with trades. During the 1940s the octogenarian Mack began to grow senile and fall asleep on the bench. By the latter part of the decade he was A's manager in name only, with coaches Jimmy Dykes, Simmons, and Earle Mack (Connie's son) doing the managing. Dignified to the end, Mack suffered through a 52–102 season in 1950. Many of those who were close to him suspected he had stayed on the job too long. On October 18, 1950, at the age of 87, Mack retired as manager of the Philadelphia Athletics, with a career tally of 3,731 wins and 3,948 losses, both easily major league records. (His mark with the A's was 3,582–3,814.) Over his 50 years as manager, Mack's A's won nine American League pennants, won five World Series (in eight tries), and finished in last place 17 times.

Mack and his sons from his first marriage, Earle and Roy, acquired nearly 80 percent of the team during the 1950 season. They bought out Ben Shibe's heirs and also Connie Mack, Jr., his son from his second marriage. The family members had squabbled over ownership for nearly a decade. Mack stayed on as team president until he, Earle, and Roy sold the franchise in November 1954 to Chicago vending machine magnate Arnold Johnson, who moved the Athletics to Kansas City.

Connie Mack died in Philadelphia on February 8, 1956, at the age of 93. Thousands of fans, friends, former players, and baseball executives turned out for the funeral and burial at Holy Sepulchre Cemetery in Montgomery County, just outside of Philadelphia. Three years before his death, Shibe Park, which the Athletics had shared with the Phillies since 1938, had been renamed Connie Mack Stadium. It remained the home of the Phillies until 1970. Today, across the street from Citizens Bank Park, where his onetime box office rivals now play, stands a statue of Mack, dressed in a business suit, waving his scorecard.

Doug Skipper

E. S. Plank

PHILADELPHIA

EDWARD STEWART PLANK
LEFT-HANDED PITCHER, 1901–1914

Eddie Plank fidgeted. On every pitch Plank went through a seemingly endless ritual: Get the sign from his catcher, fix his cap just so, readjust his shirt and sleeve, hitch up his pants, ask for a new ball, rub it up, stare at a baserunner if there was one, look back at his catcher, ask for a new sign—and start the process all over again. As if that was not enough, from the seventh inning on, he would begin to talk to himself and the ball out loud: "Nine to go, eight to go…," and so on until he had retired the last batter. Frustrated hitters would swing at anything just to have something to do. His fielders would grow antsy. Fans, not wanting to be late for supper, would stay away when he was pitching. Writers, fearful of missing deadlines, roasted him.

Somebody that annoying can hang around for only one reason—he's a winner. Plank was exactly that, winning 326 games, the most by any left-hander until Warren Spahn and Steve Carlton came along. His 69 shutouts remain the standard for southpaws. Despite all his accomplishments, however, it was Eddie Plank's fate to be second banana. He had some great seasons and many good ones, but there always seemed to be someone having a better one. Usually it was Walter Johnson, but there would occasionally be someone like Jack Chesbro, Ed Walsh, or Joe Wood, whose overall careers would not equal Plank's. Accordingly, in no season was he considered the top pitcher in the American League. He had to be satisfied with being one of the top four or five, but he was in that position year after year, and while other pitchers came and went, Plank persevered, helping the Philadelphia Athletics to five American League pennants and three world championships. "Plank was not the fastest," teammate Eddie Collins once observed. "He was not the trickiest, and not the possessor of the most stuff. He was just the greatest."

Edward Stewart Plank was born in Gettysburg, Pennsylvania, on August 31, 1875, the fourth of seven children of David L. Plank and the former Martha E. McCreary. Growing up on the family farm, Eddie never played baseball until he was 17, when a neighbor organized a team. From the very beginning the young left-hander threw with a natural crossfire motion that he called a slant ball, landing his right leg on the first base side of the pitcher's mound and then throwing across his body. For most pitchers this off-balance method resulted in wildness, but in time Plank became perhaps the greatest crossfire control pitcher in history. Eddie pitched for town teams and, at the age of 22, enrolled in Gettysburg Academy, a prep school under the auspices of Gettysburg College.

Frank Foreman, a fair to middling pitcher in the 1880s and 1890s, was the coach of the Gettysburg College team. When Foreman saw Plank's unorthodox delivery, he promised Plank, "If you follow my instructions closely, I'll make you one of the greatest southpaws in the country."

Plank never attended the college but played on the team, a common practice in an era of lax eligibility requirements. Nonetheless, Plank learned his lessons well, coming out of the academy with but one weakness: a poor move toward first (at least in the view of Ty Cobb). Foreman had turned Plank into that rarest of creatures, a crossfiring southpaw with outstanding control of his curve and fastball.

Plank signed with a minor league team in Richmond in 1900, but the Virginia League folded a few days later, so he never pitched in the minor leagues. In the spring of 1901, when Foreman told his friend Connie Mack that he ought to sign Plank, Mack telegraphed Plank, inviting him to join the Athletics in Baltimore.

Plank made his debut on May 13, 1901, finishing up a 14–5 loss at Baltimore, then returned to Gettysburg to pitch one last game. He went on to a fine rookie year: 17–13 with 28 complete games in 32 starts, a 3.31 ERA, and the first of his 69 shutouts. The 1902 season, in which the Athletics won the American League pennant, marked a first and a last for the southpaw; he won 20 games for the first time and his 3.30 ERA was his last trip north of 3.00. He also led the league in hit batters with 18 despite giving up only 1.83 walks per 9 innings. Appearing shorter and slighter than his listed 5'11" and 175 pounds, Plank obviously was not timid about pitching inside—perhaps not surprising in that his mentor, Foreman, had a reputation as a headhunter.

Plank would work in relative anonymity from 1902 through 1907, living in the shadow of Rube Waddell. Playing the tortoise to Waddell's hare, Plank won 23 games and led the league in games started in 1903, while Waddell, the prototypical screwball left-hander, struck out batters at an unprecedented rate (when he was not chasing fire engines or drinking himself blind). Rube finished the season with a 2.44 ERA; Plank at 2.38. Seven years later Rube would be out of the majors and Plank would be posting even better ERAs.

Eddie reached his career high with 26 wins (against 17 losses) in 1904, coming in a distant second to Jack Chesbro's post-1900 record 41 wins. The highlight of the year came on September 10 when Plank beat Boston's Cy Young, 1–0, in 13 innings. The shutout was one of Plank's four wins in ten decisions against the old master.

The Athletics captured the pennant in 1905, thanks in large part to Plank's 24 wins and 346⅔ innings pitched, both second in the league, and his 2.26 ERA, which in a strong pitchers' year did not crack the top ten. In his two starts against the Giants in that year's World Series, Eddie pitched 17 innings and allowed only three earned runs, but lost both games, to Christy Mathewson and Joe McGinnity, respectively. Plank's 1905 performance, in which his teammates scored zero runs for him, foreshadowed his fate in World Series play, as he would often pitch just brilliantly enough to lose in heartbreaking fashion.

In 1906 Mack worked Plank hard over the first two-thirds of the season, but the pitcher developed a sore arm and was able to start only once in the season's final 50 games. He was productive, however, going 19–6 with a 2.25 ERA; his .760 winning percentage led the American League, although his 211⅔ innings pitched were 135 fewer than the previous season.

Appearing in a league-leading 43 games in 1907, the southpaw went back to his usual chores, pitching 343⅔ innings and returning to the 20-win club, going 24–16 with a 2.20 ERA and a league-high eight shutouts. In addition, he was third in the league with 183 strikeouts. The year would be his last venture into 300 or more innings; he would never again pitch more than 268⅓ innings in any season, and that would be in the Federal League in 1915.

The Athletics were not a factor in the wild pennant race of 1908, dropping to sixth place with a 68–85 slate, just half a game ahead of Washington. Plank's won–lost record slid along with the team's, although not as far; he endured his first losing season with a 14–16 mark despite a fine ERA of 2.17. The game of September 20 shows the kind of year it was. Frank Smith of the White Sox threw the second no-hitter of his career, beating Plank, 1–0. The run scored in the bottom of the ninth when Plank was trying to walk Freddy Parent intentionally; Parent crossed things up by reaching out and swatting a sacrifice fly to short right field. As testimony of his consistency, Plank would finish with a losing record only one more time in his long career.

In 1909 Philadelphia rebounded to second place, 3½ games behind Detroit, and Plank came back with them. He finished the year 19–10 with his career-best ERA, a tiny 1.76. He had the honor of pitching the game dedicating Shibe Park on Monday, April 12, and responded by beating Boston, 8–1, giving up just six hits. The game had a tragic ending, however. A's catcher Doc Powers caught all nine innings in agonizing pain, ill with suspected food poisoning, and was taken to a local hospital afterward. Two weeks later he was dead, with "strangulation of the intestines" listed as the official cause. Powers, who was also a physician, starved to death because he could not eat. His intestines were mangled due to a hernia, which some believed he had suffered when he collided with the new park's concrete wall while chasing a foul pop-up in the seventh inning.

The Athletics team of 1910–1914 was the first of Mack's two masterpieces, a powerful unit that would win four pennants and three World Series over those five years. Plank was basically the third or fourth pitcher in the rotation, behind Jack Coombs (who would go 31–9 with a 1.30 ERA and 13 shutouts, an AL record that still stands), Chief Bender (23–5 with a 1.58 ERA, easily his best season), and Cy Morgan (18–12 with an ERA of 1.55). Next to that assemblage, Plank almost looked like an underachiever with his 16–10 mark and 2.01 ERA. Suffering from a sore arm by the end of the season, he did not even pitch in the Athletics' five-game World Series win over the Cubs, as Mack used only Coombs and Bender.

Plank bounced back in 1911, going 23–8 with a 2.10 ERA and tied for the league lead with six shutouts. His luck in the Series improved as he got his first win, a complete-game 3–1 victory over the Giants' Rube Marquard in Game Two. With Game Five tied 3–3 after nine innings, Mack brought in Plank to relieve Coombs. Plank could have closed out the Series with a win, but lasted only two-thirds of the tenth inning before surrendering the winning run.

Plank enjoyed another terrific year in 1912, posting a 26–6 record with a fine 2.22 ERA; however, the Athletics fell to 90–62, one game behind second-place Washington and 15 behind the powerful Red Sox. Indeed, the 1912 season is emblematic of a tendency to underestimate Plank's greatness. His 26–6 record jumps out at us today, but it was only the fourth highest win total in the American League, behind Joe Wood's 34–5, Walter Johnson's 33–12 (and league-best 1.39 ERA), and Ed Walsh's 27–17. In addition, Wood and Johnson each strung together league-record winning streaks of 16 games, and Marquard won a major-league record 19 straight games in the National League. Accordingly, Plank's solid performance was lost in the shuffle of one of baseball's great pitching seasons.

Still, the season had its moments. Plank dropped a 4–3 beating on Joe Wood to celebrate the Fourth of July. (Wood's next start four days later would be the first of his 16-game winning streak.) On September 27 Plank went the distance in a 19-inning loss to Washington's Bob Groom and Johnson. Collins's wild throw let in the winning run as Johnson got the win with 10 innings of scoreless relief.

Plank slipped to 18–10 with an unusually high 2.60 ERA in 1913, but the Athletics roared back to the American League throne room. The Giants were in the Series for the third straight year, having lost to the Athletics in 1911 and the Red Sox in 1912. Plank faced Mathewson in Game Two. The two aces threw shutout ball for nine innings. In a much-criticized move Mack allowed Eddie to bat for himself with the bases loaded and nobody out in the bottom of the ninth. Plank hit into a fielder's choice, the A's failed to score, and it all came apart for Plank in the tenth as he gave up three runs, including the go-ahead single to Mathewson. Everything changed in Game Five, with Mathewson and Plank once again squaring off. This time around, the southpaw threw a two-hitter and beat his nemesis, 3–1, to take the Series and send McGraw to his third consecutive Series defeat. The game was Plank's greatest career win; the only Giant run was unearned, scoring due to Plank's own error.

The Athletics remained apparently unstoppable in 1914, winning 99 games and heading back to the Series, this time against Boston's "Miracle Braves." Plank contributed a 15–7 mark, the wins being good for fourth-best on the team, as Chief Bender won 17 while Bob Shawkey and Joe Bush each chipped in with 16. Plank's mark was accompanied by a 2.87 ERA, higher than the league average and by far his highest since 1902. He could still pitch brilliantly, though, as his Game Two effort showed, a 1–0 loss (the run scored

in the ninth inning) to Bill James as the mighty Athletics were swept in a major Series upset. It was the final game of Plank's World Series career, and left him with a career 2–5 record in the fall classic despite a 1.32 ERA.

Through good times and bad, winning or losing, pitching well or not, Plank did everything the same way—quietly. He did not talk much, mostly speaking only when he had something to say. And when he did talk, as his only grandson (Edward Stewart Plank III, born much too late to know him except by reputation and memory in the family) pointed out, people listened. Moreover, he and his more outgoing teammate, Chief Bender, seem to have been patient and kind with rookies who wanted to learn. Rube Bressler made the point clearly to Lawrence Ritter: "I used to try to get near [Bender and Plank] and listen to what they were talking about, and *every question* I'd ask they'd pay attention and tell me what they thought. I used to put sticks behind my ears so they'd stand out further. Boy, I wanted to hear what those guys had to say."

Thirty-nine years old after the 1914 season, Plank had been talking about quitting baseball for several years. His workload had diminished, and Mack had nursed him along for the last two years, using him primarily against clubs he was most likely to dominate. Mack knew that Bender and Plank were talking to Federal League agents. He asked waivers on them and Coombs, and released all three pitchers. Coombs signed with Brooklyn of the National League, Bender went to the Baltimore Terrapins of the Federal League, and Plank went to the new league's St. Louis Terriers.

Plank had a good year with the Terriers, who wound up in a virtual tie for first place with the Chicago Whales, contributing a 21–11 record and 2.08 ERA. He reached a major milestone on September 11 with a 12–5 win over Newark, making him the first southpaw to attain three hundred victories.

When the Federal League folded after the 1915 season, Terriers owner Phil Ball bought control of the St. Louis Browns and retained Plank, who went 16–15 with a 2.33 ERA for a fifth-place team (albeit with a winning record of 79–75). He could go only 5–6 in 1917—just his second losing record—despite a glittering 1.79 ERA, second-best for his career. On August 6, at age 41, he hooked up with Walter Johnson, going down 1–0 in 11 innings, his seventh loss against three wins in match-ups with the Washington ace. It was Plank's last game; noting some stomach problems, he announced his retirement the next week.

Despite his announcement, Plank was still in demand. On January 22, 1918, the Yankees traded pitchers Urban Shocker and Nick Cullop, infielder Fritz Maisel, second baseman Joe Gedeon, catcher Les Nunamaker, and cash to St. Louis for second baseman Del Pratt and Plank. Now 42, Plank would have been the oldest active player in the game. He had announced his retirement, however, and had no intention of changing his plans. "I will not go to New York next season," he said from his Gettysburg farm. "I am through with baseball forever. I have my farm and my home and enough to take care of me, so why should I work and worry any longer?"

According to the *Historical Register*, in 1918 he pitched a bit for an industrial league team in Steelton, Pennsylvania, posting a 4–2 record in 52 innings. The Bethlehem Steel Company owned all six teams in the league, and offered current and former major leaguers—including Plank, Dutch Leonard, and Joe Jackson—an opportunity to play baseball while avoiding the World War I draft.

Plank had taken pretty good care of himself throughout his career, watching his money and investing it reasonably well. He spent his retirement farming, operating a Buick shop, and leading tours of the Gettysburg battlefield. Most visitors to the battlefield probably remained unaware that with their taciturn guide they were in the presence of one of the game's great pitchers.

Plank had married Anna Myers in 1915; the couple had one son, Edward Stewart Plank Jr. Having left baseball, Plank spent his time handling his various interests, even contemplating a run for public office before suffering a stroke on February 22, 1926. Plank died two days later, at the age of 50. He was buried in Evergreen Cemetery in Gettysburg. In 1946, twenty years after his death, Plank was elected to the Hall of Fame along with Waddell and nine other legends of the game.

JAN FINKEL

PHILADELPHIA

RALPH ORLANDO "SOCKS" SEYBOLD
RIGHT FIELDER, 1901–1908

At 30 years of age and the last man signed by Connie Mack for his newly organized 1901 Philadelphia team, Ralph "Socks" Seybold proved to be a durable and valuable player during the Athletics' first seven seasons, becoming one of the junior circuit's top sluggers. In spite of being somewhat maligned by the Philadelphia press for his rotund figure and voracious appetite, Seybold, at 5'11" and about 200 pounds, was a popular figure with the fans and his teammates. When he signed Seybold, Mack was unsure of his age and weight—he never did know either for sure—but Mack could see what the average fan or writer could not. He knew Seybold had deceptive quickness and speed for his size, could hit behind a runner on first, and knew how to study pitchers and batters and position himself in the outfield accordingly. "Socks was so big the fans never credited him with all the good points that he showed to me in his daily work," Mack said. Although Seybold's colorful nickname was commonly used during his playing career, its origin remains a mystery.

Ralph Orlando Seybold was born in the eastern Ohio town of Washingtonville on November 23, 1870, the second of four children of Christian and Augusta Wiggin Seybold. The family moved to Jeannette, Pennsylvania, a glass manufacturing town in the southwestern part of the state in 1889 where Christian set up shop in the hardware, tin, and slate roofing business. Playing for the Jeannette Greys in 1891, Ralph won "glory and applause for his beautiful catches in left field." In 1892 Seybold made his professional debut with Altoona of the Pennsylvania State League, batting .280; the next year he played with Johnstown in the same league. In 1894 he moved to the Franklin, Pennsylvania, independent club. In 1896 and 1897 Seybold played for Lancaster, Pennsylvania, staying with the team as it transferred from the

Pennsylvania State League to the Atlantic League. After Lancaster won the pennant in 1897, Ralph was drafted by Richmond (Pennsylvania) of the Atlantic League. He played for the Richmond Bluebirds in 1898 and 1899. On August 4, 1899, with Seybold leading the Atlantic League in home runs for the third consecutive season, his contract was purchased by the Cincinnati Reds.

Riding the bench for six weeks, he grew rusty and fat, gaining about 20 pounds, so he was out of shape when he finally made his major league debut on August 20, 1899. Appearing in 22 games he batted only .224. Cincinnati owner John T. Brush also owned the Indianapolis Hoosiers of the American League, then in its final year as a minor league, and in 1900 Seybold was demoted to Indianapolis. Despite a midseason ankle injury, Seybold played right and center field and occasionally at first base, batting .304. Reporting that Ralph might spend the winter in California with his brother, *The Sporting News* wrote, "Big Ralph is a prize that several clubs covet. A splendid fielder, a great batter and the fastest man his size in the league."

Socks's size always overshadowed his accomplishments on the field. When he arrived in Philadelphia on April 2, 1901, the *Philadelphia Record* reported, "Seybold shows points of a player. On arrival at the Hanover, before looking up Connie Mack or even bothering as to what became of his grip, he made for the dining room as though it was the first base bag." But he sometimes used his size to his financial benefit, wagering unsuspecting teammates and opponents that he could beat them in a foot race—and doing it.

Mack's 1901 opening day lineup had Seybold in left field, although right field was the position he would play most often during his career with the Athletics. With the early season failure of Charlie Carr at first base, Mack moved Seybold from the outfield to first, where he stayed through the middle of May. When Mack signed Harry Davis to play first base, Seybold was back in right field to stay. Seybold liked to play the position with a first baseman's mitt. He was able to do so only after receiving special permission from league president Ban Johnson.

The power of the 1901 team consisted mainly of Nap Lajoie, Seybold, Lave Cross, and Harry Davis. Batting behind Lajoie, Seybold finished the year with a .334 batting average, 90 RBI, and eight home runs, all figures ranking among the league leaders. From July 19 to August 14 Ralph hit safely in 27 consecutive games.

Despite the loss of Lajoie, the Athletics won the 1902 pennant by five games, with Seybold keying an offensive attack that led the league in runs scored. For the second year in a row, Ralph hit over .300, finishing with a .316 batting average. His 97 RBI were the second highest on the team, and his 16 home runs set the American League record that stood until Babe Ruth hit 29 in 1919.

In 1903 the Athletics fell to second place behind Boston. At age 32 Socks led the major leagues in doubles with 45. His .299 batting average and 84 RBI were second on the team. Injuries plagued the 1904 Athletics and they fell to the second division, even though they still finished 11 games above .500. Socks again played the majority of the games in right field, subbing for Harry Davis at first base 13 times. His .292 batting average was third highest on the team, but he hit only three home runs and his RBI total slipped to 64. The apparent drop in production, however, was an illusion of context; offense was down throughout the American League.

The 1905 Athletics won Mack's second pennant, finishing two games ahead of the White Sox and leading the league in runs scored, doubles, slugging percentage, pitching strikeouts, and shutouts. Socks played right field, finishing with a .983 fielding average, his highest ever, although his batting average slipped to .274, his lowest ever in a full season up to that point. Again, it was an illusion of context: Seybold's offensive production actually improved. Like the rest of his teammates, Seybold was stymied at the plate in that year's World Series, collecting only two singles in 16 at-bats in Philadelphia's five-game defeat at the hands of Christy Mathewson and the New York Giants.

Socks improved for the 1906 season. He batted .316, hit 23 doubles, collected 59 RBI, and slammed five home runs. He played in 116 games (his fewest since 1901), all but two in right field. The 1907 season turned out to be the last for Seybold as an everyday player. He played in a career-high 147 games, batting .271 (his lowest full-season average), but he was still among the leading power hitters in the league, and his five home runs and 92 RBI both ranked second in the league.

After the season Socks married Georgia-born Wilhelmina "Minnie" Heitz. They made their home in Jeannette until she died on March 28, 1917, of pleural pneumonia. They had no children.

While preparing for the 1908 season Socks suffered a broken leg. The *Philadelphia Record* reported on April 7, 1908, that Socks would not play at the start of the season. Even when able, his playing time was limited, for Mack had begun rebuilding with young players. Toward the end of the season, in which Seybold batted just .215 with only two extra-base hits in 130 at-bats, Mack sent Socks to Greenville, South Carolina, to collect the young outfielder Joe Jackson, who had been recently purchased by the club but was having a hard time adjusting to the big city and kept returning to his hometown. Socks found Jackson and convinced him to return to Philadelphia. On the train Seybold bought Jackson his dinner, spent the evening with him, made sure he was in his berth, and then settled in for the trip north. When Socks went to check on his companion in the morning he was gone. Jackson had gotten off the train in the middle of the night and headed back to Greenville. Socks went back for him again.

Realizing that his playing days were behind him, Socks took an opportunity to coach and play for the Toledo Mud Hens in 1909, taking over the managerial role toward the end of the season. The following year Socks was back home in Jeannette, where he coached several different industrial league teams in the area, usually known as the Seybolds. In 1912 at age 41 he played for the Richmond (Virginia) Rebels in the newly formed United States League, but the league folded by the end of June that year.

For several years thereafter Seybold worked as the steward for the local aerie of the Fraternal Order of Eagles. Just after midnight on December 21, 1921, Socks and four of his friends left town for his brother's farm in the foothills of the Allegheny Mountains. Traveling east on the Lincoln Highway past Greensburg, Pennsylvania, Socks tried to take a sharp curve at a high rate of speed and was unable to control the automobile. It plunged over an embankment, turning over four times before it stopped. When the others came to, they thought Ralph was still unconscious and waited for a passing motorist for help. After getting him to the hospital it was determined that he had died of a broken neck. Leaving behind an estate valued at $20,000, he was laid to rest on December 24, 1921, next to his wife at the Brush Creek Cemetery near Irwin, Pennsylvania.

VINCENT ALTIERI

PHILADELPHIA

BENJAMIN FRANKLIN SHIBE
OWNER, 1901–1922

Called the Edison of the Sport by James C. Isaminger in a 1922 obituary, Ben Shibe was a major contributor to the development of the national pastime. It was his business savvy that helped turn a nascent game at his birth into a multimillion dollar enterprise by his death. As co-owner of the Philadelphia Athletics, Shibe was at the forefront of baseball's greatest innovations, from the balls themselves to the stadiums. As William A. Phelon observed in *Baseball Magazine*, Shibe "is wise, shrewd, a clever calculator, a great money-maker…but it's not so many years ago that he put his money and his shoulders back of what seemed a losing venture, showed himself a grim fighter and a dead game sport—and pushed the White Elephants to the front."

Benjamin Franklin Shibe was born on January 23, 1838, on Girard Avenue in Philadelphia. Poorly educated and handicapped by a childhood accident that required him to wear a steel brace on his leg, Shibe took a job as a conductor on a Philadelphia horse car. Soon after, he worked in a leather novelty establishment with a family member. There he made things such as whips and leather watch fobs. When the Confederacy's Army of Northern Virginia briefly entered Pennsylvania in July 1863, Shibe answered the call for emergency volunteers to protect the city, joining the Pennsylvania 51st Infantry Regiment. After the crisis passed, the 51st Regiment was mustered out in September 1863. It is unlikely that Shibe saw any combat during his brief career as a soldier. By 1870 Shibe was working as a conductor on the Philadelphia City Railroad.

With baseball's popularity on the rise following the end of the Civil War, Shibe joined his brother John and nephew Dan, who had worked for a company that made cricket balls, in founding John D. Shibe & Co., which made baseballs for children and professionals. The company churned out many different brands of balls, such as the Skyrocket, Bounding Rock, Red Dead Balls, Red Stocking, and the Cock-of-the-Walk. Their company supplied others, such as Alfred J. Reach, of the firm Reach & Johnson. Reach and Ben Shibe were friends, and by 1882 the two had formed a new company, Reach & Shibe. John Shibe, however, believed the name related too closely to Ben's former affiliation (i.e., John D. Shibe & Co.), so it was changed to A.J. Reach and Company. They soon left the retailing part behind and concentrated on manufacturing. Occupying a huge factory, they had over 1,000 employees and controlled their industry. By 1883 the Reach factory was making 1.3 million baseballs and 100,000 bats per year.

Ben Shibe was not only concerned with manufacturing. He also directed the Shibe Semi-Professional Team, which produced many professional players. During the 1880s he became principal stockholder in the Athletic Club of the American Association. Although the club was bankrupt by 1890, this commitment highlights Shibe's passion for the game which his physical disability had prevented him from playing. *Baseball Magazine*'s F.C. Lane wrote in 1912, "Mr. Shibe was actuated solely by loyalty for baseball as the greatest of sports and not through any mercenary motives." The truth is that he made many investments in teams that would never produce a penny of profit—although the publicity generated by those teams certainly did not hurt his sporting goods business.

The company that Shibe helped to build was critical to baseball's development in the late nineteenth century. Throughout the mid-1800s there was a problem with the stitching on the cover of baseballs. Usually the tips of one 'S' were fitted on either side of the waist of the other, so the stitches always drew. The cover was not smooth, and the hide never had full protection. Shibe worked at the problem for many years, trying many different methods, always coming up short of the perfect design. Eventually he discovered that the nature of the spherical ball required the stitches to be grouped closer together at the end of the 'S' (to be even with those at the waist) in a decreasing space of separation. In 116 stitches, it worked perfectly. In 1889 Shibe's nephew, Daniel M. Shibe, was awarded U.S. patent no. 415,884 for the design.

In 1901 the AL awarded its Philadelphia franchise to Connie Mack. To compete with the established NL Philadelphia franchise, Mack needed a local backer who would give the newcomers instant credibility and prestige. He also needed capital. Ben Shibe was just the right man. Reach was a minority stockholder in the Phillies, and Mack made it clear that he intended to raid the Phillies for players, so Shibe hesitated to invest in the team. Still, he believed a second major league was good for baseball. Reach felt the same way, and at his suggestion Shibe agreed to buy no more and no less than 50 percent of the club. Mack had allocated 25 percent to two sportswriters, whose voting power he held, giving Mack and Shibe equal power. That way, neither man could do anything the other did not agree to. In reality they never disagreed, and Shibe left the running of the team and all the baseball decisions to Mack. When Mack wanted to buy out the two sportwriters' shares in 1912, Ben Shibe loaned him the money instead of letting his sons buy them and so put 75 percent of the stock in Shibe hands. Trusting in Mack's able leadership, Shibe's franchise captured six American League pennants and three world championships during his 21 years as team president.

Ben Shibe is probably best known for building the first steel and concrete stadium, known as Shibe Park. Weary of Columbia Park, which could scarcely hold 10,000 fans, Shibe constructed his new grounds in what was then the northern outskirts of Philadelphia, about four miles north of Independence Hall at the corner of Lehigh and Fifth. Designed in the French Renaissance style, the exterior featured terra-cotta brickwork, a dark green slate roof, and a grand rotunda at the main entrance. Universally hailed at its opening as the greatest ballpark ever built, the 23,000-seat baseball palace cost $500,000 according to some reports, $300,000 according to others. The stadium opened on Monday, April 12, 1909, with both league presidents attending and invitations sent to all owners. The National Commission thanked Shibe for being, as the *Washington Post* reported, "the first person to take advantage of the situation and realize that the fan's wishes had to be gratified; and that was accommodation." In the nearly 100 years since Shibe Park opened, every new major league stadium has been built using steel and concrete.

That same year Shibe made arguably his biggest contribution to the game with his company's invention of the cork-centered baseball. The livelier baseball—which was introduced in the 1910 World Series and used in all games beginning in 1911—led to an offensive explosion, extending base hits from singles to doubles, and doubles to triples. *The Sporting News* reported that Shibe claimed that the greatest value to the new ball was that it lasted longer.

Shibe might be remembered for his innovations, but his players remembered him for his generosity. Shibe was known to always take care of the ballplayers who helped his club to success. When Rube Waddell fell desperately ill in 1914, Shibe made sure that he was given the best available medical care to aid in his recovery (which, unfortunately, never came). Shibe's kindness was one of his most attractive characteristics. Even when the American and National leagues were still feuding, Shibe tried to put the squabbles aside for the good of the game. This was proven in 1903 when the Philadelphia Phillies needed their ballpark repaired. Shibe had no qualms about having the club play on the Athletics' grounds. The press noted that John T. Brush would never have done such a thing for the AL.

Shibe's life took a turn for the worse on August 21, 1920, when he was in a terrible car accident. He was in a car when a chauffeur, David Smith, rammed into Shibe's car, turning it over. Shibe never fully recovered from the accident and died in Philadelphia on January 14, 1922, nine days shy of his 84th birthday. He left a fortune estimated at over $1 million. With his wife, Josephine, having died many years earlier, Shibe was survived by two sons, Thomas S. Shibe (who took over as president of the Athletics) and John D. Shibe, and two daughters, Mrs. Mary A. Reach (she married A.J. Reach's son) and Mrs. Elfreda MacFarland. He was buried in West Laurel Hill Cemetery in Bala Cynwyd, Pennsylvania.

Upon hearing of his death, American League president Ban Johnson remarked, "Ben Shibe was one of the founders of the American League and its greatest pillar. During his period of active participation the organization profited by his wise counsel, and his sterling integrity helped to a large degree to maintaining the game's highest standard. There never was a man identified with baseball who commanded a greater respect. He has left an indelible stamp for good on baseball."

STUART SCHIMLER

PHILADELPHIA

TULLY FREDERICK "TOPSY" HARTSEL
LEFT FIELDER, 1902–1911

Standing just 5′5″ and a stocky 169 pounds, Topsy Hartsel used his small size to become the most effective leadoff batter of the Deadball Era. During his 10 seasons with the Athletics, Hartsel led the American League in walks five times, on-base percentage twice, and runs scored once. His 121 free passes in 1905 remained the American League record until Babe Ruth shattered it in 1920. Batting at the top of Connie Mack's order and playing a solid left field, he set the table for some of the era's best teams as his Philadelphia Athletics won four pennants during his ten-year tenure with the club. *The Sporting News* said, on reporting his death in 1944, "Though never an outstanding batsman, Hartsel, who was only 5′5″ tall, was one of the game's greatest leadoff men. He was a lefthanded hitter, very fast, with an uncanny eye at the bat. And once he got on base he was a difficult man to stop."

Tully Frederick Hartsel was born on June 26, 1874, in Polk, Ashland County, in north-central Ohio. He was the fifth of 12 children (ten surviving) born to Henry Hartsel, a laborer, and his wife, Harriet Switzer Hartsel. When he was 12 years old, the family moved to Wellington, Ohio. It was there that Tully went to school and got his start in athletic competition. He was good enough to make his high school's varsity football and baseball teams while still in the eighth grade. He was a halfback and a middle infielder and played both sports for five years. After graduating, he had an opportunity to play college football, but opted for baseball instead. In 1895 he played semipro baseball in New London, Ohio, and in 1896 continued as an infielder for several northwestern Ohio teams.

Hartsel made his professional debut in 1897 with Burlington (Iowa) of the Western Association, where he was moved to the outfield because of his left-handedness;

he also played with the independent Lima, Ohio, club that same season. The following year he started with Montgomery (Alabama) of the Southern League. When that league folded he went to Salem in the Ohio State League. That circuit folded as well and he made his way to Grand Rapids (Michigan) of the Inter-State League and was sold late in the season to the Louisville Colonels of the National League. He continued with Louisville to begin the 1899 season but was sold to Indianapolis of the Western League on June 25. Hartsel was still with the club when the league changed its name to the American League in 1900.

It was at Indianapolis that Tully Frederick Hartsel acquired the nickname Topsy. Hal Reid, an Indianapolis sportswriter, noted the young Hartsel's white hair, eyebrows and lashes, pink complexion and light blue eyes and remarked, "Say, boy, you're as light as Topsy of *Uncle Tom's Cabin* is black." He was known as Topsy for the rest of his life. One observer later remarked that Hartsel was "generally known by the fans when he steps to the plate by his shock of white hair."

In 1900 a squabble over Hartsel's services broke out between the Cincinnati Reds and Chicago Orphans of the National League, both of whom claimed to have acquired his contract from Indianapolis. Joining Cincinnati in mid-September 1900, with the dispute still raging, Hartsel batted .318 in 18 games for the lowly Reds. After the season Chicago president James Hart tried to have all Reds games in which Hartsel played forfeited. This effort was unsuccessful, but Hart did succeed in having Hartsel's contract assigned to the Orphans for 1901.

The 1901 season was Topsy Hartsel's breakout year. Playing the outfield, primarily in left, the little left-hander hit a solid .335 and was among the league leaders in almost all offensive categories. He placed second with 74 walks and 41 stolen bases, and ranked in the top seven in the league in games, at-bats, runs, hits, total bases, triples, home runs, on-base percentage, and slugging. Two of his seven home runs came on the same day at Cincinnati, both of the inside-the-park variety. Having made his mark, he was induced by Mack to jump to his American League Philadelphia Athletics for the 1902 season.

Mack immediately installed Hartsel at the top of his batting order and in left field. Hartsel did his job, leading all league batsmen in walks (87), stolen bases (47), and runs scored (109, tied) as the A's led the majors in scoring and won Mack's first pennant. Hartsel and the A's played solid, winning baseball the next two seasons and Topsy established himself as the best leadoff hitter in the game. In 1903 Hartsel batted .311 with five home runs; injuries limited him to 98 games. The following year Hartsel stayed healthy but saw his average slip to .253, although he remained an effective leadoff hitter thanks to his ability to draw walks: his 75 free passes ranked third in the league.

The A's returned to the top of the American League in 1905. Now 31 years old, Hartsel was on top of his game, too. He led the league in on-base percentage (.409) and bases on balls (121) while swiping 37 bases. The A's again led the league in scoring and won the pennant narrowly over Chicago. In a pivotal September series with the White Sox, Hartsel was involved in a very rare play. Until 1954 players left their gloves on the field when they came in to bat. Small objects in a large field, the gloves rarely came into play; one exception was a game in Philadelphia on September 28, 1905. Hartsel scored from second base on a single to left by Harry Davis when the batted ball struck Hartsel's own glove, providing just enough delay for Hartsel to score the winning run on a very close play at the plate. The A's went on to finish just two games ahead of the Sox. In that year's World Series against the New York Giants, Topsy tied for the team lead with four hits and had two walks, a pair of steals, and a run scored—that run being one third of the A's series total as they were shut down by Christy Mathewson and Joe McGinnity.

Hartsel continued to work his magic from the leadoff spot, as the A's finished a close second to the Tigers twice over the next four years. Although his batting average never again topped .300, he continued to lead the league in walks every year through 1908, and his .405 OBP topped the league in 1907. By 1909, however, the 35-year-old Hartsel was no longer playing every day. Still, he was effective as a part-time player and had a lot to do with the A's successes in 1910 and 1911, when Mack relied upon him as an assistant coach. Hartsel appeared

in just one World Series game in 1910, but was on the coaching lines in 1911. Throughout his career he had been involved in several sign-stealing schemes and was credited with stealing the Giants' signals during that Series. Long regarded by Mack as a smart player and a student of the game, Hartsel, along with fellow A's player–coach Harry Davis, developed the pregame scouting report and was instrumental in directing the A's play.

Hartsel was purchased by Toledo of the American Association in December 1911, with the hope that he would play regularly for the Mud Hens for four or five seasons—a hope never fulfilled. Cleveland and Toledo owner Charles Somers announced in January that Hartsel would manage Toledo for the coming season. In his first season at the helm, Hartsel led the Mud Hens to a solid second-place finish. The following season he was not as effective. At the end of July his Mud Hens were in seventh place with a record of 48–59. He had played little himself, hitting .303 in just 12 games. Somers became dissatisfied with Hartsel's lack of success and Topsy resigned on August 3.

To discourage the Federal League from placing a team in Cleveland, Somers moved his Toledo team there beginning in 1914, so that he would always have a game in town. Filling the void in Toledo was an entry in the Class C Southern Michigan Association, where Hartsel reappeared as part-time player and manager.

Hartsel (who usually went by the name Fred in private life) had married Angie Mae Goodwin on October 13, 1903, and the childless couple spent the post-baseball portion of their lives in Toledo. After his professional baseball days were finally over, Hartsel tried his hand as a machinist, and, for a short time, entered into business. He and another ex–Mud Hen, Harry S. Hinchman, opened a downtown Toledo business that dealt in "automatic baseball." Then he went to work as a cashier for the Community Traction Company in 1918. He continued with the public transportation company as a transfer clerk until he retired in 1941.

Hartsel stayed away from baseball until 1929 when he took over the Community Traction team and managed it. He then became a strong supporter of amateur baseball in Toledo, managed several junior teams, and was a member of the Toledo Old Timers' Baseball Association. Hartsel never lost his interest in the game and followed the 1944 World Series from his deathbed. He died on October 14, 1944, after being ill for several months. He is buried in Historic Woodlawn Cemetery in Toledo.

JOHN R. HUSMAN

PHILADELPHIA

Daniel Francis Murphy
Second baseman, right fielder, 1902–1913

For more than a decade Danny Murphy was one of the best and most powerful hitters in the American League, a fine fielder with a strong arm, a savvy baserunner, and a pioneer in the art of sign stealing. The consummate team player for Connie Mack's Philadelphia Athletics, he replaced one Hall of Fame second baseman, Nap Lajoie, and later stepped aside for another, Eddie Collins. To make way for Collins, Murphy moved from second base to right field in midcareer, thereby paving the way for one of baseball's earliest dynasties. Just 5′7″ (some sources say 5′9″) and 175 pounds, little Danny was considered a long-distance hitter. A right-hander, he ranked among the AL's home run leaders six times between 1904 and 1911, and batted .319 between 1910 and 1913. He was one of Mack's favorites; though popular with the Philadelphia fans, his teammates, and baseball writers, he was described as retiring, and was seldom quoted. After Philadelphia released him, Murphy committed an act that Mack considered betrayal, but he was eventually forgiven by the Tall Tactician and returned as a reconciled prodigal son.

Daniel Francis Murphy was born in Philadelphia on August 11, 1876, as the City of Brotherly Love celebrated the centennial of the signing of the Declaration of Independence. Although Danny was referred to as a native son throughout his career in Philadelphia, his family had moved to New England when he was a youngster. He entered professional baseball at age 20 with Fall River (Massachusetts) of the New England League in 1897. He played for the independent North Attleboro (Massachusetts) team in 1899, and landed with Norwich in the Connecticut League in 1900. The New York Giants acquired the 24-year-old that fall, and he played his first major league game on September 17. Murphy finished the season as the Giants second baseman, collecting 20 hits (only one for extra bases) in 74 at-bats. Murphy returned to New York for the first five games of the 1901 season, but after just four hits in 20 at-bats, he was returned to Norwich on May 7, and batted .336 for the Witches the rest of the way. He also led the Connecticut State League in all three types of extra-base hits, with 32 doubles, 16 triples, and 12 homers. He was even better in 1902, hitting .462 through 49 games. Mack, who was seeking a second baseman because of the Pennsylvania court decision that nullified Lajoie's contract after one game in 1902, journeyed to Norwich and purchased Murphy's contract on July 7 for $600.

Murphy's American League debut on July 8 was spectacular. Arriving after game time, Murphy entered Philadelphia's game at Boston's Huntington Avenue Grounds in the second inning and smacked six hits in six trips to the plate, including an inside-the-park three-run home run off Cy Young. He also flawlessly handled 11 chances at second base in the Athletics' 22–9 win. Although he hit no more home runs that season, Murphy batted .313, drove in 48 runs, stole 12 bases, and, in the words of *The Sporting News*, filled "the shoes of the great Lajoie" well enough to lead the Mackmen to their first American League championship. On August 22 he married Catherine Moriarty, a 17-year-old cotton mill worker from Norwich, then collected two hits that afternoon.

He played good ball again in 1903, batting .273 with 31 doubles, 11 triples, and a home run, and was dubbed the Hit Interrupter for his "brilliant and brainy" glove work at the keystone for second-place Philadelphia. The Mackmen slid to fifth place in 1904, although Murphy achieved career highs in home runs with seven (tied for second in the league) and RBI with 77, while stealing 22 bases.

Philadelphia made its first World Series appearance in 1905 as Murphy smacked 42 extra-base hits and tied for third in the AL with six home runs. The smart little second sacker batted .277 during the season, but collected just three hits in 16 at-bats as the Mackmen fell to the New York Giants in five games.

In 1906 Murphy batted .301, but the Athletics slumped to fourth. Near the end of the season, Murphy grew homesick and returned to Norwich, where Catherine was living with an older brother and two sisters. Mack himself journeyed to the Nutmeg State and convinced his second baseman to return. Although it was rumored that Mack would trade Murphy, his little sparkplug returned for the 1907 season. Early in the year he suffered a broken or badly sprained ankle, but managed to hit .271.

Late in the 1907 campaign, 20-year-old Eddie Collins played six awkward games at shortstop. In 1908 Collins played shortstop and the outfield before Mack decided he might be better suited for second base. "So I got another idea," Mack later told sportswriter Fred Lieb. "I thought, why not put my second baseman, Danny Murphy, in right field and see what Eddie could do at second base? Though Danny had been my second baseman since my first pennant winner in 1902, he didn't pivot too well on double plays, but Murphy always was a sweet hitter."

The move was unpopular with the Philly faithful and the rest of the Mackmen. Murphy was well liked, and his fresh-out-of-college replacement had already earned the moniker Cocky Collins. If Murphy himself was bitter, he did not show it. As Collins later observed, "When I replaced him in the infield, and he took over in right field, it didn't sit too well with the A's followers....Murphy wasn't resentful of the shift. In fact, unlike many players of that era, he willingly cooperated with me. I took to the position naturally and really found myself there, but Murphy played a great part in helping mold me into a good infielder, or rather a good second baseman."

For his part Murphy went from being an average second baseman to an exceptional outfielder. He led the American League in fielding percentage in 1909 and in assists in 1911. While playing the outfield, he also became a better hitter. In 1908, playing 56 games at second base early in the season before moving to the outfield for 84 games, he drove in 66 runs, sixth most in the AL. By 1909, when Mack opened baseball's first steel and concrete stadium, Shibe Park, Murphy (who recorded Shibe's first RBI, double, and inside-the-park home run) was entrenched in right field. He batted .281, stole 19 bases, and ranked among the league's top 10 with five homers and 69 RBI.

By 1910 it was apparent that Mack had strengthened the club at two positions. "That master move started a new pennant era for Mack," The Sporting News said of the switch. Collins batted .324, stole 81 bases, and drove in 81 runs. The 33-year-old Murphy, dubbed Old Reliable, played in 151 games, became the first player to hit for the cycle at Shibe Park (on August 25, 1910), batted .300 and led the team with 28 doubles, 18 triples, and four home runs (tied with Rube Oldring). The Athletics captured the AL flag by 14½ games. In the World Series he batted .400, lashing eight hits, including three doubles and the only home run of the Series, and drove in nine runs as the Athletics crushed the Cubs 4–1 for Mack's first World Series win.

With the $100,000 Infield in place, the Mackmen were every bit as good in 1911. Murphy turned 35 that year, and batted .329 with 44 extra-base hits and 66 RBI, all while leading the AL in outfield assists with 34. The Athletics returned to the World Series, where Murphy batted .304, scored four times, and drove in three runs. He smacked four hits in Game Six as the Athletics wrapped up a 4–2 Series victory over John McGraw's New York Giants. After the season, field captain Harry Davis was named manager of Cleveland, and Mack tabbed Murphy to replace him, even though Collins had been acting captain. Murphy, accompanied by Catherine, led the Athletics on a trip to Cuba for an exhibition series. Collins stayed behind, citing seasickness.

The new captain started fast again in 1912, batting .323 with two homers and 20 RBI through 36 games, but disaster struck. On June 4, while making a steal attempt, he suffered a broken kneecap and most likely structural damage to the joint. He would never be the same ballplayer. "Dan Murphy will smash no [more] base hits for the Athletics this season," the Trenton Daily Times reported. "The captain and the team's heaviest hitting outfielder has such a bad case of water on the knee that he is physically incompetent to get into another game this year. It is possible that his playing days are over for all time." His playing days were not over, but his skills were severely diminished, and a sore arm developed in spring training in 1913 hampered his return. Murphy, the eighth oldest player in the AL, appeared in only 40 games that season and made just nine outfield appearances. He could still hit, batting .322 in just 65 trips, primarily as a pinch hitter.

The Athletics returned to the World Series that fall to face the Giants. Although Murphy did not play in the Series, the Athletics won 4–1, and he returned home to a victory parade in Norwich and was named a lifetime member of the town's Elks Club.

His career with the Athletics was over, however. On March 6, 1914, Mack sold him to Baltimore in the International League. Murphy was not willing to go back to the minors. Three days later he signed with the Brooklyn team in the Federal League, owned by the Tip Top Baking Company's Ward family. Murphy was reported to be the team's new manager, but the Wards tabbed former Cleveland third baseman Bill Bradley. Murphy was signed as an outfielder and "scout."

Mack soon found out what that meant. "Danny Murphy, who had been one of my standbys, became an agent of the Federals, and he began to operate among my players," Mack said later. "He was working for the Ward Brothers of the bakeries. Murphy offered my players three times what they were getting from me." The Athletics were on their way to their fourth AL pennant in five years. But Mack later told Lieb, "I felt it was the most unhappy season I ever experienced.... The Federal League was after our players from the spring to the World Series, and the season was one of trouble and unpleasantness. What made it even more bitter was that Danny Murphy, who had played on five of my championship clubs, was the scout for the Brooklyn Federals."

The Athletics hung on to win the AL flag, but were swept by the "Miracle Braves" in the fall classic's most stunning upset. Disgruntled, Mack dismantled his team. He released three pitchers that Murphy had been in contact with (Bender, Eddie Plank, and Jack Coombs), and sold Collins to the Chicago White Sox. Over the next couple of years Frank Baker, Stuffy McInnis, Jack Barry, and others were also jettisoned.

Though blamed for his role in ending the Philadelphia dynasty, Murphy brought no players of significance to the Brookfeds. He did make a contribution on the field in 1914. In 52 games Murphy batted .304 with four home runs, 32 RBI, and four stolen bases. He was released on July 2, 1915, at age 38, after collecting just one hit in six at-bats.

Murphy became a manager in the Eastern League, at New Haven from 1916 to 1918 and Hartford in 1919, without much success. The Athletics had even less success, finishing dead last every year from 1915 to 1921. Before the 1920 season, Mack and Murphy reunited. *The Sporting News* reported that "The veteran Danny Murphy is 'home again' after six years of more or less prodigal wandering. Danny and Connie [had] something of a falling out in 1914 and Danny went astray to the Feds. Since then, he has had an uncertain career as a minor league manager." Mack later said, "I was pretty sore at the time—awfully sore.... Today, over the perspective of the years, I feel a little differently.

The players were taking advantage of a baseball war to get all they could, just as I took advantage of a baseball war to raid the National League when we first put a club in Philadelphia. I long have forgiven the players who gave me those 1914 headaches, and most of them have been back with me in some capacity."

Murphy remained with the Athletics as a coach through the 1924 season. Following his departure, he reportedly worked as a scout and then caught on as a coach for his old teammate, Stuffy McInnis, with the Philadelphia Phillies in 1927. Stuffy lasted just one season, however, and Murphy went with him, marking the end of his on-field baseball career. For a time Murphy ran a hardware store in Newark, New Jersey. While he was so engaged, a con man impersonated him in Chicago, but was nabbed on Christmas Eve, 1929. The real Murphy, by then a widower, lived with Catherine's brother and sisters in Jersey City, where he worked at the Hudson County Hospital with former major leaguer Art Devlin. He reportedly did some scouting, played in old-timers' games, spent time hunting, and attended wrestling and boxing matches.

In the early 1950s Murphy suffered a broken hip, and then a two-year illness. Murphy was living with a niece when he died on November 22, 1955, at the Jersey City Medical Center. He is buried at an unknown location in Norwich, Connecticut.

DOUG SKIPPER

PHILADELPHIA

F. Osee Schrecongost
Catcher, 1902–1908

Inexorably linked to pitcher Rube Waddell, Osee Schrecongost left his own mark as one of the Deadball Era's prominent catchers. Schreck, as his name was often truncated, hit .271 in 11 major league seasons. He also established himself as one of the best defensive catchers in the game. "Schreck could do more with his glove than any catcher that ever stood behind the plate," said Connie Mack, his manager at Philadelphia and a former big league catcher himself. "He caught 99.99 percent of balls thrown to him with one hand, his glove hand. He used his glove hand like a shortstop." Schreck held the major league catcher's record for single-season putouts for nearly 50 years. His 29 innings behind the plate on July 4, 1905, is still the top one-day workload for a major league catcher.

F. Osee Schrecongost was born on April 11, 1875, the second son of Naaman and Sarah Crotzman Schrecongost in the western Pennsylvania mining town of New Bethlehem. The family name is of German origin, and over the years a number of variations of Osee's name—first and last—have appeared. The given name has been rendered as Ossie, Ossee, Osie, and Osee, but family descendants confirm that his name was Osee (pronounced Oh-See), and that was how he signed his marriage license. Whatever he was called, Osee first received attention as a ballplayer while catching "Johnson, the crack colored pitcher" for the New Bethlehem baseball team. "Johnson and Schrecongost constituted the battery for the home team and received a hearty applause from the spectators," the *New Bethlehem Vindicator* reported in 1894. "Schrecongost caught every man but one who attempted to steal second."

The young catcher advanced through the minor leagues over the next few years with stops at Williamsport (Pennsylvania), Fall River (Massachusetts), Augusta (Maine), Cedar Rapids (Iowa), and Youngstown (Ohio). He made his major league debut for the National League's Louisville Colonels at Baltimore on September 8, 1897. By coincidence the pitcher was another western Pennsylvanian making his debut: Rube Waddell.

Osee opened the 1898 season with Cedar Rapids of the Western Association. When that league folded near midseason, Schreck hooked on with Youngstown in the Inter-State League. It was probably during this period that he met June Reed of Newcastle, Pennsylvania. A pretty spitfire of a girl who also enjoyed cards, whiskey, and cigars, Jenny June (as the family called her) married Osee in the winter of 1899. The union produced a daughter a few years later.

Schreck got a return call from the majors at the tail end of the 1898 season. He caught nine games for the NL Cleveland Spiders, batting .314 with three triples and 10 RBI in only 35 at-bats. The following year he shuttled back and forth between Cleveland and St. Louis, both owned by the Robison brothers. Overall for the season, Schrecongost hit .290 in 115 games, playing mostly catcher (64 games) and first base (43 games).

Schreck returned to the minors in 1900, but it was only a half-step back. The newly christened American League, a descendant of the Western League, was one year away from claiming major league status. Schreck hit .282 in 125 games for Buffalo's AL club, logging 95 games behind the plate. When the American League challenged the National for major league recognition in 1901, Buffalo lost its franchise. Schreck signed with the new AL club in Boston, where he batted .304 for the year.

Criger, a weaker hitter but the more consistent backstop, was the catcher of choice for manager Jimmy Collins and star pitcher Cy Young. Schreck became the odd man out, and joined the Cleveland Blues for the

1902 season. He was not even considered for catching duty with the Blues as Harry Bemis and Bob Wood were entrenched at the position. Instead, Schreck started the first 18 games of the season at first base. He hit well enough (.338) but never learned to play first base with great proficiency. The Blues released him in May.

After his release by Cleveland the Philadelphia Athletics signed Schreck. Mack, the A's manager and a shrewd judge of talent, saw Schreck as a capable backup to catcher Mike Powers. Schreck caught his first game for Philadelphia on May 28 and began to see more regular action behind the plate by mid-June. Osee enjoyed his best season at the plate, hitting .327 with career highs in RBI and slugging percentage. His throwing also received praise, with Francis Richter of *The Sporting Life* declaring, "Schrecongost's throwing is about as quick and accurate as that of any catcher now working in either League." His most significant contribution to Philadelphia's pennant-winning season, however, may have been his handling of southpaw Rube Waddell—not always an easy task.

"Often when Schreck would sign for a curve ball to be pitched, Waddell would not see the sign properly, and throw a fast ball," A's first baseman Harry Davis remembered, "but Schreck would catch it just as easily. There are very few catchers today who can catch one ball if they are crossed in this manner, particularly with the gloved hand alone, as Schreck invariably did." With Schrecongost catching most of his games, Waddell flourished in Philadelphia, winning 24 games and posting a 2.05 ERA as the Athletics captured the American League pennant.

In 1903 Schreck's batting average dipped to .255, then plummeted to a career-low .186 in 1904. A free swinger who liked to "hit it off his ear," Schreck seldom walked. In 1905 he drew only three free passes in 429 plate appearances. That year his batting average rebounded to .271, and Schrecongost caught a career-high 114 games as the Athletics once again won the American League pennant. Osee also set the single-season record for putouts by a catcher (790), a record that endured until Roy Campanella recorded 807 putouts in 1953. During a doubleheader in Boston on July 4, 1905, Schreck set a major league record by catching 29 innings in a single day. Waddell and Cy Young each went the distance in a 20-inning marathon won by the A's.

When the 1906 season opened the A's had high hopes of a repeat championship. Instead, they struggled to a fourth-place finish, 12 games behind the White Sox. Schreck and Waddell became easy targets for criticism. Like his battery mate, Schreck loved to have a good time and became known for his heavy drinking, a habit which began to wear on his teammates, even though he was batting a solid .284. "Philadelphia's oldest players are blaming Waddell and his catcher for its loss of the pennant," the *Detroit News* quoted an anonymous Philadelphia insider.

After the disappointing season Schreck agreed to clean up his act. "Schreck is too valuable a man to throw himself away on drink and he has realized that fact," Harry Davis told *The Sporting News*. "Schreck has given up drinking, and I believe for good. He has given his promise to his wife, to Connie, and to me and to his friends not to touch the stuff again." Osee reportedly weaned himself off the hard stuff with sherry-enhanced milkshakes. As Osee cleaned up his act, his relationship with Waddell reportedly deteriorated. Regardless of any personal differences, Schreck remained Waddell's usual battery partner. He caught 99 games for Philadelphia in 1907, including 29 of Waddell's 33 starts.

Waddell became increasingly unreliable during the A's tight 1907 pennant battle with Detroit. The Tigers won the flag and Mack sold Waddell to St. Louis before the 1908 season. Schreck still led the team in games caught but his batting average tumbled to .220, a 52-point drop-off from the previous year. With the A's floundering in sixth place, Mack sold Osee to the White Sox in late September. Schreck caught his last major league game on October 2, 1908, as Cleveland's Addie Joss pitched a perfect game and delivered a 1–0 victory over 40-game winner Ed Walsh.

After the end of his major league career, Schreck caught for Columbus and Louisville in the American Association. He plunged further into the minor league ranks late in the 1910 season when he signed with the Marion Diggers of the Ohio State League. When a job managing the Diggers failed to materialize the following year, Schrecongost's professional baseball career came to an end.

His health began to fail just about the same time Waddell's was in rapid decline. Despite their later squabbles, a lasting bond must have existed between them. When Osee learned of Rube's death on April 1, 1914, he reportedly told friends, "The 'Rube' is gone and I am all in. I might as well join him."

Just a few months later, Schreck collapsed in a Philadelphia café. He died on July 9, 1914, from complications of uremia. He was buried in Kittanning Cemetery in Kittanning, Pennsylvania, 20 miles southwest of where he had been born just 39 years before.

DAN O'BRIEN

PHILADELPHIA

GEORGE EDWARD "RUBE" WADDELL
LEFT-HANDED PITCHER, 1902–1907

He entered this world on Friday the 13th and exited on April Fool's Day. In the 37 intervening years Rube Waddell struck out more batters, frustrated more managers, and attracted more fans than any pitcher of his era. An imposing physical specimen for his day, the 6'1", 196-pound Waddell possessed the intellectual and emotional maturity of a child—although a very precocious and engaging one at that. "There was delicious humor in many of his vagaries, a vagabond impudence and ingenuousness that made them attractive to the public," wrote the *Columbus Dispatch*. Waddell's on- and off-field exploits became instant legends.

Known to occasionally miss a scheduled start because he was off fishing or playing marbles with street urchins, Waddell might disappear for days during spring training, only to be found leading a parade down the main street of Jacksonville, Florida, or wrestling an alligator in a nearby lagoon. Despite these and other curious distractions, Waddell's immense physical ability was undeniable. He complemented a blazing fastball with a wicked curve and demonstrated excellent control with both. His strikeout-to-walk ratio was nearly 3:1 for his career (almost 4:1 in his record-setting season of 1904).

Connie Mack, who managed Waddell for six seasons in Philadelphia, believed that Waddell had "the best combination of speed and curves" of any pitcher who played the game. Without Mack's patience and guidance, however, Rube Waddell might be nothing more than a humorous footnote in baseball history. Mack was the only manager able to tolerate Rube for any extended period, and that was for only six seasons, but Waddell always remained a Mack favorite. "Dad always had a gleam in his eye when he told stories about Rube Waddell," said Connie's daughter, Ruth Mack Clark. "Dad really loved the Rube."

Waddell's antics have become the stuff of legend, occasionally embroidered to make this larger-than-life character appear even more preposterous. No, Waddell did not regularly bolt from the mound to chase a passing fire wagon, but his fascination with fires was genuine. He regularly assisted firefighters, from a bucket brigade in Pewaukee, Wisconsin, to large metropolitan departments in Philadelphia, Cleveland, Detroit, and Washington. Yes, on occasion Waddell did direct his infielders to the sidelines and strike out the side in the final inning—but only in exhibitions, never in a regular-season game.

One of the great myths concerns Waddell's background, which helped perpetuate the rube or hayseed image that adorned his career. Contrary to popular belief, his father was not a farmer. John Waddell, a native Scotsman, labored in the Pennsylvania oil fields as an employee of the National Transit Company, a division of Standard Oil. While living in Bradford, Pennsylvania—at one time the center of world oil production—John's wife, Mary Forbes Waddell, gave birth to their sixth child on October 13, 1876. Christened George Edward, the future Rube Waddell was also known as Ed or Eddie in family circles.

In the early 1890s the Waddells relocated to Butler County, Pennsylvania, and settled in the town of Prospect. In Butler County and the surrounding area, the reputation of a burgeoning pitching talent began to grow. Teenager Ed Waddell swiftly advanced from the sandlots to play for a number of semipro baseball teams in the region. In August 1896 newspapers in Titusville and Oil City made passing mentions of an Oil City pitcher named Rube Waddell, the first known references to his famous nickname.

In August of 1897, without so much as an inning of minor league baseball, Waddell's reputation earned him a tryout with the National League's Pittsburgh Pirates. His seating assignment at a team meal, however, earned him a release before he ever appeared in a game. "Rube sat beside Manager [Patsy] Donovan," the *Louisville Courier-Journal* reported. "Patsy heard him talk and released him as soon as breakfast was over."

The visiting Louisville Colonels saw promise in the young left-hander and signed him. Rube made his major league debut on September 8, 1897, a 5–1 loss to Baltimore, the defending league champion. A week later, he relieved in a lost cause against Pittsburgh.

Louisville management believed Waddell needed more seasoning before testing the majors for a full season. Accordingly, he began the 1898 campaign with Detroit of the Western League. The relationship did not last long. Waddell pitched in nine games for Detroit before he left the team after a squabble over a fine. He pitched briefly for Chatham (Ontario), and finished the year with Homestead (Pennsylvania). Waddell returned to the Western League in 1899 with Columbus (Ohio), where he enjoyed his first successful season in Organized Baseball, as he notched a 26–8 record for Columbus and Grand Rapids (Michigan) before rejoining Louisville in the final month of the season and winning seven of nine decisions.

After the 1899 season Rube made a brief return to Columbus, where he married Florence Dunning, the first of his three marriages. To no one's surprise, Florence received a divorce from Rube in 1901 on the grounds of "gross neglect of duty."

Prior to the start of the 1900 season, the Louisville franchise was contracted from the National League, but Colonels owner Barney Dreyfuss purchased a half-interest in the Pirates and arranged for the trade of 10 of his players to Pittsburgh, including Waddell. Pitching for Pittsburgh, Waddell paced National League pitchers in 1900 in ERA (2.37) and was second in strikeouts (130), but also finished with a losing record (8–13) and missed nearly two months of the season.

Fred Clarke, the Pirates' player–manager, was a strict disciplinarian and had little use for Waddell's irresponsibility. In early July Clarke suspended Waddell, who then hooked up with a number of semipro teams in western Pennsylvania, finally landing in Punxsutawney. Mack, then manager of Milwaukee's American League team, was in need of pitching. He received permission from Pittsburgh to sign Waddell, with the stipulation that Waddell would return to the Pirates if they so desired. Mack convinced Waddell to leave Punxy, and the southpaw became an immediate sensation in Milwaukee. He won 10 games in a little more than a month, including a 22-inning doubleheader at Chicago.

Impressed by Waddell's work with the Brewers, the Pirates asked for his return.

Clarke and Rube survived the remainder of the 1900 season without major eruptions, but more problems arose the following season. In May 1901 Waddell's contract was sold to the Chicago Orphans. After winning 14 games in 28 decisions for the struggling Chicago team, Rube jumped ship again and landed with a number of semipro teams in Wisconsin. In November Rube hooked on with a barnstorming team for a tour of California. Extremely popular with West Coast fans, Rube signed with the California League's Los Angeles Looloos for the 1902 season.

Waddell stayed in Los Angeles for only a few months before Mack, now managing the Philadelphia Athletics, enticed him into leaving California to bolster the A's depleted pitching staff. When Waddell agreed, Mack sent a pair of Pinkerton escorts to ensure that Waddell made it east.

Only 87 games remained on the A's schedule when Waddell pitched his first game on June 26, yet the left-hander finished the season with a 24–7 record. Rube also led the league with 210 strikeouts, 50 more than runner-up Cy Young, who pitched 108⅓ more innings. The Athletics, only two games above .500 when Rube entered the fray, finished 30 games above the break-even mark and won their first American League pennant.

In little more than half a season, Waddell had established himself as one of the game's premier pitchers and Philadelphia's most bankable star. The Athletics attendance doubled from the previous year to a league-leading 420,000. Cigars, soap, and liquor were among the products named after Waddell. The 1902 season also saw the emergence of Osee Schrecongost as Rube's favorite catcher. Waddell and Schreck (as the catcher's name was often truncated) soon became known as baseball's wackiest battery mates, as famous for their off-field frolics as their on-field production.

The 1903 season was the most tumultuous in the erratic career of Rube Waddell. In June he was married for the second time, this time to a Massachusetts girl named May Wynne Skinner, whom he had met just three days earlier. It was the beginning of a very stormy relationship. The marriage lasted nearly seven years, but the couple only infrequently lived together and Mrs. Waddell often had her husband jailed for nonsupport. In July American League president Ban Johnson suspended Waddell for five days after he climbed into the stands to beat up a spectator, a known gambler who had baited the pitcher. Despite starting the season 13–3, Waddell limped home to a 21–16 record. Still, he struck out a record 302 batters, even though his season ended prematurely on August 25 when he failed to appear for his scheduled start in Cleveland. Mack, weary of Rube's frequent unexcused absences, suspended him for the remainder of the season. A week later, Waddell patched up his differences with Mack, signed a contract for the following season and promised to "cut out the booze and funny business."

From September to December Waddell toured with a theater company, performing as himself in a melodrama entitled *The Stain of Guilt*. Baseball's matinee idol was a big draw at the theaters as well, but critics were largely unimpressed with Waddell's acting skills. "He is let out only two minutes in each scene," wrote the *Chicago Journal*, "and the ensuing repair bills are pretty bulky for even those few minutes."

After numerous disagreements over advance pay, the company jettisoned Rube during its run in Philadelphia, unceremoniously dumping his bags in the alley. He immediately began tending bar in nearby Camden, New Jersey. His 1904 campaign progressed without serious incident. Waddell won 25 games and registered a 1.62 ERA, the second-best of his career. He also extended his post-1900 single-season strikeout record to 349, a major league total unsurpassed until Sandy Koufax whiffed 382 in 1965.

The Rube also demonstrated his more compassionate side when Athletics center fielder Danny Hoffman was knocked unconscious by a fastball to the temple. "Someone went for an ambulance, and the players crowded around in aimless bewilderment," wrote Mack. "Somebody said that Danny might not live until the doctor got there. Then the man they had called the playboy and clown went into action. Pushing everybody to one side, he gently placed Danny over his shoulder and actually ran across the field." Rube flagged down a carriage, which carted the pair to the nearest hospital. Rube, still in uniform, sat at Hoffman's bedside for most of the night, and held ice to Hoffman's head.

The 1905 season was even better for Waddell, at least statistically. He led the league in strikeouts (287), games pitched (46), ERA (1.48), and wins (27). His most spectacular victory was a 20-inning contest against Boston's Cy Young on July 4, 1905. Both Hall of Famers went the distance and Rube performed cartwheels off the mound once the A's secured the 4–2 victory. According to legend, Rube bartered free drinks with the ball he used to defeat Young in the game. Before long, the souvenir, magically multiplied, was in the possession of dozens of bartenders.

Despite this success, the 1905 season ended on a sour note for Waddell. Again, he missed most of the season's final month. After another Waddell victory over Young

at Boston on September 8, the A's headed back home to Philadelphia. While changing trains in Providence, Waddell and teammate Andy Coakley engaged in a friendly scuffle over a straw hat. Rube fell and injured his shoulder. His season was over, with the exception of two ineffective appearances in the last two days of the regular season, and he did not appear in the Athletics' five-game defeat to the New York Giants in that year's World Series. Not everybody believed the straw hat tale, however; rumors were rampant that gamblers had paid Waddell to sit out the Series.

Mack believed that Waddell was never quite the same after the straw hat incident. In 1906 Waddell's ledger sagged to 15–17. Despite this losing record, however, Waddell ranked among the league leaders with eight shutouts, including a one-hitter over the Detroit Tigers. Waddell's drinking problem escalated during the season, and a rift developed between Waddell and Schrecongost, who was giving up drinking. In 1907 Rube improved his record to 19–13, but he was ineffective down the stretch as the A's fought tooth-and-nail with Detroit for the AL pennant. In a key game against the Tigers on September 30, Waddell came on in relief of Jimmy Dygert and failed to hold a three-run lead. Although the game ended in a 17-inning deadlock, the Athletics' collapse was a crushing blow to their pennant hopes and proved to be Waddell's death knell in Philadelphia. In the "interest of team harmony," Mack sold Waddell to the St. Louis Browns on February 7, 1908—one week after Waddell's wife sued him for divorce. Shortly afterward, Waddell was accused of assault and battery against both his parents-in-law. The resulting legal difficulties prevented him from pitching in Massachusetts, where a warrant for his arrest awaited, during the 1908 and 1909 seasons.

Waddell responded with another 19-win season in 1908, helping the much-improved Browns to stay in the pennant race, although the club faded to fourth place by season's end. Not quite the dominant force he once was, Rube was still a box office bonanza. "He paid for himself in three games after he was bought," wrote *St. Louis Post-Dispatch* columnist John L. Wray. "He had added many thousands to the exchecquer [*sic*] since that time—paid admissions that would never have arrived at the gate but for the fact that Rube was scheduled to work." The Browns enjoyed a 48 percent boost in home attendance, to more than 618,000, second in the American League, while the Athletics' attendance dropped by nearly 30 percent. On July 29 Rube enjoyed a measure of revenge against his old mates when he struck out 16 Athletics, tying the American League single game record.

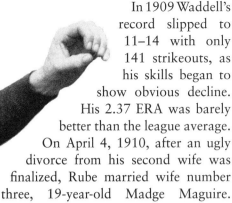

In 1909 Waddell's record slipped to 11–14 with only 141 strikeouts, as his skills began to show obvious decline. His 2.37 ERA was barely better than the league average. On April 4, 1910, after an ugly divorce from his second wife was finalized, Rube married wife number three, 19-year-old Madge Maguire. Again, the marriage was tempestuous. Rube's major league days were also numbered. He appeared in only 10 games, all but two in relief. The Browns released him in August, leaving him to finish out the year with Newark in the Eastern League.

In 1911 Waddell won 20 games for Joe Cantillon's Minneapolis Millers, helping the Millers to another American Association championship. The following winter Waddell lived with Cantillon at the manager's farm in Hickman, Kentucky, a small village situated on a bend of the Mississippi River. When flood waters threatened to swallow the town, Rube stood in icy water for hours, helping stack sandbags for the levee. As a result he contracted a severe case of pneumonia. His system weakened, Waddell soon became a victim of tuberculosis. He pitched one more season for Minneapolis and part of another with two teams in the Northern League, but by November of 1913 his health had reached the critical stage.

Cantillon paid Waddell's way to a sanatorium in San Antonio, Texas, to be close to his parents, who had moved in with Rube's younger sister in nearby Boerne, Texas. Mack and Athletics partner Ben Shibe paid for Waddell's medical care, with orders that "Waddell should have the best of medical attention and nursing, and that no expenses should be spared to either help the once mighty Rube regain his health, or to ease his sufferings if his battle is to be a losing one."

The once powerful Waddell, now down to 130 pounds, died on April 1, 1914, a few months shy of his 38th birthday. "He was the greatest pitcher in the game, and although widely known for his eccentricities, was more sinned against than sinner," said Mack. "He may have failed us at times but to him, I and the other owners of the Athletics ball club, owe much." He was laid to rest in Mission Burial Park South, in San Antonio.

DAN O'BRIEN

"Chief" C.A.Bender

PHILADELPHIA

CHARLES ALBERT BENDER
RIGHT-HANDED PITCHER, 1903–1914

Charles Albert "Chief" Bender lived a unique American life, fashioned a Hall of Fame career, and was a crucial member of modern baseball's first dynasty. Though proud of his Native American heritage, Bender resented the constant bigotry he faced and the emblematic moniker ascribed to him. "I do not want my name to be presented to the public as an Indian, but as a pitcher," he once said. The newspapermen did not listen. Even though his manager called him Albert, prevailing racial stereotypes rarely were absent from the words written about him. Bender signed his autograph as Charles or some derivative, but he was called Chief so often (and so often with affection), that he allowed the name to be etched on his tombstone.

An excellent control pitcher, several times Bender's walk rates were among the lowest in the league. He was a cerebral pitcher, who studied his opponents carefully and devised an assortment of pitches to disrupt hitters' timing. Over a 16-year major league career Bender won 212 games and posted a .625 winning percentage, but he is known foremost for a rare ability to pitch well under pressure. "If I had all the men I've ever handled, and they were in their prime, and there was one game I wanted to win above all others," said Philadelphia Athletics icon Connie Mack, who managed Lefty Grove, Herb Pennock, Eddie Plank, and Rube Waddell, "Albert would be my man."

Details about Charles Bender's childhood are sketchy. His birth certificate, created years after his birth, says May 3, 1883; other sources list May 5, 1883; in yet other sources the year given is 1884, which is probably correct. Some sources list his birthplace as Brainerd, an early error that often is repeated. It is most accurate to say Bender was born in Crow Wing County in northern Minnesota. Bender's mother, Mary Razier (or Razor) Bender, was believed to be a member of the Mississippi Band of the Ojibwe (Chippewa) tribe. His father, Albertus Bliss Bender, was a homesteader-farmer of German descent, born in Massachusetts. Charles Albert is believed to be one of 11 children. At the age of seven he took a job as a farmhand for a dollar a week.

In 1891 he enrolled at the Lincoln Institution, also referred to as the Educational Home, a government boarding school for Native Americans in Philadelphia. He later returned to Minnesota, but only briefly. He was educated at the Carlisle Indian School (Carlisle, Pennsylvania), and graduated in 1902—a few years before legendary athlete Jim Thorpe attended. The objective at both Lincoln and Carlisle was to educate students while simultaneously eviscerating any remnants of Native American culture. Bender would likely have participated in the outing program at Carlisle, which placed Native American teenagers with white families who taught them their own ("civilized") ways of living. While at Carlisle, Bender was a member of the track, football, basketball, and baseball teams. His tall frame made him a natural first baseman. Only after he pitched in spot relief for the team's regular pitcher was it apparent Bender could be something more. His coach, Glenn "Pop" Warner, who created a more notable legacy as a football coach, turned Bender into a pitcher.

In the summer of 1901, while at Carlisle, Bender accepted an offer of $5 to pitch a game for the semipro team in nearby Dillsburg. It was his first chance to get paid for playing baseball and he was brilliant, striking out 21 batters and hitting a grand slam. Unfortunately, Bender's fielders were brutal and Dillsburg lost the game in the tenth inning. When Bender went to collect his earnings, he was stiffed. He was handed a handful of coins totaling $3.20, considerably less than he was promised. He returned to school with a bitter taste in his mouth.

Bender recovered, of course, and after starting his big-league career he likely did not think much further about the matter. Then, in the late summer of 1941, long after his pitching career had ended, a 57-year-old Bender received a piece of mail containing a small sack of worn coins. Each of the coins predated 1901, and the sack contained a note from the Dillsburg baseball team, advising him that the old records indicated he was due $1.80 from his brief tenure with the team in 1901. The note went on to say that, although the team was short of revenue on the day he pitched, the postseason cabbage harvest made payment of all outstanding debts possible; Bender's records, however, had been misplaced. A final thought contained in the note advised Bender that no interest was included as the school felt he had been overpaid for his services in the first place.

Standing 6'2", weighing 185 pounds, with brown eyes and black hair, not only was Bender athletic, he looked the part. Bender's skill was quickly recognized in the area. In 1902 he attended a prep school at Dickinson College (also in Carlisle), where he played baseball and football. To make a few bucks he began pitching for the Harrisburg Athletic Club, a semipro baseball team. Bender's team played an exhibition game with the Chicago Cubs. Under the name Charles Albert he pitched his teammates to a 3–1 victory. Pitching under the name Charles, Albert allowed three runs in a loss. Soon after, Mack signed the right-hander to a $1,800 contract.

After an impressive debut in which he pitched five innings for a victory in relief, Bender hurled his first complete-game shutout on April 27, beating New York Highlanders pitcher and future Hall of Famer Clark Griffith. Bender was the youngest player in baseball by more than a year, but by the end of the 1903 season the 19-year-old rookie had 17 victories and a 3.07 ERA. After posting a mediocre 10–11 record in 1904, Bender rebounded to go 18–11 the following year.

Compared to his peers Bender did not have an inordinate level of pitching stamina, as he was plagued by poor health during several seasons and never pitched more than the 270 innings he hurled his rookie year. On October 5, 1905, however, the Athletics needed to sweep a doubleheader against Washington to clinch the pennant. Bender won the first game, 8–0, and came on as a relief pitcher in the second game and won that one as well. That day Bender pitched 15 innings and struck out 17 Senators. A fine right-handed hitter who posted a lifetime .212 batting average, he also made five hits, including a double and two triples.

Bender received his first opportunity to pitch in the World Series in 1905. Starting the second game against John McGraw's New York Giants, he delivered a masterful four-hit, 3–0 shutout in the Athletics' only victory of the Series. After the 1905 season, and after studying Christy Mathewson (who defeated him 2–0 in the fifth and final World Series game), Bender worked to further develop his control. "Without control you are like a ship without a rudder," Bender said. "No matter how much power you may have, you are unable to get results."

He developed a well-directed fastball and a sharp-breaking curve—a man named Bender has to have one—that was a precursor to the slider. The pitch, the nickel curve, became Bender's predominant out pitch. He also threw a submarine fadeaway (a pitch learned from Pop Warner that moved like the contemporary screwball, away from a left-handed hitter) and an occasional slow ball. Teammate Bob Shawkey believed Bender's knack for fooling hitters was grounded in this ability to change speeds. "The Chief had a great curveball, but I'd say his greatest success came on the change-up he threw off his fastball," Shawkey said. "They'd swing at his motion, and that ball would come floating up there. It was beautiful to watch."

"I use fast curves, pitched overhand and side arm, fast balls, high and inside, and an underhand fadeaway pitch with the hand almost down to the level of the knees," Bender told *Baseball Magazine* in 1911. "These are my most successful deliveries, though a twisting slow one mixed up with them helps at times." Bender's best pitch, however, may have been his fastball, which teammate Eddie Collins once said was no slower than Walter Johnson's. While it is unlikely that he threw quite that hard, Bender's speed made an impression. Bender "makes the baseball look like a pea," New York Giants leadoff hitter Josh Devore said. "Who can hit a pea when it goes by at the speed of light?"

Bender possessed exceptional intelligence, which was recognized by his peers and opponents, including umpire Billy Evans, who believed Bender was one of the most intelligent pitchers in the game. "He takes advantage of every weakness," Evans said, "and once a player shows him a weak spot he is marked for life by the crafty Indian." Bender possessed a keen ability to compartmentalize and focus on the task at hand, attributes that won the admiration of legendary sportswriter Grantland Rice, who once called Bender one of "the greatest competitors I ever knew." While playing a round of golf with the pitcher, Rice was struck by how Bender usually responded to questions only after giving them measured thought. "Tension is the greatest curse in sport," Bender told Rice. "I've never had any tension. You give the best you have—you win or lose. What's the difference if you give all you've got to give?"

Bender's patient, levelheaded manner was often sorely tested by the taunts and mockery he received from the fans and the press because of his Native American roots. Bender was proud of his heritage, but did not want to be portrayed as a caricature, as Native Americans often were during his lifetime. When he pitched, fans would often wear out their lungs with what they thought were authentic renditions of Indian battle cries. Displaying a sense of humor, Bender would admonish such hecklers as "foreigners" who should either quiet down or go back to Europe. Against his wishes, Bender was commonly referred to as Chief, as were other Native American baseball players during the Deadball Era. Even decades after his retirement *The Sporting News* carried this headline for his 1954 obituary: Chief Bender Answers Call to Happy Hunting Grounds. When he was voted into the Hall of Fame in 1953, *The Sporting News* wrote that it was a "long-delayed feather for the Chief."

During his first eight years in the major leagues, Bender continued to hone his craft. Although his won–lost record fluctuated over that span, his ERA dropped every year, to a career-best 1.58 in 1910. That year he also won 20 games for the first time, notching a career-best 23 victories against only five defeats, which gave him the league's best winning percentage (.821). Among his victories that season was his only no-hitter, thrown May 12 against the Cleveland Indians. He faced just 27 hitters as the lone man to reach, shortstop Terry Turner, was caught stealing after reaching on a walk. Bender won the opening game of the 1910 World Series, 4–1, and the Athletics beat the Chicago Cubs in five games.

The following year Bender helped the A's win a second World Series, and his 17–5 won–lost record was once again good enough to lead the league in winning percentage. Facing the New York Giants in the World Series, Bender enjoyed another brilliant fall classic, winning two of his three starts, posting a 1.04 ERA, and striking out 20 batters in 26 innings.

Philadelphia failed to win a third straight pennant in 1912, when injuries

limited Bender to a 13–8 record in just 171 innings, but the following year they were back, as Bender won 20 games for the second and final time in his career. He also succeeded brilliantly in a new role as the Athletics' bullpen ace, starting 21 games and finishing 21 more in relief. Although nobody realized it at the time, Bender's 13 saves in 1913 tied baseball's single-season record, which lasted until broken by Fred Marberry in 1924. In that year's World Series, again against the Giants, Bender won two more games, posting an ERA of 4.00 as the Athletics captured their third world championship in four years.

For all his success during the regular season, it was during the postseason that Bender made his mark as one of the most accomplished clutch pitchers of the twentieth century. From 1905 through 1914, Bender's last season with the Athletics, the Mackmen played in the World Series five times. In those five fall classics, Bender pitched 10 games, won six, and had a 2.44 ERA. He is the only man to complete his first nine World Series starting assignments. In 85 innings batters hit for a .212 average against him.

The worst blemish on Bender's World Series record came in 1914, when the Athletics lost four straight games to Boston's "Miracle Braves." It had been another stellar regular season campaign for Bender, who won 14 straight games before finishing the year with a 17–3 mark, good for a league-leading .850 winning percentage. His only appearance in that year's World Series, however, was a disaster: Bender started the opening game and surrendered six earned runs in 5⅓ innings. It was his last appearance in an A's uniform.

"All the Athletics were overconfident," Bender later said about that Series. "I was ill with stomach and gall bladder trouble the day of the first game. I reported this to Mr. Mack, who said, 'Oh, you can beat those fellows.'"

The next year, Bender jumped to the Federal League. Pitching for the last-place Baltimore Terrapins, he compiled a 4–16 record and was released on August 30. In the wake of the demise of the Federal League following the 1915 season, Bender was signed by the Philadelphia Phillies, where he struggled with a 7–7 record in 1916.

On February 18, 1917, Bender struck and killed a pedestrian in an auto accident. He was released by the Phillies five days later, but the club re-signed him after a coroner's jury cleared him of wrongdoing. Although Bender began the 1917 season as the Phillies' batting practice pitcher, by late May he began to show flashes of his former brilliance. He posted an 8–2 mark and sparkling 1.67 ERA, but nonetheless was released by the Phillies at the end of the season. From there Bender went to work in the Philadelphia shipyards to contribute to the war effort.

His life in baseball, however, did not end. When the war was over, Bender embarked on a career as a minor league player and manager, with considerable success. He was offered opportunities to return to the big leagues, but enjoyed managing so much that he declined. Bender managed Richmond of the Virginia League in 1919 and dominated the Class B league from the mound, if not always from the dugout, winning 29 games against just two defeats. Subsequently, he pitched and managed at New Haven, Connecticut, in the Eastern League (1920–1921, 1924), at Reading, Pennsylvania (1922), and Baltimore (1923), in the International League, and at Johnstown, Pennsylvania, in the Mid-Atlantic League in 1927. During that period he also spent five years as the baseball coach for the U.S. Naval Academy.

Bender did pitch one more time in the major leagues. In 1925, while serving as a pitching coach for the Chicago White Sox, he worked the ninth inning in a game against the Boston Red Sox—the club he had beaten for his first major league victory 22 years prior. Bender, 41 at the time, allowed two runs on a walk and a home run, but did manage to retire the side.

During the 1930s Bender managed the Eastern team of the independent House of David League. He also managed Erie (Pennsylvania) in the outlaw Continental League in 1932, Wilmington (Delaware) of the Inter-State League in 1940, Newport News of the Virginia League in 1941, and Savannah of the South Atlantic League in 1946. Thereafter he was associated with the New York Yankees, Chicago White Sox, New York Giants, and Philadelphia Athletics as pitching coach or scout. At age 60 he took a turn pitching batting practice to the Athletics.

Bender was a man of myriad talents on and off the field. A hunter and fisherman for some years in the off-season, Bender was a representative of a major American weapons manufacturer, and in later years was a Pennsylvania state champion clay pigeon shooter. For a time, after his baseball career ended, he was an outstanding golfer. He was also an excellent swimmer. Bender's favorite hobbies were gardening, playing billiards, painting landscapes in oil, and reading, especially English literature. He also occasionally served as a consultant in the diamond and textile trades.

Throughout his ventures, Bender remained married to Marie (Clement) Bender, whom he had wed in 1904. The couple's marriage, which lasted nearly 50 years, did not produce any children.

In 1953 Bender became the first Minnesota-born player enshrined in the Hall of Fame, and he remained the only one until Dave Winfield joined him in 2001 and Paul Molitor in 2004. On May 22, 1954, the year following the vote, Bender died. He had previously suffered a heart attack and was receiving treatments for cancer. He was a few weeks past his 70th birthday and did not live to attend his induction ceremony. Bender is buried in Hillside Cemetery in Roslyn, Pennsylvania.

TOM SWIFT

PHILADELPHIA

Edward Trowbridge Collins
Second baseman, 1906–1914, 1927–1930

An excellent place hitter, a slick fielder, and a brainy baserunner, Eddie Collins epitomized the style of play that made the Deadball Era unique. At the plate the 5'9", 175-pound left-handed batter possessed a sharp batting eye and aimed to hit outside pitches to the opposite field and trick deliveries back through the box. Once on base, Collins was a master at stealing, even though his foot speed was not particularly noteworthy. A believer in the principle that a runner steals off the pitcher and not the catcher, Collins practiced the art of studying pitchers: how they held the ball for certain pitches, how they looked back runners—all the pitcher's moves. He focused especially on the feet and hips of the pitcher, rather than just his hands, and thus was able to take large leads off first base and get excellent jumps.

An Ivy League graduate (Columbia University), Collins was one of the smartest players of his day, and he knew it. Saddled with the nickname Cocky from early in his career, Collins drew the resentment of teammates for his self-confidence and good breeding, which at times seemed to belong more to a ballroom than a baseball clubhouse. Whatever the origins, contradiction and complexity became a recurring theme throughout his 25-year major league career. He made his major league debut under an alias, and finished the Deadball Era as captain of the most infamous team in baseball history. He won an award recognizing him as the most valuable player in the league, only to be sold off to another club in the subsequent off-season. Despite his middle class upbringing and good education, Collins abided by a litany of superstitions—although he insisted he was not superstitious, he just "thought it unlucky not to get base hits."

Edward Trowbridge Collins was born on May 2, 1887, in Millerton, New York, the son of railroad freight agent John Rossman Collins and Mary Meade (Trowbridge) Collins. When Eddie was eight months old, the family moved to Tarrytown, New York, in the Hudson Valley 30 miles north of New York City. Young Collins registered at the Irving School in Tarrytown for the fourth grade in the autumn of 1896. According to legend he played ball there that afternoon and continued smashing hits for Irving through the spring of 1903, when he graduated from the prep school. That fall he entered Columbia University. Though a slight 135 pounds, the precocious 16-year-old quarterbacked the varsity football team, and was the starting shortstop for the college nine.

Shortly after beginning his amateur athletic career at Columbia, Collins began picking up paying gigs on the side. In 1904 he pitched for the Tarrytown Terriers for $1 per game. The following summer he performed for a Red Hook, New York, squad, drawing closer to $5 a contest. In the summer of 1906 Eddie played for a succession of semipro clubs (Plattsburgh, New York; Rutland, Vermont; and Rockville, Maryland) before his professional career was discovered, which invalidated his senior year eligibility at Columbia. The summer was not to be a total loss, however. Andy Coakley, a pitcher with the Philadelphia A's who was on his honeymoon, happened to see Collins playing for Rutland. Coakley sent word of the youngster to Connie Mack, who dispatched backup catcher Jimmy Byrnes to develop an in-depth scouting report. When Byrnes confirmed the pitcher's observations, Mack signed Collins to a 1907 contract—but not before Collins obtained a written promise that Mack would not send him to the minor leagues without his consent. John McGraw, manager of the New York Giants, had been aware of the budding prospect but declined to offer him a trial.

At Mack's suggestion Collins made his major

league debut under the alias of Eddie T. Sullivan on September 17, 1906, at Chicago's South Side Park. He played that first game at shortstop behind Rube Waddell, who completely subdued Eddie in batting practice. Nonetheless, this "Sullivan" managed to reach Chicago's Big Ed Walsh for a bunt single in his first-ever at-bat. Six fielding chances were executed flawlessly that day, though Eddie's tenure at short was not to last.

Collins was back in class at Columbia shortly after the Mackmen completed their Western tour, having played six games with the Athletics. On March 26, 1907, the day of Columbia's opening game, Collins ran out to take the field at shortstop before being informed that the University Committee on Athletics at Columbia had ruled him ineligible for the 1907 season. Still, Eddie's game smarts earned him the unprecedented position of undergraduate assistant coach for the Lions' 1907 squad. By this time the baseball bug had a firm hold on Collins, and the youngster postponed his plans for a legal career to rejoin the Athletics after graduation in 1907, appearing in 14 games for Philadelphia that summer.

Columbia took its time establishing an athletics hall of fame, but when it did, in 2006, the first class of inductees included Eddie Collins, alongside Lou Gehrig.

Collins became a regular player in the majors in 1908. That first full season he split time at five positions: short, second, and all three outfield spots, hitting .273 in 102 games. He converted to second base full-time in 1909, pushing Danny Murphy to right field, and from there his remarkable career took wing. It was no small coincidence that when Collins became the starting second baseman, the team also took off. Eddie played every game in 1909, hitting .347 as the club rose to second, chasing the pennant-winning Tigers to the wire. The young second sacker finished second in the circuit in hits, walks, steals, and batting average, and placed third in runs, total bases, and slugging. He led all second basemen in putouts, assists, double plays, and fielding average.

In 1910 the club broke through, winning the first of four pennants in a five-year stretch by a convincing 14½ games. Eddie led the American League in steals, was third in hits and RBI, and fourth in batting, while leading in most fielding categories. Philadelphia dusted the Cubs in five games to give Mack his first world title. Collins was the star of the Series, batting .429 and hitting safely in each contest.

A month after the championship was secured, Eddie married Mabel Doane, a close friend of Mack's fiancée (Mack himself had introduced them). Collins and Mack had a standing bet as to who would get married first, a bet that Mack won by a week. The Collinses remained married for more than 40 years, until Mabel's death in 1943.

In 1911, with the $100,000 Infield of Home Run Baker, Jack Barry, Collins, and Stuffy McInnis now in place, the A's repeated as world champs, besting Detroit by 13½ games and downing John McGraw's Giants in six. After finishing fourth in hitting (.365) during the year, and leading the league's second basemen in putouts, Eddie had a modest series, batting .286 with four errors. Still, the A's had successfully defended their championship and, at just 24, Collins had experienced little but success in his few years of prep, collegiate, and professional play.

Eddie's plainly evident self-confidence could rub people the wrong way. As educated and ostensibly sophisticated as he was, cockiness could lead to actions that, in hindsight at least, were not all that smart. In 1912, the only year in a stretch of five that the A's did not win the pennant, some of his teammates groused about Collins's loyalties and priorities. In the wake of the 1911 World Series triumph, Eddie accepted a $2,000 commission to write a collection of ten articles for *American Magazine* on the inner workings of the game. In one he explained how opposing pitchers had been tipping off their deliveries. The unhappiest of the A's argued that, alerted, the foes had corrected the give-away weaknesses. While Eddie led the league in runs, and posted a .348 average with 63 stolen bases, in 1912 the dissension in the clubhouse was at least in part attributable to the gifted second baseman. The anti-Collins faction in the A's clubhouse was led by backup catcher Ira Thomas, whom Mack named his field captain in spring training 1914.

The bright, confident, and successful Collins was given to a rich catalog of less than rational practices and observances. At the plate he kept his gum on his hat button until two strikes, then would remove it and commence chewing. He loathed black cats, and would walk or drive out of his way to avoid crossing paths with one. If he saw a load of barrels, he believed he would make one or two hits that day. Finding a hairpin meant a single, two hairpins a double. Scraps of paper littering the dugout steps drove him crazy. He would refrain from changing game socks during a winning streak and, as player–manager for the White Sox, is said to have fired a clubhouse man for acting in violation of this practice. He believed it lucky to have someone spit on his hat before a game. Each winter Collins soaked his bats in oil, dried them out and rubbed them down with a bone. This practice became the stuff of lore, as it has even been said that he buried his bats in cow dung piles to "keep 'em alive." On the more practical side, he would wear heavier shoes as spring approached, so that his feet would feel lighter when the season opened.

Known as a gentleman off the field, the brainy star gave grudging quarter, at best, between the foul lines. Hard-nosed play around the bag invited like responses and incurred the enmity of some. One such encounter in 1912 would have long-term consequences. An unflinching tag by Eddie broke the nose of Washington first baseman Chick Gandil. Chick's teammate Clyde Milan witnessed the play and noted that "for the rest of his playing career, Gandil was out to get even. He went into the bag against Collins 200 times I guess, and always got the worst of it."

In 1913 the A's returned to form, winning their third World Series, in five games over the Giants, as Collins hit .421 with five runs, three RBI, and three steals. His standout autumn followed a regular campaign that featured 55 steals, 73 RBI and a robust .345 average. In 1914 the A's repeated as American League champs, and Collins was honored as the Chalmers Award winner, given to the league's most valuable player. Unfortunately, the bat that had driven in 85 runs and registered a .344 clip was utterly absent in the Series. Philadelphia was stunned in four straight by the "Miracle Braves," with Collins batting .214.

In the aftermath of the upset and with his team's harmony fractured by overtures from the Federal League, Mack began to clean house. On Tuesday, December 8, 1914, Collins was sold to the Chicago White Sox for a reported $50,000. As part of the deal the White Sox agreed to pay Collins a salary of $15,000 per year (some sources say $20,000). By 1919 his salary had been trimmed to $14,500, but it was still more than double that of any of his Chicago teammates.

The White Sox had spent the first half of the 1910s languishing between fourth and sixth place. Eddie's tenure in Chicago lasted 12 years. For all 12 seasons he was a genuine star; for the last two and a half, he was player–manager. During Eddie's first year in Chicago the great Cleveland outfielder Joe Jackson joined the club through a trade, with 45 games remaining in the campaign. Although by skill they were peers, there was little evidence of friendship or social interaction between the two stars. The educated and savvy Collins may have intimidated his illiterate teammate.

A sub-.500 team in 1914, the White Sox steadily rose in the standings. The 1915 club finished third, besting the .600 mark with 93 wins. Eddie was second in the league in batting, led in walks, was third in steals and fifth in total bases, while leading second basemen in

both assists and fielding average. In 1916 the White Sox chased the Red Sox all summer, finishing a mere two games back. Eddie led the league's second basemen in double plays and fielding average, and on the offensive side of the ledger he was second in triples, third in walks, and fourth in steals. In 1917 the White Sox won the pennant by a convincing nine games, with 100 wins for a .649 percentage. Although Eddie's average dipped to .289, he led second basemen in putouts and was second in the circuit in steals and walks.

In that year's fall classic Collins enjoyed his third great World Series, posting a .409 average. He scored the first run in the sixth and final game by outthinking the Giants defense. Though immortalized as the Heinie Zimmerman boner, it was actually catcher Bill Rariden, first baseman Walter Holke, and pitcher Rube Benton who were the real goats. In a rundown between third and home plate, Rariden allowed Collins to slip past him, and Holke and Benton neglected to cover home plate. With a pursuit on foot his only option, the lumbering Zimmerman failed to catch Collins as he slid across home with what proved to be the Series winning run.

Like many other players, Collins's 1918 campaign was cut short by U.S. involvement in the Great War. On August 19, 1918, Collins joined the U.S. Marines, missing the final 16 games of the season. He served chiefly at the Philadelphia Navy Yard, received a good conduct medal, and was honorably discharged on February 6, 1919, in time for spring training.

As the great White Sox team coalesced, it became ever more socially segmented. By the time Chick Gandil arrived, ahead of the 1917 season, the calcification of some of these divisions was pretty much assured. There was resentment of owner Comiskey's penny-pinching ways, and Gandil's preexisting bitterness toward Eddie helped to focus some of the discontent on the captain. Collins came to represent management, and his status as one of the owner's favorites further poisoned the atmosphere. Of all the performers in this ill-fated cast, Collins was sharp enough to have sensed the malignant potential. Perhaps his privileged status, seemingly unbroken record of personal triumph, and the team's burgeoning success combined to help dull his sensitivity.

Even so, one might think that, if Collins were so aware and adept at the multiple dimensions of leadership, he would somehow have sensed and tried to mitigate intrasquad tensions. The superficial machismo of clubhouse camaraderie should not have been too significant a hurdle for a well-bred, broadly experienced, established star. The distinct cliques among the 1919 White Sox might have been immutable, but few were better equipped than Collins to initiate the select one-to-one rapprochements that might have modulated such tensions.

The 1919 White Sox finished with a record of 88–52 for a .629 percentage, besting Cleveland by 3½ games. Eddie hit .319 and drove in 80 runs, while leading second basemen in putouts and double plays. The 1919 White Sox were the greatest he ever saw, not least because they won despite widening dissension. The club "was torn by discord and hatred during much of the '19 season," Collins later said. "From the moment I arrived at training camp from service, I could see that something was amiss. We may have had our troubles in other years, but in 1919 we were a club that pulled apart rather than together. There were frequent arguments and open hostility. All the things you think—and are taught to believe—are vital to the success of any athletic organization were missing from it, and yet it was the greatest collection of players ever assembled, I would say."

Although Collins, like many others, heard that the fix was on during the 1919 Series, he refused to believe the rumors, and said that he was not suspicious of the actions of any of the eight players later accused. "Even today, no one realizes how subtly conceived and executed the whole thing was," Collins later marveled. "Sure, I heard that the fix was on, but I looked on it as just idle gossip and completely preposterous."

After the scandal gutted the club, Collins still starred. He was one of the few bright lights for the decimated White Sox in the early 1920s. He filled in as player–manager for 27 games during the 1924 season and assumed the role full-time for the 1925 and 1926 campaigns. The club finished fifth in each of his full years at the helm, when injuries cut into his playing time. Deposed as White Sox manager on November 11, 1926, Collins was released as a player two days later. He signed with Philadelphia six weeks later, and emerged as a solid pinch hitter in 1927. From 1928 through 1930 he mostly coached, finally playing his last game at age 43 on August 2, 1930. He concluded his career with a .333 batting average, 1,821 runs scored, 3,315 hits, and 744 steals, figures that assured his induction to the Hall of Fame in 1939 as one of the original 13 players honored by the baseball writers upon the museum's opening. That same year his son, Eddie Collins, Jr., made his debut with Mack's Athletics, where he would spend three seasons as a light-hitting outfielder. Collins's other son, the Rev. Paul Collins, officiated at his widowed father's second marriage, to Emily Jane Hall, in 1945.

Eddie coached full-time for Philadelphia in 1931 and 1932 before joining the Boston Red Sox as vice president and general manager when fellow Irving Schooler Tom Yawkey purchased the team in early 1933. Collins remained with the Red Sox for the rest of his life, but his most notable act as general manager was his decision to absent himself from Fenway Park on April 16, 1945, when Jackie Robinson and two other Negro League players tried out for the Red Sox. Facing pressure from local press and politicians, Collins and Yawkey had offered the sham tryout only reluctantly; after their failure to take Robinson and the other black prospects seriously, the Red Sox ended up as the last team to integrate instead of the first.

Due to deteriorating health, Collins turned over the general manager's reins to Joe Cronin after the 1947 season but remained as vice president. A cerebral hemorrhage in August 1950 left Eddie partially paralyzed and visually impaired. Devoutly religious throughout his life, he succumbed to complications of cardiovascular disease on March 25, 1951, Easter Day's evening, at age 63. He was buried in Linwood Cemetery in Weston, Massachusetts. He was survived by his second wife and two sons.

PAUL F. MITTERMEYER

JOHN WESLEY COOMBS
RIGHT-HANDED PITCHER, 1906–1914

For one magnificent season Colby Jack Coombs was the equal of any pitcher of the Deadball Era, Christy Mathewson, Walter Johnson, and Grover Cleveland Alexander included. Armed with an above-average fastball and a devastating drop curve, Coombs had one of the most dominant pitching seasons in baseball history in 1910, rolling up a 31–9 record to propel Connie Mack's Philadelphia Athletics to the American League pennant by 14½ games. He put together a remarkable 1.30 ERA in 353 innings pitched and completed 35 of the 38 games he started. Coombs threw 13 shutouts, an American League record that will stand for the ages; in 11 other games he held the opposition to one run.

For the last half of the 1910 season, Coombs was simply unhittable, all the more remarkable because of his heavy workload. He threw 12 shutouts, pitched 250 innings, and won 18 of 19 starts in July, August, and September. From September 5 to September 25 he racked up 53 consecutive scoreless innings to set a major league record (broken three years later by Walter Johnson). Jack then topped off his incredible year by pitching three complete-game wins against the Chicago Cubs in six days as the Athletics won their first world championship. He was nearly as good in 1911, leading the A's to their second straight pennant with a record of 28–12.

John Wesley Coombs was born on November 18, 1882, in Le Grand, Iowa, a tiny farming community some 50 miles northwest of Des Moines. The family moved to a farm near Kennebunk in southern Maine when young Jack was about four years old. He attended Freeport High School and a prep school named Colburn Classical Institute in Waterville, Maine, where he showed pitching prowess and also starred in football. Entering Colby College in 1902, he starred in baseball, basketball, football, and track, serving as captain of the first two. Jack was an outstanding runner in football and the fastest sprinter in New England, running the 100-

yard dash in 10.2 seconds. In baseball he pitched and hit Colby to several Maine collegiate championships, playing every position, including catcher in emergencies. He spent his summers playing semipro baseball in St. John, New Brunswick (1903), Northampton, Massachusetts (1904), and Montpelier, Vermont (1905).

An excellent student, Coombs majored in chemistry and had every intention of making that his life's work. In fact he had been accepted to the Massachusetts Institute of Technology for graduate work when Tom Mack (Connie Mack's brother who lived in Worcester, Massachusetts, and had been following Jack's baseball career) signed him to a big league contract in December 1905, with the understanding that Coombs would report to the Athletics after graduation in 1906. As a senior the 6'0", 185-pound right-hander led Colby to a 14–3 record, hurling a 1–0 victory over the University of Maine on his own home run. The day after his graduation he defeated traditional rival Bowdoin 6–0 for the Maine championship.

Colby Jack made his major league debut on July 5, 1906, and it was a memorable one, as he pitched a seven-hit shutout to defeat the Washington Senators 3–0. After that impressive debut Coombs had rather indifferent success for July and August and went into a September 1 start against Boston with a 5–7 record. That day's scheduled doubleheader turned into a single, epic 24-inning contest in which both rookie starters, Coombs and Boston's Joe Harris, went the distance. Coombs won the game, 4–1, striking out 18 and allowing 15 hits in 24 innings. Colby Jack threw two more complete-game victories in the next 10 days. Dogged by arm trouble in the final weeks of the season, Coombs nonetheless finished his rookie year with a solid 10–10 record in 173 innings. After a strong start in 1907, Coombs again strained his arm and struggled to a 6–9 record for the second-place Athletics, causing considerable concern that he was a flash in the pan.

When A's outfielder Socks Seybold broke his leg in

spring training the next year, Mack inserted the good hitting but still ailing Coombs in right field. Jack, who would bat .235 for his career, started the season like a house afire, hitting over .300. When he slumped to .215, however, he found himself back on the bench, replaced by veteran second baseman Danny Murphy. Still, his hitting record at season's end was better than the league average.

Back on the mound for the last half of 1908, Coombs posted a 7–5 record and an excellent 2.00 ERA in 153 innings as the Athletics slipped to sixth place. Still not completely healthy, he was 12–11 in 1909 with 18 complete games in 24 starts and an impressive 2.32 ERA as the A's rebounded and lost the pennant by only 3½ games to the Detroit Tigers. After four years, his won–lost record was an unimpressive 35–35. He began 1910 slowly, getting beaten in succession by the Senators and the Highlanders. Those efforts earned him a demotion from the starting rotation.

Two weeks later Mack inserted Coombs into the ninth inning of a 3–3 tie against Ed Walsh of the White Sox when Eddie Plank was removed for a pinch hitter. For the next three innings Jack held the Pale Hose hitless as the A's finally pushed across a run in the eleventh to win 4–3. His rediscovery of his overhand curve apparently was the key. As former catcher Malachi Kittridge observed, Coombs's devastating breaking pitch was not "one of those outdrops, but a ball that comes up to the plate squarely in the center and falls from one to two feet without changing its lateral direction."

His season revived, Coombs found himself starting two to three times a week on the way to his remarkable 31–9 season. On August 4 he again hooked up against Walsh in a 16-inning duel that ended in a scoreless tie because of darkness. Coombs considered this the best game he ever pitched. For the afternoon he struck out 18 and gave up only three hits. On September 25 Colby Jack and Big Ed found themselves in another long duel in the first game of a doubleheader. Again relieving Plank in the ninth, Coombs pitched the final six innings of the 14-inning game, starting the A's winning rally himself with a hit in the fourteenth. Coombs was spent, however, and gave up three runs to the Sox in the second inning of the second game, thereby ending his record-setting 53-inning scoreless streak. It was during Coombs's monumental 1910 year that he earned the sobriquet Iron Man.

In the World Series against the Cubs, who had swept to the National League pennant by 13 games, Coombs defeated Cub ace Mordecai "Three Fingered" Brown in Game Two, 9–3 in Philadelphia after Chief Bender had won Game One for the A's. On the train to Chicago the

following day, reporters asked Mack who would pitch Game Three. When he replied, "Why, Coombs will go for us again," they thought he was spoofing. But sure enough, Jack trotted out for Game Three with one day's rest in a sleeper car and defeated Ed Reulbach, 12–5, in another complete-game performance. After Bender lost Game Four, 4–3, Coombs pitched with two days' rest, defeating Brown for the second time, this time by a 7–2 score to wrap up the Series for the A's. All told, Coombs had pitched three complete-game victories in six days. He even hit .385 in the Series, with five hits in 13 times at bat. Mack used only two pitchers in the Series, Coombs and Bender, leaving such stalwarts as Eddie Plank (sidelined with a sore arm) and Cy Morgan on the bench.

To top off his banner 1910 year, Coombs married the former Mary Elizabeth Russ of Palestine, Texas, in November. He met his bride-to-be during a spring training trip in 1907 and fell in love not only with her but with her hometown. For the rest of his life the Coombses maintained a home in Palestine. Even when coaching college baseball at Duke after his retirement as a player, Jack would spend most of the winter in Palestine, hunting, fishing, and relaxing. (He lost a finger on his left hand in a 1936 hunting accident when a barrel of his shotgun burst as he fired at a quail.) He eventually acquired extensive land holdings in the area.

The Colby Kohinoor, as Coombs was sometimes called in the press, fell back to earth in 1911, posting an ordinary 3.53 ERA despite leading the American League with 28 wins. The Athletics won a second consecutive pennant, this time by 13½ games over the Detroit Tigers, and Coombs pitched the pennant-clinching win on September 28. Jack also flexed his muscle at the plate, batting a lusty .319 for the year. He hit two extra-inning home runs, in the fourteenth inning against the Browns on July 17 and in the eleventh on August 29 against Detroit, the last homer ever hit in old Bennett Park. (After that latter homer, however, he fumbled away the game on the mound in the bottom of the eleventh.) Among major league pitchers, only Dizzy Dean has matched Coombs's mark of two extra-inning home runs.

In the World Series against John McGraw's New York Giants, Coombs pitched the memorable Game Three against Christy Mathewson, winning the contest 3–2 in extra innings after Frank Baker had tied the game with a ninth-inning home run. Coombs allowed only three hits in his fourth World Series triumph. Following the A's Game Three victory the Series was beset by a week of rain, but Coombs started Game Five eight days later, hoping to close the Series out for the Athletics.

started the opening game for the A's at Boston on April 10. After three hitless innings, he gave way to Bender in the sixth, leading 10–5. Two days later he started again against Boston but left after facing only five batters, giving up two hits and a walk and hitting a batter.

Jack accompanied the team to Washington after the Boston series, but he was in so much pain the team sent him home to Philadelphia. There he entered the hospital and by May he was near death from typhoid fever that had settled in his spine. In early August Coombs felt well enough to work out at the ballpark, but soon landed back in the hospital for a lengthy convalescence. He endured 17 weeks of bed rest with weights hanging from his head and legs to strengthen his spine. During this ordeal his weight fell from 180 to 126 pounds.

He spent the winter resting in Palestine, but was not ready to resume his career in 1914. He worked out with the team when he felt strong enough, and started two late-season games as the A's captured their fourth pennant in five years. After the "Miracle Braves" swept the Athletics in the World Series, Mack began to disband his powerhouse team. Mack released Coombs, who signed with the Brooklyn Robins, managed by Wilbert Robinson. At 32, after missing virtually two complete seasons, Colby Jack made a remarkable comeback in 1915, winning 15 and losing 10 with a 2.58 ERA in 195⅔ innings for the third-place Robins. Facing Christy Mathewson for the first time since the 1911 World Series, Coombs twice beat him in head-to-head duels, keeping his perfect record against the Giants legend intact.

Coombs had thrown so many curveballs during his career that, according to F.C. Lane, "his arm is actually shortened by the stiffening of the cords at the elbow." Despite the heavy workload his right arm had sustained over the years, Coombs remained an effective spot starter for the Dodgers in 1916, as he went 13–8 with a 2.66 ERA to help Brooklyn to its first World Series appearance. Although the Dodgers lost the Series to the Boston Red Sox in five games, Jack started and won Game Three, 4–3 against Carl Mays for Brooklyn's only victory. It was Coombs's fifth World Series victory without a loss. Coombs continued his role as a spot starter and reliever in 1917 and 1918 with less success, compiling won–lost records of 7–11 and 8–14. He threw his 35th and last big league shutout on August 1, 1918, blanking the Cincinnati Reds 4–0. On August 30 Jack lost to Pol Perritt of the Giants 1–0, allowing the lone run in the ninth inning. The game took but 57 minutes to play. Afterward, Coombs announced his retirement.

The second-division Phillies signed Coombs to manage for 1919, but it was not a happy experience, and he resigned on July 8 with an 18–44 record. He

That seemed likely, as he came within one out of a 3–1 victory. The Giants, however, rallied to tie the score and send the game into extra innings. It turned out that Coombs had badly strained his groin in the sixth inning, catching his spikes on the mound during a pitch. Twice Mack sent Chief Bender to the mound to see if Coombs could continue and both times he refused to leave the game. In the top of the tenth Jack beat out a bunt hit, his face contorted in pain. With that, Mack put in Amos Strunk as a pinch runner. The A's lost in the bottom of the tenth on a Fred Merkle sacrifice fly against Eddie Plank. That evening, Coombs was feverish and bed-ridden.

Coombs still felt the effects of his groin pull in 1912, and after starting opening day he missed the next month of the season. He recovered enough to win 21 games while losing only 10 in 262⅓ innings, about 75 innings fewer than the year before. During spring training in 1913 Jack came down with a high fever in Montgomery, Alabama, which initially was diagnosed as ptomaine poisoning and pleurisy. After considerable rest, Coombs

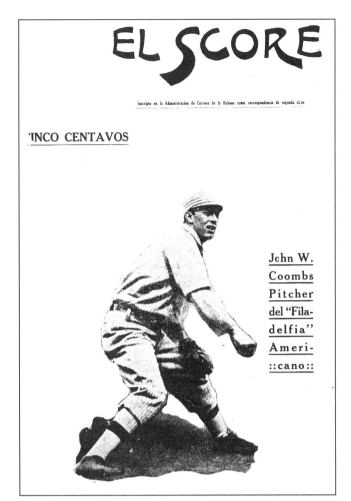

EL SCORE

Inscripto en la Administración de Correos de la Habana como correspondencia de segunda clase

'INCO CENTAVOS

John W. Coombs Pitcher del "Filadelfia" Ameri- ::cano::

served as a coach for Hughey Jennings and the Detroit Tigers in 1920 and even relieved in two games.

Coombs soon found his niche, however, as a college baseball coach, first at Williams (head coach, 1921–1924), then at Princeton (pitching coach, 1925–1928), and finally at Duke for 22 years (head coach, 1929–1952). While at Duke he authored the leading instructional book of its day, *Baseball: Individual Play and Team Strategy,* published in 1938 by Prentice-Hall. The book went through many editions and was eventually used at 187 colleges and universities and hundreds of high schools.

At Duke, Coombs led the Blue Devils to an overall 382–171 record, winning seven North Carolina state collegiate championships and five Southern Conference championships, earning the title Mr. College Baseball. Twenty-one of his players made the major leagues, including Billy Werber, Dick Groat, and his nephew, Bobby Coombs. Many more were All-Americans, including Bill W. Werber, Billy Werber's son.

Werber, who played shortstop for Coombs from 1928–1930, later described Coombs as "a great man and a great coach" and "the most beloved teacher or coach to ever walk the Duke campus." He recalled that Jack had a breezy, disarming personality that could win anyone over. Coombs and his wife, Mary, had no children and would often entertain his student-athletes at their campus apartment. Werber remembers Coombs walking up behind Duke University president William Preston Few, a scholarly, dignified man in a dark suit and felt hat, slapping him on the back in a friendly fashion and saying, "Prexy, we're having a practice game tomorrow and I'm counting on you to umpire." "I'll be there, Jack," was the reply.

As the Duke coach Coombs always wore a coat, tie, and hat in the dugout and usually a vest as well, regardless of hot weather. He made the team wear large baggy pants in the Deadball Era fashion. Bill W. Werber remembered that Coach Coombs was direct and had a sense of humor. His most common admonition to him on the field was to "get your buttocks down, Werber." He also told young Bill more than once, "Don't think, Werber. When you do you hurt the team."

After a forced retirement from Duke in 1952—university policy mandated retirement at age 70—Jack and Mary Coombs returned to live in Palestine full-time. Each spring until he died he conducted a free baseball clinic there for high school coaches and players. Coombs enlisted Ira Thomas, his old battery mate from the Athletics, and players he had coached to assist in these clinics.

On April 15, 1957, Coombs became ill while running errands in downtown Palestine. He returned home and went into the bedroom to lie down. By the time his wife, Mary, could summon the family physician, he was dead of a heart attack. He was buried in St. Joseph's Cemetery in Palestine. The baseball fields at both Colby College and Duke University are named in his honor. He is a member of the Collegiate Baseball Coaches Hall of Fame, the Duke Sports Hall of Fame, and the North Carolina Sports Hall of Fame.

C. PAUL ROGERS III

PHILADELPHIA

REUBEN NOSHIER "RUBE" OLDRING
CENTER FIELDER, 1906–1916, 1918

A prominent and popular member of the Philadelphia A's dynasty of the Deadball Era, Rube Oldring patrolled the outfield grass of Columbia Field and Shibe Park for 12 seasons. He combined power, speed, and average for Connie Mack's championship teams of the 1910s, although frequent injuries limited his playing time. Rube was described by Irwin Howe, the official statistician for the American League, as "a fast and reliable outfielder, good at laying down a bunt, and…a fast and intelligent baserunner."

Reuben Noshier Oldring was born May 30, 1884, in New York City, one of eight children and the youngest of three sons of Thomas (an English immigrant) and Sarah Oldring. Reuben took to baseball early. By the age of 15 he was traveling to New Jersey to play ball. He first played semipro ball for the Ontario team, which played at 147th Street and Lenox Avenue in New York. Rube was playing for the Hoboken, New Jersey, club in 1905, when a scout for the Montgomery, Alabama, team of the Southern Association spotted the young right-hander and offered him a contract. Oldring played 67 games in the outfield and at shortstop, first base, and third base for Montgomery in 1905, batting .272 and stealing 23 bases. Mack received a tip about Rube from Tom O'Brien, the Montgomery manager, and purchased Oldring's contract near the end of the season.

Rube reported to Philadelphia on September 23, 1905, and was told by Mack that he was ineligible for the World Series and might as well go back home to New York and get into some semipro games before reporting to the A's the following spring. Rube followed Mack's advice, and played for a Manhattan semipro team in an exhibition game against the New York Highlanders. Oldring belted a three-run home run that enabled his club to top the major leaguers, 7–5. Clark Griffith, the New York manager, was shorthanded due to injuries.

Impressed by Oldring's play that day, he invited Rube to finish the season with the Highlanders. They settled on $200 for the week. Oldring played in eight games at shortstop, batting .300 with one home run. Griffith tried to draft Oldring, only to find that he was already the property of the Philadelphia A's.

During spring training in 1906 Rube battled several players for a starting position and was told he had earned the starting third base job. The same day he received this welcome news, Oldring broke his right ankle sliding into third base and missed the start of the season. He returned to action in June, playing in 59 games, primarily at third. Rube had a powerful arm, and often overthrew first base, resulting in 16 errors in 49 games at the hot corner. When Oldring received his contract for 1907 there was a letter from Mack enclosed. "From this day on you will be my center fielder," Mack wrote. "You will have all the room you want and will not have to throw the ball over anybody's head."

For the next ten years Rube patrolled the outfield for the A's. He played primarily in center field, moving to left field later in his career. The A's were beginning to assemble their championship team and finished a close second to Detroit in 1907 and again in 1909. They finally emerged as champions in 1910, well ahead of second place New York. Rube had the best year of his career, finishing in the top ten in the American League in batting average (.308), slugging percentage (.430), hits (168), total bases (235), doubles (27), triples (14), and home runs (4).

To prepare his underdog team for the World Series against the Chicago Cubs, Mack arranged a series of exhibition games against an American League all-star team. Unfortunately for Rube, he sprained his knee trying to dodge a fly ball he had lost in the sun and so did not contribute to the A's surprising five-game upset of the Cubs.

The A's won the American League championship again in 1911, and Oldring had another fine season, batting .297 with 84 runs scored, 21 stolen bases, and 26 sacrifices. This time the A's faced the New York Giants in the World Series and Rube got his biggest thrill in baseball when he hit a three-run home run off Rube Marquard in Game Five. The A's repeated as world champions, beating the Giants in six games.

Philadelphia's string of championships stopped in 1912 as they slipped to third, 15 games behind the Red Sox. Oldring batted .301 in 99 games, but ended up suspended by Mack on September 6 for being out of condition.

In 1913 the A's and Oldring returned to their championship form. The A's finished first by 6½ games and Rube batted .283 with 101 runs scored and 40 stolen bases. Rube shifted to left field that year, and also filled in at shortstop for a week while Jack Barry was hurt. Rube himself missed several weeks with a broken nose suffered during an exhibition game to honor Harry Davis. The A's took the World Series from the New York Giants, and Oldring contributed in Game Four with one of the finest catches of the Series. With runners on the corners and one out in the top of the fifth, Oldring snagged a sinking liner off the bat of pinch hitter Moose McCormick, and then prevented the runner on third from tagging up on the play. The Athletics went on to win the game, 6–5, and the Series in five games.

The Philadelphia team won its fourth pennant in five years in 1914. Rube's statistics slipped somewhat that year, as he suffered several nagging injuries that cut his playing time to 119 games. In that year's World Series against the Braves, Rube, like most of his teammates, had a horrendous series, collecting only one hit in 15 at-bats. Unlike his fellow Athletics, however, Rube had a unique excuse for his woes at the plate. Right before the World Series began Rube announced that he was getting married. A woman who saw the news in the paper filed charges of nonsupport and desertion, claiming she was his common-law wife, Helen I. Oldring. The Braves fans picked up on the story and razzed Rube throughout the Series. Rube said, "I know I didn't play as I should, and I attribute it to this trouble."

Apparently Rube did live with this other woman at one time, as the 1910 census lists her as

his wife of two years. Rube told reporters that she was simply after his World Series money, and that he had not seen her for more than two years. The matter was settled quietly, and Rube married Hannah Thomas on October 16, a marriage that lasted almost 47 years.

After the A's stunning loss in the 1914 World Series, Mack began dismantling his championship team. Rumors had Oldring ticketed for New York, but 1915 found Rube still with Philadelphia. The team went from first to last, winning only 43 games. Rube hit a career-high six home runs—three times more than anyone else on the team—but his batting average slipped to .248 and he played in only 107 games. Rube played in 40 games in 1916 before being given his unconditional release on July 1. He returned to his farm, but was enticed to play for his hometown New York Yankees due to injuries to their outfielders. Rube played in 43 games for New York before the Yankees released him on September 9. Rube sat out the 1917 season to tend to his farm, but Mack prevailed on him to return to the A's one more time in 1918. Oldring played in 34 games before hanging up his spikes for the final time in the major leagues. Due to his age, Rube was exempt from the War Department's work-or-fight order, but he took a job playing baseball in the shipyards anyway.

After the end of the war Rube embarked on a peripatetic journey through the minor leagues. In 1919 Rube took a player–manager position with the Richmond Colts in the Virginia League, leading them to the pennant. Over the next six years Oldring spent time playing and managing in Suffolk, Seattle, New Haven, Richmond again, and Wilson (North Carolina), before finally rounding out his baseball career with a third stint in Richmond in 1926. After guiding that club to another pennant, Oldring settled into farming until he sold his farm in 1939. He then took a job with a canned vegetable manufacturer, the Phillip J. Ritter Company, evaluating crops in the New Jersey area.

Rube suffered a heart attack in 1960, and died at age 77 on September 9, 1961, at his home in Bridgeton, New Jersey, from acute blockage of the arteries.

BILL BISHOP

PHILADELPHIA

JOHN FRANKLIN "HOME RUN" BAKER
THIRD BASEMAN, 1908–1914

In an era characterized by urbanization and rapid industrial growth, Frank "Home Run" Baker epitomized the rustic virtues that were becoming essential to baseball's emerging bucolic mythology. Born and raised in a tiny farming community on Maryland's Eastern Shore, Baker developed his powerful back, arms, and hands by working long hours on his father's farm. Like the rugged president who defined the century's first decade, the taciturn Baker spoke softly but carried a big stick—a 52-ounce slab of wood that he held down at the handle and swung with all the force he could muster. One of the Deadball Era's greatest sluggers, Baker led the American League or tied for the lead in home runs every year from 1911 to 1914, and earned his famous nickname with two timely round-trippers against the New York Giants in the 1911 World Series. Baker later insisted that his hard-swinging mentality came from his country roots. "The farmer doesn't care for the pitchers' battle that resolves itself into a checkers game," he once declared. "The farmer loves the dramatic, and slugging is more dramatic than even the cleverest pitching."

John Franklin Baker was born on March 13, 1886, the second son of Franklin A. and Mary C. Baker, on a farm just outside Trappe, Maryland, a tiny community located just a few miles east of the Chesapeake Bay. Frank's mother was a distant relative of Confederate General Robert E. Lee, and though Frank's father spent his life toiling in anonymity on the farm, Baker later remembered him as a prodigiously strong and good-humored man. "He never saw a trick in the circus he couldn't perform," Frank remembered. "He [once] cartwheeled the length of the street in front of our house and finished off by landing on his feet in an upright position."

Although the younger Baker never possessed his father's flair for showmanship, he did inherit the old man's strength and athletic ability, which was first put to good use as a pitcher and outfielder for the Trappe high school baseball team. In 1905 Baker's exploits with a local amateur team caught the eye of Trappe native Preston Day, who recommended the youngster to future major leaguer Buck Herzog, then managing a semipro outfit in nearby Ridgely. After looking Baker over, Herzog signed Frank to a $5 per week contract, and moved him to third base.

The following year Baker earned $15 per week playing for the semipro Sparrows Point Club in Baltimore, and in 1907 he turned down an offer to play in the Texas League and instead signed with an independent club in Cambridge, Maryland. At the end of the season he received a tryout with Baltimore of the Eastern League, but after Baker collected just two singles in 15 at-bats, manager Jack Dunn concluded that he "could not hit" and released him. In 1908 Baker joined the Reading Pretzels of the Class B Tri-State League, where he batted .299 in 119 games. In September Connie Mack, the manager of the Philadelphia Athletics who was looking for a third baseman to replace the aging Jimmy Collins, purchased his contract.

After batting .290 in 31 at-bats at the end of the 1908 season, Baker was handed the starting job at third base at the outset of the 1909 campaign. He was an instant success, supplying a much needed dose of offense to the middle of the Philadelphia attack. On May 29 Baker became the first man to hit a ball over the right field fence at the newly constructed Shibe Park, one of his four home runs for the season. For his rookie year Baker finished with a .305 batting average and .447 slugging percentage, good for fourth best in the American League. His 85 RBI placed him third in the league, and his 19 triples led the circuit. The young slugger also proved himself to be a deft handler of the stick, finishing third in the American League with 34 sacrifices.

A left-handed batter (though he threw from the right side), Baker positioned himself with his left foot firmly planted on the back line of the batter's box, and his feet 18 inches apart in a slightly closed stance. At 5'11" and 173 pounds, Baker did not cut an imposing

figure at the plate, but the ease with which he handled his famed 52-ounce bat spoke volumes about his physical strength. Asked to explain Baker's power, Jake Daubert commented, "Frank Baker doesn't look so big, but he has big wrists." Observers noted that when Baker swung, he seemed to give the ball an extra push by violently snapping his wrists at the point of contact.

Baker also acquitted himself well on the base paths and in the field, though, like Honus Wagner, he appeared clumsy in his movements. Bowlegged and husky, the lumbering Baker ran "like a soft-shell crab" according to one observer. Nonetheless, he stole 20 or more bases every year from 1909 to 1913, and in his rookie season led all third basemen in putouts, an accomplishment he repeated six more times during his 13-year career.

Baker's outstanding rookie campaign was a major factor in the Athletics' surge in the standings. Winning 27 more games than they had in 1908, the Mackmen finished in second place, just 3½ games behind the Detroit Tigers. In late August the upstart A's had actually enjoyed a 1½ game lead in the standings, before dropping three straight at Detroit's Bennett Park. It was in the first game of this pivotal series that Baker was involved in one of the most controversial plays of the era, when Detroit superstar Ty Cobb spiked him in the forearm as Baker was attempting to tag Cobb out at third base. Frank had the wound wrapped and was able to stay in the game, but the play infuriated Mack, who went so far as to call Cobb the dirtiest player in baseball history. But a few days later, a photograph of the play taken by William Kuenzel of the *Detroit News* showed Baker reaching across the bag to tag Cobb, who was sliding away from the third baseman. The photograph vindicated Cobb, and led the *Detroit Free Press* to declare that Baker was a "soft-fleshed darling" for complaining about the play.

Although he would continue to develop into one of the league's best players, helping the Athletics win their first World Series in 1910 and batting .334 in 1911 with a league-leading 11 home runs, as a result of the Cobb spiking the mild-mannered Baker carried a reputation for being easily intimidated on the field. It was this alleged weakness that John McGraw and the New York Giants attempted to exploit in the 1911 World Series, with disastrous results.

In the bottom of the sixth inning of Game One, the Giants' Fred Snodgrass was on second and saw a chance to take third when Fred Merkle struck out on a pitch in the dirt. Following a strong throw from the catcher, Baker was blocking the base with the ball when Snodgrass went into the bag hard, spikes high, severely gashing Baker's left arm. Initially signaling an out, the

umpire called the play safe when he saw the ball rolling on the ground. The trainer came out to patch up Baker's wounds, and the Giants went on to win 2–1. But the tone had been set, and Baker took his revenge with his bat.

With the score tied 1–1 in the bottom of the sixth of Game Two, Baker came to bat with one man on base and two outs, facing Giants left-hander Rube Marquard. After running the count to 1–1, Marquard threw Baker an inside fastball, which the slugger blasted over the right field fence for a two-run home run. That proved the difference, as the A's held on to win the game 3–1 and even the Series. The following afternoon Giants ace Christy Mathewson carried a 1–0 lead into the top of the ninth inning when Baker came to the plate and again smashed a home run to right field, tying the score.

When the game moved into extra innings, the Giants once again tried to intimidate Baker. In the bottom of the tenth, Snodgrass again tried to take third, this time on a passed ball. Again, Baker blocked the base with the ball as Snodgrass came into the bag hard, spikes high, cutting into the third baseman's arm a second time. This time Baker held onto the ball. The A's went on to win the game in 11 innings, with Baker's infield hit contributing to the winning two-run rally. After the game, a Philadelphia reporter approached the "battle-scarred hero," observing the odor emanating from the bandages on Baker's wounds. When pressed, Baker finally broke his silence, and blurted out, "Yes, Snodgrass spiked me intentionally. He acted like a swell-headed busher."

The A's went on to win the Series 4–2, with Baker leading his team with nine hits, five RBI, and a .375 average. His inspired play forever dispelled the notion that he could be intimidated on the diamond, but more importantly, Baker's two dramatic home runs on consecutive days off two future Hall of Fame pitchers propelled him into the upper echelon of baseball legends. Henceforth, for the rest of his life and beyond, he would be known as Home Run Baker. The nickname would become something of a curiosity for future generations, weaned as they were on a version of the game where home runs were a routine occurrence. But in the context of Baker's time, when it was only the rare slugger who could hit as many as 10 home runs in a season, the name connoted mythic power and strength.

Despite his newfound fame, Baker remained a rugged individualist, retiring to his Maryland farm every off-season where he kept in shape by chopping wood and hunting for quail. Sportswriters who managed to track him down for a hot stove feature soon learned that the quickest way to get Frank to open up was to go hunting

with him. "Frank is the best shot in Talbot County, and he's wild about duck shooting," one friend explained. "Whenever you look at him he's either just shot fifteen or twenty ducks or is just going to, and he'll call you blessed if you save him the trouble of bringing up the subject. After that he'll discuss anything under the sun with you."

From 1912 to 1914 Baker continued to lead the league in home runs every season, and also collected his first RBI title in 1912, with a career-high 130, and a second in 1913, when he drove in 117 runs. Continuing to rank among the league leaders in assists and putouts, Baker was also widely regarded as one of the game's best fielding third basemen. His all-around superlative play helped the Athletics win two more AL pennants and another world championship in 1913, with Baker once again torching the Giants with a .450 batting average, one home run, and seven RBI in the five-game Series. After the Boston Braves shut down Baker and the Athletics in the 1914 Series, Mack began selling off his championship team. Baker, locked into a three-year contract, attempted to renegotiate for a higher salary, but Mack refused.

Both were stubborn men of principle and would not

budge from their respective positions. Baker announced he would be perfectly happy back on the farm, "batting a few out with the boys." Twenty-nine years old and at the peak of a Hall of Fame career, that is exactly what he did. In 1915 he played for the Trappe town team, the Upland club in suburban Pennsylvania, Atlantic City, and the Easton (Maryland) club of the independent Peninsula League. Many local towns held Home Run Baker Days, presenting their hero with gifts in return for his services for the day's game.

Under pressure from Ban Johnson, Mack sold Baker's contract to the Yankees for the 1916 season, ending the slugger's lengthy holdout, but after a year's absence from the major leagues Baker was no longer the dominant offensive force he had been just two years earlier. He put together four solid seasons for New York, but never led the league again in any significant offensive category. Despite his fading skills, Baker anchored an offensive attack dubbed Murderers' Row before Babe Ruth had even joined the team. In 1919, aided tremendously by the Polo Grounds, the Yankees smashed a major league-leading 47 home runs, 10 of which came from Baker's heavy stick.

Following the 1919 season, during the winter that New York became intoxicated by the news that Babe Ruth had been purchased from the Boston Red Sox, Baker was humbled by personal tragedy. An outbreak of scarlet fever struck the Baker home, killing Frank's wife, the former Ottilie Tschantre. His two infant daughters also caught the disease, though they eventually recovered. Quarantined, paralyzed by grief, and preoccupied with taking care of his family, Baker announced that he had lost interest in baseball and would not play in 1920. But within a few months Baker was itching for baseball again. He played a few games for his old Upland club, and after a trip to New York in August, agreed to return to the Yankees for the 1921 season.

The game was changing as Baker took on the role of a part-time player, and his teammate, Babe Ruth, redefined the home run. Perhaps envious of Ruth's fame, Baker bemoaned the "rabbit ball" that made the home run a more frequent occurrence. "I don't like to cast aspersions," Baker later confided to a reporter, "but a Little Leaguer today can hit the modern ball as far as grown men could hit the ball we played with." Baker decided to hang up his major league spikes after playing in just 66 games during the 1922 season. He married Margaret Mitchell of Baltimore, and returned to his Maryland farms.

Although Baker was looking to devote more time to his passions of family, farming, and duck hunting, he was pressed into service as player–manager of the Easton

Farmers of the Class D Eastern Shore League in 1924. It was there that he discovered Jimmie Foxx. After Baker sold Foxx to Mack, Baker was unceremoniously sacked as manager during the 1925 season, partly due to the "paltry" price he had received for the young slugger.

Continuing to work the family farms while raising his four children, Baker also served his community on the Trappe Town Board, acted as tax collector, was director of the State Bank of Trappe, and was active in the volunteer fire department. He never lost his love for baseball and was an avid supporter of organized Little League when it began. Inexplicably, considering that for many years Baker's record was the greatest of any third baseman in baseball history, enshrinement in the Hall of Fame eluded him. When finally selected by the Veterans Committee in 1955, Baker responded, "It's better to get a rosebud while you're alive than a whole bouquet after you're dead." Humble as ever, in his later years the man who had first popularized the home run and helped his teams win three world championships told a reporter, "I hope I never do anything to hurt baseball."

Baker died of a stroke on June 28, 1963, and was buried in Spring Hill Cemetery of Talbot County in Easton, Maryland.

DAVID JONES

PHILADELPHIA

JOHN JOSEPH BARRY
SHORTSTOP, 1908–1915

The least-known member of the Athletics' famous $100,000 Infield, Jack Barry was a .243 career hitter with little power and average speed, who nonetheless earned the respect and admiration of his peers because he did the so-called little things well: pulling off the squeeze play, turning the double play, and hitting in the clutch, among others. Playing in an era that espoused the virtues of the inside style of play, the quiet, brainy shortstop was thought by many teammates, opponents, and writers to be the most valuable member of Mack's famous infield. As *Philadelphia Inquirer* writer Edgar Wolfe (writing under the nom de plume Jim Nasium) put it in 1913, "Barry is the weakest hitter of the quartet, but his hits are always timely and his sensational fielding is something that cannot be computed in cold, soulless figures." Ty Cobb once called him the most feared hitter on the A's, and Hughey Jennings declared that "I'd rather have Barry than any .400 hitter in the business....In a pinch he hits better than anybody in our league outside of Cobb."

John Joseph Barry was born April 26, 1887, in Meriden, Connecticut, the oldest child of Patrick and Mary Doohan Barry, natives of County Kerry, Ireland. Patrick Barry owned a saloon, and his family lived atop an incline at 24 Hillside Avenue. There was a barn on the corner of the property, and young Jack developed his speed and agility by throwing a ball over the barn roof and dashing around to the other side to catch it on the way down.

Jack attended St. Rose parochial school and Meriden High, where his team twice won the state championship. His infield play prompted local Holy Cross athletic boosters to arrange for him to attend Holy Cross prep school, a division of the College of the Holy Cross. He arrived in the fall of 1902 and played every infield position during his two years at the prep school and

four years at the College. By the spring of 1908 a half dozen major league teams were eager to sign the Holy Cross senior. The White Sox asked Meriden's most prominent citizen, Ed Walsh, to talk to him. They were all too late. Connie Mack's brother, Tom, a hotel owner in Worcester, had kept his brother informed about Barry since 1905. In the fall of 1907 Tom had invited Barry to meet the Athletics' manager at the hotel. At the meeting Barry asked for a $500 signing bonus. Mack agreed, but asked Barry not to say anything about it, as it was not his policy to pay such bonuses. (Barry never mentioned it outside his family.) Barry signed a 1908 contract, and joined the A's in June after the college season ended.

Jack Barry proved to be Mack's kind of player: quiet, smart, hardworking, innovative, straight-arrow, a nondrinker until later in life. He went to Mass every morning. At first Mack intended to keep the 21-year-old rookie on the bench beside him, teaching and bringing him along slowly. But he needed a second baseman one day and put Barry in the lineup. For the rest of the year the 5'9", 151-pound Barry played second, short, and third before Mack decided that shortstop was his best position.

Barry was the second member, after Eddie Collins, to arrive in what many called the greatest infield ever assembled. Despite dissimilar personalities, Collins and Barry became lifelong friends. Given a free hand by Mack, they worked out plays that no other keystone combination could approach. Together they perfected a defense against the widely used double steal, in which the weaker-armed Collins cut in front of second to stop the catcher's throw if the runner on third broke for home, or duck and let it go through to Barry if the runner stayed near third. Chicago sportswriter Hugh Fullerton also believed that Barry was the best in the game "at taking throws, blocking the base and holding runners close to second."

Barry's enormous range enabled third baseman Frank Baker to play close to the line at third and Collins to shade toward first, even with a man on first and a potential double play in sight. His ability to cover second from deep in the hole at short and take throws from Baker, then relay to first for double plays, drew comments of amazement from the likes of shortstop Bobby Wallace. Also known for his sure hands, Barry cut a cross clear through the palm of the small, short-fingered glove he favored for digging out ground balls, using the sweat from his hand to help him grip the ball.

At the plate the weak-hitting Barry was overshadowed by his more famous teammates, as he hit with little power and never batted better than .275 in a single season. Nonetheless, the same good head that Barry brought to his play on the field, he carried with him into the batter's box, where the right-hander developed a reputation among his peers as one of the league's most dangerous clutch hitters. "If Barry's batting average was only .119 and a hit was needed to win a game for the Athletics, it's a cinch that 99 percent of the fans would rather have Barry at bat than any other man on Mack's payroll," Stony McLinn of the *Philadelphia Press* observed. An exceptional bunter, Barry was free to call a squeeze play on his own, and was the only man in the lineup who was trusted to call the double squeeze, scoring men from second and third on a bunt. It almost always worked.

Beginning in 1910, the Athletics won four of the next five pennants and three World Series. Summaries of these Series never single out Barry, but baseball people knew better. In 1910 against the Cubs, Collins batted .429, Baker .409, Barry .235, but several members of the Cubs said it was Barry who beat them with his glove, and Cubs manager Frank Chance called him the best shortstop he had ever seen, including Honus Wagner. And, despite Baker's heroics in the 1911 World Series, the four umpires who worked the games picked a Barry play that looked routine to the crowd as the best of the Series.

After the A's sweep at the hands of the Braves in 1914, Mack did not expect the team to go from first to last in a hurry, even though he sold Collins during the off-season; however, Frank Baker held out for the entire 1915 season, and by July 1 the A's had sunk into the cellar. Once Mack made the decision to cut his losses and sell Barry, several teams expressed their interest. The Yankees, Red Sox, and White Sox all wanted him, but Barry preferred to play near his home, so Mack sold

him to Boston, where he played second base, a position he considered a snap compared to shortstop. Barry would not play so much as a single game at short the rest of his career.

Thanks in part to Barry's stabilizing influence on the Boston infield, the Red Sox won back-to-back world championships in 1915 and 1916. When Bill Carrigan resigned as the Red Sox manager after the 1916 season, Barry replaced him. The only player–manager in the league, he piloted Boston to a second-place finish in 1917.

With the United States entry into World War I, Barry joined the Naval Reserve before the end of the 1917 season. In November he was called up as a yeoman at the Charlestown Navy Yard in Boston, where he managed the baseball team. He was promoted to a school for ensigns, and then was discharged in December, having missed the entire 1918 season. In his absence Barry had lost his managerial job to Ed Barrow and his second base job to Dave Shean, so in June 1919 the Red Sox traded him back to the Athletics as part of a four-man deal. Though still just 32 years old, Barry's legs and knee, injured in the Navy and abused throughout his 11-year career, felt more like 50. After weeks of mulling it over, Barry retired from baseball.

After his retirement Barry and his wife, the former Margaret McDonough, moved to Shrewsbury, Massachusetts, near Worcester, where Barry had helped coach the Holy Cross baseball team since 1912. In 1921 he became the Crusaders' full-time coach, and stayed for 40½ seasons, compiling a record of 619–147; his .806 winning percentage remains the best in baseball history. His team was unbeaten in 1924 and College World Series champions in 1952. He sent 29 players to the major leagues. In 1956 he became one of the first six inductees into the Holy Cross Hall of Fame.

At home in Shrewsbury, Jack Barry played rummy and poker, and was a member of the Knights of Columbus. A self-taught piano player, he enjoyed hitting the keys after Sunday dinner, singing "Margie" for his wife, and "Take Me Out to the Ball Game," where it was "root, root, root for the Red Sox."

Jack Barry died of lung cancer in his home on April 23, 1961, three months after his 50th wedding anniversary and three days before his 74th birthday. Survived by his wife, he left behind no children. He is buried at Sacred Heart Cemetery in Meriden. A square is dedicated to him in Shrewsbury.

NORMAN MACHT

Amos A. Strunk

PHILADELPHIA

AMOS AARON STRUNK
CENTER FIELDER, 1908–1917, 1919–1920, 1924

Moon-faced and lightning fast, Amos Strunk was one of the best defensive center fielders of the Deadball Era and a major offensive contributor to Connie Mack's powerhouse Philadelphia Athletics teams which appeared in four World Series from 1910 to 1914. A patient hitter, the left-handed Strunk placed in the top ten in the American League in slugging three times from 1913 to 1916, but his power was a derivative of his speed: though the Flying Foot never became a great base-stealer, he was one of the fastest in the league on the base paths, placing among the league leaders in doubles twice and triples four times. Strunk's exceptional speed allowed him to go from first to third on bunt plays, and his quickness led J.C. Kofoed of *Baseball Magazine* to remark: "Some call him the Mercury of the American League, but all know Amos Strunk whatever the handle they plaster on him. He is of a type one instinctively calls rangy, because he moves with the speed you would exert should you accidentally touch a red-hot range."

Amos Aaron Strunk was born on January 22, 1889, in Philadelphia, the fifth child of Amos (a carpenter) and Amanda Strunk. Young Amos learned baseball playing at Fairmount and Huntington Parks in Philadelphia, where the players were called "park sparrows" because they spent so much time on the baseball field. There, it was noted that "the lanky kid was too fast for his protagonists. He ran rings around them, and they confessed it." After playing with an amateur team in Merchantville, New Jersey, in 1907, Strunk began playing professionally with Shamokin (Pennsylvania) of the outlaw Atlantic League in 1908.

From Shamokin, Strunk was recommended by teammate Lave Cross to Mack, the Athletics manager, who brought Strunk to the major league team and played him for the first time on September 24, 1908. Strunk collected a pinch-hit single in his debut. Mack was intent on assembling a group of speedy players, and "he wanted men who could travel fast enough to burn their galoshes. Collins, Barry, Oldring, and the rest were in that class, and Amos fitted in like a drink on an August day." Strunk was sent out to Milwaukee of the American Association for some additional seasoning early in the 1909 season, but he was soon back with Philadelphia to resume a major league career that would last for 17 seasons.

In 1910, at age 21, the 175-pound Strunk was described as being "built like a panther, standing six feet in height, and without an ounce of superfluous flesh upon him." Strunk, however, played in only 16 regular season games in 1910, due to a knee injury. Strunk was plagued by injuries throughout his career, which is a major reason why he played in fewer than 100 games in eight of his major league seasons. Strunk came back late in the season and played in four of the five games in that year's World Series, collecting five hits in 18 at-bats and driving in two runs.

Strunk quickly established himself as one of the premier defensive outfielders in baseball. In 1913 one writer claimed that "Amos has justly earned the verdict of being the greatest defensive outfielder that the game has ever produced. In the matter of fielding his position on the defense, the Ty Cobbs of today and the Curt Welches of other days never even approximated the same class displayed by Amos. It is impossible to even conceive of anything in human form performing more sensational and unerring feats than Amos shows consistently day in and day out. An accurate judge of a batted ball, off at the crack of the bat, his great speed takes him to wallops that other great outfielders would never reach, and he has no weaknesses to either side, in front or back there, by the palings." *Baseball Magazine* three years later noted that "for five years now Amos has demonstrated to his fellow townsmen that, barring a few immortals like Cobb and Speaker, he need doff his chapeau to none."

High praise to be sure, but Strunk elicited it through his superlative play, leading the league in fielding percentage four times from 1912 to 1918 and regularly ranking among the league leaders in putouts per game. Despite such accolades from the press, Mack felt his center fielder was undervalued, calling Strunk "the most underrated outfielder in baseball." Mack went on to say that "Amos made his job of playing center field look a lot easier than it really was."

Strunk was also a key man in Mack's famed double squeeze play. With Strunk on second and a runner on third, Mack would have the batter bunt. The speedy Strunk would break from second base with the pitch and would follow the runner from third home, allowing the Athletics to score two runs on a single squeeze bunt. In addition to the 1910 championship team, Strunk was a major contributor to Mack's World Series teams in 1911, 1913, and 1914, though injuries kept him from appearing in more than 122 games in any of the three seasons.

During his career Strunk was considered one of baseball's great storytellers. It was said that he had a "De Wolfe [sic] Hopper way of telling stories," in reference to the legendary Broadway actor and orator. *Baseball Magazine* commented: "Some time when you're not busy get Amos to tell you stories on old John McCluskey. He'll make you laugh so hard you'll lose your wrist watch."

Strunk did not enjoy his best season in a Philadelphia uniform until after Mack had dismantled the A's dynasty, selling off most of the team's best players and sending the club plummeting in the standings. In 1916 when the A's lost an astounding 117 games—still the worst record in modern baseball history—Strunk was by far the team's best player, setting career highs in doubles (30), hits (172), and on-base percentage (.393), while ranking fourth in the league with a .316 batting average. He followed that performance with another strong campaign in 1917, scoring a career-high 83 runs while batting .281 with a .363 OBP. After the season the cash-strapped Mack completed his fire sale, sending Strunk, Joe Bush, and Wally Schang to the Boston Red Sox in

return for $60,000 cash and three players.

Strunk's average slipped to .257 in 1918, as the Red Sox captured the pennant and won the World Series. In June 1919 Strunk was traded back to the Athletics from the Red Sox, along with Jack Barry, in return for Bobby Roth and Red Shannon. Claimed off waivers by the White Sox in July 1920, Strunk had another outstanding season in 1921 with Chicago, and he went on to play primarily a part-time role with the White Sox through 1923. Although Strunk continued to be effective when he played, persistent leg injuries often kept him on the bench and chipped away at his defensive range. In 1922 Strunk batted .289 in 92 games, and in 1923 he posted a .315 batting average in 54 at-bats.

During spring training in 1924 Strunk suffered serious head injuries in an outfield collision with teammate Roy Elsh and was released by the White Sox a month later, after appearing in only one game as a pinch hitter. On May 2, 1924, the Athletics acquired him for a third time, signing the 35-year-old outfielder as a free agent. In 30 games for the Athletics, Strunk posted a .143 batting average and was released at season's end. Appointed as the player–manager of the Shamokin Shammies of the New York–Pennsylvania League in 1925, Strunk resigned in August, citing recurrent leg injuries, although he was batting .396 at the time. It was his last job in Organized Baseball.

In retirement Strunk became an insurance broker, and he remained in that business for 50 years. He was also an expert photographer. A 1958 article described how "Strunk might be taken for a retired admiral. His hair is white, and he is youthful in movement and dress." His wife, Ethel, whom he married in 1915, was a successful portrait painter, and the two were married for more than 50 years until her death in 1966.

Strunk occasionally bemoaned the lack of aggressiveness in contemporary baseball after he retired. He felt that baseball needed more of the competitive fire that teams like the Dodgers and Giants showed during Strunk's era. "Baseball needs more of that bitterness today," he said, "but it's still a wonderful game."

Amos Strunk died on July 22, 1979, at age 90 in Llanerich, Pennsylvania, after a brief illness. He was survived by two nephews. Strunk was buried in Greenmount Cemetery in Philadelphia.

JOHN MCMURRAY

John "Stuffy" McInnis

PHILADELPHIA

John Phalen "Stuffy" McInnis
First baseman, 1909–1917

The first baseman and youngest member of Connie Mack's famed $100,000 Infield, Stuffy McInnis was one of the best-fielding first basemen of the Deadball Era. During his 19-year major league career McInnis led his league in fielding percentage six times, double plays five times, putouts three times, and assists twice. At just 5'9½" and 162 pounds, McInnis was one of the smallest first basemen of his generation, but he excelled by constantly perfecting his craft. Unlike other first sackers, McInnis reached out for throws one-handed, and also perfected the knee reach, a maneuver in which he performed a full, ground-level split while stretching for a throw. During infield practice he urged his teammates to throw the ball high, low, and wide: "Make me reach for them," he liked to say. According to one report, he was also the first to wear the claw-type first baseman's glove to improve his efficiency in scooping balls out of the dirt.

At the plate the right-handed McInnis was a line-drive pull hitter who amassed more than 2,400 career hits, most of them singles. A remarkably consistent batter, McInnis batted .307 for his career and hit over .300 12 times. He was known as a consummate contact hitter, and from 1913 (when the American League began recording strikeouts) he struck out only 189 times in over 7,300 plate appearances. In 1922 McInnis struck out just five times in 537 at-bats and two years later, he whiffed just six times in almost 600 at-bats.

He hit only 20 home runs in his career, though the one he collected on June 27, 1911, at Huntington Avenue Grounds in Boston was one of the most unusual home runs of the Deadball Era. McInnis rushed to the plate to lead off the eighth inning while the Red Sox pitcher, Ed Karger, was still warming up. McInnis hit a warm-up pitch from Karger into short center field, which got by the out-of-position Boston outfielders. Standing at the plate until urged to run by his teammates, Stuffy then circled the bases for an inside-the-park home run against the unprepared Red Sox. On appeal American League president Ban Johnson upheld the home run based on a new, soon-to-be-withdrawn rule that cut off warm-up pitches as soon as the leadoff batter stepped into the batters box. The rule had been implemented due to the concern that some games were taking over two hours to play.

John Phalen McInnis was born on September 19, 1890, the fourth of five sons of Stephen and Udavilla (Grady) McInnis, in the fishing town of Gloucester, Massachusetts. His father provided a good living for the family, variously as a caretaker of a stable of driving horses, a chauffeur, and a call fireman for the Colonel Allen Hook and Ladder No. 1. All the McInnis brothers played baseball, but Stuffy stood out from an early age. He gained his unique nickname during his boyhood playing days, when teammates and spectators would shout, "That's the stuff, kid, that's the stuff!" after he had made a good play.

Playing shortstop, McInnis led Gloucester High School to championships in 1906 and 1907. In the summers of 1907 and 1908, he played for the Beverly, Massachusetts, amateur baseball club. In July 1908 McInnis joined the Haverhill (Massachusetts) Hustlers professional baseball club, and "soon became the sensation of the New England League," according to the Philadelphia Athletics 1910 Championship Season Souvenir Program. He was paid $100 per month by the Hustlers, batting .301 in 186 at-bats under the tutelage of the legendary Billy Hamilton. On the advice of Dick Madden, a member of the Beverly club who also worked as a scout for the Athletics, McInnis was purchased by Mack at the end of 1908.

Stuffy's slight stature and boyish looks were the cause of some confusion in his earlier years. Once, before a New England League game, umpire Steve Mahoney asked Hamilton when he was going to get his mascot off the field, pointing at McInnis. "Mascot nothing!" snapped Hamilton. "That's my shortstop and he's one of the best you've ever seen."

In 1909 McInnis, just 18 years old, was considered a potential rival for the starting shortstop position over Jack Barry, who had joined the Athletics a year earlier. He stuck with the Athletics out of spring training, but ended up playing only 14 games in his first season, all at shortstop. Stuffy finished the season with a .239 batting average, but made himself useful off the bench as he became particularly astute at stealing signs from opponents.

In 1910 McInnis played shortstop, second base, third base, and even the outfield, batting .301 in 38 games. During the season Mack told Stuffy to start working out at first base, despite his short stature and lack of experience at the position. Ben Houser, who was attempting to become the A's regular first baseman, tried to run McInnis off first every time he tried to take groundballs or throws, but in 1911 Mack kept Stuffy and sold Houser, who had hit only .188.

Before the 1911 season, Mack determined that McInnis would supplant regular first baseman Harry Davis, whose production had declined considerably in the previous year; however, when Jack Barry became sick early in the season, McInnis took over at shortstop instead. He played 24 games at shortstop, and with hot hitting kept Barry on the bench even after he had recovered. Eventually Barry reclaimed the position, and McInnis took over first base from Davis. Appearing in 126 games in 1911, McInnis hit .321 while driving in 77 runs and scoring 76.

On September 23, 1911, Mack included McInnis's name on a list of the 21 players eligible to represent the A's in the World Series. Two days later, however, on September 25, Stuffy sustained an injury to his right wrist when he was struck by a pitch from the Tigers' George Mullin. Although no bones were broken, McInnis's right forearm became badly swollen, and he was unable to throw even from first base to the pitcher's mound with any speed or accuracy. McInnis did not play for the rest of the regular season, and his only appearance in the World Series came as a defensive replacement in the ninth inning of the last game.

McInnis entered the 1912 season surrounded by great expectations, and with huge shoes to fill. Harry Davis, despite his declining performance over the previous season, had been one of the American League's premier power hitters and the A's regular first baseman since shortly after Mack formed the team in 1901. McInnis responded to the expectations with an excellent season, driving in 101 runs (the fourth most in the league) and scoring another 83 while batting .327. For the first time in three years, however, the Athletics failed to win the American League pennant.

In 1913 the A's got back on track, winning the American League pennant for the third time since McInnis joined the team. McInnis batted .324 with 90 RBI, which tied for second in the league. His defense also improved dramatically, providing a glimpse of his future greatness. In the World Series the Athletics beat the New York Giants for the championship. After the Series John McGraw told Mack that the A's infield was "the most perfect I ever saw, and baseball never had a first baseman in the class of McInnis."

McInnis had another strong offensive year in 1914, finishing with a .314 batting average and 95 RBI, second most in the league—although it should be noted that McInnis's annual appearances on the RBI leader boards were due more to his fifth spot in the A's vaunted batting order than to any prowess as a power hitter. Philadelphia was swept in that year's World Series, however, and in the ensuing months the A's dynasty was dismantled piece by piece, as Eddie Collins, Chief Bender, and Eddie Plank left the team and Frank Baker sat out the entire 1915 season. When Mack sold shortstop Jack Barry to Boston midway through the 1915 campaign, McInnis became the sole remaining member of the Athletics' once-feared $100,000 Infield.

Not surprisingly, McInnis's final three years with the Athletics were unhappy ones, as the A's finished in the cellar in 1915, 1916, and 1917. McInnis, however, continued to be productive, batting .314, .295, and .303 in those years to remain one of baseball's premier first basemen. After the 1917 season, in the wake of the United States' entry into World War I, a general wave of salary cuts swept through baseball, which also marked the end of McInnis's three-year contract. "I want to keep McInnis," Mack said, "and will do as much as I can for him, but it is out of the question for me to think of paying him as much money as we did in 1917....I want to say that McInnis has been fairer with me than any player I ever had. He's always been satisfied and worked his hardest even when we were shot to pieces. I hope he agrees to my terms." McInnis did not agree. Mack traded him to the Boston Red Sox for Larry Gardner, Tilly Walker, and Hick Cady on February 28, 1918.

After nine years with the Athletics, McInnis helped lead his new team to the war-shortened 1918 American League pennant. The Red Sox won the World Series over the Chicago Cubs primarily on the pitching of Babe Ruth and Carl Mays, but also with the timely hitting of McInnis and a few teammates.

Boston's fortunes fell in 1919, 1920, and 1921, as first Mays and then Ruth were jettisoned. The team finished in the bottom half of the American League each season, and McInnis again found himself on a team that had been sold for parts by its owner. McInnis hit for averages of .305, .297, and .307 in the three years, respectively. Furthermore, as the game changed around him, McInnis's hitting style remained the same. Despite hitting .300 on a nearly annual basis, McInnis's lack of walks and power made him a significantly below-average hitter during the high-octane 1920s.

It was during this period that McInnis honed his first base defense to a point of near-infallibility. In 1919 he made seven errors in 118 games for a .995 fielding average. In 1920 he again made seven errors, this time in 148 games, for a league-leading .996 fielding average. In 1921 McInnis made only one error in 152 games, for a then-record .9993 fielding average. His 1,300 chances accepted without an error in 1921 set the record for consecutive errorless chances in a season—and from May 31, 1921, to June 2, 1922, McInnis went 163 games and 1,625 chances without making an error at first base.

Before the 1922 season, McInnis was traded to the Cleveland Indians. He hit .305, making only five errors in 140 games as Cleveland finished fourth. After the season, McInnis was released. He signed with the Boston Braves, with whom he spent two seasons, batting .315 in 1923 and .291 in 1924. The Braves finished at or near the bottom of the National League in both seasons, and after McInnis refused to accept a salary cut, they released him in April 1925.

McInnis then signed with the Pittsburgh Pirates. Playing in only 59 games in 1925, he batted .368 with a .437 OBP and a .484 slugging average. Stuffy's veteran leadership was instrumental in helping the Pirates win the National League pennant. In the World Series against the Washington Senators, the Pirates lost three of the first four games. John McGraw, whose Giants had lost to the Senators the previous year, suggested to Pirate manager Bill McKechnie that he play McInnis at first base instead of the struggling George Grantham, to take advantage of Stuffy's World Series experience. McKechnie took McGraw's advice and the Pirates won three straight to come back for an improbable World Series win. McInnis's steadying hand and timely hitting were major contributors to the Pirate comeback. McInnis played part-time for the third-place Pirates in 1926, batting .299 in only 127 at-bats in 47 games.

In 1927 McInnis returned to Philadelphia as manager of the Phillies. Despite some early-season heroics by the "Flying Phils," the perpetually woeful team lost 103 games and ended up in its usual spot at the bottom of the National League. Fired after the season, Stuffy served as player–manager of the Salem Witches in the New England League. The 38-year-old batted .339 in part-time duty. He went on to coach baseball at Norwich, Cornell, and Harvard universities. After six seasons of coaching at Harvard, McInnis resigned in 1954 because of failing health.

In his private life McInnis was as steady as he was on the ball field. He married Elsie Dow in 1918. They had one daughter, Eileen, and three grandchildren. For the last 42 years of his life, McInnis lived at 11 Tappan Street in Manchester-by-the-Sea, Massachusetts, a few miles down Cape Ann from his native Gloucester. On February 16, 1960, after a lengthy illness, McInnis died in an Ipswich, Massachusetts, hospital. He was 69 years old and had been preceded in death the previous year by his wife.

AARON M. DAVIS AND C. PAUL ROGERS III

PHILA.

PHILADELPHIA

WALTER HENRY SCHANG
CATCHER, 1913–1917, 1930

A switch-hitter who was adept at getting on base, Wally Schang was considered by many of his contemporaries to be the best catcher of his time. Behind the plate, the 5'10", 180-pounder was one of the most athletic catchers of his day, so agile and alert that he occasionally played third base or in the outfield. An excellent hitter who posted a career .393 OBP, second only to Mickey Cochrane among catchers, Schang could hit for power. The energetic and likeable Schang batted better than .300 six times and caught for seven different American League pennant winners. In his six World Series appearances Schang batted .287, including a .444 mark for the Boston Red Sox in the 1918 World Series. Despite this impressive resume, however, Schang never received recognition for his accomplishments, earning only 22 votes in five appearances on the Hall of Fame ballot. In the words of one baseball writer, "the only thing Wally's career lacked is the recognition he deserved."

Walter Henry Schang was born on August 22, 1889, in South Wales, New York, a small farm community some 25 miles southeast of Buffalo, one of nine surviving children of Frank and Mary Schang. The Schangs owned and worked over 170 acres of farm land in New York, principally raising dairy cows. Despite the daily grind of schoolwork and chores around the farm, young Wally was preoccupied with baseball. As he later remembered, "From the moment I crawled out of bed my thoughts had to do with baseball, with the result that I raced the poor nag to the creamery every morning. I wanted to get my job over as early as possible so I could drive back home, walk the two miles to the school and get in forty-five minutes to an hour of baseball before the bell called us to our studies." Baseball injuries did not excuse Wally from his farm chores. Said Schang: "For a while I had to milk one-handed."

Wally was not the only member of his family obsessed with baseball. Indeed, the national game was something of a family passion. Frank Schang, a catcher for the local town team, inspired at least three of his sons to pursue the game professionally. Wally's older brother Bob enjoyed a short major league career as a catcher for Pittsburgh, New York, and St. Louis in the National League. Another brother, Quirin, spent 20 years as a catcher in the semipro circuit.

While still in high school Wally started playing semipro ball for a team in nearby Holland, New York. He played many positions (including shortstop, third base, and the outfield) before finally settling in behind the plate. Over the next three seasons Wally garnered a reputation as one of the area's best players, culminating in 1911, when he starred for the Buffalo Pullmans. George Stallings, then skipper of the Buffalo Bisons of the International League, was impressed and picked up Schang's contract near the end of the season. Appearing in 48 games for the Bisons in 1912, Schang batted .333 and cemented his excellent defensive reputation with 41 assists. Word spread quickly of the young backstop's talent and, prior to the 1913 season, 13 of the 16 major league clubs attempted to draft the 23-year-old switch hitter. The Athletics were the fortunate team to land Schang, and he traveled to Philadelphia to learn the ropes.

As the 1913 season opened Connie Mack knew he had a talented roster. With catchers Jack Lapp and the aging Ira Thomas already on board, Mack allowed the young rookie to observe his major league colleagues and slowly eased him into action. By the end of the season Schang had managed 207 at-bats, hitting a healthy .266, and ranked first among all major league backstops with three home runs and a .392 OBP. Defensively, Schang quickly developed into one of the league's best backstops, with 92 assists in 72 games behind the plate. "Schang has proved one of the wonders of the year," veteran sportswriter Hugh Fullerton observed. "Schang is steadier and works with more judgment than he did during the early part of the year, studies batters better, and works better with the pitchers."

In that year's World Series against the New York Giants, Schang performed like a seasoned veteran, batting .357 in four games and leading the team with seven RBI, including a Game Three solo home run off Doc Crandall.

With some success and money in his pocket at the conclusion of the 1913 season, the young man focused on his personal life. To cap off a fantastic year, in 1913 Schang married a Philadelphian named Marie Aubrey. Wally was ready to settle down financially, thanks to his $3,243.94 World Series paycheck, which was a very generous bonus compared to his regular $1,000 annual salary. The couple would have one child, Joan Marie, born in 1926.

The 1914 season was another good one for the Philadelphia A's, who captured another American League pennant with a 99–53 record. Once again they were aided by the continuing development of Schang, who established himself as the best offensive catcher in the game. Wally led all American League catchers in batting average (.287), extra-base hits (22), home runs (3), slugging percentage (.404), and RBI (45). Defensively, Wally struggled as he played through a broken thumb on his throwing hand, and as a result committed 30 errors, tied for the most among AL backstops.

Like most of his teammates, Schang fared poorly in the A's shocking four-game loss to the Boston Braves in that year's World Series. Starting all four games, Wally batted just .167 and struck out four times in 12 at-bats. When later asked about the team's poor performance in the fall classic, Schang was quoted as saying, "We went into [the World Series] too cocky, and we lived it up too much."

After the A's stunning defeat star pitchers Eddie Plank and Chief Bender departed for the Federal League, slugging third baseman Frank Baker held out the entire season and second baseman Eddie Collins was sold to the White Sox. Virtually overnight, the A's dynasty evaporated and the team tumbled into last place in 1915, where it would remain for the next seven years.

Schang continued to perform well for the next few years on some miserable teams. Despite Schang's growing reputation as an excellent catcher, Mack needed Wally in a utility role, playing him more in the outfield and at third base than behind the plate. Nonetheless, the 1915 *Reach Guide* described Schang as "one of

the most sensational catchers in recent years. He is a remarkably fast runner, a good hitter and a strong thrower." He finished the season with a .248 batting average, a career-high 18 stolen bases, and a team-high .385 OBP. In 1916 Schang led the 36–117 Athletics in home runs with seven, a figure he reached with the help of his historic performance on September 8 at Shibe Park, when he became the first switch hitter in baseball history to homer from both sides of the plate in the same game.

After the 1917 season, in which he batted .285 in 118 games, Schang, Joe Bush, and Amos Strunk were traded to the Boston Red Sox. Schang appeared in 88 games for Boston in 1918, batting .244 with only eight extra-base hits, but he still posted a stellar .377 OBP. With the entry of the United States into World War I, the baseball season was cut short, and the Red Sox captured their third pennant in four years with a 75–51 mark, 2½ games ahead of second-place Cleveland.

Although that year's fall classic, played in early September, was overshadowed by events overseas, Schang enjoyed a fabulous series, batting .444 over six games and making some key defensive contributions. In Game Three, with the Sox leading 2–1 with two outs in the bottom of the ninth, Chicago's Charlie Pick singled, putting the tying run on first. Pick stole second and on the next pitch broke for third on a ball that got away from Schang. Wally reacted quickly and fired to third, beating the sliding Cub to the bag. Pick's hard slide, however, had knocked the ball out of third baseman Fred Thomas's glove. As Thomas argued with the umpire, Pick raced for home. Thomas retrieved the ball and threw a strike to Schang, who was waiting for Pick to arrive. The Cub might have had more success running into a brick wall. When the dust settled, Schang was standing over the fallen Cub, ball in hand, having tagged Pick with the final out of the game. In Game Four Schang scored the winning run and in Game Six, his stellar defense, including a pickoff of Les Mann in a key situation, led to the final Red Sox victory.

After the 1919 season, in which the Red Sox finished a disappointing fifth, Boston owner Harry Frazee dismantled his team, selling Babe Ruth to the Yankees in January 1920. A year later Schang and three teammates were also sent to New York for catcher Muddy Ruel and three other players. Once again, Schang had the good fortune to be traded to a winner. Now in his thirties, Schang put together three excellent seasons in his five years with the Yankees, batting better than .300 twice and appearing in three more World Series. After hitting a disappointing .188 in the Yankees' 1922 World Series defeat, Schang batted .318 and scored three runs in the

Yankees' first World Series triumph in 1923.

Although Schang remained a productive player, by 1925 his offensive numbers began to decline, leading to rumors that his eyesight might be failing. At the end of the season Schang was traded to the St. Louis Browns for cash and pitcher George Mogridge. Determined to prove that he was not finished as a player, Wally enjoyed one of his best seasons in 1926, batting .330 with a .405 OBP and a .516 slugging percentage in 103 games. Appearing in 97 games for the Browns in 1927, Schang posted a .318 batting average. The following year his average dipped to .286, but he still managed to post a career-high .448 OBP. In 1929 his average dipped still further, to .237, but Schang adjusted by drawing 74 walks on his way to a .424 OBP. Nonetheless, at the end of the season the Browns traded the 40-year-old catcher to Philadelphia for Sammy Hale.

Back with Mack and the pennant-bound Athletics, Schang appeared in only 45 games, posting a .174 average. He did not appear in the World Series, and was released by Mack at season's end. The following year he finished out his major league career with the Detroit Tigers, batting .184 in 30 games. Even at the end, however, Schang's defensive abilities left an impression on his teammates. As one Tiger observed, "Just to watch him was an education in the art of catching. . . . I've never seen anyone so graceful behind the plate."

Released by Detroit on June 29, 1931, Schang signed two weeks later with the Chattanooga Lookouts of the Southern Association, batting .247 over the remainder of the season. Struggling financially in the early years of the Great Depression, he almost signed on with the House of David in 1932 for $230 per month, but then at the last minute George Sisler, manager of the Texas League's Shreveport Sports, offered him a roster spot. Schang batted .214 as the team's third-string catcher.

Having stretched his playing career as far as it would go, Wally returned to his Dixon, Missouri, farm, but the Great Depression continued to bring economic struggles. Farming and baseball were all Wally knew, so he headed back to the latter in 1934, as player–manager for the Joplin (Missouri) Miners of the Western Association, batting .257 in 71 games. In 1935, after failing to land a job as a Pacific Coast League umpire, Schang returned to the Western Association, batting .256 for Muskogee, Oklahoma. In 1936 the Cleveland Indians hired him as a coach, where he helped develop pitchers Denny Galehouse and Bob Feller. Indeed, he roomed with Feller that year, instructing the young phenom on the nuances of the game. Schang served as player–manager for various minor league clubs from 1938 to 1940. He finished out his career in 1942 with Owensboro (Kentucky) of the Kitty League, reaching base in five of his seven plate appearances, at age 52.

In retirement Schang was often seen at the ice cream shop in Dixon, where he would regale listeners with his stories of Ruth, Collins, and other teammates, or on the golf course, where he often played 36 holes even after he was 70 years old. He died at St. Luke's Hospital in St. Louis on March 6, 1965, at 75 years of age, and was buried in Dixon Cemetery.

DON GEISZLER

PHILADELPHIA

CLARENCE WILLIAM "TILLY" WALKER
CENTER FIELDER, 1918–1923

A powerful right-handed hitter with a legendary throwing arm, Tilly Walker spent the second decade of the Deadball Era shuffling around the American League, playing for four different teams in the span of eight seasons. After spending time with Washington, St. Louis, and Boston, Walker finally came into his own with the Philadelphia Athletics in 1918, when he tied Babe Ruth for the American League lead in home runs. Although Ruth monopolized the home run laurels for the rest of Walker's career, the red-haired Tennessean still ranked in the top five in the league every year from 1919 to 1922, when he belted a career-best 37 round-trippers.

During his playing career Tilly Walker was listed as having been born in Denver, Colorado, in 1890. Both the time and place were wildly inaccurate: Clarence William Walker was actually born on September 4, 1887, in Telford, a backwoods town in northeastern Tennessee, not far from where David Crockett grew up. Clarence was the second of three surviving children (four others died in infancy) of Nelson and Florence Desler Walker. When Clarence was still a young child, the family moved a few miles west to the tiny hamlet of Limestone, where Nelson supported his family by constructing wagons and carriages.

After finishing high school, Walker spent a few years working as a telegraph operator. In 1908 he played for the Washington College (Tennessee) baseball team, and the following year spent time with the University of Tennessee squad. That experience earned him a contract with the Spartanburg Spartans of the Class D Carolina Association in 1910. In 108 games Walker, playing the outfield, batted just .242. The following year was a different story, however, as Walker began the season with a .390 batting average. On June 2 the Washington Senators purchased his contract.

Listed at 5′11″ and 180 pounds, the right-handed Walker spent the rest of the 1911 campaign as Washington's regular left fielder, and finished the season with a respectable .278 batting average, though he collected just 12 extra-base hits (two of them home runs) in 356 at-bats. From the start of his major league career Walker dazzled observers with his powerful throwing arm. He collected 14 assists in 94 games, though he also committed 16 errors. Walker's defense became even more problematic in 1912, when he committed eight errors in 34 games in the field for a ghastly .837 fielding percentage. It was a performance bad enough to earn him a spot on the bench, despite batting a solid .273. On August 25 Washington released Walker to the Kansas City Blues of the American Association, where he spent the final month of the season.

Once again Walker's bat earned him a promotion back to the big leagues, as he batted .307 with 89 runs scored in 131 games for the Blues in 1913. On August 24, one year to the day after he had been sent down, the St. Louis Browns acquired Walker from Kansas City. In 23 games for the Browns Walker batted .294, earning himself a spot on the St. Louis roster for 1914.

Established as the club's everyday left fielder, Walker, now often called Tilly (though the precise origin of this nickname is not known), enjoyed his first standout season in 1914, batting .298 with six home runs (tied for third-best in the league), 24 doubles (tied for sixth), 16 triples (fourth-best in the league), and a .441 slugging percentage (eighth-best in the circuit). Walker was also a patient hitter: his .365 OBP (fueled in part by 51 walks) led the Browns, and his 72 strikeouts were the fourth most in the American League.

Walker distinguished himself even more with his throwing arm, as he racked up a league-leading 30 assists. According to *The Sporting News*, Walker's throwing arm was "the talk of the American League circuit." However, some observers felt that Walker's arm, while powerful, was also too wild. In 1923 *The Sporting News* observed that Walker "was famous for his throwing arm, but his throws were not always made with judgment, nor were they always well aimed." Errant throws may be why Walker led the league in errors three times during his career. Nonetheless, thanks in large part to Walker's hitting and defense, the Browns finished in fifth place in 1914, their best showing since 1908.

In 1915 the Browns slid back to sixth, and Walker regressed with the rest of the team, as his batting average fell by 29 points to .269, his on-base percentage slid 42 points to .323, and his slugging percentage dipped 76 points from his 1914 total, to .365. Playing primarily center field for the first time in his major league career, Walker led the league in outfield assists with 27, but also paced the circuit with 23 errors.

More troubling, Walker fell out of favor with some of his teammates, and the following spring the Browns' new manager, Fielder Jones, sold him to the defending champion Boston Red Sox for $3,500. The sale puzzled many observers of the game, who, according to one newspaper account, "wanted to know why a man good enough for [the] world's champions was not good enough for St. Louis." The trouble was Walker's temperament: "He is said to be quite a hitter when he feels like hitting, but grouches and sulks when he does not whang a double or a triple every few minutes. In other words he worries more about his batting average than about the club's record of games won."

Serving as Tris Speaker's replacement in center field, Walker batted .266 for the Red Sox in 1916, with 29 doubles, 11 triples, and three home runs, one of which came at Fenway Park on June 20 against New York Yankees right-hander Ray Keating. The blast, which carried over the park's 24-foot left field barrier, was the only home run hit by Boston at home all season. (Opposing teams also managed to hit only one home run at the park that year.) At the time Walker was the only player to have cleared the left field fence more than once, as he had also achieved the feat twice while playing for the Browns.

After batting .273 in Boston's five-game World Series triumph over the Brooklyn Robins, Walker spent one more season in the Hub City, finishing the 1917 campaign with a disappointing .246 average in 106 games. After the season, Walker was shipped to the Philadelphia Athletics, along with catcher Hick Cady and third baseman Larry Gardner, for first baseman Stuffy McInnis. The trade proved to be a steal for Connie Mack's ball club, as Walker took advantage of Shibe Park's more accommodating dimensions to become one of the American League's top long-ball threats. Playing for the dreadful Athletics in 1918, Walker batted .295 and tied former teammate Babe Ruth for the major league lead in home runs with 11. The following year, as the Athletics limped to a 36–104 finish, Walker batted .292 and smacked 10 round-trippers, all of them at home—but Walker had slowed perceptibly on the field.

As the curtain closed on the Deadball Era and the home run became more fashionable, Walker kept up with the times. In 1920 he finished third in the American League with 17 home runs, 12 of which came at home. That year he also led the league in assists for the third and final time in his career, with 26. In 1921 Walker smashed 23 home runs, 18 of which came at home, and drove in a career-high 101 runs. With the Athletics having finished dead last every year since 1915, Mack decided to play to his slugger's strength for the 1922 season, and moved the left field fence in by 46 feet, to a distance of 334 feet. Walker responded by hitting 37 home runs (26 at home) and driving in 99 runs.

But as good as Walker was, Philadelphia's pitching was even worse. In 1922 the staff allowed a league-worst 5.35 runs per game and the club finished in seventh place. Early in the 1923 campaign Mack benched Walker, whose diminished range had also made him a defensive liability. Explaining the move, *The Sporting News* reported that "in the eyes of Mack…the day of slugging homers is passing and…baseball is returning to normalcy. Mack figures good fast fielding of fly balls is of more value in winning ball games than smashing out homers now and then, so Walker, who has lost his speed and cunning as a fielder, goes to the bench." Appearing in only 52 games for the Athletics, Walker finished the 1923 season with a productive .275 batting average and .368 OBP. Nonetheless, the 36-year-old drew his release in December.

Walker spent the next several seasons bouncing around the minor leagues, playing for Minneapolis in the American Association, Baltimore and Toronto in the International League, and Greenville in the South Atlantic League.

After his baseball career ended, Walker lived full-time in Tennessee. His 1921 marriage to Fanella Pomeroy, which produced two children, ended in divorce. In his later years Walker worked as a highway patrolman. He died suddenly in Unicoi, Tennessee, on September 21, 1959, at the age of 72, after suffering a heart attack in his brother's home. He was buried in Urbana Cemetery in his hometown of Limestone.

DAVID JONES

CLEVELAND

Despite the inglorious end of its National League entry after the 1899 season, Cleveland soon regained a major league team. Owned by local magnates Charles Somers (who also financially aided most of the other AL clubs) and Jack Kilfoyl, the new club played in the Spiders' abandoned League Park. Sporting the blue-trimmed uniforms of the old Spiders club and with Jimmy McAleer, an old Spider, as manager, the 1901 Blues (or, more fancifully, Bluebirds) played in the first AL major league game on April 24, losing to the Chicago White Sox 8–2.

Though the 1901 Cleveland entry finished in seventh place, the Blues soon sported one of the league's most talented rosters, thanks to the defections of National League stars Napoleon Lajoie, Elmer Flick, Bill Bradley, and Bill Bernhard, and the emergence of Earl Moore and Addie Joss. Despite this impressive assemblage, the Naps (as they soon became known, after their star second baseman) consistently failed to meet expectations, finishing no better than third until the 1908 season, when they lost the American League pennant by a half game to the Detroit Tigers.

This agonizing defeat caused Kilfoyl to resign, leaving Somers in full charge of the club. Under a steady succession of managers—Nap Lajoie, Deacon McGuire, George Stovall, Harry Davis, and Joe Birmingham—the Naps continued to flounder, despite the 1910 renovation of League Park into a steel-and-concrete, box-seat-

WINNING PERCENTAGE 1901–1919

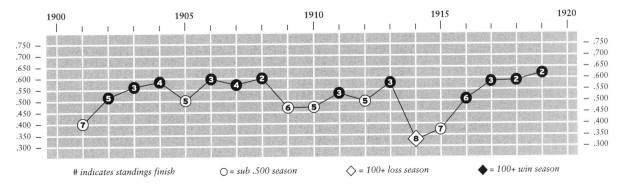

ed structure and the acquisition that year of young slugger Joe Jackson. Though Jackson developed into one of the league's best players, the club's fortunes cratered in 1914, when the team finished in last place. Before the start of the 1915 season, the aging Lajoie was dealt to Philadelphia, and a poll of sportswriters gave the team their new name, the Indians. Jackson was dealt to Chicago in midseason, and soon thereafter Somers, deep in debt, relinquished ownership of the club.

The Indians began their rise back to prominence in 1916 under new owner Sunny Jim Dunn, who quickly made his mark on the franchise by acquiring star center fielder Tris Speaker from the Boston Red Sox. With a new core of young players featuring catcher Steve O'Neill, shortstop Ray Chapman, and pitchers Jim Bagby and Stan Coveleski, Speaker's Indians inched back toward the top of the standings, closing out the Deadball Era with back-to-back second-place finishes in 1918 and 1919. One year later, the Indians captured their first world championship—but not before the franchise suffered its greatest loss on an overcast August afternoon at the Polo Grounds in New York.

STEVE CONSTANTELOS

ALL-ERA TEAM

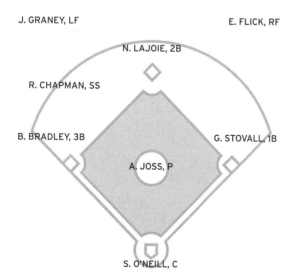

T. SPEAKER, CF

J. GRANEY, LF   E. FLICK, RF

N. LAJOIE, 2B

R. CHAPMAN, SS

B. BRADLEY, 3B   G. STOVALL, 1B

A. JOSS, P

S. O'NEILL, C

TEAM LEADERS
1901–1919

BATTING

GAMES
T. Turner	1625
N. Lajoie	1614
J. Graney	1235

RUNS
N. Lajoie	865
T. Turner	692
J. Graney	650

HITS
N. Lajoie	2046
T. Turner	1470
B. Bradley	1264

RBI
N. Lajoie	919
T. Turner	521
B. Bradley	473

DOUBLES
N. Lajoie	424
B. Bradley	237
J. Graney	205

TRIPLES
E. Flick	106
J. Jackson	89
J. Graney	78
N. Lajoie	78

HOME RUNS
N. Lajoie	33
B. Bradley	27
C. Hickman	26

STOLEN BASES
T. Turner	254
N. Lajoie	240
R. Chapman	220

BATTING AVERAGE
(2000+ plate appearances)
J. Jackson	.375
T. Speaker	.340
N. Lajoie	.339

PITCHING

GAMES
A. Joss	286
W. Mitchell	219
B. Rhoads	185

WINS
A. Joss	160
B. Rhoads	88
E. Moore	81

LOSSES
A. Joss	97
W. Mitchell	76
E. Moore	68

INNINGS
A. Joss	2327⅓
B. Rhoads	1444⅓
E. Moore	1338

STRIKEOUTS
A. Joss	920
W. Mitchell	775
E. Moore	616

WALKS
W. Mitchell	496
E. Moore	449
B. Rhoads	405

SHUTOUTS
A. Joss	45
B. Rhoads	19
S. Coveleski	16

ERA
(800+ innings pitched)
A. Joss	1.89
V. Gregg	2.32
S. Coveleski	2.33

TYPICAL LINEUPS 1901–1919

1901

1. O. Pickering, CF
2. J. McCarthy, LF
3. J. O'Brien, RF
4. C. LaChance, 1B
5. B. Bradley, 3B
6. E. Beck, 2B
7. B. Wood, C
8. F. Scheibeck, SS

1902

1. H. Bay, CF
2. B. Bradley, 3B
3. N. Lajoie, 2B
4. C. Hickman, 1B
5. E. Flick, RF
6. J. McCarthy, LF
7. J. Gochnauer, SS
8. H. Bemis, C

1903

1. H. Bay, CF
2. B. Bradley, 3B
3. N. Lajoie, 2B
4. C. Hickman, 1B
5. J. McCarthy, LF
6. E. Flick, RF
7. J. Gochnauer, SS
8. H. Bemis
   F. Abbott, C

1904

1. E. Flick, RF
2. B. Lush, LF
3. B. Bradley, 3B
4. N. Lajoie, 2B
5. C. Hickman, 1B–2B
   G. Stovall, 1B
6. T. Turner, SS
7. H. Bay, CF
8. H. Bemis, C

1905

1. J. Jackson, LF
2. H. Bay, CF
3. E. Flick, RF
4. N. Lajoie, 2B
5. B. Bradley, 3B
6. T. Turner, SS
7. C. Carr, 1B
   G. Stovall, 1B–2B
8. F. Buelow
   H. Bemis, C

1906

1. E. Flick, CF-RF
2. G. Stovall, 1B–3B
   J. Jackson, LF
3. T. Turner, SS
4. N. Lajoie, 2B
5. C. Rossman, 1B
6. B. Congalton, RF
7. B. Bradley, 3B
8. H. Bemis, C

1907

1. E. Flick, RF
2. B. Bradley, 3B
3. T. Turner, SS
4. N. Lajoie, 2B
5. N. Clarke, C
6. B. Hinchman, LF
7. J. Birmingham, CF
8. G. Stovall, 1B

1908

1. J. Clarke, LF
2. B. Bradley, 3B
3. G. Stovall, 1B
4. N. Lajoie, 2B
5. N. Clarke, C
6. B. Hinchman, RF
7. J. Birmingham, CF
8. G. Perring, SS

1909

1. W. Good, RF
2. B. Bradley, 3B
3. G. Stovall, 1B
4. N. Lajoie, 2B
5. T. Easterly, C
6. B. Hinchman, LF
7. G. Perring, 3B
8. N. Ball, SS
   J. Birmingham, CF

1910

1. J. Graney, LF-CF
   H. Niles, RF
2. G. Stovall, 1B
   A. Kruger, LF
3. T. Turner, SS
4. N. Lajoie, 2B
5. T. Easterly, C-RF
6. J. Birmingham, CF
7. B. Lord, RF
8. B. Bradley, 3B

1911

1. J. Graney, LF
2. I. Olson, SS
3. J. Jackson, RF
4. N. Lajoie, 1B–2B
   G. Stovall, 1B
5. J. Birmingham, CF
6. N. Ball, 2B
7. T. Turner, 3B
8. G. Fisher
   S. Smith, C

1912

1. J. Graney, LF
2. I. Olson, SS–3B–2B
3. J. Jackson, RF
4. N. Lajoie, 2B
5. A. Griggs, 1B
6. J. Birmingham, CF
7. T. Turner, 3B
   R. Peckinpaugh, SS
8. S. O'Neill, C

1913

1. D. Johnston, 1B
   N. Leibold, CF
2. R. Chapman, SS
3. I. Olson, 3B
4. J. Jackson, RF
5. N. Lajoie, 2B
6. B. Ryan, CF
   T. Turner, 3B
7. J. Graney, LF
8. S. O'Neill
   F. Carisch, C

1914

1. N. Leibold, CF
2. T. Turner, 3B
3. J. Jackson, RF
4. N. Lajoie, 2B
5. D. Johnston, 1B
6. J. Graney, LF
7. R. Chapman, SS
8. S. O'Neill, C

1915

1. N. Leibold, CF
2. T. Turner, 2B–3B
3. R. Chapman, SS
4. J. Jackson, RF–1B
   J. Kirke, 1B
5. J. Graney, LF
6. E. Smith, RF
   W. Barbare, 3B
7. B. Wambsganss, 2B
8. S. O'Neill, C

1916

1. J. Graney, LF
2. T. Turner, 3B–2B
   R. Chapman, SS–3B
3. T. Speaker, CF
4. B. Roth, RF
5. C. Gandil, 1B
6. I. Howard, 2B
7. B. Wambsganss, SS
8. S. O'Neill, C

1917

1. J. Graney, LF
2. R. Chapman, SS
3. T. Speaker, CF
4. B. Roth, RF
5. J. Harris, 1B
6. B. Wambsganss, 2B
7. J. Evans, 3B
8. S. O'Neill, C

1918 (first half)

1. D. Johnston, 1B
2. R. Chapman, SS
3. T. Speaker, CF
4. B. Roth, RF
5. B. Wambsganss, 2B
6. J. Wood, LF
7. J. Evans
   T. Turner, 3B
8. S. O'Neill, C

1918 (second half)

1. J. Graney, LF
2. R. Chapman, SS
3. T. Speaker, CF
4. B. Roth, RF
5. B. Wambsganss, 2B
6. D. Johnston, 1B
   J. Wood, LF–2B
7. J. Evans
   T. Turner, 3B
8. S. O'Neill, C

1919

1. J. Graney, LF
2. R. Chapman, SS
3. T. Speaker, CF
4. E. Smith, RF
5. L. Gardner, 3B
6. B. Wambsganss, 2B
7. D. Johnston, 1B
8. S. O'Neill, C

CLEVELAND

WILLIAM JOSEPH BRADLEY
THIRD BASEMAN, 1901–1910

From 1901 to 1904, Bill Bradley was arguably the best young player in the American League. Wielding a heavy bat he nicknamed "Big Bennie," the six foot, 185-pound right-hander was one of the junior circuit's most feared hitters, becoming the first player to homer in four straight games in 1902, and batting .300 or better three consecutive years. A natural power hitter who was out of place in the run-deprived Deadball Era, Bradley was not a fan of the "inside" strategies championed by many of the game's leading figures. "Brilliant coaching makes me tired," he once bluntly declared. "This idea...that coachers, teamwork, and the so-called inside ball...makes or unmakes a team, is foolishness." Yet Bradley was no simple-minded basher; he was admired throughout the league for his aggressive base running and brilliant fielding at third base, where he led the league in double plays three times and fielding percentage four times. And when a series of injuries sapped his power, Bradley transformed his game, adopting "inside" tactics to help his team win. In 1908, the man who had ranked second in the league in home runs just six years earlier laid down 60 sacrifices, the second most in baseball history.

William Joseph Bradley was born on February 13, 1878, in Cleveland, where he grew up playing pickup ball in the Payne Avenue district with the Delahanty brothers and Tommy Leach. The young Irishman got a parochial education at Immaculate Conception School for eight years. Upon leaving school, Bradley found a job with the Dangler Stove Company and earned extra money playing semipro baseball with the Galion, Ohio, club.

Hearing of an opening in the Western Association, Bill headed out to Burlington, Iowa, in September 1897, where he played third base for only 18 games before the team hit financial troubles. The day before his release,

Bradley made his mark, winning a game with a ninth-inning grand slam. After his release, he rode the rails on a freight train back to Akron and then walked the 35 miles to Cleveland, flat broke.

With the help of Leach, Bill caught on with the Auburn Maroons of the New York State League in July 1898, playing shortstop and first base. He played third the following year and posted a .312 batting average, stealing 25 bases in 88 games. On July 31, 1899, the Auburn club was transferred to Troy, and renamed the Troy Washerwomen, and 10 days later Bradley was sold to the Chicago Orphans. According to one story, upon hearing the news that he was headed for the big leagues, Bradley gave the New York State League something to remember him by, smashing a home run onto a racetrack where it proceeded to roll a quarter of a mile.

Bradley played in Chicago for $150 a month, sitting on the bench for two weeks before making his debut at shortstop on August 26, 1899. Following eight errors in five games, the Cubs shifted him to third base, where he would remain for the rest of his career. Bradley batted .310 in 1899, and in 1900 his salary rose to $300 per month. After another solid season, in which he batted .282 with eight triples, Bradley sought another raise. To his dismay, Cubs management rejected the offer and even told him he might not make the team in 1901.

After talking with teammate Clark Griffith, Bradley jumped to the American League's Cleveland franchise, which offered him a $3,500 salary (later to rise to $4,500). Bradley performed well in 1901, leading the team in slugging and scoring 95 runs. In 1902 Bradley came into his own as one of the league's top stars, homering in four straight games from May 21 to May 24, and also assembling a 29-game hitting streak. Bradley finished the season with career highs in batting average (.340) and slugging percentage (.515).

Still only 24 years old, Bradley gave every indication that he was a superstar in the making. Sensing the youngster's greatness, New York Giants manager John McGraw tried to lure him back to the National League with a three-year, $10,000 contract, plus a $5,000 signing bonus. But Bill was tired of the National League and, happy to be playing near home, he rejected the offer. For Bradley, going to New York "was the most foolish move I could have made."

Over the next two seasons, Bradley continued to make headlines with his bat. On July 28, 1903, Bradley connected for three triples, tying teammate Flick's league record. Two months later, Bradley capped off his stellar 1903 campaign by hitting for the cycle, with an extra double thrown in. For the year, he batted .313, and his .496 slugging percentage ranked second in the league. He followed that performance with another solid campaign in 1904, batting an even .300 and driving in a career-best 83 runs.

When not slamming the ball with authority, Bradley fielded with genius. He was a fearless base blocker, grinning and awaiting the incoming runner from second, and mastered fielding the bunt with a one-motion barehanded scoop and toss. His long reach, ability to judge balls, and excellent arm were also noted. Throughout his career, Bradley led the league in many fielding categories at his position and twice made seven putouts in a nine-inning game—a record that has since been tied.

Bradley was not only a dazzling fielder with clout, but also a clever and emotional player with peculiar habits of his own. Like former Cleveland shortstop Pebbly Jack Glasscock, Bradley had a mania for picking small stones out of the dust and tossing them away. He could be found whipping his head back a few times to read catchers' signals and was adept at feigning being hit by a pitch, ranking among the league leaders in that category four times. Bradley was also an aggressive base runner "who had to be carefully watched as he had the habit of stretching singles into doubles upon the slightest provocation," according to the *Cleveland Plain Dealer*.

In short, Bradley was the complete package—a powerful hitter and excellent base runner who was among the league's best fielders at a position where good offense remained a rare commodity. Still only 26 years old following the 1904 season, Bradley appeared to have a long and prosperous future ahead of him, a fact his contemporaries were quick to acknowledge. In 1904, when a fan asked Boston's standout third baseman, Jimmy Collins, who was the game's best third sacker, Collins simply replied, "Well, if I could field and bat like Bradley, I should lay claim to that title myself."

But things began to unravel for Bradley during the 1905 season, when he was diagnosed with "autotoxicity, a stomach ailment." Weakened by the illness, Bradley's batting average plummeted to .268, and for the first time in his career he failed to hit a single home run. Things went from bad to worse the following year, when he missed half the season after his right wrist was broken by a pitch from New York hurler Bill Hogg, who according to one account then spat, "The big Frenchman [Nap Lajoie] is next on my list." Bradley returned the following year, but was struck with fever in July and finished the year with an abysmal .223 batting average. In May 1908, the ill-starred third baseman tore a ligament in his side. Though he remained in the lineup despite the injury, Bradley finished the year with a .243 batting average.

Even his personal life had taken a turn toward the macabre. In November 1905, a 36-year-old bookmaker, Christian Schlather, entered the Bradley home, fondled Bradley's 14-year-old sister, Alice, and threatened to kill her if she would not elope with him. When she met the man later, Bill jumped out and thoroughly thrashed Schlather, who was later convicted of intoxication, carrying concealed weapons, and assault and battery. The would-be kidnapper and rapist was almost lynched by a hostile crowd of Bradley supporters before police arrived.

With his reduced effectiveness at the plate, Bradley found other ways to contribute. In 1907 he set an American League record with 46 sacrifices, which he broke the following year when he amassed 60 sacrifices, still the second highest total in history. Even as Bradley's batting average plummeted still further in 1909 and 1910, as he failed to reach .200 in both seasons, Bradley was still celebrated for his fielding. When Cleveland finally released him in August 1910, the *Cleveland Plain Dealer* declared "there is not a third baseman in either big league today who is as accurate a thrower as Bradley with his famous underhand whip."

Bradley landed on his feet, joining Toronto's Eastern League team and turning in three strong seasons as a playing manager. He batted .294 with 13 triples and eight home runs in 1911, and in 1912 his Maple Leafs team won the inaugural International League pennant as he posted a .292 average with 17 triples. In 1914, Bill was summoned back to a slightly larger stage when the Federal League made a bid to become a third major-league. Signed to a three-year contract for $7,000 per season, he managed the Brooklyn Tip Tops to a .500 record and fifth-place finish, only playing in a pinch-hitting role.

Bradley was not invited back for the next season, and he sued the league for breach of contract in New York State Supreme Court. Meanwhile, he played the 1915 season for former teammate George Stovall's Kansas City Packers, also of the Federal League. He could still field third base pretty well, but his hitting had gone even further south, as he finished the year with a .187 batting average in 203 at-bats.

After a brief tenure managing Erie of the Inter-State League in 1916, Bill did not return to Organized Baseball until 1928, when he rejoined the Indians as a scout. He remained in that capacity through the 1945 season, went to Detroit for 1946, and returned to Cleveland in 1947. Bradley was a notable scout, responsible for recommending such talent as Denny Galehouse, Tommy Henrich, Ken Keltner, Frankie Pytlak, and Gene Woodling. In 1950, Bradley suffered a heart attack, ending his days of traveling to scout players, though he continued to look over young talent brought up by the team until 1953. Bill Bradley died at Cleveland's Ingleside Hospital on March 11, 1954, following a three-week bout with pneumonia. He was survived by his wife of 50 years, Anna, and two children. Buried in Cleveland's Calvary Cemetery, Bradley was posthumously elected to the Cleveland Indians Hall of Fame.

STEVE CONSTANTELOS

CLEVELAND

EARL ALONZO MOORE
RIGHT-HANDED PITCHER, 1901–1907

Nearly forgotten today amid the pantheon of great Deadball Era hurlers, Earl "Crossfire" Moore—so nicknamed for his unorthodox method of shooting a sidearm pitch from the very end of the rubber—ranked as one of the American League's most promising young players during the first five years of its existence. Six-feet tall, square-jawed, and with his cap pushed low over his eyes, Moore cut a striking figure on the mound, and he answered to an assortment of nicknames. When he racked up 79 victories by the age of 28—at times out-dueling Cy Young, Rube Waddell, Jack Chesbro, Chief Bender and Eddie Plank—Earl appeared poised for greatness. But a drive through the box on an afternoon late in 1905 tore apart Moore's left foot. The injury so debilitated him that he managed only six big-league victories over the next three seasons, yet it would not be the end for the self-proclaimed "Steam Engine in Boots." After regaining his form in the minors, Earl became an 18 and 22-game winner for the Philadelphia Phillies in 1909 and 1910, respectively, before tapering off and finishing with the Federal League in 1914.

Although most sources state that Earl Alonzo Moore was born in Pickerington, Ohio, on July 29, 1879 or 1878, official birth records from Fairfield County, Ohio, for Violet Township indicate that the future major-leaguer actually began life on July 29, 1877, under the name of Alonzo Moore. One of 14 children of Reason G. and Martha Ann (Claybaugh) Moore, Earl was called both Lonzo and Lon growing up. The phonetics of the name Lon Moore gave rise to one of Earl's first nicknames, "Lon Mower," an appropriate sobriquet for a teenager who once stepped out of the crowd at a game in nearby Dayton to strike out 17, substituting for an injured pitcher. Later, he drew the attention of professional scouts while playing semipro baseball at Bushnell Park in Columbus. Now going by

"Earl," Moore earned a spot with Dayton of the Inter-State League in 1899. The next season, making $85 a month, he overwhelmed hitters with his exceptional velocity and registered a 24–11 record (including a no-hitter) to help lead the team to a league title. His rise perfectly coincided with the formation of the American League in 1901, and the newly born Cleveland club snapped up the local prodigy for $1,000.

Moore started the second game in Cleveland AL history—a 7–3 loss at Chicago. Following his home debut—a 6–3 victory over Milwaukee—the *Cleveland Plain Dealer* remarked, "He showed wonderful speed—almost up to the quality possessed by Cy Young in his best days, and fairly good control." The Ohioan often relied on his fast ball against opponents, but he mixed in some "speedy benders," too. Perhaps most aggravating to hitters was Moore's signature "crossfire" pitching technique. In this unusual delivery, Moore cleverly toed the side edges of the rubber and, augmenting his wide mound position with a sidearm throwing motion, hurled pitches plate-ward at puzzling angles. Earl lamented his peers' reluctance to try the method: "They rely absolutely on curves and change of pace. Both are essential to success, but how much better they might succeed if they would only change from one side of the pitcher's plate to the other. That is what constitutes the crossfire, in addition to the ability to stand with one foot on the extreme corner of the plate and step out and deliver the ball at the same time."

In just his fourth outing, the 23-year-old soared to prominence by spinning the American League's first-ever nine-inning no-hitter on May 9 against the Chicago White Sox, though he lost both the no-hitter and the game in the tenth frame. Moore overcame other setbacks in 1901—his father once angrily refused to contact him for two weeks after an 11–5 embarrassment to Philadelphia on July 30, author Franklin A. Lewis recalled—and fashioned a solid rookie season. Despite poor control (107 walks, 13 wild pitches), he went 16–14, fired four shutouts, and even vanquished Cy Young, 2–1, on July 19. Not surprisingly—considering his age and burgeoning reputation as an overpowering pitcher—Earl let the success go to his head, though he did so in typically endearing fashion. "Moore carries the title of 'Steam Engine in Boots,'" noted the *Washington Post*, "and after his name in the hotel registers always appears the letters 'S.E.I.B.'"

The cockiness may have been justified, given the amount of attention paid him by National League clubs. Cincinnati and New York took turns trying to pry the talented fireballer loose from Cleveland in 1901–1902. So certain did Earl's defection to the National League seem in late July 1902 that *The Sporting News* felt compelled to print a front page sub-head declaring, MOORE HAS NOT JUMPED.

On the diamond, Moore overcame a spring-training bout with pleurisy to produce a mixed-bag of a season in 1902. He finished in the top 10 in wins (17), ERA (2.95), games (36), innings (293), strikeouts (84), and shutouts (4), but continued to be plagued by wildness, leading the league in walks (101) and finishing fifth in losses (17). Life was bursting at the seams for the young ballplayer that year. On July 10, he wed Cleveland school teacher Blanche G. Patno, a marriage that would last 53 years. During the off-season, Moore stayed in the area and resided a short distance from League Park. He and Blues third baseman Bill Bradley became fierce rivals on the bowling alleys and billiard tables of the Forest City. "Both come downtown every afternoon and settle their disputes in bowling and pool," wrote the *Cleveland Leader*. "Moore is an excellent bowler, and when he defeated Bradley three times, the third baseman suggested a pool match. Then Bradley had his revenge. Moore would not call quits until Bradley had won five games. Moore is an excellent pool player himself and was deeply chagrined at his defeat." So enamored of the lanes did Moore become that he eventually managed a bowling alley. But he soon gave it up, calling the work "too strenuous for me."

By comparison, throwing a baseball seemed easy for Earl in 1903. Adding twenty pounds to his frame (bringing him close to 200) and a $3,000 salary to his wallet, he enjoyed his greatest season in the AL, going 19–9 with a league-leading 1.74 ERA. He placed in the top 10 of nearly every major pitching category, though at the outset it appeared the year might be a disaster, after he got off to a terrible 1–4 start. Employing his scythe-like delivery, Earl captured 18 of his next 23

decisions—including 11 out of 12 from mid-July until the end of August. He beat every club in the circuit at least twice. He completed all 27 of his starts, and in 22 of those, allowed eight hits or fewer. His sub-2.00 ERA easily outpaced runner-up Cy Young's by a third of a run and he notched wins over future Hall of Famers Jack Chesbro (twice), Eddie Plank and Chief Bender.

Moore's skein would have been even more impressive, except that twice within a month, the right-hander absorbed line drives off his pitching arm—one of them from the bat of teammate Charlie Hickman on July 24, while throwing batting practice. The damage to Earl's arm caused him to miss the final month of the season and would be a bad omen for "Crossfire."

Shrugging off a mediocre 1904 season—marred by rheumatism and a sliding injury—Earl broke to an excellent 13–7 start in 1905 and helped propel Cleveland into first place by late July. Then Moore's career came instantly crashing down. In a game against the Highlanders at New York on August 1, a line drive ricocheted off of the "Steam Engine's" foot, damaging muscles and ligaments. The severity of the injury apparently was not recognized right away, because he finished the contest and continued to take his regular turn in the rotation until early September, possibly hurting the foot further. But, clearly, Earl was not right the final two months of the season: he was regularly shelled and went 2–8 the rest of the way.

As the 1906 season drew near, the dire nature of Moore's injury became publicly known. The renowned sports osteopath, Bonesetter Reese, issued a statement from Youngstown, saying, "pitcher Earl Moore will be of no use to the Cleveland Americans this year. The muscles of Moore's left foot…have been torn loose, allowing the instep bone to drop down and making the pitcher flat-footed." Earl and his Cleveland physicians disputed Reese's claim and predicted a return to the hill in 8–10 weeks. But it proved to be wishful thinking and Reese's prognosis was right on: the Naps hurler saw action in just five games for the year.

Not yet 30 years old, the right-hander's career slid off the major league map. Struggling to mend his foot and regain form early in 1907, Moore was dealt to the New York Highlanders for Frank Delahanty and Walter Clarkson. But the fresh start in Gotham failed to resurrect Earl; he finished the campaign at just 3–7 in 15 games. Finally, a minor league stint with Jersey City of the Eastern League beginning in August 1907 turned out to be just the right elixir. He went 13–12 for the Skeeters in 1908 and performed so well that the Philadelphia Phillies acquired him at the end of that season.

Moore astounded major league baseball in 1909

with an amazing comeback. Still utilizing his rapid crossfire delivery, he became the ace of the Phillies staff and quickly ascended to the top echelon of National League hurlers. Despite persistent control problems—his 108 walks led the NL—Earl went 18–12 with a 2.10 ERA for a 74–79 team that finished in the second division. Known variously in the Philadelphia press as "Big Earl," "Big Moose," and "Big Ebbie," Moore made it all the way back to the big time on August 19 by defeating Christy Mathewson, 1–0, at the Baker Bowl. He followed it up with an electrifying 1910 campaign, pacing the league in shutouts (6) and strikeouts (185), and finishing third in wins (22). Phillies catcher–manager Red Dooin used Moore wisely, yanking him at the first sign that his pitches weren't finding the plate (he lasted just one inning in a loss to the Cubs on September 16). Other times, he permitted him to go the distance and even well into extra innings when Earl found a groove. Like fellow workhorses Mathewson and Three Fingered Brown, he also received occasional relief assignments.

Future Hall-of-Fame umpire Bill Klem marveled at Moore's mound mastery. "I believe that Earl Moore, of the Phillies, has more stuff on his ball than any other pitcher I worked behind during the summer," he said in January 1911. "Really, I never saw a more deceptive ball to judge than Moore's cross-fire. It comes up to you at a peculiar angle, and if it's half as hard to hit as it is for an umpire to judge, then I can easily understand why the batters don't fatten their averages when Moore is working. His speed is tremendous, and his curves fast breaking. There are a lot of great pitchers in the National League, but Moore is the one best bet to me."

Even when he wasn't on the hill, Earl could be tough on opponents. While coaching first base one April afternoon against New York in 1911, he drew the rage of John McGraw when, at the conclusion of an umpire dispute, he called the Giants manager a "wife killer." (In 1899, McGraw's first wife had died tragically at age 22 of a burst appendix.) Already irked that Moore had shut out his Giants twice that season, McGraw grabbed a bat and went after him. Before McGraw could get to the "Big Moose," the Philadelphia police broke up the skirmish.

Moore's pitching renaissance turned out to be short-lived. En route to a disappointing 15–19 record

in 1911, he began to fall out of favor with Philadelphia management due to his wildness on the mound—and off it, too. Reports ran rampant that he regularly broke team rules, failed to stay in condition, and didn't give his best on the mound. The Phillies tried to peddle him to various NL clubs—Chicago, Brooklyn, New York, and Pittsburgh showed interest—but to no avail. They kept him for 1912, and he was injured by a hit ball yet again, this time breaking his finger. The Phillies finally unloaded him to the Cubs in 1913, and Earl's major league career culminated in 1914 when, at long last, he jumped to an outlaw team and league—the Buffalo Federals. He went 11–15 with a horrendous 4.30 ERA to close out his topsy-turvy ride in the big leagues at 162–154.

Following his playing days, Moore remained close to the game of baseball (records show both he and his wife Blanche had a season pass to the Indians for 1933). He occasionally participated in Indians old-timers' games and frequently indulged his love of golf. Professionally, he held jobs selling both oil and real estate. Earl retired to his native Pickerington, the "Violet Capital of Ohio," and became identified later in life primarily as the man who threw the first American League no-hitter. (This distinction, however, was taken away from Moore in 1991 by MLB's rules committee, which ruled that only a complete hitless game of nine innings or more counts as a no-hitter.) As Moore entered his twighlight years, a youngster named Gary Taylor—now a member of the Pickerington–Violet Township Historical Society—delivered the Columbus, Ohio, newspaper to the aging ex-ballplayer's residence. "I remember going to him and asking him how to grip the ball to throw a curve," he said. "We sat on his front porch swing and talked a lot about how to pitch. He was very kind to me. He was always very accommodating to the kids in Pickerington."

Appropriately, when Earl Moore passed away due to complications from heart disease at 84 on November 28, 1961, in Columbus, Ohio, the death certificate listed his business or industry in life as "Base Ball." Under the heading "Usual Occupation," he was identified simply as "Pitcher." Earl is buried beside his wife Blanche at Glen Rest Memorial Estate in Reynoldsburg, Ohio.

TONY BUNTING

CLEVELAND

HARRY ELBERT BAY
CENTER FIELDER, 1902–1908

Once clocked on a stopwatch from plate-to-first in 3.5 seconds, Harry Bay was considered by many contemporary baseball authorities to be the fastest man in the American League. A photographer experimenting with a motion picture camera filmed "Deerfoot" in full stride and newspaper reports commonly referred to the speedster as "a ten-second man in the 100 yard dash." Bay utilized this blazing foot speed to forge a reputation marked by splendid base running, spectacular catches, and acrobatic dives. At the plate, he mastered the "chop swing" to further exploit his natural talents. A left hander, Bay played both sides of the game—offense and defense—with reckless abandon. He was especially adept at sliding headlong into first base on particularly close plays. One account mused that Bay was so slender—5′8″ and 138 pounds— that he didn't even cast a shadow on sunny days. His thin build earned Bay a second nickname, "Sliver," and surely qualified him as one of the slightest men in professional baseball.

Harry Elbert Bay was born on January 17, 1878, in Pontiac, Illinois, to George and Martha (Springer) Bay. At five years of age, Harry's family relocated to Peoria where he learned how to play sandlot baseball. Later, he became an all-around athlete at Peoria High School. After graduation, Bay barnstormed the Midwest on a team that included a young pitching prospect from Rock Island—future Hall of Famer Joe McGinnity. His stellar fielding and base running attracted the attention of local minor league clubs, and Bay signed his first professional contract with the independent Lincoln (Illinois) Bronchos in 1898.

Bay rose quickly through the ranks of the minor circuits. Playing for Rock Island of the Western Association and Troy of the New York State League in 1899, he moved on one year later to play for Detroit in the American League—one year before that circuit

declared major league status—and Marion (Indiana) of the Inter-State League. His break came in 1901 with a great performance for the Indianapolis Hoosiers of the Western Association, where he hit .303, stole 24 bases, and fielded .949. By midsummer, the Cincinnati Reds opened a roster spot for the fleet-footed outfield prospect. Bay appeared in his first major league contest on July 23, 1901, against Pittsburgh. He normally batted lead-off and played centerfield, but saw limited action in 41 games and hit a disappointing .210. Cincinnati sportswriters labeled the rookie "a thirty-center," a disparaging reference to ordinary skills.

Bay received his release from the Reds in May 1902, and he promptly signed with the Cleveland Bronchos, who were in a desperate position because of injuries sustained by left fielder Jack McCarthy and right fielder Elmer Flick. Bay auspiciously starred in his first game when he collected a pair of singles, a double, stole one base, and initiated a double play from the outfield. The following day he hit safely in three appearances. Although the ailing outfielders returned to the Blues lineup, Bay had earned a spot when he replaced Ollie Pickering in center field. Appearing in 108 games, he batted a respectable .290 and swiped 22 bases. At one point, "Deerfoot" produced a 26-game hitting streak. Moreover, he led all American League centerfielders with a .973 fielding percentage. In his first season with the Blues, the likable Bay also made an impression upon the Washington, D.C. police, who fined the Cleveland player $25 for placing his signature on the Washington Monument.

1903 promised to be Bay's breakout season. He remained consistent in the leadoff role with a .292 average, and pilfered 45 "pillows" to lead the American League. He also placed high in other categories as well: 579 at-bats (second), 169 hits (fourth), 94 runs scored (fifth), 201 times on base (ninth), 18 sacrifice hits (ninth), and 12 triples (tenth). Bay's personal life also began to take off with his marriage to Lelia Ballinger. In the off season, Harry and Lelia joined the vaudeville act of Guy Kibbee, who would later become well known as a character actor in Warner Brothers western and gangster films. A natural entertainer, Harry was widely recognized as an accomplished cornet player.

By his own admission, Bay suffered from the effects of running on hard base paths. When he suffered an injury to one of his "underpinnings" (legs) in 1904, Harry slumped to a .241 average. The nimble one still managed to steal 38 bases and dazzle crowds with his athleticism in the field. On July 19, Bay registered 12 outfield putouts in a 12-inning contest against Boston to set a major league record.

Bay returned to form in 1905 to post some of the most impressive numbers of his career. He batted a personal best .301 and nabbed 36 bases. Harry also banged out 166 hits (fifth in the AL), and twice tallied five hits in a single game. On the same day that he became the first American Leaguer to reach the coveted mark of 100 hits (July 27), he injured his left shoulder while diving into a bag. Several days later, he aggravated his right knee while slipping and sliding for fly balls on a muddy field. The lame "Deerfoot" never returned to top form; indeed, the damaged knee plagued Bay for the remainder of his baseball life.

Sidelined for much of the last year of his career in Cleveland, a frustrated Bay asked on June 13, 1907, to be traded to the Boston Americans. "Maybe there can be torture more acute to an ambitious ball player than sitting stock still while his team mates are out there hustling for victory," revealed Bay, "but I've yet to learn what it can be." The trade never

materialized, and when adoring fans sent Bay a loving cup in appreciation of his efforts in Cleveland flannels, it signaled the end of his career. He literally limped through his last major league game on May 3, 1908.

When Cleveland skipper Nap Lajoie shipped Bay to Nashville in the spring of 1908, the recuperating outfielder was reunited with his former Bronchos teammate and current manager of the Vols, Bill Bernhard. Bay played left field and appeared in 123 games for the Vols while batting a crisp .283. Bay remained a crowd favorite in Nashville for three more seasons, as he posted consistent offensive and defensive numbers despite being hampered by the bum knee. Once Bernhard departed for Memphis, Bay left Nashville and decided to try his own hand as a minor league player–manager. He worked mostly in the Three-I League: Bloomington (1912), Madison (1913–1914), Rock Island (1916), and Alton (1917), and Mason City of the Central Association in 1915.

When Bay retired, he returned to his hometown to work as a state automobile license examiner. Bay's musical career held equal prominence in his life. "His fame as a trumpet virtuoso almost equaled that of his big league ball playing," claimed the *Peoria Journal*. For years, Bay was a featured soloist with the Peoria Municipal Band, and performed regularly with the Shriners' Marching Band.

During the frosty winter of 1952, Bay slipped on an icy sidewalk and fractured several ribs. He was in considerable discomfort and bedridden for five weeks. On March 20, 1952, Harry Elbert Bay passed away at age 74 from a coronary occlusion. He was buried alongside his wife, who preceded him in death, at Parkview Cemetery, Peoria.

JOHN A. SIMPSON

Elmer Flick

CLEVELAND

Elmer Harrison Flick
Right fielder, 1902–1910

At 5'9" and only 168 pounds, Elmer Flick was not the prototypical slugger. But he was one of the American League's most feared hitters in the century's first decade, placing in the top five in slugging percentage five times from 1901 to 1907, and leading the league in 1905. Throughout his 13-year career, the left-handed-hitting Flick wielded a thick-handled bat that he turned out on his own lathe, and used it to muscle extra-base hits over outfielders' heads. A confident hitter, Flick was unafraid of even the game's most intimidating hurlers. "I loved to hit against Cy Young and Walter Johnson," Flick later recalled, "because they were fastball pitchers and they couldn't fool me with that inside stuff that everyone today pops up in the air, or breaks his bat." Though he was at times clumsy in the field, Flick also possessed enough foot speed to occasionally move to center from his customary position in right field. On the base paths, Flick used his speed to great advantage, leading the league in triples three times and stolen bases twice. Flick was so highly regarded that in 1907 Cleveland declined an offer to trade him to the Detroit Tigers for a young Ty Cobb. However, soon thereafter, Flick's Hall of Fame career ended prematurely when he came down with a mysterious gastrointestinal ailment.

Elmer Harrison Flick was born in Bedford, Ohio, on January 11, 1876, the third of five children of Zachary Taylor and Mary Flick. Elmer's father, an American Civil War veteran, was a farmer and skilled mechanic who operated a chair-making shop in Bedford, and gained notoriety because of his failed attempt or attempts (the stories vary) to fly without using an airplane.

A natural athlete, Elmer boxed, wrestled, and played football, but his favorite sport was baseball, something that he first excelled at as a slugging catcher on the Bedford high school team, though some locals considered

his younger brother, Cyrus, a better player. Sometime in 1891, the Bedford town team was embarking on a trip to play a neighboring team when the manager noticed that he had only eight players. Not wanting to forfeit the game, he began looking for someone with baseball skills in the crowd that had gathered at the train station to wish the team well. Among the crowd, Elmer was invited to join the team, an offer that he eagerly accepted despite not having a uniform or even any shoes. The result was that Bedford lost both games of a doubleheader, but "Shoeless Elmer" made a name for himself with his good hitting.

Flick continued to play for the Bedford team until he joined the Youngstown Puddlers of the Inter-State League in 1896 after the manager agreed to hire him sight unseen. Not wanting to disappoint himself or his manager, Flick prepared for his sojourn into the professional ranks through an exercise program that consisted of running and bouncing a ball off the side of a building, and by making his own bat on his father's lathe, something that he would do more than once during his baseball career.

At Youngstown, Flick moved to right field because the Puddlers already had a catcher. This was the position that Flick would play for most of the rest of his career, though the transition was not easy for him and his fielding percentage was an atrocious .826 for the 31 games he played. His biggest difficulty was judging fly balls. However, the change did not affect his hitting, as he pounded the ball for a .438 average with five doubles, nine triples, and six home runs among his 57 hits. As Flick described his Youngstown days to Brian Williams of the *Cleveland Record* in January 1963, "The manager told me that as an outfielder, I wasn't so hot . . . then he added: 'But you can sure sting that ball.'"

The following year Flick took his talents to Dayton, another member of the Inter-State League. While playing there, Flick improved his fielding to a .921 mark and continued to hit the ball at a torrid pace, finishing with 183 hits—including 42 doubles, 10 homers, and a league-leading 20 triples—and a .386 average. Added to those figures, he stole 25 bases, scored an incredible 135 runs in only 126 games, and topped the league with 295 total bases. His offensive exploits prompted the youngsters who came to see him perform to chant, "Elmer Flick, you are slick / Hit a homer pretty quick."

Flick's performance with Dayton caught the eye of George Stallings, then manager of the Philadelphia Phillies, who signed the 22-year-old outfielder to a major league contract for the 1898 season. Stallings hoped to use Flick as the club's fourth outfielder, but when starting right fielder Sam Thompson was sidelined with a back injury, Flick was pressed into service, and he quickly established himself as one of the team's best players, becoming a fixture in right field for the next four seasons. After batting .302 and finishing fourth in the league with a .430 OBP his rookie season, Flick improved to .342 in 1899, scoring and driving in 98 runs. Flick's walk rate, however, took a precipitous nosedive from which it would never recover, inexplicably falling from 91 walks per 600 plate appearances to 46. In 1900, he put together his best season with the Phillies, placing second in the league with a .367 batting average and .545 slugging percentage, smashing 11 home runs, and pacing the circuit with 110 RBI.

While in Philadelphia, Flick improved his defensive skills and learned to take advantage of the short dimensions of Baker Bowl's right field by playing shallow and ranking among the league leaders in assists, often by fielding would-be singles and then tossing the batter out at first base. As he established himself as one of the league's best hitters, Flick also showed that he had the toughness necessary to command respect from opponents and his own teammates. Twice in a game in 1899, he got angry at Nap Lajoie for going back into shallow right field to catch fly balls that Flick thought should have been his chances. Then, during a game in 1900, he and Lajoie got into a fistfight over who owned a bat. Despite giving away about four inches and 30 pounds to the larger Lajoie, Flick held his own and settled for a draw when Lajoie missed with a punch, struck a grate or a wall (the sources disagree), and broke his thumb.

With the coming of the American League, Flick remained loyal to the Phillies in 1901, but jumped to their Philadelphia rivals, the Athletics, the following year. There he played for only 11 games before his former franchise got a court injunction to prohibit his teammates Bill Bernhard, Chick Fraser, and Nap Lajoie, who had jumped to the A's the previous year, from playing in Pennsylvania for any team except the Phillies. Flick was not mentioned by name in the injunction, but the results affected him as well. In order to keep Bernhard, Lajoie, and Flick in the American League (Fraser decided to return to the National League), Ban Johnson made arrangements with the Athletics and the Cleveland club to transfer the contracts of the three league jumpers to the Bronchos, soon to be renamed the Naps. The move cost Flick a chance to play on a pennant winner with the Athletics, but Cleveland was glad to have a local boy to boost attendance, and Flick was delighted.

Although falling a little short of his usual .300 batting average, "the demon of the stick" (a nickname Flick had acquired while playing at Youngstown) lived up to advance billing when he set an American League record that has since been tied but not broken by hitting three triples in a game against Chicago on July 6. He then followed that performance by walking five times in a game against Boston on July 18.

The next five seasons marked Flick's heyday with the newly named Naps. Batting first or third in over half the games in which he appeared, he led the American League three times in triples (consecutively), twice in stolen bases, and once each in runs scored, batting average, and slugging percentage. Arguably Flick's finest season in a Cleveland uniform came in 1905, when he topped the league in slugging percentage (.462), triples (18), and batting average (.308, which remained the lowest mark for a batting champion until Carl Yastrzemski won the 1968 title with a .301 mark). Even Flick's defense improved enough for him to become Cleveland's primary center fielder for the 1906 season. Flick acquitted himself well at his new position, committing only five errors in 150 games, 86 of them in center field.

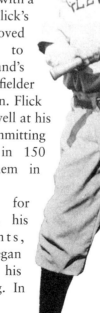

Unfortunately for Flick, despite all his accomplishments, baseball life began to take its toll on his physical well-being. In a revealing article published in the July 22, 1907, issue of the *Cleveland Press*, Flick disclosed that "playing the game day in and day out [was] ruining his health," that he was "on the verge of physical collapse," and that "the time of his retirement [was] not far distant." Almost prophetically, less than eight months later, Flick came down with a mysterious gastrointestinal illness that caused him to miss most of the 1908 season and play in a total of only 90 games during the 1909 and 1910 seasons. He lost weight, his power and speed declined, and the pain was so severe there were times when he thought that he would die. "My last three years—from 1908 to 1911 [*sic*]—were awful," Flick later admitted. "I shouldn't have played at all....There was a time in 1908 I was positive I wouldn't live another week." Initially, Flick's doctors were mystified as to what was ailing him, but later they decided that it was acute gastritis and prescribed pills for him which he kept taking for the rest of his life.

Whatever the cause of Flick's misery, the ailment brought an end to his major league career. From 1908 to 1910, Flick batted just .254 in 338 at-bats. In July 1910, the Naps finally released him to Kansas City of the American Association—a move Flick negated by refusing to report. Instead, Flick spent the 1911 and 1912 seasons playing for another American Association team, Toledo, before retiring from professional baseball

and returning to Bedford. There, he farmed, hunted (Flick was an outstanding shot with a rifle), raised trotting horses, built houses and office buildings, and, according to an article in the January 28, 1963, issue of the *Cleveland Record*, "dickered in real estate." Also, he scouted for the Cleveland franchise and spent more time with his wife, Rose, and his five daughters.

Despite his short but outstanding career, Flick remained largely forgotten by the baseball community in general and the Hall of Fame voters in particular until Ty Cobb's death in 1961. Some articles written about the Georgia Peach mentioned the aborted 1907 trade and thus revived interest in who Flick was and what made him worthy of being suggested in a trade for Cobb. The renewed attention, in turn, led to Flick being voted into the Hall of Fame by the Veterans Committee in 1963, an honor he treasured until his death from congestive heart failure at 8:25 A.M. on January 9, 1971, only two days before his 95th birthday. Flick also suffered from mycosis fungoides, a cancerous disease of the skin, which contributed to his death. He was buried in Crown Hill Cemetery in Twinsburg, Ohio. In 1977 "the demon of the stick" was posthumously inducted into the Greater Cleveland Sports Hall of Fame, and 10 years later, into the Ohio Baseball Hall of Fame. Today the baseball park in Bedford bears his name.

ANGELO LOUISA

CLEVELAND

CHARLES TAYLOR HICKMAN
FIRST BASEMAN, 1902–1904, 1908

Known as Piano Legs and Cheerful Charlie, the ponderous clubber Charlie Hickman possessed one of the Deadball Era's most potent bats. In 1903, the 5′9″, 215-pound Hickman hit one ball 100 feet over the left field fence at Cleveland's League Park, and another completely out of New York's Hilltop Park. "If we had the lively ball in our day, we would have had five Babe Ruths," former Hickman teammate and gifted scout Bill Bradley said in 1926. "Buck Freeman, Charlie Hickman, Larry Lajoie, Ed Delahanty and Sam Thompson. They could hit as hard as Ruth; they could hit as far as Ruth; they could hit as often as Ruth." Though Hickman's powerful bat was constant during his 12-year major league career and he possessed good speed, he struggled to find a defensive position at which he could excel. Perhaps because of his defensive shortcomings, he was shuffled among five American League teams (including Cleveland twice) during his seven years in the league. Through it all, he was always a fan favorite. His genial nature, outgoing personality, and friendliness were hallmarks throughout his life. In reporting his passing, the Morgantown *Post* said, "It could be safely said he had no personal enemies."

Charles Taylor Hickman was born in Taylortown, Pennsylvania, on March 4, 1876, to Isaac Newton Hickman and Josephine Estelle Taylor Hickman. He was the second of the couple's three children. His mother's family was so prominent in the area that Hickman's hometown (a tiny village near the college town of Morgantown, West Viriginia) was named after them. From family lore, we know that Charlie's father, a carpenter and farm hand, played baseball and taught the game to his son. Throughout his career, Charlie returned to his father's land to personally select trees for use in his bats, shipping the lumber off to Louisville

for manufacture. He was educated in his home county's public schools and went on to nearby West Virginia University in 1895. There he studied law, played baseball and was a classmate and friend of legendary football coach Fielding Yost. Hickman was an early student-athlete and was compensated with board, books and $10 dollars per month. Though West Virginia was on the other side of the Mason-Dixon Line, a few miles from Hickman's hometown, Charlie would make Morgantown his home for the rest of his life.

Hickman started at college as a catcher but was switched to the box when his pitching skill was realized. He turned professional in 1896 as a pitcher and part-time outfielder for New Castle in the Inter-State League. The following season, then as a full-time pitcher, he split among West Virginia University, New Castle, and the Boston Beaneaters after being signed by Frank Selee on July 19. He tried the outfield as well as pitching, but saw little action in three years at Boston, during which the right hander also spent time with Rochester and Providence of the Eastern League. His arm failed midway through the 1899 season, essentially ending his pitching days. These were championship years in Boston and his club traveled to Cuba to support United States troops fighting in the Spanish-American War. While there Charlie met and formed a lasting friendship with Teddy Roosevelt.

In 1900, Hickman moved to New York, where the Giants installed him at third base, his first regular position as a professional. He responded by blossoming as a strong hitter, though he also became a defensive liability. He once hit in 27 straight games for the Giants, but also committed 86 errors in just 120 games at the hot corner, still the major league record. His offensive production dropped a bit in 1901 as he was tried at every position except catcher for the cellar-dwelling Giants, including nine games as a pitcher. Before the 1902 season, Hickman jumped to the Boston Americans, but spent less than two months there before he was traded to Cleveland for first baseman Candy LaChance.

It was at Cleveland that Charlie Hickman came into his own, as he established his reputation as a talented hitter and became a favorite of the fans. He had perhaps his finest season at the bat in 1902, leading the American League in hits and total bases and becoming the team's regular first baseman. Though still not sure-handed—he committed 40 errors—his miscues were forgiven because of his hitting. He had a career best .361 average and ranked among the league's leaders in most offensive categories, including home runs (tied for second with 11), RBI (second with 110), and slugging percentage (third at .539). During that season he, along with mates Bill Bradley and Nap Lajoie, became the first American League trio to hit consecutive home runs. The following year, Hickman enjoyed another outstanding season, batting .295 with 12 home runs and 97 RBI (the latter two figures each ranked second in the league).

But fielding woes would always bring Hickman back to earth. There was talk by some that many of shortstop Johnny Gochnauer's staggering 98 errors were thanks to Charlie's poor first base play. Although Hickman fielded decently when installed at second base in 1904, manager Bill Armour continued a running feud with him, finding fault with his fielding, his batting stance, and so on. Hickman claimed he got along with Armour at first, but then became his whipping boy. "Still I persevered," Hick later related, "for the Cleveland fans appeared to appreciate my work. They called me 'Cheerful Hick,' but no one can tell of the misery that I had to put in with this man Armour."

Late in the 1904 season Cleveland sent the popular Hickman off to Detroit for Charlie Carr and Fritz Buelow. After struggling at the plate and in the field there, and again tangling with Armour (now managing the Tigers), he was sold to Washington, where he remained for one complete season and parts of two others. He was the team's leading hitter, but his defensive woes continued. On September 29, 1905, Hickman entered the record books again when he had a five-error game at second base. While playing in the nation's capital he continued his friendship with Roosevelt and often visited the White House. He co-owned and operated a sporting goods store during these years that was frequented by the president's sons, and also attended classes at George Washington University.

Though still an effective hitter who batted .284 with nine home runs for the Senators in 1906, Hickman's inability to play defense limited his value. During spring training in 1907, Hickman suffered a knee injury that would hamper him the rest of the season. On August 1, 1907, he was sold to the White Sox, where the knee problems limited him to pinch-hitting duties. At the end of the 1907 season, Hickman's contract was once again sold, this time back to Cleveland. He managed to hit only .234 in 65 games for the Naps in 1908. His major league career ended when Cleveland sent Hickman to Toledo of the American Association. Overall, Hickman played 1,081 games in the big leagues, batted .295, and appeared at every position except catcher.

Charlie impressed immediately at Toledo as he hit .409 to finish out the 1908 campaign. He still possessed power and thrilled fans by hitting an over-the-fence home run the day Toledo's spacious park, Swayne Field, opened in 1909. He led the American Association in doubles, total bases, and uncharacteristically, outfield assists (35) that year, and in triples the following year. He was playing the best baseball of his career. In spite of hitting .355 in 1911 at age 35, Toledo let him go in mid-season, because, the *Washington Post* reported, "his legs have gone back on him" and he "was unable to cover any territory in the field." He latched on with the Milwaukee Brewers, also of the American Association, for 13 games, before they too let him go, ending his professional playing career after 16 seasons.

Hickman returned to Morgantown and began a new phase of his life, still involved in baseball. He continued his relationship with the Cleveland club, beginning a 14-year (not continuous) scouting career with them in 1912. He also assumed the coaching reins for the University of West Virginia baseball team in 1913. He held that job for five seasons, winning 70 percent of his games and capturing the West Virginia state championship in 1916. On November 1, 1913, Charlie married Pearl Taylor, his mother's first cousin. They had three children, but only Harriet and Charles Jr. survived infancy.

Hickman was elected Recorder of the City of Morgantown. He became mayor in 1918 and served three terms. In 1932, he was elected Sheriff of Monongalia County. He died due to heart-related problems in his home on April 19, 1934, at age 58, and was buried in East Oak Grove Cemetery, in Morgantown.

JOHN R. HUSMAN

CLEVELAND

ADRIAN JOSS
RIGHT-HANDED PITCHER, 1902–1910

For nine seasons Addie Joss was one of the best pitchers in the history of the American League, posting four 20-win seasons, capturing two ERA titles, and tossing two no-hitters (one of them a perfect game) and seven one-hitters. Of Joss's 160 career victories, 45 were shutouts, and his career 1.89 ERA ranks second all-time only to his long-time rival Ed Walsh among players with 1,000 innings pitched. An exceptional control pitcher with a deceptive pitching motion, the right-handed Joss had a corkscrew delivery, turning his back entirely to the batter before coming at him with a sidearm motion that confused most hitters. "Joss not only had great speed and a fast-breaking curve," *Baseball Magazine* observed in 1911, "but [also] a very effective pitching motion, bringing the ball behind him with a complete body swing and having it on the batter almost before the latter got sight of it." After nearly pitching the Naps to their first pennant in 1908, illness and injury limited Addie's endurance during his final two major league seasons, before his life was tragically cut short at the age of 31 by a bacterial infection.

Adrian Joss was born April 12, 1880, in Woodland, Wisconsin, the only child of Jacob and Theresa Joss. Jacob was a native of Switzerland who had emigrated to Wisconsin to take up the cheese-making trade, eventually owning his own factory in Woodland. He died in 1890, apparently of liver disease caused by alcoholism, when Addie was only 10 years old. Theresa was a well-educated woman whose father had ties to politics in Caledonia, Wisconsin. After her husband's death, Theresa opened a millinery shop and sewing school in Juneau, Wisconsin, which provided her family with some financial support.

As he grew, Addie developed into a tall, skinny boy with noticeably long arms. These attributes would one day earn him the nicknames "Human Slat" and "Human Hairpin." It was an ideal physique for a pitcher, but Joss's first ventures in baseball came as a second baseman, on the Juneau high school team. After graduating in 1896, he entered the teaching profession in Horicon, Wisconsin. In the summer he joined the town baseball team as a pitcher, developing the unusual pitching motion that would eventually bring him fame in the major leagues. Despite turning his body toward second base and kicking his leg high into the air, Joss did not fall off the mound in his follow-through, but rather completed his motion upright, ready to field any ball that came his way.

In 1899, Joss joined the Oshkosh, Wisconsin, baseball team after he was offered $10 a week to play for them. There was little interest in the team, however, and repeated financial crises caused the owners to freeze the players' salaries. After the initial Oshkosh team was disbanded, Addie accompanied a second team to Manitowoc, Wisconsin, as the second baseman. Soon after, he joined the premier Manitowoc team as a pitcher, and won four games against only one defeat. At the end of the season, he was offered his first professional contract, by the Toledo Mud Hens of the Inter-State League.

On April 28, 1900, he started Toledo's opening day game, holding on to win his first professional start 16–8. (Among those in attendance was a young woman named Lillian Shinavar; two years later, on October 11, 1902, Addie and Lillian were married in Monroe, Michigan.) Joss went 19–6 in his first season, and the following year won 25 games and struck out 216 batters. It was a performance good enough to merit an invitation to spring training with the Cleveland Bronchos of the American League. At 6′3″ and 185 pounds, the Human Slat impressed Cleveland management with his performance and made the team out of spring training.

Joss burst onto the major league scene with one of

the greatest debuts of any pitcher in history. On April 26, 1902, against the St. Louis Browns, he set down batter after batter, taking a no-hitter into the sixth inning. The Browns' Jesse Burkett led off the sixth with a short bloop fly to right field. Outfielder Zaza Harvey tried to make a sliding catch, but the play was ruled a base hit by home plate umpire Bob Caruthers, sparking a heated protest from Cleveland. At the plate, Joss, who would finish his major league career with a .144 batting average, added what appeared to be a home run, but it was ruled a double by Caruthers—who nevertheless allowed a runner to score from first base. In the end, Joss allowed only the one scratch hit and beat the Browns easily, 3–0. Addie won 17 games during his rookie season, led the league with five shutouts, and finished with a 2.77 ERA. He was subsequently invited to play for the All-Americans, a team made up of American League All-Stars who played a similar team from the National League during a winter tour.

Joss continued to show improvement during the 1903 season, finishing the year with 18 victories and a 2.19 ERA, but he really came into his own in 1904, when he led the league with a 1.59 ERA (although illness limited him to just 24 starts and 14 wins). In 1905, a healthy Joss achieved his first 20-win season, posting a 20–12 ledger with a 2.01 ERA, a performance that earned him a $500 bonus. Joss's stellar work in the 1906 season, in which he went 21–9 with a 1.72 ERA, third best in the league, earned him another bonus. After the 1906 campaign, Joss took an off-season job with the *Toledo News Bee* as the writer of a Sunday sports column. In his column, Addie spoke of serious baseball issues and related humorous stories from his own experiences in the game, and covered the Mud Hens and other local baseball teams. He would become known as an extremely talented and popular sportswriter, especially for his coverage of the World Series. Joss's familiar voice in the column gave him greater fan support during his holdout for a salary increase before the start of the 1907 season. He finally settled for a $4,000 contract.

In 1907 Joss won his first 10 starts in a row. That year he would tie for the American League lead with 27 victories. One of those victories was on September 4, when he threw a one-hitter against the Detroit Tigers. Three weeks later, on September 25, Joss fired another one-hitter, this time against the New York Highlanders. The following day, teammate Heinie Berger followed with his own one-hitter, marking the second time since 1900 that teammates threw back-to-back one-hitters.

On his way to a second ERA title, Joss pitched brilliantly for the Naps in 1908, keeping them in a tight three-way pennant race. He saved his best performance

for October 2, when he squared off against Big Ed Walsh of the Chicago White Sox at Cleveland's League Park. Going into the contest, Chicago trailed the Naps by one game, and Cleveland stood half a game behind the front-running Detroit Tigers. Walsh matched Joss pitch for pitch, striking out 15 Naps while holding the team to only four hits. In the third inning, a passed ball by Chicago catcher Osee Schrecongost allowed Cleveland outfielder Joe Birmingham to score. Joss kept the White Sox in check and had a 1–0 lead and a perfect game as the contest rolled into the ninth frame. Of the tension in the ballpark, one writer said that "a mouse working his way along the grandstand floor would have sounded like a shovel scraping over concrete." After Joss retired the first two batters, pinch hitter John Anderson smashed a would-be double down the line that barely went foul. Anderson then grounded harmlessly to third baseman Bill Bradley, who added to the tension by bobbling the ball and then throwing it low, but first baseman George Stovall dug out the throw to preserve the 1–0 perfect gem. Joss needed only 74 pitches to out-duel Walsh and retire all 27 White Sox batters. It was only the second perfect game in American League history.

Although the win put the Naps two games ahead of Chicago, the Detroit Tigers would prevail over both the Naps and the Sox, capturing the pennant with a win over the Sox on October 6. The Naps finished the season just half a game behind the Tigers, the closest to a World Series that Joss came during his career. Joss finished the season with 24 wins, his last 20-win season, and the eighth-lowest single-season ERA in baseball history, 1.16. He also walked only 30 batters in 325 innings pitched.

Joss spent the 1908–09 off-season hitting the civil engineering books, designing an electric scoreboard that would allow fans to keep track of balls and strikes. Joss successfully marketed the device to Cleveland management, who installed the Joss Indicator on a new,

larger scoreboard at League Park, which also posted the lineups of both teams on either side of the balls and strikes. Unfortunately, Addie struggled with fatigue throughout the season, and he was relegated to the bench for much of September as the Naps finished a disappointing sixth.

Joss seemed to have regained his strength at the beginning of the 1910 season. On April 20, he tossed a no-hitter, once again against the White Sox. The only drama from the White Sox came in the second inning, when shortstop Freddy Parent lightly topped a ball to Cleveland third baseman Bill Bradley. Bradley raced toward the ball, but juggled it and failed to get Parent before he crossed first base. The initial ruling on the play was a base hit, but the official scorer later changed it to an error on Bradley. Luckily for Joss the ruling stood, as he allowed only two walks on his way to throwing his second career no-hitter. He also aided his own cause with a fine defensive effort, fielding 10 balls from the mound flawlessly and earning 10 assists. It was the last great performance of Addie Joss's career. A torn ligament in his right elbow limited Addie to only 13 total appearances in 1910. His final career regular-season appearance came on July 25, pitching five innings against the Athletics before leaving with complications from the elbow injury.

Joss continued to report arm trouble in early 1911, although he expected to be able to pitch by May after some rest. On April 3, however, before an exhibition game in Chattanooga, Tennessee, he fainted on the field while talking to his friend, Chattanooga shortstop Rudy Hulswitt. His condition continued to worsen, and Joss returned to Toledo. His personal physician, Dr. George Chapman, diagnosed an attack of pleurisy. In the early morning hours of April 14, two days after his 31st birthday (which fell on Opening Day), Joss died suddenly of tubercular meningitis. Later that day, devastated teammates spoke highly of Addie: "No better man ever lived than Addie," said George Stovall, and Napoleon Lajoie added, "In Joss's death, baseball loses one of the best pitchers and men that has ever been identified with the game."

Joss's funeral was held in Toledo on April 17, a day when Cleveland had a scheduled game against Detroit. Despite orders from American League president Ban Johnson for the Naps to play the game, all of Joss's Cleveland teammates insisted on attending the funeral. George Stovall, the Naps team captain, declared his team on strike, proclaiming, "I may be captain, but I'm still a ballplayer." Finally Johnson relented, and the game was postponed. Former ballplayer turned evangelist Billy Sunday delivered Addie's eulogy at the funeral, which at the time was the second-largest in Toledo's history. "Joss tried hard to strike out death, and it seemed for a time as though he would win," Sunday proclaimed. "The bases were full. The score was a tie, with two outs. Thousands, yes, millions in a nation's grandstands and bleachers sat breathless watching the conflict. The great twirler stood erect in the box. Death walked to the plate."

Joss was buried at Woodlawn Cemetery in Toledo, Ohio. Two months later, on July 24, a group of all-stars from throughout the American League played the Cleveland Naps in an exhibition game to benefit Joss's widow, Lillian, and their two children. Walter Johnson and Joe Wood pitched for the all-stars against Cleveland's Cy Young. Some of the other stars in the game included Ty Cobb, Sam Crawford, Eddie Collins, and Tris Speaker. Over 15,000 tickets were sold for the game, which saw the all-star team win 5–3, but more importantly, the game raised $12,914 for Joss's family.

In 1978, the Veterans Committee of the Baseball Hall of Fame sidestepped the minimum 10 seasons played rule and elected Joss to the Hall of Fame, 67 years after his untimely death.

ALEX SEMCHUCK

Napoleon Lajoie

CLEVELAND

NAPOLEON LAJOIE
SECOND BASEMAN 1902–1914; MANAGER 1905–1909

The first superstar in American League history, Napoleon Lajoie combined graceful, effortless fielding with powerful, fearsome hitting to become one of the greatest all-around players of the Deadball Era, and one of the best second basemen of all time. At 6′1″ and 200 pounds, Lajoie possessed an unusually large physique for his time, yet when manning the keystone sack he was wonderfully quick on his feet, threw like chain lightning, and went over the ground like a deer. "Lajoie glides toward the ball," noted the *New York Press*, "[and] gathers it in nonchalantly, as if picking fruit." During his 21-year career, Lajoie led the league in putouts five times, assists three times, double plays five times, and fielding percentage four times.

But he was even more memorable in the batter's box, where the right-hander captured four (or five) batting titles, including a modern-era record .426 mark for the Philadelphia Athletics in 1901. He also won the first Triple Crown in American League history, and finished with a lifetime .338 batting average. An expert bunter who was capable of hitting the ball to all fields, Lajoie was nonetheless completely undisciplined at the plate, regularly swinging at pitches down at his ankles or up at his eyebrows, and occasionally thwarting attempts to intentionally walk him by reaching out for those pitches, too. For years, the conventional wisdom among American League pitchers was to try to upset Lajoie's timing with off-speed stuff, but Francis Richter thought this strategy ineffective, noting that no pitch could fool Lajoie for long. "Good Old Ed Delahanty could clout the horsehide some," Hugh Duffy once observed, "but [Lajoie] seemed to be just as powerful, if not more so." Indeed, Lajoie swung so hard and met the ball with such force that on three separate occasions in 1899 he literally managed to tear the cover off the ball.

Napoleon Lajoie (typically pronounced LAJ-way, though Nap himself is supposed to have preferred the French pronunciation, Lah-ZHWA) was born on September 5, 1874, in Woonsocket, Rhode Island, the youngest of eight surviving children of Jean Baptiste and Celina Guertin Lajoie. The Lajoie clan traced its origins to Auxerres, France, though Jean Baptiste was born in Canada, and immigrated with his family to the United States in 1866, initially settling in Rutland, Vermont, before relocating to Woonsocket. During Napoleon's early years, Jean worked as a teamster and a laborer, but his premature death in 1881 forced his children to find employment as soon as they were physically able. After attending school for only eight months, Napoleon was obliged to forsake his formal education in 1885, when he found work as a cardroom sweeper in a local mill.

About the same time, the young lad was seized by the baseball craze sweeping the country. His mother did not approve of his ball playing and so his teammates gave the dark-haired Lajoie the nickname "Sandy" to hide his presence on the diamond. By 1894 Lajoie was clerking for an auctioneer named C. F. Hixon and playing part time with the semipro "Woonsockets." As word of his ability spread, Lajoie discovered that other semipro teams wanted him to play for them in critical games. He obliged them all and his rate of pay ranged from two to five dollars per game, plus round trip carfare. Off the diamond, Nap followed in his father's footsteps and became a teamster. He drove a hack out of the Consolidated Livery Stable, providing him with the nickname, "The Slugging Cabby." In 1896, Lajoie joined the Fall River club in the Class B New England League, which offered him $500 for the five-month season. Lajoie was making $7.50 per week as a cabby and his words of acceptance served as his slogan for his entire career: "I'm out for the stuff."

Lajoie's tenure with Fall River lasted only until August 9, when he and teammate Phil Geier were purchased by the Philadelphia Phillies. With his .429 batting average and .726 slugging percentage, Fall River had no trouble soliciting offers for Lajoie, but Philadelphia was the only franchise that agreed to the asking price of $1,500. During his abbreviated minor league career, Lajoie had played mostly center field, but upon joining the Phillies manager Billy Nash installed the rookie at first base, which had been manned on an emergency basis by Ed Delahanty. This allowed Del to return to his best position, left field. In 1898, Phils manager George Stallings made several sweeping defensive changes. The most important was shifting Lajoie to second base, where he would achieve his enduring fame. Stallings later explained this move by saying, "He'd have made good no matter where I positioned him."

Over his final three seasons with Philadelphia, Lajoie matured into one of the game's best second basemen, using his excellent speed, quick reflexes, and soft hands to adeptly handle all the position's tasks. "He plays so naturally and so easily it looks like lack of effort," Connie Mack would later observe. "Larry's reach is so long and he's fast as lightning, and to throw to at second base he is ideal. All the catchers who've played with him say he is the easiest man to throw to in the game today. High, low, wide—he is sure of everything." Unlike his contemporaries, Lajoie preferred to break in a new fielding mitt each season, and he also parted from accepted practice by cutting the wrist strap off his glove, providing his large hands with added flexibility and control.

At the plate, Lajoie wasted little time demonstrating that his gaudy minor league numbers had been no fluke. From 1896 to 1900, he never batted lower than .324, and led the league in slugging percentage in 1897 and doubles and RBI in 1898. He posted a .378 batting average in 1899, though an injury following a collision with Harry Steinfeldt limited him to just 77 games played. It was the first of several seasons in which Nap would miss significant playing time, though the causes of his absences from the starting lineup rarely owed themselves to typical injuries. In 1900, Lajoie lost five weeks after breaking his hand in a fistfight with teammate Elmer Flick. Two years later, legal squabbles between the American and National Leagues cut into his playing time, and in 1905, Nap's leg nearly had to be amputated after the blue dye in his socks poisoned a spike wound. The leg recovered, but the incident led to a new rule requiring teams to use sanitary white socks.

During his career, Lajoie also had some famous run-ins with umpires. In 1904, he was suspended for throwing chewing tobacco into umpire Frank Dwyer's eye. After one ejection, Lajoie had to be escorted from the park by police after Nap stubbornly refused to leave the bench. And in 1903, Lajoie became so infuriated by an umpire's decision to use a blackened ball that he picked up the sphere and threw it over the grandstand, resulting in a forfeit.

But Lajoie's most famous battle came off the field, when he jumped his contract with the Phillies to join the insurgent American League in 1901. Prior to the 1900 season, Lajoie had been assured by Philadelphia owner John Rogers that he and teammate Ed Delahanty would receive equal pay. After the season began, however, Lajoie discovered that his salary of $2,600 was actually $400 less than Delahanty's pay. As Lajoie later explained, "I saw the checks." Incensed, Lajoie exacted his revenge on Rogers in the offseason, when he jumped to Connie Mack's Philadelphia Athletics of the American League.

When he abandoned the National League in favor of the new organization Lajoie almost single-handedly legitimized the AL's claim to major league status, but Rogers immediately moved to block the deal, suing for the return of his "property." While the case worked its way to the Pennsylvania Supreme Court, Lajoie, a major star at the peak of his powers, capitalized on the golden opportunity of playing in a newly-formed league with a diluted talent pool by putting together one of the most impressive seasons in major league history. Nap punished the American League's overmatched pitchers in 1901, becoming just the third Triple Crown winner in baseball history with a .426 batting average (the highest posted by any player in the twentieth century), 14 home runs, and 125 RBI. Lajoie also led the league in hits (232), doubles (48), runs scored (145), on-base percentage (.463), and slugging percentage (.643). Despite those figures, the Athletics could finish only in fourth place.

Ironically, Connie Mack's team would win the pennant the following year, but they would do so without Lajoie, who moved to the Cleveland franchise after Rogers succeeded in getting an injunction from the Pennsylvania Supreme Court, which prevented Nap from playing ball in the state for any team other than the Phillies. Lajoie was able to circumvent the ruling by signing with Cleveland, and skipping all of the club's games in Philadelphia. (The fact that the A's never had to face the league's best hitter in their home park undoubtedly helped them capture the pennant; indeed, the .339 difference between Philadelphia's home and road winning percentages in 1902 remains the second-highest differential in baseball history.) In the peace agreement brokered between the two leagues following the 1902 season, Rogers dropped his claim on Lajoie, and Nap remained with Cleveland through the 1914 season. During his 13 years with the club, Lajoie becoming such a powerful symbol of the franchise that the press soon took to calling the team the "Naps," thus making Lajoie the only active player in baseball history to have his team named after him.

With his legal status secured, in 1903 and 1904 Lajoie solidified his reputation as the league's best hitter, winning his third and fourth consecutive batting titles. In 1904 he batted .376, led the league in on-base percentage (.413), slugging percentage (.552), hits (208), and RBI (102). Despite that performance, and despite the considerable offensive contributions of teammates Bill Bradley and Elmer Flick, the Naps finished a disappointing fourth, and in September manager Bill Armour tendered his resignation. Following the end of the season, Lajoie formally accepted the position as field manager.

Though he would finish his managerial career with a .550 winning percentage, Lajoie was not a successful manager. When he assumed control of the team in late 1904, Lajoie inherited one of the league's most talented rosters. In addition to himself, the Naps featured several promising players under the age of 30: Bradley, Flick, shortstop Terry Turner, and center fielder Harry Bay. Their pitching rotation was anchored by a trio of young pitchers, none of whom were older than 25: Addie Joss, Earl Moore, who had won 52 games in his first three seasons, and Bob Rhoads, who would post a record of 38–19 for the Naps in 1905–06.

Despite this assortment of talent, under Lajoie's leadership the Naps only twice challenged for the AL pennant, losing out to the White Sox by five games in 1906 and the Detroit Tigers by .004 in 1908. Lajoie blamed himself for the team's second-place finish that year, as he batted just .289 for the season and failed in the clutch in two critical games down the stretch. In fact, there is much evidence to suggest that Lajoie's managerial responsibilities detracted from his on-field performance. After winning four consecutive batting titles from 1901 to 1904, Lajoie put together only one comparable season during his managerial career, posting a .355 batting average in 1906.

As manager, Lajoie was criticized for his rudimentary method of relaying signals to the outfielders. He had a way of wiggling his finger behind his back, as notice to his outfield, when his pitcher was going to throw a fast ball, and wiggling two fingers for a curve. Enemy pitchers in the bullpen often could read Nap's signals, and they were never a mystery to Connie Mack. One contemporary observed of Lajoie, "The great player-artist rather disdained the subtleties of the game and responsibility sat heavily upon him. He failed to lift up lesser players to the batting and fielding heights that he had attained so easily. He knew how to do a thing, but to impart to another how it should be done eluded him."

Midway through the 1909 season, with the team once again languishing in the standings, Lajoie resigned as manager. Free to focus once again exclusively on his on-field performance, Nap batted over .300 every year from 1909 to 1913. From 1910 to 1912, he batted bet-

ter than .360 every season, with his .384 mark in 1910 finishing second, or first, depending on your point of view, in the American League batting race.

In one of the most famous episodes of the Deadball Era, Lajoie and Ty Cobb entered the closing days of the season neck-and-neck for the American League batting crown, with the winner set to receive a brand new Chalmers automobile, one of the finest makes of the day in a time when automobiles were still scarce commodities. On the season's final day, the Naps faced the St. Louis Browns in a doubleheader, with Lajoie, now trailing Cobb, needing a base hit in virtually every at-bat to secure the batting crown. The Browns manager, Jack O'Connor, no fan of the ill-tempered Georgia Peach, ordered rookie third baseman Red Corriden to play deep, well behind the bag throughout both games. Seizing the opportunity, Lajoie dropped seven straight bunts down the third base line for hits, though an eighth bunt was recorded as a sacrifice. His eighth and final hit was a triple belted over the centerfielder's head. O'Connor was fired for his actions, and Lajoie received a congratulatory telegram from eight of Cobb's teammates, but one week later American League president Ban Johnson declared Cobb the batting title winner, by a .000860 margin. (Subsequent research would determine that Cobb had been erroneously credited with two extra hits, and when this clerical error was corrected, Cobb's average dropped to .383, giving Lajoie the higher batting average. Nonetheless, in 1981 Commissioner Bowie Kuhn rejected an appeal to declare Lajoie the true 1910 batting champion.) The Chalmers company reacted to the controversy by giving both players free automobiles, but according to Lajoie's nephew, Nap "didn't want to accept it," though his wife insisted that he do so. "He just thought that he, not Cobb, had won that championship and was angry that Cobb had been ruled the winner."

In 1914, Lajoie struggled to a .258 batting average, as bad eyesight gradually diminished his effectiveness.

Following the 1914 season, Lajoie's contract was purchased by the Philadelphia Athletics, and Nap was reunited with his old friend and manager, Connie Mack. Unfortunately, Nap arrived one year too late to get his first shot at winning a pennant. In 1915 and 1916, Lajoie played out the string as Eddie Collins's replacement at second base, posting batting averages of .280 and .246, respectively, while the A's plummeted into the American League cellar. Following Philadelphia's dismal 36–117 performance in 1916, Lajoie announced his retirement from the majors. On January 15, 1917, he signed as playing manager of the International League's Toronto Maple Leafs. Toronto won the pennant and Lajoie captured the batting title with a resounding .380 mark. The following year he signed as player–manager for Indianapolis of the American Association, batting .282 and leading the Indians to a third-place finish in the war-shortened campaign. One month away from his forty-fourth birthday, Lajoie offered his services to his draft board. They declined with thanks.

Lajoie married the former Myrtle I. Smith, a divorcee, on October 11, 1906. They purchased a small farm of about 20 acres in the Cleveland suburb of South Euclid and it remained their residence until they moved to a smaller home in Mentor, Ohio, in 1939. Long popular in Cleveland, Lajoie was put up as the Republican candidate for Sheriff of Cuyahoga County. Failing election, he was named commissioner of the old Ohio and Pennsylvania League. He also dabbled around in a rubber company, sold truck tires, and finally set up a small brass manufacturing company. These businesses were merely diversions to occupy his time. Lajoie had been careful with his money and he and Myrtle lived a comfortable life.

In 1943, the Lajoies made a permanent move to Florida and finally settled in the Daytona Beach area. Myrtle passed away of cancer in 1954. Nap died on February 7, 1959, of pneumonia. The couple left behind no children.

DAVID JONES AND
STEVE CONSTANTELOS

Geo. T. Stovall

CLEVELAND

GEORGE THOMAS STOVALL
FIRST BASEMAN, 1904–1911; MANAGER, 1911

At one time there was probably no figure more popular in the American League than the outspoken but amicable George Stovall, a gifted fielding first baseman and team leader who would later go on to a stormy managerial career culminating in a prominent role in the establishment of the upstart Federal League. F.C. Lane of *Baseball Magazine* accurately described him: "There is a homely grace in his six feet-one of solid tendon and muscle.... There is an impressive power in his firm, protruding jaw, a seasoned endurance in his entire physical makeup. He has a keen brain, ready wit, a blunt philosophy. But he is no man to be trifled with."

George Thomas Stovall was born on November 23, 1877 (reported in his playing days as 1881), in Leeds, Missouri, a town now part of Kansas City. He grew up on a farm and was brought up by his sister after his American-born Scotch-Irish parents died while he was a youngster. After a public school education, he went to work for his butcher brother and continued to work the family farm. Another brother, Jesse Stovall, would go on to pitch briefly in the American League from 1903 to 1904.

Legends would later tell of Stovall playing baseball with the descendants of Jesse James, and his having pitched and caught for the local Leeds Train Robbers on weekends did nothing to quell the rumors. In 1901 he toured Kansas and Nebraska pitching for the J. J. Foster's company team. That same year he pitched for Seattle of the Northwestern League, and won his first game 6–0. He injured his arm in his second game and was released, never to pitch again.

George returned to the West Coast in 1902, now a first baseman. The lean 6'2", 180-pound Stovall threw and batted right handed, and played for Pendleton of the Inland Empire League, supposedly wearing an Indian blanket for promotion. He then moved on to Portland of the Pacific Northwest League, who released him on the first day of training in 1903. From there he

rapidly played for a succession of four teams, and then barnstormed his way back east with a team called the Mormons. When this pick-up team reached Atlantic, Iowa, they defeated the local team and the Mormons were adopted wholesale by their opponents' manager.

1904 brought Stovall stability and much more. Playing for Burlington of the Iowa State League, Stovall hit .299 and fielded .986 in 47 games. He was made manager in June, and was sold to Cleveland in July for a figure reported between $700 and $1,000. Stovall was proud to debut on July 4, and on October 7 hit his first big league home run—off his brother Jesse, pitching for Detroit in his last game. It was the first time a player had homered off of his brother. George hit .298 for the Naps, playing five positions. After his season ended, he capped off his meteoric year by marrying Burlington's Emma Senn on October 19.

Stovall was an excellent fielding first baseman who sometimes played second and third when the starters were injured. On August 7, 1912, Stovall made seven assists at first base, an AL record that still stands. He hit .265 for his career, but his power and patience at the plate were problematic. Fielding and leadership were his talents. Stovall was also clever, perpetrating six documented hidden-ball tricks.

Stovall played beside Nap Lajoie, the eponymous manager of the team. In later years, Stovall praised Lajoie's hitting, but added, "He wasn't what I would call a good manager. 'Bout all he'd ever say was let's go out and get them so-and-so's today. He knew he could do his share but it didn't help the younger fellows much." Stovall also criticized Nap's lack of on-field managing savvy, including not having any signs worth mentioning. In 1907, on a road trip in Philadelphia, Lajoie dined with a fan and reporter who had no end of managing advice for the Cleveland skipper. Lajoie stayed quiet, and later at the hotel, Stovall (already upset with being juggled in the batting order) confronted Lajoie for not sticking up for his players. Nap fined George $50, and George

CLE.

662

dared him to double it, which Nap promptly did. "This angered Stovall more, and picking up a heavy oak chair, he let fly with it, the chair just grazing Larry's head." Stovall was suspended, but was quickly reinstated. Some were mystified by this, but the placid Lajoie said, "Why not? He's a good player and we need him. That chair episode was just one of those things." An older Stovall related that "it never amounted to as much as they said. Guess we'd be good friends now if we met." In 1908, when Stovall enjoyed his best season with a career-high .292 batting average, Lajoie confided to the *Washington Post* that he would not trade his first baseman for star Hal Chase, a comment the *Post* thought to be a "needless declaration on the part of Napoleon."

Stovall's salary rose steadily from $1,500 to $3,500 a season as the years passed and he developed into a popular team leader. When Joe Jackson joined the team in 1910, Stovall became his roommate, and mentored him about matters on and off the field. Jackson, who had endured an awful time when first called up by Philadelphia two years earlier, joined others in calling the popular Stovall "Brother George."

Cleveland ace Addie Joss passed away right after the start of the 1911 season. Stovall, now team captain, defied Ban Johnson and his manager, Deacon McGuire, who wanted the club to play their scheduled game in Detroit on April 17, the day of Joss's funeral in Toledo. Stovall declared his team on strike, proclaiming, "I may be captain, but I'm still a ballplayer." In the end, Johnson approved their funeral attendance, postponing the game for one day. Naps owner Charles Somers even paid the team's fares to Toledo. It was the first time the ballplayers had budged the Great Ban, and it would not be the last time Stovall would try.

The unsuccessful McGuire resigned after a 6–11 start, and on May 3, Brother George was summoned to replace him. Stovall immediately cancelled morning practices, which he felt took an edge off the team. He gave his players more latitude off the field, figuring out that no one could compel a player to take care of himself if he didn't want to. He was friendly with his men, something he saw as a necessity for a playing manager. In the *Los Angeles Times*, Stovall explained how he set his team up with drinks, so they'd be less inclined to go out behind his back. This was in keeping with his oft-quoted slogan: "Two kegs of beer if we win, boys, and one keg anyway."

All of this led to results on the field, as his inexperienced charges struggled and learned to play together as a unit, free from McGuire's "incessant tinkering." Brother George led his mates from seventh to third place with a record of 80–73, their best showing since the near-miss of 1908. "The team lacked pepper, but Stovall got them all up on their toes, and today they jabber away like a lot of poll parrots," the *Cleveland Plain Dealer* remarked at the end of the season. "They are full of fight, back up each other like champions, and you can look for them to be very much in next year's pennant race."

But 1911 would be Stovall's only year at the Cleveland helm. During the year it was well-known throughout the league that Stovall was only a temporary replacement, as Somers had his sights set on Philadelphia's Harry Davis to manage in 1912. Despite the fans sending a petition to Somers, Stovall was let go. His appreciative parting letter to the fans and his teammates only enhanced his popularity.

Stovall hoped to buy his release outright, possibly with money provided by Cubs owner Charles Murphy, who could use Stovall in case first baseman Frank Chance did not last the season. Somers, on the other hand, wanted Stovall to manage his Toledo American Association club in 1912. Stovall could not buy his outright release, and Somers could not get Stovall through waivers, so the first baseman was traded to St. Louis for pitcher Lefty George, who went 0–5 for the Naps and was dropped after 11 games.

Stovall stabilized an infield that in 1911 had used 10 first basemen. Beleaguered Bobby Wallace, who had administered the team to a 45–107 cellar finish in 1911, had never wanted the job, and after the 1912 Browns started at 12–27, Stovall took the reins on June 2. He was well paid at $6,250 and began shaping the team he envisioned. He liked fast, young players with good arms, and emphasized defense and pitching. He waived ineffective veteran pitchers and by 1913 the whole pitching staff was under thirty years of age.

The 1912 season was not without its controversies. Stovall once again delved into the unprecedented by joining managers Jimmy Callahan and Harry Davis against Frederick Westervelt, an umpire they felt to be incompetent. The three conferred in New York in July, after Stovall had been suspended due to an argument with Westervelt, who had been moved from Chicago to Cleveland games when Ban Johnson had given in to protests earlier in the season. Westervelt, who had been promoted to the majors in 1911, "was not asked to continue" in the majors after the 1912 season. Stovall led the Browns to a seventh-place finish, and there was reason for optimism in "that Siberia of the ball players, St. Louis." Owner Robert Hedges raised his salary to $7,500.

Controversy continued to stalk Brother George during the 1913 season. On May 3, Stovall was ejected from a game for grabbing the cap of umpire Charlie Ferguson and throwing it on the ground. When Stovall took too long retrieving his glove, Ferguson told George to hurry it up. As teammate Jimmy Austin later recalled for Lawrence Ritter's *The Glory of their Times*, "I guess that was the straw that broke the camel's back, because George let fly with a big glob of tobacco juice—p-tooey!—that just spattered all over Ferguson's face and coat and everywhere else. Ugh, it was an awful mess. It was terrible. George always did chew an uncommonly large wad, you know."

Stovall had, as Austin put it, "expectorated himself right out of a job"—but it would take some time. Ban Johnson, trying to preserve his league's reputation for clean baseball, deposed and indefinitely suspended him on May 5. "When the suspension will be lifted, if ever, or whether or not he will ever be allowed to resume his place at the head of the club, is a question I cannot answer now," Johnson told the press. Stovall was contrite, but it did nothing to alter Johnson's course—and Johnson would not meet with him in person. On May 22, though, Stovall was reinstated on condition that he write Ferguson a letter of apology, and was fined a mere $100 by Johnson.

Meanwhile, the Browns had improved but were still mired in or near last place. Up-and-coming Branch Rickey was seen consulting with Hedges. Stovall complained that he had not been given enough control of the club. He was disappointed with what he considered to be Hedges' amateurish approach to finding talent, not letting Stovall get the men he wanted. "I wasn't running

a primary school of baseball in connection with my work as manager of a big league club," said Stovall. Hedges countered that Stovall would not develop the players sent to him, particularly college boys recommended by Rickey. After two months of the cold shoulder from Hedges, Stovall was finally discharged on September 6.

Although relieved of his managing duties, Stovall was still under contract as a player. Told by Hedges that his salary would be forwarded if he returned home, the mistrusting Stovall asked the owner to put this in writing, offending Hedges. Stovall reported every morning, despite new manager Rickey asking him not to. There was some talk that Stovall was courting other players to consider joining him in a new rival circuit, the Federal League.

Hedges refused to release him, and Stovall refused to be sold "like furniture," arguing, "No white man ought to submit to be bartered like a broken-down plow horse." He claimed an unconditional release was his right after 10 years in the AL and two managerial "unfortunate experiences." He was denied by Ban Johnson. As Stovall later explained, "I had contempt for the reserve clause as a barbaric and unjust rule."

Despite his protests, spitting on an umpire, and hurling a chair at his manager, George Stovall was not called "Firebrand" until he became the feared incarnation of the upstart Federal League. The firebrand was "the red symbol of insurrection and anarchy," and the papers of late 1913 and early 1914 were full of rumors of Stovall scouring the country for baseball talent that could be taken from the two established leagues.

CLE.

In October 1913, he participated in the meeting in Indianapolis that organized the FL's run at major league status. Ignoring the reserve clause he so despised, Stovall signed to manage an unspecified club, with a generous contract for $7,000 a season for three years, plus a signing bonus of $5,000 to $10,000 dollars. "No player had yet broken his reserve contract to go with the Federal League. But I argued that somebody had to be the first and it might as well be I," he said. Joe Tinker came along two months later, followed by Mordecai Brown, both at the urging of "The Jesse James of the Federal League," Firebrand Stovall. It was announced that Brother George would be back in his home town, as player–manager of the Kansas City Packers.

It was Stovall and Tinker who landed more than half the FL players for the 1914 season. Though failing to sign big stars, Stovall got a kick out of costing teams money by forcing them to pay players more to stick with the established leagues. He usually went after unsigned and reserve list players, but was also known to loiter around hotels at spring training sites. He especially delighted in aggravating Hedges, Rickey, and Ban Johnson while courting hurler Earl Hamilton, who committed to Stovall, but jumped back to the Browns after they offered him a substantial raise. Stovall commented in his usual homespun way, "I can go out and get these ball players, but I can't chain 'em down."

With the Packers, Stovall was reunited with some former Naps, and played well, tagging seven home runs. The team finished in sixth place, with a 67–84 record, but helped foil the Chicago team's pennant hopes by taking two of four from them at season's end, thus handing the pennant to Indianapolis.

In October 1914, an article by Stovall appeared in *Baseball Magazine* defending the FL. He admitted that three of the eight teams were losing money, including his own, but that the league was here to stay. He defended the league's backers: "The money that stands behind the Federal League is clean money, made by legitimate businessmen, which is more than can be said of a lot of the boodle back of the two other major leagues." That winter Stovall served as the Federal League's recruiting agent on the West Coast, where, according to one newsman, "his presence here is relished by Coast League magnates about as much as a German spy would be in Paris."

Not one to alter his habits, Stovall had the occasional run in with league officials and umpires, but a suspension he earned in July 1915 was lifted a couple of days later as the Packers held a Stovall Day on July 31. After the season Stovall revealed that he had been offered money not to start pitcher Nick Cullop in a season-ending series against St. Louis, which was fighting for the pennant. Stovall started Cullop anyway and he defeated St. Louis, and the Chicago Whales went on to tie the Terriers for the pennant. Again, Stovall's team had played spoiler down the stretch, improving to an 81–72 record and fourth-place finish. The FL dissolved after the 1915 season, and Stovall praised the league's officials as square dealers. Ban Johnson had declared that he would not allow FL players back into the AL, and this was true for many, including Stovall.

After playing and coaching for Roger Bresnahan's Toledo Iron Men of the American Association in 1916, there were rumors Stovall might manage in the majors again. Brother George ended up working out west, though, where he had settled and taken up orange farming. He managed the Vernon Tigers of the Pacific Coast League, starting spring training with a bang by climbing a fence with a ladder to get his men onto the field after a miscommunication with management. "The Human Torch," as he was dubbed by the *Los Angeles Times*, lasted only one season with Vernon, finishing in last place with an 84–128 record.

In 1918 Stovall began swinging a sledgehammer for the L.A. Shipbuilding Company as part of the war effort. He played and managed independent semipro teams in California and Arizona from 1918 to 1921 and did the same for Jacksonville of the Florida State League in 1922. In the 1920s Stovall was featured in popular annual old-timers' games at LA's Wrigley Field. Stovall's Sons of the Revolution played against Cap Dillon's 49ers, the latter team later managed by Mike Donlin and Charlie Deal. Brother Jesse played too, along with many top-notch old-time stars. The games raised money for the Association of Professional Ballplayers of America (APBA), helping injured and indigent players, and took place throughout the 1930s. Stovall also served as president of APBA, stepping down in 1937.

From 1931 to 1932, Stovall managed a well-drawing Houghton Park semipro team, coached the Loyola University team in LA from 1933 to 1934, and then scouted for Pittsburgh from 1935 to 1940. During World War II Stovall returned to the shipyards, working as a foreman throughout the war. Afterwards, he would visit the Pittsburgh spring training camps in San Bernardino to meet up with his old pal Honus Wagner. Even in old age Stovall was still "spry and straight as a poker."

George Stovall died on November 5, 1951, back in Burlington, Iowa, his wife's hometown. His wife, Emma, had died on October 11 the year before.

STEVE CONSTANTELOS

CLEVELAND

TERRENCE LAMONT TURNER
INFIELDER, 1904–1918

Known for his fielding prowess and head-first slides, Terry "Cotton Top" Turner is Cleveland's all-time leader in games played with 1,619. The quintessential utility player, the 5'8", 149-pound Turner was, in the words of sportswriter Gordon Cobbledick, "a little rabbit of a man with the guts of a commando." He was also one of the era's finest practitioners of the inside game; his 264 sacrifices are tied for the second most in franchise history, and his career total of 268 ranks 26th on the all-time list. "Inside work is a big factor in modern baseball," Turner declared in 1906. "You will observe, if you look closely, that winning teams are the ones that have developed this feature of the game. Inside work does not permit individual playing as much as where every man is a unit, but it brings results, and, after all, that is what counts."

Terrence Lamont Turner was born on February 28, 1881, in Sandy Lake, Pennsylvania, the oldest of two children of a blacksmith, Clarence Turner, and his wife, Alta. After completing his schooling, Terry began his professional baseball career at the age of 19 with the Wheeling Stogies of the Inter-State League, where he batted .307 with 21 steals while manning first base. In 1901, Turner joined Ashtabula, Ohio, of the outlaw Oil and Iron League and moved with the rest of the team to Dubois, Pennsylvania, for most of the 1901 season. Terry reportedly drew interest from both the Athletics and the Reds that season, but the Pittsburgh Pirates got there first, purchasing his contract near the end of the 1901 campaign. Appearing in two games for the Pirates, Turner gathered three hits in seven at-bats. His debut performance caught the eye of the press, which remarked that he was "the greatest factor both inside and out in downing the [Cincinnati] Reds," on his first day in the majors.

Nonetheless, at season's end the Pirates released him to Columbus of the American Association. Playing third base for Columbus in 1902 and 1903, Turner batted .295 and .310, respectively, and led the team with 41 stolen bases in 1902. It was also in Columbus that Turner began to utilize his patented head-first slide. In a 1955 *Cleveland Press* article, Cotton noted, "I discovered at Columbus that sliding feet-first wasn't for me. I caught my spikes too often and hurt my ankles. Yes, I suppose head-first was dangerous, too, and I still have scars on my hands where I got stepped on. But for me, it was better."

Late in the 1903 season, Terry was traded to Cleveland for infielder Billy Clingman and pitcher Gus Dorner, but remained with Columbus for the duration of that season. He opened the 1904 season at shortstop for Cleveland, a position that had been a major weakness for the club during its first three seasons in the American League. Over the next four seasons, Turner developed into a respectable hitter by Deadball Era standards, batting .291 with 27 doubles and 85 runs scored in 1906. A .253 lifetime hitter, Turner nonetheless had a knack for breaking up no-hitters, something he did three times in his career. In a May 12, 1910, game against Chief Bender and the Philadelphia Athletics, Turner was the only Cleveland batter to reach base, gathering a walk in the fourth inning to deprive Bender of a perfect game.

Fielding was his specialty, though. At shortstop, the position he played more than any other during his career, he led the league in assists, double plays, and fielding percentage in 1906. After he switched to third base later in his career, Turner led the league in fielding percentage at that position two times. Turner's defensive ability and versatility elicited comparisons with the greatest player at the position in baseball history, Honus Wagner. Just as Tommy Leach called Wagner the best first baseman, second baseman, third baseman, shortstop and outfielder in *The Glory of their Times*, in 1913 Cleveland manager Joe Birmingham called Turner "the most valuable infielder in the American League… as he can play third base, second base, and shortstop equally well." Birmingham continued, "It is only once in a lifetime that you find one of these players who is brilliant wherever you play him....He is too valuable a man to tie at one position when he is so good at several."

F.C. Lane of *Baseball Magazine* also acknowledged Turner's outstanding ability at the three infield positions in a 1913 article about third basemen. Dubbing him "a performer who is superior to the regular incumbent at third and short," Lane added that "Turner, in his prime, was a shortstop who for brilliancy of fielding has never been surpassed." Terry did some filling in for Cleveland's star second baseman Nap Lajoie in 1913, and Lane judged that he "covered second as ably as Lajoie." For his part, Turner thought the most difficult position to field was shortstop, noting, "Third basemen are sometimes applauded for catching line drives hit right at them. The fans seem to think the play good because the ball is hit hard. Liners are the easiest to catch of all batted balls. The meanest kind are pop flies. They twist and are liable to twist out of a fielder's glove. A fielder is generally hooted for muffing a pop fly, when he should be given credit for getting his hands on the ball."

Of course, Turner's arsenal also included speed. His 256 career steals rank him third in Indians history. His aggressive style on the base paths contributed to his propensity for injury, however. Various injuries and illnesses often kept him out of the lineup, including a bout with typhoid fever in 1904 and a serious beaning that took place in 1908. When Ray Chapman was killed by a pitched ball in 1920, several observers compared the incident to Turner's frightening experience 12 years earlier. "I can still remember vividly how I was fascinated by seeing that ball coming towards my head," Turner later told the *Cleveland Press*. "I was paralyzed. I couldn't make a move to get out of the way, though the ball looked as big as a house....The ball crashed into me. It sounded like a hammer striking a bell. Then all went dark." Though Turner recovered from that injury, because of his various ailments he managed to play in 140 or more games only four times during his career.

What Turner lacked in durability, he made up for with longevity. Besides being Cleveland's career leader in games played and ranking third in steals, Turner tied for second in sacrifices (264), third in at-bats (5,787), ninth in hits (1,472) and ninth in triples (77). His 38 sacrifices topped the league in 1914.

Terry's long run in Cleveland officially came to an end when he was given his unconditional release on August 25, 1918. He signed with Cleveland again in 1919, but never got into a game and was released on July 3, 1919. Some two weeks later Connie Mack signed him, but he appeared in only 38 games for the miserable last-place A's. Turner's sub-par performance (.189 batting average with only two steals and seven runs scored) marked the end of his major league career. Sadly, the Tribe's all-time games played leader was not around to taste a World Series triumph just one season later in 1920.

After baseball Turner returned to Cleveland, where he lived with his wife, Jo, and worked as a chief superintendent in the Cleveland Street Department until 1952. He died in Cleveland on July 18, 1960, at the age of 79, after suffering a stroke.

SCOTT TURNER

CLEVELAND

Frederick Peter "Cy" Falkenberg
Right-handed pitcher, 1908–1911, 1913

Cy Falkenberg was perhaps the most unlikely pitching star of the Deadball Era. Nothing special for most of his career, he developed a deadly emery ball at age 32 in 1913, and rocketed to the forefront of major league pitchers. "Falkenberg has upset all possible existing dope, has broken preconceived notions into a million scattered fragments,[and] has set a high-water mark that will stand as long as records stand," F.C. Lane declared during Falkenberg's breakout campaign. Just four years later, however, Falkenberg was out of the majors for good after a dalliance with the ill-fated Federal League. A tall, gawky hurler with a peculiar delivery, Falkenberg's three-year stretch as a dominant pitcher (1912–1914) is often obscured by the fact that one of the three seasons occurred in the Federal League and another in the minors.

Frederick Peter Falkenberg was born in Chicago on December 17, 1879 (although he would later fudge his baseball age by one year, claiming to have been born in 1880). The blue-eyed boy was the oldest of seven children, "all better looking than myself," he later insisted. According to census records, Falkenberg's mother, Agnes, emigrated to the U.S. from Norway at age seven in 1868; his father, Frederick A., did the same at age 20 in 1873. They were married in 1879 and settled in Chicago, where the elder Falkenberg worked as traffic manager for a publishing company.

From 1899 to 1902 young Fred Falkenberg attended the nearby University of Illinois, where he joined fellow future big league stars Jake Stahl and Carl Lundgren on the baseball team. Under the guidance of coach George Huff, later manager of the Boston Americans, the Illini posted a 36–13 overall record during Falkenberg's three years on campus. Falkenberg's dream was to become an engineer and build public works like the Panama Canal (then under construction in Central America), and he

earned his mathematics degree in just three years. But then baseball got in the way.

The Worcester Hustlers in the Eastern League tried to sign Fred's teammate Lundgren, but when Lundgren signed with the Chicago Cubs, Worcester settled for Falkenberg instead. He pitched a shutout in his first professional game on June 7, 1902, and won 18 games over the remainder of Worcester's season. That performance was impressive enough for Falkenberg to begin the 1903 season with the defending National League champion Pittsburgh Pirates, but he was seldom used, posting a mediocre 3.86 ERA in 56 innings. By August, he was back pitching in Worcester. Years later Falkenberg attributed his struggles in Pittsburgh to the fact that he had heretofore skated by on speed alone, but in the majors, his lack of a good breaking pitch was a handicap. He summed up his Pirate experience thusly: "I regretted it, and so far as I know, I'm sure they did also."

Falkenberg pitched for Toronto in 1904 and Harrisburg in 1905, and during the latter year enjoyed a stroke of good fortune when his old college battery mate, Jake Stahl, was named manager of the Washington Senators. Purchased by the Senators, Falkenberg got his second major league opportunity in 1905. He pitched poorly again; the most notable thing he did was give up the first major league home run of 18-year-old Ty Cobb's career, an inside-the-park job at National Park on September 23.

Falkenberg returned to the Senators in 1906, and in a 6–3 win over Chicago on July 18, became the first post-1900 major league pitcher to hit a grand slam. It was the only home run of his career, and a complete accident. With the bases loaded in the sixth inning, Falkenberg lofted a Texas Leaguer that dropped in front of the outfielders and then, to the amazement of all, took a wacky hop and ended up rolling around under the stands down the right-field line. All four runners, including Falkenberg, scored on a hit that barely made it past the infield.

In almost every news item written about Falkenberg, the first thing mentioned was his height. Falkenberg was tall and lanky—at about 6′5″ and 178 pounds (published reports range between 6′4½″ and 6′6″), he was the tallest regular major leaguer of his era. In those pre-Randy Johnson days, however, such a build was actually considered a drawback for a pitcher. "No one could call Falkenberg 'ideal' as to formation," a *Sporting News* scribe observed in 1911. "He is built on bean-pole lines, stands several inches over six feet, and carries just enough flesh to knit his bones together." Considered a physical curiosity, "the human obelisk" even posed for a bare-chested anatomical illustration in the October 1913 issue of *Baseball Magazine*. As recorded by the magazine, Falkenberg's wingspan measured 79 ½ inches, or one inch longer than that of the famously long-armed Walter Johnson. "Falkenberg is not the handsomest man in the world," F.C. Lane wrote. "Neither was Abe Lincoln. But pitchers are not hired on their looks."

In both 1906 and 1907, Falkenberg gave Washington 200-plus innings of league-average starting pitching, posting records of 14–20 and 6–17. But his patron, Stahl, was gone by 1907, and when Falkenberg started off the 1908 season with a 6–2 record, the Senators sold him (along with utility man Dave Altizer) to Cleveland for $5,000. After the season, Falkenberg returned to the nation's capital to marry Edna Russell, a telephone operator he had met there.

Like many pitchers of his day, Fred Falkenberg probably got his nickname by reminding someone, somewhere, of Cy Young. Although it is tempting to speculate that the name dates from Falkenberg's days as Young's teammate in Cleveland (1909–11), the moniker "Cy Falkenberg" appeared in the *Washington Post* as early as 1906. Whatever the case, Falkenberg in Cleveland continued his career as a well-established mediocrity, posting records of 10–9, 14–13, and 8–5 from 1909–1911. After the latter season he came into conflict with new Naps manager Harry Davis, who was unsympathetic to an illness that had limited Falkenberg's time on the mound. In December 1911 Davis dispatched Falkenberg to Toledo, an unofficial Cleveland farm team.

Sometime before 1913, Falkenberg learned the trick pitch that would soon rocket him to unexpected major league success: the emery ball. Until then, Falkenberg's repertoire had consisted of an average fastball, an average curveball, and a seldom-used spitball. The emery ball, meanwhile, was the secret weapon of Yankee hurler Russ Ford. The pitcher kept a small piece of emery board hidden in his glove, and when the occasion called for it, he would use the board to scuff one side of the ball, which caused remarkable dips and dives over the 60 feet the ball traveled toward home plate. Although the emery ball was not technically an illegal pitch, Ford, upon reaching the majors in 1910, tried his best to keep it a secret by disguising it as a spitball. However, the emery ball was soon discovered and employed successfully by a handful of other pitchers, including Falkenberg, who was said to have learned it from Toledo infielder Earle Gardner, an ex-teammate of Ford's. "Russ Ford of the Yankees started it and I improved upon it," Falkenberg was once quoted as saying of the emery ball. "None of us had any qualms of conscience." Presumably working on his new emery ball during his lone season as a Toledo Mud Hen, Falkenberg posted a sparkling 26–8 minor league record in 1912 and was re-purchased by Cleveland before the 1913 season. The stringbean got healthier during his year in the minors, too, gaining about 20 pounds while also giving up smoking.

Then in 1913, at age 32, Falkenberg enjoyed one of the best breakout seasons in the game's history, going 23–10 with a 2.22 ERA after not pitching a single major league game the previous season. Like Houston's Mike Scott nearly 75 years later, the aged Falkenberg's transformation from mediocrity into marvel was due largely to the addition of a single dynamite pitch to his repertoire. "The main thing that makes Falkenberg's record so out of the ordinary is that he was considered a has-been, never very brilliant in his prime," *Baseball Magazine* wrote. Falkenberg "was always ranked as a fair or indifferent workman at his craft."

According to *Baseball Magazine*, Falkenberg's new emery ball made it seem like he "could make a ball almost stop at will in midair about where he wished to," then change directions. Like Ford before him, Falkenberg went to considerable lengths to hide the identity of the pitch, calling it "my fall-away" in interviews.

Falkenberg won these raves by starting the 1913 season with complete game victories in each of his first eight starts—and after a no-decision, he won two more to stretch his record to 10–0. This streak, of course, paled in comparison to the 16-game win streaks turned in by Walter Johnson and Joe Wood the previous year, but was still impressive enough to establish Falkenberg as one of the league's top hurlers. Falkenberg's streak was finally snapped on June 9 by the World Champion Red Sox, who beat him 4–1. Falkenberg slumped in June, going 1–5, but rebounded to post a 6–1 mark in July and ended the season at 23–10. His record was compiled mostly against the league's weak sisters—he went 12–1 combined against the three worst teams in the league, and only 4–6 against the two best. But such details went unnoticed as the Naps rode Falkenberg's right arm to an 11½ game improvement in 1913, staying in pennant contention most of the season after a second-division finish the previous year.

Because of the unusual movement on his emery ball, Falkenberg became known as something of a lefty-killer despite being a right-handed pitcher. In June 1913, Frank Baker declared Falkenberg's "fadeaway" to be superior to Mathewson's. "I would like to see how many hits a team composed entirely of left-handed batters could make against Fred," Baker said. "I'll bet he would come mighty close to pitching a no-hit game." Cy also stood out for his unusual pitching motion. "Players who have batted against Falkenberg have always contended that his delivery is the most peculiar they have ever faced," the *Washington Post*'s Ed Grillo noted in 1908.

During his offseasons, Falkenberg worked 48-hour weeks as a seat upholsterer for the Overland Automobile Co., and was a member of the Machinists' Union, Local No. 68. Falkenberg operated a tufting machine, "a contrivance for making back and seat cushions," he said. "Day by day I thumped and pounded the long curled bale into that machine, getting a great deal more of good, solid exercise for my throwing arm than if I were pitching a game every day." Although someone with a university mathematics degree might reasonably hope to find a better job than manual labor, Falkenberg appears to have found his work rewarding.

In 1913 Falkenberg gave the first hint that he might be interested in baseball labor issues, becoming a director of the Base Ball Players' Fraternity, the nascent forerunner of the players' union. Before the 1913 season he had negotiated a raise to $3,250 per season, after making between $1,800 and $2,800 in every previous year of his career. After his tremendous 1913 success Falkenberg seemed in line for even a bigger raise, but could not reach agreement with Cleveland on a contract. This was good news for proponents of the outlaw Federal League, which, in its bid to become a major league, spent that offseason raiding as many players as it could from American and National League rosters. In January 1914 one of Falkenberg's old teammates, Larry Schlafly, became manager of the Buffalo Feds and visited Cleveland to try to recruit Cy for the new league. Falkenberg was then given a train ticket home to Chicago, where he was wined and dined by Federal League president James Gilmore. Eventually, Falkenberg agreed to a three-year contract worth about $15,000, almost twice what he had been making in Organized Baseball. "All told," he said, "I feel assured

of terminating my baseball career, under circumstances far more profitable to myself than I ever hoped for."

With the Indianapolis Hoosiers, Falkenberg quickly established himself as one of the finest pitchers in the Federal League, going 25–16 with an ERA of 2.22, fourth-best in the league. He also led the fledgling circuit in innings pitched (377⅓), strikeouts (236), and shutouts (9). He also pitched the best game of his career that year, a one-hitter against Buffalo on August 12. Thanks to the stellar performances of Falkenberg and Bennie Kauff, the league's top hitter, the Hoosiers won the inaugural FL pennant by a game and a half over Chicago. Their offer to take on the World Series champion Boston Braves was politely declined.

In 1915, Falkenberg got off to a poor start with the Newark Peppers (as the newly renamed and relocated Indianapolis team was called). That August, with Newark in a tight pennant race, they shipped Falkenberg off to the woeful Brooklyn Tip-Tops in exchange for a younger pitcher, Tom Seaton. The trade backfired in a big way, as Falkenberg threw 48 innings with a 1.50 ERA for Brooklyn the rest of the year, while Seaton posted a 2–6 record for Newark. The Peppers finished in fifth place.

When the Federal League folded after just two seasons, there was still one year remaining on Falkenberg's three-year contract. Federal League magnate Harry Sinclair was still legally obligated to pay, but the record is unclear on whether Falkenberg ever got his money. But that wasn't the worst news for Falkenberg that winter. The emery ball—Falkenberg's bread and butter pitch, and the only reason he was even in the majors—was now banned from the American League. On September 12, 1914, umpire Tommy Connolly had found a piece of emery paper hidden in the glove of Yankees pitcher Ray Keating. Although there was officially no rule against this, Connolly sent the emery paper and a pair of scuffed balls to Ban Johnson for a ruling. Ten days later came the official decree: The emery ball would henceforth be illegal, with violators subject to a $100 fine and 30-day suspension. In effect, it wasn't just the emery ball banned from the American League—Cy Falkenberg was, too. Unable to hook on with a major league team as a result, Falkenberg signed to pitch the 1916 season in the city of his greatest major league success—Indianapolis. Cy posted a 19–14 record for the Indians of the American Association, and led the league with 178 strikeouts.

The next spring, 1917, Falkenberg beat Connie Mack's Athletics 3–1 in a spring exhibition game, renewing hopes that the Cy of 1913 and 1914 had returned. "Mack told newspapermen that Falkenberg never looked better in his life and, even with the Indianapolis team behind him, he could win lots of games in the American League," one newsman reported. Indeed, shortly thereafter, Falkenberg got one last chance in the majors when Mack traded pitcher Jack Nabors to Indianapolis for him. One report from that season noted that Falkenberg "is one pitcher who improved tremendously with age. Formerly erratic, he acquired steadiness and poise through experience and is now a smooth, consistent toiler on the tee."

However, Falkenberg pitched poorly in 15 games with Philadelphia, and on July 6 the Athletics returned him to Indianapolis for "failure to make good." The stint with Mack's men was the last major league action Falkenberg would ever see. He spent two more seasons at the highest levels of the minors—Indianapolis in 1918, Oakland and Seattle in 1919—before calling it a career. During the 1918–19 offseason he also worked in a shipyard in Superior, Wisconsin, in order to help the war effort and, presumably, stay out of the draft.

During his playing career Falkenberg had expressed his desire to someday become a pecan farmer in Florida, but after spending a season in the PCL he had other ideas. Falkenberg instead moved his family to San Francisco, where he turned his concentration to managing a bowling alley. (Even during his magical 1913 season, Cy, who boasted a 200-per-game average, had been quoted as saying, "I like to bowl better than I like to pitch.") In 1934 Falkenberg founded the Diamond Medal Tournament, sponsored by the *San Francisco Chronicle*, which according to his 1961 obituary "has run without a break ever since and has become one of the most popular [bowling competitions] on the West Coast." Falkenberg continued to follow baseball as a fan, but according to one obituary, "Cy often spoke with scorn about the 'coddled, pampered modern-day pitcher.'"

Cy Falkenberg died at age 80 in San Francisco on April 15, 1961; he was survived by Edna, his wife of 52 years, and their children, Frederick A. Falkenberg and Doris Bisler. Falkenberg was interred at Holy Cross Cemetery in Colma, California, where in later years he would be joined by fellow ballplayers Joe DiMaggio, Frank Crosetti, George Kelly, Ping Bodie, and Hank Sauer.

ERIC ENDERS

CLEVELAND

John Gladstone Graney
Left fielder, 1910–1922

Today Jack Graney is best remembered as the man of the firsts. Graney was the first hitter Babe Ruth faced as a pitcher in the major leagues for the Boston Red Sox, one of the first major leaguers to take the field with a number on his uniform, and in 1908 was part of the first All-Star team to tour the Orient. After his career was over, Graney also became the first former player to become a baseball radio broadcaster. Never one to hit for power or for a high average, Graney generated offense by working the count and drawing walks, earning the nickname "Three-and-two Jack" in the process. "I believe the waiting game is the most effective batting system that could possibly be devised," Graney once explained. "The batter can do the pitcher far more damage by waiting him out than he can possibly do by hitting safely. And isn't that what the batter is supposed to do; disrupt the pitching defense in every legitimate way?" Graney's hitting philosophy worked: despite posting a career batting average of just .250, the left-hander registered a .354 on-base percentage, and twice led the league in walks.

John Gladstone Graney was born in St. Thomas, Ontario, on June 10, 1886, the sixth of nine children of James S. Graney and Mary Ann McFeely, who had moved their family to St. Thomas from Buffalo in 1880. Jack's father, a baseball enthusiast who played much amateur ball in his day, supported the family as an operator and later chief train dispatcher on the Canadian Southern Railway. From an early age, Jack displayed an unusual aptitude for sports, starring at both baseball and hockey. As early as 1897, when Graney was just 11 years old, his exploits on the baseball fields of St. Thomas caught the eye of area scouts. Ten years later, Bob Emslie, a Canadian native and National League umpire for 34 years, spotted Jack as a semipro pitcher and recommended him to the Chicago Cubs. In

1907 Jack pitched for Rochester of the Eastern League and Wilkes-Barre of the New York State League, where he won 24 games prior to being sold to the Cleveland Naps at the end of the season.

Blessed with an extraordinary fastball, though little ability to control it, the 5'9", 180-pound left-hander joined the big club at the start of the 1908 season. He appeared in two games, giving up two runs in 3⅓ innings before breaking his finger on a line drive off the bat of future teammate Neal Ball. Sidelined for a month following the injury, Graney was sent to Columbus of the American Association, where he remained until returning to Cleveland in mid-July. This time, Graney did not last long enough with the Naps to appear in any games; he was quickly shipped out to Portland for the remainder of the season. Rumors circulated that Cleveland manager Nap Lajoie didn't like the wild left-hander, who had hit him in the head with a pitch during spring training. Years later, Graney confirmed that he had hit Lajoie during a spring practice, but denied that he was sent back to the minors because of the incident.

Graney joined the Portland Beavers midway through the 1908 season, finishing the season with a 12–13 record, 146 strikeouts, and 111 walks. Though he had a better season the following year for Portland, posting a 17–9 record in 31 games, management decided to make the wild Graney a left fielder. Jack finished the 1909 season with a .252 batting average in 385 at-bats, good enough to earn him a trip to Cleveland's spring training in 1910, where he made the team.

Graney's offensive skills matured slowly. In his rookie season, he managed only a .236 batting average with 37 walks in 116 games. Installed as the club's leadoff hitter, Graney was instructed not to swing until he had two strikes on him. The strategy was successful:

in 1911, Graney's batting average improved to .269, and he drew 66 walks. Though he played in an era when followers of the game exalted high batting average while mostly ignoring a player's ability to get on base through means other than a hit, Graney became an enthusiastic proponent of his style of play. Perhaps because of his own struggles with wildness on the mound, Graney recognized the damage that could be done to a pitcher's arm by working the count. "Not only does waiting a pitcher out impair his confidence and his control, but it also makes him work harder," Graney argued. "A safe hit may be made on the first ball pitched. A pass is much more wearing on the pitcher's arm."

From 1911 to 1919, Graney never batted higher than .269, yet never posted an on-base percentage lower than .335. In 1916, he batted just .241, yet tied for the team lead with five home runs and led the league with 41 doubles, all while drawing 102 walks, second most in the league. In 1917, he batted just .228, yet led the league with 94 walks. Two years later he again led the league in free passes, with 105, despite posting just a .234 average and connecting for only 31 extra-base hits. F.C. Lane, comparing Graney's walk totals to the man who challenged him that year for the league lead in walks, concluded, "could any contrast be clearer than the contrast between the massive, fence-smashing Ruth and the unimpressive, slender, and meagre-hitting Graney? Ruth's passes were gifts. Graney's passes were earned."

In the field, Graney was considered an excellent outfielder, particularly adept at negotiating the tricky sun field at Cleveland's League Park. Charged with patrolling the park's spacious left field, which extended as far as 505 feet just left of center, Graney displayed above-average range and—not surprising for a former pitcher—a strong arm. As he established himself as a mainstay on the Cleveland roster, Graney also became something of a fan favorite in Cleveland, known for his sense of humor and attachment to the franchise. In a 1919 exhibition game against Tulane University, Graney took his position in left field on the back of a horse.

In 1920 the first of two tragedies hit Graney. On August 17, 1920, Graney's roommate and best friend, Ray Chapman, died after being hit in the head the previous day by a Carl Mays pitch. No one was more devastated by Chapman's death than Graney. Upon viewing his friend's body at the hospital, Graney broke down sobbing and had to be forcibly removed from the room. Two days later, Graney fainted during the viewing of Chapman's casket. Graney was so distraught over the loss of his friend that he couldn't make it to the funeral. To the day he died he never forgave Mays for the fatal beaning. In 1962, writer Regis McAuley asked Graney about the incident. The old ballplayer's words were as bitter as they had been more than forty years earlier: "People ask me today if I still feel Mays threw at Chappie. My answer has always been the same—yes, definitely." The second great tragedy in Graney's life occurred more than two decades later, in May 1943, when his only son was killed in an airplane training accident at Fort Bragg, North Carolina.

By the time the Indians appeared in their first World Series in 1920, Graney was only a part-time player, and had just three plate appearances in the Series win. Two years later, the 36-year-old Graney gathered only nine hits in 37 games and finished the season managing the Indians' farm team in Des Moines.

From 1923 to 1927, Jack operated a successful Ford automobile dealership in Cleveland. When Henry Ford changed his design from the Model T to the Model A, the Ford plant closed for a year and Graney, with no cars to sell, moved into investments. But like other Americans he lost everything in the 1929 stock market crash. He went back to selling cars, though he still struggled to make ends meet. Fortunately in 1932 radio station WHK won the broadcasting rights for the Cleveland baseball games and hired Graney as an announcer. Although he had a high-pitched voice, Graney's clear and smooth delivery and sound knowledge of the game made him a popular choice. From 1932 to 1953 he was the voice of Cleveland baseball every year except 1945. "He was a careful reporter and observer," *Cleveland Plain Dealer* reporter Bob Dolgan later remembered. "His voice dripped with sincerity and crackled with vitality. He wasn't bored with baseball, you could tell he loved his job. He made baseball sound like sport."

Jack Graney died of natural causes in a Missouri nursing home on April 20, 1978, at the age of 91, and was buried in Memorial Gardens Cemetery in Bowling Green, Missouri. His wife, Pauline, died five years later. In 1984, Graney was inducted into the Canadian Baseball Hall of Fame.

ADAM ULREY

CLEVELAND

Joseph Jefferson Jackson
Right fielder, 1910–1915

Shoeless Joe Jackson, a country boy from South Carolina, never learned to read or write much ("It don't take school stuff to help a fella play ball," he once said) but is widely hailed as the greatest natural hitter in the history of the game. A left-handed batter and right-handed thrower, Jackson stood 6'1" and weighed 178 well-built pounds. He belted sharp line drives to all corners of the ballpark, and was fast enough to lead the American League in triples three times. He never won a batting title, but his average of .408 in 1911 still stands as a Cleveland team record and a major league rookie record. Unfortunately, after Cleveland traded him to the Chicago White Sox, Jackson's career ended ignominiously due to his involvement in the infamous Black Sox Scandal of 1919. He was expelled from the game in his prime; for that reason, he has never received a plaque in the Baseball Hall of Fame at Cooperstown.

Joseph Jefferson Wofford Jackson was born in rural Pickens County, South Carolina, on July 16, 1888 (or 1889). His father George was a laborer who settled in nearby Greenville soon after Joe's birth and found employment at Brandon Mill, a textile factory that paid $1.25 a day. Joe, the oldest of eight children, began working at the mill at age six or seven. He never attended school, but learned to play baseball. Brandon Mill sponsored a team that faced squads from other mills and factories, and Joe earned a spot in the lineup when he was 13 years old. He soon became renowned throughout the Carolinas as an outfielder, pitcher, and home-run hitter. Joe played for factory teams and semipro clubs until 1908, when Greenville obtained a franchise in the Carolina Association, a new Class D league at the lowest level of organized ball. Jackson signed a contract with the Greenville Spinners for $75 a month.

The strong, agile 19-year-old quickly became the biggest star in the Carolina Association, leading the league with a .346 average, making phenomenal throws and catches in center field, and serving as mop-up pitch-

er. A reporter for the *Greenville News* tagged him with his nickname that season, when Joe played a game in his stocking feet because his new baseball shoes were not yet broken in. For the rest of his life, he was known as Shoeless Joe Jackson. He also gained a wife that year, marrying the 15-year-old Katie Wynn on July 19, 1908.

In August of that year, Philadelphia Athletics manager Connie Mack bought Jackson's contract. Joe made his first major league appearance on August 25, and singled in his first trip to the plate. However, Joe was homesick, and three days later he boarded a train back to Greenville. He returned in early September, but Philadelphia, a city of two million people, frightened the illiterate country boy. He jumped the team once more before the 1908 season ended, finishing his first major league stint with three hits in 23 at-bats.

Jackson bounced between Philadelphia and the minors for the next two years. He won batting titles at Savannah in 1909 and at New Orleans in 1910, but did not hit well in Philadelphia in a 1909 late-season call-up. Joe did not get along with his Philadelphia teammates, many of whom teased him mercilessly about his illiteracy (which he tried to hide) and lack of polish. Connie Mack reluctantly decided that Joe would never succeed in Philadelphia, and traded him to the Cleveland Naps for outfielder Bris Lord and $6,000 in July of 1910. In mid-September, at the conclusion of New Orleans' season, Joe reported to Cleveland.

Cleveland was a smaller city than Philadelphia, and as many of Jackson's new teammates were either southerners or had played in the South, Joe fit in well there. Playing in right and center field, Joe batted .387 in the final month of the 1910 season and claimed a permanent place in the Cleveland lineup. In 1911 he made a major leap to stardom, battering American League pitching for 233 hits, 45 doubles, 19 triples, and a .408 batting average. He did not win the batting title, as Detroit's Ty Cobb batted .420, but set Cleveland team records for hits, average, and outfield assists (32) that stand to this day. His torrid hitting helped lift the Naps to a third-place finish.

Jackson swung the bat harder than most of his contemporaries, and players swore that his line drives sounded different than anyone else's. Many other players held their hands apart on the bat and punched at the ball, but Joe put his hands together near the bottom of the handle and took a full swing. "I used to draw a line three inches from the plate every time I came to bat," said Jackson many years later. "I drew a right angle line at the end of it, right next to the catcher, and put my left foot on it exactly three inches from home plate." He stood in the box, feet close together, then took one long step into the pitch and ripped at it with his left-handed swing. "I copied my swing after Joe Jackson's," said Babe Ruth to Grantland Rice in 1919. "His is the perfectest."

Though the Naps fell from third place to sixth in 1912, Jackson batted .395, with 121 runs scored, 226 hits, and 30 outfield assists. He also set a new American League record with 26 triples, a mark that was tied by Sam Crawford in 1914 but has never been surpassed. However, Joe once again finished second in the batting race to Cobb, who batted .409 for the Tigers. "What a hell of a league this is," wailed Jackson to a reporter. "I hit .387, .408, and .395 the last three years and I ain't won nothing yet!"

Jackson displayed his power on June 4, 1913, when he belted a fastball from the Yankees' Russ Ford; the hit bounced off the roof of the right-field grandstand at the Polo Grounds and into the street beyond. The newspapers claimed that the blast traveled more than 500 feet. Jackson's .373 average that year trailed Cobb once again, but he led the league in hits with 197 and doubles with 39, finishing second in the Chalmers Award balloting.

Joe turned down offers from the new Federal League in early 1914, though two Cleveland pitchers joined the new circuit and left the Naps short-handed on the mound. Federal League raids and the sudden decline of Lajoie caused the Naps to drop from contention, and injuries to Jackson and shortstop Ray Chapman doomed them to last place for the first time in their history. Forced to miss 35 games with a broken leg, Joe's average dipped to .338 with only 61 runs scored and 53 runs batted in, and he posted new career lows in the speed-dependent categories of triples and stolen bases.

Controversy swirled around Jackson during the 1915 season. He had spent the winter months headlining a vaudeville show that drew curious crowds throughout the South. Joe enjoyed the theatrical life so much that he refused to report for spring training, threatening to quit baseball and begin a new career on the stage. Katie Jackson reacted poorly to that idea, and filed for divorce that March (though she and Joe soon reconciled). In May, team owner Charles Somers ordered manager Joe Birmingham to move Jackson to first base to make room for rookie Elmer Smith in the outfield. Joe played 30 games at first, but the experiment ended when Joe left the lineup with a sore arm. Somers became incensed when Birmingham blamed the position switch for Jackson's injury, and the team owner soon fired Birmingham and appointed coach Lee Fohl to succeed him.

In 1915, Somers, teetering on the edge of bankruptcy, decided that he could not afford to keep his two best players, Jackson and Chapman. He needed to trade one and rebuild the ballclub (which was renamed "Indians" after the team sold Lajoie to Philadelphia that spring) around the other. Somers' mind was made up when the newspapers reported that the Federal League had offered Jackson a multi-year contract at a salary of $10,000 per year. Somers feared that Jackson would bolt for the new circuit, leaving the Indians with nothing in exchange, so the Cleveland owner solicited offers for his cleanup hitter.

Jackson, who at the time was in the second season of a three-year contract for $6,000 per annum, was not opposed to a trade. "I think I am in a rut here in Cleveland," Jackson told local sportswriter Henry Edwards, "and would play better somewhere else." Indeed, Jackson's batting average had now declined for four consecutive years. The Washington Senators offered a package of players for Jackson, but Somers rejected the bid to await a better one, which soon came from the Chicago White Sox. Owner Charles Comiskey coveted Jackson, and sent his secretary, Harry Grabiner, to Cleveland with a blank check. "Go to Cleveland," ordered Comiskey, "watch the bidding for Jackson, [and] raise the highest one made by any club until they all drop out." On August 20, 1915, Grabiner and Somers reached an agreement. Somers signed Joe to a three-year contract extension at his previous salary, then sent him to Chicago for $31,500 in cash and three players (outfielders Bobby Roth and Larry Chappell and pitcher Ed Klepfer) who collectively cost the White Sox $34,000 to acquire. In terms of the total value of cash and players, this $65,500 transaction was the most expensive deal ever made in baseball up to that time.

Jackson joined a contending team, one that featured four future Hall of Famers in second baseman Eddie Collins, catcher Ray Schalk, and pitchers Red Faber and Ed Walsh. He hit poorly (for him) in the last six weeks of the 1915 season, and some observers believed that Joe's career was on the downslide. However, he rebounded

in 1916, batting .341 with a league-leading 21 triples as the White Sox challenged Boston for the league lead. Chicago finished second that season, but roared to the pennant in 1917 despite a subpar performance by Jackson, who was hobbled all year long after he sprained an ankle in spring training. Joe's average dipped to .278 in early September, but he finished with a flurry of hits that lifted his final mark to .301. During the World Series, New York Giants manager John McGraw used left-handed starting pitchers in four of the six games in a bid to neutralize the hitting of Collins and Jackson, but Joe batted .304 and saved the first game with a circus catch in left field. Red Faber won three decisions as the White Sox defeated the Giants, four games to two, for their second World Series championship.

The White Sox were rocked by the entry of the United States into World War One. Several Chicago players enlisted in the military, while others were drafted in the early months of 1918. Joe, as a married man, was granted a deferment by his hometown draft board in Greenville, South Carolina, but after Jackson played 17 games with the White Sox the board reversed its decision and ordered him to report for induction. Instead, Jackson found employment at a Delaware shipyard, where he helped build battleships and played ball in a hastily assembled factory circuit, the Bethlehem Steel League. Jackson was the first prominent player to avoid the draft by opting for war work, and was severely criticized in the sporting press, especially in Chicago. He won the factory league batting title with a .371 average, but the controversy permanently damaged his relationships with the local sportswriters.

At war's end, Jackson signed a new one-year contract for $6,000 (the same salary he had been receiving since 1914) and returned to the White Sox. He was healthy again, and led the club in batting as the White Sox grabbed first place and held it for most of the 1919 season. Joe finished fourth in the league in batting with a .351 mark, his best average since 1913, with 202 hits and 96 runs batted in. Faber, Chicago's leading pitcher, was sidelined late in the season with a sore arm, but Eddie Cicotte (29–7) and Lefty Williams (23–11) picked up the slack and pitched the White Sox into a comfortable lead in the standings. On September 24, Jackson drove home the winning run in the pennant-clinching game against the St. Louis Browns.

The White Sox were considered the most talented team in baseball, but they were also the unhappiest. Charles Comiskey was a tough negotiator, and some of the players grew embittered by their low salaries and Comiskey's take-it-or-leave-it approach. First baseman Chick Gandil, the leader of this resentful

group, concocted a plan to fix the upcoming World Series against the Cincinnati Reds. Jackson, according to his own later admissions, agreed to help Gandil and several other White Sox lose the Series in exchange for $20,000, an amount more than three times his annual salary. Jackson, who ultimately received only $5,000, batted .375 against the Reds but failed to drive in a run in the first five games, four of which the White Sox lost (it was a best-of-nine Series that year). Chicago won the sixth and seventh games, but fell behind quickly in the eighth contest. Jackson belted a homer, the only one of the Series, and drove in three runs in Game Eight, but his production came too late. Cincinnati defeated the favored White Sox by a 10–5 score and won its first World Series title. Jackson tied a record with his 12 hits in the Series, but eight of the 12 came during the four games the White Sox tried to win. In the four games Chicago threw, Jackson went 4-for-16.

Gandil, who reportedly pocketed $35,000 for his involvement in the crooked World Series, did not return to the White Sox in 1920. However, Jackson signed a three-year deal for $8,000 per annum and rejoined the team, despite the cloud of suspicion that hovered over him and several of his teammates. Jackson gave one of his finest performances in 1920, with a .382 average, a career-best 121 runs batted in, and a league-leading 20 triples. However, his season ended abruptly on the morning of September 28 when newspapers published allegations by gambler Billy Maharg claiming that eight members of the White Sox had helped Maharg and other gamblers fix the World Series. Comiskey immediately suspended Jackson and the six other accused players who were still with the team. Eddie Cicotte and Jackson both later appeared before a Cook County grand jury investigating the matter and confessed their involvement. Despite being acquitted by a trial jury, all eight accused players, including the retired Gandil, were eventually expelled from baseball for life by new Commissioner Kenesaw Mountain Landis. The scandal brought a sad and untimely end to Joe Jackson's brilliant baseball career.

Jackson, whose lifetime batting average of .356 is the third-highest in the game's history, played semipro and "unorganized" ball, mostly in the South, for many years thereafter. He gave a few newspaper interviews in which he made his case for reinstatement, but mostly stayed out of the public eye during the last three decades of his life. He eventually moved back to his old neighborhood in Greenville, near the Brandon Mill textile factory, where he operated a restaurant and a liquor store until his death on December 5, 1951, at the age of 63.

DAVID FLEITZ

CLEVELAND

SYLVEANUS AUGUSTUS GREGG
LEFT-HANDED PITCHER, 1911–1914

At 6'2" and 180 pounds, Vean Gregg was a lanky, loose-jointed southpaw who had a world of confidence, a wicked curve ball, and a roller coaster career hampered by arm injuries. As a 26-year old rookie for the 1911 Cleveland Naps, Gregg was only three years removed from pitching in the deepest bush of the remote Pacific Northwest when he won 23 games and led the American League with a 1.80 ERA. Both Ty Cobb and Eddie Collins called him the best left-hander in the league, and Hall of Fame umpire Billy Evans said Gregg was "one of the greatest southpaws I ever called balls and strikes for." The only twentieth century pitcher to win at least 20 games in his first three years in the major leagues, Gregg is Cleveland's career won-loss percentage leader. Traded by the Naps in 1914 to the Boston Red Sox, where he floundered and was eventually demoted to the minors, Gregg retired after pitching for the Philadelphia Athletics in 1918. Out of the game for three years, he staged a comeback, and after a six-year absence made a miraculous return to the American League at the age of 40. A legendary minor league pitcher, Gregg won 224 games in 15 seasons of organized professional baseball.

Sylveanus Augustus Gregg was born on April 13, 1885, near the town of Chehalis in Washington Territory, the third of nine children born to Charles Carroll and Mary Adelia Gregg. Charles Gregg pioneered west in 1876 from his native Pennsylvania to Chehalis, a small town south of Olympia near Mount Rainier. There he met and married Chehalis native Mary Phillips in 1880. The Greggs were farmers, although Charles supplemented his income by engaging in plastering jobs. In 1896, the Greggs moved their farming and plastering operations first to Lewiston, Idaho, and then eight months later across the Snake River to Clarkston, Washington. By the time Charles died in 1913, his Clarkston cherry orchard was one of the largest in the Lewis-Clark valley.

Though Vean attained a bookkeeping diploma from the Clarkston Commercial School in January 1904, he instead chose to follow in his father's footsteps and make his living as a plasterer. He later credited years of "trowel wielding" for developing the strong hands that snapped-off his sharp-breaking curve ball.

Gregg initially made a name for himself as a pitcher by winning amateur and semipro games in the Palouse region of eastern Washington. By the time he was 23 years old, he was a sandlot star, a hired gun pitching for numerous town, semipro and college teams. (He remains the only major leaguer to pitch for South Dakota State University.) An obvious candidate for organized professional baseball, Gregg delayed pursuing it because he felt he could earn more money plastering and pitching for $25 a game on weekends. "I did not go into professional baseball any sooner because I could make more money outside than I could inside," Gregg later explained. "In my semipro days I played baseball all over Washington, Montana and Idaho. On these barnstorming tours a player can often make more money than he could as a member of a regular league."

In March 1908, Gregg relented and attended a tryout with the Spokane Indians Northwestern League team. Impressing the Indians' management, Gregg apparently did not care for the team's offer. After pitching a few early season games for an industrial league team in Spokane, he finally made his organized professional baseball debut in the short-lived Class D Inland Empire League in June. Pitching for the Baker City (Oregon) Nuggets, Gregg won seven of eight games, dominating a circuit that included future major leaguers Jack Fournier, Pete Standridge, Les "Tug" Wilson, and Tracy Baker.

In 1909, Spokane manager Bob Brown was able to sign Gregg to a $185 a month contract. In a season where the Spokane team won 100 games and finished 34 games over .500, Gregg's won-loss record was a mysterious 6–13. He had a knack for losing close contests, but mainly was ineffective due to arm problems suffered from "practicing too much." However, after watching two of Gregg's better games, Cleveland scout Jim "Deacon"

McGuire, outbidding Pittsburgh and Detroit, bought Gregg from Spokane for $4,500 and two players. It was reported that this was the largest amount ever paid for a player from the West Coast. At the time his contract was purchased on July 8, 1909, Gregg's record was just 3–6 but he had struck out 82 batters over his past eight games.

Seeming a bit indignant and unappreciative of an opportunity, Gregg refused to sign a $250 a month contract offered by Cleveland for 1910. Sold on option to Portland, Gregg had a breakout, historic season. He won 32 games, including a record 14 shutouts, struck out 379 batters in 387 innings, and hurled four one-hitters and a no-hitter. His best game came on August 16 against Portland's main pennant rival, the Oakland Oaks, when Gregg struck out 16 batters in a 12-inning, one-hit shutout. In the no-hitter at Portland's Vaughn Street Ballpark on September 2, Gregg won 2–0 and struck out 14 Los Angeles Angels, including eight men in a row, only one of which was even able to foul a pitch. Behind the strong arm of Gregg, the Beavers won the PCL championship. Years later, whenever old West Coast sportswriters or ballplayers were asked to pick their all-time PCL teams, inevitably they would include Vean Gregg based upon his dominating 1910 season. Even the local census taker was impressed; that year he listed Gregg's occupation as "star pitcher."

In 1911, Gregg joined a "disorganized" Cleveland team that included a very old Cy Young, an aging but still productive Napoleon Lajoie, and a 21-year-old Joe Jackson, who hit an astounding .408 that year. Finishing under .500 and in the second division the year before, the Naps lost revered right-hander Addie Joss when he took ill and died on April 14. However, the team overcame that setback and improved under interim manager George Stovall, finishing the season with a winning record and in third place.

One day shy of his 26th birthday, Gregg came out of the bullpen and made his major league debut on April 12, 1911, at St. Louis, giving up three runs in four relief innings while also hitting a double. After striking out Detroit's Sam Crawford twice in a second relief appearance six days later, Gregg moved into the starting rotation and won his first start, 5–2, against Chicago. By mid-July, he was the talk of the American League. When he beat Philadelphia on July 27, he won his tenth consecutive game and ran his record to 18–3. After winning a July game against New York, Hal Chase called Gregg "the leading pitcher of the league, and in my opinion, the most marvelous southpaw I have ever looked at."

Gregg's pitching motion was described as "a free and easy delivery, and his wind-up is a graceful sweep above the head that bothers the batters not a little." In addition to throwing overhand, he would mix-in "an under-hand toss and cross-fire for variety." While his fastball was described as "good," he was known for his curveball, a pitch that "drops between three and four feet in a space of eight or 10 feet, possibly less." Gregg had such good control of his curveball that he would not hesitate to throw it with the sacks loaded and a full count on the batter.

Whether it was the strain of throwing too many curveballs, or "practicing too much," or throwing too many innings for Portland, Gregg experienced annual, recurring arm pain. He would have periods where the arm "never felt better," but would also suffer through entire seasons where he was a shadow of his former self. With a good arm, he was very, very good. With a bad arm, he sat on the bench and lost opportunities.

Gregg's arm was sore the latter part of his rookie season, and after beating Chicago 9–2 on September 4 he did not pitch again. He went home to Clarkston in early October, missing the Naps post-season series with Cincinnati. In addition to leading the league in ERA, Gregg also led the circuit in fewest hits per nine innings. He was especially adept at beating Chicago, besting the White Sox seven times without a loss during the 1911 campaign, including three wins where he matched up against Sox ace Ed Walsh. Named in *The Sporting News* as a member of the "all-American League" team, Gregg received a $500 bonus from the Naps, bringing his total 1911 salary to $2,600. "Unless something unexpected happens," the *Chicago Tribune* wrote, "he promises to take a place among the great left-handers of baseball history."

After much off-season dickering, Gregg finally agreed to a 1912 contract calling for $3,500, plus a $1,500 bonus should he win 25 games. With sporadic arm soreness and visits to the noted chiropractor Bonesetter Reese, Gregg only managed to win 20 games. While Cleveland retrograded to a sub-.500 fifth place team in 1912, Gregg continued to impress, even with a sore arm. Naps manager Harry Davis, who tired of a bickering, faction-torn team and resigned a month before the end of season, claimed, "That fellow Gregg is an exact duplicate of Waddell when the Rube was at his best."

Gregg had his last outstanding season in the major leagues in 1913. He started the season underweight, the result of contracting an illness during spring training, but by June he had regained his strength and ran off 32 consecutive scoreless innings, beating Boston, Philadelphia, Washington and Detroit during the streak.

When Gregg beat the league-leading A's and Chief Bender on August 17 in front of the largest crowd in League Park history, the Naps were in second place, only 5½ games back of Philadelphia. However, arm soreness again crept its way into Gregg's season. He struck out Ty Cobb three times on September 4, only to lose when Cobb drove in Sam Crawford with the game winner in the twelfth inning. With his arm growing lamer as the season entered its final stages, Gregg became a 20-game winner for the third time on October 1, beating the Tigers 8–1. But it was too little, too late, and the Naps ultimately faded to a third-place finish under new manager Joe Birmingham.

That fall, in a post-season series with Pittsburgh, Gregg's arm came back to life. He beat the Pirates in the second game, 2–1, in 11 innings, striking out nine. Then, on October 13 at Forbes Field, he may have pitched the best game of his career. In a pitcher's duel with Claude Hendrix that went 13 innings and tied the best-of-seven series at three games apiece, Gregg scattered five singles, struck out the unheard of total of 19, including Honus Wagner twice, and doubled and scored the game's only run. Cleveland manager Birmingham and former manager Lajoie called it the greatest game a Cleveland pitcher had ever thrown, including Joss's perfect game and Bob Rhoads's no-hitter. Home plate umpire Bob Emslie said, "I have seen all of the great ones; Rusie,

Radbourne, Mathewson; but I am confident that I never saw any pitcher show the stuff that Gregg had." Pirates first baseman Dots Miller said, "I can't understand how anyone ever hits that fellow."

In the spring of 1914, the Federal League war wreaked havoc on the diminishing finances of Cleveland owner Charles Somers. Losing ace right-hander Cy Falkenberg to the Feds, Somers didn't want to lose Gregg, too, and signed him to a reported three-year, $8,000 a year contract in March. When Gregg's balky left arm reared its head and his disposition turned surly playing for a poor team, Somers decided to reduce his risk and on July 28 traded Gregg to the Boston Red Sox for three players. On a last-place team which had won only 30 of 91 games, the sore-armed Gregg had still managed a 9–3 record, ranking fourth in the American League.

Gregg, while well paid, spent the next 2½ seasons dealing with his sore arm and stewing on the Red Sox bench. He won a total of nine games for Boston during that time and had become such an afterthought that his teammates voted him only a three-quarters share of the player winnings from the 1915 World Series. In 1917, he was optioned to Providence and had one of the finest seasons in International League history when he won 21 games and led the league in ERA and strikeouts.

In one of Connie Mack's infamous sell-offs, Gregg,

who had been brought back to Boston after the 1917 season, was traded with two players and $60,000 cash to the Philadelphia A's for Joe Bush, Wally Schang and Amos Strunk. Making his first comeback to the majors, Gregg suffered along with a poor A's team in 1918, posting a 9–14 record. When the season was cut short by the World War I work-or-fight order, Gregg, who was too old to serve, went to the Alberta, Canada, ranch he had purchased in 1912 and dropped out of the game for three years.

When crop prices hit rock bottom in 1921, Gregg abandoned the farm and decided to get back into baseball, returning to the league where he never failed. Pitching for the Seattle Indians, he solidified his esteemed standing in Pacific Coast League history when he won 19 games in 1922, led the league in ERA in 1923, and won 25 games and led Seattle to its first-ever PCL championship in 1924. Pitching as he had for Cleveland over 10 years earlier, the 39-year-old Gregg became the object of a bidding war. Clark Griffith won the war, paying $10,000 and giving three players to Seattle. In a repeat performance from his halcyon days with Cleveland, Gregg was a hold-out in the spring of 1925.

Gregg was described as "attempting an experiment that is absolutely original. No other hurler ever attempted a major league comeback—his second at that—at such an advanced age." Working mostly out of the bullpen for the Senators in 1925, Gregg pitched in 26 games for the repeat pennant-winners, winning two, losing two, and saving two games. While he performed admirably in the role he was assigned, Gregg was optioned to the New Orleans Pelicans of the Southern Association before the end of the season, and did not participate in the 1925 World Series against Pittsburgh. In nine games at New Orleans, Gregg won three and lost three.

Traded to Birmingham for the 1926 season, Gregg chose to retire rather than play for the Barons. Except for a brief comeback in the spring of 1927 with the Sacramento Senators of the PCL, the remainder of his pitching career, which lasted until 1931, took place in his home state of Washington in the highly competitive semipro Timber League. When he wasn't dazzling the fans of the Timber League towns with his famous curveball, he was exploring the great Pacific Northwest outdoors where he was known as an expert hunter and fisherman. "I am especially interested in hunting and spend a part of each year looking for game," he said. "It is a great sport. There is none like it, not even baseball." After his first wife divorced him in 1926, Gregg remarried and raised a family in Hoquiam, Washington, where he owned and operated "The Home Plate" for 37 years, a multi-purpose establishment that featured sporting goods, cigars and a lunch counter.

Suffering from prostate cancer, Gregg died at the age of 79 on July 29, 1964, in a convalescent home in Aberdeen, Washington. He is a member of the Pacific Coast League Hall of Fame, the Portland Beavers Hall of Fame, the Washington State Sports Hall of Fame, the Inland Empire (eastern Washington) Sports Hall of Fame, the Northwest Baseball Old-timers Association Hall of Fame, and in 1969 was voted by the Cleveland fans as the greatest left-handed pitcher in Indians history.

ERIC SALLEE

CLE.

CLEVELAND

STEPHEN FRANCIS O'NEILL
CATCHER, 1911–1923; MANAGER, 1935–1937

With a flattened nose and the grim jaw of a heavyweight boxer, Steve O'Neill looked like he was born to be a catcher, and for much of his 17-year career he was arguably the best all-around backstop in the game. An extremely smart catcher, O'Neill did all the things a good catcher is supposed to do, and he did them better than almost anyone else. His legendary throwing arm stymied would-be base stealers, his agility behind the plate made him one of the game's best at blocking pitches in the dirt, and he was universally regarded as a great pitch-caller. "He was one of the few who had the guts to call for a curve ball with the tying or winning run on third base," teammate George Uhle said. "'Don't worry bout throwing it in the dirt,' he'd say. 'I won't let it get by me.' And he wouldn't." After spending several years in the majors as the prototypical great-defense, no-offense catcher, by the end of the era O'Neill had also matured into a fine hitter.

Stephen Francis O'Neill was born on July 6, 1891, the tenth of thirteen children of Mike and Mary O'Neill, and the fifth of the clan born in America. The first five were born in Ireland; the rest, including himself, in the coal mining town of Minooka, Pennsylvania, located three miles southwest of downtown Scranton. Like most children who grew up in mining towns around the turn of the century, Steve started working in the mines after his tenth birthday, separating slate and other refuse from the anthracite coal, receiving a few pennies a day for his troubles.

As a youngster, Steve could box and wrestle, and he admired athletes of any description, but baseball was the only sport he ever really cared about. As a boy he played it from snow season to snow season. Steve had three other brothers that carved out small major league baseball careers. In fact his two eldest brothers, Mike and Jack, became one of the first brother batteries in major league history. Mike pitched for the Cardinals for four years, posting a 32–44 record with a 2.73 ERA. Jack was a catcher for five years with the Cardinals, Cubs, and Beaneaters. Steve's younger brother Jim played just two years with the Senators as a shortstop before injuries cut his career short. The oldest brother, Pat, might have made it five O'Neills in the majors, but he hurt his hand in a mining accident.

After years playing for the semipro Minooka Blues, Steve O'Neill received his first professional contract in 1910, when the Elmira Colonels, then managed by his older brother Mike, offered him a contract. Actually, Mike didn't think much of his little brother as a baseball player, but he needed a second-string catcher and figured Steve would fit the bill.

Steve received little playing time until an injury to the starting catcher opened the door. He batted only .200, but handled himself behind the plate as though he was born there, and attracted the attention of a friend of Connie Mack's, who talked so much about the youngster that Mack signed him. Steve reported to the Athletics at spring training in 1911 with a beat-up catcher's mitt and spiked shoes with holes in them. The first thing Mack did was send him to a sporting goods store to get new equipment. Mack said, "If you want to play big league baseball you must have big league tools."

Prior to the start of the 1911 season, Mack sent O'Neill to Worcester of the New England League, where he played for Jesse Burkett, who owned and managed the team. He caught all but a few games, again handled himself like a pro, and won the confidence of the whole pitching staff. Just before the end of the season Mack got his first baseman, Harry Davis, a job as manager of the Cleveland Naps. Davis knew that Mack had Wally Schang available in the minors and that O'Neill was expendable. So as a favor to Davis, Mack sold O'Neill to Cleveland for $3,000.

682

Cleveland is where Steve would make his home for the next 12 years, though he would not become the team's full-time catcher until 1915, at which point he began a string of nine consecutive seasons catching 100 or more games. His defense was so outstanding that it offset several years of anemic hitting. In 1917, for instance, the right-handed O'Neill batted only .184, yet caught 127 games. Despite his struggles at the plate, nobody ever thought to relieve him of his job because of his poor hitting. "When you have a catcher like Steve O'Neill," one of his managers said, "you don't care whether he hits or not." But that all changed in 1919 with the appointment of Tris Speaker as his manager. Speaker agreed that Steve was one of the best catchers in the business, but saw no reason why he shouldn't be a good hitter as well. "Nobody with your guts and determination should be such an easy mark at the plate," Speaker told O'Neill. "Instead of floundering around .240 you should be a .300 hitter every year." "That would suit me fine," Steve said. "Only how do I do it?" "Well," said Speaker, "in the first place go up there figuring you'll get a hit, not that you won't. In the second, try to outthink the pitcher. And in the third, stop swinging at bad pitches."

The advice paid off, as O'Neill's walk totals began to climb while his strikeout rate declined. In 1919, O'Neill batted .289 in 125 games, knocked in 46 runs and pasted 35 doubles, fourth best in the league. From 1920 to 1922, he batted over .310 every year, and ranked in the top 10 in on-base percentage each season. During the Indians championship 1920 campaign, O'Neill was behind the plate for 100 straight games, and played every inning of 148 of the Indians' 154 games, yet still finished the year with a .321 average and .408 on-base percentage. O'Neill might have played in more games, but for Speaker giving him five days off to tend to his ailing wife, Mary, who gave birth to twins in midseason. O'Neill and Mary would have four children.

As the games behind the plate mounted and O'Neill's 5′10″, 165-pound frame endured more punishment, his offensive production began to slacken. In 1923, his average plummeted to .248 (although his on-base percentage was a robust .374), and after the season the Indians traded him to the Boston Red Sox along with Dan Boone, Joe Connolly and Bill Wambsganss for George Burns,

Roxy Walters and Chick Fewster. In 1924 O'Neill appeared in 100 games for the last time in his career, batting just .238 with 16 extra-base hits, but still getting on base proficiently with a .371 OBP. He was picked up off waivers at the end of the season by the New York Yankees, but played only 35 games in pinstripes in 1925 before drawing his release. After spending the 1926 season with Toronto of the International League, O'Neill returned to the majors with the St. Louis Browns the following year. During his last season with the Browns in 1928, O'Neill was almost killed when the New York City cab he was riding in was hit by a truck. The police and medics who rushed to the scene took one look at Steve (without realizing his identity) and summoned a priest to give him the last rites of the Catholic Church. O'Neill not only lived through the night, but despite critical injuries, rallied so magnificently that he amazed the specialists attending him.

After retiring as a full-time player in 1928, O'Neill stayed in baseball as a manager for the next 23 years. Though not typically thought of as a manager, O'Neill became one of the most consistent field generals in baseball history. After managing in the minor leagues for several seasons, O'Neill was hired to replace Walter Johnson as manager of the Cleveland Indians. Steve managed his old team for the next 2½ years, guiding the team to back-to-back winning seasons, though the club never finished higher than fourth. After four more years managing in the minors, O'Neill took over the managerial reins of the Detroit Tigers prior to the 1943 season. During his six seasons in Detroit O'Neill enjoyed the greatest success of his managerial career, guiding the Tigers to three second-place finishes and the 1945 World Championship. Following his tour of duty with the Tigers, O'Neill managed the Red Sox for two years, then the Phillies for three seasons. Over 14 seasons with four different franchises, O'Neill's clubs posted a 1,040–821 record, good for a .559 winning percentage. He also never had a losing season; only Joe McCarthy did that over a longer career.

Following his last managerial position, O'Neill worked as a scout, and later, for the Cleveland Recreation Department. He was still working in that position when he died of a heart attack on January 26, 1962.

ADAM ULREY

CLEVELAND

RAYMOND JOHNSON CHAPMAN
SHORTSTOP, 1912–1920

Ray Chapman, star shortstop for nine seasons with the Cleveland Indians, might have ended up in the Hall of Fame had he not been fatally injured by a Carl Mays fastball at the Polo Grounds on August 16, 1920. An ideal number two hitter who crowded the plate, the 5′10″, 170-pound Chapman led the league in sacrifice hits three times. His total of 67 sacrifices in 1917 is a major league record, and he stands in sixth place on the all-time career list with 334. Chapman was also a legitimate offensive force in his own right: the right-handed batter led Cleveland in runs scored three times during his career, and paced the entire American League in runs and walks in 1918, with 84 of each. He also led the Indians in stolen bases five times, and his 52 thefts in 1917 remained the franchise record until 1980. In addition to his offensive skills, Chapman was also an excellent fielder who led the AL in putouts three times and assists once. Put it all together and Chapman was, in the view of the *Cleveland News*, the "greatest shortstop, that is, considering all-around ability, batting, throwing, base-running, bunting, fielding and ground covering ability, to mention nothing of his fight, spirit and conscientiousness, ever to wear a Cleveland uniform."

But as good as Chapman was on the field, he was even more beloved for his infectious cheerfulness and enthusiasm off it. One of the most popular players in Cleveland Indians history, Chapman was a gifted storyteller who played the piano and once won an amateur singing contest. The good-humored shortstop also had a wide circle of admirers outside the game—his show business friends included Al Jolson, William S. Hart and Will Rogers. One newspaper described Chapman as a man who "was as much at home in the ballroom as on the ball diamond." His tragic demise in 1920 sparked one of the largest spontaneous outpourings of grief in Cleveland history.

Raymond Johnson Chapman was born to Everett and Barbara Chapman on January 15, 1891, on a farm near Beaver Dam, Kentucky, about 80 miles southwest of Louisville. The family settled in Herrin, a town in southern Illinois, in 1905. Ray, the middle of three surviving children, did odd jobs as a boy and sometimes worked in the mines. Young Chapman played his first professional ball in 1909 for the semipro club in Mt. Vernon. In 1910, he went to Springfield, Illinois, where he played every position except pitcher and catcher. "He was a very flashy player," recalled a Springfield teammate. "And he could run. He was a beautiful runner, the way he could pick up his knees. He was very fast, had a good arm, and was a good fielder, although at times a little erratic. And he was very jolly, a jolly guy. Always laughing, talking, singing." From Mt. Vernon Chapman went on to Davenport of the Three-I League, where he hit .293 with 75 runs scored and 50 stolen bases in 1911. Cleveland purchased Chapman's contract toward the end of the season and assigned him to Toledo of the American Association.

Chapman faced a traffic jam at shortstop when Cleveland brought him up to the big club in August 1912. The Naps had two promising shortstops in addition to Chapman, who had been batting .310 for the Mud Hens in 140 games, with 49 steals and 101 runs scored. One rival, Roger Peckinpaugh, had played 15 games for Cleveland in 1910 but spent 1911 in the minors. The second, Ivy Olson, was the team's regular shortstop the previous year (third baseman Terry Turner had played shortstop for the team from 1904 to 1910). Cleveland began the 1912 season with Olson at shortstop and Peckinpaugh, a favorite of manager Harry Davis, in reserve. Just two days after Chapman's arrival, however, Davis was replaced as manager by centerfielder Joe Birmingham, who doubted Peckinpaugh's ability to hit big league

CLE.

pitching. Birmingham also benched Olson, who had 27 errors at shortstop in 56 games and was nagged by minor injuries. Birmingham then turned to Chapman, who, though shaky in the field, took advantage of his opportunity by hitting .312, as Cleveland won 22 of the 31 contests he appeared in.

Chapman hit .258 in 1913, his first full season with Cleveland, and led the American League with 45 sacrifice hits, to form a strong middle infield with the Naps' legendary 38-year-old second baseman, Napoleon Lajoie. In 1914, Chapman broke his leg in the spring and only played in 106 games. With Lajoie no longer on the club, the team collapsed. Chapman bounced back the next season to hit .270, and his 101 runs scored were nearly three times more than anyone else on the team. However, he was again plagued by leg ailments in 1916, when he hit only .231 in 109 games. Despite his physical problems, Chapman's prowess was widely recognized. In 1915, the Chicago White Sox tried to obtain him from Cleveland, but, after being rebuffed, had to settle for acquiring outfielder Shoeless Joe Jackson instead.

In 1917, Cleveland finished well back of Chicago in the standings, but Chapman blossomed. Sparked by his all-round play, the Indians won 32 of their last 47 games to finish 88–66, in third place. From August 31 to September 24, they won 17 of 20 games, including a 10-game winning streak in which Chapman hit .517 with four steals of home. In an exhibition game against the Braves in Boston on September 27, Chapman won a loving cup for the fastest time circling the bases, fourteen seconds. Chapman finished the year with a .302 batting average and 98 runs scored to go along with his club-record 52 stolen bases.

Chapman's production declined in 1918, as he finished the year with just a .267 average and 28 extra-base hits. Despite those numbers, Chapman led the American League in runs scored with 84, thanks in large part to his league-leading 84 walks, which helped him post a career-high .390 on-base percentage. After the season ended in September, Chapman complied with the War Department's work-or-fight order and enrolled in the Naval Auxiliary Reserve as a second-class seaman. He spent three months as a deckhand on the steamer *H. H. Rogers*, which sailed on the Great Lakes, and was captain of the Naval Reserve baseball and football teams. Chapman was also a sprinter on the track squad, where he specialized in the 20- and 100-yard dash. His best time in the latter event was 10.0 seconds. His service ended with the armistice in November 1918. The following year, Chapman rebounded to hit .300 in 115 games for the Indians, who finished in second place with an 84–55 record, their best showing in franchise history.

After the season, Chapman married Kathleen Daly, daughter of the millionaire president of the East Ohio Gas Company. Tris Speaker, Ray's closest friend on the Indians, was the best man. Before the 1920 season began, Chapman gave some thought to retirement from baseball—he was already secretary-treasurer at the firm Pioneer Alloys. Speaker was the new Indian manager, however, so Chapman decided to play at least one more year to help his pal and owner James Dunn win the team's first pennant.

During the thrilling 1920 season the scrappy White Sox were again contenders for the AL pennant, though they would soon be gutted for having thrown the 1919 World Series to the Cincinnati Reds. The surging New York Yankees, who like the Indians had never won a pennant, were led by Babe Ruth's unprecedented slugging. In mid-August, however, Speaker's club clung to slim leads over both teams and Ray Chapman was having one of the best seasons of his career. On the morning of August 16 he had a batting average of .304, with 97 runs scored, 52 walks, 27 doubles, and 49 RBI.

That afternoon, rainy and dark, the Indians were in New York for a game against the Yankees at the Polo Grounds. The Yankees' starting pitcher, right-hander Carl Mays, was a surly man unpopular with both his teammates and other players. One of the few hurlers who threw underhand, Mays had a reputation as someone who liked to pitch batters tight.

Chapman was 0-for-1 when he led off the fifth inning with Cleveland ahead 3–0. With a count of one ball and one strike, Chapman, who batted and threw right-handed, hunched, as usual, over the plate, waiting for the next pitch. He always popped back when the ball was thrown. Mays looked in and, detecting that Chapman was slightly shifting his back foot—probably to push the ball down the first base line—released a fastball, high and targeting the inside corner. The gray blur sliced through the heavy, humid air, possibly a strike. Chapman did not move.

Many of the players and 20,000 fans heard an "explosive sound"—Babe Ruth said it was audible where he stood far out in right field. Sportswriter Fred Lieb, sitting in the downstairs press box about fifty feet behind the umpire, heard a "sickening thud." The ball dribbled out toward the pitcher's mound on the first base side. Mays fielded it and threw it to first baseman Wally Pipp for the out, apparently thinking the ball had struck the bat. Pipp turned to throw the ball around the infield, but froze when he glanced home. Chapman had sunk to his knees, his face contorted, blood streaming from his left ear. Yankee catcher Muddy Ruel tried to catch Chapman as his knees buckled. Umpire Tommy Connolly ran toward the grandstand yelling for a doctor. Speaker rushed over from the on-deck circle to tend to his stricken friend, who was trying to sit. Speaker thought Chapman wanted to get up and rush Mays. Finally, two doctors, one the Yankee team physician, arrived, applied ice and revived Chapman. He walked under his own power across the infield toward the clubhouse in center field, but his knees gave way again near second base. Two teammates grabbed the shortstop, put his arms around their shoulders, and carried him the rest of the way.

Mays remained near the mound, showed the ball to Umpire Connolly, and told him that the fateful pitch had been a "sailer"; a rough spot on its surface had caused it to move further inside than he expected. (That summer AL owners had complained to league president Ban Johnson that umpires were running up expenses by throwing out too many balls unnecessarily, so Johnson issued a notice ordering umpires to "keep the balls in the games as much as possible, except those which were dangerous." Thus, teams often played with balls that were scuffed and browned by dirt and tobacco juice.) The game continued, eventually a 4–3 Indian victory.

After the game New York manager Miller Huggins, a lawyer, took Mays to the police station nearest the Polo Grounds to file a report on the incident. Mays was later cleared of all wrongdoing in the incident. The stricken Chapman, meanwhile, was at St. Lawrence Hospital nearby on 163rd Street, where doctors—operating on Speaker's authority—made a three-inch incision in the base of Chapman's skull, finding a ruptured lateral sinus and plenty of clotted blood. They removed a small piece of his fractured skull. Kathleen Day Chapman, pregnant with the couple's first child, was immediately summoned to New York. Chapman rallied briefly, but he died early the next morning before his wife's arrival. Kathleen, Speaker, and Joe Wood accompanied the body back to Cleveland; Chapman was seen off on his final journey by a large crowd of mourners at Grand Central Station. As word of Chapman's death spread around the League, players on the Boston, Washington, St. Louis, and Detroit rosters—with Ty Cobb among the loudest—demanded that Carl Mays be banned from baseball. A few Indians players warned Mays that he should not show his face in Cleveland again. Many newspaper editorials railed against the bean ball and *The New York Times* called for batting helmets to be required. The league soon took steps to keep cleaner balls in play.

Chapman's funeral at St. John's Cathedral on August 20, Cleveland's largest in years, was attended by many baseball dignitaries and thousands of Indians fans. Thirty-four priests participated in the service. A blanket made of more than 20,000 blossoms purchased by mourning fans was placed on his grave. Flags in the city were flown at half-staff. Tris Speaker and Jack Graney were so overwhelmed by grief they did not attend.

The Cleveland-New York game of August 17 was cancelled because of Chapman's death. (Cleveland's victory in the tragic game had kept the Indians in first place). The demoralized Indians lost to the Yankees 4–3 when play resumed on August 18 and dropped seven of nine games after the incident. Graney said, "We feel as if we did not care if we ever played baseball again. We cannot imagine playing without Chappie." But Speaker, almost too weak to hold a bat, rallied the club when he returned on August 22. With the addition of pitcher Walter (Duster) Mails, and future Hall of Famer Joe Sewell, who took Chapman's place at shortstop, the Indians won 24 of their final 32 games and defeated Brooklyn in the World Series. The team awarded Mrs. Chapman a full World Series share of $3,986.34.

Speaker never blamed Mays for Chapman's death, but many others, including Graney, held him responsible. Miller Huggins left Carl Mays at home during the Yankees' September road trip to Cleveland. "It is an episode which I shall always regret more than anything that has ever happened to me," Mays said, "and yet I can look into my own conscience and feel absolved of personal guilt. I have long ceased to care what most people think about me."

Kathleen Daly Chapman, once a baseball fan, never attended another game. On February 27, 1921, she gave birth to a daughter, Rae-Marie. She married a cousin two years later. The former Mrs. Chapman died in Los Angeles on April 21, 1928, after swallowing a poisonous fluid. She was accompanied at the time by her mother, who said her daughter had been recovering from a nervous breakdown. The Daly family insisted that Kathleen had taken the poison accidentally. The Chapmans' daughter went to live with her grandmother, but died a year later during a measles epidemic.

Ray Chapman is buried in Section 42, Lot 16, of Lake View Cemetery in Cleveland. Chapman's younger sister Margaret Joy visited the site for many decades afterward to pay her respects. "Ray is there all by himself," she told the *Cleveland Plain Dealer* in 1995. "Ray loved Cleveland. He thought it was such a wonderful place. So did I. I still look in the papers to see how the Indians are doing."

Don Jensen

Robert Roth

CLEVELAND

Robert Frank "Braggo" Roth
Right fielder, 1915–1918

Bobby Roth, sometimes called "Braggo," was an often insufferable self-promoter who bounced around among six American League teams in the years surrounding the First World War. Roth was on the wrong side of two of the most lopsided trades of the Deadball Era: he was dealt to the Cleveland Indians for the legendary Joe Jackson, and then, three years later, away from Cleveland for third baseman Larry Gardner, who would eventually help the Indians to their first world championship. A player with diverse skills, Roth won a home run title and also stole home as many as six times in a season. But he was hampered by what one source called "the unhappy faculty of gaining enemies—apparently with cold deliberation."

Robert Frank Roth was born in the southern Wisconsin town of Burlington, on August 28, 1892. At the time of his birth, Roth's parents resided in Chicago, but spent several weeks each summer in Burlington, at the home of his mother's brother. Situated on the banks of the Fox River, the tranquil village served as a summer playground for Bobby during his childhood. Fourteen years in age separated Bobby from his older brother Frank, but the two shared a love of baseball, which was a pursuit encouraged by their father. Frank would enjoy a six-year career in the majors as a catcher, ending in 1910.

In 1910, when he was just 17 years old, Bobby signed his first professional contract with Green Bay of the Class-D Wisconsin-Illinois League. But after less than three months of underwhelming play, Roth was released and latched on with the Red Wing Manufacturers of the Minnesota–Wisconsin League (Class-D). The next season, with the Racine Belles, Roth displayed a strong throwing arm at third base, despite enough errant throws to accumulate 44 errors in 114 games.

Roth was a stocky 5'8" right-handed batter, described as "small, but with fine forearms and the wrist action that poles a ball such long distances." In 1912, he was optioned to St. Joseph (Missouri) of the Western League, where he played 39 games and made 14 errors at third. Four times that season his contract was bought and sold. His frequent travels from team to team earned him the nickname "The Globetrotter."

In 1913, after being released twice, Roth caught on with the Virginia (Minnesota) Ore Diggers of the Class C Northern League. Roth improved his defense and hit .362 in just under two months of action, and his contract was purchased by the Class AA Kansas City Blues. He appeared in 123 games for the Blues in 1914, batting .293 with eight home runs and 91 runs scored. A quick runner, Roth earned a reputation as a "fleet-footed master" capable of "dismantling the enemy club with his spikes."

Two important changes occurred in Kansas City in 1914 for Roth. First, he was made an outfielder by manager Bill Armour, former skipper of Cleveland and Detroit. Second, he earned a label that haunted him the rest of his career. In Kansas City, bolstered by his successes on the field, Roth began to acquire a taste for self-promotion. As author Tom Meany noted, Roth was "an entertaining talker and more often than not the hero of his stories was himself." Based in large part on his boastful clubhouse attitude, Roth earned the nickname "Braggo."

Helped by a recommendation from Armour, Roth was purchased by the White Sox in August of 1914. Playing regularly for the final month of the season, Roth performed well, hitting .294 in 34 games with six triples. In 1915, Roth switched to third base, where he stayed for the first six weeks of the season. But Roth's inconsistent defensive play, and the purchase of outfielder Eddie Murphy from the A's, severely reduced Braggo's playing time. On August 21, Chicago dealt Roth and two others to the Indians for Joe Jackson. As part of the swap, the Sox sent more than $30,000 in cash to Cleveland.

With Cleveland, Bobby struggled at first, but gradually his bat warmed up, as he hit .299 with an impressive .507 slugging mark in 39 games with the

Indians to close out the 1915 campaign. Overall for the season, Roth ranked fifth in the league in slugging, third in triples, and eighth in OPS. Despite having been dealt for the popular Jackson, Cleveland fans took a liking to Braggo, who delighted them with flashy, though often unnecessary, diving catches. In the last week of the season, Roth slugged three homers to give him a total of seven, enough to edge Rube Oldring for the American League lead. Roth became the first man in the American League, and the first player since Bill Joyce in 1896, to capture a home run title while playing for more than one team. The much-traveled Roth hit all seven of his homers on the road.

On the eve of the 1916 season, Cleveland acquired center fielder Tris Speaker from the Red Sox, and Roth was nudged from center to right field, a position where he was far more comfortable. Batting in the cleanup position directly behind Speaker, Roth enjoyed a fine season, hitting .286 with 29 steals and four home runs. In April, Roth was at the center of an ugly incident at Sportsman's Park in St. Louis. As an unruly partisan crowd grew strident during a lopsided game in their favor, fans began hurling objects onto the diamond. Roth was hit with a bottle, and retaliated by hurling the object back into the crowd. A ruckus ensued, which resulted in Roth's ejection for his own safety. As a result,

CLE.

Roth became a villain in St. Louis and suffered taunting in that city for the remainder of his career.

In 1917, after a brief holdout, Roth displayed a different specialty, as he increased his stolen base total to 51, often swiping third on the front end of double steals with Bill Wambsganss. Though he was not credited with it at the time, Roth stole home six times in 1917, tying a major league mark. In 1918, Roth hit .283 in a season abbreviated by the war. Despite a back injury that plagued him most of the year and kept him from the Cleveland lineup for nearly three weeks, Bobby banged out 12 triples and was among the league leaders in extra-base hits and RBI. After a mediocre start, the Indians inched to a second-place finish. Cleveland entered the off-season determined to acquire pitching. Their primary bait was Roth. With his talent for socking extra-base hits and swiping bases, Roth was coveted by nearly every team in the league. Eventually, it came down to the Yankees and the A's, and Connie Mack won the sweepstakes, sending veteran third baseman Larry Gardner, pitcher–outfielder Charlie Jamieson, and pitcher Elmer Myers to the Indians for Roth.

Playing in right field and batting cleanup, Roth missed action early, suffering an injury in the first week of the season. Then in mid-May, Bobby shot his average above the .300 mark. But the colorful Roth found it difficult to relate to the stoic Mack, and in short order Bobby was in the doghouse. More importantly, Mack was receiving offers from the Yankees and Red Sox, who still wanted Braggo in their uniform. Trying to turn around his franchise, Mack ignored Roth's .323 average and 26 extra-base hits in 48 games and dealt Braggo to the Red Sox on June 27.

The Red Sox moved Roth to center field, where he replaced Strunk and played alongside Babe Ruth, who was stationed in left when not pitching. In Boston, "The Globetrotter" struggled, batting .256 with no homers, 23 RBI, and eight errors. The Red Sox slumped to sixth place and in the off-season dealt Roth to the Senators for three players. It was Braggo's fourth team in less than two years. Playing under Clark Griffith in Washington in 1920, Roth was used in right field and rebounded at the plate, batting .291 with nine homers, 92 RBI and 80 runs scored, all career bests. He also took more pitches, walking 75 times to post a .395 OBP. Despite Braggo's fine season, Griffith dealt the outfielder to the Yankees on January 20, 1921 (one year to the day after he had last been traded), for Duffy Lewis and George Mogridge.

With the Yankees in 1921, Bobby joined his older brother Frank, who served as New York's pitching coach. Though Miller Huggins had tried to acquire Roth for nearly three years, the Yankee skipper showed little confidence in his new outfielder. Hampered by nagging injuries, Roth appeared in just 43 games for the Yankees, and was used primarily as a pinch-hitter in the last month of the season. In his eighth and final year in the big leagues, Roth batted .283 with 10 RBI and 29 runs scored, many of them as a pinch-runner. In January of 1922, the Yankees released Roth, whose star had faded in quick fashion. His failing legs were a part of the reason, but his big mouth was a larger factor. The *Reach Guide* reported: "[Roth] is known as a tempermental [sic] player, who serves no club satisfactorily for any length of time."

Just 29 years old in the spring of 1922, Roth found himself without a team and with few options. He spent the year at home in Burlington, playing sparingly for local semipro teams, before returning to the Kansas City Blues in 1923. Roth was hitting .339 for Kansas City when his stay with the club came to an abrupt end on August 3, when Roth was released from the team for "indifferent play." According to the *Sporting News*, "only with a hit in sight would [Roth] put his best leg power in motion and in the field it was a crime."

Despite the negative publicity surrounding his release by the Blues, a few weeks later Roth was signed by St. Paul, the team chasing Kansas City in the standings. With St. Paul, Roth hit .313 for the balance of the season, but could not help the club overtake his former teammates. In total, Roth had batted .324 in 133 games, and scored 110 runs with 32 doubles, eight triples, 12 home runs, 97 RBI, and 19 stolen bases. In spite of his production, Roth was not invited back by St. Paul the following spring, having worn out his welcome once again. As the *Kansas City Bulletin* put it, Roth "was the exasperating grain of dust in the eye of whatever ballteam he became associated with."

After spending several years playing for semipro teams in the Chicago area, in 1928 Roth reemerged with the Hollywood Stars of the Pacific Coast League. Under his shaky 35-year-old legs, Braggo hit .283, but his foot speed and power had abandoned him. He returned to Wisconsin and never played Organized Baseball again. On September 11, 1936, Roth was the passenger in a car driven by a friend when they were struck by an oncoming vehicle. Roth's friend was killed instantly and Roth died later that day in a Chicago hospital from severe head injuries. He was 44 years old. Ironically for Roth, a man who had spent much of his life promoting himself, his car had been struck by a newspaper truck.

DAN HOLMES

CLEVELAND

STANLEY ANTHONY COVELESKI
RIGHT-HANDED PITCHER, 1916–1924

With one of the finest spitballs in baseball history, Stan Coveleski baffled American League hitters from the final years of the Deadball Era into the 1920s. To keep hitters off balance, Coveleski went to his mouth before every pitch. "I wouldn't throw all spitballs," he later explained. "I'd go maybe two or three innings without throwing a spitter, but I always had them looking for it." Though he led the American League in strikeouts in 1920, Coveleski prided himself on his efficient pitching. "I was never a strikeout pitcher," he recalled. "Why should I throw eight or nine balls to get a man out when I got away with three or four?" The right-hander often boasted of his control, once claiming he pitched seven innings without throwing a ball; every pitch was either hit, missed, or called a strike. During his 14-year career, Coveleski ranked among the league's top 10 in fewest walks allowed per nine innings pitched seven times.

Stan Coveleski was born Stanislaus Anthony Kowalewski to a family of Polish descent on July 13, 1889, in Shamokin, Pennsylvania, a coal mining town located 60 miles north of the state capital in Harrisburg. "Covey" later recalled working in the local mines by the time he was 12 years old, from seven in the morning to seven at night six days a week for $3.75 per week. The youngest of five boys—four of whom would play professional baseball—Stanley, like his older brother Harry, who won 81 games for the Phillies, Reds, and Tigers, anglicized his name to Coveleskie when he moved into Organized Baseball (at some point after retirement the final "e" came off his name). His oldest brother, Jacob, died during the Spanish-American War. Frank spent time with an outlaw club in Pennsylvania but fell victim to rheumatism that ended his career. John, a third baseman and outfielder, played in the minor leagues but could never quite break through.

As a young boy Coveleski built up his strength by hauling timber for the miners, stopping every now and then to throw rocks at birds. When he got home, Stan continued to practice by throwing rocks at tin cans; he later claimed he could even hit them blindfolded. It was while throwing at the cans that Covey remembered being approached by a local school teacher to pitch on the school team.

In 1909 Coveleski signed with Lancaster of the Tri-State League. Stanley and his brother John were watching a movie when someone went to the front of the theatre and announced, "If Mr. Coveleski is in the house, he is wanted at the box office." Neither knew which brother was wanted so both went and found the Lancaster manager waiting for them. It turned out he was looking for Stanley, but the unworldly and shy youngster was reluctant to sign. Only when the manager agreed to sign older brother John as well would Stan agree to join the club. By that time Coveleski had graduated to hauling and sawing wood for the miners, and his weekly pay had grown to $9.00 per week, well below the $250 dollars per month Lancaster offered him.

Coveleski hurled admirably in his first season in the league; in 272 innings pitched he led the league with 23 wins while losing only 11. His next two years, also in Lancaster, proved satisfactory if not as spectacular as his rookie season. In 1912 he moved to Atlantic City in the same league and continued pitching well, finishing the season with 20 wins and a 2.53 ERA. Near the end of the 1912 season Coveleski caught the eye of manager Connie Mack from the nearby Philadelphia Athletics. Signed to a contract and given a couple of late-season starts, the 23-year-old Coveleski acquitted himself well, but Mack believed he needed additional seasoning. Accordingly, the manager sent Covey to Spokane in the Northwestern League, apparently believing he had a gentleman's agreement with Spokane to retain the rights to the promising young pitcher.

Coveleski played two years in Spokane, hurling over 300 innings each year. In his stellar sophomore campaign Coveleski won 20 games and led the league in strikeouts. After the 1914 season, Portland of the Pacific

Coast League traded five players to Spokane to acquire Coveleski, now considered the Northwestern League's top pitcher. According to one story Mack had forgotten about his "rights" to Coveleski and failed to take up his claim for the player. Later, upon inquiring about Covey, Mack was sent a box of big red apples as thanks and told his rights had expired.

Despite not being particularly large at 5′11″ and 166 pounds, Coveleski was bestowed the nickname "the Big Pole." He typically threw overhand, but would drop down to a sidearm delivery once in a while. While at Portland Coveleski developed the spitball for which he later became famous. Coveleski felt that in order to become a top flight hurler he needed an additional pitch to supplement his fastball, curve and slowball. Covey developed excellent control of his spitball which he could make break in three directions depending on his wrist action: down, out, or down and out.

When he first started experimenting with the spitball he tried using tobacco juice. Later, at the suggestion of Joe McGinnity and Harry Krause, he switched to alum, which worked much better. Covey kept the alum in his mouth where it became gummy; he would wet his first two fingers to throw the spitter. With his newly developed spitball, Coveleski led the PCL in games pitched and finished the 1915 season 17–17 with a

respectable 2.67 ERA. Despite his .500 record, Covey remained favorably regarded and prior to the 1916 season the Cleveland Indians, who enjoyed a close relationship with Portland, purchased his contract.

Coveleski was scheduled to pitch during the 1916 season's first week against the Detroit Tigers and his brother Harry, a star coming off two straight 20-win seasons. Harry demurred from pitching against his younger brother and the much-heralded matchup never occurred. Coveleski lost his first start, but went on to a respectable rookie season, finishing 15–13 with an ERA of 3.41. Cleveland won 77 games in 1916, 20 more than the club's 1915 total.

In 1917 Cleveland and Coveleski both continued to improve. The team jumped to 88 wins and a third-place finish; Coveleski won 19 of those games, finished third in the league with a 1.81 ERA, and led the circuit with nine shutouts. During the war-shortened 1918 season, Coveleski was even more brilliant, ranking second in the league in ERA (1.82) and wins (22). One of those victories was a complete game, 19-inning 3–2 victory over the New York Yankees on May 24. Thanks to Coveleski's strong pitching, the Indians finished in second place, 2½ games behind the Boston Red Sox. Cleveland finished second again in 1919, and Coveleski once again turned in a stellar performance, posting a 24–12 record with a 2.61 ERA.

Though he could be taciturn and ornery on days when he pitched, off the field Coveleski was generally considered friendly, though not particularly talkative. Stan also indulged a lively but sometimes malicious sense of humor. At spring training in 1921 in Dallas, manager Tris Speaker invited the team down to his nearby home for a barbeque. Coveleski and shortstop Joe Sewell took a rowboat out on the lake. Once out a ways from shore, Covey asked Sewell if he could swim. The rookie replied in the negative, whereupon Coveleski shoved him into the lake and rowed away. A rescue party saved Sewell; Coveleski never explained himself, thinking the prank very funny.

The year 1920 would prove to be a year of tragedy and triumph for both Coveleski and the Cleveland Indians. Covey, one of the 17 pitchers allowed to continue throwing the banned spitball under the "grandfather" clause, started the season hot by winning his first seven starts. On May 28, however, he received the tragic news that his wife of seven years, Mary Stivetts, had died. Although she had been sick for some time, her death was unexpected. Coveleski returned to Shamokin, where the broken-hearted pitcher grieved with his family before returning to the team on June 4. A couple of years after his wife's death, Coveleski married her sister, Frances, who had been helping care for his two children, William and Jack. Covey's second marriage would last until his death many years later.

On August 17, 1920, tragedy again struck the Cleveland Indians, with the death of shortstop Ray Chapman following a beaning at the hands of New York pitcher Carl Mays. Coveleski, who had been the opposing pitcher in the game, later recalled that he did not think Mays was purposely trying to hit Chapman but "at that time if we saw a fellow get close to the plate, we'd fire under his chin."

Despite these tragic circumstances, both Coveleski and the Indians persevered to narrowly win the American League pennant. Once again, Coveleski was a big reason for the Tribe's success, winning 24 games, finishing second in the league with a 2.49 ERA and leading the league with 133 strikeouts. But he saved his best work for that year's best-of-nine World Series against the Brooklyn Robins, pitching three complete-game victories, including a shutout in the series-clinching Game Seven. For the Series Covey posted a 0.67 ERA, while walking only two batters in 27 innings.

From 1921 through 1924, Cleveland gradually fell out of contention as ownership did little to improve the ball club. In 1921 Covey won 23 games, marking his fourth straight year of at least 22 victories. Although his win totals declined thereafter as the fortunes of the team waned, Coveleski continued to pitch well, winning his first ERA title in 1923.

After a sixth-place finish in 1924, the Indians traded Coveleski, coming off a subpar year (13–14, 4.04 ERA), to the world champion Washington Senators. Despite having spent nine years of his career there, Coveleski had no regrets about leaving Cleveland behind. "I never did like Cleveland," he later explained. "Don't know why. Didn't like the town. Now the people are all right, but I just didn't like the town." He even admitted that his dissatisfaction with his surroundings had come to affect his performance. "You know I got to a point where I wouldn't hustle no more," Covey remembered. "See, a player gets to be with a club too long. Gets lazy, you know."

True to form, Coveleski rebounded strongly for the Senators in 1925, finishing the season with a 20–5 record and capturing his second ERA title with a 2.84 ERA, though he lost both of his starts in Washington's World Series defeat to Pittsburgh. After turning in another good year in 1926, Coveleski came down with a sore arm in 1927, and the Senators gave him his unconditional release. Covey caught on with the Yankees for the 1928 season, but pitched poorly and was released in August.

Now out of baseball and with the opportunity to coach a boys' amateur team, Coveleski moved his family to South Bend, Indiana, where he and his wife purchased a home on Napier Street from the Napieralskis, one of the city's founding pioneer families. Coveleski then acquired and ran the Coveleski Service Station on the city's west side. During the Great Depression, however, both gas and business became hard to come by, and Covey quit the business. Coveleski, now retired, spent his time hunting and fishing—often driving to a nearby lake at 6:00 A.M.—and generally enjoying life, although he had to endure the death of his son Jack in 1937.

On the strength of his 215 career wins and lifetime .602 winning percentage, Coveleski was elected to the Baseball Hall of Fame in 1969. In his own stoic way he expressed both his appreciation and frustration for having to wait so long: "It makes me feel just swell," he said. "I figured I'd make it sooner or later, and I just kept hoping each year would be the one." Coveleski passed away at the age of 94 on March 20, 1984, in a nursing home after a lengthy illness, and was buried in St. Joseph's Cemetery in South Bend. At the time of his death he was the oldest living Hall of Famer.

DAN LEVITT

NEW YORK

lthough the live-ball era would see them become the most successful franchise in baseball history, the New York Highlanders were largely a puzzle during the Deadball Era. Despite playing in the nation's most populous and media-friendly city, the team never won a pennant, and finished as high as third place only four times in the whole era.

The franchise began play in 1901 as the Baltimore Orioles, a new team named after the 1890s NL juggernaut and featuring one of that team's stars, John McGraw, as manager. One of McGraw's first moves was an unsuccessful ploy in March 1901 to break the color line by signing star black second baseman Frank Grant and passing him off as an Indian. The ruse failed, and McGraw managed the team to a pedestrian fifth-place

finish. In July 1902, amid a dispute with Ban Johnson, McGraw jumped to the NL's New York Giants, taking Orioles stars Joe McGinnity, Roger Bresnahan, and Dan McGann with him. The wrecked Baltimore franchise finished in last place, and moved to New York before the 1903 season.

The new team was dubbed the New York Highlanders because their home field, Hilltop Park in upper Manhattan, was located on the island's highest point. In 1904, behind the 41 victories of Happy Jack Chesbro, the Highlanders came as close as they ever would to winning a pennant. In the ninth inning of a tie game on the last day of the season, however, Chesbro threw a spitball over his catcher's head. A runner scored from third on the infamous wild pitch, handing both the

WINNING PERCENTAGE 1901–1919

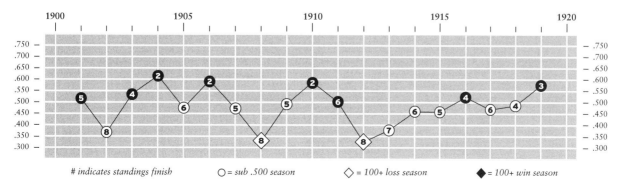

693

game and the pennant to the Boston Americans. It was the first dramatic moment in what has since become the most celebrated rivalry in sports.

In 1912 the Highlanders began wearing the pinstripes that would become their signature. A year later, in 1913, they changed their name to the Yankees.

During the Deadball Era five future Hall of Famers (McGraw, Wilbert Robinson, Clark Griffith, Frank Chance, and Miller Huggins) tried their hand at managing the franchise, but year after year the team proved unable to win. Their best finish during the second Deadball decade was an 80-victory, third-place showing in 1919. By then, owners Jacob Ruppert and Cap Huston, using money loaned to them by other magnates, had begun to build the framework of the first great Yankee dynasty, capping off a series of signings with the acquisition from the Boston Red Sox of slugger Babe Ruth. The sale, completed on January 3, 1920, provided a fitting conclusion to the Deadball Era, paving the way for the new brand of long ball that would dominate the sport for decades to come.

ERIC ENDERS

ALL-ERA TEAM

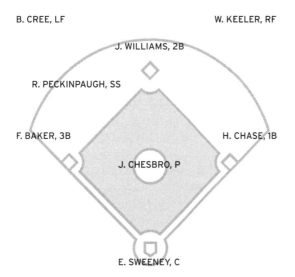

C. HEMPHILL, CF

B. CREE, LF   W. KEELER, RF

J. WILLIAMS, 2B

R. PECKINPAUGH, SS

F. BAKER, 3B   H. CHASE, 1B

J. CHESBRO, P

E. SWEENEY, C

TEAM LEADERS 1901–1919

BATTING

GAMES
H. Chase 1061
J. Williams 940
R. Peckinpaugh . . . 931

RUNS
H. Chase 551
J. Williams 487
W. Keeler 482

HITS
H. Chase 1182
J. Williams 978
W. Keeler 974

RBI
J. Williams 537
H. Chase 494
B. Cree 332

DOUBLES
J. Williams 176
H. Chase 165
R. Peckinpaugh . . . 123

TRIPLES
J. Williams 87
H. Chase 62
W. Conroy 59

HOME RUNS
W. Pipp 34
F. Baker 32
J. Williams 31

STOLEN BASES
H. Chase 248
W. Conroy 184
F. Maisel 183

BATTING AVERAGE
(2000+ plate appearances)
W. Keeler 294
B. Cree 292
F. Baker 289

PITCHING

GAMES
J. Chesbro 269
R. Caldwell 248
J. Warhop 221

WINS
J. Chesbro 128
R. Caldwell 95
R. Fisher 76

LOSSES
R. Caldwell 99
J. Chesbro 93
J. Warhop 93

INNINGS
J. Chesbro 1952
R. Caldwell 1718⅓
J. Warhop 1412⅔

STRIKEOUTS
J. Chesbro 913
R. Caldwell 803
R. Fisher 583

WALKS
R. Caldwell 576
J. Chesbro 434
J. Warhop 400

SHUTOUTS
J. Chesbro 18
R. Caldwell 17
A. Orth 14

ERA
(800+ innings pitched)
G. Mogridge 2.50
B. Shawkey 2.51
R. Ford 2.54

TYPICAL LINEUPS 1901–1919

1901 (as Baltimore)

1. J. McGraw
   J. Dunn, 3B
2. M. Donlin, LF
3. J. Williams, 2B
4. B. Keister, SS
5. C. Seymour, RF
6. J. Jackson, CF–LF
   S. Brodie, CF
7. B. Hart, 1B
8. R. Bresnahan
   W. Robinson, C

1902 (as Baltimore)

1. H. McFarland, CF
2. K. Selbach, LF
3. J. Williams, 2B
4. D. McGann, 1B
5. C. Seymour
   H. Arndt, RF
6. R. Bresnahan, 3B
7. B. Gilbert, SS
8. W. Robinson, C

1903

1. L. Davis, LF
2. W. Keeler, RF
3. K. Elberfeld, SS
   D. Fultz, CF
4. J. Williams, 2B
5. J. Ganzel, 1B
6. W. Conroy, 3B
7. H. McFarland, CF–LF
8. M. Beville
   J. O'Connor, C

1904

1. P. Dougherty, LF
2. W. Keeler, RF
3. K. Elberfeld, SS
4. J. Anderson, OF–1B
5. J. Williams, 2B
6. J. Ganzel, 1B
   D. Fultz, CF
7. W. Conroy, 3B
8. D. McGuire, C

1905

1. P. Dougherty, LF
2. W. Keeler, RF
3. K. Elberfeld, SS
4. J. Williams, 2B
5. H. Chase, 1B
6. J. Yeager, 3B
   W. Conroy, INF–LF
7. D. Fultz, CF
8. R. Kleinow, C

1906

1. W. Keeler, RF
2. K. Elberfeld, SS
3. H. Chase, 1B
4. F. LaPorte, 3B
5. J. Williams, 2B
6. F. Delahanty, LF
   W. Conroy, CF–SS–LF
7. D. Hoffman, CF
8. R. Kleinow, C

1907

1. D. Hoffman, CF
2. W. Keeler, RF
3. K. Elberfeld, SS
4. H. Chase, 1B
5. F. LaPorte, 3B–RF
6. J. Williams, 2B
   G. Moriarty, 3B
7. W. Conroy, LF
8. R. Kleinow, C

1908

1. H. Niles, 2B
2. W. Keeler, RF
3. H. Chase, 1B
4. C. Hemphill, CF
5. J. Stahl, LF
6. W. Conroy, 3B
7. N. Ball, SS
8. R. Kleinow, C

1909

1. R. Demmitt
   B. Cree, CF
2. W. Keeler, RF
3. H. Chase, 1B
4. C. Engle, LF
5. F. LaPorte, 2B
   K. Elberfeld, SS
6. J. Knight, SS
7. J. Austin, 3B
8. R. Kleinow, C

1910

1. B. Daniels, LF
   C. Hemphill, CF
2. H. Wolter, RF
3. H. Chase, 1B
4. F. LaPorte, 2B
   J. Knight, SS
5. E. Gardner, 2B
6. B. Cree, CF
7. J. Austin, 3B
8. E. Sweeney
   F. Mitchell, C

1911

1. B. Daniels, CF
2. H. Wolter, RF
3. R. Hartzell, 3B
4. B. Cree, LF
5. J. Knight, SS
6. H. Chase, 1B
7. E. Gardner, 2B
8. W. Blair
   E. Sweeney, C

1912

1. B. Daniels, LF
2. H. Chase, 1B
3. D. Sterrett, CF
4. G. Zinn, RF–CF
5. H. Simmons, 2B
6. R. Hartzell, 3B–RF
7. J. Martin, SS
8. E. Sweeney, C

1913

1. B. Daniels, RF
2. H. Wolter, CF
3. B. Cree, LF
4. R. Hartzell, 2B
5. R. Peckinpaugh, SS
6. J. Knight, 1B
7. E. Midkiff, 3B
8. E. Sweeney, C

1914

1. F. Maisel, 3B
2. R. Hartzell, LF
3. D. Cook, RF
4. B. Cree, CF
5. C. Mullen, 1B
6. R. Peckinpaugh, SS
7. E. Sweeney
   L. Nunamaker, C
8. L. Boone, 2B

1915

1. H. High, CF
2. R. Peckinpaugh, SS
3. F. Maisel, 3B
4. W. Pipp, 1B
5. D. Cook, RF
6. R. Hartzell, LF
7. L. Boone, 2B
8. L. Nunamaker, C

1916

1. F. Gilhooley, RF
2. H. High, LF
3. R. Peckinpaugh, SS
4. W. Pipp, 1B
5. F. Baker, 3B
6. L. Magee, CF
7. J. Gedeon, 2B
8. L. Nunamaker, C

1917

1. T. Hendryx, RF
2. H. High, LF
3. F. Maisel, 2B
4. W. Pipp, 1B
5. F. Baker, 3B
6. E. Miller, CF
7. R. Peckinpaugh, SS
8. L. Nunamaker, C

1918 (first half)

1. F. Gilhooley, RF
2. R. Peckinpaugh, SS
3. F. Baker, 3B
4. D. Pratt, 2B
5. W. Pipp, 1B
6. P. Bodie, LF
7. E. Miller, CF
8. T. Hannah, C

1918 (second half)

1. F. Gilhooley, RF
2. B. Lamar, CF
3. F. Baker, 3B
4. D. Pratt, 2B
5. W. Pipp
   J. Fournier, 1B
6. P. Bodie
   H. Hyatt, LF
7. R. Peckinpaugh, SS
8. T. Hannah
   R. Walters, C

1919

1. S. Vick, RF
2. R. Peckinpaugh, SS
3. F. Baker, 3B
4. D. Lewis, LF
5. W. Pipp, 1B
6. D. Pratt, 2B
7. P. Bodie, CF
8. M. Ruel
   T. Hannah, C

NEW YORK

JAMES THOMAS WILLIAMS
SECOND BASEMAN, 1901–1907

One of the best hitting middle infielders of the Deadball Era, Jimmy Williams was a powerful, free-swinging right-handed batter who led his league in triples three times during his 11-year major league career, and ranked among his league's top ten in RBI seven times. Sure-handed defensively, Williams was nicknamed "Buttons" because of his small stature, though his listed size of 5'9" and 175 pounds was about average for his day. Possessing only average speed and adequate range in the field, Williams was nonetheless described in one article by the *Washington Post* as an accurate thrower, one who "can put the ball knee-high nearly every time." During his career, he led American League second basemen in assists and double plays twice each, and fielding percentage once.

James Thomas Williams was born on December 20, 1876, in St. Louis, one of five children of David L. and Mary A. Williams, both Welsh immigrants. Within three years the family relocated to Denver, with breadwinner David first running a coffee and spice shop. As a teenager, Jimmy made his way 110 miles south to Pueblo where in 1892 he joined a semi-pro club called the Rovers, an offshoot of the town's Rover Wheel and Athletic Club. By 1895 Jimmy was the Rovers' regular third baseman on a squad that played on weekends and featured the keystone duo of Zack and Bill Dean, African-American brothers who had been playing for the Pueblo Blues, a black team. The Rovers ended the 1895 season at 19–2, and Jimmy established himself as one of the team's best players.

Though Williams rejoined Pueblo for the 1896 season, the league disbanded in midseason, and Williams spent the rest of the year playing ball with the Leadville Blues and Albuquerque Browns. The following year, he caught on with the St. Joseph (Missouri) Saints of the Western Association. Switching to shortstop, Jimmy became known as "Homerun" Williams to Saints rooters, after he blasted a dozen home runs in his first twenty May games and added ten more blasts by July 1. He finished the season with 31 home runs.

James Manning, veteran manager of the Kansas City Blues, secured Williams's bat for the 1898 season, and it helped power the Blues to the Western League pennant with an 88–51 record. Williams finished the season with a sparkling .343 batting average. Now a legendary hitter everywhere he had played, Williams was acquired by the Pittsburgh Pirates prior to the 1899 season.

Under manager Patsy Donovan, the 1899 Pirates won only four more games than they had the previous season to finish in seventh place in the 12-team National League, but Williams put on one of the greatest rookie hitting displays in baseball history. Playing in 152 games at third base, Williams compiled separate hitting streaks of 27 and 26 games, both of which were stopped by fellow rookie and future Pirate Deacon Phillippe. Williams also finished fifth in the National League with a .355 average (behind four future Hall-of-Famers), ranked third in the league in home runs (9) and RBI (116), and led the league with 28 triples. (Though statistical reference sources list Williams with 27 three-baggers, recent research conducted by this author indicates that Williams was not properly credited for a three-bagger he hit off Cincinnati's Bill Dammann in the season's second game.) His .532 slugging percentage also ranked third in the league. In one late July five-game sweep of the Phillies, Williams went 13-for-20 with 10 runs scored, five triples, two home runs, and 18 RBI. The 27-game hitting streak remains the Pirates franchise record, and his 28 triples still stand as baseball's rookie record, and tied for fifth all-time.

The following year Williams remained the club's third baseman, as the Pirates brought in the players who would form the foundation of their great teams of the Deadball Era, including new player-manager Fred Clarke and shortstop Honus Wagner. With the eight-team National League more competitive than ever before, Williams suffered through a dreadful sophomore slump, finishing the year with a .264 average and .389 slugging percentage. He also missed a month of the season after injuring his ankle on July 13. The Pirates finished in second place, however, and after the season Williams celebrated the coming turn of the century by marrying Nannie May Smith on December 5.

In late March 1901 Williams boarded a train in Denver bound for Hot Springs, Arkansas, the Pirates spring training area. He never made it because the shrewd and persuasive John McGraw, manager of the newly-formed American League Baltimore Orioles, was on a talent safari. He "kidnapped" Williams (and soon Cardinal Mike Donlin) and talked him into jumping his Pittsburgh contract to sign with the Orioles.

Jimmy started his AL career at Baltimore's newly built American League Park on April 26, 1901. Since McGraw himself played third base, Williams was moved to second, where he would spend the rest of his career. Though he went hitless in his first game, by the end of the year the .317-hitting Williams led the Orioles in doubles (26), home runs (7), RBI (96), runs (113), and tied teammate Bill Keister with 21 triples to lead the majors.

During the Orioles' tumultuous 1902 campaign, when John McGraw resigned and carried several players with him to the New York Giants, Williams continued to provide stellar offense, batting .313 with 27 doubles, eight home runs, and 83 RBI. Once again, he topped the American League with 21 triples.

With the relocation of the Baltimore franchise to New York prior to the 1903 season, American League president Ban Johnson tried to ensure the success of the rechristened Highlanders by orchestrating the acquisition of several star players. By the start of the 1903 campaign, Williams was joined in the New York infield by third baseman Wid Conroy and shortstop Kid Elberfeld, to go along with an outfield that included Willie Keeler and a starting rotation anchored by Jack Chesbro, Jesse Tannehill, and Clark Griffith. The club finished in fourth place with a 72–62 record, as Williams, despite a .267 batting average, continued to hit with power, leading the team with 30 doubles, 12 triples (tied with Conroy), and 82 RBI. Among his 1903 feats were batting in the first run in Highlanders history in the team's first game, and driving in its first run on Manhattan soil one week later. His production sagged

in 1904, as he finished the year with a .263 average and .354 slugging percentage, both career lows to that point—though he did distinguish himself with his glove, leading all AL second basemen in assists and double plays. The Highlanders' loss to Boston on the season's final day marked the closest Williams would ever come to winning a major league pennant.

In 1905, Williams's production cratered, as he batted just .228 and the Highlanders stumbled into sixth place. They rebounded in 1906 to finish in second with a 90–61 record, and Williams improved along with the team, batting .277 with a team-high 77 RBI. The following year New York fell back into the second division, but Williams continued his consistent offensive production, batting .270 with 11 triples and 63 RBI. In the 1907–08 offseason he was traded to the St. Louis Browns along with Hobe Ferris and Danny Hoffman for Fred Glade, Harry Niles, and Charlie Hemphill.

"Williams is a classy fellow and dangerous at the plate," said Browns manager Jimmy McAleer in March 1908. "He is a smart ballplayer and will report lighter than in five years." In fact, Jimmy reported to spring training a bit chunky and never got in good shape. McAleer's faith in Williams looked good in the season opener, as Williams's RBI and run helped St. Louis beat Cleveland ace Addie Joss 2–1 in ten frames. St. Louis played well all season and reversed its 1907 record to 83–69. Williams's contribution was a .236 batting average with 53 RBI. The following year, Williams batted only .195 before McAleer finally pulled him from the lineup on August 28. Williams appeared in his last major league game in the season-ending doubleheader against Cleveland.

Joe Cantillon, owner and manager of the Minneapolis Millers of the American Assocation, signed Williams prior to the 1910 season. Jimmy spent the next six seasons in Minneapolis, batting over .300 twice and helping the Millers capture four AA pennants. After he retired from the Millers, Williams remained in Minneapolis for the rest of his life, working first in the insurance business and later as a health inspector for the city. During the early 1930s he also worked as an area scout and coach for the Cincinnati Reds, and was one of the instructors at a Reds-sponsored baseball school in Bartlesville, Oklahoma. During the 1940s he worked as an assembler and elevator operator for the Honeywell Company. Following the death of his wife Nannie in 1949, Williams began spending his winters in St. Petersburg, Florida, where he died following a short illness on January 16, 1965, at age 88.

RICHARD DIXIE TOURANGEAU

NEW YORK

John D. Chesbro
Right-Handed Pitcher, 1903–1909

Jack Chesbro's success with the spitball revolutionized the art of pitching during the Deadball Era, as countless hurlers followed his example in the wake of his brilliant 1904 campaign. That year, the broad-shouldered, sandy-complexioned right-hander established twentieth century records for games started (51) and wins (41), while amassing 454⅔ innings pitched, the century's second highest total. Unlike many of his fellow spitballers, Chesbro relied exclusively on his wet one after he began using it in 1904. By his own estimate, over the final 30 games of the 1904 campaign he threw no more than six balls that weren't spitters, and claimed after the season that the heavy regimen did not affect his arm. "The ball is not hard on the arm," he declared. "I pitched in 54 [*sic*] games last season and my arm never bothered me. Speed must be used to make the ball effective; at least, I always used speed, but the exertion is no greater than that of pitching fast straight balls." In fact, the workload proved too much for the pitcher's 5′9″, 180-pound frame, and by 1906 Chesbro was an average pitcher; three years later he was out of baseball.

He was born John D. Cheesbro on June 5, 1874 in Houghtonville, a village in North Adams, Massachusetts, the fourth of five children of shoemaker Chad Brown and Martha Jane (Fratenburgh) Cheesbro. He would eventually write his name as "Chesbro," but he never legally changed it from the birth spelling. The family name was pronounced "Cheez-boro," but he became known as "Chez-bro" early in his major league career. Throughout his youth, family members called him "Chad."

After starring for amateur teams, Chesbro and three other locals, including future big league teammate Art Madison, moved to Middletown, New York, in 1894 to play for the Asylums, a team representing the state mental hospital. While he did work with patients, his primary purpose was to pitch for the ball club. His pitching skills were honed by Asylums coach and catcher Pat McGreevy who, noting Chesbro's long fingers, predicted great success for the pitcher. Chesbro also acquired the nickname Happy Jack while working at the hospital after a patient noted his cheery disposition and friendly grin.

Chesbro joined the professional ranks with Albany of the New York State League in 1895, posting a 5–1 record before the club folded on May 20. Over the next two years, Chesbro pitched for Johnstown of the New York State League, Springfield of the Eastern League, and Roanoke of the Virginia League. He even found time to play some semipro ball in, of all places, Cooperstown, New York.

Signing with Richmond of the Atlantic League in 1897, Chesbro went 16–18 with a 1.82 ERA. The following year he went 23–15, helping Richmond to the league championship. At season's end, he was drafted by Baltimore's Ned Hanlon, but Hanlon moved to Brooklyn, Baltimore was nearly contracted, and Chesbro never signed. Back with Richmond in 1899, he began the season 17–4 before being sold July 7 to Pittsburgh for $1,500. Starting 17 games for the Pirates the rest of the season, Chesbro was unimpressive, posting a 6–9 record with a 4.11 ERA. After the season, the Pirates traded Chesbro along with three other players to Louisville for twelve players, including Honus Wagner, Fred Clarke, and Rube Waddell. Soon after the trade, however, the Louisville club was dissolved and Chesbro's contract was reassigned to Pittsburgh.

With an above-average fastball and curve that he threw with an over-the-top motion, Chesbro improved to 15–13 in 1900, but he really hit his stride the following year, when he won 21 games and registered a 2.38 ERA, fifth-best in the league, as Pittsburgh won its first of three consecutive NL pennants. In 1902, the Pirates enjoyed one of the greatest seasons in baseball history, winning 103 games against only 36 losses. Anchoring a pitching staff that included Deacon Phillippe, Sam Leever, and Jesse Tannehill, Chesbro led the league in wins (28), winning percentage (.824) and shutouts (8), while also hitting a league-high 21 batters.

Following the 1902 season, Chesbro jumped to the New York Highlanders of the American League. Because Chesbro did not report to the team until April 1, he missed a spring training series in which New York faced New Orleans right-hander Elmer Stricklett, who had begun to experiment with a spitball in exhibition games. Nonetheless, Chesbro enjoyed another standout season, leading the Highlanders to a fourth place finish with a 21–15 mark, good for his third consecutive 20-win season. He reported earlier the next spring, and saw Stricklett and his spitball first-hand in a spring training game. When Chesbro questioned Stricklett about the pitch, the diminutive right-hander refused to divulge his secret. Chesbro thus set out to master the pitch on his own.

Learn it he did. As he discovered, the moisture on the ball simply allowed the sphere to leave the fingers before the thumb. "The thumb, and thumb alone, directs the spit ball," he later explained. "The saliva on the ball does not make it drop. In fact, the saliva does not affect the ball in any way." Chesbro declared that his control of the pitch was so sure that he could make the spitball drop anywhere from two to eighteen inches. By the end of the 1904 season, Chesbro signaled his catchers how much of a break he was going to put on the ball.

New York manager Clark Griffith disliked the spitball because it was difficult to catch and he was worried he would run out of catchers due to hand injuries. But after Chesbro began the 1904 season with a mediocre 4–3 record, Griffith gave permission for his ace to use the new pitch as his primary weapon. He promptly won his next 14 starts, and finished the season with a 41–12 record and career-best 1.82 ERA. Becoming an amazing workhorse, Chesbro completed 48 of his 51 starts and relieved in four others while amassing a staggering 454⅔ innings pitched. Twenty-five of his starts came with less than three days of rest.

On the strength of Chesbro's pitching, New York challenged for the pennant, trailing defending champion Boston by a half-game entering a five-game showdown to end the season. Pitching on two days rest, Chesbro beat Boston for his 41st win to put New York a half-game up with four to play. Griffith's plan was to have Chesbro rest for the double-header on the final day. However, Chesbro talked his way into a start with no days rest and was knocked out of the box for only the third time all season as New York suffered a 13–2 loss. Cy Young hurled a 1–0 shutout in the following game to put Boston up by a game and a half with two to play. New York would need to sweep the doubleheader scheduled for the final day to take the flag.

Making his eighth start in fifteen days, Chesbro held a 2–0 shutout through six innings of the first game of the twinbill. Aided by two errors by second baseman Jimmy Williams, Boston scored twice in the seventh to tie. Lou Criger led off the Boston ninth with a single and advanced to third on two outs. With a 2–2 count on Freddy Parent, Chesbro unleashed a wild pitch that sailed over the glove of catcher Red Kleinow and ricocheted off the press box, scoring Criger. Though Parent singled on the next pitch, Chesbro would be forever remembered as the man who lost the pennant on a wild pitch. No banner season has ever ended on a more sour note, and some commentators even traced the pitcher's subsequent decline to his costly mistake.

Despite his protests to the contrary, Chesbro's heavy workload in 1904 probably did permanent damage to his arm. In one indication of the added strain, Chesbro changed his delivery from over-the-top to a round-house fling. His offseason conditioning also didn't help matters, as he stayed north during 1905 spring training to coach Harvard and reported to New York weighing 200 pounds. His effectiveness curtailed by a sore arm, Chesbro pitched more than 150 fewer innings,

Amid rumors he was to be farmed out to Indianapolis in 1909, Chesbro skipped spring training and refused to report to New York, causing the National Commission to place him on the ineligible list. He was reinstated May 24, but reported to New York out of shape. One newspaper described him as being "decidedly fat." After posting an 0–4 record in nine appearances, Chesbro was waived September 11 to the Boston Red Sox. Under the terms of the agreement, Boston had until May 1 of the following year to decide whether to keep him or return him to New York. He made just one appearance for Boston, losing to the Highlanders on the final day of the season. It would be his last major league game.

Deciding he was not even worth taking to training camp, the Red Sox announced they were returning Chesbro to New York in January 1910. The Highlanders had no plans for him on the major league roster, but he would not report to the minors, which again caused him to be placed on the ineligible list. He stayed on his farm and pitched nearby semipro Whitinsville to a championship.

Chesbro coached Massachusetts Agricultural College (now the University of Massachusetts) in 1911 and continued to pitch for semipro clubs, though with less success. One reporter who watched Chesbro get mauled by a Massachusetts semipro outfit sadly observed, "It was pitiful. Time was when any major league club would have paid a fabulous price for Chesbro. Now they wouldn't give him $25 a year for pitching." Nonetheless, Highlanders manager Harry Wolverton did agree to give Chesbro a look at 1912 spring training, but before leaving for camp he reconsidered and released him. Deciding to pay his own way to Hot Springs, Chesbro worked out for Brooklyn and Pittsburgh, but both clubs passed on him. He returned to Conway and continued to pitch and coach semipro teams. In 1924, Chesbro was hired by his old friend Clark Griffith to coach third base for the Washington Senators. However, when Al Schacht was hired June 1 to be reunited with coach and fellow clown Nick Altrock, Chesbro was trimmed from the coaching staff. It was his last job in Organized Baseball.

Jack Chesbro died November 6, 1931, on his Conway chicken farm. He had climbed a hill to determine the problem with a water pipeline when he succumbed to a heart attack at age 57. He is buried in Conway's Howland Cemetery. Chesbro was survived by his wife, the former Mabel Shuttleworth, a Conway resident he had married in 1896. In 1946, Chesbro was selected to the Hall of Fame by the Old-Timers Committee.

WAYNE McELREAVY

and finished the 1905 season with a 19–15 mark. He reported to spring training on time in 1906 and won 23 games, but also lost 17 and led the league in earned runs allowed.

When his contract for 1907 arrived in the mail, Chesbro mailed back his intention to retire to tend to his business interests, which included the Conway, Massachusetts, farm he had purchased at the turn of the century, as well as a sawmill and timber land. All told, he was making more money on the farm than on the ball field. Griffith eventually convinced Chesbro to return for another season, but the pitcher managed only a 10–10 record in 25 starts. The following year he was even worse, losing 20 games and posting an ERA nearly one-half run above the league average.

NEW YORK

WILLIAM EDWARD "WID" CONROY
THIRD BASEMAN, 1903–1908

An adept base stealer known for taking unusually large leads from first base, Wid Conroy used his raw speed and acrobatic skills to earn a reputation as one of the most versatile defensive players of the Deadball Era. During his eleven-year major league career, Conroy played a significant number of games at third base, shortstop, and left field, eliciting praise for his keen intelligence, sure-handedness, and leaping catches. One writer declared that Conroy's movements around third base were "as graceful as a dancing master," while another observed that "no matter in what position he is played, Conroy is generally recognized as a heady, hard-working ball player of much natural ability."

William Edward Conroy was born on April 5, 1877, the fifth child of Irish immigrants Bridgit and John Conroy. Most sources list Camden, New Jersey, as William's place of birth, but throughout his life census records indicated that he was born in neighboring Pennsylvania. In either event, William spent his childhood in Camden, where his father was employed in a shoe factory. From an early age, William demonstrated a love for baseball, spending much of his free time playing on Camden's sandlots, and earning the nickname "Widow," which would later be shortened to "Wid" during his playing career. Conroy pleaded ignorance as to the origin of his peculiar moniker, but fellow Camdenites asserted that he earned the name because of "his motherly interest in youngsters smaller and younger than himself, who used to number themselves in his 'gang.'"

Conroy's first professional baseball experience came in 1896, when the 5'9", 158-pound right-hander earned $75 per month plus board playing for Carlisle, Pennsylvania, of the Cumberland Valley League. The following season, Conroy played for a club in Milton, Pennsylvania, staying there until the final month of the 1898 season, when the Paterson Silk Weavers of the Atlantic League signed him to play shortstop. Wid appeared in just 23 games for the Silk Weavers before contracting malaria. He was too weak to suit up, but Paterson manager Sam LaRoque accused Conroy of feigning illness and handed him his release. The following season found Conroy with the Cortland Wagonmakers of the New York State League, where he led all shortstops in fielding percentage. That performance caught the eye of Connie Mack, then managing the Milwaukee Brewers of the American League, and Mack signed Conroy for the 1900 season. In 1901 the American League attained major league status and Mack departed for Philadelphia, but Conroy remained with the Brewers, playing a solid shortstop while batting .256 with five home runs and 64 RBI in 131 games.

The following season the Brewers franchise moved to St. Louis and a legion of National Leaguers jumped to the junior circuit, but Wid left Milwaukee and became one of the few American Leaguers to jump over to the National League, signing with the defending league champion Pittsburgh Pirates. The Pirates initially pegged Conroy as a backup for Honus Wagner, but Wagner eventually moved to the outfield and Conroy assumed the starting shortstop role.

Appearing in 99 games for one of the best teams in history, Conroy was the weakest hitter in the vaunted Pittsburgh lineup, collecting only 17 extra-base hits in 365 at-bats and posting a .299 on-base percentage. He played commendable defense however, and earned the respect and loyalty of his teammates for his take-no-prisoners approach to the game. In the fourth inning of a contest against the Chicago Cubs on June 23, Conroy got into a fistfight with the Cubs star shortstop, Joe Tinker, after Conroy had blocked Tinker on the base paths and spiked another Cub the previous day. Thirsty for revenge, Tinker got his chance when he moved from first to second on an infield hit. According to the *Chicago Tribune*, "Tinker tore down to second" and seeing Conroy covering the base, "pushed the Pirate off the bag…Conroy wheeled quickly and started toward the cushion as if to strike Tinker, whereupon the latter pushed his open hand over the greater part of Conroy's face in the manner so irritating to belligerents." A scuffle ensued, in which Conroy landed blows on Tinker's shoulder and the Cub shortstop struck Wid on the neck, before the pair could be separated. The fracas upset Pirates secretary Harry Pulliam, who declared in the days following the fight that he was "so disgusted by that row between Tinker and Conroy that I couldn't go out to the grounds."

But the ensuing punishments upset the Pirates even more, as the chairman of the league's executive committee, John T. Brush, suspended Conroy for 20 days, while benching Tinker for only three. Pittsburgh manager Fred Clarke blasted the ruling, noting that "if Conroy had not covered the bag he would have stamped himself an incompetent of the worst kind. Yet he is suspended for 20 days, because he did his duty." Owner Barney Dreyfuss appealed the ruling, but Brush dismissed the complaint.

Following the 1902 season, Conroy jumped leagues again, signing with the New York Highlanders. He was also accused of working as a spy for the American League, convincing teammates Tommy Leach and Harry Smith to jump leagues with him, while also attempting to persuade other Pirates to break their contracts. In the peace agreement between the two leagues that ensued prior to the start of the 1903 season, Leach and Smith were returned to the Pirates, while Conroy was awarded to the Highlanders.

Wid spent the next six seasons with New York, never batting higher than .273, but finishing among the league's top ten in home runs twice, triples four times, slugging percentage once, and stolen bases four times. In 1907, Conroy's 41 steals tied for second, behind only Ty Cobb's league-leading 49. Consistently praised for his deft handling of the bat (like many players of the era, Conroy choked up on the bat several inches and found his base hits by punching the ball to all fields), Conroy was also known as a smart, speedy base runner, routinely taking "the biggest leads off base of any player in the big show."

Though he had proved himself to be a fine defensive shortstop with Pittsburgh, Conroy agreed to play third base for New York, as the Highlanders already boasted a standout defensive shortstop in Kid Elberfeld. In 1903

and 1904, Wid emerged as a reliable third baseman with excellent range and sure hands. He proved his defensive versatility in 1905, when injuries to other players forced him to play every position on the field except pitcher and catcher. When rookie third baseman Frank LaPorte joined the starting lineup in 1906, Conroy moved to the outfield and schooled the youngster on the fundamentals of the hot corner. After LaPorte was traded to the Boston Red Sox prior to the 1908 campaign, Conroy returned to his old position at third and continued to field well, though by then his batting skills had begun to decline.

Following the 1908 season, in which he batted just .237 with a .296 slugging percentage, Conroy was sold to the Washington Senators for $5,000. Reflecting his solid standing within the game, Conroy's acquisition was greeted with delight by Washington fans, who took it as a sign that "the local owners are sincere in their efforts to build up a winner." Now 32 years old, Conroy failed to live up to the high hopes that had been set for him, and finished the year with a .244 batting average and career-low .293 slugging percentage. He spent the following offseason "boiling out" in Hot Springs, Arkansas, and his offensive production improved slightly in 1910, but the following year he finished with a .232 batting average, the lowest of his career, while stealing just 12 bases.

Before the 1912 season, Washington released Conroy to Rochester of the International League, where he played for two years. Prior to the 1914 campaign, Wid accepted a job as manager of the Elmira Colonels of the New York State League, where he enjoyed two winning seasons and claimed one league championship. Following his dismissal from the Elmira job after the 1916 campaign, Wid played for Wichita of the Western League in 1917. He spent his last season as an active player with Hutchinson of the Western League in 1918, though shortages caused by the U.S. entry into World War I forced that circuit to suspend its season in July. Conroy's last job in baseball came in 1922, when he briefly served as a coach for the Philadelphia Phillies.

Following baseball, Conroy worked as a security guard, and later as a messenger for the Burlington County Trust Company in Moorestown, New Jersey. Living with his wife, Mary, and their six children, Wid suffered personal tragedy in 1945, when his second oldest son, William Conroy, Jr., was killed in the battle of Okinawa. Wid died fourteen years later, on December 6, 1959, in Burlington County Hospital, after suffering a stroke. He was buried in Mt. Carmel Cemetery in Moorestown.

SAM BERNSTEIN

NEW YORK

Norman Arthur "Kid" Elberfeld
Shortstop, 1903–1909; Manager, 1908

Kid Elberfeld, called "the dirtiest, scrappiest, most pestiferous, most rantankerous [sic], most rambunctious ball player that ever stood on spikes" for his vicious arguments on the diamond, patterned his combative style after that of his favorite team, the Baltimore Orioles of the mid-1890s. He believed, like those Oriole players, that an umpire should be kept in his place, and that what happened behind an arbiter's back was none of his business. But when Elberfeld kept his volatile temper in check, he was also an "ideal infielder—full of ginger." Called by George Stallings one of the two best shortstops in baseball, his throwing arm was "cyclonic," and, though only 5′7″, 158 pounds, he was fearless in turning the double play. Not surprisingly, he was frequently spiked, and by 1907 wore a whalebone shin guard on his right leg for protection. He was also one of the best hitting shortstops of his day, with a career .271 average, and a master at getting hit by close pitches. He perfected the art of angling his body in toward the plate, holding his arms in such as way as to take only a glancing blow while simultaneously appearing to make an honest attempt to avoid the pitch, and then, for effect, shouting and gesticulating at the pitcher. He became so adept at this that he still ranks 13th on the career hit by pitch list, with 165.

Norman Arthur Elberfeld was born on April 13, 1875, in Pomeroy, Ohio, on the Ohio River, between Cincinnati and Pittsburgh. His parents, Philip Elberfeld, a shoe merchant, and Katherine Eiselstein, were German immigrants who had settled in Meigs County, Ohio, in the mid-nineteenth century. Norman was the tenth of eleven children—six boys and five girls—though the youngest child died when Elberfeld was six years old. In 1878 the family moved to Cincinnati. Called "Kid" from his earliest days, Elberfeld had only a few years of formal schooling, and as a youngster played mainly hockey and baseball. From 1892 to 1894 he captained local baseball teams in the Norwood and Bond Hill neighborhoods of Cincinnati and played nearly every position, including catcher. In 1895, Elberfeld joined an independent team in Clarksville, Tennessee, managed and partly owned by former major leaguer Billy Earle.

Elberfeld's first professional job came the next season when he and Earle joined the Dallas Navigators of the Texas Southern League. A pre-season contract dispute with Montgomery was settled in Dallas' favor, but Elberfeld's season with the Navigators ended abruptly in May due to a leg injury. Jumping his contract with Dallas (possibly under the influence of Earle, who left at the same time), he recovered enough to latch on with a club in Lexington, Kentucky, where Jake Wells of the Richmond Bluebirds spotted him. Elberfeld played with Richmond of the Atlantic League in 1897. His .335 batting average and 45 stolen bases attracted the attention of the Philadelphia Phillies, who purchased his contract in September.

Elberfeld didn't play for Philadelphia in 1897, and his 1898 major league debut was delayed by knee injuries caused by a spring training bathtub fall. Finally, on May 30, he started the first game of a doubleheader against Louisville at third base and belted two doubles, got hit by a pitch, and committed two errors in the field. He quickly became a favorite with the Philadelphia fans, but poor fielding and a penchant for interfering with opposing runners left the local writers less impressed. One wrote: "Elberfeld might as well learn now that Philadelphia ballcranks will not stand for his minor league methods. What we want [are] ball players, not toughs." He played only 14 games for Philadelphia, and, though presented with a gold watch during a late-June game at Cincinnati by his hometown fans, was sold to the Western League Detroit

Tigers in July, where he was ejected and fined in one of his first games. He finished the year with a lowly .237 average.

In 1899 Elberfeld hit .308 and stole 23 bases, earning him another chance in the majors. The Cincinnati Reds purchased his contract in August, but he injured his back, batted and fielded poorly, and was generally overshadowed by another rookie acquired around the same time, Sam Crawford. He jumped back to Detroit in 1900, where, as the "most aggressive" player on the "most aggressive and scrappiest" team in the newly renamed American League, he was ejected from three games during one eight-game stretch in June. Though he batted only .262, he led all shortstops with an astonishing average of over seven successful chances per game. He also married Emily Grace Catlow on October 10, settling in Chattanooga, where he raised chickens on his farm during off seasons, and, later, tended to his apple orchard.

Elberfeld remained with Detroit for the next 2½ years. In 1901, as the Tigers staked their claim to major league status, he batted .308 with 11 triples and three home runs, all of which would remain his major league career highs. Near the end of the 1902 season, New York Giants owner John T. Brush and manager John McGraw attempted to beef up their last place team by securing several Detroit players, and reportedly signed Elberfeld to a two-year contract for $4,500 per year. McGraw's personality appealed to Elberfeld. "McGraw always liked me," Elberfeld said. "I played his aggressive style of ball. And I would have liked to have played for him." But the 1903 peace agreement returned Elberfeld to Detroit, and when Ed Barrow was suddenly named to replace suicide-victim Win Mercer as new Detroit manager, Barrow inherited an unhappy shortstop. Though Elberfeld started fast, batting .431 during the first three weeks of the season, his hitting soon tailed off and his fielding was shoddy. On June 2, Barrow fined and suspended him for "loaferish conduct," suspecting Elberfeld of playing poorly to force a trade to the St. Louis Browns. Eight days later, Barrow did trade him, not to St. Louis, but to the New York Highlanders.

The move nearly derailed the nascent peace treaty between the leagues. Brush, opposed to peace in the first place, viewed the trade as an attempt by AL president Ban Johnson to siphon fans from the Giants. Brush badgered NL president Harry Pulliam into declaring that Johnson had violated the "spirit if not the letter" of the treaty and persuaded Pulliam to let McGraw use George Davis—then the subject of a dispute between the Giants and the Chicago White Sox—at shortstop. The case dragged on for weeks. In the meantime, Elberfeld

got himself charged with disorderly conduct and fined for throwing a bottle (some reports say a knife) at a hotel waiter. Ultimately, the other NL owners decided they could not afford another interleague war, and on July 20 repudiated Brush's position. One of Elberfeld's career highlights came a short while later, on August 1, in a 3–2 Highlander victory over Philadelphia ace Rube Waddell. Elberfeld made all four New York hits and drove in all three runs as Waddell struck out 13 New Yorkers. It was after his arrival in New York, too, that sportswriter Sam Crane dubbed Elberfeld Tabasco Kid, referring to Elberfeld's now infamous temper and "peppery" style of play.

Over the next three years with New York, Elberfeld solidified his reputation as one of the best-hitting short-stops in baseball. From 1904 to 1906, he had the highest batting (.275) and on-base-plus-slugging (.688) percentages of any shortstop in the American League, and was second in the majors only to Honus Wagner. But injuries and suspensions continued to dog him; the Highlanders might have won pennants in 1904 and 1906 had Elberfeld not missed 89 games during those years. In late 1906 he also had two memorable run-ins with umpire Silk O'Loughlin. The first, on August 8, occurred when Elberfeld was denied first base after being hit by a pitch, prompting him to menace the umpire with a bat. Then, on September 3, the two went at it again in a brawl described by the *New York Times* as "one of the most disgraceful scenes exhibitions of rowdyism ever witnessed on a baseball field." The Highlanders were in a close pennant race with Chicago, and when Elberfeld was suspended for only seven games by Johnson, some viewed it as an act of favoritism toward the Highlanders.

Elberfeld's last years in New York were difficult. He feuded with teammates Wid Conroy, Jimmy Williams, Ira Thomas, and Hal Chase, and, in July 1907, was suspended by Highlander owner Frank Farrell for what the *New York Times* called "indifferent work in the field and at the bat." Elberfeld, harboring unrealized managerial aspirations, again sought to force a trade (this time with Washington) through sulking and lacka-daisical play. When it was announced between games of a July 26 doubleheader that Conroy would replace Elberfeld, 8,000 fans greeted the news with "tumultu-ous" applause. After Elberfeld apologized to manager Clark Griffith, Farrell lifted the suspension on August 15 and, before 1908, Elberfeld was even offered a con-tract for $2,700—with a $1,000 bonus if he behaved himself.

On May 1, 1908, with the New Yorkers tied for first place, Elberfeld was severely spiked by Washington outfielder Bob Ganley, essentially ending Elberfeld's season. The team continued to play well without him through May, but won only seven games during June. On June 24, Farrell finally forced Griffith to resign, and Elberfeld got his chance to be manager. His tenure was a disaster. New York lost 15 of their next 18 games and the *Washington Post* soon quoted an unnamed Highlander saying: "We are...playing under the direction of a crazy man. It won't take Elberfeld more than two weeks to make us the most demoralized ball team that the American League has ever known. He thinks he is a manager, but he can't convince any one but himself that he has the first qualification for the place. It's a joke." Even Elberfeld himself apparently harbored doubts about his qualifications; some years later *Baseball Magazine* reported that he wouldn't select the team's starting pitchers without first consulting his wife. Regardless of who picked the pitchers, the Highlanders sank to last place, Chase jumped the team in early September, and Elberfeld's sole stint as a major league manager ended with a dismal 27–71 record.

Though replaced by George Stallings as manager after the season, Elberfeld remained with the team, reluctantly, as a player in 1909; his nasty reputation, high salary, and history of injuries made him difficult to trade. His battered legs forced him to play more at third base, a familiar position from his early days and one for which he was well-suited because of his strong arm. Rusty from his long layoff, Elberfeld batted only .237 that year, but showed enough life to enable Stallings to sell him to Washington in December. The next spring, he began coaching young players from D.C.-area town and high school teams, an occupation that would dominate his activities after his playing days ended.

Elberfeld remained with Washington for two years, and manager Jimmy McAleer twice selected Elberfeld to play on post-season "all-star" teams formed to keep the pennant-winning A's sharp for their upcoming World Series appearances. In 1911, Elberfeld played through ankle, hip, and back injuries. Though he batted a solid .272 and posted a career high .405 OBP, in 1912 new Senators manager Clark Griffith was determined to go with younger players, and, prior to the season, Elberfeld was sold to Montgomery of the Southern Association. He batted .260 in 78 games for the Rebels, then moved on to the Chattanooga Lookouts in 1913 as player–manager, where he batted .332 in 94 games. He was then hired to manage New Orleans, but after a change in team ownership left him jobless, Brooklyn signed him as a coach and utility player. Elberfeld played his final major league game on September 24, 1914, entering the game, ironically,

as a late-inning defensive replacement when starting shortstop Dick Egan was ejected for arguing a call.

His big league days over, Elberfeld forged a second career as a minor league player and manager, primarily in the Southern Association. He spent three more years at Chattanooga, taking over as manager in July 1915. In 1918 he managed Little Rock, playing sporadically, and worked briefly at Camp Shelby, Mississippi, as a YMCA director, teaching soldiers to throw hand grenades like baseballs. Two years later he managed Little Rock to a league championship, though they were upset by the Class B Texas League champions Fort Worth in the post-season series. He stayed with Little Rock for four more seasons, followed by stints in Mobile, Chattanooga, and Little Rock again, and Springfield in the Western Association. After scouting for Little Rock and Atlanta, he finished his minor league managerial career in 1936 with the Fulton (Kentucky) Eagles in the Class D Kitty League, even appearing in one last game as a 61-year-old pinch hitter.

Though an utter failure as a leader of mature major league players, Elberfeld was highly successful working with younger athletes. He discovered or helped develop many major league players, including Casey Stengel, Travis Jackson, Bill Terry, Cecil Travis, and Jim Turner, though his influence wasn't uniformly positive—Burleigh Grimes blamed his own notoriously bad temper on his early exposure to Elberfeld. Beginning in the 1920s, he ran or participated in baseball schools throughout the South, even managing the female pitcher Jackie Mitchell on his 1931 barnstorming team, the Lookout Juniors. He had a lot of experience tutoring female athletes; of his six children, five were girls, and during the mid-1920s they competed as boxers, held state and national amateur championships in tennis and swimming, and even formed a basketball team around Chattanooga called the Elberfeld Sisters.

In the early 1940s, Elberfeld ran annual baseball camps sponsored by Coca-Cola in Minden, Louisiana. He would regale the boys with reminiscences of his career and show off the scars crisscrossing his legs. Though patient with his more uncoordinated charges, traces of the Tabasco Kid of old still remained: he called them "rock" or "hardhead" when they botched a play, and passed along tips on the finer points of bench jockeying.

Early in 1944, Elberfeld caught a cold and on January 13 died of pneumonia at Erlanger Hospital in Chattanooga. He was buried in Chattanooga Memorial Park.

TERRY SIMPKINS

NEW YORK

William Henry Keeler
Right Fielder, 1903–1909

A diminutive lefty who was one of baseball's biggest stars in the 1890s, Wee Willie Keeler continued "to hit 'em where they ain't" through the first decade of the Deadball Era. The tiny right fielder—he stood just 5′4½″ and weighed 140 pounds—capped a stellar career with several solid seasons after the turn of the century. Wee Willie, also known as "Billy Keeler," played in 19 big league campaigns, and in 13 of them—every year from 1894 to 1906—he hit .300 or better and ranked in his league's top 10 in hits. Eight straight times he collected more than 200 safeties, and his .424 average in 1897 is the highest single season mark by a left-handed hitter in baseball history. For his career, Keeler compiled a .341 batting average and racked up 2,932 hits—86 percent of them singles—in 2,123 big league games. A Brooklyn native, Wee Willie played for all three New York teams of the day, and was a key member of the rollicking Baltimore Orioles dynasty of the 1890s. He was gregarious and friendly, and when asked why he smiled so much, he replied, "Because I get paid for playing baseball."

A two-time batting champion and a three-time league leader in hits, he had the speed to leg out infield singles, the bat control to drop down bunts, chops, and rollers in front of infielders, and when they moved in, the ability to loft a base hit over their heads. "Keeler could bunt any time he chose," Honus Wagner remembered. "If the third baseman came in for a tap, he invariably pushed the ball past the fielder. If he stayed back, he bunted. Also, he had a trick of hitting a high hopper to an infielder. The ball would bound so high that he was across the bag before he could be stopped." Wee Willie wielded a bat that was just 30 inches long, but weighed 46 ounces. He choked up nearly halfway, and snapped at the ball with a short stroke. He once said, "Learn what pitch you can hit good, then wait for that pitch," but he is best remembered for his description of his hitting style to *Brooklyn Eagle* writer Abe Yager. "I have already written a treatise and it reads like this: 'Keep your eye clear and hit 'em where they ain't; that's all.'"

William Henry O'Kelleher, Jr., was born on March 3, 1872, in Brooklyn. The son of William, Sr., a trolley switchman, and Mary, Willie served as captain for his PS 26 team, but quit school at age 15 to play for the semipro Acmes for $1.50 a game. He toiled locally for Flushing and Arlington, and in 1890 joined the Crescents of Plainfield, New Jersey, where he drew $60 per month as a pitcher and third baseman. Keeler broke into Organized Baseball in 1892 with Binghamton, and led the Eastern League in batting with a .373 average, but made 48 errors in 93 games as a left-handed third baseman.

Keeler made his big league debut with the New York Giants on September 30, 1892, with a single off Philadelphia's Tim Keefe at the Polo Grounds. He appeared in 14 games as a third baseman and stroked 17 hits, including three doubles in 53 at-bats, for a .321 average. He was back with the Giants to start the 1893 season, and smacked eight hits in 24 at-bats, including his first triple and home run, and played second base, shortstop and the outfield. He injured his leg sliding on May 10, missed two months, and served a stint back at Binghamton, where he made 11 errors in 15 games at third base. Late in the season, the Giants shipped him to the Brooklyn Grooms, where Willie finished out the season batting .312 for his hometown team.

In one of history's most lopsided trades, on January 1, 1894, Baltimore manager Ned Hanlon acquired Keeler and star first baseman Dan Brouthers from Brooklyn in exchange for journeymen Bill Shindle and George Treadway. Installed as the regular right fielder in a lineup

that included John McGraw, Hughey Jennings, and Wilbert Robinson, Wee Willie blossomed in Baltimore. Keeler collected more than 200 hits each year he played with the Orioles. During that five-year span, he batted .388, and averaged 219 hits, 74 RBI, 48 steals and 278 total bases per year. In 1897, he led the National League with a .424 average, the highest ever by a left-handed hitter, and collected 46 extra-base hits and 64 steals. He also hit safely in 44 consecutive games, a major league record until 1941, when Joe DiMaggio hit safely in 56 straight, and still the National League record, though one he now shares with Pete Rose. A year later, Keeler won another batting crown with a .385 average.

Batting atop the Baltimore lineup, McGraw and Keeler perfected the "Baltimore Chop," driving the ball into the infield dirt and beating out the resulting high hop, and though they didn't invent the hit-and-run, Muggsy and Wee Willie turned it into an art form. Keeler was also an excellent bunter, possessed great bat control and was a master at fouling off pitches. He was a fleet and instinctive outfielder: McGraw later referred to Keeler's diving, barehanded catch into a barbed wire fence in Washington in June 1898 as the greatest he ever saw. However, McGraw often needled Keeler for his defensive lapses, and during the 1897 season, the two teammates brawled naked in the shower room of

the Baltimore clubhouse as teammate Jack Doyle, a Muggsy antagonist, stood guard to prevent interference. As Doyle had predicted, McGraw was the first to "squeal." Despite the incident, Keeler, who didn't drink or swear, was generally regarded as the genteel, friendly, and cheerful member of the rough-and-tumble Orioles dynasty.

By 1899, Hanlon and Harry Von der Horst jointly owned both the Baltimore and Brooklyn franchises and sought to combine their best players on one team. Keeler and several key Orioles moved to Brooklyn with Hanlon, though McGraw and Robinson chose to stay in Baltimore. Back home, Keeler led the Superbas to the NL pennant in 1899, batting .379, and again in 1900, when he hit .362. He finished the nineteenth century with a .381 lifetime batting average, the best in baseball history up to that point. In 1901, he opened the Deadball Era with his eighth straight 200-hit season, though his average dipped to .339 thanks in large part to the National League's adoption of the foul strike rule. "His hitting along the foul line was the chief cause of adopting the foul strike rule," *Chicago Daily Tribune* writer Hugh Fullerton reported. Prior to the 1902 campaign, Keeler turned 30 years old, was named the Superbas team captain, and started to show signs of age. He rapped out 186 hits, batted .333, drove in 38 runs, scored 86, and stole 19 bases, all nine-year lows.

In 1903, the American League's Baltimore Orioles relocated to Hilltop Park in Manhattan, and New York owners Frank Farrell and Bill Devery sought out Keeler, who had been limited by the NL's $2,400 salary cap for several seasons. Willie jumped to the junior circuit and became baseball's first $10,000 player. "We can count on our fingers the number of years we will be able to play," Keeler had told the *New York Clipper* earlier in his career. "That makes it plain that we must make all the money we can during the short period we may be said to be star players."

In his first season with Clark Griffith's Highlanders, Wee Willie batted .312, collected 160 hits, stole 24 bases, and played 128 games in the outfield and four at third base. He improved the next year to hit .343, second only to Cleveland's Nap Lajoie. The Highlanders fell just short of an AL flag despite Keeler's stellar season and 41 wins from Jack Chesbro. Commuting to Hilltop Park from his Brooklyn home, Keeler batted .302 in 1905, and made his final infield appearances when he played three games at third and 12 at second base, making him one of the last lefties to play either position in the major leagues.

The 1905 season also saw Lajoie leapfrog Keeler as the man with the highest lifetime batting average in baseball history, .361 to .359. Keeler hit .304 in 1906, his final season as a full-time player, and the Highlanders finished second again under Griffith. In 1907 New York fell to fifth, and at age 35, Wee Willie batted just .234 in 107 games as his declining speed took a toll on his ability to beat out infield hits. He revived his career in 1908 by batting .263 in 91 games, but New York slipped into the cellar and Griffith resigned early in the season. The owners wanted Keeler to take the helm, but when Wee Willie declined, shortstop Kid Elberfeld finished out the season. Keeler considered retirement prior to the 1909 season, but decided to stay on, serving as team captain and batting .264 in 99 games as the Highlanders climbed to fifth place under new manager George Stallings. At 37, Keeler was now the sixth-oldest player in the American League.

In 1910, Willie moved to the other side of Manhattan to reunite with McGraw and finish his big league career where it started. That season he played in 19 games, but just two in the field, collecting three hits in 10 at-bats and stealing a base, the 495th of his career. The fact that he was just 68 hits shy of 3,000 at the time of his retirement went virtually unnoticed. Wee Willie played one more year of Organized Baseball, collecting 43 hits in 39 games for Toronto in the International League in 1911. He returned to his hometown as a coach with the Brooklyn Tip-Tops of the Federal League in 1914, and served as a scout for the Boston Braves in 1915.

After his retirement, Keeler invested his baseball earnings in real estate, and purchased commercial lots in New York City. He was regarded as a millionaire, but when the real estate market lost its speculative value after World War I, Willie was forced to rely on his family for financial support. Although he worked briefly as a scout for the Yankees, by 1921 he was forced to accept a joint gift of $5,500 from the National and American leagues to save his mortgage.

Keeler suffered from heart disease in the early 1920s, was too ill to attend a Baltimore Orioles team reunion, and after two years of suffering, was losing the battle for his life during the holiday season of 1922. He vowed to live to see 1923, and on New Year's Eve, several well-meaning friends stopped by his home on Gates Avenue in Brooklyn to congratulate him and cheer him up. When Willie became exhausted, they left him alone, rang in the New Year, and returned to find him celebrating by ringing the tiny bell that he used to summon his attendant. Hours later, he passed away at age 50. Keeler, a lifelong bachelor and a member of the fraternal order of the Elks, was laid to rest in Queens' Calvary Cemetery next to his father and siblings, and at his request, in the same grave with his beloved mother, who had died in 1901. In order to place a memorial to the former baseball star, her headstone was moved to become a footstone. Among the pallbearers were a number of old Orioles, including McGraw, Robinson, Jennings, Joe Kelley, and Kid Gleason. On June 12, 1939, Wee Willie Keeler was one of 25 legends inducted into the Baseball Hall of Fame at its formal opening.

DOUG SKIPPER

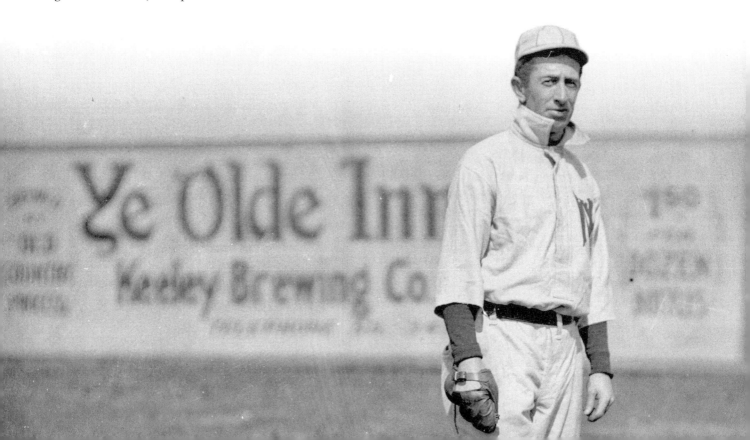

NEW YORK

ALBERT LEWIS ORTH
RIGHT-HANDED PITCHER, 1904–1909

A typical Al Orth pitch was once described in a poem by W.A. Phelon as a "glistening ball…but little speed, and scarce a curve at all." During his 15-year major league career, the "Curveless Wonder" won 204 games, yet struck out just 948 batters in more than 3,300 innings pitched. The burly six-foot, 200-pound right-hander threw with a seemingly-effortless delivery, and relied on pinpoint control to overcome batters. "To the spectators Orth pitched a ball that it seemed must be easy to hit," J. E. Wray observed in 1928, "yet year after year he kept on 'fooling' the batsmen." Though some reports indicate he had a good fastball early in his career, and once even tinkered with a curve, by the late 1890s his success on the mound was the result of his "slow ball." During the Deadball Era, Fred Lieb later related, Osee Schrecongost of the Philadelphia Athletics once caught one of Orth's pitches barehanded while batting against him. Nonetheless, Orth remained an effective pitcher during the early years of the new century, and posted career highs in wins (27) and strikeouts (133) for the New York Highlanders in 1906.

Albert Lewis Orth was born on September 5, 1872, and raised in Danville, Indiana. Orth attended DePauw University in Greencastle, Indiana, and after his stay there the right-hander's baseball career began to take shape. Some reports have Orth playing in Lebanon, Indiana, before making his professional debut with a club in Indianapolis, but it was not until he joined the Lynchburg Hill Climbers of the Virginia League that he began to make a name for himself. By mid-August 1895, Orth was pitching well for Lynchburg, putting together a 24–7 record and attracting attention from major league scouts. Lynchburg rejected a $500 offer from the Pittsburgh Pirates before selling Orth's services to the Philadelphia Phillies for $1,000. Orth appeared in

a major league uniform for the first time as the seventh-place Phillies (48–41 and eight games back of NL-leading Cleveland) hosted New York at the new Philadelphia home park (later known as the Baker Bowl).

In a game described by the *Washington Post* as a "travesty on baseball" Orth saw his teammates rack up a 20–9 lead after seven innings. When he came in to mop up in the eighth inning, Orth was greeted by the home crowd with cheers. He kept New York scoreless over the next two innings, allowing just two singles and walking none while helping the Phillies pad their lead by hitting a double off the fence on the first pitch he saw as a major league batter, and later coming around to score in the Phils' 23–9 win. Two days later, on August 17, Orth made his first major league start against Boston and managed to get the win despite giving up seven runs on 12 hits as his teammates scored 17 runs in the new hitter-friendly Philadelphia ballpark.

Orth's early success and overwhelming run support (the Phillies averaged more than 11 runs per game in his 10 starts) continued through the rest of the 1895 season. He strung together eight consecutive wins (one start ended in a tie) before spoiling his perfect record in his last start of the season, a 6–3 loss to Brooklyn. Orth finished the year at 8–1 with a solid 3.89 ERA, displaying excellent control by yielding only 22 walks in 88 innings of work.

During his next six seasons with the Phillies, Orth won at least 14 games every year, ranked third in the NL with a 2.27 ERA in 1901, and brought his victory total to an even 100 wins against 72 losses. On October 13, 1898, Orth pitched and won both ends of a doubleheader against Brooklyn. In 1901, Orth won 20 games for the first time in his career and led the league in fewest walks per nine innings, as he surrendered just 32 free passes in 281⅔ innings of work.

Like many of his Philadelphia teammates, following the 1901 season Orth jumped to the American League, signing with the Washington Senators. Orth again posted the lowest walk rate in his league in 1902, with just 40 bases on balls allowed in 324 innings. Orth struck out just 76 batters for the year, however, finishing with a 19–18 record and a subpar 3.97 ERA. He was even worse in 1903, winning 10 games against 22 losses while posting a horrendous 4.34 ERA. After starting the 1904 campaign 3–4 with a 4.76 ERA, Orth was traded to the New York Highlanders for Tom Hughes and Barney Wolfe.

Shortly after his arrival with the Highlanders, Orth turned his season around, helping to keep New York in the pennant race until the last day of the season with an 11–6 record and league-average 2.68 ERA. Orth's turnaround was probably due in part to teammate Jack Chesbro, who rode the spitball to a 41-win season that year. Orth himself said he first used the spitball at the end of the 1904 season and considered the pitch "more effective than a curve" with a "quicker break." Orth threw it "regularly" during the 1905 season, as he posted an 18–16 record with a 2.86 ERA for the sixth-place Highlanders.

Perhaps because of his growing familiarity with the new pitch, in 1906 Orth set a career high in victories. His 27 wins and 36 complete games led the American League, and he registered a career-high 133 strikeouts in 338⅔ innings. The Highlanders finished the year in second place, three games out, but the campaign would mark the last time in Orth's career that he would come close to winning a pennant. In 1907, the Highlanders dropped to fifth place, and Orth tied for the league lead with 21 losses, making him the first pitcher in baseball history to lead his league in wins one season and in losses the next.

In 1908 Orth was even worse, posting a 2–13 record with a miserable 3.42 ERA before drawing his release in August. Orth returned to Lynchburg, where he made his off-season home, and purchased a share in the local franchise in the Virginia League, assuming the role of player–manager. He had begun the 1909 season in that capacity when reports emerged of an offer from George Stallings, the new manager of the struggling Highlanders, to rejoin the club.

Rather than letting him pitch—Orth appeared on the mound in only one game for the Highlanders in 1909, surrendering four runs in three innings of work—Stallings kept Orth on the roster for his offense. Orth had always been one of the best-hitting pitchers in the game, finishing his career with a .273 batting average and 12 home runs, and batting over .300 in five

different seasons. In his last stint in the majors, however, the 36-year-old finished the year with a .265 batting average and only one extra-base hit in 34 at-bats. After initially appearing as a pinch-hitter, Orth played at second base in six games, committing no errors in 26 chances but impressing no one with his range. As Ring Lardner observed after one contest, the "game must have convinced George Stallings of one thing if he was watching it closely, and that is that Al Orth has much to learn about playing second base."

Following his stint with the Highlanders, Orth signed with the Indianapolis Indians of the American Association for the 1910 season, but didn't last long there and rejoined Lynchburg in July of that year. By 1912 he had signed on with the National League as an umpire, a role foreshadowed in 1901 when Orth, while still playing for the Phillies, was one of three players who replaced umpire Bob Emslie after the latter had become ill between games of a doubleheader. Orth served as an NL ump until 1917. Orth also worked as a baseball coach for Washington and Lee University and the Virginia Military Institute, and spent time with the YMCA as an athletic director for American troops stationed in France during World War I.

Orth died in Lynchburg, Virginia, on October 8, 1948, at the age of 76. He was survived by two sons and his wife, the former Jimmie Allen, whom he had married following his rookie season with the Phillies in 1895. He was buried in Spring Hill Cemetery in Lynchburg.

CHRIS HAUSER

Hal Chase

NEW YORK

HAROLD HOMER CHASE
FIRST BASEMAN, 1905–1913; MANAGER, 1910–1911

Hal Chase, whose big league career lasted from 1905 to 1919, was the most notoriously corrupt player in baseball history. He was also, according to many of those who saw him play, the greatest defensive first baseman ever. A cocky, easygoing Californian, Chase was the first homegrown star of the New York Highlanders (later the Yankees), but he wore out his welcome with them, as he did with just about every other team he played for during his fifteen years in the major leagues.

Yet there was something about "Prince Hal," as he was perhaps inevitably nicknamed, some combination of athletic grace, back-slapping charm, and apparent sincerity, that convinced any number of hard-bitten baseball men—men who should have known better—to take a chance on him. Long after his alleged transgressions had come to light, moreover, he was recalled by many of his peers—including Babe Ruth, Pants Rowland, Ed Barrow, Cy Young, and Bill Dinneen, to name just a few—as the best first baseman they had ever seen. Yet when he died, a penniless derelict, in 1947, he left behind two shattered marriages, an estranged son, and one of the great unfulfilled careers in baseball history. Today he is remembered as the poster boy for an era when gambling and throwing games seem to have been much more common than anyone was willing to admit.

Harold Homer Chase always marched to the beat of a different drummer. He was born in Los Gatos, California, on February 13, 1883, the fourth son of James and Mary Chase, natives of Maine who had emigrated to California, where a number of relatives had already settled, in the late nineteenth century. The Chase family was involved in the lumber industry, but young Hal never evinced much interest in the family business. Instead, at an early age, he decided that his remarkable athletic skills would be his meal ticket. As a youth he played on various semipro teams in and around San Jose and eventually enrolled in nearby Santa Clara College, which at that time was a West Coast collegiate baseball power.

At Santa Clara, Chase supposedly studied engineering, though there is no evidence to suggest he ever set foot in a classroom. He was something of an oddity in that he frequently played second base and catcher even though he threw left-handed, but his athletic ability was obvious—so much so that in 1903 the Los Angeles Angels of the Pacific Coast League signed Chase to his first professional contract.

Chase spent the 1904 season with the Angels, playing first base, batting a solid but unspectacular .279, and catching the eyes of scouts from the eastern major league clubs. When the Highlanders drafted him, the Angels threatened to rupture the newly-signed peace agreement between the PCL and the rest of Organized Baseball rather than give up their promising young star-in-the-making, but eventually cooler heads prevailed. Chase reported to the Highlanders and was immediately installed as the starting first baseman.

The Highlanders were an appropriate team for Chase, if only because their owners personified the dubious morality of early twentieth century New York. Frank Farrell was the proprietor of the most famous illegal casino in the city; his partner Big Bill Devery was a notoriously corrupt police captain and Tammany Hall functionary. Their young star took to New York like the proverbial duck to water. He quickly became a fixture in Broadway's sporting and theatrical demimonde, rubbing shoulders and raising glasses with the likes of George M. Cohan, Al Jolson, and Willie Hoppe.

It took eight and a half seasons for Chase to wear out his welcome in New York, but during that time he established himself as one of the biggest stars in baseball.

Those seasons had highs, though they were mostly individual rather than collective: the Highlanders went through six managers, including Chase himself, and only twice posted winning records, but Prince Hal finished among the AL top ten four times in RBI, three times in batting average, and twice in stolen bases. In addition, he earned a reputation as perhaps the best batter in the league at executing the hit-and-run. For the most part, though, Chase was better known for his defense, and his relaxed ethical standards, than his offense.

Right from the start, his glovework was a revelation. Longtime baseball men were astonished at how far off the bag he played, his casual one-handed catches, and his catlike pounces on sacrifice bunt attempts. Soon, however, the whispers began that Chase, while undeniably talented, was a selfish prima donna who was a disruptive force on the ballclub. Once, when a reporter complimented him on a particularly outstanding play, he grinned and replied, referring to his less-talented teammates, "I could make plays like that every day, only I am afraid to turn the ball loose because I might hit one of those dopes in the head."

More seriously, in 1907 he threatened to jump to the outlaw California State League until Farrell raised his salary. In September 1908 he left the Highlanders and returned to California, reportedly upset that shortstop Kid Elberfeld, rather than Chase, had been named to replace Clark Griffith as interim manager of the struggling Highlanders. Two years later he left the team during a Midwestern road trip and returned to New York to demand that Farrell fire manager George Stallings. The fiery Stallings responded by accusing Chase of "laying down" on the team. The owner sided with his star player, dismissing Stallings and appointing Prince Hal in his stead. His teammates were less than thrilled; recalling the episode years later, Jimmy Austin commented, "God, what a way to run a ballclub!"

Chase's tenure as manager was not a success, and he was allowed to resign following the 1911 season. He managed to stay out of trouble until early in the 1913 campaign, when he ran afoul of the Yankees' new manager, Frank Chance. "The Peerless Leader," whom Farrell had hired with great fanfare, told two reporters that Chase was "throwing down me and the team." Farrell finally agreed that Prince Hal had to go, and traded him to the White Sox for first baseman Babe Borton, who batted .130 in 33 games as Prince Hal's replacement, and infielder Rollie Zeider, who was troubled by foot problems. Both were gone after the season; reporter Mark Roth wrote caustically that "The Yankees traded Chase to the White Sox for an onion and a bunion."

Chase spent scarcely more than one full season in Chicago before jumping to Buffalo of the upstart Federal League. He turned the tables on the White Sox by invoking the standard baseball contract's "ten-day clause," by which clubs were required to give an unwanted player ten days' notice before terminating his contract. Chase saw no reason why the ten-day clause shouldn't work the other way. Organized baseball, needless to say, was outraged, but the ensuing legal wrangle ended with a judge declaring that the structure of Organized Baseball was "a species of quasi-peonage unlawfully controlling and interfering with the personal freedom of the men employed."

Chase was one of the biggest stars in the Federal League, batting .347 over the remainder of the 1914 campaign and leading the league with 17 home runs in 1915, but when the Feds went belly-up following the 1915 season his reputation as a troublemaker ensured that no American League team would have him. He finally caught on with the National League Cincinnati Reds as the 1916 season began and went on to enjoy his finest season in the majors, leading the NL in batting (.339) and hits (184), finishing second in RBI (82) and slugging percentage (.459), and third in total bases (249).

Two years later, however, he was in trouble again. Christy Mathewson had become manager of the Reds, and Matty suspended his old friend in August 1918 for offering bribes to teammates and opponents, including Giant pitcher Pol Perritt, to influence the outcome of games on which he had bet.

At a postseason hearing before NL president John Heydler, three Reds players—Jimmy Ring, Greasy Neale, and Mike Regan—testified against a defiant Chase. But neither Mathewson, serving with the military in France, nor Perritt was present, and McGraw himself testified that he could not confirm the allegation that Chase had offered Perritt a bribe. A frustrated Heydler had no choice but to let Chase off the hook.

To the surprise of practically no one, the newly exonerated Prince Hal quickly signed on with McGraw's Giants, who were in dire need of a first baseman. "I have found him a most agreeable chap, and I am sure we will get along without a hitch," predicted the manager in the spring. (Adding to the intrigue, Mathewson returned from France and also joined the Giants as a coach.)

McGraw's optimism was, to put it mildly, misplaced. By September 1919 Chase was on the sidelines, ostensibly because of an injured wrist but in reality because he had once again, along with Giant third baseman Heinie Zimmerman, been attempting to bribe teammates. Chase never played in the majors again.

In the spring of 1920 he was back in California playing semipro ball when his former Cincinnati teammate Lee Magee revealed that he and Prince Hal had conspired to throw games during the 1918 season. In August Chase was also accused of attempting to bribe Pacific Coast League players, for which he was banned from Organized Baseball in his native state. But even these bombshells were overshadowed when news of the Black Sox scandal began to leak out in September. Chase was eventually indicted as an alleged middleman in the fix, though he avoided extradition to Chicago, and thus his role in the scheme was never definitively established. Rube Benton testified that Chase had won $40,000 betting on the 1919 World Series, though his testimony was later called into question. Curiously, however, baseball commissioner Kenesaw Mountain Landis never officially expelled Chase from Organized Baseball.

Prince Hal spent most of the 1920s playing semipro ball in Arizona, bouncing among teams representing Nogales, Williams, Jerome, and Douglas, to which he lured Black Sox pariahs Chick Gandil, Buck Weaver, and Lefty Williams. He was in the latter town in 1926 when the radio evangelist Aimee Semple McPherson turned up there, claiming to have been abducted by Mexican bandits. It was eventually revealed that she had run off with her radio engineer, and reporter S. L. A. Marshall later claimed that Chase had contemplated blackmailing Sister Aimee, threatening to reveal that she had disappeared to have an abortion, though no evidence exists to corroborate this story. Chase moved on to an El Paso, Texas, team in 1927, and spent the rest of the 1920s playing for various semipro clubs in California while also prospecting for gold in the Sierra Nevada mountains.

Eventually, of course, the years of carousing began to take a toll, as did a 1926 car accident which severed an Achilles tendon. By December 1933, when he was rediscovered in Tucson by the New York writers accompanying the Columbia football team to the Rose Bowl, Chase seems to have been little more than a shambling derelict.

The last fifteen years of his life were miserable. Chase ended up living on the Williams, California, ranch of his sister Jessie and her husband, Frank Topham. Topham so loathed his brother-in-law that he refused to allow him in the house and built him his own cabin on the property. Chase granted interviews that were published in *The Sporting News* while he was hospitalized with various health problems in 1941 and again in 1947. He must have sensed that he was running out of time, for in these interviews he seemed desperate to clear his name. He again denied having had a role in arranging the Black Sox fix, though he admitted that he had known about it in advance and expressed regret at having kept silent about it: "I did not want to be what I then called a 'welcher.' I had been involved in all kinds of bets with players and gamblers in the past, and I felt this was no time to run out." He added, "I'd give anything if I could start in all over again.... I was all wrong, at least in most things, and my best proof is that I am flat on my back, without a dime." But, he still insisted, "I never bet against my own team." He died on May 18, 1947, and was buried in Oak Hill Memorial Park in San Jose.

MARTIN KOHOUT

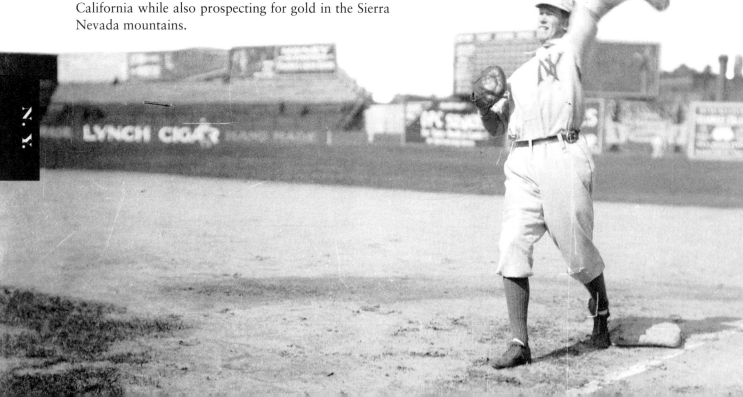

N. F. Cree

NEW YORK

WILLIAM FRANKLIN "BIRDIE" CREE
OUTFIELDER, 1908–1915

A school teacher, a football player, a Penn State graduate, a professional ball player, and finally, a bank cashier, Birdie Cree spent his major league career with only one team, while witnessing the rise and fall of managers Kid Elberfeld, George Stallings, Hal Chase, Harry Wolverton, Frank Chance, and Roger Peckinpaugh. Batting and throwing right-handed, the speedy 5′6″, 150-pound Cree was described as a "robust walloper," and one who could "throw as far as anyone his size." During his eight-year major league career, Cree established the Yankees franchise record (later broken) for most triples in a season, with 22 in 1911, and his 48 stolen bases that year remain the eighth-highest figure in franchise history.

Born on October 23, 1882, 50 miles south of Pittsburgh in the small town of Khedive, Pennsylvania, William Franklin "Birdie" Cree was the adopted son of Levi Cree. After finishing public school, he attended Southwestern State Normal School at California, Pennsylvania in 1901, and graduated two years later as a fully qualified teacher. He began teaching eighth grade in the California city public schools, while also playing shortstop and third base with the Normal School baseball team. He also starred as a quarterback for the football team, figuring it would improve his speed. Word of his football skills spread and Cree received a scholarship to Penn State in the fall of 1904 after being discovered by Penn State athletic director "Pop" Golden.

That summer before attending Penn State, Cree played baseball for the Washington (Pennsylvania) Patriots of the outlaw Ohio-Pennsylvania League. While sliding head first into second base, he dislocated his collarbone. Then in the fall after only three days of football practice, he again dislocated the same collarbone and was out for the year.

During the spring of 1905, Cree began to play baseball for the State team. It was here he first earned his nickname of "Birdie." Cree recalled, "In my first game for State, I hit everything but the umpire, getting a home run, triple, double and single. A classmate jumped up and yelled: 'he's a bird—that's what he is.' The name stuck and eventually became 'Birdie,' possibly also because I was so small."

To make extra money, Cree began playing baseball for a team in Sunbury, Pennsylvania. Still in school, and not wanting to appear under his own name, he played under the name "Burde" and was the top hitter on the team. While in Sunbury, Cree met his future wife, Mary Edna Keefer.

The following summer Cree played in Burlington, Vermont, along with several other future major leaguers. In 1907, Cree was persuaded by Penn State coach Jimmy Sebring, an outfielder for the Williamsport club of the Tri-State League, to join the Millionaires. Cree played shortstop and batted .297 over the season, helping lead Williamsport to the championship.

At the end of the season, Cree, still known as Bill Burde, was purchased by Connie Mack of the Philadelphia Athletics, but was left in Williamsport for another year. With a surplus of shortstops, Manager Harry Wolverton moved Cree to the outfield. Before the 1908 season was over, the Detroit Tigers acquired Cree from the Athletics and traded him to the New York Highlanders on condition that George Moriarty would be sold to the Tigers before the beginning of the next season. On September 17, center fielder Birdie Cree made his major league debut, playing center field and batting third.

On June 24, 1909, while facing Cy Morgan, Cree hit his first home run. It was also the first home run ever hit out of Shibe Park in Philadelphia by a right-handed batter. "I drove that ball over the right field wall and into Matt Kilroy's saloon on the corner of Twentieth Street and Lehigh Avenue," Cree recalled. "I know it bounced into the barroom because that is where I got the ball. I still have it." Cree finished the year with a .262 batting average in 104 games.

On April 22, 1910, Cree was hit in the head by a

N. Y.

Walter Johnson fastball. Knocked unconscious, he was carried from the field, yet returned to the lineup the next day. Finishing the season with a .287 batting average, he led his team with 16 triples, and tied for the team lead with four home runs and 73 RBI.

With an abundance of outfielders in 1911, new manager Hal Chase tried Cree at shortstop, declaring that "he must have Cree on the big team somewhere when the players return north." But Cree soon moved back to the outfield—playing left now instead of center—and had the best season of his career. He not only led his team in almost every category, but was in the top five of the American League in batting average (.348), slugging (.513), total bases (267), triples (22), stolen bases (48), and extra-base hits (56). His four home runs, all solo shots, again tied for the team lead. In one game against the Browns, Cree stole four bases. As the season wound down, Cree once again tried playing shortstop for a couple days, but proved a failure, declaring that he would never again try his hand in any infield work. Cree finished sixth in the Chalmers Award voting for most valuable player that year.

After contracting a severe cold in Atlanta during spring training in 1912, Cree was sent home in advance of the team. He played the opening series with Boston, but Cree was so ill he was taken to a hospital. Upon his return, Cree continued his pace of 1911, batting .332 with 12 stolen bases and six triples after only 50 games. Then, on June 29, Cree's wrist was broken on a pitch thrown by Buck O'Brien of Boston, forcing him to miss the remainder of the season.

With his wrist still bothering him, Cree's batting suffered throughout the 1913 season, dropping his average to .272. However, he led the league in fielding percentage for the first time, making only three errors in 259 chances while also recording five double plays as a left fielder. His only home run was a grand slam, one of only five hit that year in the American League.

As the team trained in Bermuda for 1914, Cree reported out of shape and was unable to play to his ability. "I was overweight and patrolling the outfield in a rubber shirt, a sweat shirt and a sweater," Cree later recalled. "The grass in the outfield was up to my knees. Somebody hit a fly my way and I went after it, but before I had gone ten feet I was tangled up in the bulrushes and the ball fell safe. After the inning was over, I went to the dugout. Manager

Chance was sitting on one end of the bench. I knew he was angry but he didn't say anything for a minute or two. Then, looking over at me, he rasped: "Birdie, why in the hell don't you lay down out there? You'd cover more ground than you do standing up!"

Unable to trade him, Cree was released to Baltimore of the International League. Manager Jack Dunn signed Cree to a $4,500 contract, teaming him up with other former major league players Bert Daniels, Neal Ball, Freddy Parent, and future stars Babe Ruth and Ernie Shore. Cree claimed that he had been offered $30,000 over three years by the Pittsburgh club of the Federal League, and had been presented a certified check for half the amount in advance. But after realizing that Cree was out of shape, the Feds broke off negotiations.

By the middle of the 1914 season, the Orioles were ahead by 17 games with a revived Cree batting .356 along with his usual collection of extra-base hits. But the team was suffering badly at the gate due to competition from the local Federal League team, and Dunn began to sell off his players. Cree was sold back to New York on July 9—two days before teammate Ruth was sold to the Red Sox—and finished the season batting .309 in 77 games.

As in 1912, Cree was again injured after an outstanding season. In April 1915, while warming up before a game, Cree was hit in the face by a ball, breaking his nose. This injury, along with his weight gain, eventually forced Cree into retirement. He finished the 1915 campaign with a .214 average, but posted a robust .353 on-base percentage in 74 games.

After being released in February 1916, Cree began working as a mail clerk at the First National Bank in Sunbury, Pennsylvania. Although his salary was a lot less than during his ball playing days, he "didn't mind beginning at the bottom." Eventually he moved on to the bookkeeping department, then teller, and finally cashier. He continued his love of sports, playing tennis and learning golf. Becoming the leading golfer at his country club, Cree won the club championship five years in a row. He was also an outstanding billiards player for the Masonic Temple Club. An avid pinochle player, he also enjoyed the music of Franz Liszt and Irving Berlin. Cree died on November 8, 1942, after a ten-week illness. He was buried in Pomfret-Manor Cemetery in Sunbury.

PAUL SALLEE

NEW YORK

RUSSELL WILLIAM FORD
RIGHT-HANDED PITCHER, 1909–1913

The first major league player born in the western Canadian province of Manitoba, Russ Ford burst into the spotlight in 1910, winning 26 games for the New York Highlanders with a baffling new pitch never before seen in professional baseball. Using a piece of emery board hidden in his glove, Ford roughed up one side of the ball, causing it to break at odd angles depending on how he threw it. For two seasons, Ford used the emery ball to dominate the American League, all the while hiding the origin of his new discovery. "He kept his secret a long time by pretending he was pitching a spitter," Ty Cobb later recalled. "He would deliberately show his finger to the batter and then wet it with saliva." Though Ford's signature pitch was banned by 1915, his invention set the precedent for a long line of scuff ball artists, including contemporaries Cy Falkenberg and Eddie Cicotte and Hall of Famers Whitey Ford and Don Sutton.

Russell William Ford was born in Brandon, Manitoba, on April 25, 1883, the third of five children of Walter and Ida Ford, a second cousin of future U.S. President Grover Cleveland. When Russell was three years old, his family immigrated to the United States, eventually settling in Minneapolis, where Walter worked as a clerk. Following high school, Russ spent several years pitching in the minor leagues. In 1905 the 5'11", 175-pound right-hander debuted with the Cedar Rapids Rabbits of the Three-I League. That same year, Ford's older brother Gene, who had been born in Nova Scotia, briefly appeared in the major leagues as a pitcher for the Detroit Tigers. After winning 22 games for Cedar Rapids in 1906, Russ moved up the professional ladder to the Atlanta Crackers of the Class A Southern Association, where he won a total of 31 games in 1907 and 1908. His success in Atlanta led the New York Highlanders to draft him prior to the 1909 season. Primarily a spitball pitcher, Ford made his major league debut against the Boston Red Sox on April 28, 1909, pitching three innings in relief, surrendering four runs,

three of them earned, on four hits, four walks, and three hit batsmen. The *New York Times* noted that "the cold weather seemed to affect" Ford, but the Highlanders, unimpressed, farmed the 26-year-old out to the Jersey City Skeeters of the Eastern League.

In a 1935 interview with *The Sporting News*, Ford explained that he first discovered the secret behind the emery pitch in 1908, when he was still with Atlanta. On a rainy spring morning Ford was warming up under the stands with catcher Ed Sweeney when he became wild. One pitch struck a wooden upright; another sailed sideways about five feet. When Sweeney returned the ball, Ford examined it and saw that it was rough where it had hit the upright. He wondered if the roughened surface was responsible for the ball's odd movement, so he gripped the sphere on the side opposite its roughened surface and when he pitched it, the ball shot through the air with a sailing dip. "It never occurred to me that I had uncovered what was to become one of the most baffling pitches that a Cobb, Lajoie, Speaker or Delahanty [*sic*] would be called upon to bat against in the big leagues," Ford told *The Sporting News*.

After being demoted to Jersey City in 1909, Ford returned to his discovery and conducted additional experiments during batting practice. At first he used a broken pop bottle to scuff the ball deliberately. After his teammates missed hitting the ball by as much as 12 to 18 inches in practice, Ford began employing the scuff ball during games, using a small piece of emery he carried in his glove. Throughout the season, Ford worked on various ways of concealing the pitch, which helped him strike out 189 Eastern League batters.

Ford's solid performance in Jersey City earned him another shot with the Highlanders at the start of the 1910 season. Now armed with the emery pitch—which he continued to disguise as a special kind of spitball called the "slide ball"—Ford authored one of the finest rookie pitching seasons in baseball history. In his first major league start, Ford struck out nine batters, walked

none, and shut out the Philadelphia Athletics, 1–0. By the end of the season, Ford ranked second in the league in wins (26) and tied for second in shutouts (8), while posting a brilliant 1.65 ERA, seventh-best in the league. With 209 strikeouts and 70 walks, he also boasted the fourth-best strikeout-to-walk ratio in the league. Ford's 26 victories also established the American League rookie record, which still stands. Thanks in large part to Ford's dominating performance, the Highlanders finished in second place with an 88–63 record, their best showing in four years.

Ford continued to guard the secret of his new pitch, boasting to the press that he had 14 different versions of his "spitball." "Ford worked cleverly," umpire Billy Evans recalled. "He had the emery paper attached to a piece of string, which was fastened to the inside of his undershirt. He had a hole in the center of his glove. At the end of each inning he would slip the emery paper under the tight-fitting undershirt, while at the start of each inning he would allow it to drop into the palm of his glove."

In 1911 the Highlanders slumped to sixth place, but Ford continued to rank among the best pitchers in the league, posting a 22–11 mark with a 2.27 ERA. On July 24 Ford also pitched for the all-star team that played a benefit game against the Cleveland Naps in the wake of pitcher Addie Joss's death, hurling four innings in relief

of Joe Wood and Walter Johnson. Another measure of respect came the following spring, when Ty Cobb spoke to a *Baseball Magazine* reporter about his participation in a vaudeville tour through the South. A month of one-night stands was worse than facing Walter Johnson or Russ Ford 154 games in the season, Cobb said.

But opposing batters had a much easier time handling Ford's deliveries in 1912, as the pitcher lost a league-high 21 games, though his 3.55 ERA was still slightly better than the league average. By the following year, the secret behind the emery pitch had also made its way around the league, and the delivery was picked up by Cleveland right-hander Cy Falkenberg, who used it to win 23 games in 1913. That year, Ford battled through a fatigued right arm to post a 12–18 record with a solid but unspectacular 2.66 ERA. In a sign of his reduced strength, Ford struck out just 72 batters in 237 innings, a distant cry from the dominance he displayed as a rookie three years earlier.

When New York offered him a cut in pay in 1914, Ford moved to the new Federal League, where he went 21–6 and posted a 1.82 ERA (second-best in the league) with Buffalo. Ford's .778 winning percentage led the league, as did his 3:1 strikeout-to-walk ratio and his six saves. It proved to be the last great season of his career, however, as the emery ball, already illegal in the American League, was banned by FL president James Gilmore in 1915. Deprived of his signature pitch and again nursing a sore arm, Ford struggled to a 5–9 record for Buffalo before the club released him on August 28, ending his major league career.

Following his release from the Federal League, Ford pitched two more seasons in the minors with Denver of the Western League and Toledo of the American Association. After his baseball career ended, Ford lived with his wife, Mary Hunter Bethell, whom he had married in 1912. The couple had two daughters, Mary and Jean. Ford worked in Newark, New York City and in Rockingham, North Carolina, near his wife's hometown. He died of a heart attack in Rockingham on January 24, 1960, at age 76. His cremated remains were buried in Rockingham's Leak Cemetery. In 1989, Ford was inducted into the Canadian Baseball Hall of Fame; his 2.59 career ERA remains the best of any Canadian-born pitcher.

T. Kent Morgan
and David Jones

NEW YORK

RAYMOND BENJAMIN CALDWELL
RIGHT-HANDED PITCHER, 1910–1918

Ray Caldwell was a pitcher of immense talent who had an enormous appetite for the nightlife and a weakness for alcohol. As the ace of the New York Yankees in the early 1910s, the slender right-handed hurler was at times so dominant that Washington once reportedly offered Walter Johnson for him in a trade. But Caldwell's flashes of brilliance were usually followed by frustrating "outbreaks of misbehavior," and he never realized his immense potential. Yet by the time his professional baseball career ended in 1933, Caldwell had won almost 300 games, 133 of them in the major leagues.

Raymond Benjamin Caldwell was born on April 16, 1888, in Corydon, a small shantytown in northwestern Pennsylvania that was later abandoned for the construction of Kinzua Dam and the Allegheny Reservoir. Before, during, and after his baseball career, Ray worked as a telegrapher for the Buffalo, Rochester, and Pittsburgh Railway. Ray was a latecomer to baseball: 1910 was his first professional season at age 22. After winning 18 games for McKeesport of the Ohio-Pennsylvania League, Caldwell was acquired by the New York Yankees. He appeared in six games for New York in 1910, posting a 1–0 record with a poor 3.72 ERA, though he struck out 17 batters in 19⅓ innings of work.

With a lanky 6′2″, 190-pound frame and an elongated face, Caldwell quickly earned the nickname "Slim." Ray threw with an effortless delivery that matched his easygoing temperament and masked the explosiveness of his fastball and sharp-breaking curve. In 1911 he showed glimpses of his promise with a 14–14 record and 145 strikeouts in 255 innings. The *Detroit News* even went so far as to call him "the second Matty."

It was a comparison Caldwell would never live up to. Over the next two seasons, Ray was hampered by a shoulder injury and plagued by inconsistency. In 1912, Caldwell won just eight games against 16 losses, and posted a poor 4.47 ERA in 26 starts. The following year he notched his first winning season with a 9–8 record and lowered his ERA by more than two runs, but recurring pain in his shoulder limited him to just 16 starts.

While he struggled to find his groove on the mound, Caldwell found other ways to make himself useful. Yankee manager Frank Chance contemplated moving Caldwell—who had batted .272 his rookie season while appearing in 18 games as an outfielder and pinch hitter—to the outfield permanently in 1913. Ray had a staggering .421 batting average in late July 1913 and finished with a .289 mark. He appeared in the outfield in three games that season, but was used many times as a pinch hitter.

In 1914, Ray finally solidified himself in the Yankee rotation, as he began the season with three consecutive shutouts. To compensate for his sagging arm strength, Caldwell began to rely more on finesse than raw speed. As the *New York Times* reported of his April 17 gem against the Philadelphia Athletics, "Caldwell teased the champs with a slow hypnotic floater, which dipped over the plate so easily that spectators in the grand stand could read Ban Johnson's signature on the leather." By mid-August, Caldwell's record stood at 17–9, and his ERA was a sparkling 1.94. His season, however, came to an abrupt end soon thereafter, when the pitcher disappeared during a road trip to Boston. Chance, who had already warned Caldwell that he wouldn't tolerate his drinking or his "Broadway training," fined Ray $300 and removed him from the starting rotation.

As the tension mounted between the wayward pitcher and his stern manager, in early September the Buffalo Bisons of the Federal League announced that they had signed Caldwell to a contract for 1915.

However, Caldwell offered to return to New York if owner Frank Farrell rescinded the fine. Farrell agreed, and when Chance received word that his authority had been undermined by the team's owner, he promptly resigned. During the 1914–15 offseason, the Yankees' new owners, Jacob Ruppert and Til Huston, signed Ray to a three-year contract at $8,000 or $9,000 per year. At the same time, Washington ace Walter Johnson was flirting with the Federal League, and, as both Fred Lieb and Joe Vila later reported, Washington owner Clark Griffith offered to trade Johnson for Caldwell. American League president Ban Johnson reportedly advised the New York owners not to accept the deal because Ray had so much talent and potential.

In 1915, Caldwell stayed healthy all season, and pitched a career-high 305 innings en route to a 19–16 record and 2.89 ERA, approximately the league average. Caldwell also put on an impressive hitting exhibition in June, when he smashed three homers in three consecutive days, two as a pinch hitter. Though he had only 144 at-bats during the season, Caldwell's four home runs were tied for ninth-best in the American League with, among others, rookie Babe Ruth. Summing up Caldwell's still mostly unrealized potential, *New York World* sports editor Walter Trumbull observed, "Certain men, such as Ty Cobb and John McGraw, cannot bear to lose. If it is only pitching pennies at a crack, they put their whole heart into it. If the soul of Caldwell ever burns with this flame; if he ever acquires this fierce ambition to be better than the best, he will make a name for himself that will last as long as the game endures."

Instead, Caldwell continued to distinguish himself more through his off-field exploits. On July 3, 1916, Caldwell pitched an 11-inning shutout to defeat Walter Johnson 1–0, but two weeks later his kneecap was shattered by a comebacker that ended his season. As the Yankees fell out of the pennant race, the pitcher fell off the wagon, and was fined and suspended by manager Bill Donovan. Ray took "French leave" and was nowhere to be found. On September 21, *The Sporting News* reported that Ray had been admitted to a St. Louis hospital in order to dry out. The paper wrote that his cure was complete. Starting only 18 games for the season, Caldwell finished the year with a 5–12 mark. He then surfaced in Panama, where he pitched that winter under an assumed name.

The following year "the pearl of Panama," as the press dubbed Ray, managed to stay in the rotation most of the season, but finished the year with a disappointing 13–16 record. As always, flashes of brilliance interspersed with periods of dissipation and distraction. As Joe Vila of *The Sporting News* wrote in the spring of

1917, "This fellow Caldwell is a most peculiar chap. He is sensitive and boyish, although he is 29 years old. He is good natured, intelligent and nervy when he faces the opposing batsmen. But he lacks self control when temptation is near at hand—and for that reason he has fallen from grace on several occasions."

On June 23, Ray beat the Athletics twice, prompting Connie Mack to say, "Put Ray Caldwell on a winning team and he would be one of the greatest pitchers of all time." Upon returning from a suspension on July 10, Caldwell pitched 9⅔ innings of shutout ball in a relief win. That very night, Ray was arrested by St. Louis police and charged with grand larceny, stealing a $150 ring from a Mrs. Lucy Dick while visiting her in her home. Two months later he was arrested again at the Polo Grounds after his wife Nellie charged abandonment and sued for support, demanding more than $100 of his monthly salary for herself and their seven-year-old son. The Yankees offered to turn over the day's gate receipts to cover the $1,000 bond and keep Caldwell out of jail, but the attendance was not big enough to cover the cost, and Caldwell eventually had to raise his own bail.

When Miller Huggins took over as Yankee manager in 1918, he assigned two private detectives to Ray, to keep him out of trouble and away from bars, yet Ray was often able to elude them. He developed a lame arm, and in mid-August left the Yankees without notice and joined the Tietjen and Lang Drydock Company, in order to enter an "essential service" and thus avoid the war draft.

Huggins and the Yankees had finally had enough of Caldwell, and in December 1918 traded him to the Boston Red Sox as part of a deal for Ernie Shore and Duffy Lewis. Upon the announcement of the trade, Fred Lieb wrote in the *New York Sun*, "Caldwell might have been the Mathewson of the Yankees, but he turned out to be the Bugs Raymond of the local Americans…His irregular habits destroyed his effectiveness."

After posting a 7–4 record for the Red Sox in 1919, Caldwell was released that August 4 and picked up by the Cleveland Indians two weeks later. As Indians historian Franklin Lewis later related, Cleveland manager Tris Speaker employed a fascinating strategy of reverse psychology on Caldwell. The Grey Eagle had his new pitcher agree to a contract which stated, "After each game he pitches, Ray Caldwell must get drunk. He is not to report to the clubhouse the next day. The second day he is to report to Manager Speaker and run around the ball park as many times as Manager Speaker stipulates. The third day he is to pitch batting practice, and the fourth day he is to pitch in a championship game." It worked. With Cleveland, Caldwell enjoyed a brief renaissance, as he learned the spitball (probably from teammate Stan Coveleski) and won five games with a 1.71 ERA. Two of the wins were remarkable. On August 24, in his first game with Cleveland, Ray led the Philadelphia Athletics 2–1, with two outs in the ninth. Suddenly, he was hit by lightning and knocked down, unconscious. The bolt may have entered the metal button on the top of his cap and exited the metal spikes on his shoes. Ray later told the *Cleveland Press*, "It felt just like somebody came up with a board and hit me on top of the head and knocked me down." A few minutes later, he arose and retired the final batter. Then, on September 10, in what the *New York Times* called a "shocking occurrence," Ray tossed a 3–0 no-hitter against his old team, the New York Yankees.

Named as one of the 17 spitball pitchers who were allowed to continue throwing the banned pitch under the "grandfather clause," Caldwell posted a mediocre 3.86 ERA in 1920, but thanks to strong run support won 20 games for the only time in his career. Given the nod to start Game 3 of that year's World Series, Caldwell failed to make it out of the first inning, and didn't appear again in the Series. In 1921, Caldwell was used as a reliever and spot starter, and he struggled with a 6–6 record and 4.90 ERA. After Tris Speaker suspended Ray for "violating rules of discipline" in September, Caldwell was released by the Indians at the end of the season, thus ending his major league career.

Improbably, the pitcher who had squandered much of his talent during his days in the majors embarked on a prosperous 12-year minor league career. From 1922 to 1924, he pitched for Kansas City, winning 22 games in his first year and 16 games in 1923, when the Blues won the American Association pennant and beat the Baltimore Orioles in the Little World Series. In 1925, Ray moved on to Little Rock for three seasons, where he led the Southern Association in losses in both 1926 and 1927. After brief stays with Milwaukee, Memphis and Akron, the Birmingham Barons felt that Ray could still pitch and signed him late in the 1929 season. He responded with a 4–2 record and a 1.79 ERA. The Barons won the pennant and beat Dallas in the Dixie World Series, with Ray winning twice.

Despite advancing age, in 1930 he continued his impressive comeback with a 20–12 record. In 1931, Caldwell went 19–7, and his Barons won their second pennant in three years. Their opponents in the Dixie Series were the Houston Buffaloes, led by 21-year-old pitcher Dizzy Dean. Ray, 43 and a grandfather, had just gotten married for the third time. He beat Dean 1–0 in Game 1, before 20,000 fans at Rickwood Field. Dean came back to beat Ray in Game 4, 2–0. With the series tied at three games apiece, the Barons called on "old man Caldwell" in the ninth inning of the deciding game. He struck out the Texas League's home run and RBI leader, Joe Medwick, and preserved the win for Birmingham.

In April 1933, the Barons released him. He finished his playing career that year with Atlanta, Charlotte, and Keokuk. He had pitched more than 2,200 innings with 133 wins in the majors and 2,200 innings with 159 wins in the minors. He was named to the Birmingham Barons Hall of Fame in 1943.

After retiring from baseball, Ray settled in the Jamestown, New York, area, where he once again worked for the railroads, and tended bar at a gun club and tavern. In 1939, he married Estelle Sheppard of Lorraine, Ohio, and helped raise her four stepdaughters. In his later years, Caldwell also conducted free baseball clinics in Fremont, Ohio. In one of his last jobs, he worked as a greeter at the Golden Nugget Casino in Las Vegas. Ray Caldwell died of cancer in Salamanca, New York, on August 19, 1967, aged 79, and was buried in Randolph Cemetery in Randolph, New York.

Steve Steinberg

NEW YORK

RAY LYLE FISHER
RIGHT-HANDED PITCHER 1910–1917

Boasting an exceptional curveball and a spit-ball that was favorably compared to Jack Chesbro's wet one, right-hander Ray Fisher emerged as a workhorse for the New York Yankees pitching staff from 1913 to 1915, before poor health sapped his strength and limited his effectiveness. An intelligent pitcher who once spent his offseason teaching Latin, Fisher was known as "The Vermont Schoolmaster," after his native state. As one of his managers put it, "[Fisher] is an intelligent workman, studies every batsman and usually succeeds in putting the ball where the maceman doesn't like to have it." After the 1920 season, Fisher jumped his contract with the Cincinnati Reds to coach the University of Michigan baseball team, a move that landed him on baseball's ineligible list but also resulted in one of the greatest coaching tenures in Big Ten history, as Fisher managed the Wolverines for 38 seasons, winning 14 Big Ten Championships and the 1953 College World Series title.

Ray Lyle Fisher was born in the shadow of the Green Mountains on October 4, 1887, in Middlebury, Vermont, the fourth and youngest son of Albert and Emerette M. Fisher. Working on his father's Middlebury farm and attending school occupied the early years of a boy who longed to spend his spare moments playing sports. In 1906, Ray enrolled at Middlebury College, where the 5'11", 180-pound youngster established a new school shot-put record and played varsity football, basketball, and baseball. Ray's coach at Middlebury encouraged him to try pitching and he swiftly made his mark on the college diamond. He played semipro ball in Valleyfield, Quebec, in 1907 and signed on with Hartford of the Connecticut League in 1908. Ray compiled a 12–1 record in his first partial season in the minors and went 24–5 the following year with 243 strikeouts. Scouts were quick to look at Fisher after his second year at

Hartford, and his contract was sold to the Yankees in 1909, with the Yanks granting Ray's request that he finish college before reporting.

Ray, or "Pick," as he had been known in college, joined the Highlanders at Hilltop Park in the summer of 1910 and, to the amusement of his new teammates, brought along his homemade bat from off the farm. He made his major league debut against Philadelphia on July 2, pitching three innings in relief. Players who saw Ray pitch report that he had a marvelous curveball, but he also relied on the spitter when he came up to the majors. According to a contemporary report, Ray's spitball "had a very good break, and his control of it was such that he could keep it at the knee almost constantly." By the end of his first season Ray was being compared to Jack Chesbro, who was just winding up his years in the major leagues: "He laughs, talks, acts, and pitches with the same motion as the North Adams farmer," wrote one reporter. "He has a spit ball which, according to Ed Sweeney, is just as dangerous as the one Chesbro exhibited."

Ray had largely abandoned the spitball by 1914, however, even though he would later be one of the 17 players exempted from the 1920 ban on the pitch. The reason, according to one reporter, was that Ray was concerned that the pitch might cause the early loss of his pitching arm. Ray had hardly used the spitball prior to coming to New York. "I was a little country boy and I read about big leaguers and never expected to be amongst them," Fisher explained. "I'd wake up and realize I was 2–0 or 3–1 and had to come in, but I knew I could throw a spitter so I threw a spitter and it helped me. When I got acclimated and knew more about how to handle myself, I would just sneak it over for a strike now and then. I kept slippery elm in my mouth anyway, just in case."

In his second season with New York, Ray was

the team's fourth starter. The newspapers by then had christened the college-educated pitcher The Vermont Schoolmaster. Ray was getting a reputation as a real workhorse for the team and the paper reported that, "The Vermont schoolmaster pitches with all might and main. He seems to use every ounce of strength behind every ball he sends over. Of course this strength-spending style is bound to tell, but in a single game like yesterday, Fisher appeared to be stronger at the finish than at the start and the expected giving out of strength did not occur during the afternoon."

From 1913 to 1915 Ray was one of New York's most reliable starters, posting a 40–39 record for a team that won just 42 percent of its games over that span. His best season came in 1915, when he posted a 2.11 ERA, fifth-best in the American League, and notched 18 wins for the fifth-place Yankees. "That Ray Fisher, the New York Yankee's [sic] pitcher, has won respect in the proper circles is evidenced by the fact that both Ty Cobb and Larry Lajoie picked him as one of the dozen best hurlers in the American League," one observer noted. "Fisher is often overlooked when fans are studying the stars. But he is a star and belongs right in the Ford–Wood–Walsh class. His fastball is a beauty, and he has a curve that few others can boast of."

Ray's dreams of stardom began to crumble in 1916, however, when the rugged pitcher was struck with what was then diagnosed as pleurisy, though it may actually have been tuberculosis. After posting a mediocre 3.16 ERA in the 1916 season, Fisher battled his way to a team-best 2.19 ERA in 144 innings in 1917.

At the end of 1917 Ray was drafted into the military and eventually placed in a physical training program run for the Army at Fort Slocum near New Rochelle, New York. Fisher left the Army at the end of 1918, and in March of the following year the Cincinnati Reds selected him off waivers. The Yankees released Fisher believing that his time away from the game had sapped whatever strength remained in his right arm, but as the 1919 season progressed, Ray's surprising performance demonstrated the Yankees' folly. Perhaps inspired by his cut in salary (after earning as much as $6,666 with the Yankees, Fisher received only $3,500 from Cincinnati), Fisher finished the season with a 14–5 record and 2.17 ERA over 174⅓ innings pitched, helping the Reds to their first National League pennant. Cincinnati manager Pat Moran was duly impressed, noting to a reporter that "Fisher's speed is fine, his curves are all that could be desired. But, beyond all else, is his headwork. Fisher knows a lot of baseball, far more than the average pitcher." In that fall's World Series, Fisher started only one game, losing 3–0 to White Sox rookie Dickie Kerr in Game 3. He also recorded two outs in a mop-up role in Game 7, and posted an overall 2.35 ERA for the Series.

Ray put in one more season with the Reds, but his dissatisfaction with his salary and his wife Alice's desire to see him settle down, after their daughter Janet's birth in 1919, caused Ray to start looking for a college coaching position. A brief conversation with Branch Rickey in 1920 led to Rickey recommending Fisher for the head coach post at the University of Michigan the following year. In accepting the Michigan job after having signed his 1921 contract with Cincinnati, Ray incurred the displeasure of Reds management. He had expected to be classified as "voluntarily retired," but as events progressed and he was approached by other teams inquiring as to his availability to play following the Michigan season, Ray found himself declared ineligible by Commissioner Landis, a ruling that would stand for the next sixty years.

Aside from his position as head baseball coach at the University of Michigan, Fisher also served for 25 years as freshman football coach and as assistant basketball coach, thus returning to the three sports that he had played as an undergrad at Middlebury College. Fisher led Michigan's baseball team for 38 seasons, compiling a 636–295–8 record with only two losing seasons. Nineteen of his players at Michigan later signed with major league teams, and Ray mentored Robin Roberts while coaching summers in the Northern League.

Ray retired as Michigan coach in 1958 at age 71, but his love for the sport kept him active in the game. Under his successors he continued to work with pitchers at Michigan, and in the 1960s he spent five seasons training pitchers for the minor league teams of the Milwaukee Braves and Detroit Tigers, despite his official ineligibility. In 1970 Fisher received his greatest tribute when the University of Michigan named its baseball stadium Ray L. Fisher Stadium; in 1980 Commissioner of Baseball Bowie Kuhn finally lifted Ray's banishment, declaring the 92-year-old Fisher to be a "retired player in good standing" with professional baseball.

Ray lived until age 95, making him both the oldest former New York Yankee and the oldest former World Series player in the last years of his life. In his final year Ray attended the annual Old Timers Day at Yankee Stadium on August 7, 1982. It was his first visit to the "House That Ruth Built," and the crowd of 43,000 gave him two standing ovations. He passed away three months later, on November 3, 1982, and was buried at Washtenong Memorial Park, in Ann Arbor, Michigan.

JOHN LEIDY

NEW YORK

ROGER THORPE PECKINPAUGH
SHORTSTOP, 1913–1921; MANAGER, 1914

Roger Peckinpaugh was one of the finest defensive shortstops and on-field leaders of the Deadball Era. Like Honus Wagner, the 5'10", 165-pound "Peck" was rangy and bowlegged, with a big barrel chest, broad shoulders, large hands, and the best throwing arm of his generation. From 1916 to 1924, Peckinpaugh led American League shortstops in assists and double plays five times each. As Shirley Povich later reflected, "the spectacle of Peckinpaugh, slinging himself after ground balls, throwing from out of position and nailing his man by half a step was an American League commonplace." The even-tempered Peckinpaugh was equally admired for his leadership, becoming the youngest manager in baseball history when he briefly took the reins of the New York Yankees in 1914.

Roger Thorpe Peckinpaugh was born February 5, 1891 in Wooster, Ohio, the third child of John and Cora Peckinpaugh. From an early age, Roger took an interest in baseball, and probably received special instruction from his father, who had been a semipro ball player. When Roger was a boy his family moved to the east side of Cleveland, taking up residence in the same neighborhood as Napoleon Lajoie, the manager and biggest star of the Cleveland Naps. Roger grew up idolizing Lajoie, and matured into a fine all-around athlete, starring in football, basketball, and baseball at East High School. Lajoie noticed Peckinpaugh's talent, and upon the youngster's graduation from high school in 1909, offered him a $125 per month contract to play pro ball. Roger's father was against his turning pro, so he asked his high school principal, Benjamin Rannels, for advice. Probably aware of Roger's love for baseball, Rannels urged Peck to sign the contract, advising him to allow himself three years to make it to the majors. If he didn't make it, then he should go to college. Peck was a regular in two years.

In 1910 the Naps sent Peckinpaugh to the New Haven Prairie Hens of the Connecticut State League for some seasoning before calling him up to the big league club in September. Peckinpaugh hit only .200 over 15 games in his first major league trial, and was farmed out to the Pacific Coast League's Portland Beavers for the entire 1911 season. Peck made the big club to stay in 1912, but the right-hander only hit .212 in 70 games. Based on that poor showing, the Naps gave the starting shortstop job to another youngster, Ray Chapman, and in May 1913 traded Peck to New York for Bill Stumpf and Jack Lelivelt. Yankees manager Frank Chance installed Peck at shortstop, where he would stay for the next eight and a half years.

Given a chance to play regularly, Peck hit a respectable .268 in 1913, as the Yankees finished seventh. In 1914, Peckinpaugh's average dipped to .223, though he played all 157 games, swiped a career-high 38 bases, and displayed the strong arm and superior range that would soon win him plaudits as one of the league's finest defensive shortstops. Though he was only 23 years old, Peckinpaugh also emerged as one of the steadying influences in a distracted clubhouse. When Chance resigned with three weeks left in the season, the Yankees made Peck the manager for the rest of the season. He still holds the record as the youngest manager in major league history.

Jacob Ruppert and Cap Huston bought the New York franchise after the 1914 season and started turning the Yankees into winners. Ruppert hired Wild Bill Donovan to take the managerial reins but he kept Peck as captain. With the Federal League dangling big money in front of established stars, the Yankees signed Peck to a three-year contract at $6,000 per year. While he continued to post pedestrian batting averages over that span—topping out at .260 with 63 runs scored in the final year of his contract—Peckinpaugh repaid the

Yankees' loyalty with his glove, leading the league in assists in 1916 and double plays the following year.

According to Tris Speaker, opponents were able to cut down on Peckinpaugh's batting average by cheating to the left side, where the right-handed dead pull hitter found the vast majority of his base hits. "Peck usually hits a solid rap when he does connect with the ball," Speaker explained to *Baseball Magazine* in 1918. "But he has the known tendency to hit toward left field. Consequently at least four men are laying for that tendency of his…. A straightaway hitter whose tendency was unknown might hit safely to left field where the very same rap by Peckinpaugh would be easily caught." But after hitting just .231 in 1918, Peck began hitting the ball with more power, posting a career-high .305 average in 1919 with seven home runs. He followed up that performance with back-to-back eight-homer seasons in the lively ball seasons of 1920 and 1921, drawing a career-high 84 walks in the latter season. As further evidence of his expanding offensive versatility, Peckinpaugh also laid down 33 sacrifices, fifth-best in the league. Two years later, he would lead the league with 40 sacrifices, and would eventually finish his career with 314 sacrifices, eighth most in baseball history.

In his first World Series in 1921, Peckinpaugh played poorly in the Yankees' eight-game loss to the New York Giants, as he batted just .194 and his crucial error in the final game allowed the Giants to win 1–0 on an unearned run. In the off-season Babe Ruth complained about the managerial skills of Miller Huggins (not for the first or last time) and said the Yanks would be better off if Peck managed them. Probably to avoid more conflict, New York traded Peck and several teammates to the Red Sox for a package that included shortstop Everett Scott and pitcher Joe Bush. However, three weeks later, Senators owner Clark Griffith, sensing that his team was one shortstop away from contention, managed to engineer a three corner trade in which the Red Sox received Joe Dugan and Frank O'Rourke, Connie Mack's Athletics received three players and $50,000 cash, and the Senators received Peckinpaugh.

The veteran shortstop teamed with the young second baseman Bucky Harris to form one of the best double play combinations in the American League. Everything fell into place by the 1924 season when owner Griffith appointed Harris the manager. Harris considered Peck his assistant manager, and together they led the Senators to back-to-back pennants in 1924 and 1925. Peck was the hero of the 1924 World Series, batting .417 and slugging .583, including a game-winning, walk-off double in Game 2. However, while running to second base (unnecessarily) on that hit, Peckinpaugh strained a muscle in his left thigh, which sidelined him for most of Game 3 and all of Games 4 and 5. But in what Shirley Povich called "the gamest exhibition I ever saw on a baseball field," Peckinpaugh took the field for Game 6 with his leg heavily bandaged and went 2-for-2 with a walk before re-aggravating the injury making a brilliant, game-saving defensive play in the ninth inning. Although Peckinpaugh had to sit out Game 7, he had already done more than his share to bring the Senators their first world championship.

Peckinpaugh came back strong in 1925 and had a fine season. He batted .294 (approximately the league average) as the Senators won their second straight pennant. In a testament to his fielding and leadership abilities, the sportswriters voted Peck the American League MVP in a narrow vote over future Hall of Famers Al Simmons, Joe Sewell, Harry Heilmann, and others. Despite his strong performance, Peck's legs continued to give him trouble, and by the start of the World Series they needed to be heavily bandaged. After carrying the Senators in the 1924 World Series, Peckinpaugh sabotaged them in 1925, turning in one of the worst performances in Series history. He committed eight errors, a Series record that still stands, although Peckinpaugh later groused that "some of them were stinko calls by the scorer." Three of Peck's errors led directly to two Senators losses, including an eighth-inning miscue in Game 7 that allowed the Pirates to come from behind to capture the championship.

Peck's legs were giving out, and he would only play two more years in the big leagues. After retiring from the game following the 1927 season, Peckinpaugh accepted the managerial post for the Cleveland Indians. In five and a half seasons with Cleveland, Roger guided the club to one seventh-place finish, one third-place finish and three consecutive fourth-place finishes before being fired midway into the 1933 season. After stints managing Kansas City and New Orleans in the minor leagues, Peck returned to skipper the Indians again in 1941, finishing in fifth place before moving into the Cleveland front office, where he remained until he retired from Organized Baseball after the 1946 season.

After leaving the Indians, Peck worked as a manufacturer's rep for the Cleveland Oak Belting Company, finally retiring in 1976 at the age of 85. He passed away on November 17, 1977, in Cleveland, of cancer and heart disease. He was buried in Acacia Masonic Memorial Park in Mayfield Heights, Ohio. Roger's wife, Mildred, had preceded him in death five years earlier. He was survived by two sons.

PETER GORDON

NEW YORK

WALTER CLEMENT PIPP
FIRST BASEMAN 1915–1925

Tall, lithe-limbed and broad-shouldered, the 6'2", 180-pound Wally Pipp carried himself with an unmistakable air of confidence and distinction, befitting one of the Deadball Era's premier sluggers. Whether disembarking from a train, haggling with management over bonus money, scooping up grounders around first base, or swatting home runs, Pipp "was a high-class specimen of the ball player," *New York Times* reporter James R. Harrison observed. "On and off the field, he was a prime favorite." A harbinger for the style of play that would grip the game beginning in the 1920s, in 1916 the left-handed, free-swinging Pipp became the first player in American League history to lead the league in both home runs and strikeouts. In addition to his batting exploits, Pipp was one of the finest defensive first basemen of the Deadball Era; in 1915, he led all American League first basemen in put-outs, assists, double plays, and fielding percentage. Yet despite these achieve-ments, today Pipp is most remembered as the man whose nagging headache per-suaded him to accept a day off on June 2, 1925, a decision that—along with his poor hitting that year—led to his permanent displace-ment from the starting lineup by a young Lou Gehrig. For that, Wally Pipp has found a permanent place in the American lexicon, as an object lesson in the pitfalls that may await any athlete who takes a day off. As Los Angeles Dodgers outfielder Dave Roberts told reporters after leaving a game during the second inning with an injured hamstring on April 25, 2003: "I don't want to be Wally Pipp."

Walter Clement Pipp, the son of William H. Pipp and the former Pauline Stauffer, was born into an Irish-Catholic family in Chicago on February 17, 1893. He grew up in Grand Rapids, Michigan, and studied architecture at Catholic University of America

in Washington, D.C., before entering professional baseball. In 1912, Pipp batted .270 in 68 games for the Kalamazoo Celery Champs of the Southern Michigan League before the Detroit Tigers purchased his contract late in the season.

Pipp did not get into any games with the Tigers in 1912, and spent the first three months of the 1913 sea-son with Providence of the International League and Scranton of the New York State League. As Scranton reporter Chic Feldman later recalled, the youngster already had a big league air about him, arriving at the modest Scranton train station wearing a 10-gal-lon Texas wide-brimmed hat and appearing "sartorially neat in a gray suit, white shirt, and dark blue tie." Though he batted just .220 with Scranton, Pipp was recalled by Detroit and made his big league debut on June 29, 1913, going 0-for-3 against Roy Mitchell of the St. Louis Browns. In all, he appeared in twelve games for Detroit and batted just .161, which earned him a trip back to the International League. Playing for the Rochester Hustlers, Pipp was the league's best player in 1914. He bat-ted .314 and led the International League with 15 home runs, 290 total bases, and a .526 slug-ging percentage. Surprisingly, or so it seemed in light of his outstanding season, on February 4, 1915, the Tigers sold him and outfielder Hugh High to the New York Yankees for $5,000 each.

On opening day 1915 at Washington, Pipp singled off Walter Johnson in his first at-bat as a Yankee. He went on to hit .246 with four home runs, one of only a handful of players to hit that many in 1915. The following year Pipp became the first player in franchise history to lead the American League in circuit clouts, batting .262 with 12 home runs. Pipp became the first in a long line of standout longball artists to play in pinstripes. "When [Pipp] swings that long heavy bat of his and gets his 180 pounds of rugged bone and muscle well behind the swing," *Baseball Magazine's* J.J. Ward observed, "that little horsehide pellet usually describes a long, beautiful arc over the outfielders' heads." The free-swinging Pipp also struck out 82 times in 1916, a league-high. In 1917 he cut his strikeouts to 66, but retained his home run title, hitting nine four-baggers.

The following year, Pipp slugged just two home runs, but lifted his average to .304, before the government's "work or fight" order caused him to leave the Yankees and accept a job as a naval aviation cadet at the Massachusetts Institute of Technology. He returned to New York in 1919, batting .275 with seven home runs. Though those figures were in line with his previous efforts, Pipp's status as the AL's top home run hitter had already been supplanted by Babe Ruth, who blasted a major league record 29 four-baggers that year.

Upon joining the Yankees in 1920, Ruth quickly became the sport's biggest star, as his unprecedented power barrage signaled the end of the Deadball Era and the emergence of the Yankees, who won three consecutive American League pennants from 1921

to 1923. By 1921 Pipp's maturation as a hitter was complete, as the former strikeout leader fanned only 28 times in 667 plate appearances. Though completely overshadowed by Ruth's exploits, Pipp was a vital cog in the Yankee juggernaut, batting a career-best .329 in 1922, and driving in 108 runs in 1923. In 1924, Wally led the league with 19 triples and drove in a career-high 114 runs, enough to lead the league most years during the Deadball Era, but only third-best on his own team in the offense-saturated environment of the 1920s.

Pipp's large, agile frame also helped him become a standout defensive player. Playing deeper than most first basemen of the era, Wally used his excellent range and soft hands to anchor the New York infield. While Pipp's fielding skills are reflected in his own numbers (during his 15-year-career, he led the league in double plays and putouts five times each, fielding percentage three times, and assists twice), his ability to reach errant throws also cut down on his teammates' miscues. As *Baseball Magazine* observed, "anything that is aimed in the general direction of Pipp is pretty sure to find a safe landing place in his spacious glove."

Throughout his life and during his baseball career, Pipp suffered recurring headaches, the result, he later explained, of a schoolboy hockey injury that had also left him with reduced vision in his left eye. He was suffering one of those headaches on June 2, 1925, and asked trainer Al "Doc" Woods for a couple of aspirin. Yankee manager Miller Huggins strolled by and suggested Pipp take the day off. "The kid can replace you this afternoon," he said, referring to Lou Gehrig. Heading into that day's game, the Yankees were 15–26, had lost five in a row, and were only a half game from the American League cellar. Pipp had started slowly too, batting just .244 with three home runs and 23 RBI.

When Gehrig got his opportunity to start, he took full advantage of it. And a month later, when Pipp suffered a brain concussion, the changeover was complete. Rookie pitcher Charlie Caldwell, later the head football coach at Princeton, beaned Pipp in batting practice, and Wally spent the next two weeks at St. Vincent's Hospital in Manhattan. When he returned, Gehrig had won the first baseman's job, and Pipp's role for the rest of the season was as a pinch-hitter.

The Yanks tried to trade him to several American League clubs, but couldn't come to terms with any of them. So, after getting waivers on him, they sold Pipp to the National League's Cincinnati Reds. The Reds, still badly in need of a first baseman more than a year after the untimely death of Jake Daubert, paid what was said to be much more than the $7,500 waiver price.

Now 33, Pipp bounced back with a strong performance in 1926, posting a .291 average and finishing fourth in the National League in both RBI (99) and triples (15). A less productive year followed—.260 with 41 runs batted in—before he ended his major league career in 1928, batting .283 in 95 games. After batting .312 for the 1929 Newark Bears of the International League, Pipp retired from baseball. He devoted the next few years to playing the stock market in Depression-era America, and even wrote a book on the subject called *Buying Cheap and Selling Dear*. Often jobless during these difficult times, he organized baseball programs for the National Youth Administration, tried his hand at publishing, worked as an announcer on a pre-game baseball broadcast, and even wrote scripts for a Detroit radio announcer. But money remained scarce. "We kneeled down and said prayers at night that Dad would get a job," his son, Walter Jr., later remembered. "Those were rough times."

During World War II, Pipp worked producing B-24 bombers at Henry Ford's Willow Run plant near Ypsilanti, Michigan. After the war, he went to work for the Rockford Screw Products Corporation, selling screws and bolts to the major automotive companies in the Detroit–Grand Rapids area, a job he held for the rest of his working life. In poor health for the last 15 months of his life, Pipp died of a heart attack on January 11, 1965. He was survived by his wife, the former Nora Powers, and four children. He was buried in Woodlawn Cemetery, in Grand Rapids.

LYLE SPATZ

WASHINGTON

It was during the first decade of the Deadball Era that Chicago sportswriter Charles Dryden coined the expression, "Washington: First in war, first in peace, and last in the American League." Inheriting the remnants of the Western League's Kansas City franchise, Washington finished sixth in 1901 and 1902 but ended up last or next-to-last in each of the next nine seasons. The low point was 1904 when the club finished 38–113 (.252), the AL's second-worst record of the entire Deadball Era behind only the 1916 Philadelphia Athletics (36–117, .235). To improve their luck, the Senators changed their official nickname in 1905 to the "Nationals," in honor of the old Washington National League teams of the 1880s and

'90s, but fans used both nicknames interchangeably into the 1950s.

Despite the development of a solid core of young players—fireball pitcher Walter Johnson and speedy center fielder Clyde Milan made their debuts in 1907, good-field, no-hit shortstop George McBride signed on in 1908, and the talented but erratic Bob Groom joined the pitching staff in 1909—the Nats' fortunes did not improve until the arrival of new manager Clark Griffith in 1912. In a youth movement that saw new players at every position except two—right fielder Danny Moeller, third baseman Eddie Foster, first baseman Chick Gandil, left fielder Howard Shanks, second baseman Ray Morgan, and catcher John Henry, all of

WINNING PERCENTAGE 1901–1919

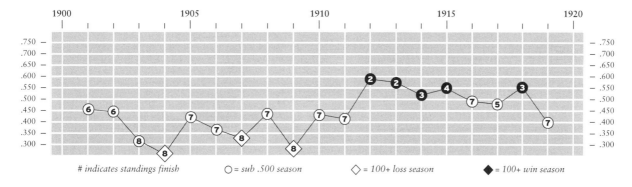

# indicates standings finish   ○ = sub .500 season   ◇ = 100+ loss season   ◆ = 100+ win season

them rookies or second-year players, joined holdovers Milan and McBride in the regular lineup—the "Little Fox" (the 42-year-old Griffith did not become known as the "Old Fox" until later) built the team in his own image: small, but smart and quick. With Johnson at his peak, "My Little Ballclub," as Griff fondly referred to his team, reeled off 17 consecutive victories, 16 of them on the road, en route to a 91–61 record and a second-place finish.

Those eight everyday starters set a record for consistency by holding together for four full seasons, during which the Nats finished in the first division every year. "Griff's Little Ballclub" started to break up in 1916, when Joe Judge replaced Gandil as the first baseman and the Nats slid to seventh. But with the addition of pitcher–outfielder Sam Rice in 1915 and second baseman Bucky Harris in 1919, the Little Fox was already assembling the core of the team that would bring Washington its first World's Championship in 1924.

TOM SIMON

ALL-ERA TEAM

C. MILAN, CF

H. SHANKS, LF   S. RICE, RF

R. MORGAN, 2B

G. McBRIDE, SS

E. FOSTER, 3B   C. GANDIL, 1B

W. JOHNSON, P

G. STREET, C

TEAM LEADERS
1901–1919

BATTING

GAMES
C. Milan 1701
G. McBride 1445
E. Foster 1121

RUNS
C. Milan 871
E. Foster 579
G. McBride 455

HITS
C. Milan 1803
E. Foster 1177
G. McBride 1059

RBI
C. Milan 531
G. McBride 390
H. Shanks 382

DOUBLES
C. Milan 194
E. Foster 145
G. McBride 126

TRIPLES
C. Milan 89
E. Foster 59
H. Shanks 53

HOME RUNS
W. Johnson 16
D. Moeller 15
B. Coughlin. 13
C. Milan 13
J. Ryan 13

STOLEN BASES
C. Milan 481
E. Foster 166
D. Moeller 163

BATTING AVERAGE
(2000+ plate appearances)
C. Gandil 293
C. Milan 283
J. Judge 270

PITCHING

GAMES
W. Johnson 544
T. Hughes 285
C. Patten 269

WINS
W. Johnson 297
C. Patten 105
T. Hughes 83

LOSSES
W. Johnson 191
C. Patten 127
T. Hughes 125

INNINGS
W. Johnson 4090⅔
C. Patten 2059⅓
T. Hughes 1776

STRIKEOUTS
W. Johnson 2614
T. Hughes 884
C. Patten 757

WALKS
W. Johnson 818
J. Shaw 584
T. Hughes 567

SHUTOUTS
W. Johnson 86
J. Shaw 17
T. Hughes 17
C. Patten 17

ERA
(800+ innings pitched)
W. Johnson 1.65
D. Ayers 2.64
J. Shaw 2.73

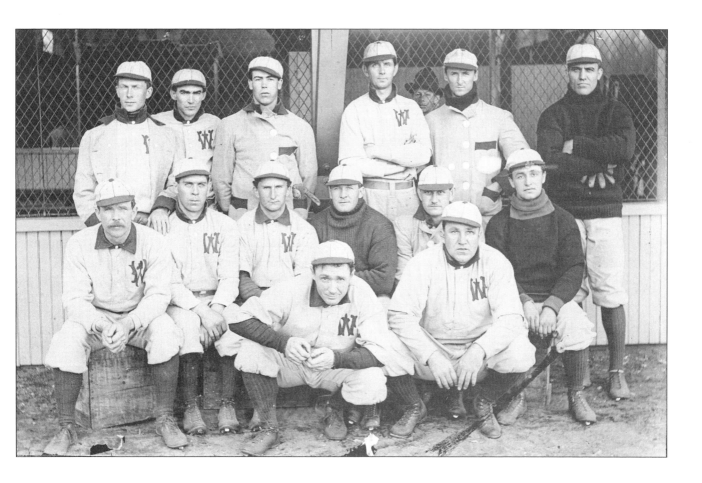

TYPICAL LINEUPS 1901–1919

1901

1. I. Waldron, CF
2. J. Farrell, 2B–CF
3. S. Dungan, RF
   J. Quinn, 2B
4. B. Clarke, C
5. M. Grady, 1B
6. P. Foster, LF
7. B. Coughlin, 3B
8. B. Clingman, SS

1902

1. J. Ryan, CF
2. J. Doyle, 2B
   H. Wolverton, 3B
3. E. Delahanty, LF
4. B. Keister, RF
5. B. Coughlin, 3B
6. S. Carey, 1B
7. B. Ely, SS
8. B. Clarke, C

1903

1. C. Moran, SS
2. K. Selbach, LF
   J. Hendricks, RF
3. B. Clarke, 1B
4. J. Ryan, CF
5. W. Lee, RF
6. B. Coughlin, 3B
7. B. McCormick, 2B
   R. Robinson, UT
8. M. Kittridge
   L. Drill, C

1904

1. B. O'Neill, CF
   B. Coughlin, 3B
2. H. Hill, 3B
3. J. Stahl, 1B
4. F. Huelsman, LF
5. B. McCormick, 2B
6. J. Cassidy, SS
7. P. Donovan, RF
8. M. Kittridge, C
   B. Clarke, C–1B

1905

1. C. Jones, CF
2. H. Hill, 3B
3. C. Hickman, 2B
4. J. Anderson, RF
5. F. Huelsman, LF
6. J. Stahl, 1B
   R. Nill, 3B–2B
7. J. Cassidy, SS
8. M. Heydon
   M. Kittridge, C

1906

1. R. Nill, INF
2. C. Jones, CF
   L. Schlafly, 2B
3. D. Altizer, SS
4. L. Cross, 3B
5. J. Anderson, LF
6. C. Hickman, RF
7. J. Stahl, 1B
8. H. Wakefield
   M. Heydon, C

1907

1. O. Clymer, LF–RF
2. B. Ganley, RF–LF
3. J. Delahanty, 2B
4. J. Anderson, 1B
5. C. Jones, CF
6. D. Altizer, SS
7. B. Shipke, 3B
8. J. Warner
   M. Heydon, C

1908

1. C. Milan, CF
2. B. Ganley, LF
3. J. Delahanty, 2B
4. O. Pickering, RF
5. G. Street, C
6. J. Freeman, 1B
7. G. McBride, SS
8. B. Shipke, 3B

1909

1. G. Browne, LF
2. C. Milan, CF
3. B. Unglaub, 1B–RF
4. J. Delahanty, 2B
   J. Donahue, 1B
5. J. Lelivelt, LF–CF
6. W. Conroy, 3B
7. G. McBride, SS
8. G. Street, C

1910

1. C. Milan, CF
2. J. Lelivelt, LF
3. K. Elberfeld, 3B
4. D. Gessler, RF
5. G. McBride, SS
6. R. Killefer, 2B
7. B. Unglaub, 1B
8. G. Street, C

1911

1. C. Milan, CF
2. G. Schaefer, 1B
3. K. Elberfeld, 2B–3B
4. D. Gessler, RF
5. T. Walker, LF
6. G. McBride, SS
7. B. Cunningham, 2B
   W. Conroy, 3B
8. G. Street, C
   J. Henry, C–1B

1912

1. D. Moeller, RF
2. E. Foster, 3B
3. C. Milan, CF
4. C. Gandil, 1B
5. R. Morgan, 2B
6. H. Shanks, LF
7. G. McBride, SS
8. J. Henry
   E. Ainsmith, C

1913

1. D. Moeller, RF
2. E. Foster, 3B
3. C. Milan, CF
4. C. Gandil, 1B
5. R. Morgan, 2B
6. H. Shanks, LF
7. G. McBride, SS
8. J. Henry, C

1914

1. D. Moeller, RF
2. E. Foster, 3B
3. C. Milan, CF
4. C. Gandil, 1B
5. H. Shanks, LF
6. R. Morgan, 2B
7. G. McBride, SS
8. J. Henry, C

1915

1. D. Moeller, RF
2. E. Foster, 3B–2B
3. C. Milan, CF
4. H. Shanks, LF
5. C. Gandil, 1B
6. R. Morgan, 2B
7. J. Henry, C
8. G. McBride, SS

1916

1. R. Morgan, 2B
   D. Moeller, RF
2. E. Foster, 3B–2B
3. C. Milan, CF
4. S. Rice, RF
5. H. Shanks, LF
6. J. Judge, 1B
7. J. Henry, C
8. G. McBride, SS

1917

1. J. Judge, 1B
2. H. Shanks, SS
3. C. Milan, CF
4. S. Rice, RF
5. E. Foster, 3B
6. R. Morgan, 2B
7. M. Menosky, LF
8. E. Ainsmith, C

1918 (first half)

1. B. Shotton, RF
2. E. Foster, 3B
3. C. Milan, CF
4. H. Shanks, LF
5. J. Judge, 1B
6. R. Morgan, 2B
7. D. Lavan, SS
8. E. Ainsmith, C

1918 (second half)

1. B. Shotton, LF
2. E. Foster, 3B
3. J. Judge, 1B
4. C. Milan, CF
5. F. Schulte, RF
6. H. Shanks, 2B
7. D. Lavan, SS
8. E. Ainsmith, C

1919

1. J. Judge, 1B
2. E. Foster, 3B
3. C. Milan, CF
4. S. Rice, RF
5. P. Gharrity, C–LF
6. V. Picinich, C
   M. Menosky, LF
7. H. Shanks, SS
8. H. Janvrin, 2B

WASHINGTON

EDWARD JAMES DELAHANTY
LEFT FIELDER, 1902–1903

One of the greatest right-handed sluggers of all time, Ed Delahanty dominated the 1890s like no other hitter, batting better than .400 three times, leading the league in slugging percentage four times, and capturing three RBI crowns on his way to a lifetime batting average of .346, the fifth best mark in baseball history. Known as Big Ed, or the King of Swat, the muscular Delahanty was more than a one-dimensional slugger; he was also a fleet-footed, rifle-armed left fielder who was good enough to play center, and an excellent base runner who once led the league in stolen bases. "Delahanty is an awfully even, well balanced player all around," *The Sporting Life* once observed. "You look at his batting and say well, that chap is valuable if he couldn't catch the measles, and then you look at his fielding and conclude that it wouldn't pay to let him go if he couldn't hit a bat bag." Despite such versatility, the temperamental star was destined to make more headlines off the field than on it, and his death, less than two years into his tenure with the Washington Senators, remains one of the most fascinating mysteries in the annals of the sport.

The eldest and most talented of five major league brothers, Edward James Delahanty was born on October 30, 1867, in Cleveland, to Bridget and James, Irish immigrants who had arrived in the United States two years earlier. Ed was their second child, and the first to survive infancy. To support his family James Delahanty took on a variety of blue-collar jobs in Cleveland, while his wife converted the family's spacious Phelps Street home into a boardinghouse. Young Edward and his brothers managed to steer clear of the crowded family home by playing a variety of sports, but especially baseball, in the neighborhood's vacant lots. Ed's impressive hitting caught the eye of local scouts, who recruited him to play for the Cleveland Shamrocks, a semipro club.

His success there led to a $50 per month contract with Mansfield of the Ohio State League, where Delahanty spent the 1887 season, batting .351 with 90 runs scored in 83 games. After appearing in 21 games and posting a .412 batting average for Wheeling (West Virginia) of the Tri-State League in 1888, Delahanty's contract was picked up by the Philadelphia Phillies of the National League for approximately $2,000.

A strapping 6'1" tall and 170 pounds, Delahanty was not an instant success in the majors, as opposing pitchers took advantage of the youngster's free-swinging approach at the plate, holding him to a .228 batting average. He improved to .293 in 1889, then jumped to Cleveland of the Players League in 1890, where he batted .296 in 115 games. After that league failed, Delahanty returned to Philadelphia, struggling to a .243 average, although he scored 92 runs and drove in another 86, eighth best in the circuit. Having failed to live up to his potential after more than three years in the major leagues, Delahanty rededicated himself to his profession in the off-season, working out every day and reporting to camp in 1892 in the best shape of his life. He responded with his finest season to date, batting .306 while leading the league in triples (21) and slugging percentage (.495). It was a performance that drew praise from *The Sporting Life*, which credited Delahanty for his "hard and timely" batting, but the slugger was just getting started.

From 1892 to 1901 Delahanty anchored a powerful Philadelphia lineup that featured the likes of Billy Hamilton, Sam Thompson, Napoleon Lajoie, and Elmer Flick. During that span he led the National League in a major offensive category 24 times. In 1899, when he led the league with a .410 mark, Delahanty became the first player in baseball history to bat better than .400 three times. Among the league-leading 238 hits he collected that season were a career-high 55 doubles. He also captured two home run titles during the decade, blasting 19 round-trippers in 1893 and 13 in 1896. That season he became just the second player in history to hit four home runs in a single game, turning the trick on July 13 against the Chicago Colts. Two of the four homers were inside the park. Three years later, on May 13, 1899, Delahanty hit four doubles in a single game, making him the only player to achieve both feats.

A pull hitter who kept opposing defenses honest by occasionally hitting to the opposite field, Delahanty once confided to a reporter that he often liked to swing at the first pitch, because a pitcher with good control usually tried to "do his business" with the first offering. Nonetheless, Delahanty could be a patient hitter too, as evidenced by his ranking among the league's top ten in walks four times during his career. When outfielders, fearing the legendary slugger's power, played him deeper, Delahanty responded by place-hitting the ball over the infielders' heads. Delahanty's ability to adjust his hitting approach to confound opposing defenses made him, in the estimation of Cincinnati Reds pitcher Red Ehret, "the hardest man in the league for pitchers to puzzle." Longtime catcher Jack O'Connor concurred, noting, "If Del had a weakness at the bat I never could discover it."

Delahanty left an impression in the field as well, where he developed into one of the game's finest outfielders. After spending his first years in the majors as a subpar infielder, Delahanty found his home in the outfield in 1892, displaying enough range to merit the occasional start in center field. At his accustomed position, left field, Delahanty ranked among the league's best. He became known for his strong arm, which he used to collect 243 career assists, and for his hustling style of play, which helped him to reach balls that lesser outfielders would allow to drop in for base hits. That same aggressiveness carried over to the basepaths, as Delahanty swiped 455 bases in his career, including a league-best 58 in 1898.

Blessed with the ability to hit for average and power, exceptional range in the field, a strong arm, and excellent speed, Delahanty was a five-tool player long before the term came into use. Arguably the game's greatest player in the 1890s, Delahanty nonetheless failed to win a pennant with the Philadelphia Phillies, who, despite a robust offense, often found themselves hampered by injuries and short on pitching. While the club struggled, Philadelphia owner John Rogers also managed to suppress the salaries of his top stars. At the beginning of the twentieth century, the great Delahanty was earning $3,000 per year, only a slight increase over the pay he

had received when he entered the major leagues over a decade earlier. Nearing 34 years of age at the conclusion of the 1901 campaign, in which he batted .354 with 108 RBI for the Phillies, Delahanty decided to join many of his teammates in seeking higher pay and better treatment with the rival American League.

Indeed, during the final two months of the 1901 season, reports circulated that Delahanty had become an agent for the upstart league, selling his fellow players on the merits of the new circuit. Delahanty's success can be measured by the number of players for the 1901 Phillies who donned uniforms for the American League the following year—a total of nine players, including Elmer Flick, Red Donahue, Ed McFarland, Monte Cross, Harry Wolverton, Al Orth, and Delahanty himself, who signed a $4,000 contract with the Washington Senators, including a $1,000 signing bonus.

Coming in after the club's disappointing sixth-place finish in 1901, Del gave Washington instant baseball credibility, both to the fans and to the players. He was named captain of his new club, and joined friend Jimmy Ryan in the outfield. As a result of a judge's ruling, any players from the Phillies were forbidden from playing in the state of Pennsylvania, thus preventing Delahanty and his fellow Philadelphia jumpers from playing against the Athletics. To deal with the court order, Del and the other jumpers would typically get off the Philadelphia train in Delaware and head to the team's next destination.

Big Ed battled former Phillies teammate Lajoie of the Cleveland club for the batting crown in 1902, finishing the season with a .376 mark. At the time this was believed to lead the league, which would have made Delahanty the only player ever to win a batting title in both the American League and the National League. Subsequent research, however, established that Lajoie actually bested Delahanty with a .378 average. By today's standards Delahanty would have been declared champion anyway, because Lajoie had only 381 plate appearances.

Despite his continued on-field success, by the end of the 1902 season Delahanty's personal life was beginning to unravel. His wife, Norine, became ill, and Delahanty squandered the couple's financial resources by gambling on horses and binge drinking. Looking to pay off his mounting debts, Delahanty signed a three-year contract with the New York Giants, reported at either $6,000 or $8,000 per season. The deal also included a $4,000 advance.

The contract was never fulfilled. Prior to the 1903 season the leagues agreed to honor each other's contracts, with the result that Delahanty's deal with the Giants was declared void and the rights to his contract were returned to Washington. Even worse news for Delahanty, he was ordered to pay back the $4,000 advance he had already received. Delahanty's 1903 contract with Washington called for a salary of $4,500, of which $600 had already been advanced, so in effect the already cash-strapped Delahanty would have had to pay out $100 to play the 1903 season for the Senators. For a man suddenly on the brink of personal and financial ruin, it was the worst possible outcome. A few days prior to the start of the 1903 season, Delahanty ended a lengthy holdout when Washington agreed to pay the $4,000 he owed New York, but in return $2,000 per year would be deducted from the slugger's salary in 1903 and 1904. Even after reporting, however, Delahanty continued to seek opportunities to jump from the Senators, including a dalliance with Denver of the Western League which never came to fruition.

Delahanty was out of shape when he returned to the Senators, and soon injured his back and ankle. Washington manager Tom Loftus sent him to a health spa in Michigan to shape up, and Del rejoined the team on May 29. Although he continued to bat well upon his return to the lineup, posting a .333 average in 156 at-bats, Delahanty feuded with Loftus, who ordered him to play right field, while Del adamantly insisted on left. Amidst the turmoil, Delahanty's drinking again increased, and his behavior became more erratic. He started giving away precious keepsakes, including his gold watch, to teammates, and it was even rumored that he had once attempted suicide by turning on the gas in his room in Washington.

Prior to embarking on a lengthy road trip with the Senators on June 17, Delahanty took out a life insurance policy on himself, naming his daughter Florence as the beneficiary. On June 25, Delahanty played the last game of his career in Cleveland. When the following morning's newspapers reported that NL president Harry Pulliam had decided to violate the nascent peace agreement by allowing contract-jumping shortstop George Davis to play for the Giants, Delahanty presumably saw his opportunity to finally join the New York club. He abandoned the Senators that morning and went on a drinking binge which left him angry, disoriented, and in no condition to play. He reportedly threatened to kill himself, and several teammates, fearing for his safety, felt it necessary to keep a close watch on him at the team hotel. Delahanty chased one of them away with a knife.

Del accompanied the Senators to their next stop in Detroit, where his mother and two brothers were summoned to help straighten him out. He continued to drink heavily, however, and again abandoned the team on July 2. By this time he knew he would be unable to jump to the Giants, as a court order issued the previous day prohibited Davis from playing for New York. Delahanty nonetheless boarded a train to New York that afternoon but, perhaps tellingly, left his belongings in his Detroit hotel room. Del misbehaved on the train, smoking when he was not supposed to, drinking to excess, and accidentally breaking the glass in front of the emergency tool cabinet. Finally, he fell asleep. When the train made a scheduled stop in Bridgeburg (now Fort Erie), Ontario, a disoriented Del tried to enter an already occupied berth. The commotion seemed to confuse him more, and he had to be subdued by three men. The conductor, John Cole, had understandably had enough of him for the evening and ordered Del off the train.

The train crossed the International Railway Bridge over the Niagara River into Buffalo. In the darkness Big Ed walked out onto the 3,600 foot long bridge and was standing still at its edge, staring down into the water, when he was accosted by night watchman Sam Kingston, on the lookout for smugglers. A scuffle ensued, with Kingston dragging Delahanty back to the middle of the wide bridge, but Kingston then fell down and Delahanty got away. Moments later, according to Kingston—who claimed it was too dark to see what happened—Del either jumped or drunkenly stumbled off the edge of the bridge, falling 25 feet into the 40-foot-deep Niagara River.

His body (naked except for tie, shoes, and socks) was found 20 miles downstream at the base of Horseshoe Falls—the Canadian portion of Niagara Falls—seven days later. Dead at the age of 35, he was buried in Calvary Cemetery in Cleveland.

JOHN T. SACCOMAN

WASHINGTON

THOMAS JAMES "LONG TOM" HUGHES
RIGHT-HANDED PITCHER, 1904–1909, 1911–1913

Long Tom Hughes mixed a happy-go-lucky lifestyle with a Chicago-tough pitching moxie. Tall for his time at 6′1″, he stayed at about 175 pounds throughout his career. A heavy smoker and drinker who took no particular care of his body, he nonetheless managed to stay in the major leagues until nearly age 35 and in the semipro ranks past age 40.

Hughes loved being on the mound, at the center of the game. He had an outstanding drop curveball, a good change of pace that helped his fastball, and a rubber arm. After throwing 200 or more innings every year from 1903 to 1908, Hughes's arm finally gave out, and he spent the 1910 season in the minors. Nonetheless, in an age before reconstructive surgery, Hughes then succeeded in doing what few pitchers of his era could: he came back from a lame arm and pitched three more seasons in the major leagues, winning 28 games for the Senators from 1911 to 1913. "Prize fighters might not be able to come back," Alfred Spink observed prophetically in 1910, "but good, old, sturdy, big-hearted athletes like the grand old man, Hughes, can."

Thomas James Hughes was born in Chicago on November 29, 1878, the fifth surviving child of Patrick and Bridget McNally Hughes, Irish immigrants who had arrived in the United States as children prior to the end of the Civil War. The son of a common laborer, Tom escaped the same fate by honing his skills as a pitcher on the city's sandlots around Ashland and Wabansia avenues. A younger brother, Ed, also became a pitcher, eventually spending parts of two years with the Boston Americans.

Purchased by the Chicago Orphans from Omaha (Nebraska) of the Western League in 1900, Tom pitched a major league career-high 308⅓ innings for the Orphans the following year. Despite a lackluster 10–23 record, Hughes's occasional brilliance on the mound (including

a 1–0, 17-inning victory over Bill Dinneen) aroused the interest of two American League managers, Connie Mack of the Philadelphia Athletics and John McGraw of the Baltimore Orioles. McGraw outbid Mack for Hughes's services, and Tom reported to Baltimore for the 1902 season.

Long Tom's stay in Baltimore was brief. In July 1902 McGraw returned to the National League, and the syndicate of National League managers that controlled the Baltimore franchise set about selling off much of the Orioles roster. Hughes, nursing a sore arm, was released to the Boston Americans. For the final two and a half months of the season, Hughes started eight games for the Americans, going 3–3 with a 3.28 ERA. When Boston charged to the pennant in 1903, Hughes became, along with Cy Young and Dinneen, the third axis in Boston's trio of standout starting pitchers. For the year, Hughes posted a 2.57 ERA and finished with a career-high 20 wins against only 7 losses. Picked to start the third game of that year's World Series, Hughes fared poorly, lasting only two innings in a 4–2 defeat to the Pirates.

That off-season manager Jimmy Collins traded his young 20-game winner to the New York Highlanders for Jesse Tannehill. According to one writer, Collins made the deal because he "had some trouble in holding Tom in the straight path." Hughes started just 18 games for New York before being traded once again. On July 20, 1904, the Highlanders shipped Hughes and fellow pitcher Barney Wolfe to the Washington Senators for Al Orth. In going to Washington, Hughes joined one of the worst teams in baseball history. On their way to a 38–113 record in 1904, the Senators would finish no higher than seventh place for the rest of the decade. From 1904 to 1909 Hughes pitched in 184 games for this feeble outfit; he lost 86 of them.

Although a subpar defense and lack of run support

consistently hampered his efforts, Hughes was much admired in Washington, where his intimidating mound presence and electric assortment of pitches set him apart from his teammates. Armed with an above-average fastball and a willingness to throw it near a batter's head to make a point, Hughes kept opposing hitters off-balance, sprinkling in the occasional insult for good measure. Hughes "is one of the most original 'goat getters' in the business," one writer observed. "When pitching he keeps up a verbal broadside against every batter he faces."

In 1905 Hughes enjoyed one of his best seasons in Washington, finishing the year with a 2.35 ERA in 291⅓ innings, although his 17 wins were offset by 20 losses. He pitched six shutouts, five over the same team, the Cleveland Naps. "His one ambition this season has been to be the master of that team of heavy-hitters at Cleveland," the Washington Post reported. "And now that he has succeeded...the baseball world is talking about his achievement. Hughes is regarded by ball players as one of the most skilled pitchers in either big league. They claim he has no superior when he wants to exercise all his pitching talents. But Tom doesn't always feel that way." At season's end, one Washington paper collected money for a fan testimonial for Long Tom. In appreciation for his efforts, the fans presented Hughes with a diamond scarf pin in the shape of a fleur-de-lis.

But the love affair was not mutual. Frustrated by pitching for the league's doormats, Hughes slumped in 1906, as he posted a 7–17 record with an awful 3.62 ERA. Late in the season, Hughes quit the team, declaring, "The American League is a joke. I am tired of being the scapegoat of the Washington club for the past two years....Rather than come back to Washington, I will join an amateur club or play with the outlaws. This proposition of being the fall guy for the bunch is not what it is cracked up to be....I am through with Washington for good." The Washington Post reported that manager Jake Stahl had already suspended Hughes, for "being too friendly with the cup that cheers."

In the off-season Stahl was replaced as manager by Joe Cantillon, and Hughes returned to the Senators for spring training. It turned out to be another rough year for Hughes and the Senators, as Long Tom posted a 7–14 record and articles about the club featured headlines such as TEAM DOES BEST IT CAN and SHOULD PRACTICE BUNTING. Washington finished the year with a 49–102 record, 43½ games out of first place.

With the emergence of Walter Johnson the Senators improved to 67 wins in 1908, and Hughes enjoyed his first winning season in a Washington uniform: 18–15 with a 2.21 ERA. Tom re-signed for the 1909 season and felt sufficiently hopeful about Washington's prospects that he specifically asked not to be traded. "I want it understood...that I don't want to figure in any deals," he told the Washington Post. "I want to stay right here in Washington as long as I can pitch ball. No trades for mine. I like this old town, and now that the team has some prospects of being in a race, I am more anxious than ever to stay here."

Unfortunately for Hughes and the Senators things did not work out as planned. The Senators won only 42 games, and chronic soreness in his pitching arm limited Tom to just 13 starts and four victories before he was sold on waivers to the Minneapolis Millers of the American Association. For the Deadball Era, it was a familiar story: the sore-armed pitcher who quietly disappears from the league, never to be heard from again. But Hughes would be different. By July 1910 the Washington Post was reporting that Hughes was "mowing down" batters for Minneapolis, striking out as many as ten in one outing and winning two-thirds of his games. Hughes finished the season as the league leader in wins (31), strikeouts (222), and winning percentage (.721); the Millers won the pennant going away with a 107–61 record. That September the Senators repurchased Hughes, and the following spring he was back with Washington.

Arm trouble continued to plague Hughes during his comeback, however. In 1911 he battled his way through 223 innings for the Senators, finishing with a respectable 3.47 ERA. The following year he was better, lowering his ERA to 2.94 and posting a 13–10 record.

Though advancing in years, Hughes never lost his combative spirit. When a crank challenged his pitching effectiveness in a Chicago saloon, Hughes invited him to settle their differences outside. It took five police detectives to separate the two men, who bloodied each other so badly that one passer-by incorrectly assumed they were slashing each other with knives. Both Hughes and his fellow pugilist spent the night in jail, where they shook hands and declared the matter settled.

Tom's arm gave out again in 1913. After finishing the year with a 4–12 record and 4.30 ERA, Hughes was released to the Los Angeles Angels of the Pacific Coast League. Upon examining their new pitcher the Angels were delighted to find that in addition to now being a crafty veteran, Hughes still had plenty of movement and zip on his pitches. In 1914 he was 24–16 with an ERA of 1.91 in a career-high 348 innings. With the Angels again in 1915, Tom pitched well in the early part of the season, posting a record of 19–16 as his team competed for first place. The Angels, however, faded badly and management decided to clean house, releasing the malcontent Hughes in the process. Tom caught on with the Salt Lake City Bees in 1916 and went 9–11 with a 3.87 ERA in 209 innings. Hughes ended his Pacific Coast League career the following year, going 9–14 for the Bees.

Following his retirement, Tom returned to his native Chicago. He was married to Ida Elletsen in 1904, and the couple had seven children: six sons and one daughter.

After pitching in the semipro circuit for several years, Hughes worked in a tavern, and later as a groundskeeper for the Chicago park system. He spent the rest of his life in his beloved hometown and died there at age 77 on February 8, 1956, of pneumonia. He was buried in St. Joseph Cemetery, in nearby River Grove, Illinois.

JOHN STAHL

WASHINGTON

JOHN JOSEPH ANDERSON
OUTFIELDER, 1905–1907

Throughout his 14-year major league career John Anderson had to be accustomed to change. As one of the era's few switch-hitters, one might say he even had a knack for it. From 1894 to 1908, Anderson played for six different franchises in seven different cities. He played for winners, such as the pennant-winning 1899 Brooklyn Superbas (101–47), and for losers, such as the dreadful 1907 Washington Senators (49–102). During his baseball life Anderson may have accumulated more nicknames than any other player of his generation. He was known as Honest John, because he rarely protested umpires' calls; Long John, because of his 6′2″ frame; the Swedish Apollo, for his Scandinavian roots, handsome appearance, and muscular build; and also Big John, in case anyone had forgotten that he was one of the tallest players in the game. A consistent hitter who typically batted fourth or fifth in the lineup and who once led the National League in slugging percentage, Anderson was also an aggressive base runner—his 39 stolen bases tied for the American League lead in 1906. Unfortunately Anderson's reputation took a hit in 1903, when he reportedly attempted to steal an already-occupied second base. Although the evidence shows he was merely picked off first base, stealing an already-occupied base—or any other mental blunder—became known as a "pulling a John Anderson."

John Joseph Anderson was born on December 14, 1873, in Sarpsborg, Norway, one of only three players in the history of major league baseball to come from this European country. Sarpsborg, in southeastern Norway, is about 20 miles from the border with Sweden, and while Anderson's father was Norwegian by birth, his mother was Swedish. At age five John and his parents emigrated to the United States, settling in Worcester, Massachusetts, which contained the country's largest concentration of Swedish immigrants. (Anderson would become an American citizen in 1900.) After starting the 1894 season as a pitcher for Worcester in the New England League, he was released in May and signed by the Haverhill, Massachusetts, club in the same league. He was too wild, though, and after one game in which he walked 13 batters and hit three others, he was moved to left field. Anderson played 86 games with Haverhill, batting .354 and attracting the attention of the National League's Brooklyn Grooms. Late in 1894 he was purchased by Brooklyn and finished the season with the club, hitting .302 in 17 games.

For the rest of the decade Anderson established himself as a solid run producer, batting better than .300 in both 1896 and 1897, driving in an average of 80 runs per season, and leading the National League with a .494 slugging percentage in 1898. Thanks to his power and above-average speed, Anderson also frequently ranked among the league leaders in extra-base hits, connecting for nine home runs in both 1895 and 1898 and leading the league with 22 triples in 1898.

On the field Anderson debuted as a subpar outfielder, posting a woeful .882 fielding percentage in 101 games for Brooklyn in 1895. His defensive play quickly improved, however, as Anderson used his excellent foot speed to track down fly balls in Brooklyn's expansive outfield. By 1897 one publication noted that "Anderson is improving in his fielding and his batting is good, but on the bases he is in the primary class of ball players." Anderson also demonstrated his versatility in the field, filling in at first base for 42 games in 1896, after Brooklyn's regular first baseman suffered a season-ending hand injury. For the rest of his playing career Anderson would alternate between all three outfield positions and first base.

After spending his first three full seasons with

Brooklyn, Anderson was sold to the struggling last-place Washington Senators on May 19, 1898. Although Washington finished in 11th place with a 51–101 record, manager Tom Brown praised Anderson as "one of the best natural batsmen in the league, and a power at the bat for his team." Anderson played 78 games in center field for the Senators that year, and impressed the locals with acrobatic catches.

Anderson's glory days in Washington were short-lived, however. That September, Brooklyn manager Charlie Ebbets announced that Anderson had not been sold to Washington but had merely been "loaned" to the struggling team, so Anderson went back to Brooklyn. In 1899 Brooklyn, now called the Superbas, finally assembled a championship baseball team. Anderson appeared in 41 games at first base and 76 games in the outfield, as Brooklyn finished with a 101–47 record. Though not the star of the team, Anderson hit .269 with 92 RBI, second highest on the club.

Following the 1899 season Connie Mack, who had signed on to manage the Milwaukee club of Ban Johnson's American League, approached Brooklyn about Anderson. After negotiating directly with John, Connie signed him. Playing for the Brewers in 1900 Anderson finished the season with a .309 batting average and a league-leading 63 stolen bases. An open recruiting war erupted between the National and American leagues after the 1900 season, and Anderson opted to remain with Milwaukee. Playing first base for the struggling Brewers in 1901, Anderson had one of his best seasons as a professional, finishing the year with a .330 batting average, eight home runs, 99 RBI, and 35 stolen bases. His 46 doubles in 1901 remained an American League record by a switch-hitter for more than 100 years.

Following the 1901 season Ban Johnson shifted the Brewers to St. Louis, where they became the Browns, and Anderson had another good season, finishing the year with a .284 average, 29 doubles, a team-leading 85 RBI, and 15 stolen bases. The veteran Anderson also became something of a team leader on the Browns. His teammates later characterized him as a warm and friendly person who was extremely generous when contributing to collections made for newly wedded teammates. With his size and strength, he was also known as an outstanding wrestler, able to pin most of the team in pregame wrestling contests.

The following year John hit .284 again and played in 138 of the Browns' 139 games. He led the team in RBI (78), doubles (34), and extra-base hits (44). The Browns, however, faltered, finishing the year in sixth place with a 65–74 record. Late in the season, on September 24, 1903, Anderson made the mistake for which he would forever be remembered. During the first game of a doubleheader against the New York Highlanders, the Browns trailed 6–0 going into the eighth inning. They rallied, loading the bases with one out and John on first base via a walk. With the count full on St. Louis hitter Bobby Wallace, Anderson broke with the pitch. Wallace struck out and the catcher threw to first. The first baseman tagged Anderson, completing the double play. The press reported that Anderson had attempted to steal an already-occupied second base, mistaking his aggressive lead for an attempted steal. Unfortunately this non-attempted steal became Anderson's most famous play. At the end of the season, however, the very same New York Highlanders traded for John, giving up utility man and St. Louis native Jack O'Connor.

Playing with New York in 1904 John found himself reunited with former Brooklyn teammate Willie Keeler. Managed by Clark Griffith, the Highlanders finished second, 92–59 and 1½ games behind Boston. The season came down to the last Boston series. Although New York lost, John made a spectacular relay throw from center field nailing a Boston runner at the plate. John played 143 games, over 100 games in the outfield and 33 games at first base. He hit .278 and drove in a team-leading 82 runs.

Thirty-six games into the 1905 season and with John hitting a lowly .232, the Highlanders sold him to Washington. John spent 1905, 1906, and 1907 with the Senators, hitting .290, .271, and .288, respectively. In August 1907, with the hopeless Senators on their way to a 49–102 record, John deserted the team. Disgusted with the overbearing tactics of the team's new manager, Joe Cantillon, Anderson simply left for home and announced his retirement from baseball. He was suspended and subsequently sold in December 1907 to the Chicago White Sox. Playing his final big league season for the White Sox in 1908, Anderson batted .262 with 21 stolen bases. In 1909 he joined the Providence Grays of the Eastern League; playing first base, he hit .262 and stole 31 bases.

Beginning in 1907, Anderson served with the Worcester police force for about five years, and later worked on his Worcester farm. Married since 1898, he and his wife, Emma, had two children. In 1920, he briefly coached the Buffalo Bisons of the International League. Fifteen years later, John received a silver lifetime pass to all major league games, presented jointly by the presidents of the American and National leagues. He died at age 75 on July 23, 1949, in Worcester, the place where his baseball odyssey began.

JOHN STAHL

WASHINGTON

WALTER PERRY JOHNSON
RIGHT-HANDED PITCHER, 1907–1927; MANAGER, 1929–1932

On August 2, 1907, a young man later described by Frank Graham as "beyond doubt, the greatest pitcher that ever scuffed a rubber with his spikes" made his big league debut for the Washington Senators, losing a 3–2 decision to the pennant-bound Detroit Tigers. The great Ty Cobb later admitted that his fastball "made me flinch" and "hissed with danger." By the time he hung up his spikes 20 years later, Walter Johnson had recorded statistics which seem beyond belief: 417 wins and 279 losses, 3,509 strike-outs, 110 shutouts, twelve 20-win seasons, eleven seasons with an ERA below 2.00, and—what seems almost incomprehensible a century later—531 complete games in 666 starts. And, as superlative as his pitching record was, in Shirley Povich's words, "Walter Johnson, more than any other ballplayer, probably more than any other athlete, professional or amateur, became the symbol of gentlemanly conduct in the heat of battle."

Walter Perry Johnson traveled a circuitous and improbable route to his major league debut and subsequent stardom. He was born on November 6, 1887, on a farm in Allen County, Kansas, the second of six children of Minnie (née Perry) and Frank Edwin Johnson. As a child he helped his parents scratch out a living on their 160-acre farm and found time for hunting and fishing, which became his lifelong passions. Other than occasional schoolyard pick-up games, baseball had no place in his early life.

At the turn of the century Frank Johnson was forced to give up his farm as a result of the persistent Kansas droughts. The family moved into the town of Humboldt, where Frank worked at odd jobs and Walter attended the eighth grade. At this time, Minnie's parents and siblings were all moving to the oil fields of southern California, attracted by the good weather and plentiful jobs. After years of poverty in Kansas, a move

to the Golden State seemed very appealing to Frank and Minnie. They joined the migration in April 1902, settling in Olinda, where Frank found work with the Santa Fe Oil Company as a teamster.

Working on the Kansas farm and then in the oil fields, Walter developed a strong, muscular, 6′1″ frame which eventually filled out to 200 pounds. At 16, he gained his first baseball experience with a sandlot team. Shortly afterward he started his first game against adults, pitching for a semipro team sponsored by the local oil company. Soon he was a permanent member of the oil company team, and was so impressive that a reporter commented, "Johnson was presented as a high school kid, but he is certainly a graduate in the science of delivering the ball."

The unorganized baseball action of southern California continued year-round, pitting town teams, company teams, and barnstorming teams against one another. During winter the rosters were augmented by major and minor leaguers who needed to pick up some extra cash. Over the next three years, it was in this environment that the young Walter honed his pitching skills—if indeed they needed honing.

As Johnson readily admitted, his gift for pitching was not of his own doing, but God-given: "From the first time I held a ball," he explained, "it settled in the palm of my right hand as though it belonged there and, when I threw it, ball, hand and wrist, and arm and shoulder and back seemed to all work together." His signature pitching motion was unique—a short windmill-style windup followed by a sweeping sidearm delivery. During the first part of his career he relied almost exclusively on a fastball (he developed a good curve around 1913), which inspired Ring Lardner to comment, "He's got a gun concealed on his person. They can't tell me he throws them balls with his arm."

In April 1906 a former teammate arranged a job for

Walter with Tacoma in the Northwestern League. After one exhibition outing Walter was released, but another ex-teammate landed him a job playing for the Weiser (Idaho) team in the semipro Southern Idaho League. In Weiser he was paid $90 a week, ostensibly to work for the local telephone company but actually to play baseball on weekends. There was plenty of time to enjoy hunting and fishing in the nearby mountains during the week. Pitching until July for Weiser, Johnson racked up a 7–1 record, then returned to his California home.

It was not until after Walter returned for a second season in Weiser and was on his way to a 14–2 mark that his pitching prowess came to the attention of major league baseball. "The Weiser Wonder" posted a 0.55 ERA while striking out 214 batters in 146 innings. Manager Joe Cantillon of the Washington Senators began receiving telegrams touting Johnson's feats and the wire services were spreading far and wide the story of the young pitcher's string of 77 scoreless innings, which included back-to-back no-hitters. Cantillon eventually sent an injured catcher, Cliff Blankenship, west on a scouting trip. Blankenship persuaded the young phenom to accept a Washington contract. The 19-year-old was so reluctant to accept the offer that he demanded a train ticket to return home to California in case he did not make good, and he insisted on wiring his parents to obtain their permission to sign.

On July 22, 1907, a large crowd came to the Weiser depot to see him off. As Johnson said goodbye to his pals, there were tears in his eyes. A group of appreciative Weiser fans had tried to convince him to stay, offering to set him up with a cigar store on the town square. Johnson thanked them sincerely, but declined the offer. "You know how you are at 19," he explained later. "You want to see things."

The team to which Walter Johnson reported had never finished higher than sixth in the American League, but their highly touted youngster was an immediate success. After Johnson's debut game against the Tigers, Detroit hurler Bill Donovan called him "the best raw pitcher I have ever seen." The rookie posted a 1.88 ERA in 110⅓ innings, but it wasn't enough to save the Senators from a 49–102 mark, 43½ games behind Detroit.

For the next two seasons Walter's presence in Washington's pitching rotation made scant difference. After improving to seventh place in 1908, the woeful Nats returned to the cellar in 1909, finishing 42–110, 56 games out of first and 20 games behind the seventh-place St. Louis Browns. This is not to say that Johnson pitched badly, although he must have been extremely disappointed with his 13–25 won–lost mark in 1909.

His 2.22 ERA that year was better than average, and his 164 strikeouts ranked second in the league. In 1908 Walter recorded one of the greatest pitching performances of his life over the Labor Day weekend. With his pitching staff in shambles, manager Cantillon sent the sturdy Johnson to the mound in New York for three consecutive starts over a four-day period. Walter did not disappoint, shutting out the Highlanders on six, four, and two hits, in a feat that electrified the baseball world.

On March 9, 1910, the *Fullerton Tribune* noted, "Mr. and Mrs. F.E. Johnson, accompanied by their son, Walter, left for Coffeyville, Kansas." Frank Johnson had just returned from a trip there to buy a farm, and now his family was moving back to Kansas, permanently. Walter had never gotten completely used to the constant climate of southern California, and he and his father wanted to be Kansas farmers again. Now, after two and a half years of major league pay, he was in a position to do something about it, settling near the Oklahoma border where he raised grain and blooded Holstein cows and White Orpington hens. He told a reporter that he "could be here all the year round and be contented."

In 1910, with Johnson posting a 25–17 record with a 1.36 ERA and 313 strikeouts, the Washington team improved to seventh place. This marked the beginning of a ten-year run of 20-victory seasons for the big right-hander—a time when Johnson acquired his nickname the Big Train for the blinding speed of his fastball; for his flamboyant motoring habits, he was also called Barney, after race car driver Barney Oldfield. During this decade the Senators achieved some degree of respectability, finishing second in 1912 and 1913. In 1918 they were closing in on the Red Sox and Indians when the government's "work or fight" order brought the curtain down on the baseball season on Labor Day with Washington four games out, in third place.

Washington's improved performance during the second decade of the twentieth century was due mostly to Walter Johnson's pitching. This can

be illustrated by a breakdown of the won–lost record into games where Walter was awarded the decision and games won or lost by other pitchers. The Johnson decisions come to 265 wins and 143 losses, for a .650 winning percentage. For other pitchers, it is 490, 594, .452 and for the team overall it is 755, 737 and .507.

That Johnson recorded as many losses as he did was due to the mediocre quality of his team's batting and fielding. This lack of support is reflected by the fact that he holds major league records for number of 1–0 wins (38) as well as for 1–0 losses (26).

Walter's peak years were 1912 and 1913, when he went 33–12 and 36–7, winning a Chalmers automobile as American League MVP during the latter year. He was now admired all over America not only for his pitching exploits and his fierce competitiveness, but also for the modesty, humility, and dignity with which he conducted himself, never arguing with umpires, never berating his teammates for their errors, never brushing back hitters or using foreign substances on the baseball. At a time when many ballplayers were ruffians and drunkards, Walter was never in a brawl and did not patronize saloons.

During the summer of 1913 Walter Johnson met the love of his life, Hazel Lee Roberts, the daughter of Nevada's congressman. They renewed their acquaintance when Walter returned from Kansas in 1914 and their romance soon became the talk of Washington society. The couple was married June 24, 1914, with the chaplain of the U.S. Senate officiating. They had six children, five of whom lived to adulthood.

Walter's string of 20-win seasons was broken in 1920 when a combination of a bad cold, a sore arm, and pulled leg muscles limited him to an 8–10 mark in only 21 appearances. Although his health returned in 1921 and he posted a 17–14 record, tragedy struck twice that year, when his father died of a stroke in July and his two-year-old daughter Elinor died from influenza in December. Burdened with the memories of these losses, Walter and Hazel sold their farm and moved away from Coffeyville, eventually making Bethesda, Maryland, their year-round home.

Johnson decided to make 1924, his 18th major league season, his last hurrah, and planned to become the owner of a team in the Pacific Coast League following the season. Meanwhile, Washington owner Clark Griffith finally had assembled a team worthy of its pitching ace and the Senators captured their first American League pennant. A rejuvenated Walter Johnson was the key to their victory and was the league's MVP, delivering a 23–7 record and leading the league in wins, ERA, strikeouts, and shutouts.

Facing John McGraw's New York Giants in the opening game of one of the most dramatic World Series of all time, Walter pitched well but lost 4–3 in 12 innings at Griffith Stadium. Perhaps still tired from that 165-pitch effort, he turned in a lackluster performance in Game Five, losing 6–2 in the Polo Grounds. The Senators were now one game away from elimination and it looked as though Walter Johnson might never have another chance at World Series glory.

In Game Six, however, Washington rallied for a 2–1 win behind Tom Zachary, setting the stage for a seventh game. On a beautiful Indian summer afternoon, as the Giants and Senators battled to the finish, an ovation

echoed across Griffith Stadium when Johnson headed for the bullpen in the sixth inning. In the top of the ninth, manager Bucky Harris, who had just singled in two runs to tie the score at 3–3, called the Big Train in to pitch. He handed him the ball with the words, "You're the best we've got, Walter. We've got to win or lose with you."

Walter did not disappoint his manager, nor his millions of fans, holding the Giants scoreless for four innings, pitching his way into and out of one jam after another. Twice after intentional walks to Ross Youngs, he fanned major league RBI champ George Kelly. Washington secured its only world championship in the bottom of the 12th inning, when Muddy Ruel scored on an Earl McNeely ground ball that hit a pebble and bounced over the head of Giants third baseman Fred Lindstrom.

Following his World Series triumph, Johnson traveled to California, visiting his boyhood home in Olinda, pitching an exhibition game against Babe Ruth, visiting Hollywood movie studios, and trying to wrap up ownership of a Pacific Coast League franchise. After

the purchase fell through, he decided to return to Washington for yet another big league campaign.

Although 1925 was a superb season for Washington—the Senators won the pennant handily and Walter delivered his final 20-win season while setting a record for the highest batting average by a pitcher, at .433—the World Series that year turned out to be the exact opposite of the 1924 triumph. After Walter notched 4–1 and 4–0 wins, disaster struck in Game Seven on a muddy, rainy day in Pittsburgh. In a game that should never have been played under such conditions, Walter and his team went down to a 9–7 defeat.

After 1927, his final season, Johnson managed for a year at Newark in the International League, then returned to Washington, where he served as manager for four seasons. He also managed at Cleveland from 1933 to 1935, where he was constantly under attack by the local press. Although his managerial style was criticized as too easy-going, it should be noted that his teams had an overall winning percentage of .550.

The biggest tragedy of Walter's later years, however, was Hazel's death at age 36 on August 1, 1930, apparently the result of exhaustion from a cross-country drive during one of the hottest summers on record. After he lost the woman he idolized, a cloud of melancholy descended over the rest of Johnson's life, darkening what should have been tranquil, happy years of retirement on his Mountain View Farm in the Maryland countryside.

During his later years Walter kept busy on the farm, served as Montgomery County commissioner, was brought back by the Senators in 1939 as their broadcaster, and made an unsuccessful run as a Republican for a seat in the U.S. Congress. On June 12, 1939, along with such other greats as Babe Ruth, Ty Cobb, and Honus Wagner, Johnson was inducted into the newly created Baseball Hall of Fame in Cooperstown, New York. During World War II he made several brief playing appearances in war bond games, including serving up pitches to Ruth in Yankee Stadium.

After suffering for several months from a brain tumor, Walter Johnson died in Washington, DC, at age 59 on December 10, 1946. He was buried next to Hazel at Union Cemetery in Rockville, Maryland.

CHARLES CAREY

WASHINGTON

JESSE CLYDE MILAN
CENTER FIELDER, 1907–1922; MANAGER, 1922

He was a left-handed hitter who batted .285 over the course of 16 seasons, and Clark Griffith called him Washington's greatest center fielder, claiming that he played the position more shallow than any man in baseball—and yet Clyde "Deerfoot" Milan achieved his greatest fame as a base stealer. After Milan supplanted Ty Cobb as the American League's stolen-base leader by pilfering 88 bases in 1912 and 75 in 1913, F.C. Lane of *Baseball Magazine* called him "Milan the Marvel, the Flying Mercury of the diamond, the man who shattered the American League record, and the greatest base runner of the decade." It was hyperbole, of course. Cobb reclaimed the American League record in 1915 by stealing 96 bases and went on to swipe far more bases over the decade than Milan, but Deerfoot stole a total of 481 during the Deadball Era, ranking third in the American League behind only Cobb (765) and Eddie Collins (564).

The son of a blacksmith, Jesse Clyde Milan (pronounced "Millin") was born on March 25, 1887, in Linden, Tennessee, a quiet hamlet of some 700 residents nestled in the hills above the Buffalo River, 65 miles southwest of Nashville. He was one of eight children (four boys and four girls), and his younger brother Horace also took up professional baseball, briefly joining him in the Washington outfield in 1915 and 1917. Another younger brother, Frank, became a noted Broadway actor, co-starring alongside Humphrey Bogart in the famed original staging of *The Petrified Forest*. Baseball was almost unknown in rural Middle Tennessee where the Milans grew up, and Clyde told Lane that he did not play much of the sport as a youngster. "To show what little experience I really had, I will say that in 1903 I played in just nine games of baseball, and the following season I didn't play the game at all," he recalled. Clyde's chief sporting interest in those years was hunting for quail and wild turkey with his two setters, Dan and Joe.

In 1905 Clyde traveled several days to join a semipro team in Blossom, Texas, after reading an advertisement that the manager of the club was looking for players. There was a great rivalry that year between Blossom and the neighboring town of Clarksville. "Dode Criss, now with St. Louis, was the star pitcher and batter of the Clarksville team, and he surely was some hitter," Milan told a reporter in 1910. "Well, we played Clarksville and I not only hit Criss hard, but in the ninth inning, with the bases full, I guess I made the most remarkable catch off of his bat that I have ever made in my life. I don't know today how I ever got near the ball, but I nailed it and was a hero in Blossom thereafter." Milan ended up joining Blossom's rivals, but he was not with the Clarksville team very long before the North Texas League disbanded in mid-July due to an epidemic of yellow fever. Milan then finished up the season in the Missouri Valley League, with the South McAlester Miners in Indian Territory (now Oklahoma).

During his short stint in Clarksville Clyde managed to meet his future bride, Margaret Bowers, whom he visited each off-season for the next eight years. The couple ended up marrying after the 1913 season and eventually made their home in Clarksville, where they raised two daughters.

Milan began the 1906 season by hitting .356 for Shawnee (Indian Territory) of the South Central League, but the team again disbanded before Milan received his pay. Disgusted with professional baseball, he was thinking about quitting when he received an invitation to join Wichita (Kansas) of the Western Association. "I felt none too sure that I could make good there, for the company was much faster," Clyde recalled. That partial season in Wichita saw him hit just .211, but he returned in 1907 and batted .304 with 38 stolen bases in 114 games, attracting the attention of Washington manager Joe Cantillon, who had seen him in a spring exhibition. That summer Cantillon dispatched injured catcher Cliff Blankenship to Wichita with orders to purchase Milan's contract, then go to Weiser, Idaho, to scout and possibly sign Walter Johnson. In later years Clyde loved to relate Blankenship's remarks during his contract signing: "He told me that he was going out to Idaho to look over some young phenom. 'It looks like a wild goose chase and probably a waste of train fare to look over that young punk,' Blankenship said." Milan cost the Nats $1,000; Johnson was secured for a $100 bonus plus train fare.

Milan and Johnson had a lot in common: they were the same age, they both hailed from rural areas—Washington outfielder Bob Ganley started calling Milan "Zeb," a common nickname for players from small towns—and they were both quiet, reserved, and humble. They became natural hunting companions and inseparable friends, and eventually they became the two best players on the Senators team. "Take Milan and his roommate, Walter Johnson, away from Washington, and the town would about shut up shop, as far as base ball is concerned," wrote a reporter in 1911.

For Milan, stardom was not immediate. After making his debut with the Senators on August 19, 1907, he played regularly in center field for the rest of the season and batted a respectable .279 in 48 games. In 1908, however, Milan batted just .239, and the following year he slumped to .200, with just 10 stolen bases in 130 games. Cantillon wanted to send him to the minors and purchase an outfielder who could hit, but the Senators were making so little money that they could not afford a replacement. Fortunately for Washington, Jimmy McAleer took over as manager in 1910 and immediately recognized the young center fielder's potential. Under McAleer's tutelage, Milan bounced back to hit .279 with 44 steals, and in 1911 he became a full-fledged star by batting .315 with 58 steals.

Milan's peak was from 1911 to 1913, when he played in every game but one, batted over .300 each season, and averaged almost 74 stolen bases per season. In 1912 he finished fourth in the Chalmers Award voting, and his American League record-breaking total of 88 steals would have been 91 if Washington's game against St. Louis on August 9 had not been rained out in the third inning.

Running into Milan on a train that summer, Billy Evans, who had umpired Milan's first game back in 1907, remarked on his wonderful improvement in every department of the game, base running in particular. "When I broke in, I thought all a man with speed had to do was get on in some way and then throw in the speed clutch," Milan told the umpire. "I watched with disgust while other players much slower than me stole with ease on the same catcher who had thrown me out. It finally got through my cranium that a fellow had to do a lot of things besides run wild to be a good base runner. I used to have a habit of going down on the second pitch, but the catchers soon got wise to it and never failed to waste that second ball, much to my disadvantage. Now I try to fool the catcher by going down any old time. Changing my style of slide has also helped me steal many a base that would have otherwise resulted in an out. I used to go into the bag too straight, making it an easy matter for the fielder to put the ball on me, but I soon realized the value of the hook slide."

In 1914 Milan suffered a broken jaw and missed six weeks of the season after colliding with right fielder Danny Moeller. He rebounded to play in at least 150 games in each of the next three seasons, 1915 to 1917, and he continued to play regularly through 1921, batting a career-high .322 in 1920. Griffith appointed Milan to manage the Nats in 1922 but the job did not agree with him; he suffered from ulcers as the club finished sixth, and he was fired after the season amidst reports that he was "too easy-going."

That marked the end of his major league playing career, but he continued to play in the minors while managing in Minneapolis in 1923, and serving as player–manager in New Haven in 1924 and Memphis in 1925 and 1926. After retiring as an active player, Milan coached for Washington in 1928 and 1929 and managed Birmingham from 1930 to 1935 and Chattanooga from 1935 to 1937. He also scouted for Washington in 1937 and served as a coach for the Senators from 1938 through 1952.

On March 3, 1953, Clyde Milan died from a heart attack at a hospital in Orlando, Florida, two hours after collapsing in the locker room at Tinker Field. Three weeks short of his 66th birthday, he had insisted on hitting fungoes to the infielders during both the morning and afternoon workouts, despite the 80-degree heat. He was buried in Clarksville Cemetery in his adopted hometown.

TOM SIMON

WASHINGTON

George Florian McBride
Shortstop, 1908–1920; Manager, 1921

Like his contemporary in the National League, Mickey Doolan, George McBride was the prototypical "good-field, no-hit" shortstop during the Deadball Era. Widely viewed as the best defensive shortstop in his league, McBride struggled mightily at the bat. A relatively large shortstop, standing 5′11″ and weighing 170 pounds, McBride was described in the press as an "aggressive, alert, and quick-witted" fielder. He led the American League in fielding percentage five times, including four times consecutively from 1912 to 1915, and was near the lead in most other years. Meanwhile he achieved only a .218 lifetime batting average, never exceeding .235 for a single season. He was an iron man during his days as the regular shortstop for the Washington Senators, and was recognized as one of the smartest players of his day.

George Florian McBride was born in Milwaukee on November 20, 1880, to the former Mary Frommell and Peter McBride, an Irish immigrant, Milwaukee city supervisor, policeman, shoemaker, and saloon keeper. George became enchanted with baseball at an early age and spent much of his youth engaged in schoolyard and sand-lot games. In 1901, at the age of 21, he headed west to play third base for the Sioux Falls Canaries, an independent team participating in a loosely structured South Dakota baseball circuit. After completing the season there in early September, George returned to Milwaukee, where the local entry in the fledgling American League was mired in last place and missing the services of its starting shortstop, Wid Conroy, who had sprained an ankle. According to McBride, he had been alerted by local newspapermen that there might be an opportunity for him to play for the Brewers in Conroy's absence. He appeared at Lloyd Street Grounds prior to a game on September 12, and was invited by manager Hugh Duffy to suit up. McBride played in three games for the Brewers, handling 12 chances flawlessly in the field while collecting two hits in 12 at-bats.

The local American League franchise was transferred to St. Louis following the 1901 season, leading Milwaukee to field a team in the American Association. McBride re-signed with the Brewers for the 1902 season, but after the franchise moved to St. Louis, he became one of the few players ever to jump a major league contract for a minor league one, signing with Milwaukee's team in a new outlaw league, the American Association. He split time that year between Milwaukee and Kansas City, also of the American Association, as a third baseman, then rejoined Organized Baseball in 1903 with Peoria (Illinois) and St. Joseph (Missouri), both of the Western League, as a second baseman. He achieved the highest single-season batting mark of his professional career in 1903, averaging .286 for the year. He remained at St. Joseph in 1904, returning to the shortstop position.

In August 1904 the Pittsburgh Pirates purchased McBride for $1,000, but he wasn't asked to report until spring 1905. He served as a utility infielder, playing in 27 games, sometimes subbing at short for an injured Honus Wagner. On July 5 he was traded to the St. Louis Cardinals for Dave Brain and cash. With St. Louis McBride finally settled into the position he would call home for the rest of his career, playing 80 games at shortstop for the Cards in 1905 and playing 90 games at the position in 1906.

Although his fielding ranked among the best in the National League, McBride's hitting was abysmal. He averaged only .217 in 1905, and in 1906 was batting only .169 when he was sold to Kansas City to finish out the season. He continued his strong play at short for the Blues through the end of 1907, while also showing improvement at the plate, raising his average to .269 in his final year with the club.

McBride's nomadic baseball wanderings ended following the 1907 season when he was purchased by the Washington Senators of the American League. Beginning in 1908 McBride played 13 seasons with the Senators, holding down the regular shortstop position for the first nine of those years. He was considered an iron man for his time. From 1908 to 1914 he played in at least 150 games a season, including every Senators game during the 1908, 1909, and 1911 seasons. He was the American League leader in fielding percentage in 1909 and in each of the four seasons between 1912 and 1915, and always among the league leaders in putouts and assists. His defense was such that he received votes for the Chalmers Award in 1913 and 1914 despite batting .214 and .203 in those respective years. In addition to his superior glove work, McBride was also noted for the good head he had for the game. He was named field captain of the Senators in 1911, a title he held throughout the remainder of his playing days.

Never strong from the plate, McBride did not hit for either average or power. He compiled a paltry .218 lifetime batting average with just seven home runs, and never collected more than 26 extra-base hits in any season. His most productive and consistent offensive seasons in the American League were from 1908 through 1911, a four-year period during which he averaged between .230 and .235 a season. His hitting declined in the years following, as his average dipped to only .203 and .204 in 1914 and 1915, respectively, while still playing full time. Relegated to part-time duty after that, McBride mustered only a .185 mark over his final four seasons. Like many bad hitters during the Deadball Era, McBride acquired a reputation as a good hitter in the clutch. Incredibly, F.C. Lane of *Baseball Magazine* once declared that there were "few worse men for the pitcher to face with men on base than this same quiet, flawless fielder."

Though considered relatively even-tempered and easygoing, McBride was a fiery competitor, subject to sudden bursts of temper. The most prominent of these occurred on June 30, 1916. McBride was facing Carl Mays of the Boston Red Sox, a notorious head hunter. Following some verbal jostling between the two, McBride was struck in the arm while protecting himself from a pitch that was tracking perilously close to his head. McBride stepped to the side of the plate, waited a few seconds, then wheeled and fired his bat at the Bosox pitcher, missing him by only a couple of feet. A lively altercation between the two teams ensued. McBride was suspended for two games.

As the Deadball Era wound down, so did McBride's playing career. He was replaced as the Senators' regular shortstop in 1917 by Howard Shanks, reducing his playing time to 50 games that season. He remained on the roster through 1920, but saw his playing time further curtailed, never again playing in more than 18 games in a season. However, his primary role with the Senators during these final seasons was not as a player, but as a manager in training under the watchful eye of Clark Griffith. During this time he served as an instructor to the team's younger infielders, as a base coach, and as a fill-in manager when Griffith was away from the team scouting or tending to other front-office duties. Prior to the 1921 season Griffith stepped away from his on-field duties and appointed McBride the new team manager, the first in a long line of ex-Washington players to take the reins for Griffith.

McBride's appointment as manager was popular throughout the baseball world, but ill fortune scarred the ex-shortstop's first and only season as the club's manager. On July 27, 99 games into the 1921 season, McBride was struck above the temple by a ball thrown by outfielder Earl Smith during practice prior to a scheduled contest with the Chicago White Sox. He reportedly suffered a slight concussion and partial paralysis of the face. He was confined to his bed for almost a week and returned to the club on August 4, but continued dizziness and fainting spells hampered his efforts to lead his squad. Nevertheless, McBride guided the 1921 Senators to a fourth-place finish, with an 80–73 record, the best winning percentage achieved by the club during the 1919–1923 period. McBride continued to feel the ill effects of his injury during the off-season, and on December 6 he resigned his post as manager. Griffith offered him a job with the club as a scout, but McBride did not feel his health was good enough to accept the offer.

McBride stayed out of baseball until 1925, when he returned as a coach with the Detroit Tigers, serving as Ty Cobb's first lieutenant during the 1925 and 1926 seasons. Thereafter he spent one year as a coach with Newark in the International League, and another year back with the Tigers, coaching under manager Bucky Harris, who had previously played for McBride in 1921. George retired from baseball for good following the 1929 season, at the age of 48.

After leaving the game McBride returned to his hometown of Milwaukee, supporting himself primarily from the returns on successful investments he made during and following his playing days. He died at age 92 on July 3, 1973, after a brief illness. His grave is in Holy Cross Cemetery, in Milwaukee.

STEPHEN ABLE

WASHINGTON

NICHOLAS ALTROCK
COACH, 1909, 1912–1957

For three years at the turn of the last century, Nick Altrock was arguably the best left-handed pitcher in the game. His talent, pitching smarts, and extraordinary fielding ability helped him to win 62 games for the Chicago White Sox from 1904 through 1906, and to beat Mordecai Brown in Game One of the 1906 World Series. However, Altrock's baseball prowess was overshadowed by his second career as one of the most-popular and longest-working baseball clowns of all time. At his clowning peak, Altrock enjoyed a salary that rivaled Babe Ruth's.

Nicholas Altrock was born in Cincinnati on September 15, 1876. He used to joke, "the country was born in 1776 and Nick Altrock was born in 1876. But somehow my parents slipped up. I should have been born on the Fourth of July." Nick's parents were part of Cincinnati's burgeoning German population and he, like many children of immigrants in the city's Over-the-Rhine neighborhood, took up America's game. As a young man in Cincinnati he established a reputation as a good pitcher in the semipro leagues around the city while working as an apprentice cobbler. Altrock soon realized that getting paid for baseball was more fun than getting paid to fix shoes, but his father initially disapproved of the boy's priorities. "I thought he was a hopeless case the way he stuck to baseball," Christian Altrock later told the *Chicago Tribune*. "I was discouraged and thought he would never amount to a row of pins."

In 1898 Altrock got his first job in Organized Baseball pitching for Grand Rapids (Michigan) in the Inter-State League. He won 17 games against just three losses, leading Barney Dreyfuss of the Louisville Colonels to purchase the left-hander's contract near the end of the season. Nick went 3–3 for the Colonels, but he spent more time drinking and partying than preparing

for games and manager Fred Clarke sent him back to Grand Rapids in 1899.

From 1899 to 1902 Nick knocked around the minors, pitching and partying. He threw for Oswego and Binghamton in the New York State League, Syracuse and Toronto in the Eastern League, and Los Angeles in the California League. With Milwaukee of the American Association in 1902 Altrock finally put it all together, finishing the season with a 28–14 record in 338 innings of work. Impressed, the Boston Americans acquired him near the end of the season. Despite posting an ERA of 2.00, Altrock lost both his starts.

Boston was the best team in the league in 1903, but manager Collins preferred his veteran aces Cy Young and Bill Dinneen to the young Altrock. Collins sold Nick to the White Sox midway through the 1903 season. The trade cost Altrock an opportunity to pitch in that year's World Series, but he quickly established himself in the Chicago rotation, going 4–3 with a 2.15 ERA to close out the season. The following year he was even better, posting a 19–14 record in 307 innings of work (second most innings on the staff).

The White Sox under fiery manager Fielder Jones were one of the best teams in the new American League, and in 1905 Nick almost pitched them to a pennant with a fine 23–12 record and 1.88 ERA, the fifth best in the American League. Altrock's 315⅔ innings pitched were a career high, and Chicago finished in second place, two games behind the Philadelphia Athletics.

The following year Chicago stormed to the top of the league, winning 93 games and holding off a late charge by the New York Highlanders to capture the American League pennant. Altrock was once again a key factor in the club's success, finishing the year with a 20–13 record and 2.06 ERA in 287⅔ innings of work. With their .230

team batting average, few observers gave the Hitless Wonders much of a chance in that year's World Series against the powerhouse Chicago Cubs, but manager Fielder Jones remained confident in his team's ability to compete. For any clutch situation, Jones said, "I would send Nick Altrock to the slab, and show me any pitcher in the league who is better acquainted for just such an emergency."

Nick rewarded Jones's faith by tossing a four-hitter to beat Cubs' ace Mordecai Brown in the first game, 2–1. Brown took the honors in their Game Four rematch 1–0, but Nick posted a 1.00 ERA for the series. In the second game Altrock set a Series record for chances handled by a pitcher in one game with 11—eight assists and three putouts. Nick also set a record for most chances in a six-game Series with 17. Hippo Vaughn later tied that mark in the 1918 series, but pitched three games to Nick's two.

It was a fitting accomplishment, given Altrock's reputation as one of the finest fielding pitchers of his or any other generation, thanks in large part to an extraordinarily deceptive pickoff move. In 1901, while pitching for Los Angeles in the California League, Nick reportedly walked seven men intentionally and picked off six of them. Altrock still holds the all-time record for most chances accepted by a pitcher in a nine-inning game (13).

Despite his considerable talent and success on the mound, Nick never took his playing very seriously. His contemporaries as often described him as "carefree" and "eccentric" as they did "tough." Nick was known to take a drink or three after a game, and some writers blamed Nick's love for malt brew for his decline after the 1906 Series. Altrock himself once said, "I never took but two things seriously in my life. My clowning and my golf." In February 1908 Altrock married Hannah Weddendorf, but she soon grew weary of Nick's late night habits and the couple was divorced in 1912. Two years later, he married Eleanor Campbell.

Nick's inattention to training may have contributed to his poor 1907 season. He hurt his arm, and his record fell to 7 wins and 13 losses as the Sox slipped to third place. In 1908 Altrock's record was only 5–7, and the Sox lost the pennant on the last day of the season to the Tigers. In May 1909 Chicago owner Charles Comiskey traded Altrock, outfielder Gavy Cravath, and first baseman Jiggs Donahue to the Washington Senators for Bill Burns. Nick did not pitch well for Washington, and later that year found himself back in the minors, playing for the Minneapolis Millers. Nick's career as a major league pitcher may have been finished by 1909, but his second career was just beginning.

Altrock barely hung on in the minors for three years of pitching and coaching. Then one day in 1912, when Nick was coaching third base for Kansas City in the American Association, he decided to imitate a film he had seen the previous night of a shadow-boxing exhibition featuring featherweight champion Johnny Kilbane. Altrock opened with a roundhouse right to his own chin and fell to the ground. Then he picked himself up and went at himself again, as the crowd roared in bemused delight. Nick finished by knocking himself out to raucous applause.

Unfortunately Nick's comic routine did not amuse Kansas City's owner, Patsy Tebeau. Altrock later liked to tell the story of how Tebeau called Nick into his office to say that he was releasing him. "Don't worry about me, Mr. Tebeau," Nick told the owner. "Why, with my face, I might break into movies."

And what a face it was. With a big wide nose spread out to his cheeks and two jug handles for ears, his face looked like an iron had flattened it. With his cap sitting sideways and slightly askew on his head, and usually with a big grin on his face, Altrock looked like a born comic. He always enjoyed fooling around, and now Nick was about to make a career of it.

Nick took his release from Kansas City in stride because he already had an offer from manager Clark Griffith to join the Washington Senators as a "comedy coacher." The Senators already enjoyed the services of Germany Schaefer, one of the most colorful eccentrics ever to play baseball. In his first few days with the club, however, Nick was buried deep on the bench. Then one day the Senators were losing to a strong Cleveland pitcher named Vean Gregg. Griffith turned to his rubber-faced acquisition and said, "What good are you?"

Nick replied, seriously, "I'm the king's jester." Then he asked, "Do you really want to win this game?" Griffith said, "With your pitching I suppose?" Altrock said, "No. With my coaching."

Altrock talked Griffith into sending him to the first base coaching box. The next time Griffith looked out to the field he saw Nick in a heap on the ground finishing a pantomime of a man who spiked himself with his own shoe. Gregg was laughing so hard he started heaving the ball over the middle and the Senators starting hitting. Altrock morphed the routine into a full wrestling pantomime, pinning himself for a victory. Finally, home plate umpire Silk O'Loughlin, himself doubled over with laughter, ordered him to stop.

Naturally the newspapers reported this strange behavior and more fans started to turn out for Senators games. American League president Ban Johnson attended one of Nick's early games and decided to

allow his antics so long as they did not interrupt play. Nick was funny enough by himself, but his routines really began to soar when he added a partner. At first he did routines with Schaefer, until Schaefer signed with Newark of the Federal League in 1915. Altrock then teamed with reserve Carl Sawyer for two seasons, then worked solo until 1919, when the Senators acquired another washed-up pitcher, Al Schacht.

Altrock and Schacht became the Martin and Lewis of baseball comedy. They created a series of pantomimes that they performed at games, including bowling, juggling, golf tricks, rowing boats during rain delays, mocking umpires, and other tricks. The two of them regularly headlined vaudeville bills, and became part of the eagerly anticipated entertainment for the World Series and All-Star games. Altrock made more money at his peak in the 1920s than almost any other ballplayer. His salary from all his various appearances was reported in the $180,000 range.

Ironically, in the midst of this success Altrock and Schacht stopped speaking to each other in 1927. Although Altrock never spoke about the specific reasons for it, their rift was often attributed to a fake prizefight routine that got a little too real. The story is that Schacht thought it would be funnier if he actually hit Nick and so punched the older comic unexpectedly and knocked him to the ground. Altrock got revenge a few days later, during a routine where he would normally fire a hard baseball at Schacht for him to dodge and follow it with a soft baseball that Schacht took on the head. Altrock

switched the baseballs, and Schacht took a hard blow to the skull and hit the turf.

They nonetheless continued their successful performing partnership until 1934, when Schacht joined the Red Sox. Nick continued as a coach and clown for the Senators until 1957, when he was 81. Until the 1930s the Senators would often let Nick play in one of the games at the end of the year. Thanks to such opportunities Nick became, and remains, the oldest player ever to hit a triple, doing it in 1924 when he was 48. The newspaper accounts claimed the outfielders were not running very fast after the ball, but Nick still whaled it a long way. He hit a clean single in 1929 at the age of 53, and made his last appearance in 1933 at the age of 57. That makes Nick the third oldest man to appear in a major league baseball game; the only older players are Satchel Paige, 59, and Minnie Miñoso, 57. Altrock is also one of the very few major leaguers to play in five different decades.

Nick spent his baseball seasons in Washington, DC, and his winters in Sarasota, Florida. He died on January 20, 1965, in Washington at the age of 88. After Nick's death Al Schacht said of his former partner, "Nick was a great comedian....I have never seen anyone with better facial expressions. And we should all remember that he was a fine big league pitcher as well as an exceptional entertainer." Altrock was survived by his wife of 50 years, Eleanor, and was buried in Vine Street Hill Cemetery, in Cincinnati.

PETER GORDON

WASHINGTON

ROBERT GROOM
RIGHT-HANDED PITCHER, 1909–1913

One of the taller pitchers of his day, 6'2", 175-pound Bob Groom possessed a lively fastball and an assortment of breaking pitches (including a spitball moistened with tobacco juice) which he struggled to control during his 10-year major league career. Recalling Groom, umpire Billy Evans noted, "He was plenty fast and inclined to be wild." During his career the right-hander ranked among the American League leaders in walks five times and led the league in losses three times. Nonetheless, Groom was a consistent workhorse, throwing more than 200 innings in nine consecutive seasons and striking out enough batters to consistently post excellent strikeout-to-walk ratios. Caught in the large shadow of Washington's top starter, according to Evans Groom never received full credit for his ability. "He happened to be on the same team as Walter Johnson, who overshadowed the whole staff," said Evans. "If he had been with some other club, I dare say Groom would have been regarded as a speed marvel."

Robert Groom was born on September 12, 1884, in Belleville, Illinois, the oldest of four children of John and Mary Katherine Dickinson Groom. His father and grandfather were successful coal mine owner–operators in southern Illinois. As a teenage semipro pitcher in the St. Louis area, Bob caught the attention of Jake Bene, a noted St. Louis baseball man. In early 1904 Bene bought the Fort Scott (Kansas) Giants of the Missouri Valley League and added the 18-year-old Groom to his roster. The Giants struggled to a terrible 35–89 record, and Groom finished the season with an 8–26 mark, although he did provide the highlight of the season in July when he started and won both ends of a doubleheader.

Following the 1904 campaign Groom joined the Springfield (Illinois) Hustlers of the Western Association, signing for $150 per month. Although Springfield finished the 1905 season with just a 54–80 record, Groom posted a solid 21–21 ledger to lead the staff. The following year Springfield posted a winning record, as Bob won 20 games against 18 losses and earned a promotion to Portland of the Pacific Coast League.

The 1907 Portland Beavers were not a good team, particularly early in the season. Groom pitched well but his fielding support often betrayed him. As the Beavers fell into last place, one writer characterized their lousy playing as "cheap horsehide vaudeville." In summing up the Beavers' 1907 pitching, Bob was described by a West Coast writer as having "the curves, speed and other attributes to win fame" but was "too erratic and wild." Groom finished with a 20–26 record, leading the league with 158 walks, 28 hit batsmen, and 22 wild pitches.

The 1908 Beavers were a much better team, finishing in second place with a 95–90 mark. Groom was their best pitcher, recording a league-leading 29 wins against 15 losses. He was sold to Washington after the season for $1,750. In his five years in the minor leagues, Groom had won 98 games and lost 106.

Groom began his major league career with the woeful 1909 Washington Senators, who despite the presence of Walter Johnson, lost a staggering 110 games. Groom absorbed a league-leading 26 of those defeats, while Johnson lost 25. Groom had a 2.87 ERA and also led the league with 105 walks. In his first start for the Senators, Groom was a disaster, walking or hitting the first three batters before surrendering a two-run double that drove him from the game. After the game, one local sportswriter joked that Groom "could not locate the plate with a search warrant." Groom's season was also marred by a 15-game losing streak—although even during this abysmal stretch the young pitcher showed flashes of brilliance, including a relief appearance in which he pitched 9 innings of shutout ball against the Detroit Tigers.

Washington continued to flounder through the 1910 and 1911 seasons, and the team finished in seventh place both years. Groom struggled along with them, posting a combined record of 25–34 with ERAs of 2.76 in 1910 and 3.82 in 1911. Nonetheless, he continued to show signs of promise, cutting his walk rate by nearly 30 percent from his 1909 total and notching the sixth best strikeout-to-walk ratio in the league in 1911.

Both Groom and the Senators enjoyed breakout seasons in 1912, as Washington recorded its best record in franchise history (91–61) with a second-place finish, and Groom ranked in the top five in the league in wins (24), strikeouts (179), and innings pitched (316). The major highlight of the season was the Senators' 17-game winning streak from May 30 to June 18, during which Groom started and won four games. The most impressive of these victories was the last. Prior to a game against the Philadelphia Athletics, doctors discovered a painful abscess in Groom's back, between his shoulders. The team physician advised Groom to undergo a debilitating operation but Bob refused and instead had the doctor insert a drainage tube in his back. With the tube in his back, Groom pitched the Senators to a complete-game victory over Philadelphia.

In 1913 Washington won 90 or more games for the second consecutive season, but Groom struggled to a 16–16 record with a subpar 3.23 ERA. Prior to the 1914 campaign Bob jumped to the St. Louis Terriers of the newly formed Federal League. He pitched 280⅔ innings in 42 games, going 13–20 and tying a teammate for the most losses in the league. The Terriers finished last (62–89), scoring the fewest runs per game in the league. The next year, bolstered by some new players, the Terriers made a run for the pennant and finished second (87–67), just .001 behind the league leaders. Bob pitched 209 innings in 37 games for an 11–11 record.

Following the collapse of the Federal League after the 1915 season, Groom and several of his Terrier teammates were transferred to the St. Louis Browns. He started and won the 1916 opener with a complete game victory. After a shaky beginning, he finished strong, winning 10 of his last 11 decisions for a 13–9 record and 2.57 ERA, the last time in his career he would post an ERA lower than the league average.

In 1917 Groom led the league in losses (again tied with a teammate) for the third

time in his career, dropping 19 games against just eight victories. In a sign of his declining skills, for the second consecutive season Groom walked more batters than he struck out. However, Groom also contributed to the season's highlights by tossing a 1–0, 11-inning no-hitter against the Chicago White Sox in the second game of a May 6 doubleheader. The previous day, Browns left-hander Ernie Koob had also no-hit Chicago, who would go on to win the World Series that fall. Groom received a $100 bonus for his no-hitter. The following February, he was selected off waivers by the Cleveland Indians, where he finished his professional career in 1918, going 2–2 in 43 atrocious innings of work, posting a 7.06 ERA.

In retirement, Groom lived in Belleville, where he ran the family coal business and lived with his wife, Katherine, and their son Robert. He also sat on the board of a Belleville bank and for many years coached Belleville's Junior American Legion baseball team. He was a doting grandfather, sending his granddaughters to the local store to buy some candy and a bag of Mail Pouch or Horseshoe Plug so he could have a chew and reflect on his pitching career.

Groom died in Belleville at age 63 on February 19, 1948, of pneumonia. He is buried in Walnut Hill Cemetery in Belleville.

JOHN STAHL

WASHINGTON

ARNOLD "CHICK" GANDIL
FIRST BASEMAN, 1912–1915

Prior to his involvement in the 1919 Black Sox scandal, Chick Gandil was one of the most highly regarded first basemen in the American League, both for his play on the field and his solid work ethic. In 1916 a Cleveland newspaper described Gandil as "a most likeable player, and one of excellent habits." From 1912 to 1915 the right-handed Gandil starred for the Washington Senators, leading the club in RBI three times and batting .293. On the field Gandil paced American League first sackers in fielding percentage four times and assists three times. He continued his strong work with the Chicago White Sox from 1917 to 1919, helping the club to two American League pennants before forever tarnishing his legacy by helping to fix the 1919 World Series. Gandil himself may have been the only banished player who gained more than he lost from the fix, as after the 1919 Series the first baseman retired from major league baseball, reportedly taking $35,000 in cash with him.

Arnold Gandil was born on January 19, 1887, in St. Paul, Minnesota, the only child of Christian and Louise Bechel Gandil. The family relocated to Berkeley, California, where Gandil grew up. As a youngster, Gandil loved baseball, splitting his time between pitcher, catcher, and the outfield. By all accounts he was a problem child, and after two years at Oakland High School Gandil left home to make it on his own.

After playing some semipro ball in Los Angeles and Amarillo, Texas, Gandil migrated in 1907 to Humboldt, Arizona, becoming the catcher for a semipro team sponsored by the local copper smelter. The club experienced financial problems, however, and Gandil moved on to a team in Cananea, Mexico, 40 miles from the U.S. border in Sonora. It was with Cananea that Gandil became a first baseman. In addition to his work as a baseball player, Gandil worked as a boilermaker in the rugged copper mines. He also did a bit of professional boxing, reportedly receiving $150 per bout.

Gandil made his debut in Organized Baseball in 1908, the same year he married Laura Kelly. He spent the season with Shreveport (Louisiana) in the Texas League, batting a solid .269. After the season he was drafted by the St. Louis Browns, but failed to make the club for that following year. The Browns ordered him back to Shreveport, but Gandil refused to report, instead joining the Fresno team in the outlaw California State League. Faced with being blacklisted by Organized Baseball, Gandil joined Sacramento of the Pacific Coast League for the 1909 season. He was soon arrested for absconding with $225 from the Fresno team coffers, but had good success in Sacramento, batting .282. Late in the season he was sold to the Chicago White Sox, but was not required to report until the following season.

Gandil's rookie season was by far the worst of his career. A part-time performer, he appeared in 77 games, hitting an anemic .193. Reportedly, he had trouble hitting major league curveballs. In 1911 Gandil was sold to Montreal in the Eastern League, and he responded with a solid season, batting .304. Following the season several major league clubs wanted to draft him, but the rules at the time stated that only one player could be drafted from each team, so Gandil returned to Montreal to begin the 1912 season.

Gandil got off to a solid start with Montreal in 1912, batting .309 in the season's first 29 games, after which he was sold to the Washington Senators. This time the big first sacker was ready for the major leagues, and in 117 games with Washington he hit .305 and led American League first basemen in fielding percentage.

Gandil was highly regarded by Washington. In 1914 Senators manager Clark Griffith wrote, "He proved to be 'The Missing Link' needed to round out my infield.

We won seventeen straight games after he joined the club, which shows that we must have been strengthened a good bit somewhere. I class Gandil ahead of McInnes [sic] as he has a greater range in scooping up throws to the bag and is just as good a batsman."

Gandil continued to perform well with Washington both at bat and in the field. In 1913 he hit for a career-high average of .318. He was also tough and durable, averaging 143 games during his three full seasons with Washington, despite knee problems which haunted him throughout his career. When asked by a reporter after the 1912 season what was his greatest asset, he replied, "plenty of grit." He reportedly used the heaviest lumber in the American League, as his bats weighed between 53 and 56 ounces.

Gandil was sold to Cleveland before the 1916 season for a reported price of $5,000. One of the main reasons for the sale was supposedly the fact that Gandil was a chain smoker, occasionally lighting up between innings, which annoyed Griffith. In any event, the Indians also picked up Tris Speaker for that season, and things were looking bright in Cleveland. Although the Indians climbed only from seventh place to sixth, the team won 20 more games than the previous season, reaching the .500 mark. Gandil was unspectacular, batting only .259.

In March 1917 Gandil was sold to his original major league team, the Chicago White Sox. A headline in the *Chicago Tribune* prophetically announced GET YOUR SEAT FOR '17 SERIES! WHITE SOX PURCHASE GANDIL. Manager Pants Rowland pushed Comiskey to make the deal, and *Tribune* writer John Alcock described Gandil as "the ideal type of athlete—a fighter on the field, a player who never quits under the most discouraging circumstances, and so game that he is one of the most dangerous batters in the league when a hit means a ball game."

Gandil appeared in 149 games for the 1917 World Champion White Sox, batting .273 with little power. He then hit .261 in the Series win over New York, leading the team with five RBI. Exempt from the draft because he had a wife and daughter, Gandil had a similar year in the war-shortened 1918 season, when the White Sox fell to sixth place.

In 1919 the owners, fearing a continued slump in attendance, cut back on costs wherever possible, especially salaries. Given that Comiskey was miserly with his players under the best of circumstances, and that the Chicago team was rife with internal dissension, the atmosphere in the clubhouse was far from happy. Meanwhile, attendance was booming (contrary to preseason fears), and the players asked manager Kid Gleason to demand

WAS.

raises from Comiskey. The tight-fisted owner refused to even discuss the subject, and the players grew more discontented.

No one knows the full story of the Black Sox scandal—few of the participants were willing to talk, and the whole plot was confused and poorly managed. By all accounts Gandil, furious with Comiskey's miserly ways, was one of the ringleaders. Most accounts agree that it was Gandil who approached gambler Sport Sullivan with the idea of fixing the Series, and that he also served as the players' liaison with a second gambling syndicate that included Bill Burns (a former teammate of Gandil's) and Abe Attell. Chick was also the go-between for all payments—and reportedly kept the lion's share of the money. Although none of the other fixers took home more than $15,000 from the gamblers, Gandil reportedly pocketed $35,000 in payoffs.

Interestingly, Gandil had a reasonably good Series. Although he hit only .233, that was the fourth best average among Sox regulars. He was second on the team with five RBI, and he had a game-winning hit. However, he made several suspicious plays in the field, and all but one of his seven hits came in games the Sox were trying to win, or in which they were already losing comfortably. Rumors of a Series fix began to circulate, with Gandil's name prominently mentioned.

The next spring Gandil demanded a raise to $10,000 per year. When Comiskey balked, Gandil and his wife decided to remain in California. Flush with his financial windfall from the Series, Gandil announced his retirement from the majors, instead spending the season with outlaw teams in St. Anthony, Idaho, and Bakersfield, California. Thus, Gandil was far away from the scene as investigations into the 1919 World Series began during the fall of 1920.

Following the players' acquittal on conspiracy charges in August 1921, Gandil said, "I guess that'll learn Ban Johnson he can't frame an honest bunch of ball players." The players' joy was short-lived, however, as almost immediately Commissioner Kenesaw Mountain Landis announced that the eight Black Sox were permanently expelled from baseball.

Gandil, who had retired from the major leagues anyway, continued to play baseball after his expulsion. A month after the trial he was in contact with Joe Gedeon, Swede Risberg, Joe Jackson, and Fred McMullin, attempting to put together a team in Southern California. In 1925 Gandil played with Hal Chase and other banished players in the Frontier League in Douglas, Arizona. In 1926 and '27 he ended his playing career with semipro clubs in the copper mining towns of Bayard and Hurley, New Mexico.

In 1952 Gandil and his wife moved to Calistoga, California, in the Napa Valley, where he worked as a plumber. He had carbuncles, and the town's mud baths and mineral springs aided his health. To the end of his life, Gandil denied any role in fixing the 1919 World Series. In a 1956 *Sports Illustrated* article he told writer Mel Durslag that the players had planned to fix the Series, but abandoned the scheme when rumors began to circulate. In an interview with Dwight Chapin published in the *Los Angeles Times* on August 14, 1969, Gandil again denied that he threw the Series, stating, "I'm going to my grave with a clear conscience."

Chick Gandil died at age 83 in Calistoga on December 13, 1970, and was buried in St. Helena Cemetery in the nearby town of the same name. The cause of death was listed as cardiac failure. People in town had no idea of his fame, and his death reached the sports wires only due to the efforts of Tom Hufford, SABR cofounder.

DAN GINSBURG

WASHINGTON

CLARK CALVIN GRIFFITH
MANAGER, 1912–1920; OWNER, 1920–1955

Few individuals in baseball's long history can boast of a career to rival Clark Griffith's. As a player, manager, and executive, it was one of the longest ever, spanning nearly 70 years, and he is the only man in major league history to serve at least 20 years in each capacity. From his earliest days as a pitcher for money in Hoopeston, Illinois, to his last breath, the Old Fox, as he became fondly known, dedicated his life to baseball. A fiery competitor, he was outspoken, innovative, crafty, and resourceful. He played with and against some of the pioneers of the game, was a star during its rowdiest era, managed for two decades, and was the face of baseball in the nation's capital for over 40 years. Along the way he won 237 games as a major league pitcher, helped to establish the American League, brought Washington its only World Series title, and could name eight U.S. presidents among his many friends.

Clark Calvin Griffith was born on November 20, 1869, in Clear Creek, Missouri, to Isaiah and Sarah Anne (née Wright) Griffith. The family, including Clark's four older siblings, moved from Illinois before he was born. Intent upon farming in Oklahoma, they ended up settling in Missouri, staking out 40 acres near a settlement called Nevada, close to the Kansas border. Isaiah Griffith planned to farm, but soil in the Clear Creek watershed was not conducive to productive farming and he was forced to rely upon hunting to provide for his family.

In February 1872, when Clark was just two, his father was killed in a hunting accident, mistakenly shot by a neighbor. His mother, at the time of the accident expecting once more, struggled to raise six children in the rugged frontier. For several years she persevered, farming the land, while her eldest son Earl hunted for game to feed the family. Adding to their hardship, as he grew older, Clark became afflicted with a persistent

ailment, eventually diagnosed, informally, as malarial fever. He was forced to bed for long periods, unable to assist with chores. Ultimately, the hard life, coupled with Clark's health problems, prompted the Griffiths to move back to Illinois in 1882, where they found a home in the town of Normal, near Bloomington. Clark was about 13 at the time.

During his early years in Missouri he was introduced to baseball, made popular there by soldiers returning from the Civil War. Too small and sickly to play for the local teams, Clark nonetheless developed a love for the game and acted as mascot and water boy for his hometown club. Upon moving to Illinois he found a more sophisticated version of baseball played there and, though still considered too small to play for his high school club in Normal, he played wherever possible in pick-up games, earning a reputation first as a catcher and then as a pitcher.

At 17, he was offered $10 to pitch for the Hoopeston, Illinois, club against hated rival Danville. Clark took the money and won the game, and by the end of 1887 he had entered organized ball, pitching for the Bloomington Reds. He became that club's star pitcher in 1888 when it joined the Central Inter-State League. At this time, he was also enrolled at Illinois Wesleyan University, but never completed his studies there. In July, Bloomington played an exhibition game against Milwaukee, a Western Association team, and Clark so impressed Milwaukee manager James Hart (later owner of the Chicago Cubs) that he was offered a contract for $225 a month.

Griffith starred for Milwaukee during the next three seasons, until he caught the eye of St. Louis Browns manager Charlie Comiskey. Comiskey convinced him to jump to the American Association in 1891, where he pitched well, going 11–8 for the Browns, but was released in mid-July when he developed a sore arm.

He caught on with the Boston club near season's end, but when the Association disbanded, Clark was again looking for work.

He toiled successfully the next two years in places like Tacoma (Washington), Missoula (Montana), and Oakland (California), but the leagues, like many in that era, were unstable, and the paychecks uncertain. With Oakland in 1893 Clark led the California League with 30 wins, but when owners were tardy with payroll in August, he led the players in a strike which resulted in the league disbanding. Temporarily out of a job, he won 30 games while also performing in Wild West skits on stage in San Francisco's Barbary Coast neighborhood after the league disbanded in August. By early September, however, he was signed by Cap Anson's Chicago National League club. There he found lasting fame as a pitcher, made numerous friends, and learned about both showmanship and gamesmanship from the legendary Anson. Over the next eight seasons, Griffith won 152 games, six consecutive times winning over 20, and became a star.

Never a power pitcher, Clark relied on his wiles and control, using a variety of breaking balls, trick pitches, and deceptive deliveries to befuddle his opponents. He was a master of the quick pitch and claimed to have invented the screwball while pitching on the West Coast in the early 1890s. Often experimenting with the effects of friction on a pitches, one of his favorite tricks was to openly deface a new ball by gouging it on his spikes. Although the umpires often did nothing to discourage this, the Detroit club, after one particularly destructive game, presented Griff with a bill for 11 new baseballs.

After his playing days were over, he claimed to have never thrown a spitball during his career, but it is difficult to believe he would have ignored any opportunity to gain advantage over a batter. "He was the first real master of slow ball pitching, of control reduced to a science, of using his head to outwit batters," said long-time New York sportswriter William B. Hanna. Chicago teammate Jimmy Callahan opined, "I will hand it unreservedly to [Christy] Mathewson as one of the greatest pitchers who ever lived. But I think that old Clark Griffith, in his prime, was cagier, a more crafty, if not a more brainy, proposition."

A popular myth about Griffith was that he was superstitious about throwing shutouts, often allowing a late run to avoid bad luck. Clark himself said, however, the story was bunk, started by longtime Chicago teammate Bill Lange after a Lange error broke up a shutout. According to Griffith, Lange said he muffed the play to accommodate his pitcher. Griffith snorted, "That's all pipe about my being afraid to shut out a club. Why, I'll fan 'em all out, any time, if they'll let me!"

Besides becoming a star pitcher, Clark also learned about the business and politics of baseball and developed into a leader. He was a catalyst in the April 1900 formation of the Ball Players Protective Association, an organization that did not accomplish much in the area of players' rights but did play an important part in the successful launching of the American League. Near the end of the 1900 season, in which he won only 14 games, Clark met with Ban Johnson and his old friend Comiskey to discuss the possibility of Johnson's American League challenging the National League as a new major league. Comiskey and Johnson were clearly supportive of the notion, but feared it would fail for lack of players. Griff assured them he could get the players and advised them to wait until the owners meeting in December to do anything.

When the National League turned down an Association petition for better pay, he had the ammunition he needed to recruit players for the new league. Immediately going to work, he single-handedly convinced many National League stars to sign American League contracts. Of 40 players targeted by the American League to form the foundation of its rosters, Clark claimed to have signed all but one: Honus Wagner. Comiskey, in turn, signed Clark to manage his Chicago White Sox.

As White Sox manager, and the franchise's star pitcher, he won 24 games and led the club to its first major league pennant in 1901. The following year he won only 15 games, as the team slipped to fourth place, but the new league was a success. Following the 1902 season Johnson moved the Baltimore franchise to New York and named the Old Fox as manager of the newly rechristened Highlanders.

Hope was fervent that Griff could bring a pennant to Gotham, but the Highlanders finished a disappointing fourth in their inaugural season. Clark won 14 games in what would be his last season of full-time pitching and, although he would log about 100 innings pitched in each of the next two seasons, his appearances increasingly were in relief.

In 1904, mainly through the machinations of Ban Johnson, New York was fortified by the additions of Jack Powell and John Anderson, and the pick-up of Smiling Al Orth in July helped to solidify the team in its run for the pennant. On the season's final day, however, a wild pitch by Jack Chesbro denied the Highlanders a championship. It was the closest Griff would come to a flag in New York.

The club was up and down in the standings over the next several seasons, sagging to sixth place in 1905, finishing second in 1906, and falling back again to fifth in 1907. In June 1908, as the team was beset with injuries and spiraling downward, losing 12 of 13 games, Clark announced his resignation. He blamed the bad luck that followed the club, intimating that perhaps it was he, himself, who was the hoodoo. A disheartened Griffith stated, "It [is] simply useless for me to continue....I have tried everything, but it [is] fighting against fate."

Over the next few months Griff was deluged by offers to manage other clubs. He made no secret of his desire to assume an ownership role, even in the minor leagues, and for several months he carefully considered all of his options. Finally, in December, in something of a surprise move, he signed a contract to manage the Cincinnati Reds and was back in the National League.

Under Griffith Cincinnati finished fourth in 1909, just nosing into the first division, distantly behind perennial leaders Pittsburgh, Chicago, and New York. After three straight losing seasons, the campaign was considered a success. It would mark the high point of Clark's brief stay in the Queen City, however, as the Reds dropped a notch in the standings each of the next two years. Although managerial success eluded him, Clark received credit during this time for managing the NL's first Cuban ballplayers, Armando Marsáns and Rafael Almeida. He still longed to be an owner, however, and when the opportunity arose in 1911, he was ready to do whatever was necessary to avail himself of it.

In September 1911 Washington manager Jimmy McAleer became president of the Boston Red Sox, leaving a vacancy in the capital. Griffith's interest in the Senators job was enormous, for several reasons: he wanted to be an owner, he enjoyed managing, and he wanted to return to the American League. It was a natural fit, even if it meant going to a franchise that had never finished higher than sixth place. All he had to do was come up with the money. Turned down for loans by Ban Johnson and Charlie Comiskey, Clark risked everything by mortgaging the Montana ranch he owned with his brother to raise the necessary funds. He purchased a one-tenth interest in the Washington club, becoming its largest stockholder, and signed a contract in October 1911 to manage the Senators in 1912.

The other Washington owners wanted a manager to develop new talent, thereby ensuring future success, instead of trying to make a winner out of the current roster of veterans. Clark was equal to the task, immediately releasing or trading several older players, and heading into spring training with few certainties. The Senators were unanimous second-division picks by preseason prognosticators and did nothing in the early going to dispel those predictions. In early June, howev-

er, after the pickup of first baseman Chick Gandil from Montreal, the club caught fire and reeled off 17 straight wins, all but one on the road. Walter Johnson began a personal string of 16 consecutive victories on his way to a new career high of 33, and the Nats vaulted into the first division. They remained there, never seriously challenging for the flag, but arousing Washington fandom nonetheless. Their second-place finish was by far the best performance to date in franchise history.

Hopes were high for 1913, but despite a Herculean effort (36–7) from Johnson, the club spent much of the first half in a double-digit deficit behind Connie Mack's Athletics. A good second half salvaged another second-place finish, with 90 wins, but that was as high as a Griffith-led team would finish during the remainder of his managerial career. The Senators slipped to third in 1914 and would finish no higher than that for the next nine years.

With the U.S. entry into the war against Germany in April 1917, Griffith launched an imaginative plan to involve the nation in supporting troops overseas by raising money to purchase enough athletic equipment, mainly baseball gear, to outfit every U.S. military training camp. By limiting donations to twenty-five cents, everyone could contribute, and the campaign was an enormous success. Ballparks around the country, major and minor league alike, held Griffith Days and collected money for the effort. President Wilson contributed his two bits, and donations poured in from every state. By July over $7,500 had been raised and the first shipment of equipment sailed for France. On July 11, however, the steamship *Kansan*, carrying outfits for 150 teams in General John J. Pershing's army, was torpedoed by a German U-boat and sunk in the Atlantic. Everything was lost. Undeterred, the Old Fox mounted another campaign almost immediately. In addition to equipment, Griff also bought mass quantities of *The Sporting News* and sent them to France to keep the troops updated on the pennant races.

Ironically enough for a former ball-scuffing pitcher, one of Clark's other contributions to the game during this period was leading the charge to abolish "freak" pitches, including the spitball and the shine ball, which helped eventually to bring an end to the Deadball Era. Although he penned essays against the spitter, the shine ball in particular prompted a personal crusade by Griff, who claimed as early as 1917 that it was unfair and should be outlawed.

Griffith managed the Senators through 1920. In December 1919 he partnered with a Philadelphia grain broker, William M. Richardson, to purchase 80 percent of the team's stock, again mortgaging the family ranch to borrow his half of the required $400,000. With this move he became free to make whatever changes he felt necessary to strengthen the club. There was talk for a while of running the club for a few more years from the bench, as well as from the front office, but he lasted only one season in the dual capacities before ending his managing career.

During his 20 years as a manager, Clark was credited with inventing the squeeze play and with leading the revolution toward more frequent use of relief pitchers. A vocal leader, it was estimated he was thrown out of more games than anyone in the era outside of John McGraw.

Within four years, despite hiring four different managers, Griffith molded a club which brought the first and only World Series title to the nation's capital in 1924. Proving that it was no fluke, the Senators won the American League crown again in 1925. Washington would win only one other pennant, in 1933, over the next 30 years.

During his years as owner of the Senators, and as he grew older, Clark was perceived by turns as a shrewd judge of talent, a frugal and resourceful owner, a sentimentalist, a curmudgeon, a horse trader, a silent and generous benefactor, and a stubborn, outspoken voice against change—unless it was on his own terms. He is often remembered for trading his niece's (and adopted daughter's) husband, Joe Cronin, to the Red Sox in 1934 for Lyn Lary plus a record price, and for selling his nephew and adopted son, Sherry, to the A's for $10,000 in 1952. Both deals, however, had underlying reasons other than the bottom line and were made, ultimately, because Clark knew they would benefit the players involved. Griffith also a became a pioneer in signing Cuban players, whom he valued both for their skills and the fact that they could be acquired cheaply by his confidante in Havana, scout Joe Cambria. In Griffith's 44 years at Washington's helm, 63 Cubans reached the major leagues—35 of them with the Senators.

Active well into his eighties, Clark was married to the former Anne Robertson for nearly 55 years. Although they had no children together, when Anne's brother Jimmy died in 1922, the Griffiths adopted his two eldest children, Mildred and Calvin. By 1925, Clark had a full house as the family unofficially adopted the other five Robertson children. Over the years all of them were employed in some capacity by the Washington ball club, most notably Calvin, who eventually took over the club's day-to-day operations in the early 1950s and became team president upon Clark's death.

On October 19, 1955, Clark was admitted to Georgetown Hospital in Washington, DC, for treatment of neuritis. He died of lung congestion on October 27, less than a month before his 86th birthday. President Dwight Eisenhower, speaking for his family and the nation, said, "Clark was a good friend of ours and we shall personally miss him greatly." Griffith was buried at Fort Lincoln Cemetery in Brentwood, Maryland, just outside of Washington.

MIKE GRAHEK

ST. LOUIS

The first two decades of the twentieth century were rough times to be a baseball fan in St. Louis. The National League Cardinals finished above fourth place only twice, ending up last six times. The AL's Mound City representatives were even worse.

The 1901 Milwaukee entry in the AL finished last, then moved to St. Louis, retaining just one starter (first baseman John Anderson). To replenish the roster, the AL upstarts "stole" seven Cardinals players: infielders Dick Padden and Bobby Wallace, outfielders Jesse Burkett and Emmet Heidrick, and hurlers Jack Harper, Willie Sudhoff, and Jack Powell. With his team stocked with familiar locals, owner Robert Hedges then adopted the name of the great Browns American Association clubs of the 1880s.

Not that it helped much; the Browns finished a relatively close second in 1902, then fell to sixth in 1903 and finished above .500 only three more times (and never higher than fourth place) for the remainder of the Deadball Era.

While shortstop Wallace carved out a Hall of Fame career, and others, including George Stone, Barney Pelty, Del Pratt, Burt Shotton, and even an aging Rube Waddell, enjoyed fine seasons in Brownie garb, managers Jimmy McAleer (on the job until 1909) and his successors lacked front-line talent. Even Albert Schweitzer couldn't help—not the scientist and humanist, but rather an unremarkable St. Louis outfielder who played from 1908 to 1911.

The Browns played their games at Sportsman's Park, and—influenced by new parks going up in Philadephia

WINNING PERCENTAGE 1901–1919

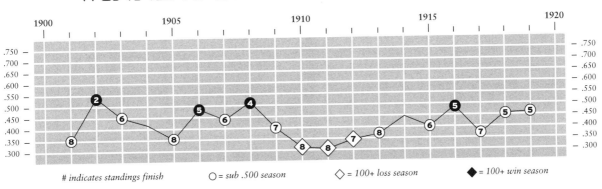

# indicates standings finish   ◯ = sub .500 season   ◇ = 100+ loss season   ◆ = 100+ win season

and Pittsburgh—refurbished it in 1909, replacing the wood grandstand with concrete and steel and building outfield bleachers the next year. The new structure, which seated about 24,000 fans in June 1909 and was upgraded several times over the years, housed major league baseball in St. Louis until 1966.

Though St. Louis was the fourth-largest city in the major leagues when the Browns arrived in 1902, by the end of the Deadball Era St. Louis had fallen behind Cleveland and Detroit in population. Hedges sold to Phil Ball (owner of the defunct local Federal League team, the Terriers) prior to the 1916 campaign.

In 1920, the Cardinals moved into Sportsman's Park, as tenants of the Browns. Behind the strong hitting and sparkling defense of the greatest player in Browns history, George Sisler, the Browns had their greatest decade during the 1920s, but the Cards, under the control of ex-Browns player and manager Branch Rickey, would be even better, soon eclipsing the Browns on the field and at the box office.

STU SHEA

ALL-ERA TEAM

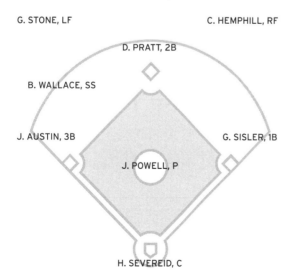

B. SHOTTON, CF

G. STONE, LF

C. HEMPHILL, RF

D. PRATT, 2B

B. WALLACE, SS

J. AUSTIN, 3B

G. SISLER, 1B

J. POWELL, P

H. SEVEREID, C

TEAM LEADERS 1901–1919

BATTING

GAMES
B. Wallace 1569
J. Austin 1182
B. Shotton 1041

RUNS
B. Wallace 609
B. Shotton 600
J. Austin 525

HITS
B. Wallace 1424
B. Shotton 1070
J. Austin 1029

RBI
B. Wallace 607
D. Pratt 455
G. Sisler 281

DOUBLES
B. Wallace 236
D. Pratt 179
J. Austin 135

TRIPLES
D. Pratt 72
G. Stone 70
B. Wallace 65

HOME RUNS
G. Stone 23
D. Pratt 21
G. Sisler 21

STOLEN BASES
B. Shotton 247
J. Austin 187
D. Pratt 174

BATTING AVERAGE
(2000+ plate appearances)
G. Sisler 331
G. Stone 301
D. Pratt 282

PITCHING

GAMES
J. Powell 294
B. Pelty 255
E. Hamilton 233

WINS
J. Powell 117
B. Pelty 91
H. Howell 78

LOSSES
J. Powell 143
B. Pelty 113
H. Howell 91

INNINGS
J. Powell 2229⅔
B. Pelty 1864⅓
H. Howell 1580⅔

STRIKEOUTS
J. Powell 884
H. Howell 712
B. Pelty 678

WALKS
B. Pelty 522
J. Powell 486
E. Hamilton 478

SHUTOUTS
J. Powell 27
B. Pelty 23
H. Howell 16

ERA
(800+ innings pitched)
H. Howell 2.06
C. Weilman 2.42
F. Glade 2.52

TYPICAL LINEUPS 1901–1919

1901 (as Milwaukee)

1. I. Waldron, RF
   G. Hogriever, LF
2. B. Gilbert, 2B
3. B. Hallman, RF-LF
4. J. Anderson, 1B
5. W. Conroy, SS
6. H. Duffy, CF
   B. Friel, 3B
7. J. Burke, 3B
8. B. Maloney, C

1902

1. J. Burkett, LF
2. C. Hemphill, RF
3. E. Heidrick, CF
4. J. Anderson, 1B
5. B. Wallace, SS
6. B. McCormick, 3B
7. D. Padden, 2B
8. J. Sugden
   M. Kahoe, C

1903

1. J. Burkett, LF
2. E. Heidrick, CF
3. C. Hemphill, RF
4. J. Anderson, 1B
5. B. Wallace, SS
6. H. Hill, 3B
7. B. Friel, 2B
8. M. Kahoe
   J. Sugden, C

1904

1. J. Burkett, LF
2. E. Heidrick, CF
3. B. Wallace, SS
   C. Hemphill, RF
4. P. Hynes, RF
5. T. Jones, 1B
6. D. Padden, 2B
7. C. Moran, 3B
8. J. Sugden
   M. Kahoe, C

1905

1. G. Stone, LF
2. I. Rockenfield, 2B
3. E. Frisk, RF
4. B. Wallace, SS
5. T. Jones, 1B
6. H. Gleason, 3B
7. B. Koehler, CF
8. J. Sugden, C

1906

1. H. Niles, RF
2. T. Jones, 1B
3. G. Stone, LF
4. C. Hemphill, CF
5. B. Wallace, SS
6. P. O'Brien, 2B
7. R. Hartzell, 3B
8. B. Rickey
   J. O'Connor
   T. Spencer, C

1907

1. H. Niles, 2B
2. C. Hemphill, CF
3. G. Stone, LF
4. O. Pickering, RF
5. B. Wallace, SS
6. J. Yeager, 3B
7. T. Spencer
   J. Stephens, C
8. T. Jones, 1B

1908

1. G. Stone, LF
2. R. Hartzell, RF
3. J. Williams, 2B
4. B. Wallace, SS
5. C. Jones, CF
   D. Hoffman, RF-CF
6. T. Jones, 1B
7. H. Ferris, 3B
8. T. Spencer, C

1909

1. R. Hartzell, RF–SS
2. G. Stone, LF
3. D. Hoffman, CF
4. A. Griggs, 1B–LF
5. B. Wallace, SS
6. J. Williams, 2B
   T. Jones, 1B
7. H. Ferris, 3B
8. L. Criger
   J. Stephens, C

1910

1. G. Stone, LF
2. R. Hartzell, 3B
3. B. Wallace, SS
4. A. Griggs, INF-RF
   P. Newnam, 1B
5. A. Schweitzer, RF
6. D. Hoffman, CF
7. F. Truesdale, 2B
8. J. Stephens, C

1911

1. B. Shotton, CF
2. J. Austin, 3B
3. A. Schweitzer, RF
4. F. LaPorte, 2B
5. W. Hogan, LF
6. N. Clarke
   J. Stephens, C
7. J. Black, 1B
8. B. Wallace, SS

1912

1. B. Shotton, CF
2. W. Hogan, LF
3. G. Stovall, 1B
4. D. Pratt, 2B
5. G. Williams, RF
6. J. Austin, 3B
7. B. Wallace, SS
8. J. Stephens, C

1913

1. B. Shotton, CF
2. J. Johnston, LF
3. D. Pratt, 2B
4. G. Williams, RF
5. G. Stovall, 1B
6. J. Austin, 3B
7. M. Balenti
   D. Lavan, SS
8. S. Agnew, C

1914

1. B. Shotton, CF
2. J. Austin, 3B
3. D. Pratt, 2B
4. T. Walker, LF
5. G. Williams, RF
6. J. Leary, 1B
7. D. Lavan
   B. Wares, SS
8. S. Agnew, C

1915

1. B. Shotton, LF
2. J. Austin, 3B
3. D. Pratt, 2B
4. T. Walker, CF
5. D. Walsh, RF-CF
   G. Williams, RF
6. J. Leary
   I. Howard, 1B
7. D. Lavan, SS
8. S. Agnew, C

1916

1. B. Shotton, LF
2. J. Austin, 3B
3. W. Miller, RF
4. G. Sisler, 1B
5. D. Pratt, 2B
6. A. Marsáns, CF
7. H. Severeid, C
8. D. Lavan, SS

1917

1. B. Shotton, LF
2. J. Austin, 3B
3. G. Sisler, 1B
4. D. Pratt, 2B
5. T. Sloan, RF
   A. Marsáns, CF
6. B. Jacobson, RF-CF
7. H. Severeid, C
8. D. Lavan, SS

1918 (first half)

1. J. Tobin, CF
2. J. Austin, 3B
3. G. Sisler, 1B
4. R. Demmitt, RF
5. E. Smith, LF
6. J. Gedeon, 2B
7. L. Nunamaker, C
8. W. Gerber, SS

1918 (second half)

1. J. Tobin, LF-CF
2. F. Maisel, 3B
3. G. Sisler, 1B
4. R. Demmitt, RF
5. T. Hendryx, CF-LF
   E. Smith, CF
6. J. Gedeon, 2B
7. J. Austin, SS
8. H. Severeid
   L. Nunamaker, C

1919

1. J. Austin, 3B
2. J. Gedeon, 2B
3. J. Tobin, LF
4. G. Sisler, 1B
5. B. Jacobson
   K. Williams, CF
6. E. Smith, RF
7. W. Gerber, SS
8. H. Severeid, C

ST. LOUIS

JESSE CAIL BURKETT
LEFT FIELDER, 1902–1904

crafty hitter and disputatious competitor, Jesse Burkett won three National League batting titles from 1895 to 1901 before finishing his 16-year-career in the American League with a lifetime .338 batting average. Twice a .400 hitter, Burkett stands larger in the record books than he did in real life. Upon his election to the Hall of Fame in 1946, one writer called the left-handed Burkett a "terrible and fearsome foe," adding, "We've often wondered what he would have done had they used in his day that rabbit ball with which Babe Ruth set his records." But the 5′8″, 155-pound Burkett bore a closer resemblance to Willie Keeler than Ruth, and his offensive accomplishments owed themselves to finesse, not brute strength. Like contemporaries John McGraw and Roy Thomas, Burkett was a master at fouling off pitches, and was thought by many observers to be the era's greatest bunter. Of his 2,850 career hits, nearly 80 percent were singles, hardly the mark of a powerful slugger.

On and off the field, "The Crab"—as his Cleveland Spiders teammates dubbed him—was cranky and unsociable, prone to challenging opponents with his fists and insulting fans and umpires with strings of expletives so creative that sportswriters of the day could only reprint his repartee by omitting all the bad language, which usually made his harangues incomprehensible. In 1906, one publication rendered a Burkett tirade this way: "Why you blank, blankety blank, do you know what I think of you? I think you are the blankest blank blank that ever came out of the blank blankest town in the blank blank land. You ought to be put in a museum." Burkett's most notorious achievement may have come in 1897, when he was ejected from both ends of a doubleheader.

Jesse Cail Burkett was born on December 4, 1868, in Wheeling, West Virginia, the oldest of two sons of Granville and Eleanor Burkett. Throughout Jesse's childhood Granville worked a variety of jobs to support his family, including stints as a day laborer, painter, and repairman on the Wheeling Suspension Bridge, which was at one time the longest suspension bridge in the world and the first to span the Ohio River. As a young boy, Jesse learned to swim in the river, and was on hand one afternoon in 1881 when a little girl fell off a skiff into the currents. Jesse quickly dove into the water and began scouring the muddy bottom in a desperate attempt to find her. "Finally one of my hands touched her," he later recalled, "and I brought her to the surface. Her heart was still beating but they couldn't bring her to." More than 70 years later, the memory of the girl's death still brought tears to the eyes of the typically brusque, unsentimental Burkett.

His first success on the diamond came on the pitcher's mound, where he won plaudits pitching for local town teams before signing a contract with Scranton of the Central League in 1888 for $85 a month. After spending one season with the Miners, the southpaw was signed by Worcester of the Atlantic Association on the recommendation of fellow Wheeling native and star major league shortstop Jack Glasscock, who was also rumored to be Burkett's distant cousin. Actually, Burkett, with his piercing blue eyes, slender frame, and light, reddish hair, closely resembled Glasscock, a fact which hecklers delighted in reminding Burkett, much to the ire of the temperamental star.

Burkett enjoyed a banner season with Worcester in 1889, leading the league with 30 wins and 240 strikeouts while batting .267. Although he only played one year in Worcester, Burkett's experience in the city proved so enjoyable that he would call it home for the rest of his life.

At season's end, Burkett's contract was acquired by the Indianapolis Hoosiers of the National League, then managed by Glasscock. But the Indianapolis franchise folded prior to the start of the 1890 season, and Burkett's contract was picked up by the New York Giants. Going into the season, the young left-hander hoped to join the Giants' stalwart pitching staff, which already included an 18-year-old Amos Rusie and 30-year-old veteran Mickey Welch. But Burkett struggled on the mound, winning just three games against ten losses while posting a miserable 5.57 ERA. Fortunately for Burkett, he hit well enough to gain a starting job in right field, and finished the season with a .309 average in 401 at-bats.

With the collapse of the Players League at the end of the 1890 season, competition for jobs in the National League became stiffer, with the result that Burkett was squeezed out of New York and picked up by the second-division Cleveland Spiders prior to the 1891 campaign. Burkett struggled initially in Cleveland, finishing the season with a .269 batting average in part-time duty. But as the decade progressed, Burkett steadily improved his production at the plate, raising his batting average every year from 1892 to 1896. Beginning in 1892, Burkett was also shifted from right to left field, where he would remain for the rest of his career. Never more than average defensively thanks to limited range and a weak arm, Burkett was at first considered incompetent in the field. One observer later declared his clumsy defensive play "was as awkward as the bovine in a china shop on any kind of ball." But, the reporter hastened to add, "constant practice and familiarity with the position eradicated the weakness and Burkett, while by no means a star, is today one of the most consistent outfielders in the major leagues." Perhaps, but Burkett never accumulated many outfield assists during his career, and three times led all outfielders in errors.

Cleveland manager Patsy Tebeau was more than willing to put up with Burkett's defensive struggles, thanks to his stellar offense. After raising his batting average from .275 in 1892 to .358 in 1894, Burkett really hit his stride in 1895, when he captured his first batting title with a .409 average. Burkett's offensive explosion came via a sudden barrage of singles. Never ranking among the top five in doubles, Burkett became the best singles hitter in the game in 1895, thanks in large part to his improved bunting technique, the result of constant practice. "Burkett seldom failed to drop a bunt just where he wanted to," one reporter later remarked. "He could lay it down either side of the plate, stop it dead if need be or drag it as the occasion required." In fact, Burkett became so good at laying one down that at least one knowledgeable observer, longtime scout Frank Shaughnessy, thought Burkett was the greatest bunter who ever lived.

In an era before fouls counted as strikes, Burkett also became a master at fouling off pitch after pitch until he found an offering to his liking, or worked a walk (he ranked among the league's top ten in free passes 12 times during his career). Indeed, as one commentator later observed, Burkett seemed to take special pleasure in fouling off tough pitches: "He would do a snappy little jig after tipping off a good pitch, or snapping one on a low line into the left field section of the grandstand or the left field bleachers, very well pleased with himself."

But the hot-tempered, sharp-tongued Burkett could also become easily unsettled by opposing players, fans, and umpires who delighted in getting his goat. New England sportswriter Dan Parker, who watched Burkett play in the New England League following the end of his major league career, remembered an incident when Burkett came into the game as a pinch-hitter and was asked by the umpire who he was batting for. Burkett responded, "None of your blankety blank business." The umpire, Red Rorty, then turned around and announced to the crowd, "Burkett batting for exercise." A red-faced Burkett proceeded to strike out, much to the delight of the crowd.

During his major league career, Burkett was once benched for throwing a baseball at a crowd of hecklers in the stands. On the field, "The Crab" was regarded by many as the meanest player on the infamously rowdy Cleveland Spiders, "and Crab Burkett's claws were in every rhubarb," one writer recalled. "Even when he was hitting .400, he played ball with a perpetual scowl." On August 4, 1897, the Spiders were forced to forfeit the opening game of a doubleheader to the Louisville Colonels after Burkett refused to leave the field following his ejection from the game. In the second game of the doubleheader, Burkett was again ejected for arguing with the umpire, who then called two policemen to have Burkett forcibly removed from the grounds.

Despite such incidents, Burkett continued to excel as one of the game's best hitters. He won a second consecutive batting title in 1896 with a .410 batting average and 240 hits, which remained the major league record until Ty Cobb collected 248 safeties in 1911. In 1899, Burkett finished second in the batting race with what was believed to be another .400 season, but subsequent research downgraded his batting mark to .396. His performance that year marked his first in St. Louis, following his transfer along with most of his teammates from the doomed Cleveland franchise. In 1901, Burkett captured a third batting title with a .376 mark for the Cardinals, and also led the league with 142 runs scored and a .440 on-base percentage. His ten home runs, a career high, ranked third in the league.

Nearing the age of 33, Burkett decided in October 1901 to jump to the newly-arrived St. Louis Browns of the rival American League in 1902. While the change netted Burkett a heftier salary, it also hurt his batting, as his average slumped to .306, the last time he would bat better than .300 in the major leagues. Despite his lowered average, Burkett remained an effective hitter. In 1903, he batted .293 and ranked fourth in the league with 52 walks. When his average dipped further in 1904, the resourceful Burkett responded by placing second in the league with 78 free passes, and his .363 on-base percentage was fifth-best in the circuit. Along with his reputation as a great hitter, it was a performance good enough to allow the Browns to trade Burkett to the Boston Americans at the end of the season for George Stone, who would briefly emerge in 1906 as one of the game's best hitters. Burkett, on the other hand, was nearly finished. Playing in 148 games for Boston in 1905, Jesse batted just .257. Combined with his ability to get on base, it was still an above-average offensive performance, but for Burkett it marked the end of his major league career.

The move to Boston had brought Burkett closer to his home in Worcester, where he lived with his wife, the former Ellen McGrath, and their three children. Despite his cantankerous personality, Burkett had always been sober in his habits and careful with his money. In 1906, he purchased a franchise in the New England League and moved it to Worcester, where he became the new team's manager and best player. In his first year, he won the NEL batting crown with a .344 average and guided Worcester to the first of four consecutive pennants.

After selling his ownership in the franchise, Burkett became the head coach at Holy Cross in 1917, remaining in that position through the 1920 season, when he accepted a coaching job with John McGraw's New York Giants. Burkett, as caustic as ever, proved unpopular with the Giants players, who voted not to give Jesse a share of their winnings when they won the Fall Classic in 1921 and 1922. Burkett's most notable assignment during his tenure with the Giants was to chaperone the club's alcoholic pitcher, Phil Douglas, to ensure that he did not get into any trouble. Burkett completely failed at this task, as Douglas succeeded in escaping from Burkett in 1922 and embarking on a drinking binge that landed him in a sanitarium.

Following his stint with the Giants, Burkett returned to the minor leagues, where he managed the Worcester entry in the Eastern League in 1923 and 1924 and Lewiston of the New England League from 1928 to 1929. During the Great Depression he worked occasionally as a scout and spring training instructor, while also holding down a job with the Massachusetts State Highway Department. He was hospitalized in 1935 after being struck by a car while directing traffic in Southbridge, Massachusetts, though he eventually recovered.

Ever with a chip on his shoulder, Burkett felt he had been forgotten by the game he loved. After his election to the Hall of Fame in 1946, Burkett told a reporter, "It took them a long time and I thought they weren't going to because everybody had forgotten me." Still unsparing in his judgments, even when it came to members of his own family, Burkett also told reporters that his greatest disappointment was that his son, Howard, who spent several years playing in the minor leagues, never reached the majors. "Curveball pitching is what beat him," Burkett told the *New York Herald Tribune* in 1947. "They never could get curves past me, but I guess the boy just didn't have the knack."

Jesse Burkett died of heart disease on May 27, 1953, at the age of 84. He was buried in St. John's Cemetery, in Worcester.

DAVID JONES

ST. LOUIS

Robert Lee Hedges
Owner, 1902–1915

The first owner of the St. Louis Browns, Robert Hedges was a visionary leader and a shrewd businessman who maximized the value of his baseball franchise. He saw his club through two great baseball wars and played a critical role in settling those conflicts. While his team struggled to remain competitive on the field, "Tail-end Bob" drew the envy of his fellow owners with his ability to consistently turn a profit. "He always had players who cost little, to trade for players who were worth much," the *Sporting News* observed in 1915. "In this way he saved his club hundreds of thousands of dollars." A frequent seller on the player market, Hedges expertly turned his players into cash which he deposited in the bank or used to upgrade Sportsman's Park.

Despite his business acumen and full treasury, Hedges also railed against the danger of money taking over the sport. As he remarked in 1916, "The chief menace to baseball...is the presence of so much big money behind certain clubs...Until some system of shackling the millionaires...is devised...the moneyed fighters of the game will always be able to strengthen at the expense of the weaker....Baseball is a big, big business and the open sesame is 'Lots of money.'"

Robert Lee Hedges was born in 1869 near Kansas City, Missouri. His father died when he was ten, and two of his brothers, both civil servants, were killed soon afterward when the famed Lathrop School Tornado of 1886 destroyed Kansas City's courthouse. In the early 1890s, he started a buggy manufacturing company in Hamilton, Ohio, near Cincinnati. There he met and married Pauline Davis, daughter of a local millionaire businessman. Hedges sold his carriage business in the boom times of 1900, in part because he saw the emergence of the auto industry and the threat it posed. American League president Ban Johnson, also from

Cincinnati, persuaded Hedges to buy the Milwaukee franchise of the fledgling American League after the inaugural 1901 season. Hedges paid around $35,000 for the team and moved it to St. Louis. He called the team the Browns and refurbished the nineteenth century Browns' Sportsman's Park. "I went into baseball purely as a matter of business," Hedges explained in 1912. He started out as a minority stockholder and grew his share of the club both slowly and cheaply. He acquired a team with modest talent; the Milwaukee Brewers had finished the 1901 season in last place.

In his first season as owner Hedges undertook the most spectacular raid of one team by another in baseball history. His manager, Jimmy McAleer, a former star of the Cleveland Spiders, signed virtually every star from the 1901 Cardinals (most of whom had played with McAleer in Cleveland) for the 1902 Browns. The "jumpers" included Bobby Wallace, Jesse Burkett, Jack Powell, and Jack Harper.

The Cardinals sued to stop their players from jumping, but the judge denied their injunction. The Browns contended for most of the season, only to be outlasted in September by the Philadelphia Athletics. During that giddy summer of 1902, Hedges said, "We are in a position to pay as much as anyone for those we want." That summer, Hedges demonstrated his financial independence by signing the rising star pitcher of the New York Giants, Christy Mathewson, to an "ironclad" contract, which included a cash advance.

When the assignment of disputed players became the main sticking point at the January 1903 peace conference between the two leagues, Hedges played a critical conciliatory role by agreeing to relinquish his rights to Mathewson, thereby placating New York owner John T. Brush, one of the American League's most intractable foes. As Sid Keener, sports editor for the *St. Louis Times* later observed, "Hedges was the one who held the key to the famous peace treaty of 1903."

The Browns did not come close to that first year's performance during the next five seasons. They sunk to the second division and stayed there until 1908. That year, key trades for veteran players—including famous pitchers Bill Dinneen and Rube Waddell—propelled the Browns into a spectacular pennant race. The two aging hurlers had great comeback seasons, and the Browns were in the hunt for the pennant until late September. The club drew more than 600,000 fans that year (more than the pennant-winning season of 1944 and second only to the great 1922 season), and Hedges made a spectacular profit of $165,000.

Hedges took a significant portion of that profit and plowed it back into the ballpark. He modernized and expanded Sportsman's Park, reinforcing its structure with steel and concrete in 1908 and adding an upper deck the following year. Outfield bleachers were added in 1912. The new ballpark was simply one of many innovations that Hedges introduced. During his tenure with the club he popularized Ladies' Day, and became one of the first owners to use an electric scoreboard and public address system at games. He also took steps to clean up the game's image. Hedges hired security guards to control rowdyism and prevent gambling in the stands, and banned the sale of alcohol at the park. In 1915, sportswriter John Sheridan poked some fun at Hedges' Browns, who were then managed by the straight-laced Branch Rickey: "First in morals, first in sobriety, first in bed, first in the field, first in the front bench at church, and last in the American League."

Most of Robert Hedges's seasons with the Browns were losing ones record-wise, yet most were also profitable ones. Even in 1908, when he "splurged" on veteran players, his expenditure of $25,000 netted him the profit of $165,000. His financial success with losing teams created resentment from other owners. They referred to Hedges as "Tail-end Bob" and said he was "too canny a businessman for the good of the game" since "he wouldn't gamble for profit."

After suffering through four losing seasons with four different managers from 1909 to 1912, Hedges hired Branch Rickey as his top advisor early in 1913, and by the end of the campaign made him manager of the team, replacing the fiery George Stovall. "I have had enough of the man who relies on vitriolic language to win ball games," Hedges explained. "What I want is a man of learning, a student of human nature, psychology and, incidentally, baseball."

In addition to using him as manager, Hedges also planned to have Rickey execute the owner's vision of a farm system. Hedges had grappled with the challenge of competing with wealthier teams that could outbid him for promising players for years, and his solution was to formalize an arrangement that clubs occasionally used to develop talent. Rather than simply loaning players to minor league clubs, Hedges wanted to *buy* minor league teams and develop his own stars. The concept that Rickey later executed so brilliantly with the St. Louis Cardinals began with the vision Robert Hedges shared with him in 1913.

Two developments prevented Hedges and Rickey from pursuing the farm system in 1914. First, that January major league baseball passed a law banning the ownership of minor league teams by big league clubs. Second, the upstart Federal League declared war on Organized Baseball and placed a team in St. Louis. With player salaries quickly escalating, the farm system would have to wait.

Now facing competition from two other clubs within his city, Hedges tried to strengthen his team by bringing a big star to the Browns, but his attempts to acquire Joe Jackson from Cleveland and Frank Baker from Philadelphia were unsuccessful. Hedges managed to thwart Federal League attempts to raid his roster, but the beleaguered Browns finished in the second division in both 1914 and 1915, and attendance suffered.

Weary of struggling to balance the franchise's slumping finances, Hedges sold the Browns and Sportsman's Park to Phil Ball, the owner of the doomed St. Louis Federal League franchise, following the 1915 season as part of the settlement with the Federal League. Ball paid Hedges around $525,000, an enormous return on Hedges's initial investment. At one point during the final negotiations, the deal got hung up over $40,000 of outstanding liabilities that showed up on the Browns' books. It turned out that the compassionate Hedges had been regularly making advances and loans to his players.

After selling the Browns, Hedges remained in St. Louis, where he lived with his wife, Pauline, and their son, Robert, Jr., who later married the daughter of Cardinals owner Sam Breadon. In his later years, Hedges worked as the president of a bank. He died of lung cancer on April 23, 1932, at 63 years of age.

STEVE STEINBERG

ST. LOUIS

CHARLES JUDSON HEMPHILL
OUTFIELDER, 1902–1904, 1906–1907

At his best, Charlie Hemphill was a strong-armed, fleet-footed outfielder and solid hitter who drew walks. In 1910, Alfred Spink described him as "a cracking good batsman and when right is a hard man to beat." At his worst, however, Hemphill was a poor fielder known to misjudge balls in the air and an inattentive base runner. Hemphill's career was also marred by several bouts with dissipation. After his major league career was over, Hemphill's drinking cost him his managerial post with the Atlanta Crackers and his chance for a long career in the minor leagues.

Charles Judson Hemphill was born in Greenville, Michigan, on April 20, 1876, to Frederick and Louisa, natives of Canada and probably recent immigrants. During Charlie's childhood Frederick worked as an engineer, while his wife stayed at home, raising the couple's four sons. Two of them, Charlie and Frank, would play in the major leagues.

Charlie played for Saginaw in 1895–96, missed the 1897 season with Dayton because of illness, but was reserved for 1898 and played with Grand Rapids late that year until June 1899 when he was acquired by St. Louis. Batting third and playing center field in a June 27 game against the Phillies, Hemphill fouled out, then homered off Wiley Piatt in a 6–4 win. In eight games he posted a .389 on-base percentage, but was benched due to his terrible fielding—playing three times more that season, he finished with five errors in 10 games as an outfielder for a glaring .750 fielding average. In August, Hemphill was transferred to the Cleveland Spiders, en route to the worst record (20–134) in major league history. When judged against the low standards set by his teammates, he acquitted himself well in Cleveland, batting .277 in 55 games, of which the Spiders won only four. His fielding remained problematic; for the year he posted an abysmal .837 fielding percentage.

With the contraction of the Cleveland franchise at the end of the season, Hemphill was transferred back to St. Louis for the 1900 campaign. But with the St. Louis roster overcrowded with players, Charlie sat on the bench for the first three weeks of the season before the Cardinals loaned him to the Kansas City Blues of the American League, then in its final season as a minor league. Hemphill joined the team on May 10 and soon established himself as the club's leadoff batter and center fielder. Despite his late arrival, Hemphill led the league in triples and ranked fourth in runs scored and batting average.

St. Louis reserved him for the 1901 season, but Charlie jumped his contract to sign with the Boston Americans. The *Boston Globe* introduced Hemphill as "the poorest outfielder in the league," but it was his hitting that proved to be the biggest disappointment. Dropped from second to fifth in the batting order in early June, he finished the year with a .261 batting average and .332 slugging percentage, both figures worse than all but two of the 24 AL outfielders who played more than half their team's games that season.

Despite standing 5'9" and weighing 160 pounds, no better than average size for his day, Hemphill was often described as big by contemporary sportswriters, perhaps by some illusion of build or the way he wore his uniform. A left-handed batter and thrower with good speed but no special talent for using it either on the base paths or in the field, Hemphill boasted below average power at the plate and failed to distinguish himself as a hitter, a shortcoming which, coupled with his defensive failures, made him expendable. He went unsigned after the 1901 season, became a free agent, and the following February joined the Cleveland Bronchos, a bad team rapidly on the rise. At the start of the season, Hemphill was used as a fourth outfielder. Hemp batted .266 in 25 games before drawing his release. He quickly signed on with the St. Louis Browns, where he became the club's regular right fielder and number three hitter. Hemphill enjoyed one of his best seasons with the 1902 Browns, leading the team in batting average (.317), slugging percentage (.447), triples (11), home runs (6) and steals (23).

The following spring, Hemphill reported to Sportsman's Park "a trifle fat" according to one reporter. During a four game pre-season series with the Cardinals, Charlie could be seen running around the park "five or six times as a flesh reducer." Following the series, one writer noted that "Hemphill is a hard worker who is often guilty of stupid baserunning." And weak hitting. By August, Hemphill was benched, then suspended, for "dissipation," and finished the year under a doctor's care in Youngstown, Ohio. For the season he batted .245 with only 12 extra-base hits in 383 at-bats.

Despite spending part of his off-season boiling out in Hot Springs, Arkansas, in 1904 Hemphill again reported for duty out of shape, and finished the year with a .256 batting average in 114 games. The following off-season St. Louis farmed him out to the St. Paul Apostles of the American Association, where the left-hander rediscovered his hitting stroke. At season's end, Charlie led the circuit in batting average (.364) and hits (204), a performance which earned him another chance with the Browns in 1906.

Batting in the top third of the St. Louis order, Hemphill showed significant improvement at the plate over his 1904 totals, and finished the year with a .289 batting average, 62 RBI, 33 stolen bases, and a career-best 90 runs scored. In better shape, Hemphill also spent 114 of his 154 games patrolling center field, where he used his improved foot speed to offset his other defensive shortcomings. The following year, however, Hemphill was mediocre at best, batting .259 with 38 RBI and 66 runs scored in 153 games. That November the Browns traded him, along with Fred Glade and Harry Niles, to the New York Highlanders for Jimmy Williams, Hobe Ferris and Danny Hoffman.

Joined by Jake Stahl and Willie Keeler in the outfield, Hemphill played center for the Highlanders and put in the best season of his major league career. In addition to his .297 batting average, Hemp swiped a career-high 42 bases and drew 59 walks, also a career-best, to give him a .374 on-base percentage, third-best in the American League.

Hemphill's 1909 campaign was marred by illness. Vaccinated twice that spring for smallpox after teammate Hal Chase was quarantined in Atlanta, Hemphill played the opening game of the season, then went home with a sore throat. Sidelined with an illness rumored to be, by various media accounts, smallpox, tonsillitis, tuberculosis, and diphtheria, Charlie eventually returned to the lineup but batted poorly and finished the season as the team's fifth outfielder. Despite his .243 batting average, however, Hemphill posted a solid .357 on-base percentage in 216 plate appearances.

Back in the starting lineup in 1910 following Keeler's retirement, Hemphill split his time between right and center and held the leadoff spot for three months before his poor hitting again relegated him to the bench. He finished the year with a .239 batting average, but once again posted an excellent on-base percentage (.350) thanks to 55 walks. In 1911, his last season in the major leagues, Hemphill played in only 69 games but batted .284 with a .397 on-base percentage, thanks to 37 walks in 244 plate appearances.

Hemphill started out the 1912 campaign as player-manager of the Atlanta Crackers of the Southern Association. After a fair start, the team slipped into last by July 15. Everything unraveled for Hemphill during a weekend series with New Orleans, when Charlie drank too much to play in the Saturday game. When he did not report for the Monday July 22 game in Montgomery, he was summoned home, deposed as manager, suspended as player, and peddled to clubs in the American Association. Kansas City was interested; Columbus made the purchase.

He lasted only a week with the Senators before management suspended him "for failure to get into condition." Hemphill spent the rest of the season playing for Youngstown of the Central League, though he remained Columbus property. Sold to St. Paul in the off-season, Hemphill spent the winter boiling out in Hot Springs. After a hot start, Hemphill faded during the summer and was suspended again on August 27 for "failure to keep in condition" and "failure to report at the park for that day's game."

Many old ballplayers moved up during the Federal League years but Charlie Hemphill moved briskly down. In 1914 he batted .277 for St. Paul and .225 for New Orleans. In 1915 he appeared in 15 games for the local club, batting .119. By then Hemphill was also making his offseason home in Youngstown with wife Theresa (whom he had married in 1905) and their three children.

By 1930, the family had moved to Detroit, where Charlie worked as an automobile iron master. He died there on June 22, 1953, at the age of 77.

PAUL WENDT

ST. LOUIS

JAMES ROBERT MCALEER
MANAGER, 1902–1909

Jimmy McAleer was not much of a hitter, but this brilliant defensive outfielder was a smart, clever, and ambitious man who helped create two of the original eight franchises of the American League. In 1900 he became the first manager of the Cleveland franchise now known as the Indians, and two years later league president Ban Johnson chose McAleer to assemble and manage a new team in St. Louis in direct competition with the established Cardinals of the rival National League. McAleer's new club, the Browns, nearly won the pennant in its first year of operation. Though the Browns soon fell to the second division, McAleer led the team for eight years, winning more games than any manager in team history. He then moved on to manage the Washington Senators, where he started Walter Johnson on the road to stardom, and ultimately became president and part-owner of the Boston Red Sox in 1912. His Red Sox won the World Series that year, but a series of disputes with his business partners drove him from the game and deprived the American League of one of its most talented leaders and organizers.

James Robert McAleer was born in Youngstown, Ohio, on July 10, 1864. He began his playing career with minor league teams in his hometown during the early 1880s before advancing to Charleston of the Southern League in 1886. After a season and a half with Memphis of the same circuit, he moved to Milwaukee of the Western Association in 1888. His stellar fielding drew the attention of the Cleveland Spiders of the National League, which he joined in 1889. He switched to Cleveland's Players League entry in 1890, but returned to the Spiders at season's end, remaining with the team for eight more years.

McAleer, who stood six feet tall and weighed 180 pounds, was the prototypical good-field, no-hit outfielder.

One of the weakest batters in the National League (in 1898, 84 of his 87 hits were singles), his brilliance in the field more than compensated for his shortcomings at the plate in the eyes of many of his contemporaries. He was considered the best defensive outfielder of the 1890s, and some say that McAleer was the first center fielder to take his eyes off a fly ball, run to the spot where it would fall to earth, and catch it.

Following the 1898 season, McAleer announced his retirement as a player and returned to Youngstown, where he purchased and managed the local Inter-State League team and waited for a chance to manage in the majors. The opportunity came in 1900, after the NL folded the Spiders and three other poorly performing franchises. Ban Johnson, president of the newly-renamed American League, then placed a team in Cleveland and hired Jimmy McAleer to manage it. His Cleveland ballclub finished sixth in 1900 and seventh in 1901, after the upstart circuit assumed major status and declared war against the National League.

The Cleveland manager played an important role in the battle between the leagues. He proved to be one of Ban Johnson's leading recruiters, convincing many National League stars to cast their lot with the new circuit. In late 1901, Johnson moved the struggling Milwaukee franchise to St. Louis and asked McAleer to manage the ballclub, which was named the Browns, and recruit players for it. The new leader scored a coup when he induced seven members of the St. Louis Cardinals, including future Hall of Famers Jesse Burkett and Bobby Wallace, to join his Browns. McAleer's raid devastated the Cardinals, who did not reach the first division again until 1914, and made the Browns the most popular team in St. Louis. Burkett batted .306 in 1902, while Jack Powell and Red Donahue won 22 games apiece as McAleer led the Browns to a strong second-place finish.

His playing career was virtually over by this time. McAleer played in only two games for the 1902 Browns, and (except for two pinch-running appearances in 1907) was a non-playing manager from 1903 onward. Many teams in that era employed a bench manager and appointed a player as field captain, but McAleer directed the team from the coaching lines, assuming full responsibility for the club on the field and off.

Though McAleer managed the team for eight seasons, St. Louis never surpassed its 1902 performance under his leadership. The Browns dropped to sixth place in 1903, remained there in 1904, and fell to last place in 1905, though they drew more fans than the rival Cardinals.

McAleer tried to improve the Browns through trades. In December 1904, he sent the fading Burkett to the Boston Americans for George Stone, an outfielder who had been the talk of the minors with Milwaukee in 1904. Stone blossomed in St. Louis, leading the league in hits in 1905 and winning the 1906 batting title. McAleer traded Jack Powell to the New York Highlanders for pitcher Harry Howell and cash in March 1904, then repurchased Powell the following year and restored him to the rotation. In 1908, McAleer purchased the erratic left-hander Rube Waddell, who had worn out his welcome with the Philadelphia Athletics. Though Waddell quit the team briefly that spring when McAleer refused him an advance on his salary, Rube won 19 games and teamed with Howell, Powell, and Bill Dinneen to form a formidable pitching corps. All four starters posted earned run averages of 2.11 or better for McAleer that season.

The Browns battled the Tigers, Naps, and White Sox for the 1908 pennant, leading the league in July before fading to a fourth-place finish. McAleer expected the Browns to challenge again in 1909, but injuries and the protracted illness of George Stone knocked them out of contention. The team suffered through a 2–20 skid in May and June and fell to seventh place as the St. Louis newspapers produced a steady stream of condemnation. "There are things a manager should be held accountable for, and I am willing to get my share of criticism," said a defiant McAleer, "but unforeseen accidents and a steady run of ill luck are not among the causes for criticism." Owner Robert Hedges did not agree, so McAleer resigned in September 1909, accepting an offer of $10,000 per year to manage the Washington Senators.

Washington was a last-place team, but featured the most promising young pitcher in the major leagues. Walter Johnson, a 22-year-old fastballer, had compiled a 32–48 record in his first three seasons. His previous managers had used him irregularly, alternating flurries of activity with periods of inaction. McAleer gave Johnson a more regular workload, and the pitcher responded with a 25-win season. The Senators, led by Johnson, finished seventh in 1910 but posted a 23½-game improvement over the previous year.

Washington finished in seventh place again in 1911, and McAleer was ready to move on when the owners of the Boston Red Sox put their team up for sale. McAleer's longtime friend and hunting companion, Ban Johnson, arranged a deal in which McAleer and Robert McRoy, Johnson's personal secretary, bought a half-interest in the Red Sox. The deal was consummated in September 1911, and McAleer took over as president of the club.

The 1912 season, McAleer's first as club president, was an unqualified success. The team opened its new stadium, Fenway Park, on April 20, coasted to the pennant by 14 games over the second-place Senators, and defeated the New York Giants in the World Series. Unfortunately, McAleer and manager Jake Stahl clashed often, and their differences came to a head during the Series when McAleer ordered his manager to pitch Buck O'Brien instead of Joe Wood in Game Six, which the Red Sox lost 5–2, with all five runs scoring off O'Brien in the first inning. The manager resented McAleer's interference, while the team president complained when Stahl, who batted .301 in 1912, decided to withdraw from active play and manage from the bench the following year. The Red Sox stumbled in the early part of the 1913 campaign, and on July 15, McAleer fired Stahl and appointed catcher Bill Carrigan to succeed him.

This move angered Ban Johnson and his coterie of investors, making McAleer's position as club president untenable. Johnson's refusal to support McAleer drove a wedge between the two old friends, and at the end of the 1913 season, McAleer sold his stock in the Red Sox and retired from baseball. McAleer married at least three times, the first time by 1908; 1920 census records show McAleer with a wife six years his junior, Hannah B. McAleer. He later married a widowed Youngstown grocery clerk named Anna Durbin. He pursued business interests in Youngstown until becoming ill with cancer in the early 1930s. On April 28, 1931, four months after his second wife, Anna Durbin, passed away, and two months after marrying singer Georgianna Rudge, Jimmy McAleer shot himself in the head with a handgun, and died the next day. He was 66 years old, and was buried at Oak Hill Cemetery in Youngstown.

DAVID FLEITZ

Jack Powell

ST. LOUIS

JOHN JOSEPH POWELL
RIGHT-HANDED PITCHER, 1902–1903, 1905–1912

Jack Powell, a stocky right-hander who pitched for the St. Louis Browns in ten of his 16 major league seasons, was labeled a "nothing" pitcher because neither his fastball nor his curve impressed many people. He threw the ball with an easy sidearm motion that caused many fans to say, "I could hit Jack Powell," but his delivery put little strain on his arm and helped him earn a reputation as a workhorse. Powell led the National League with 40 complete games in 1899, and pitched more than 300 innings in six of seven seasons from 1898 to 1904. He played much of his career for mediocre teams, but won nearly 250 major league games by changing speeds, hitting the corners, and trusting his defense to make plays behind him. He lost more games than he won and never played for a pennant winner, but made a valuable contribution to pitching staffs that included such Hall of Famers as Cy Young, Rube Waddell, and Jack Chesbro.

John Joseph Powell was born in Bloomington, Illinois, on July 9, 1874, the fourth of five children of Elijah and Mary Powell, English immigrants who had arrived in the United States prior to the Civil War. The Powell family was working class—Elijah worked a number of blue-collar jobs during his life, including stints as a boilermaker and coal miner, and his children left school early to help support the family. At some point during Jack's childhood, the family moved to Chicago, where young Jack starred in the semipro ranks during the mid-1890s, and often threw batting practice for Cap Anson's Chicago Colts at the West Side Grounds. Powell dreamed of pitching for the Colts, but Anson was unimpressed with Powell's fastball. The Chicago manager declared, "He hasn't anything," and declined to sign the young pitcher.

In 1896, George Tebeau, manager of the Fort Wayne Farmers of the Inter-State League, signed Jack to his first professional contract. Powell, with future major leaguer Lou Criger catching most of his games, helped the Farmers to a second-place finish. At the conclusion of that season, the National League's Cleveland Spiders, managed by George Tebeau's brother Patsy, bought Powell's contract.

Perhaps no player in history experienced a more difficult major league debut than Jack Powell. He joined the Spiders in May 1897, and saw action at first base in a game at Cleveland on Sunday, May 16. Sunday baseball was illegal in the city of Cleveland at that time, but team owner Frank Robison defied the local ordinance and scheduled the game on the Christian Sabbath. The local authorities called Robison's bluff, and after one inning was completed, police invaded the field and arrested all the players on both teams, plus umpire Tim Hurst. They were soon released on $100 bail each, but the authorities decided to prosecute one participant in the contest to test the validity of the law. Powell, an easily expendable rookie, was the only Spider charged with violating the ban on Sunday ball, and remained in Cleveland to await trial while his teammates embarked on a road trip. In June, Powell was tried and convicted of playing ball on Sunday. He was fined five dollars, with an additional $153 tacked on for court costs.

Following the trial, Tebeau put Jack into the starting rotation for the injury-riddled Cleveland ballclub. He made his pitching debut for the Spiders on June 23, 1897, and threw a three-hitter, "two of them of the scratch order," in an 18–1 romp over the Louisville Colonels. He also pitched the first two legal Sunday games ever played in Cleveland, on July 11 and July 18. Powell made 26 starts and compiled a 15–10 record in his rookie season. In 1898, a sore arm drove Nig Cuppy to the sidelines, but Powell solidified his position as Cleveland's number two starter behind Cy Young with a 23–15 mark for a fifth-place team.

Powell, who stood 5'11" and weighed about 200 pounds, bore a physical resemblance to Young, though Young was taller and threw a harder fastball. Powell was one of the few pitchers of the Deadball Era who threw without a windup, and his quick delivery caught some batters napping at the plate. Umpire Billy Evans, an admirer of Powell's, stated, "All he seems to do is make a quick hitch, and the ball is on top of the batter before he realizes it." He could warm up quickly, and his managers often called on him to finish games.

When Cleveland owner Robison bought the St. Louis ballclub (soon to be renamed the Cardinals) in early 1899, he transferred Jack Powell and all the other Cleveland stars to St. Louis. Jack threw 373 innings and won 23 games that year, second on the team behind Cy Young's 26 wins. After compiling a 17–16 record for the 1900 Cardinals, Powell became the team's leading pitcher when Young signed with the Boston club of the new American League in 1901. Powell led St. Louis in starts and innings pitched, posting a 19–19 mark.

After the 1901 season, Powell's former Cleveland teammate, Jimmy McAleer, induced Jack and six of his teammates to leave the Cardinals and join the new St. Louis Browns of the American League. Powell won 22 games in 1902 for McAleer's second-place Browns.

Jack made his home in St. Louis for the remainder of his life. In 1902 he married Nora O'Connor, the sister of former and future teammate Jack O'Connor, and the two brothers-in-law opened a saloon in St. Louis. The Powells had a son named Jim before the marriage ended in divorce in 1907. Jim Powell eventually followed his father into professional ball, playing for and managing several minor league teams, though he never advanced to the majors.

The Browns turned a profit in 1902, and Jack demanded a substantial raise for the following season. Browns owner Robert Hedges demurred, prompting Powell to hold out during the spring of 1903. He threatened to sign with an independent team in Sheboygan, Wisconsin, rather than return to St. Louis, but the threat proved hollow, and Jack rejoined the Browns shortly before the season began. The Browns fell to sixth place in 1903 as Jack posted a 15–19 mark.

Powell's holdout caused some hard feelings between the pitcher and team owner Hedges, and on March 5, 1904, the Browns traded Jack to the New York Highlanders for pitcher Harry Howell and $8,000 cash. Clark Griffith, manager of the Highlanders, put the hard-working right-hander to the test. Powell, who made a career-high 45 starts that season, and spitballer Jack Chesbro, who started a league record 51 games, nearly pitched New York to the pennant by themselves. Chesbro won 41 games, losing only 12, while Powell posted a 23–19 log as the Highlanders challenged for the flag in a wild race with the Boston Americans. The New Yorkers lost the flag to Boston on the last day of the season when Chesbro's wild pitch let in the winning run in the penultimate contest. Powell never again came close to playing for a pennant winner.

Jack Powell pitched 390⅓ innings in 1904, but the heavy workload took its toll, and he began the 1905 campaign with a sore arm (as did Chesbro, who threw 454 innings in 1904). Powell fell to an 8–13 mark for New York and was sold back to the Browns in September of that year. He never again pitched more than 256 innings in a season, and struggled to stay above the .500 mark for a weak St. Louis team. He went 16–13 in 1908 as the Browns, sparked by 19 wins from left-hander Rube Waddell, rose to fourth place, but Powell's won-lost records fell as the Browns sank to the bottom of the standings in the next few seasons. In 1910 Jack's former brother-in-law Jack O'Connor succeeded Jimmy McAleer as manager of the Browns, but the team dropped to last place as Powell struggled to a 7–11 mark. Another of Powell's old Cleveland teammates, Bobby Wallace, became manager of the Browns in 1911, but Wallace was unable to lift the Browns out of last place. Powell posted a record of 8–19 in 1911, leading the American League in losses, and closed his major league career with a 9–17 mark in 1912.

Powell's lifetime won-lost record stood at 209–191 after the 1908 season, but his total of 36 wins and 63 losses from 1909 to 1912 dropped his career mark to 245–254. No other pitcher in history has won as many games as Powell while losing more often than he won.

Powell pitched for Louisville in the American Association in 1913, winning 17 games at the age of 38, and played for Venice of the Pacific Coast League in 1914. He pitched semipro ball for several years afterward, and made an unsuccessful comeback attempt with the Browns in 1918 when major league rosters were depleted by the military draft of World War I. Jack Powell was 70 years old when he died in Chicago on October 17, 1944. He was buried at Mount Carmel Cemetery in suburban Hillside, Illinois.

DAVID FLEITZ

ST. LOUIS

Rhoderick John "Bobby" Wallace
Shortstop, 1902–1916; Manager, 1911–1912

Perhaps the greatest defensive shortstop of his generation, Bobby Wallace was a fair right-handed hitter whose spectacular glove work catapulted him to the Hall of Fame. Wallace began his major league career as a pitcher, where his dazzling fielding soon convinced management to find a position that better suited his unique combination of skills. After spending two seasons at third base, Wallace moved to shortstop in 1899, where his strong arm, spectacular range, and fluid motion revolutionized the way the position was played. His defensive play was so outstanding that in 1911, a year in which Wallace batted only .232, Pittsburgh Pirates owner Barney Dreyfuss declared, "The best player in the American League, the only man I would get if I could, plays on a tail-end team, and few people pay any attention to him. I mean Bobby Wallace of St. Louis. I wish I had him." On June 10, 1902, Wallace accepted 17 chances in a game against Boston, a mark which has stood as the American League record for more than 100 years.

Rhoderick John Wallace was born in Pittsburgh on November 4, 1873, but spent most of his youth in nearby Millvale. Rhoderick's mother, Mary, was a native-born Pennsylvanian of German extraction, and his father, John, was a Scottish immigrant who supported his family as a grocery clerk. The first serious money Bobby earned from playing baseball came in 1893, when the 19-year-old was paid the princely sum of $25 to pitch for the Clarion Eagles in an independent league in Pennsylvania. "I had to pinch myself on the train to make sure I was awake and was really going to get 25 smackers, which was big dough in those days, for doing something I'd have been willing to pay $25 for doing if, at the time, I had been loaded," recalled Bobby.

He pitched so well against a squad from Franklin, Pennsylvania, that the Franklin team hired him the following season for $45 a month. By the summer of 1894, however, the Franklin team and the independent league in which it played went under. Bobby asked Connie Mack (then manager of the Pittsburgh Pirates) for a big league tryout, but Mack told the 5'8", 170-pound right-hander that he was too little for a big league pitcher. Even after Bobby had become a big league star, he did not hold a grudge against Mack, stating that, "For years I never met Connie on or off the field without saying 'Too little?' It was a standing joke between us and later I noticed that Connie found you could get good pitching in other than the big economy size package."

Soon after he was turned away by Pittsburgh, Bobby signed a contract with the Cleveland Spiders. Cleveland's manager, Patsy Tebeau, had learned about Wallace from Bobby's old catcher with the Clarion Eagles. Bobby's pitching debut on September 15, 1894, was anything but Hall of Fame material, as he surrendered 13 hits and seven runs to Boston in a rain-shortened six-inning game. He appeared in just four games that season, but showed the Spiders enough that he was given 28 starts and two relief appearances in 1895 en route to a 12–14 record. In 1896, Bobby made 16 starts and six relief appearances while compiling a record of 10–7 with an outstanding 3.34 ERA.

As a pitcher, Bobby exhibited above-average fielding skills to the extent that, after a short-lived experiment as an outfielder in 1896, manager Tebeau switched him to third base in 1897. Bobby logged over 300 games at the hot corner until June 5, 1899, when he finally moved to the position that earned him the nickname "Mr. Shortstop." By then, thanks to syndicate ownership, Wallace and Tebeau had been transferred from the hapless Spiders to the St. Louis Perfectos, the first of three seasons Bobby would spend with the franchise. "We were in Philadelphia when Manager Pat shifted me from third to short and right off the bat I knew I had found my dish," said Wallace. "Footwork was more a part of the new position than it had been at third. I suddenly felt I had sprouted wings. A world of new possibilities opened for me."

Even in the Deadball Era, however, baseball was a business as well as a game, and the National League's salary cap of $2,400 limited what Senior Circuit teams could pay star players like Bobby. The new American League, however, had no such constraints and gave Bobby the chance to earn substantially more. He seized that opportunity by jumping to the cross-town St. Louis Browns of the junior circuit in 1902. His contract totaled $32,500 over five years, with $6,500 paid at signing, making Wallace for a time the highest-paid player in baseball. Remarkably for contracts of that era, it also contained a clause providing that Wallace could not be traded without his consent. In another unusual move, the Browns also took out a life insurance policy on Wallace in case he met an untimely death before the contract's expiration.

During his prime years with the Browns, Bobby was a fearsome hitter; though his batting average never surpassed .285 during his 15-year stay with the club, Wallace at various times ranked among AL leaders in hits, walks, total bases, doubles, triples, and slugging percentage. He was also almost annually among the RBI leaders, ranking in the top ten during eight out of 12 seasons from 1897–1908.

It was on defense, though, that Bobby really earned his salary. He led the AL in assists twice and fielding percentage three times. Wallace's defensive prowess resulted not only from his physical skills but also from his mental approach to playing shortstop. "As more speed afoot was constantly demanded for big league ball, I noticed the many infield bounders which the runner beat to first only by the thinnest fractions of a second," noted Bobby. "I also noted that the old-time three-phase movement, fielding a ball, coming erect for a toss and throwing to first wouldn't do on certain hits with fast men…it was plain that the stop and toss had to be combined into a continuous movement."

The toughest play for Wallace was the ball hit directly at him. He explained that "when you were going either way, you could gauge the length, height and speed of the hit as you moved over to get it. But you had to play the ones straight at you by ear."

When Jack O'Connor was fired as Browns manager following his role in the 1910 batting race scandal, Wallace was named as his replacement. The quiet, colorless Wallace was not cut out for managing a big league ball club, and he knew it. "I never had the slightest desire to be a major league manager and all knew it," said Wallace. "But Ban Johnson, Bob Hedges, and Jimmy McAleer persuaded me that the Browns were in a sort of a jam and it was up to me, as an old standby, to do what I could. Part of my reluctance to act as boss was based on my knowledge that a once fighting team had gone steadily downhill through lack of business office know-how."

Wallace piloted the woeful Browns to a 45–107 record in 1911 and a 12–27 record in 1912 until, on June 1, he was succeeded by Browns first baseman George Stovall.

Bobby continued as a player with the Browns until May 17, 1915, when, after two consecutive sub-par seasons at the plate, he decided to give umpiring a go. "If I disliked managing, I liked umpiring even less," said Wallace. Consequently, the 42-year-old Wallace returned to the Browns in 1916, but only for 22 games as a coach and substitute player. After a brief stint with Wichita in the Western League, he closed out his career in 1917 and 1918 back in the National League as a part-time player with his old team, the St. Louis Cardinals. He got his final big league hit on September 1, 1918, against Jimmy Ring of the Reds.

Away from the diamond, Bobby enjoyed fishing, billiards and golf. But baseball remained his life and career. He managed in the minor leagues, coached for the Reds (managing them for 25 games in September 1937), and scouted for Cincinnati for the final 33 years of his life. Wallace's stellar career was capped off with his election to the Baseball Hall of Fame in 1953 by the Veterans Committee, along with pitcher Chief Bender, managers Harry Wright and Ed Barrow, and umpires Bill Klem and Tommy Connolly.

Wallace had no children, but had no doubts that he would have wanted a son to play baseball. Reasoned Bobby, "Where else could he lead a cleaner and healthier life in sunshine and fresh air? Or bring so much pleasure to so many people? And be paid for it too?"

Bobby Wallace died in a nursing home in Torrance, California, on November 3, 1960, one day before his 87th birthday. He was buried in Inglewood Park Cemetery, in Inglewood, California.

SCOTT E. SCHUL

ST. LOUIS

BARNEY PELTY
RIGHT-HANDED PITCHER, 1903–1912

Starting 217 games as a Browns pitcher and relieving in 49 more, Barney Pelty was, along with shortstop Bobby Wallace, the common thread on a team that flirted with destiny and fell into oblivion. Armed with an excellent curveball that kept opposing hitters off-balance, the 5'9", 175-pound right-hander recorded 22 career shutouts, but also was shut out 32 times, meaning that fully a quarter of his decisions ended as a shutout, one way or the other. In his best season, 1906, Pelty finished with a 1.59 ERA, which still stands as a record for the lowest single season ERA in Browns/Orioles franchise history, and a league-best .202 opponents batting average, but still won only 16 games. A man of cautious intelligence, with handsomely broad features and prominent ears that made him seem slightly older than he was, Pelty was often used by his managers as a field coach, and after his baseball career dabbled in trade and politics. One of only a handful of Jewish ballplayers during the Deadball Era, "the Yiddish Curver" made no attempt to hide his heritage, but was also not a religious person. If he faced anti-Semitism, he certainly never complained publicly or let it be known that it bothered him. He was a proud man who dealt with life the way he dealt with the hard-luck team he played for, with a quiet and dignified professionalism.

Barney Pelty (not Peltheimer, as is often reported) was born in Farmington, Missouri, on September 10, 1880, the youngest of six children of Samuel and Helena Pelty. Samuel, a Prussian Jew, had immigrated to the United States at age seventeen to avoid conscription into the Prussian Army. He arrived in St. Louis, married Helena (who was also Jewish), and pursued a career as a cigar maker.

Barney was an athletic boy who grew up playing football and baseball and served as shortstop for the "Little Potatoes" children's baseball team in Farmington. His baseball talent began to manifest itself in grammar school, and he received a scholarship to pitch for the varsity team at Carleton College, which was located in Farmington until its closure in 1916. Although he left to play for Blees Military Academy in Macon, Missouri, two years later, Carleton is where he met Eva Warsing, who would later be his wife. His first offer from Organized Baseball came from Nashville of the Southern Association in 1902, but he injured his arm in practice. He wound up playing for Nashville that season as a catcher. Unhappy in this new role, he quit the team and went home.

After his arm recovered, he joined a semi-pro team in Cairo, Illinois, again as a pitcher, and finished out the 1902 season there. In 1903, he signed to play for the Cedar Rapids Rabbits in the Three-I League. Both the Red Sox and Browns scouted and tried to acquire him over the course of the summer. Unfortunately for Pelty, the Browns won the contest, purchasing his contract from Cedar Rapids in August. Pelty made his major league debut on August 20, 1903, in relief against New York, and two days later started and won 2–1 against Bill Dinneen and the Boston Red Sox, who were on their way to the first modern World Series Championship. Starting six games for the Browns in 1903, Pelty proved himself with a 3–3 record and 2.40 ERA. The following season, Pelty became a workhorse for the Browns, hurling 301 innings en route to a 15–18 record and mediocre 2.88 ERA.

At some point, Pelty acquired the nickname the "Yiddish Curver," and indeed, his curve ball was the most impressive pitch in his repertoire. Newspaper reports of Pelty's starts frequently indicated that opposing hitters "failed to solve his curves," even in games which he lost.

In 1905 Pelty finished with a 14–14 record despite pitching for a Browns club which lost 99 games and featured three other pitchers who lost 20 games apiece. Pelty came into his own during the 1906 campaign. Throughout the 1906 season, Pelty dominated the champion "Hitless Wonders," shutting them out for 33 consecutive innings before finally allowing his first run of the season to them on October 1, in the 13th inning of a 1–0 loss to Nick Altrock.

Despite that loss, the Browns finished the year above .500 in fifth place, their best showing since 1902. With outfielder George Stone leading the league in batting average, Pelty received better run support than in years past and finished the season with a 16–11 record and career-low 1.59 ERA, second-best in the league. No doubt thanks in part to the excellent defense playing behind him, Pelty also allowed the fewest hits per nine innings of any pitcher in the league, despite striking out just 92 batters in 260⅔ innings of work.

Hopes were high for Pelty and the Browns heading into the 1907 campaign, but both Barney and the club fared poorly. The Browns finished the year in sixth place, 14 games under .500, and Pelty fell with them, starting the year 1–7. Though he recovered to finish the year with 12 victories, his 21 losses led the league, and his 2.57 ERA was nearly a full run higher than the mark he had posted the previous year.

In 1908 the Browns reversed their 69–83 mark, finishing in fourth place. Pelty, however, struggled with reduced velocity and a lame arm, throwing just 122 innings for the season while striking out only 36 batters. When he did pitch, he was very good, notching a 7–4 record and 1.99 ERA for the season.

On April 23, 1909, Pelty bested Cy Young 3–1 on a six-hitter. But with much of the bite gone from his curveball, the sore-armed Pelty required extensive rest between starts to remain effective. In 199⅓ innings of work, Pelty posted an 11–11 record, including five shutouts, to finish the year with a 2.30 ERA. Ominously, Pelty was shut down for the season after making his last start on September 12, and spent the last weeks of the campaign filling in at first, second, shortstop, and right field. Undoubtedly, Pelty was given this opportunity because of his sterling fielding ability. The lifetime .143 hitter batted just .165 for the season.

In 1910 and 1911, Pelty continued to pitch occasionally for the Browns, who were now quickly sinking into the American League cellar. Starting only 41 games over the two seasons, Pelty compiled a lackluster 12–26 record, and for the first time in his career began walking more batters than he struck out. Still showing flashes of brilliance, Pelty tossed three shutouts in 1910,

including the first game ever played at Comiskey Park in Chicago, as Pelty outdueled White Sox ace Ed Walsh 2–0 to christen the new grounds on July 1. Pelty finished the 1910 season at 5–11 with a terrible 3.48 ERA for the 47–107, last-place Browns. In 1911 the Browns again lost 107 games, but Pelty finished the year with a 7–15 record and 2.83 ERA, the best mark on the club.

Despite optimistic reports out of spring training in 1912, Pelty fared poorly out of the gate for the Browns, dropping five of his six starts. In June he was sold to the Washington Senators for $2,500. Though he pitched well enough for the Senators splitting time between the rotation and the bullpen, Pelty lost four of five decisions and in August was sold to the Baltimore Orioles of the International League. *Washington Post* columnist Joe S. Jackson's prediction that Pelty was "not done yet, and is one of the wisest pitchers in the game," proved inaccurate, as Pelty was bombed in his first outing with the Orioles, then relegated to mop-up duty. At the beginning of the 1913 season, Pelty was sold to the Minneapolis Millers of the Northern League (not to be confused with the American Association team of the same name), then sent back to the Orioles. But Pelty never pitched for them again; manager Jack Dunn lamented that he was useless.

After his playing days ended, Pelty dabbled in scouting, once recommending a pitcher who had lost his leg. Pelty continued his involvement in sports, coaching local area football and several semipro baseball teams including the Farmington Blues. He had also been coaching the Farmington High School baseball nine since at least 1906.

Much of his post-major league life he spent in Farmington with his wife, Eva, and their son, while running the book and merchandise store that had been started by his parents and continued by his older sister Gertrude. He also participated in local Republican party politics, serving as alderman of Farmington for several terms. Appointed in 1921 by governor Arthur Hyde as an inspector for the Missouri State Pure Food and Drug Department, he remained in that post through two successive Republican administrations, until 1933. Later, he became plant foreman for the Hafner Rock and Construction Company in Farmington. He died on May 24, 1939, shortly after suffering a cerebral hemorrhage in his hometown. He was buried in the Masonic cemetery in Farmington, where today a downtown mural pays tribute to him as one of six significant figures in the town's history.

CHRISTOPHER WILLIAMS
AND ROBERT W. BIGELOW

ST. LOUIS

HARRY TAYLOR HOWELL
RIGHT-HANDED PITCHER, 1904–1910

A stocky 5'8" right-hander who threw one of the wettest spitballs in baseball history, Harry Howell was the St. Louis Browns' best pitcher during the Deadball Era, establishing a franchise record for career ERA (2.06) that has never been equaled. Howell learned his singular pitch from spitballing legend Jack Chesbro in 1903, and subsequently relied on it almost exclusively. Indeed, Howell's method of loading-up the ball disgusted those who thought it uncouth and unsanitary. Eddie Collins once said, "Howell used so much slippery elm we could see the foam on his lips and on hot days some of the boys thought he was about to go mad."

Harry Taylor Howell was born somewhere in New Jersey on November 14, 1876, the fourth child of Edward and Helen Howell. Harry learned the baseball craft on the sandlots of Brooklyn, and was employed as a plumber when the Meriden Bulldogs of the Connecticut League signed him for the 1898 season. Unofficially, Howell ran up an 18–13 twirling record in addition to a .209 batting mark as an extra outfielder for the defending champion Bulldogs.

Sold to the Brooklyn Bridegrooms of the National League, Howell debuted as a pitcher in the major leagues by defeating Philadelphia twice within a six-day period in mid-October 1898. The convenience of playing for his hometown team was short-lived however, and over the next five seasons Howell bounced between Brooklyn and Baltimore, operating as a pawn in high stakes games played by baseball's magnates. In 1899, Howell pitched for Baltimore of the National League, registering a 13–8 record. At the end of the season the Orioles were contracted, so Howell went back to Brooklyn, winning six and losing five in 1900 before jumping back to Baltimore when that city was awarded an American League franchise in 1901. Playing for John McGraw again, Howell displayed his versatility, hurl-ing 294⅔ innings, and also appearing at first, second, shortstop, and in all three outfield positions, batting .218 with two home runs and 26 RBI. He continued in the utility role with the 1902 Orioles, playing in 96 games, including 52 in the infield and 18 in the outfield, batting .268 in 347 at-bats, and leading the last-place, poorly supported, and soon-to-be-relocated Orioles in innings pitched.

When Ban Johnson moved the failed Baltimore franchise to New York after the 1902 campaign, Howell went along, and was credited with the first victory in New York Highlanders history on April 23. Up to that time, Howell had relied exclusively on a fastball and curve, and was never better than an average major league pitcher. But thanks to the instruction of teammate Jack Chesbro, Howell began to experiment with the spitter. The initial results were mixed, as Howell finished the year with a 9–6 record and mediocre 3.53 ERA.

Traded by manager Clark Griffith to the Browns on March 5, 1904—along with $8,000 cash—in exchange for pitcher Jack Powell, Howell began a productive five-year run in St. Louis for manager Jimmy McAleer. Now armed with a nasty spitball which he featured regularly, Howell averaged 308 innings a season from 1904 to 1908 and yielded earned runs at a rate of 2.02 per nine innings, a half run below the league average. In 1905 he led the AL in complete games with 35. Playing for the floundering Browns franchise, however, hurt Howell's record, as he lost 13 more games than he won in a Browns uniform. Twice a 20-game loser with St. Louis, Howell's best season with the Browns came in 1908, when he registered 18 wins against 18 losses with a 1.89 ERA. In contrast to his time with New York, Howell only rarely appeared at other positions for the Browns, posting his best average with the club in 1907, when he batted .237 with two home runs.

The spitter became both a source of Howell's success and also a contributing factor in his failures. An enthusiastic proponent of the spitball, Howell, according to one report, "simply loves to throw the 'spitter' and tries his hardest to retire every batter on strikes. When pitching, Howell always has a mouth full of slippery elm and he simply covers the ball with saliva. When Howell is pitching, the infielders always complain about handling the ball." The infielders' difficulty may have contributed to his uneven record, as Howell typically gave up more unearned runs than the average Browns pitcher. In 1905, for example, when Howell went 15–22 despite a 1.98 ERA, he surrendered 38 unearned runs, 35 percent of his total runs allowed. The league average that year was 29 percent, a figure in line with the rest of the St. Louis pitching staff.

Occasionally a springtime holdout and always a tough salary negotiator, Howell was nonetheless very popular in St. Louis with his teammates, the sportswriters, and the fans, particularly women. "Handsome Harry" became separated from his wife, Susie, in August 1907 after she found a letter in Howell's coat pocket from a Detroit woman that called him "the dearest and sweetest of men" and asked why he had not kept a promise to see her. Mrs. Howell also contended that a woman living near the St. Louis ballpark had received Harry's attentions. The Howells could not reconcile and divorced on December 23, 1907, after six years of marriage.

Due to injury, Howell's career as a baseball player soon wound down. In the spring of 1909, Howell threw out his arm taking infield practice at third base. Something tore loose in his shoulder, putting him on the shelf for most of the 1909 season. After 12 months of failed rehabilitation, Howell had surgery on his ailing wing in March 1910. The surgery was not successful and he was forced to retire from the mound.

Howell's association with the American League came to an unfortunate conclusion in October 1910, when he was implicated in the scandal surrounding the Ty Cobb-Napoleon Lajoie batting race. On the final day of the season, Browns manager Jack O'Connor instructed rookie third baseman Red Corriden to play deep on Lajoie, in order to allow the Cleveland second baseman to boost his batting average with bunt hits. After tripling in his first at bat, Lajoie dropped down eight bunts, seven of which were ruled as hits. When one of the bunts was ruled a sacrifice, Howell went up to the press box to try to convince the official scorer, Victor Parrish, to change his ruling. Parrish refused, but Howell remained around the press box for some time attempting to plead his case. At one point, a local bat boy brought an unsigned note promising a suit of clothes if Parrish would change his ruling. Reports conflicted as to whether or not Howell was the author of the note, but in either event once the affair was brought to light both O'Connor and Howell were fired by St. Louis owner Robert Hedges. Neither man ever worked again in the American or National leagues. When asked, Howell claimed he "acted merely as the emissary of friends and had no interest in the controversy."

His major league career over, Howell played 89 games at second base for Louisville and St. Paul of the American Association in 1911, batting a solid .260. His arm was still wrecked by the 1909 injury however, and he made no pitching appearances in his final playing season. From 1912 to 1914, Howell worked as an umpire in the International and Texas leagues, before winning a spot as a Federal League umpire for the 1915 season. This appointment lasted only a few months, until late July, when Howell was released after an on-field brouhaha with St. Louis Federals manager Fielder Jones. After that Howell umpired in the Northwestern League for a time. Howell's former manager, McAleer, called him "one of the best umpires that ever stood behind the bat."

Following his baseball career, Howell migrated to Seattle, where by 1920 he was living in a downtown boarding house with his new wife, Marie, and working as a steamfitter in the shipyards. He later moved to Spokane, Washington, where he worked as a mining engineer, and later, as a bowling alley manager, hotel manager, plumber, and truck driver. Howell also served as a trusted advisor to Spokane team owner Bill Ulrich, and in 1941, Howell and Ulrich created the Star Baseball card game and published a book, *Ulrich's Baseball Manual: All Baseball Plays For the Young Ball Players and Baseball Fans of America*, which Howell described as a "guide to show [young players] the right way to develop themselves." Despite this activity, Howell and Marie struggled financially in their later years, and for a time lived rent-free at a Spokane hotel owned by Ulrich.

In May 1956, Howell developed gangrene in his left foot. After an operation at St. Luke's Hospital in Spokane, he died on May 22 from heart failure. He was six months shy of his 80th birthday and left no known descendants. Howell is buried next to Marie, in the non-endowed section of the Greenwood Memorial Terrace Cemetery in Spokane.

ERIC SALLEE
AND DAVID JONES

ST. LOUIS

WESLEY BRANCH RICKEY
CATCHER, 1905–1906; MANAGER, 1913–1915

Long before he became one of the most important figures in baseball history, Branch Rickey spent his early major league years crouched anonymously behind the plate for the St. Louis Browns and New York Highlanders of the upstart American circuit. Rickey saw action in a scant 120 games (117 of those coming in 1906 and 1907), sported a confidently upturned collar, and supplied a constant barrage of chatter to go with a powerful throwing arm. "He is a high-strung youngster with ability and enthusiasm," noted *The Sporting News* in 1906, "but barring a disposition to hit the first ball without regard to the conditions of the game, behaved like a veteran. He earned the plaudits of [American League] President Johnson, Umpires Sheridan and Klem, the players of both teams and the spectators." Ironically, it was when the young catcher injured his magnificent arm that he achieved his only playing career notoriety—surrendering a record 13 stolen bases in a 1907 game.

Managing in the majors also proved to be as difficult as a wild pitch for Rickey. Piloting the second-division St. Louis Browns from late 1913 through 1915, Branch drew a mixture of jibes and praise for his "blackboard" or "theoretical" brand of baseball, novel approach to training players, and refusal to set foot inside a ballpark on Sundays. The perceived strangeness of his personality—combined with continual losing—led Rickey to be regarded more as a curiosity than an innovative genius during the Deadball Era.

Wesley Branch Rickey was born on December 20, 1881, the second of three surviving sons of devout Methodist parents Jacob and Emily Brown Rickey near the town of Flat (now Stockdale) in south-central Ohio. Branch grew up honing his physique on his father's farm at Duck Run, and quickly developed a passion for the diamond. Determined to forge his own identity, he dropped his first name of Wesley because two cousins claimed the same moniker.

Thanks to a phenomenal arm and good speed, Branch found a spot on the Lucasville town team in the 1890s as a catcher. Yet it was his super-charged spirit and ability to take command of a game that caught the attention of fans. Future New York Giant Al Bridwell, who squared off against Branch's Lucasville club as a member of the Portsmouth, Ohio, team, recalled Rickey's inexhaustible energy in Lawrence Ritter's *The Glory of Their Times*: "They beat us, and after the game Branch wanted to wrestle all comers. He got three or four challengers, and had them all in the dust. All in good fun, you know. And from that time on, he was a kind of hero of mine."

Branch had brains to match, enrolling in 1901 at Ohio Wesleyan University in nearby Delaware, where he eventually earned bachelors degrees in literature and art. After a seemingly innocuous $25-a-week summer stint in semipro baseball wiped out his college eligibility in 1902, Rickey played football for the Shelby Steel Tube Company team, making as much as $100 a contest. He also coached OWU athletic teams, and while guiding the baseball squads of 1903–1904, he befriended Charles Thomas, a black player on the team whose frequent encounters with racial bigotry later proved to be a turning point in the development of Rickey's social consciousness.

Rickey's rise to the majors was swift. The 5'9", 175-pound backstop played 41 games for LeMars, Iowa, of the Iowa-South Dakota League in the summer of 1903, then landed with Dallas of the Texas League a year later. There he signed a contract for $175 a month, which stated that he would not play baseball on Sundays—a private decision Branch had made to honor his mother's lifelong observance of the holy day. Rickey's .261 batting average in 41 games, 14 stolen bases, and strong work behind the plate soon captured the notice of the Cincinnati Reds, who purchased the minor leaguer's contract late in the 1904 season. But the Ohio native would never play a regular season contest with Cincinnati. A clubhouse confrontation with cranky Reds manager Joe Kelley erupted one Saturday when Rickey casually mentioned he would be missing the following day's game. Kelley threatened to banish him from the team and ordered him to see Reds president Garry Herrmann. Sympathetic, though a bit perplexed, Herrmann allowed Rickey to stay with the club, permitting him to rest Sundays, as outlined in the Dallas contract. Kelley retaliated by refusing to play Branch and, with the matter at an impasse, the youngster parted company with the Reds. He received $306.50 from Herrmann—"more money than I had ever seen in my life"—and his contract was returned to Dallas.

Branch resuscitated his major league career in 1905, this time with the St. Louis Browns, who had obtained his playing rights. The left-handed hitting Rickey debuted on June 16 against the Philadelphia Athletics and future Hall-of-Fame left-hander Rube Waddell. He went 0-for-3 with two strikeouts. "I never saw the first three pitches on which Waddell struck me out," he remembered decades later. "The next time I did a little better—sending up a feeble pop fly which the first baseman gathered up with thinly disguised contempt." The game turned out to be another false start to Rickey's career. Back in Ohio, his mother had become seriously ill and Branch returned to help take care of her. Following her recovery, he got a ticket back to the minor leagues for the remainder of the season, again catching for Dallas. Finally, he began his big league career in earnest with the Browns in 1906, at a salary of $1,800.

Still skipping Sundays, the animated rookie assumed one third of the catching duties for the Browns. Although signed for his terrific defense, Branch provided some pop at the plate. Batting mostly eighth, he hit a robust .284 in 201 at-bats (the league average was just .249) and smacked three home runs, enough to tie for eighth-best in the league. Yet Rickey struggled at times, most notably from the end of May through early July, after he ate a noxious batch of oysters in Cleveland. *The Sporting News*, however, cynically attributed his slump to another factor: "He married on his recovery, and since he became a benedict has not been batting, catching or throwing as well as he did in his bachelor days. He is sure to come on again." Branch had wed childhood sweetheart Jane Moulton on June 1, a union that would last 59 years and produce six children (five of them girls). Rickey did "come on again" in 1906. The rookie mounted a late season surge, hitting a Lajoie-like .375 over the final two months of the season.

The fall marked a return to Ohio Wesleyan University, where the newlywed coached football, baseball, and basketball. The job furnished Rickey with an extra source of income, but ultimately wound up costing him the remainder of his playing career. While putting the OWU baseball team through the paces, he severely injured his arm throwing in the school's gymnasium. A story later claimed that he damaged it experimenting with trick pitches.

He was never the same as a player. In the off-season, the Browns had traded Rickey to the New York Highlanders and, despite Branch's grim report on the condition of his arm, manager Clark Griffith summoned the catcher to his new team. Rickey's presence set the stage for one of the strangest occurrences in the early part of the Deadball Era, and produced a rare slapstick episode in Branch's illustrious baseball life. On June 28, 1907, he filled in behind the plate for the ailing Red Kleinow in a game at Hilltop Park against the visiting Washington Senators. With his arm clearly limp, Rickey proceeded to give up an American League record 13 stolen bases to the opposition in a 16–5 loss. He nevertheless tried to gun down the first few Washington baserunners and wound up throwing one "where they ain't," causing legendary outfielder Willie Keeler to track it down just beyond the infield in right. "That's how erratic the arm was," he said years later. "Actually, I never made another throw to second base. They all ran down as soon as they got on…[Griffith] knew about my arm, but that made no difference." Rickey received considerable help in achieving the mark: "[rookie pitcher Lew] Brockett was slow [to the plate]," said one Senator, "and we took full advantage of him."

Branch spent much of his spare time that season waging battle with—and finally besting—a mechanical checkers player in New York City. On the diamond, he endured an awful campaign. Rickey hit an abysmal .182 in 137 at-bats, playing mostly in left field and filling in at first and catcher. With no hope of his arm recovering—and eager to pursue a career in law—he retired from the game at the age of 25.

After a frightening bout with tuberculosis in 1909, Branch obtained his law degree from the University of Michigan in 1911 and coached the college's baseball team from 1910 to 1913. Rickey's Wolverines posted a 68–32–4 record over his four seasons; the 1913 squad, which went 21–4, featured Doc Lavan and George Sisler, both of whom would later play for Rickey in the majors. When a law partnership in Idaho failed miserably, Rickey returned to major league baseball as an assistant to St. Louis Browns owner Robert Lee Hedges for $7,500. Throughout the second half of 1913, the press speculated that Rickey had actually been hired as Hedges's handpicked successor to lame-duck skipper George Stovall, a suspicion that was confirmed when Branch officially took over as manager on September 17, 1913.

At the start of the 1914 season, major league baseball was completely unprepared for Branch Rickey, manager. "Just what bitter formula has been compounded by Messrs. McGraw and Mack in building championship teams is nothing to Rickey," wrote Hunt Stromberg of *The Sporting News* prior to the 1914 campaign. "He has ideas, suggestions, plans, schemes, and a system which is oceanwide different from any system employed by a major league manager." The fledgling skipper confounded some of his old-guard peers by introducing handball courts (to "brighten" his players' eyes, he said), sprinter's tracks, batting cages, and a sliding pit—new to baseball training then—at the Browns' camp in Florida. Falling back on his college experience, he held daily classroom-type sessions regarding strategy with his team. In the parlance of today, he was "cutting edge." The press, sometimes derisively, labeled his approach to the game as "theoretical," "educated," or "blackboard" baseball. Rickey bristled at such characterizations. "I want no theoretical base ball," he said. "In plain words—to hell with that report. I have never made such a statement. I know absolutely nothing regarding the 'law of averages,' but if it is thought that playing an intelligent game and watching closely the fine points, call it that if you wish."

His methods worked, at least temporarily. The 1914 Browns raced to a 36–29 record and a second-place spot, before cooling off the rest of the way to finish 71–82 in fifth place—a 14 game improvement over the cellar-dwelling outfit of the previous year. If there was a star or media lightning rod on the Browns, it was Rickey. Eschewing the raunchy expletives of the day, he astonished the press, fans and players with his exasperated shouts of "Judas Priest!" He urbanely initiated an argument over a close play with "Mr. Umpire." His steadfast continuation of "no Sunday baseball"—Browns third-baseman Jimmy Austin stood in for him on the Sabbath—drew both supporters and critics alike. One observer colorfully dubbed the Sunday version of the St. Louis Browns the "Rickeyless Rickeyites." But Branch wasn't a complete prude: he furnished his players cigars, so long as they gave up cigarettes.

The tremendous strides made in 1914 vanished the following year. The lone highlight of 1915 for Branch and the St. Louis organization was the signing of future Hall-of-Famer George Sisler—an event that became one of the most bitter playing rights disputes of the Deadball Era. Rickey stood at the center of it. As a 17-year-old high-schooler in 1911, Sisler had signed a contract with the minor league Akron club, then decided instead to enroll and play baseball at the University of Michigan. The Pittsburgh Pirates eventually purchased the contract, yet the National Commission held off ruling on Sisler's playing status until his college career neared completion. As Sisler finally prepared to enter the professional ranks in 1915, the Commission declared the star collegian a free agent, with the understanding that he give owner Barney Dreyfuss and the Pirates every opportunity to sign him to a contract. But by this time, Sisler's former college coach, Branch Rickey, was now manager and vice-president of the St. Louis Browns. Sisler signed with the Browns in June 1915, prompting a livid Dreyfuss to charge that Rickey "tampered and interfered" with his efforts to secure the prospect. The Commission dismissed the charges—Branch simply had offered George a sweeter deal—and Sisler remained with St. Louis for most of his career.

Sisler provided minimal help to the sputtering Browns in 1915. St. Louis suffered a relapse, going 63–91. When the Browns were sold to Federal League owner Philip Ball after the season, Branch was replaced as manager, though he was retained in the club's front office. Rickey soon jumped to the St. Louis Cardinals in 1917, taking over the presidency of the ball club. It began an affiliation with the National League that would last most of the rest of his life. He left baseball briefly in 1918 to serve in France during World War I as a major with the Chemical Warfare Service, then returned to the Cardinals in 1919 as field manager.

It was only after the sun had set on the Deadball Era that Rickey's star began to rise in the majors. Although more successful in his second go-around as a skipper—he went 458–485 for the Cardinals from 1919 to 1925—Rickey's true genius began to emerge as an executive. Branch's ability to scout proved exceptional, and his conception and installation of the modern farm system in the late teens and 1920s not only produced nine pennants and six world championships for the St. Louis Cardinals, it completely overhauled major league baseball's method of developing players.

Following his exit from the Cardinals in 1942, Rickey took over as general manager and president of the Brooklyn Dodgers for eight years, winning pennants in 1947 and 1949. But his most significant act as a Dodger executive—and indeed in his entire baseball career—was the signing of Jackie Robinson on August 28, 1945. Though made under outside pressure from sportswriters and activists, Rickey's courageous move began the dissolution of baseball's color line. So monumental in stature did the older Rickey become that the rich blend of his personal and physical characteristics—broad grin, round glasses, immense eyebrows, tousled hair, bow ties, ever-present black book of prospects, cigars, and amplified voice—attained a larger than life quality. His elevated style of speaking earned him the nickname "The Mahatma."

Branch spent almost the entire 1950s helping lead the Pittsburgh Pirates organization. In 1959, he became president of the Continental League, a prospective third major circuit. The enterprise ultimately failed, but his efforts to bring baseball to more cities spurred major league expansion in the early 1960s.

Branch Rickey suffered a heart attack while speaking at his induction to the Missouri Sports Hall of Fame on November 13, 1965, and died weeks later, on December 9, at the age of 83. He was enshrined in the Baseball Hall of Fame in 1967. Branch is buried beside his wife Jane in Rushtown Cemetery in Rushtown, Ohio, not far from where his extraordinary life began.

TONY BUNTING

ST. LOUIS

GEORGE ROBERT STONE
LEFT FIELDER, 1905–1910

From 1901 through 1928, a future member of the Baseball Hall of Fame won the American League batting title in every season but one. The exception was in 1906, when outfielder George Stone of the St. Louis Browns hit .358 and beat out four-time batting champion Napoleon Lajoie for the AL batting crown. Stone's great 1906 season is often forgotten, likely because his team finished in the second division, but in that year, Stone led the league in batting average, hits, total bases, and slugging percentage, while finishing second in triples, third in RBI, and seventh in home runs. In spite of his batting success, Stone was self-effacing and reticent, and he acquired the nickname "Silent George" because of his understated disposition. According to a 1906 article, Stone "never talks loud and is one of the most inconspicuous men on the team outside of the fact that he is a man way above the average in physical development and has a head and face that indicate a man of business or one following a profession rather than a ball player. Stone's taste runs to reading and his hobby is violin playing. In fact, he would rather be a great violinist with a limited income than he would a great ballplayer with a handsome salary."

George Robert Stone was born on September 3, 1877, in Lost Nation, Iowa, to George and Hannah Stone. As a 16-year-old, while working as a clerk in Coleridge, Nebraska, Stone got five hits in a local game along with three home runs. That performance led Stone to take baseball more seriously, and in 1902, he played with Peoria and Omaha, both in the Western League, and led the circuit with 198 hits. He soon was purchased by the Boston Americans, for whom he debuted on April 20, 1903. Stone's time with Boston was short-lived, however, as he made just two pinch-hitting appearances, striking out both times, before getting farmed out to the Milwaukee Brewers of the American Association, a team owned and managed by Hugh Duffy.

Remaining with the Brewers for the 1904 season, Stone enjoyed one of the best seasons in minor league history—his .406 batting average remained the league record until the circuit folded in 1997, and he also belted out a league-best 254 hits that year. "He is so highly regarded in Milwaukee that the press there claims he is the premier batter of the world," the *Washington Post* reported. On August 9, 1904, Milwaukee sent Stone to the Washington Senators in a three-way deal, in exchange for a sum "as large as was ever paid for a minor league player." But when the Philadelphia Athletics reneged on their end of the bargain, refusing to send Ollie Pickering to Milwaukee, the deal fell through. Later in the 1904 season, Boston re-purchased Stone from Milwaukee, but he refused to report. That December, the Americans promptly shipped Stone to the St. Louis Browns for Jesse Burkett and cash.

In his 1905 rookie season, Stone made an immediate impact, leading the American League in at-bats, hits, and total bases. "He is a clever bunter as well as a clean hitter and his speed allows him to beat out an infield fumble," said one contemporary writer. "He covers a great deal of territory and is a reliable fielder."

Stone's batting style was the subject of considerable fanfare. "When [Stone] first joined the Browns he was let go by Boston because Jimmy Collins did not like his style and considered him a doubtful batter owing to it," *The Sporting News* remarked in 1906. "Stone crouched down over the plate, with his bat tight against his shoulder, took two steps and soaked the ball for all he was worth…His explanation of the advantages of the crouch is that it gets the eyes in a better position to follow the ball, as they are almost on a direct line with any delivery that comes over the plate. Secondly, the crouch sets the muscles so that a quick chop can be taken at the ball instead of the longer swing employed by most players. As a matter of fact, Stone can and does hit the ball with terrific force, when it looks as though he is going to let it pass without attempting to hit it, so close is the leather to him before he starts his stroke."

The 5'9", 175-pound, left-handed throwing and batting outfielder enjoyed his best season in 1906. At age 28, Stone set career highs in hits, triples, and stolen bases, in addition to winning the American League batting title. At the end of the season, though, Stone commented to *The Sporting Life* that he thought his major league career might be fleeting: "I realize that each year I continue in base ball sets me just that much further back in a business career. I am still a young man and believe it should be the ambition of every young man to get in business for himself…No, in a few years, you will see me hustling for myself in my Nebraska home, trying to work up a business that by and by will work for me."

After his great initial success, Stone held out for $5,000 to start the 1907 campaign. In order to make sure that team owner Robert Hedges met his demands, Stone did not report to the team until right before the start of the season. The holdout, as one publication put it, "seems to have been the turning point of his career." On one level, "the papers aired the case and naturally by some Stone was censured for what was termed unreasonable demands." Moreover, "when he was finally granted the amount he asked, the fans figured that a player getting such big money should never fail to deliver the goods. Any time Stone failed, and unfortunately for him he had a rather tough year in

1908, he was roasted to a turn by the fans. Stone began to show signs of slowing up that year."

Stone's statistics fell off in both 1907 and 1908, though he was still an outstanding hitter. One account indicates that he contracted malaria in 1908, and Stone's production plummeted in 1909 when he suffered an injury to his ankle. That injury cost Stone his speed, which had enabled him to beat out many infield hits. He also had problems with his arm, and "any time a ball was hit into his territory the opposing base runners advanced almost at will. The worry over all these things caused Stone's batting to suffer and as a result the sensation of the American League of 1906 was a near joke in 1910." Stone never hit higher than .300 after 1907, and his average fell to .256 in 1910, his last season in the major leagues. Stone returned to the Milwaukee Brewers in 1911, batting .282, but injuries led him to retire from professional baseball just 12 games into the 1912 campaign. He wrote to manager Duffy "that he has retired from the game for good and will spend all of his future time attending to his business in Nebraska."

Stone soon entered the banking industry in Coleridge, Nebraska, and retirement afforded him more time to play the violin. He also owned a Western League franchise in Lincoln, Nebraska, in 1916. In 1940, he and his wife Pearl (Moore) moved to Clinton, Iowa, near his birthplace.

George Stone died of a heart attack in Clinton at age 67 on January 3, 1945. He was survived by his wife and son, Dr. Vean M. Stone. He is buried at Coleridge Cemetery in Coleridge, Nebraska.

JOHN MCMURRAY

ST. LOUIS

BURTON EDWIN SHOTTON
CENTER FIELDER, 1909, 1911–1917

Despite suffering from poor eyesight and a chronic condition that caused him pain in his legs and lower back, Burt Shotton carved out an impressive 14-year career in the major leagues as a speedy leadoff hitter who compensated for his lack of power at the plate by drawing walks and bunting for base hits. Given the physical disabilities which impeded success on the diamond, Shotton relied heavily on his wits to gain an advantage over his adversaries. A patient hitter who liked to work deep into the count, Shotton prided himself on his strategic approach to the game. As he once explained, "It requires not only a keen eye, but the proper mental poise to enable a batter to restrain his natural inclinations and to follow a set formula in his work." After his playing days ended, Shotton built on his experience to become a successful manager, gaining a reputation as a superior in-game strategist who could orchestrate a game with the proficiency of a master.

Burton Edwin Shotton was born on October 18, 1884, in Brownhelm, Ohio, the second of four children of John and Alice Shotton, native Ohioans of French and Irish descent. John supported his family as an engineer. Like many young men of his generation, Burt developed his baseball skills in high school and on factory teams. A pitcher in the beginning, his swiftness of foot soon designated him for the outfield where he could track down a batted ball with dizzying speed. Sometime early on he gained the handle "Barney" after a renowned racecar driver, Barney Oldfield, a fellow Ohioan who reportedly was the first ever to drive around a mile track in less than a minute.

It was Shotton's swiftness around the bases, as well as in the outfield, that captured the attention of scouts. In 1908, he signed with the Erie Sailors of the Ohio-Pennsylvania League for $125 a month, his first professional stint in baseball. Although he spent most of that season on the bench due to an elbow injury, Steubenville of the same league bought his contract the following year. There, his league-leading batting average of .347 earned him a ticket to the majors late in the season with the St. Louis Browns, where Shotton hit .262 in 61 at-bats. Although Burt spent the next season in the minors, he was back with the Browns in 1911, batting .255, stealing 26 bases and tying for the team lead with 84 runs scored.

Over the course of the next six seasons, Shotton emerged as one of the most dependable players on a team that finished in the second division every year. Though his quickness afoot helped him patrol center field, Shotton was not a good defensive player. The 5′11″, 175-pound, right-handed thrower led the league in putouts in 1912, but also paced the circuit in errors, something he would do four more times over the course of his career. Recognizing his limitations, the Browns shifted Shotton to left field in 1915. At the plate, however, the left-handed batter matured into one of the game's most patient hitters. From 1912 to 1918 he ranked among the league's top ten in free passes six times, and led the league twice, in 1913 and 1916. Shotton prided himself on his ability to work the count and draw walks, going so far as to call the base on balls "the corner stone of the game. The very name baseball is almost the same as base on balls."

Shotton's skill at working a walk constituted a large part of his game. Never a .300 hitter, Shotton nonetheless posted on-base percentages of .400 or higher twice during his career, in 1913 (.405) and 1915 (.409). For his career, the .271 hitter boasted a .365 OBP, thanks to his 713 walks. When Shotton did put the ball in play, he rarely hit with power, preferring instead to slap at the ball or beat out bunts for base hits. At .333, Shotton boasts one of the lowest slugging percentages in history by a player with a .270 average or better: only Muddy Ruel (.332), Maury Wills (.330), and Otis Nixon (.314) are lower. Once on base, Shotton continued to pester opposing defenses with his excellent speed, ranking among the league leaders in stolen bases every year from 1912 to 1916, including a career-high 43 thefts in 1913 and again in 1915.

He accomplished all this despite poor eyesight and nagging soreness in his legs and lower back caused by sciatica, a degenerative neurological condition not diagnosed until his later years. The fact that he played and managed with acumen despite these afflictions affirms the ideology of baseball as the thinking man's game—Shotton clearly compensated with intellect and sheer determination, an asset noted by his manager with the Browns, Branch Rickey, who sometimes designated Shotton as his "Sunday manager," because Branch had promised his mother never to work on the Sabbath.

A freak clubhouse injury sidelined Shotton for part of the 1917 season, and his performance on the field degenerated. By the next season, he found himself traded to the Washington Senators along with Doc Lavan for Bert Gallia and $15,000. He played well for Washington in 1918, but when baseball cut the season short because of the entrance of the United States into World War I, and owners responded by abbreviating players' salaries, Shotton was among those players who sued for the balance owed. He demanded $1,400 from the club, a controversial stance which inspired one reporter to write "something or other turned him Bolsheviki." The Senators owner then put Shotton on the trading block, and the outfielder was soon waived out of the American League. But by then his old friend Branch Rickey managed the National League Cardinals, and Burt returned to St. Louis in 1919. Although he came to the Cards in an advisory capacity, he played in some games during his stay there, and also resumed his position as Sunday manager for Rickey. Though he batted a solid .285 for St. Louis in 1919, Shotton's performance quickly worsened: in 1920, he batted just .228, and was confined to part-time duty until his playing days finally came to an end with a lone appearance as a pinch runner in 1923.

With his experience directing the game from the bench, Shotton found a place in the Cardinal organization, managing the Syracuse Stars of the International League in 1926. Though the club finished a disappointing seventh, Shotton was offered the managerial post with the Philadelphia Phillies. In 1928, his first season as a big league manager, Shotton helmed one of the worst teams in baseball history, finishing 43–109. He remained in Philadelphia six seasons, posting only one winning record, a fourth-place finish in 1932, though he also exhibited his eye for baseball talent, personally scouting Hall of Fame outfielder Chuck Klein, whom the Phillies purchased for $7,000. Let go after the 1933 season, Shotton briefly coached the Cincinnati Reds, then accepted a job managing the Columbus Senators of the American Association in 1936. He remained there for six seasons and won two pennants.

From there he accepted a coaching position with the Cleveland Indians in 1942, staying there for four years. Though he officially retired from baseball after the 1945 season, Rickey, now president of the Brooklyn Dodgers, convinced him to do some scouting work for the Dodgers in Bartow, Florida, where he lived. Shotton's greatest opportunity arrived in 1947, when commissioner Happy Chandler suspended Brooklyn manager Leo Durocher for a year. Rickey named Shotton as replacement, just in time for the arrival of Jackie Robinson with the big league club. When Robinson got off to a slow start in his rookie season, Shotton ignored advice to bench the talented first baseman, and Brooklyn won the National League pennant by five games. In 1948, Durocher resumed his position with the Dodgers, but in July abandoned the club to manage the New York Giants. For the second time in two years, Shotton was called upon as his replacement, and again performed admirably, guiding the Dodgers to another pennant in 1949. Regularly wearing a suit and bow tie to work, Shotton was only one of two managers in baseball— Connie Mack being the other—to wear civilian clothes on the field. Shotton's tenure in Brooklyn came to an end after the 1950 season, when Rickey was replaced as club president by Walter O'Malley, who quickly fired Shotton in favor of Charlie Dressen. On October 1, 1950, Shotton managed his final game, a dramatic extra-inning contest in which the Dodgers lost the pennant to the Phillies on Dick Sisler's famed home run. As fate would have it, that was also Connie Mack's last day as a major league manager, and by virtue of the A's game ending 35 minutes earlier than the Dodgers game, Shotton became the last big league manager to wear civilian clothes in the dugout.

His baseball career finally over, Burt spent the remainder of his days with his wife, Mary, enjoying their Florida home at Camp Lester (still a fishing camp today), 15 miles east of the town of Lake Wales. In that community, he helped organize Little League baseball. On July 29, 1962, while seated at the table at home, he suffered a fatal heart attack. His final resting place is at the Lake Wales Cemetery.

Joan M. Thomas

ST. LOUIS

JAMES PHILIP AUSTIN
THIRD BASEMAN, 1911–1923, 1925–1926, 1929

One of the most energetic players of his era, Jimmy Austin was a sparkplug for the New York Highlanders and St. Louis Browns over an 18-year career spent entirely in the American League. A speedy switch-hitting third baseman, Austin stole at least twenty bases in each of his first six major league seasons, and he was regularly among the league leaders in sacrifice hits. What he lacked in stature, the 5′7½″ 155-pound Austin made up for in hustle, leading his manager with New York, George Stallings, to give Austin the nickname "Pepper." Even during his coaching tenure with the Chicago White Sox in the 1930s, Austin was still known throughout baseball for being vocal and jumping around with the energy of a young man. In fact, one contemporary sportswriter reflected that, "If pepper had not been discovered some years before James Austin was born, those who know him well would have been prone to assert that the condiment was named after 'Jimmy' instead of 'Jimmy' being named after it. He surely is the essence of pepper."

James Philip Austin was born on December 8, 1879, in Swansea, Wales. His father, Alfred, was a shipbuilder who decided to come to the United States in 1885 in search of higher wages. Alfred Austin began work with the Cleveland Shipbuilding Company, and he was able to bring his family to Ohio in 1887.

Unlike many future major leaguers, Jimmy didn't see a baseball game until he was 14 years old. Although he had initially wanted to teach his young friends the game of rugby, Jimmy said later that, "I forgot all about rugby in my eagerness to learn how to catch and hit a baseball." Soon, Austin formed a team of neighborhood kids who were eager to play. The team called itself the Franklin Athletic Club, and, while playing against other neighborhood teams, Jimmy first tried switch-hitting.

Austin was the shortstop on the team, while Dode Paskert, who later starred for the Philadelphia Phillies, was an outfielder.

After finishing school, Austin went to work as a machinist-apprentice at Westinghouse in Cleveland. Shortly after his four-year apprenticeship ended in 1903, however, the union went on strike, leaving Jimmy without a job. In a stroke of luck, Austin was soon approached to play independent league ball in nearby Warren, Ohio, at a salary of $40 per month. In need of work and hoping to follow in the footsteps of fellow Clevelanders such as Ed Delahanty and Tommy Leach, Austin jumped at the opportunity.

Jimmy recruited Paskert to play with him, and the two were teammates with the Warren team. In the spring of 1904, they were both offered the opportunity to play Organized Baseball with Dayton, Ohio, of the Central League, on the strength of a recommendation from a traveling salesman with the White Chewing Gum Company. The following year, Austin switched to third base, the position he would play in the major leagues. In 1906, Austin stole 59 bases for Dayton, and the next spring, both Austin and Paskert were picked up by the Atlanta Crackers of the Southern Association. Paskert went, but Jimmy asked that he be sent elsewhere because he didn't like Atlanta's intense summer heat. Austin was shipped to Omaha of the Western League, where he stole a total of 160 bases over two seasons and caught the eye of the New York Highlanders, who purchased his contract following the 1908 season.

Jimmy made his major league debut with New York on April 19, 1909, at the advanced age of 29. Despite his age, Austin played with the joy and exuberance of a younger man. His love for the game was so infectious that it even won over the veteran whose job he was trying to take. As Austin later related in Lawrence Ritter's

The Glory of Their Times, Kid Elberfeld treated him well even though Austin was competing for Elberfeld's third base job. When Elberfeld was suspended and Austin replaced him at third, Jimmy continued to sleep in his upper berth on the train, normally reserved for the substitutes. Elberfeld, according to Austin, would have none of it: "Put the youngster down in a lower berth," Elberfeld ordered. "Take mine if you have to. He's playing every day, hustling like the devil out there, and he needs his rest."

Austin's hustle helped him steal 30 bases during his rookie year with New York. It was during this time that manager George Stallings gave Austin the nickname "Pepper," which took on other formulations over time, including "Pepper Jim" and "Peppery Jimmy." During the 1910 season, Austin also appeared in what is perhaps the most famous baseball photograph of all-time. Jimmy was the third baseman sent sprawling by Ty Cobb in the photograph, taken at Hilltop Park by photographer Charles Conlon, that has since been published thousands of times. "Jimmy and I were very close friends," Conlon later wrote. "Jimmy turned, backed into the base, and was greeted by a storm of dirt, spikes, shoes, uniform—and Ty Cobb. My first thought was that my friend, Austin, had been injured. When Cobb stole, he *stole.* But in a moment I realized [Austin] wasn't hurt... then I began to wonder if by any chance I had snapped the play."

Jimmy's second season in New York was less successful than the first. His batting average fell from .231 to .218, and George Stallings, whom Jimmy had admired, was replaced as manager by Hal Chase. The new manager wanted to purge the team of players loyal to his predecessor. Accordingly, in February 1911, Austin was traded to the St. Louis Browns with second baseman Frank LaPorte for third baseman Roy Hartzell and cash. Though now 31 years old, and reaching the age when many players begin to decline, Austin's career in the major leagues was just beginning.

Jimmy's first season with the Browns was his best year as a player. In 1911, Austin achieved his career bests in hits (141), doubles (25), and RBI (45), while leading the American League with 34 sacrifices. An athletic fielder who was blessed with quick reflexes and superior range, Austin also led all American League third basemen in putouts, assists, and double plays. Over the course of the decade, he would lead the league in double plays three more times. In 1913, Jimmy set a career high with 37 stolen bases. During that same season, Austin served the first of three stints as temporary manager of the Browns, guiding the club for eight games in September

between the firing of George Stovall and the naming of Branch Rickey as his replacement.

From 1914 to 1919, he played in more than 100 games with St. Louis in each season, never posting higher than a .266 batting average but registering a career-best .359 on-base percentage in 1918, when he led the club in walks. Austin also solidified his reputation as one of the league's best third basemen, though his powerful but erratic arm caused problems. As John Kieran of the *New York Times* later recalled, "What an arm! Every fourth heave he made across the diamond went into the right field bleachers."

In 1920, the 40-year-old Austin became a part-time player, posting a career high .271 batting average in 83 games. Still, as J. Roy Stockton of the *St. Louis Post-Dispatch* reflected, "Austin, of course, can go in there any time and deliver, but his eyes cannot perform as well as his arms and hands." Jimmy became a full-time coach with the Browns beginning in 1923, but he did come back to play in exactly one game in the 1923, 1925, 1926, and 1929 seasons, before officially finishing his playing career at age 49. Austin remained with the Browns through the 1932 season, when Depression-era belt-tightening forced the franchise to let him go. He then joined the Chicago White Sox for an eight-year coaching career. With Chicago, Austin continued to display unbridled enthusiasm for the game he loved. "Jimmy yells and jumps around more than any other player on the team," one newspaper reported during Austin's first year coaching with the White Sox. "He'll pitch batting practice, wipe off the balls on days the muddy field gets them in that condition, handle the catcher's glove in spare moments, hit to the infield and outfield, race to the clubhouse on an errand and chip in with countless other chores."

After 32 years in the major leagues, Austin finished his coaching career in 1940 at age 60. Following his retirement, he returned to Laguna Beach, California, where he had made his home since 1913. A popular figure, Austin served as mayor of the town during the 1940s. Married to Josie for 45 years, the couple had no children. After Josie's death, Jimmy remarried and retired from politics. He was still living in Laguna Beach when Lawrence Ritter tracked him down and interviewed him for *The Glory of Their Times.* Jimmy died before the book was published, passing away from congestive heart failure on March 6, 1965, at the age of 85. Austin was buried three days later in Melrose Abbey Memorial Park in Anaheim, California.

JOHN MCMURRAY

ST. LOUIS

DERRILL BURNHAM "DEL" PRATT
SECOND BASEMAN, 1912–1917

After Eddie Collins, Del Pratt was the best second baseman in the American League during the second decade of the twentieth century, and one of the few bright spots on a St. Louis Browns team that finished in the second division every year from 1912 to 1917. During his six seasons in St. Louis the speedy, powerful Pratt used Sportsman's Park's spacious confines to his advantage, placing among the league leaders in doubles, triples, and home runs many seasons, and leading the league in RBI in 1916. A notorious bad ball hitter, during his prime Pratt was known to get good lumber on pitches far out of the strike zone. Sportswriter John B. Sheridan described Pratt as a "notoriously unstylish, yet most viciously effective hitter…He violates all the rules of good hitting…he hits the bad ball to any field…Pratt, to my mind, is one of the most dangerous hitters I have ever seen. You can't pitch to him." In the field, Pratt struck observers as almost nonchalant in his pursuit of ground balls and pop-ups, but he got to more balls than any other second baseman in the league, and as a result frequently led the league in putouts, assists, and errors. Feisty and temperamental, Pratt also made his share of enemies among teammates and management, leading John Kieran of the *New York Times* to call him "the greatest clubhouse lawyer baseball ever knew."

Derrill Burnham Pratt was born into a well-off family on January 10, 1888, in Walhalla, South Carolina, a town near Greenville founded in 1849 as a German-American colony. His father, George Walker Pratt, was an industrialist in the cotton business, and his mother, Mary Dawson Pratt, was a homemaker. In 1906 Del left for college at Georgia Tech, playing on the baseball team for two seasons. In 1908, the family moved to Tuscaloosa, Alabama, where George became a cotton broker. Del transferred to the University of Alabama, where he studied textile engineering for two years and earned varsity letters in both baseball and football. On the baseball team, Pratt played shortstop and served as team captain both years.

After graduating from Alabama in 1909, Pratt entered professional baseball in 1910 with the Montgomery Climbers of the Southern Association. He hit only .232 and was sent to Hattiesburg of the Class D Cotton States League that same year. His .367 average in 20 games brought him back to Montgomery in 1911. Not only did Del continue his solid hitting—.316 in 139 games—but he also showed his speed with 36 stolen bases. Montgomery finished in second place, and Pratt led the league in batting average, hits, and runs.

During the offseason, the St. Louis Browns acquired Del for players and cash, along with a $250 signing bonus. Early in 1912, John McGraw of the New York Giants offered St. Louis $8,000 for Pratt, to no avail. Del had a sparkling rookie season, posting a .302 batting average with 26 doubles, 15 triples, and a .426 slugging average. He also hit five home runs, including the first ever in Detroit's new stadium, Navin Field. A year later, he ended Walter Johnson's scoreless inning streak at 55, by driving in a run with a single. In 1916, when Pratt's batting average dropped to .267, he led the league in runs batted in with 103. During his first five seasons with St. Louis, the right-handed Pratt batted between .283 and .302 four of the five years, and averaged 31 doubles, 13 triples, 80 RBI, 69 runs scored, and 31 stolen bases per year. A remarkably durable player, Pratt also led the league in games played every year from 1913 through 1916.

Del was a solid fellow, standing 5'11" and weighing 175 pounds. In the field he was not flashy, and had an easygoing way of covering a lot of ground and getting to the ball. Initially he was not known for his defense.

In 1913, the *Globe-Democrat* wrote that he would have to work on his fielding to become a star, and the *Post-Dispatch* said later that season that he was a "juggler," not an infielder. Just a few years later, *The Sporting News* called him the best defensive second baseman in the game.

The numbers reflected the maturation of his glove skills. Del led the American League in chances and put-outs five times, and double plays and assists three times. From 1913 to 1919, his chances per game were more than those of Eddie Collins, often by a large margin. As a consequence of reaching more balls than any other second baseman in the game, Pratt also led the league in errors three times, even though his fielding percentage often exceeded the league average.

Off the field, Pratt became known for being outspoken and temperamental. His manager, Branch Rickey, described Pratt as "a high-strung Southern gentleman," and Pratt's nephew James later remembered that Del was "Not bashful…said his part." When Dave Foutz was organizing the Players' Fraternity, the rookie Pratt became the Browns' team representative. A year later, during a Browns-Cardinals game in the October 1913 City Series, Del punched the Cards' Zinn Beck and was tossed from the game. Cardinal bench jockeys had been riding Del, suggesting he was revealing union secrets to ownership. There was such animosity that the City Series ultimately was called off and ended in a 3–3 (in games) tie.

In 1916 the Browns new owner Phil Ball installed Fielder Jones as manager. The astute and caustic Jones praised Pratt as one of the best natural hitters he had ever seen, but also gave him a hard time over his performance on the field. A rift developed between the manager and his star player. John B. Sheridan of *The Sporting News* reported that Jones liked to "ride" Pratt, "a boyish Southerner, extremely sensitive, but garrulous, though a self-bred gentleman of education and manners."

1917 was a difficult year for Del, who, seriously hampered by injuries for the first time in his major league career, batted just .247 for the season with one home run. Early in the season, he broke a bone in his wrist and missed three weeks. A week after returning to the lineup, he was sidelined again with a bad knee. Then, after a 13–6 September 4 loss to the league-leading Chicago White Sox, Ball accused his players of "laying down" on the job.

In reality, Ball did not single out any guilty parties. Yet Del, shortstop Doc Lavan and outfielder Burt Shotton took issue with the remarks. All three were hampered by injuries and having poor years. The Browns owner soon backed down, explaining that his friends were telling him that the players were "laying down."

Was Ball suggesting that the players were "dogging it" as the end of the season approached, or was he implying something more sinister? "Damn lie," Del would tell his friends and family. "I played 100 percent every day." Fifty-five years after the incident, Alabama sportswriter Morris Frank wrote, "An athletic contest was a contest to Del whether it was in Detroit or Dime Box."

Pratt and Lavan soon each filed $50,000 libel lawsuits against Ball. Del suggested that he would call ballplayers as character witnesses to testify about his efforts on the ball field. *The Sporting News* referred to Del as the team's "Trotsky." Manager Jones, while publicly defending his players from Ball's charges, privately pressured business manager Bob Quinn to dump the malcontents. A few months later, Lavan and Shotton were traded to the Washington Senators. Soon after, on January 22, 1918, Pratt and 42-year-old pitcher Eddie Plank were traded to the Yankees for Fritz Maisel, Joe Gedeon, Les Nunamaker, pitchers Nick Cullop and Urban Shocker, and $15,000 in cash.

Many observers thought the Browns had gotten the better of the deal, especially after Plank retired to his Gettysburg farm. *Baseball Magazine*'s W.A. Phelon wrote, "it looks like five pretty good men for one ageing infielder." Yankees owner Jacob Ruppert admitted he "had to pay all out of reason" for Pratt, but he and Huggins desperately wanted Del to strengthen the team's middle infield.

As it turned out, the Yankees did not do so poorly. Besides his solid glovework, Del averaged .295 over the next three seasons, with both extra-base hitting and speed on the base paths. He continued to show his durability: he played in all but one game from 1918 through 1920. Miller Huggins told reporter Bozeman Bulger that Pratt was "the man who put the ball club on its feet." As early as 1918, Fred Lieb coined the phrase "Murderers' Row" to describe the heart of the New York offense, which he characterized as "the greatest collection of pitcher thumpers in baseball today." As the Deadball Era came to an end, the Yankees began to inch their way up the standings in the American League, finishing in third place with an 80–59 record in 1919, their best showing in nine years.

Off the field, however, Pratt became a constant headache to New York management. First came his holdout in his first spring as a Yankee, when he used an offer from the University of Alabama to coach their football team as leverage in salary negotiations. He went public with his dispute before settling for more money. Del also expressed concern that he might be railroaded out of baseball because of his ongoing legal battle with

Phil Ball. He even asked the Yankees to put a clause into his contract that they would not waive him out of the league because of it. The lawsuits with Phil Ball were settled in late March 1918. While some newspapers reported that the cases were settled in the plaintiffs' favor, they probably got far less than $50,000. *The Sun* reported that Del received $5,400.

In late March of 1920, a controversy erupted in the Yankee clubhouse over the distribution of third-place money among the team members. Pratt led the protesters and even suggested that the players would strike over the matter. The Yankees owners settled the dispute with money out of their own pockets. Del then went on to his finest season in a Yankee uniform, batting .314 with 84 runs scored, 97 RBI and a then career-high 37 doubles.

In a year when Miller Huggins battled critics both in the press and in the Yankee clubhouse, Pratt became one of the central anti-Huggins agitators, and did not discourage suggestions that he would make a good successor to the little skipper. That fall, Del was again considering a college coaching career, this time as the University of Michigan baseball coach, thanks to Branch Rickey's recommendation. Miller Huggins told the *New York Times* that Del could leave for Michigan if he wanted to. The Yankee skipper, who possessed a law degree from the University of Cincinnati, would later crack, "Two lawyers on one team do not make a great combination." On December 15, 1920, Pratt was included in an eight-player trade with the Boston Red Sox. Following the trade, the *Boston Globe* reported that "Pratt and the Yankee management have been at swords points for more than a year...a club now famous for its cliques." The *Boston Herald* noted that Pratt and Huggins had almost come to blows a few times that past season.

And so Del Pratt was sent from the Yankees, just as they were about to embark on a decade of dominance, to the Red Sox, a team entering a decade of despair. Del would have no more worries about how third-place money would be distributed. When the dust settled, he once again decided to remain a player rather than pursue a career in coaching. Boston owner Harry Frazee sent Del a blank contract and let him fill in the salary amount. He inserted $11,500 a year for two years, making him one of baseball's highest-paid players.

Pratt had two terrific seasons with Boston. His eye was better than ever: in 1921, he struck out only ten times in 521 at-bats, drove in 102 runs, and posted career-highs in batting average (.324), on-base percentage (.378) and slugging percentage (.461). After another stellar campaign in 1922, when Pratt batted .301 with 86 RBI and a career-high six home runs, Del was traded to the Detroit Tigers in another multi-player deal. Detroit player-manager Ty Cobb had long admired Del's hitting skills and durability. But Pratt, who turned 35 shortly after the trade, missed 89 games for the Tigers from 1923 to 1924. Though he batted better than .300 both seasons, it was not much better than the league average, and on the bases and in the field he "had slowed down to a walk," in the judgment of Fred Lieb. Following the 1924 season, Del was released by the Tigers and waived out of the league. He finished his major league career with just under 2,000 hits, of which 26 percent were doubles or triples, and a .292 career batting average.

Following his departure from the majors, Pratt embarked on a career as player-manager for the Waco Cubs of the Texas League. From 1925 to 1927, he averaged 28 home runs after hitting just three homers a year in the preceding five years. In 1927, Del put together one of the greatest seasons by a player-manager in minor league history, winning the Texas League Triple Crown with a .386 batting average, 32 home runs and 140 RBI. In 1930 Del had only 91 at-bats, though he still saw the ball well enough to hit .374. In 1931, Del became the manager of the Galveston Buccaneers for two seasons. In 1932, he had his last plate appearances at the age of 44, when he hit .293 in 41 at-bats. After operating a bowling alley in Galveston for one year, Pratt returned for his final stint in the minors in 1934, as manager of the Fort Worth Cats. He lasted just one season, guiding the team to a poor seventh-place finish.

With his baseball days behind him, Del now had more time for two of his passions, hunting and fishing. In the late 1930s, he coached the Kirwin High (now O'Connell High) football team in Galveston. Del stayed in Galveston for the rest of his life, where he lived with his wife, Leontine, with whom he had four children. For many years he owned a beachfront gas station. In the early 1960s, he managed the sporting goods department of a Thrifty Discount Store.

When Del Pratt was inducted into the Alabama Sports Hall of Fame in 1972 at the age of 84, he told the *Galveston Daily News*, "I've got a pretty good record. But I don't talk about it much." Pratt died on September 30, 1977, at age 89.

STEVE STEINBERG

ST. LOUIS

GEORGE HAROLD SISLER
FIRST BASEMAN, 1915–1922, 1924–1927; MANAGER, 1924–1926

Arguably the first great first baseman of the twentieth century, George Sisler was the greatest player in St. Louis Browns history. An excellent baserunner and superb fielder who was once tried out at second and third base even though he threw left-handed, Sisler's primary asset was his left-handed swing, which he used to notch a career .340 batting average. From 1916 to 1925, Sisler batted over .300 nine consecutive times, including two seasons in which he batted better than .400, making him one of only two players in American League history (the other was Ty Cobb) to post multiple .400 batting marks. Though Sisler's greatest feats occurred in the years immediately following the end of the Deadball Era, by 1919 he had already established himself as one of the game's top young stars, placing in the top three in batting average every year from 1917 to 1919, and leading the league with 45 stolen bases in 1918. That year one writer declared that Sisler possessed "dazzling ability of the Cobbesque type. He is just as fast, showy, and sensational, very nearly if not quite as good as a natural hitter, as fast in speed of foot, an even better fielder, and gifted with a versatility Cobb himself might envy."

George Harold Sisler was born on March 24, 1893, the youngest of three children of Mary Whipple and Cassius Clay Sisler in Manchester, Ohio, 45 miles south of Cleveland. Like many rural communities of the day, baseball was a passion that united the town. Sisler's extended family owned and populated much of the surrounding countryside, and young George quickly gained a reputation as a sterling ballplayer without sacrificing the educational values stressed by his parents, both graduates of nearby Hiram College.

While Sisler excelled on the athletic fields and in the classroom, his life turned as he entered his teenage years. Manchester had no high school, and at age 14 he

moved to Akron, Ohio, to live with his brother Bert and advance his education. At Akron High, Sisler played football as a slender end, basketball as a smooth forward, and baseball as a southpaw pitcher noted for his speed and curveball. Sisler also played on several pickup and semipro squads, and the local newspapers soon referred to the handsome boy as "Gorgeous George."

Upon graduating from high school, Sisler followed the wishes of his parents and curbed plans to enter the professional ranks in order to pursue a college education. Rejecting scholarship offers from Penn and Western Reserve, Sisler decided to follow his high school catcher Russ Baer to Michigan. Sisler departed Akron with his sights set on law school, but upon his arrival in Ann Arbor enrolled in the engineering program due to his affinity for math.

With no firm plans to play collegiate baseball, Sisler didn't act on the notion until several months after he arrived on campus. By that time, the Wolverines had filled their vacant coaching position with the man who would significantly impact Sisler's life, Michigan law school grad Branch Rickey. In the late winter of 1912, the confident freshman reported for baseball tryouts at Waterman Gym. Although the session was only for upperclassmen, Rickey was persuaded by a team member to give the green freshman a chance, and by the end of the session Sisler was regarded as a top performer. Freshmen were not eligible for varsity competition, but by leading the first-year engineering students to the school baseball title over a strong group of junior law students, Sisler made his mark on campus.

Sisler's career continued to gather momentum as he pitched in Akron's industrial league that summer. He and his older brother Cassius, a catcher, comprised the core of the Babcock and Wilcox Boilerworks company team, and the local press chronicled his strikeout total and mound success. On one memorable Sunday afternoon, with the immortal Cy Young perched behind the plate as umpire, Sisler twirled a no-hitter against the Amherst Grays.

A full-fledged member of the Wolverine varsity nine during his sophomore year, Sisler's fast start on the mound was interrupted by arm trouble, but his batting averaged remained around .500 most of the campaign. Rickey left the squad to join the Browns front office after the season, but Michigan finished 22–4–1, and Sisler's .445 batting average and pitching success earned him All-America honors. Still plagued by a sore arm, Sisler starred at the plate for Akron's B&W team again in the summer of 1913 before turning to famed sports medical professional John "Bonesetter" Reese for treatment. Despite a sore arm, the following season Sisler split time between the mound and the outfield, and finished the year with a .451 average. Once again, he was named to the All-America team.

At some point during the summer of 1910, before his senior year in high school, Sisler had signed a contract to play for the Akron Champs of the Ohio & Pennsylvania League. Sisler received no bonus money and never reported to the club, and Lee Fohl's Champs eventually sold the contract to Columbus. Acting on a tip from Cubs infielder Artie Hofman, Pittsburgh owner Barney Dreyfuss scouted Sisler in a sandlot game in Akron in the summer of 1912, purchased his contract, and insisted that Sisler report to the National League club. The story leaked to the press, and Sisler's contract became public knowledge.

Confronted with the problem, Rickey's keen mind soon found the loophole. Because Sisler was 17 when he signed, the contract was void without his father's signature, and Rickey recognized that immediately. Rickey took the case to the National Commission, and after a protracted battle Cincinnati owner Garry Herrmann cast the deciding vote on January 9, 1915, granting Sisler free agency upon entering the professional ranks.

Sisler then turned his eyes toward professional baseball, and toward his former mentor, the man he called "Coach" for the rest of his life, Branch Rickey. After entertaining an offer from Pittsburgh, Sisler signed with the St. Louis Browns for $300 a month, less than Dreyfuss offered him, though the Browns also paid Sisler a $5,000 bonus. Dreyfuss filed a complaint with the National Commission. At 22 years old, Sisler joined the Browns as a left-handed twirler in 1915. The rookie pitched 15 games that summer for the Browns, starting eight and throwing six complete games. In 70 innings he compiled a 2.83 ERA. While Sisler experienced mound

success that summer, it took Rickey only a few days to start working him at first base and the outfield. His hitting came in spurts, but he ended the season with a solid .285 batting average, three homers and 29 RBI. The highlight of his rookie season was a 2–1 win over Walter Johnson on August 29 in which he limited the Senators to six hits and struck out three, winning the game thanks to Del Pratt's successful execution of the hidden ball trick. For the remainder of his life, Sisler spoke of that game as his greatest thrill in baseball. "Sisler can be counted a baseball freak," the *Washington Post* reported the next day. "[Rickey] plays him in the outfield and he makes sensational catches…he plays him on first base and actually he looks like Chase when Hal was king of the first sackers, and then on the hill he goes out and beats Johnson."

Incoming St. Louis owner Phil Ball replaced Rickey with Fielder Jones during the 1916 season, but despite the changes Sisler consolidated his hitting gains and took over as the club's first baseman. He hit .305, the first of nine straight seasons over .300, and rapped out 11 triples and four homers, as the Browns finished in fifth place with their first winning record in eight years. On June 10, 1916, the National Commission finally issued its ruling on Dreyfuss's grievance, turning it down and declaring Sisler's contract with St. Louis legitimate.

As war loomed on the national horizon in 1917 the newlywed Sisler, who had married his college sweetheart Kathleen Holznagle the previous fall, became a star. Limited to three mound appearances in 1916, none in 1917, and just two in 1918, Sisler's grace around first base drew him accolades as one of the league's top defensive players. He was also an offensive star, finishing second in the league in hits, fourth in doubles and fifth in stolen bases in 1917, and third in hits in 1918 with a league-leading 45 steals. The national press took to calling him "the next Cobb."

From 1919 to 1922, Sisler largely fulfilled that promise, as he batted .407 to win his first batting title in 1920, collecting 257 hits, a major league record that would last 84 years. He captured his second batting crown in 1922 with a .420 mark, which still stands as the third-best season average in modern baseball history. After the 1922 season, Sisler was given the inaugural American League Trophy as the league's MVP, voted on by a league-appointed panel of sportswriters.

Sisler finished second in the league in stolen bases in 1919 and 1920, and led the league in 1921 and 1922. Though Sisler often ranked among the league leaders in doubles, triples, and home runs, he was primarily a place hitter, adept at finding the gaps in opposing defenses. Like Cobb, Sisler stood erect at the plate, and relied on his superior hand-eye reflexes to react to a pitch's location and lash out base hits. "Except when I cut loose at the ball, I always try to place my hits," he once explained. "At the plate you must stand in such a way that you can hit to either right or left field with equal ease." Unlike Cobb, who shifted his feet while hitting, Sisler was an advocate of the flat-footed swing.

At the peak of his powers following his historic 1922 performance, Sisler missed the entire 1923 season with a severe sinus infection that impaired his optic nerve, plaguing him with chronic headaches and double vision. Though he was able to return to the field in 1924, when he also agreed to serve as manager of the Browns, Sisler was never again the same player. He batted .305 in 1924—below the league average—improved to .345 the following year, but then batted just .290 in 1926 with a .398 slugging percentage. Under his management, the Browns finished fourth in 1924 and third a year later. After falling to seventh place in 1926, Sisler was removed as manager, and later admitted that he "wasn't ready" for the post. In 1927, his last season with the Browns, he hit .327 and knocked out 201 hits. He was shipped to Washington before the 1928 season, but was traded to the Boston Braves early in the campaign. He finished his major league career in strong fashion, hitting .326 in 1929 and .309 in '30.

After spending the 1931 campaign with Rochester of the International League and 1932 with Shreveport-Tyler of the Texas League, Sisler retired from baseball. He launched several private ventures, including a sporting goods company, and founded the American Softball Association. Sisler engineered the first lighted softball park, and that sport boomed throughout the 1930s. In 1939, Sisler was elected to the Baseball Hall of Fame by the writers' panel, and was among the first four classes of inductees enshrined that summer.

In 1942, Branch Rickey hired the 49-year-old Sisler to scout for the Brooklyn Dodgers. Sisler served in this capacity throughout the decade, but his greatest contribution may have come in preparing Jackie Robinson to break baseball's color barrier. He scouted Robinson prior to his signing with the Dodgers, and helped the future Hall of Famer make the transition to first base during his first year in the majors. Sisler moved to Brooklyn to assume an expanded role with the Dodgers in 1947, and in addition to scouting and

player development helped tutor several of the players that would serve as the foundation of the outstanding Dodgers teams of the 1950s. When Rickey moved to the Pirates before the 1951 season, Sisler again went with him. There he helped bring Bill Mazeroski into the fold, and also worked with Roberto Clemente, teaching him to keep his head still during his swing.

Sisler remained with the Pirates after Rickey left, but after serious abdominal surgery in 1957 he and Kathleen moved back to St. Louis. Despite the move, Sisler remained with the Pirates as a roving hitting coach, and instructed such players as Willie Stargell, Gene Alley, and Donn Clendenon. Sisler passed away on March 26, 1973, in Richmond Heights, Missouri. Kathleen survived him by 17 years. The couple had three sons, one of whom, Dick, spent eight years in the major leagues and later managed the Cincinnati Reds. Another son, Dave, had a seven-year career as a big league pitcher. George Sisler is buried at the Old Meeting House Presbyterian Church Cemetery in Frontenac, Missouri.

BILL LAMBERTY

SOURCES

Note: This list is not comprehensive, but rather represents the key sources used by the authors in compiling this book.

INTERVIEWS

Phone Interview with Bud Cole (ballplayer with the Farmington Blues), November 19, 2004.

Phone and email Conversations with Lawrence Paul Pelty (grandson of Barney Pelty), November 2004.

Interview with Ann L. Hickman, July 19, 2004.

Phone Interview with Edward Stewart Plank III in November 2002.

Phone Interview with Milwaukee Historian John Gurda, November 5, 1999.

Phone Interview with Donald Pratt (son of Del Pratt), October 22 and November 17, 2003.

Phone Interview with James B. Pratt (nephew of Del Pratt), October 22 and November 12, 2003.

Interview with Charles Dundas (Osee Schrecongost's grandson).

Interview with Christine Crawford-Oppenheimer (Schrecongost family genealogist).

ARCHIVAL SOURCES

Clippings files from the National Baseball Hall of Fame Library:

Nick Altrock, John Anderson, Jimmy Austin

Frank Baker, Jimmy Barrett, Ed Barrow, Jack Barry, Harry Bay, Chief Bender, Bill Bradley, Jesse Burkett, Donie Bush

Ray Caldwell, Jimmy Callahan, Bill Carrigan, Ray Chapman, Hal Chase, Jack Chesbro, Eddie Cicotte, Ty Cobb, Eddie Collins, Jimmy Collins, Ray Collins, Charles Comiskey, Tom Connolly, Wid Conroy, Jack Coombs, Harry Coveleski, Stan Coveleski, Sam Crawford, Birdie Cree, Lou Criger

George Dauss, George Davis, Harry Davis, Ed Delahanty, Jim Delahanty, Bill Dinneen, Patsy Dougherty

Kid Elberfeld, Billy Evans

Red Faber, Cy Falkenberg, Happy Felsch, Hobe Ferris, Ray Fisher, Elmer Flick, Russ Ford, Buck Freeman

Chick Gandil, Larry Gardner, Jack Graney, Vean Gregg, Clark Griffith, Bob Groom

Topsy Hartsel, Robert Hedges, Charlie Hemphill, Charlie Hickman, Harry Hooper, Harry Howell, Tom Hughes

Frank Isbell

Joe Jackson, Hughey Jennings, Ban Johnson, Walter Johnson, Davy Jones, Fielder Jones, Addie Joss

Willie Keeler, Ed Killian

Nap Lajoie, Dutch Leonard, Duffy Lewis

Connie Mack, Carl Mays, Jimmy McAleer, George McBride, Stuffy McInnis, Matty McIntyre, Clyde Milan, Earl Moore, George Moriarty, George Mullin, Danny Murphy

Frank Navin

Rube Oldring, Silk O'Loughlin, Steve O'Neill, Al Orth

Freddy Parent, Roger Peckinpaugh, Barney Pelty, Wally Pipp, Eddie Plank, Jack Powell, Del Pratt

Branch Rickey, Swede Risberg, Bobby Roth, Reb Russell, Babe Ruth

Germany Schaefer, Ray Schalk, Wally Schang, Osee Schrecongost, Jim Scott, Socks Seybold, Ben Shibe, Burt Shotton, George Sisler, Frank Smith, Charles Somers, Tris Speaker, Chick Stahl, Jake Stahl, Oscar Stanage, George Stone, George Stovall, Amos Strunk, Billy Sullivan

Jesse Tannehill, Terry Turner

Bobby Veach

Rube Waddell, Tilly Walker, Bobby Wallace, Ed Walsh, Buck Weaver, Doc White, Jimmy Williams, Lefty Williams, Joe Wood

Cy Young

CLIPPINGS FROM THE SPORTING NEWS LIBRARY

Doc White, Harry Bay, Jim Scott, John Anderson

OTHER ARCHIVAL SOURCES

George D. Weaver vs. American League Baseball Club of Chicago in the United States District Court, Northern District of Illinois, Filed 11/26/1921. Case No. 33870.

George D. Weaver vs. American League Baseball Club of Chicago in the United States Municipal Court of Chicago. Case No. 855871

Del Pratt Family Scrapbook and Clippings

Earl Moore Collection. Pickerington-Violet Township Historical Society, Pickerington, Ohio.

Elmer Harrison Flick, 1876-1971 File. Bedford Historical Society Manuscript Collection. The Bedford Historical Society Archives, Bedford, Ohio.

Fielder Jones Family Album and Papers, Portland, Oregon.

Fielder Jones Papers, Potter County, Pennsylvania, Historical Society.

Harry Hooper Papers, Capitola, CA and Baytown, TX.

Joe Wood Papers, Keene, NH.

Ray Fisher Family Papers.

Vean Gregg Family Scrapbooks.

NEWSPAPERS AND PERIODICALS

Atlanta Constitution, Baltimore Sun, Baseball Digest, Baseball Magazine, Boston American, Boston Globe, Boston Post, Brooklyn Eagle, Buffalo Evening News, Chicago Daily Tribune, Chicago Evening American, Chicago Examiner, Cincinnati Enquirer, Cleveland Plain Dealer, Detroit Free Press, Detroit News, Evening Times (Pawtucket), Fort Wayne Journal-Gazette, Illustrated Sporting News, Indianapolis Star, Los Angeles Times, Milwaukee Journal, Milwaukee Sentinel, Newark Daily Advocate, New York Herald, New York Times, New York World, Oneonta Star, Philadelphia Daily News, Philadelphia Inquirer, Philadelphia North American, Philadelphia Public Ledger, Philadelphia Record, Pittsburgh Sunday-Post, Portland Oregonian, Reno Evening Gazette, The Republic (St. Louis), St. Louis Globe-Democrat, St. Louis Post-Dispatch, The Saturday Evening Post, Sporting Life, The Sporting News, The Toledo Blade, The Toledo Times, Washington Post

WEB SITES

www.baseball-almanac.com
www.baseballlibrary.com
www.baseballprospectus.com
www.baseball-reference.com
www.bioproj.sabr.org
www.thedeadballera.com
www.retrosheet.com

BOOKS

Alexander, Charles. *John McGraw* (New York: Viking Penguin, 1988).

Alexander, Charles. *Ty Cobb* (New York: Oxford University Press, 1984).

Anderson, David. *More Than Merkle* (Lincoln, NE: University of Nebraska Press, 2000).

Asinof, Eliot. *Eight Men Out* (New York: Henry Holt, 1987).

Barrow, Ed. *My Fifty Years in Baseball* (New York: Coward-McCann, 1951).

Brown, Warren. *The Chicago White Sox.* (New York: Putnam, 1952).

Browning, Reed. *Cy Young: A Baseball Life* (Amherst, MA: University of Massachusetts Press, 2000).

Casway, Jerrold. *Ed Delahanty in the Emerald Age of Baseball* (South Bend, IN: University of Notre Dame Press, 2004).

Cobb, Ty with Al Stump. *My Life in Baseball: The True Record* (New York: Doubleday, 1961).

Creamer, Robert W. *Babe: The Legend Comes to Life* (New York: Simon & Schuster, 1992).

DeValeria, Dennis and Jeanne Burke DeValeria. *Honus Wagner* (New York: Henry Holt, 1996).

Dewey, Donald and Nicholas Acocella. *The Black Prince of Baseball: Hal Chase and the Mythology of the Game* (Toronto: Sport Classics Books, 2004).

Elfers, James E. *The Tour To End All Tours: The Story of Major League Baseball's 1913–1914 World Tour* (Lincoln, NE: University of Nebraska Press, 2003).

Enders, Eric. *100 Years of the World Series* (New York: Barnes & Noble, 2003).

Evers, Johnny. *Touching Second* (New York: Reilly and Britton, 1910).

Fleitz, David. *Shoeless: The Life and Times of Joe Jackson* (Jefferson, NC: McFarland, 2001).

Ginsburg, Dan. *The Fix Is In* (Jefferson, NC: McFarland, 1995).

Golenbock, Peter. *The Spirit of St. Louis: A History of the St. Louis Cardinals and Browns* (New York: William Morrow, 2000).

Graham, Frank. *The New York Yankees: An Informal History* (New York: Putnam, 1945).

Hirschberg, Al. *Baseball's Greatest Catchers* (New York: Putnam, 1966).

Ivor-Campbell, Frederick, Robert L. Tiemann and Mark Rucker eds. *Baseball's First Stars* (Cleveland: The Society for American Baseball Research, 1996).

James, Bill. *The New Bill James Historical Abstract* (New York: Free Press, 2001).

James, Bill and Rob Neyer. *The Neyer/James Guide to Pitchers* (New York: Fireside, 2004).

Kashatus, William. *Connie Mack's '29 Triumph* (Jefferson, NC: McFarland, 1999).

Kashatus, William. *Diamonds in the Coalfield* (Jefferson, NC: McFarland, 2001).

Kohout, Martin. *Hal Chase: The Defiant Life and Turbulent Times of Baseball's Biggest Crook.* (Jefferson, NC: McFarland, 2001).

Labenski, Scott. Unpublished Biographical Sketch of Buck Freeman (2004).

Lewis, Franklin. *The Cleveland Indians* (New York: Putnam, 1949).

Lieb, Fred. *The Baltimore Orioles* (New York: Putnam, 1955).

Lieb, Fred. *Baseball As I Have Known It* (Lincoln, NE: University of Nebraska Press, 1977).

Lieb, Fred. *The Boston Red Sox* (New York: Putnam, 1947).

Lieb, Fred. *Connie Mack* (New York: Putnam, 1945).

Lieb, Fred. *The Detroit Tigers* (New York: Putnam, 1946).

Longert, Scott. *Addie Joss: King of the Pitchers* (Cleveland, OH: SABR, 1998).

Lowry, Philip J. *Green Cathedrals* (New York: Addison-Wesley, 1992).

Mack, Connie. *My 66 Years in the Big Leagues* (New York: Universal House, 1950).

Masur, Louis. *Autumn Glory: Baseball's First World Series* (New York: Hill and Wang, 2003).

McGraw, John. *My Thirty Years in Baseball* (Lincoln, NE: University of Nebraska Press, 1995).

Muchlinski, Alan. *After the Blacksox: The Swede Risberg Story* (Bloomington, IN: Authorhouse, 2005).

Murdoch, Eugene C. *Ban Johnson: Czar of Baseball* (Westport, CT: Greenwood Press, 1982).

Neft, David S. and Richard M. Cohen. *The World Series: Complete Play-by-Play of Every Game 1903–1989* (New York: St. Martin's Press, 1990).

Porter, David. ed. *The Biographical Dictionary of American Sports: Baseball* (Westport, CT: Greenwood Press, 1987).

Povich, Shirley. *The Washington Senators: An Informal History* (New York: Putnam, 1954).

Reisler, Jim. *Before They Were the Bombers* (Jefferson, NC: McFarland, 2002).

Ritter, Lawrence. *The Glory of Their Times* (New York: William Morrow, 1992).

Santry, Joseph M. *Grazing Through Columbus Baseball* (Columbus OH: Self Published, 2004).

Seymour, Harold. *Baseball: The Golden Age* (New York: Oxford University Press, 1971).

Smelser, Marshall. *The Life That Ruth Built* (Lincoln, NE: University of Nebraska Press, 1975).

Sowell, Mike. *July 2, 1903* (New York: Macmillan, 1992).

Sowell, Mike. *The Pitch That Killed* (New York: Macmillan, 1989).

Spink, Alfred H. *The National Game. 2nd ed.* (Carbondale: Southern Illinois University Press, 2000).

Stein, Irving M. *The Ginger Kid: The Buck Weaver Story* (Dubuque, IA: Brown & Benchmark, 1992).

Stout, Glenn and Richard A. Johnson. *Red Sox Century* (New York: Houghton Mifflin, 2000).

Stump, Al. *Cobb: A Biography* (Chapel Hill, NC: Algonquin Books, 1996).

Thomas, Henry W. *Walter Johnson: Baseball's Big Train* (Washington, DC: Phenom Press, 1995).

Tiemann, Robert L. and Mark Rucker eds. *Nineteenth Century Stars* (Kansas City, MO: Society for American Baseball Research, 1989).

Wood, Allan. *Babe Ruth and the 1918 Red Sox* (Lincoln, NE: IUniverse, 2000).

Wright, Marshall D. *The International League: Year-by-Year Statistics, 1884–1953* (Jefferson, NC: McFarland, 1998).

Wright, Marshall D. *The Southern Association in Baseball, 1885–1961* (Jefferson, NC: McFarland, 2002).

Wright, Marshall D. *The Texas League in Baseball, 1888–1958* (Jefferson, NC: McFarland, 2004).

Zingg, Paul J. *Harry Hooper: An American Baseball Life.* (Champaign, IL: University of Illinois Press, 1993).

ARTICLES

Christensen, Chris. "Chick Stahl: A Baseball Suicide," *Elysian Fields*. Vol. 20. No. 2. 2003.

Gough, David. "A Tribute to Burt Shotton," *The National Pastime*. No. 14. 1994.

Lamb, William F. "George Davis: Forgotten Great," *The National Pastime*. No. 17. 1997.

Longert, Scott. "Bill Bradley," *The National Pastime*. No. 16. 1996.

Murphy, J.M. "Napoleon Lajoie: Modern Baseball's First Superstar," *The National Pastime*. No. 1. 1988.

Stump, Al. "Ty Cobb's Wild Ten Month Fight To Live," reprinted in *The Third Fireside Book of Baseball*, Charles Einstein ed. (New York: Simon and Schuster, 1968).

Tholkes, Robert. "Chief Bender: The Early Years," *Baseball Research Journal*. No. 14. 1983.

Thompson, Dick. "Stahl's Suicide," *Baseball Research Journal*. No. 28. 1999.

CREDITS

Photographs are used with permission from the following collections.

BRACE PHOTO: pp. 529, 544, 639, 677, 695, 751, 755

CHICAGO HISTORICAL SOCIETY: pp. 383, 384, 389, 395, 398, 403, 406, 408, 409, 411, 414, 417, 420, 422, 424, 426, 428, 432, 442, 443, 445, 449, 451, 457, 459, 462, 471, 473, 477, 479, 480, 483, 486, 488, 490, 491, 493, 496, 497, 499, 500, 504, 507, 510, 512, 514, 516, 519, 520, 530, 538, 542, 549, 553, 563, 570, 577, 589, 595, 597, 600, 602, 605, 610, 625, 629, 632, 634, 640, 642, 644, 647, 648, 649, 651, 652, 657, 660, 664, 668, 670, 675, 680, 682, 683, 688, 696, 697, 699, 702, 708, 710, 711, 714, 731, 733, 736, 738, 749, 763, 764, 765, 776, 778, 780, 783, 786, 795, 797

DETROIT PUBLIC LIBRARY: p. 401

THE LIBRARY OF CONGRESS: p. 693

NATIONAL BASEBALL HALL OF FAME AND MUSEUM, COOPERSTOWN, NY: pp. 390, 393, 399, 402, 418, 430, 433, 438, 441, 448, 455, 464, 467, 469, 470, 474, 485, 495, 502, 506, 517, 523, 525, 527, 532, 533, 535, 537, 540, 546, 550, 551, 555, 559, 561, 567, 568, 572, 575, 578, 579, 581, 583, 584, 587, 593, 599, 606, 608, 612, 614, 616, 618, 619, 621, 624, 627, 631, 635, 637, 641, 643, 650, 654, 655, 656, 658, 661, 667, 673, 684, 691, 700, 701, 704, 707, 712, 718, 719, 722, 727, 728, 732, 741, 742, 743, 744, 745, 747, 753, 754, 757, 759, 768, 770, 782, 788, 790, 792

THE SPALDING COLLECTION: p. 571

THE SPORTING NEWS: p. 774

TRANSCENDENTAL GRAPHICS: pp. 404, 434, 439, 453, 482, 524, 531, 548, 556, 566, 573, 610, 613, 616, 623, 672, 708, 716, 720, 724, 726, 729, 739, 761

Note: The pagination for *Deadball Stars of the American League* picks up where the companion volume, *Deadball Stars of the National League*, left off. This index serves as a guide to both volumes.